TOTAL QUALITY

Management, Organization, and Strategy

Fourth Edition

James R. Evans
University of Cincinnati

THOMSON

SOUTH-WESTERN

Australia · Canada · Mexico · Singapore · Spain · United Kingdom · United States

THOMSON

SOUTH-WESTERN

Total Quality Management, Organization, and Strategy, 4e

James R. Evans

VP/Editorial Director:
Jack W. Calhoun

Publisher:
Rob Dewey

Senior Acquisitions Editor:
Charles E. McCormick, Jr.

Acting Developmental Editor:
Alisa Madden

Senior Marketing Manager:
Larry Qualls

Production Editor:
Lora Arduser

Manufacturing Coordinator:
Diane Lohman

Technology Project Editor:
Christina A. Wittmer

Web Coordinator:
Kelly Reid

Art Director:
Tippy McIntosh

Production House:
Pre-Press Company, Inc.

Compositor:
Cadmus Professional
Communications

Cover Designer:
Tippy McIntosh

Cover Images:
©GettyImages/PhotoDisc, Inc

Internal Designer:
Patti Hudepohl

Printer:
Webcom
Toronto, Ontario

For permission to use material
from this text or product, submit
a request online at
http://www.thomsonrights.com
Any additional questions
about permissions can be
submitted by email to
thomsonrights@thomson.com

For more information
contact South-Western,
5191 Natorp Boulevard,
Mason, Ohio, 45040.
Or you can visit our
Internet site at:
http://www.swlearning.com

BRIEF CONTENTS

CONTENTS

PREFACE

Total Quality Management or "TQM" reached a pinnacle in the early 1990s, after which corporate America began to lose interest. There's an old cliché that "history repeats itself," and we are seeing it in business today. "Why is quality still so bad?" laments Scott Paton, editor-in-chief of *Quality Digest*, a major trade publication for the quality profession, in his April 2002 editorial. Although he notes that the quality of U.S. products as a whole is better now than it was in 1972, it is worse than it was in 1992 (after quality was the buzzword among businesses). And it's not just in manufacturing. Paton states, "If you've had a truly high-quality experience on a recent flight or with your loan application or buying a car or with your hospital, you're in the minority." He places the blame squarely on senior management, who fail to see the simple but essential relationship between customers' needs and expectations and designing, building, and delivering great products and services.[1]

Customer dissatisfaction with many goods and services is causing managers to rethink their commitment to quality. Many organizations are returning to the concepts and principles that were credited with bringing U.S. industry from near demise in the 1970s. Some are taking the first step toward learning about total quality (TQ) and implementing it. But, for many other organizations, the principles of TQ have become ingrained in the way organizations conduct their daily affairs. These organizations expect that their new employees (college graduates) understand not only the importance of providing quality products and services to customers but also the principles and tools of TQ. Students starting their working lives unfamiliar with total quality will indeed be one step behind.

It is difficult for students to learn about TQ on their own, because there are so many different approaches to the topic. Although these approaches are similar, each has its own jargon and acronyms, which makes trying to penetrate the subject for the first time a difficult experience. Furthermore, most books about TQ are not written with the needs and experiences of students in mind.

1. Scott Paton, "Grading Quality," First Word, *Quality Digest*, April 2002.

This book has three objectives:

➤ to familiarize students with the basic principles and methods associated with total quality;

➤ to show students how these principles and methods have been put into effect in a variety of organizations; and

➤ to illustrate the relationship between TQ principles and the theories and models studied in management courses.

The book presents the basic principles and tools associated with TQ and provides many illustrations and end-of-chapter cases that can be used as the basis for class discussion. Many cases focus on large and small companies in manufacturing and service industries in North and South America, Europe, and Asia–Pacific.

This book is organized so that it can be used as a supplement to textbooks for courses in management, organization theory, organizational behavior, and/or strategic management. The book also can be used as a freestanding introduction to TQ in an elective course on quality management.

CHANGES IN THE FOURTH EDITION

Drawing on insightful comments and suggestions from reviewers and adopters of previous editions, the general organization of the chapters in this edition has been changed somewhat to place quality first in a broader strategic context before delving into the details. However, considerable flexibility remains to meet the individual needs of instructors. Except for the first two chapters, all others can be sequenced in almost any order. More significantly, the content of several chapters has been rearranged to provide a clearer focus on quality principles, process management, quality tools and techniques, and organizational change. Specific changes include:

• Incorporation of Six Sigma, which has garnered considerable attention among business and academics alike, as a key approach for improving quality in organizations. Six Sigma is introduced in Chapter 2 and integrated as appropriate in other chapters.

• New sections on quality and e-commerce, comparison of Baldrige, ISO and Six Sigma, CRM technology in customer relationships, process design and control, lean thinking, Kaizen blitz, statistical process control, Six Sigma project teams, situational leadership, self-assessment and follow-up, knowledge management, and organizational change for Six Sigma have been added.

- New boxed vignettes that illustrate the concepts and themes of TQ in real, and sometimes unusual, circumstances; and new stories of quality concepts in action (all of which provide an appreciation for the application and universality of the principles of TQ); and new end-of-chapter cases have been added.

ORGANIZATION OF THE BOOK

Unlike most books on TQ, this one is organized according to traditional management topics. This organization helps students to see the parallels between TQ and management theories in areas such as organizational design and leadership. TQ often is presented as new or different, which it clearly is not. Many TQ ideas are based on management theories that are familiar to teachers and students. The organization of this book enables students to appreciate the ways in which TQ really is different.

The book has four parts. Part 1, Introduction to Total Quality, presents the core principles of TQ and begins to explain how they relate to familiar management concepts. It also positions TQ within general business management frameworks and strategy.

Chapter 1 introduces the concepts of TQ, their applicability to manufacturing, services, and the increasingly important e-commerce sector; the evolution of TQ principles deriving from the philosophies of Deming, Juran, and Crosby; the modern principles of TQ and its relationship with agency theory.

Chapter 2 describes three major frameworks for pursuing TQ in organizations: the Malcolm Baldrige National Quality Award, ISO 9000:2000, and Six Sigma, focusing on the value of these approaches in building performance excellence and evaluating their similarities and differences.

Chapter 3 addresses the role of quality in achieving competitive advantage, particularly in differentiating organizations from their competitors, and its relationship to strategic management. An important aspect of strategic management is the use of a "balanced scorecard" of metrics and information for data-driven decisions. This topic is also addressed.

Part 2, Total Quality and Organization Theory, introduces the idea of customer-supplier relations and shows how TQ relates to such topics as organization-environment relations, organizational design, and process improvement. A separate chapter on tools and techniques for design and improvement supports the organizational emphasis.

Chapter 4 discusses the importance of customers and suppliers in a total quality organization. It presents principles of customer-supplier relationships, practices for dealing with customers and suppliers, and examples of customer-supplier relationships in action and how they relate to organization theory.

Chapter 5 focuses on designing organizations to support a quality focus. It explains how TQ organizations must differ from traditional functional organizations, approaches to organizational design, examples of organizations that have successfully redesigned themselves with a TQ focus, and comparisons with organizational design theory.

Chapter 6 focuses on process management—the design, control, and improvement of organizational processes. Principles underlying each of these key managerial responsibilities are discussed, along with approaches for implementing them in organizations. These include Kaizen, the Deming Cycle, Six Sigma DMAIC, lean thinking, benchmarking, reengineering, and organizational learning. The chapter presents several examples of process management in action.

Chapter 7 summarizes the most important tools and techniques for quality planning, design, and improvement. It also discusses the role of creativity and innovation in quality, and statistical thinking and effective use of such tools as statistical process control.

Part 3, Total Quality and Organizational Behavior, discusses the themes of teamwork and empowerment and relates TQ to the topics of groups and motivation.

Chapter 8 focuses on teamwork. It highlights the importance of teams in TQ, and describes the various types of teams commonly found in TQ organizations, including Six Sigma project teams. It also discusses what teams must do to work effectively from an organizational viewpoint, presents some examples of teamwork in action, and compares TQ team concepts to organizational behavior theories.

Chapter 9 develops the important TQ concepts of empowerment and motivation. This chapter describes why empowerment is important in organizations, principles for successfully introducing and sustaining empowerment, and examples of organizations that have done so successfully. Motivation is discussed in the context of organizational practices that support TQ efforts. These concepts also are discussed in the context of popular organizational theories of motivation.

Part 4, Leadership and Implementation, deals with practices for making TQ a part of today's modern organizations, focusing on leadership and organizational change.

Chapter 10 is devoted to leadership, the roles of a quality leader, examples of leadership in action, and relationships with traditional theories of leadership.

Chapter 11 concludes the book with a discussion of organizational change, organizational culture, and approaches for sustaining TQ for the long run. It also illustrates some examples of organizational change in action and how TQ change relates to organization theory.

The bibliography at the end of the book provides a number of references for students who wish to deepen their understanding of various aspects of TQ.

ACKNOWLEDGMENTS

Users of previous editions of this book will notice a significant change on the front cover. My friend and colleague, Dr. James W. Dean, Jr., is no longer associated with this book. Jim was instrumental in defining the design and character of this book from its inception, and for integrating the concepts of total quality with traditional theories of management and organizations. I have learned much from working with him and wish him continued success in his career at the University of North Carolina.

For this edition, we are especially grateful to the many reviewers who provided comments and suggestions for improvement. They are:

Benjamin Abramowitz, University of Central Florida
Dr. Phyllis C. Alderdice, Jefferson Community College
John Alderson, East Arkansas Community College
Mohsen Attaran, Ph.D., California State University, Bakersfield
Uttarayan Bagchi, University of Texas at Austin
Janet Barnard, Rochester Institute of Technology
Stephen Beckstead, Utah State University

George D. Bertish, University of Central Florida–Daytona Beach

Allen Bluedorn, University of Missouri–Columbia

Elia Chepaitis, Fairfield University

Arthur Darrow, Bowling Green State University

Dr. Lou Firenze, Northwood University

Marjorie Mathison Hance, Chair, Business Administration Department, The College of St. Catherine

Jodi L. Harrison, Northwood University

Karen Hawley, University of Minnesota

Yunus Kathawala, Eastern Illinois University

Jim Kling, Niagara University

Patrick Lee, Fairfield University

Cynthia Lengnick-Hall, Wichita State University

Kenneth Paetsch, Cleveland State University

Barbara Price, Wayne State University

Charles Schrader, Iowa State University

Robert Scott Stevens, Eastern Illinois University

Oya I. Tukel, Cleveland State University

David A. Waldman, Concordia University

Finally, we greatly appreciate the help of our editor at South-Western, Charles McCormick, as well as our former editors at West Publishing Company, Richard Fenton and Esther Craig.

We believe, like many business and academic leaders, that quality is an absolute essential not only for competitive success in business, but also for meaningful work and integrity in many aspects of life. If this book helps students to contribute to the quality of their organizations' products and services and to understand the importance of quality in all their endeavors, then our efforts will have been worthwhile.

If you have any suggestions for improvement or perhaps a good story or case to contribute to the next edition, we would love to hear from you and acknowledge your contribution in the next edition. Please feel free to contact the author via e-mail at James.Evans@UC.edu.

James R. Evans

PART 1

Introduction to Total Quality

CHAPTER 1

Introduction to Total Quality in Organizations

Joseph Juran, one of the most respected leaders of quality in the 1900s, suggested that the twentieth century would be defined by historians as the century of productivity. He also stated that the twenty-first century should be designated the century of quality. "We've made dependence on the quality of our technology a part of life."[1]

In this chapter we will introduce you to the basic principles of total quality (TQ). Specifically, we will

➤ provide reasons why attention to quality should be a part of every organization's culture and management systems;
➤ provide a brief history of the "quality revolution";
➤ describe philosophies of Deming, Juran, and Crosby as a basis for TQ approaches;
➤ provide an overview of the key principles of TQ;
➤ compare and contrast quality-focused management with traditional management practices; and
➤ discuss relationships of total quality with organizational models in management theory.

THE IMPORTANCE OF QUALITY

Today, we generally do not hear much about quality in business, except when things go wrong. Here is one example:

Spend $25,000 on a car that doesn't run the way you expect it to, and you get pretty angry. Spend $50,000 or $100,000, and you get really angry. Just listen to the anguished howls of Mercedes-Benz owners on Web sites . . . as they vent about the latest mishap to afflict their Benzes. Depending on the model, the complaints range from faulty key fobs and leaky sunroofs to balky electronics that leave drivers and their passengers stranded. Regardless of the severity, a single sentiment runs through the gripes: this shouldn't be happening to a Mercedes.[2]

Quality was THE buzzword among businesses during the 1980s and into the 1990s. Nevertheless, Jeffrey E. Garten, dean of the Yale School of Management, observed just a few years ago: "Whatever happened to the hoopla surrounding quality control in Corporate America? Has the issue slipped from the front page because the war against big-time defects has been won? Or could Corporate America be deluding itself into thinking that quality no longer is the huge problem it once was?" Dean Garten points to the Firestone tire fiasco, recalls of circuit boards by Intel, automobile recalls, poor customer-service quality, the lack of a quality framework for e-business, and the need for higher quality standards in biotechnology as reminders that quality problems still abound.[3] Although Mercedes' longtime CEO noted, "Quality is part of our heritage, one of our core values," without a continuous and relentless focus on it, it is easy for quality to slip by the wayside. Consumers today are intelligent enough to recognize quality issues that firms face today (see the box "You Can Fool Some of the People Some of the Time"), and the organization that doesn't heed its customers is in for a rude awakening, or, at worst, a quick demise. This is why an understanding of quality is vital to every employee in every organization.

Stories of successful organizations generally end up in publications dedicated to quality professionals, which basically "preach to the choir." Here are just a few highlights of the results achieved by companies that have

---

You Can Fool Some of the People Some of the Time . . .

Letters to the editor of *Business Week* show that quality is an important concern to consumers, and that quality guides their purchasing decisions: "[Robert A.] Lutz and the other big hires will have to do more than spruce up GM's designs in order to regain market share. The new Cadillac CTS and other model changes will have very little effect unless GM buckles down to improve the quality of its products. As a longtime GM customer . . . I have watched GM fall behind in product reliability and durability and just never quite get with it. Finally this year, I threw in the towel and reluctantly invested in a Lexus" (September 17, 2001, p. 16). "'Can the Nordstroms find the right style?' summarizes, in part, what my wife has been telling me for several years: The company has lost touch with its customer base. When a salesperson responded to an observation my wife made by telling her to write the company a letter—while telling her they had "100 letters on the same subject"— that tells you something" (September 10, 2001, p. 22).

embraced quality as a basic business principle but that have never made the pages of *Fortune* and *Business Week*.

1. Among associates at Clarke American, overall satisfaction improved from 72 percent in 1996 to 84 percent in 2000. Rising associate satisfaction correlates with the 84 percent increase in revenue earned per associate since 1995. Annual growth in company revenues increased from a rate of 4.2 percent in 1996 to 16 percent in 2000, compared to the industry's average annual growth rate of less than 1 percent over the five-year period.
2. The Spicer Driveshaft Division of Dana Corporation lowered internal defect rates by more than 75 percent. Employee turnover is below 1 percent, and economic value added increased from $15 million to $35 million in two years.
3. Texas Nameplate Company increased its national market share from less than 3 percent in 1994 to 5 percent in 1997, reduced its defects from 3.65 percent to about 1 percent of billings, and increased on-time delivery from 95 to 98 percent.
4. Region Americas of STMicroelectronics, Inc., reduced lost-day injuries from 1.01 per 100 workers in 1996 to 0.65 in 1999, which is 74 percent below the industry average, and employee satisfaction levels in 1999 exceeded the industry composite in 8 of 10 categories.
5. Pal's Sudden Service, a privately owned quick-service restaurant chain in eastern Tennessee, garnered customer quality scores averaging 95.8 percent in 2001, compared with 84.1 percent for its best competitor, and improved order delivery speed by more than 30 percent since 1995.
6. Parent satisfaction at Pearl River School District increased from 62 percent in 1996 to 96 percent in 2001.
7. KARLEE, a contract manufacturer of precision sheet metal and machined components, reduced waste from 1.5 percent of sales to less than 0.5 percent of sales while nearly doubling productivity from 1995 to 2000.
8. SSM Health Care's share of the St. Louis market increased substantially while three of its five competitors lost market share. They achieved a AA credit rating by Standard and Poor's for four consecutive years, a rating attained by fewer than 1 percent of U.S. hospitals.

Many more statistics like these can be cited, and other empirical evidence exists that firms implementing effective total quality approaches improve their performance on measures of income, sales growth, cost control, and growth in employment and total assets.[4] Nevertheless, scores of companies have either failed to take the first step in a quality journey, or have let initial successes fade away because of lack of commitment and sustainability.

Total quality—a comprehensive, organization-wide effort to improve the quality of products and services—applies to all organizations—large and small, manufacturing and service, profit and not-for-profit (see the box "Quality Starts with a Vision").

Quality Starts with a Vision[5]

Unless you live in Webster, New York, you probably have never heard of Trident Precision Manufacturing, Inc. The privately held company was formed in 1979 with three people, and today manufactures precision sheet metal components, electromechanical assemblies, and custom products, mostly in the office equipment, medical supply, computer, and defense industries with a workforce of about 170. In 1995, revenues totaled $14.5 million. Trident has established quality as its basic business plan to accomplish short- and long-term goals for five key business drivers: customer satisfaction, employee satisfaction, shareholder value, operational performance, and supplier partnerships.

Employee turnover declined dramatically, from 41 percent in 1988 to 5 percent in 1994 and 1995. Defect rates fell so much that Trident offered a full guarantee against defects in its custom products. On-time delivery performance increased from 87 percent in 1990 to 99.94 percent in 1995. Rates of return on assets consistently exceeded industry averages, customers rated the quality of their products at 99.8 percent or better, and the company never lost a customer to a competitor. In 1996, Trident received the Malcolm Baldrige National Quality Award, the highest level of recognition in the United States for organizations demonstrating outstanding business results and management approaches to achieving performance excellence.

How did Trident achieve such success? Trident's total quality quest began in 1988, when CEO Nicholas Juskiw attended a symposium offered by Xerox Corporation about its Leadership Through Quality strategy. When Juskiw wrote his vision statement he said: My Vision for Trident is one in which each of us shares in the responsibility, growth, and benefits of becoming a world-class organization. How will we, as a team, achieve this? Through quality! Not just the quality of each individual part but through Total Quality—in everything we say and do. . . . As a strong team, with each headed in the same direction, we can become the unquestionable leader that our Customers, Industry, and Community look up to.

A BRIEF HISTORY

To understand the importance of quality in business today, we need to review some history. Before the Industrial Revolution, skilled craftspeople served both as manufacturers and inspectors, building quality into their products through their considerable pride in their workmanship. Customers expected quality, and craftspeople understood it.

The Industrial Revolution changed everything. Thomas Jefferson brought Honore Le Blanc's concept of interchangeable parts to America. Eli Whitney mistakenly believed that this idea would be easy to carry out. The government awarded him a contract in 1798 to supply 10,000 muskets in two years.

He designed special machine tools and trained unskilled workmen to make parts according to a standard design, measure them, and compare them to a model. Unfortunately, Whitney grossly underestimated the effect of variation in the production process and its impact on quality. It took more than 10 years to complete the project, perhaps the first example of cost-overrun in government contracts! This same obstacle—variation—continues to plague American managers to this day.

Frederick W. Taylor's concept of "scientific management" greatly influenced the nature of quality in manufacturing organizations. By focusing on production efficiency and decomposing jobs into small work tasks, the modern assembly line destroyed the holistic nature of manufacturing. To ensure that products were manufactured correctly, independent "quality control" departments assumed the tasks of inspection. Thus, the separation of good from bad product became the chief means of ensuring quality.

Statistical approaches to quality control had their origins at Western Electric when the inspection department was transferred to Bell Telephone Laboratories in the 1920s. The pioneers of quality control—Walter Shewhart, Harold Dodge, George Edwards, and others—developed new theories and methods of inspection to improve and maintain quality. Control charts, sampling techniques, and economic analysis tools laid the foundation for modern quality assurance activity and influenced the thinking of two of their colleagues, W. Edwards Deming and Joseph M. Juran, both of whom also worked at Western Electric in the first half of the twentieth century.

Deming and Juran introduced statistical quality control to Japanese workers after World War II as part of General MacArthur's rebuilding program. Although this was not much different than what was being done in America, there was one vital difference. They convinced top Japanese managers that quality improvement would open new world markets and was necessary for the survival of their nation. The managers believed in, and fully supported, the concept of quality improvement. The Japanese were in an ideal position to embrace this philosophy. Their country was devastated from the war, and they had few natural resources with which to compete, except their people. During the next 20 years, while the Japanese were improving quality at an unprecedented rate, quality levels in the West remained stagnant. Western manufacturers had little need to focus on quality. America had a virtual monopoly in manufacturing, and the postwar economy was hungry for nearly any kind of consumer good. Top managers focused their efforts on marketing, production quantity, and financial performance.

During the late 1970s and early 1980s, many businesses in the United States lost significant market share to other global competitors, Japan in particular. By 1987 *Business Week* posed a stern warning to American management:

Quality. Remember it? American manufacturing has slumped a long way from the glory days of the 1950s and '60s when "Made in U.S.A." proudly stood for the best that industry could turn out. . . . While the

Japanese were developing remarkably higher standards for a whole host of products, from consumer electronics to cars and machine tools, many U.S. managers were smugly dozing at the switch. Now, aside from aerospace and agriculture, there are few markets left where the U.S. carries its own weight in international trade. For American industry, the message is simple. Get better or get beat.[6]

The "quality revolution" in America can be traced to 1980, when NBC aired a white paper titled "If Japan Can . . . Why Can't We?" This program introduced the 80-year-old Deming, who was virtually unknown in the United States, to corporate executives across America. Ford Motor Company was among the first to invite Deming to help transform its operations.

Within a few years, Ford's earnings were the highest for any company in automotive history, despite a 7 percent drop in U.S. car and truck industry sales, higher capital spending, and increased marketing costs. In 1992 the media celebrated the fact that the Ford Taurus outsold the Honda Accord to become the leader in domestic sales. Former CEO Donald Petersen stated: "The work of Dr. Deming has definitely helped change Ford's corporate leadership. . . . Dr. Deming has influenced my thinking in a variety of ways. What stands out is that he helped me crystallize my ideas concerning the value of teamwork, process improvement and the pervasive power of the concept of continuous improvement." Ironically, by the turn of the new century, Ford's quality dropped to last place among American car companies, demonstrating that sustaining quality efforts is indeed a difficult challenge.

America woke up to quality during the 1980s as most major companies embarked on extensive quality improvement campaigns. In 1984 the U.S. government designated October as National Quality Month. In 1987—some 34 years after Japan established the Deming Prize—Congress established the Malcolm Baldrige National Quality Award, spawning a remarkable interest in quality among American businesses. By the end of the decade Florida Power and Light became the first non-Japanese company to win Japan's coveted Deming Prize for quality. After the publicity that quality received from the manufacturing sector, the quality movement shifted to services. Companies such as FedEx, The Ritz-Carlton Hotel Company, and AT&T Universal Card Services (now a part of CitiBank) demonstrated clearly that quality principles can be applied effectively in the service sector.

During the 1990s, health care, government, and education began to pay increased attention to quality. As more public and government attention focuses on the nation's health care system, its providers turn toward quality as a means of achieving better performance and lower costs.[7] One hospital, for example, lowered its rate of postsurgical infections to less than one fifth of the acceptable national norms through the use of quality tools. In 1993, Vice President Al Gore spearheaded the National Performance Review, an initiative driven by the need to improve quality, which made 384 recommendations and indicated 1,214 specific actions that the federal government should take to improve operations and reduce costs. In 1991 a consortium of professional associations, business associations, and individual businesses and universities incorporated a nonprofit group called the National Education Quality Initiative to improve educational processes through quality principles. Many local school systems, colleges, and universities have made considerable progress.

Although quality initiatives focused initially on reducing defects and errors in products and services through the use of measurement, statistics, and other problem-solving tools, organizations began to recognize that lasting improvement could not be accomplished without significant attention to the quality of the management practices used on a daily basis. Managers began to realize that the approaches they use to listen to customers and develop long-term relationships, develop strategy, measure performance and analyze data, reward and train employees, design and deliver products and services, and act as leaders in their organizations are the true enablers of quality, customer satisfaction, and business results. In other words, they recognized that the "quality of management" is as important as the "management of quality." Many began to use the term **Big Q** to contrast the difference between managing for quality in all organizational processes as opposed to focusing solely on manufacturing quality (**Little Q**). As organizations began to integrate quality principles into their management systems, the notion of total quality management, or TQM, became popular. Quality took on a new meaning of organization-wide performance excellence rather than a narrow engineering- or production-based technical discipline and permeated every aspect of running an organization.

Today, the term TQM has virtually disappeared from business vernacular; however, the underlying principles of quality management are recognized as the foundation of high-performance management systems and an important factor for competitive success. Perhaps it is unfortunate that a three-letter acronym was chosen to represent such a powerful management concept. It is equally unfortunate that people point to the demise of faddish terminology as a generalization of the concepts themselves. Many organizations have integrated quality principles so tightly with daily work activities that they no longer view quality as something special. In contrast, many other organizations have barely begun.

Reasons for failure of quality initiatives are rooted in organizational approaches and systems, many of which this book addresses. As a former editor of *Quality Digest* put it: "No, TQM isn't dead. TQM failures just prove that bad management is still alive and kicking." The most successful organizations have found that the fundamental principles of total quality are essential to effective management practice, and continue to represent a sound approach for achieving business success.

The real challenge today is to ensure that managers do not lose sight of the basic principles on which quality management and performance excellence are based. The global marketplace and domestic and international competition has made organizations around the world realize that their survival depends on high quality.[8] Many countries, such as Korea and India, are mounting national efforts to increase quality awareness, including conferences, seminars, radio shows, school essay contests, and pamphlet distribution.

Spain and Brazil are encouraging the publication of quality books in their native language to make them more accessible. These trends will only increase the level of competition in the future. Even the tools used to achieve quality a decade ago are no longer sufficient to achieve the performance levels necessary to compete in today's world. Many organizations are embracing sophisticated, statistically based tools as part of popular "Six Sigma" initiatives, which we highlight in Chapter 2. These require increased levels of training and education for managers and frontline employees alike, as well as the development of technical staff. As Tom Engibous, president and chief executive officer of Texas Instruments, commented on the present and future importance of quality in 1997: "Quality will have to be everywhere, integrated into all aspects of a winning organization."

THE CONCEPT OF QUALITY

People define quality in many ways. Some think of quality as superiority or excellence, others view it as a lack of manufacturing or service defects, still others think of quality as related to product features or price. A study that asked managers of 86 firms in the eastern United States to define quality produced several dozen different responses, including:

1. perfection
2. consistency
3. eliminating waste
4. speed of delivery
5. compliance with policies and procedures
6. providing a good, usable product
7. doing it right the first time
8. delighting or pleasing customers
9. total customer service and satisfaction.[9]

Today most managers agree that the main reason to pursue quality is to satisfy customers. The American National Standards Institute (ANSI) and the American Society for Quality (ASQ) define quality as "the totality of features and characteristics of a product or service that bears on its ability to satisfy given needs." The view of quality as the satisfaction of customer needs is often called *fitness for use*. In highly competitive markets, merely satisfying customer needs will not achieve success. To beat the competition, organizations often must *exceed* customer expectations. Thus, one of the most popular definitions of quality is *meeting or exceeding customer expectations*. This definition is reflected in the vision statement of Hollywood Casino Resort in Tunica,

Mississippi: "Hollywood Casino Resort/Tunica is a place where guests feel invited and welcome. We provide the highest levels of personalized service and products for our guests, who always enjoy a fun-filled experience. Everyone at Hollywood Casino does the right thing right the first time, and puts the needs and wants of our guests in the forefront of every decision we make." Deer Valley Resort is another example of an organization dedicated to exceeding customer expectations (see box "At Deer Valley, Quality Is Not a Snow Job").

Customer-driven quality is fundamental to high-performing organizations. The president and CEO of Fujitsu Network Transmission Systems, a U.S. subsidiary of Fujitsu, Ltd., stated, "Our customers are intelligent; they expect us to continuously evolve to meet their ever-changing needs. They can't afford to have a thousand mediocre suppliers in today's competitive environment. They want a few exceptional ones."

Managers of manufacturing and service functions deal with different types of quality issues; the following sections provide a brief overview of these issues. Although the details of quality management differ between manufacturing and service industries, the customer-driven definition eliminates these artificial distinctions and provides a unifying perspective.

At Deer Valley, Quality Is Not a Snow Job[10]

Deer Valley Resort in Park City, Utah, is viewed by many as The Ritz-Carlton of ski resorts, providing exceptional services and a superior ski vacation experience.

The resort offers curbside ski valet service to take equipment from vehicles, parking lot attendants to ensure efficient parking, and a shuttle to transport guests from the lot to Snow Park Lodge. Guests walk to the slopes on heated pavers that prevent the pavement from freezing and assist in snow removal. The central gathering area by the base lifts is wide and level, allowing plenty of room to put on equipment and easy access to the lifts. At the end of the day, guests can store their skis without charge at each lodge. The resort limits the number of skiers on the mountain to reduce lines and congestion, and offers complimentary mountain tours for both expert and intermediate skiers. Everyone is committed to ensuring that each guest has a wonderful experience, from "mountain hosts" stationed at the top of the lifts to answer questions and provide directions, to the friendly workers at the cafeterias and restaurants, whose food is consistently rated number one by ski enthusiast magazines. "Our goal is to make each guest feel like a winner," says Bob Wheaton, vice president and general manager. "We go the extra mile on the mountain, in our ski school, and throughout our food-service operation because we want our guests to know they come first."

Quality in Manufacturing

Well-developed quality systems have existed in manufacturing for some time. However, these systems focused primarily on technical issues such as equipment reliability, inspection, defect measurement, and process control. The transition to a customer-driven organization has caused fundamental changes in manufacturing practices, changes that are particularly evident in areas such as product design, human resource management, and supplier relations. Product design activities, for example, now closely integrate marketing, engineering, and manufacturing operations. Human resource practices concentrate on empowering workers to collect and analyze data, make critical operations decisions, and take responsibility for continuous improvements, thereby moving the responsibility for quality from the quality control department onto the factory floor. Suppliers have become partners in product design and manufacturing efforts. Many of these efforts were stimulated by the automobile industry, which forced their network of suppliers to improve quality.

Manufactured products have several quality dimensions[11] including the following:

1. *Performance*: a product's primary operating characteristics.
2. *Features*: the "bells and whistles" of a product.
3. *Reliability*: the probability of a product's surviving over a specified period of time under stated conditions of use.
4. *Conformance*: the degree to which physical and performance characteristics of a product match preestablished standards.
5. *Durability*: the amount of use one gets from a product before it physically deteriorates or until replacement is preferable.
6. *Serviceability*: the ability to repair a product quickly and easily.
7. *Aesthetics*: how a product looks, feels, sounds, tastes, or smells.
8. *Perceived quality*: subjective assessment resulting from image, advertising, or brand names.

Most of these dimensions revolve around the design of the product. In designing the initial Lexus automobile for instance, Toyota bought several competitors' cars—including Mercedes, Jaguar, and BMW—and put them through grueling test track runs before taking them apart.[12] The chief engineer decided that he could match Mercedes on performance and reliability, as well as on luxury and status features. He developed 11 performance goals. The final design had a drag coefficient smaller than any other luxury car (resulting in higher aerodynamic performance), a lighter weight, a more fuel-efficient engine, and a lower noise level. Sturdier materials were used for seat edges to maintain their appearance longer. The engine was designed with more torque than German models to give the car the quick start that Americans prefer. Ford's director of North American interior design called the instrument cluster "a work of art."

Quality control in manufacturing is usually based on conformance, specifically *conformance to specifications*. Specifications are targets and tolerances determined by designers of products and services. Targets are the ideal values for which production strives; tolerances are acceptable deviations from these ideal values. For example, a computer chip manufacturer might specify that the distance between pins on a computer chip should be 0.095 ± 0.005 inches. The value 0.095 is the target, and ± 0.005 is the tolerance. Thus, any pin distance between 0.090 and 0.100 would be acceptable. A lack of defects has constituted quality in manufacturing for many years. Many studies comparing domestic and foreign products focus on statistical measures of defects. However, the lack of defects alone will not satisfy or exceed customer expectations. Many top managers have stated that good quality of conformance is simply the "entry into the game." A better way to achieve distinction and delight customers is through improved product design. Thus, manufacturers are turning their attention toward improved design for achieving their quality and business goals.

Quality in Services

Service can be defined as "any primary or complementary activity that does not directly produce a physical product—that is, the non-goods part of the transaction between buyer (customer) and seller (provider)."[13] A service might be as simple as handling a complaint or as complex as approving a home mortgage. Service organizations include hotels; health, legal, engineering, and other professional services; educational institutions; financial services; retailers; transportation; and public utilities.

Today services account for nearly 80 percent of the U.S. workforce. The importance of quality in services cannot be underestimated, as statistics from a variety of studies reveal:[14]

- The average company never hears from more than 90 percent of its unhappy customers. For every complaint it receives, the company has at least 25 customers with problems, about one fourth of which are serious.
- Of the customers who make a complaint, more than half will do business again with that organization if their complaint is resolved. If the customer feels that the complaint was resolved quickly, this figure jumps to about 95 percent.
- The average customer who has had a problem will tell nine or ten others about it. Customers who have had complaints resolved satisfactorily will only tell about five others.
- It costs six times more to get a new customer than to keep a current customer.

So why do many companies treat customers as commodities? In Japan the notion of customer is equated with "honored guest." Service clearly should be at the forefront of a firm's priorities.

The service sector began to recognize the importance of quality several years after manufacturing had done so. This can be attributed to the fact that service industries had not confronted the same aggressive foreign competition that faced manufacturing. Another factor is the high turnover rate in service industry jobs, which typically pay less than manufacturing jobs. Constantly changing personnel makes establishing a culture for continuous improvement more difficult.

The production of services differs from manufacturing in many ways, and these differences have important implications for managing quality. The most critical differences are:

1. Customer needs and performance standards are often difficult to identify and measure, primarily because the customers define what they are, and each customer is different.
2. The production of services typically requires a higher degree of customization than does manufacturing. Doctors, lawyers, insurance salespeople, and food-service employees must tailor their services to individual customers. In manufacturing, the goal is uniformity.
3. The output of many service systems is intangible, whereas manufacturing produces tangible, visible products. Manufacturing quality can be assessed against firm design specifications, but service quality can only be assessed against customers' subjective, nebulous expectations and past experiences. Manufactured goods can be recalled or replaced by the manufacturer, but poor service can only be followed up by apologies and reparations.
4. Services are produced and consumed simultaneously, whereas manufactured goods are produced prior to consumption. In addition, many services must be performed at the convenience of the customer. Therefore, services cannot be stored, inventoried, or inspected prior to delivery as manufactured goods are. Much more attention therefore must be paid to training and building quality into the service as a means of quality assurance.
5. Customers often are involved in the service process and present while it is being performed, whereas manufacturing is performed away from the customer. For example, customers of a quick-service restaurant place their own orders, carry their food to the table, and are expected to clear the table when they have finished eating.
6. Services are generally labor intensive, whereas manufacturing is more capital intensive. The quality of human interaction is a vital factor for services that involve human contact. For example, the quality of hospital care depends heavily on interactions among the patients, nurses, doctors, and other medical staff. Hence, the behavior and morale of service employees is critical in delivering a quality service experience.
7. Many service organizations must handle very large numbers of customer transactions. For example, on a given business day, the Royal Bank of Canada might process more than 5.5 million transactions for 7.5 million

customers through 1,600 branches and more than 3,500 banking machines, and FedEx might handle more than 1.5 million shipments across the globe. Such large volumes increase the opportunity for error.

These differences made it difficult for many service organizations to fully understand and apply total quality principles when it was the rage in manufacturing, although many have caught up admirably.

Many service organizations have well-developed quality assurance systems. Many of them, however, are based on manufacturing analogies and tend to be more product-oriented than service-oriented. Many of the key dimensions of product quality apply to services. For instance, "on time arrival" for an airline is a measure of service performance; frequent flyer awards and "business class" sections represent features. A typical hotel's quality assurance system focuses on technical specifications such as properly made-up rooms (see the box, "Knock Three Times"). However, service organizations have special requirements that manufacturing systems cannot fulfill. The most important dimensions of service quality include the following:[15]

- *Time:* How much time must a customer wait?
- *Timeliness:* Will a service be performed when promised?
- *Completeness:* Are all items in the order included?
- *Courtesy:* Do frontline employees greet each customer cheerfully?
- *Consistency:* Are services delivered in the same fashion for every customer, and every time for the same customer?
- *Accessibility and convenience:* Is the service easy to obtain?

Knock Three Times[16]

Marriott has become infamous for its obsessively detailed standard operating procedures (SOPs), which result in hotels that travelers either love for their consistent good quality or hate for their bland uniformity. "This is a company that has more controls, more systems, and more procedural manuals than anyone—except the government," says one industry veteran. "And they actually comply with them." Housekeepers work with a 114-point checklist. One SOP: Server knocks three times. After knocking, the associate should immediately identify themselves in a clear voice, saying, "Room Service!" The guest's name is never mentioned outside the door.

Although people love to make fun of such procedures, they are a serious part of Marriott's business, and SOPs are designed to protect the brand. Recently, Marriott has removed some of the rigid guidelines for owners of hotels it manages, empowering them to make some of their own decisions on details.

- *Accuracy:* Is the service performed right the first time?
- *Responsiveness:* Can service personnel react quickly and resolve unexpected problems?

Service organizations must look beyond product orientation and pay significant attention to customer transactions and employee behavior. Several points that service organizations should consider are as follows:[17]

- The quality characteristics that a firm should control may not be the obvious ones. Customer perceptions are critical, although it may be difficult to define what the customer wants. For example, speed of service is an important quality characteristic, yet perceptions of speed may differ significantly among different service organizations and customers. Marketing and consumer research can play a significant role.
- Behavior is a quality characteristic. The quality of human interaction is vital in every transaction that involves human contact. For example, banks have found that the friendliness of tellers is a principal factor in retaining depositors.
- Image is a major factor in shaping customer expectations of a service and in setting standards by which customers evaluate that service. A breakdown in image can be as harmful as a breakdown in delivery of the service itself. Top management is responsible for shaping and guiding the image that the firm projects.
- Establishing and measuring service levels may be difficult. Service standards, particularly those relating to human behavior, are often set judgmentally and are hard to measure. In manufacturing, it is easy to quantify output, scrap, and rework. Customer attitudes and employee competence are not as easily measured.
- Quality control activity may be required at times or in places where supervision and control personnel are not present. Often work must be performed at the convenience of the customer. This calls for more training of employees and self-management.

These issues suggest that the approach to managing quality in services differs from that used in manufacturing. However, manufacturing can be seen as a set of interrelated services, not only between the company and the ultimate consumer but also within the organization. Manufacturing is a customer of product design; assembly is a customer of manufacturing; sales is a customer of packaging and distribution. If quality is meeting and exceeding customer expectations, then manufacturing takes on a new meaning, far beyond product orientation. Total quality provides the umbrella under which everyone in the organization can strive to create customer satisfaction.

Quality and E-Commerce

Without a doubt, e-commerce has transformed our lives dramatically over the past decade. Customers can research information, shop for almost any product; configure, price, and order computer systems; and take virtual test drives of automobiles and select from thousands of possible combinations of options on the Internet in the convenience of their homes. However, as many businesses found out, just setting up a Web site will not guarantee instant success. Several perceptive writers observed quality issues associated with e-commerce shortly before the dot-com crash in 2001.[18] They noted that two out of three online shoppers abandoned their transactions after placing items in their shopping cart, and that 27 percent of people in the United States who tried e-banking stopped because the services were too complicated or time-consuming, whereas another 25 percent stopped because they were unhappy with customer service. Without a good understanding of customer needs and how to create simple, bulletproof processes to meet those needs, many virtual businesses failed. E-commerce is about providing quality information, goods, and services rapidly and accurately.

One consultant identified a simple set of quality characteristics on which e-tailers should focus by analyzing customer behavior of various Web sites and through customer satisfaction surveys. He concluded that customers return to e-commerce sites because of:

- Valuable content that is intuitive and understandable, accurate, and current. This means that the design of the site must meet the customers' requirements, not the company's. If customers misinterpret information and make a wrong purchase, expect returned products and nonreturning customers. Product offerings and price data change quickly, and need to be kept accurate and current. One of the author's unfortunate experiences involved purchasing an accessory listed as compatible with a PDA only to find out that it didn't work, leading to wasted time getting a return authorization, repackaging, and returning the product (the Web site was corrected a few weeks later).
- Speed and reliability as reflected by page loading rates, and the number of clicks required to navigate through the site, and server uptime.
- Ease of use and the ability to meet expectations, meaning no confusion in navigating the site and finding the required information, eliminating the need to input duplicate data, and providing any needed assistance.[19]

These lessons were difficult to grasp initially, but many dot-coms have done it successfully. In fact, they have exploited information technology to develop and enhance customer relationships far beyond what traditional service organizations typically do. Amazon.com, from which many readers have probably ordered, has been extremely successful at this. They provide extensive information about products, such as reader reviews to help customers evaluate books, search used bookstores for out-of-print books, and even provide e-mail thank you letters a month or so after purchase.

However, although information technology reduces labor intensity and increases the speed of service, it can have adverse effects on other dimensions of quality. Some people, including some customers, will argue that customer satisfaction is decreased when less personal interaction takes place. However, consumers accustomed to the speed, efficiency, and superior customer service of e-commerce are demanding the same in retail transactions, simply adding more pressure to improve quality.

EVOLUTION OF TOTAL QUALITY PRINCIPLES

W. Edwards Deming, Joseph M. Juran, and Philip B. Crosby are regarded as true "management gurus" in the quality revolution. Their insights on measuring, managing, and improving quality have greatly influenced the practices that organizations use today. In this section we review their thinking as the foundation for modern concepts of TQ.

The Deming Philosophy[20]

Deming was trained as a statistician and worked for Western Electric during its pioneering era of statistical quality control development in the 1920s and 1930s. During World War II he taught quality control courses as part of the national defense effort. Although Deming taught many engineers in the United States, he was not able to reach upper management. After the war, Deming was invited to Japan to teach statistical quality control concepts. Top managers there were eager to learn, and he addressed 21 top executives who collectively represented 80 percent of the country's capital. They embraced Deming's message and transformed their industries. By the mid-1970s, the quality of Japanese products exceeded that of Western manufacturers, and Japanese companies had made significant penetration into Western markets. Deming received Japan's highest honor, the Royal Order of the Sacred Treasure. The former chairman of NEC Electronics once said, "There is not a day I don't think about what Dr. Deming meant to us."

Deming was virtually unknown in the United States until 1980 when NBC aired a white paper entitled "If Japan Can . . . Why Can't We?". This program made Deming a household name among corporate executives, and companies such as Ford invited him to assist them in revolutionizing their quality approaches. Deming worked with passion until his death in December 1993 at the age of 93, knowing he had little time left to make a difference in his home country. When asked how he would like to be remembered, Deming replied, "I probably won't even be remembered." Then after a long pause, he added, "Well, maybe . . . as someone who spent his life trying to keep America from committing suicide."[21]

Unlike other management gurus and consultants, Deming never defined or described quality precisely. In his last book, he stated, "A product or a service possesses quality if it helps somebody and enjoys a good and sustainable market."[22] Deming stressed that higher quality leads to higher productivity, which in turn leads to long-term competitive strength. The Deming "chain reaction," shown in Figure 1.1, summarizes this view.

The Deming philosophy of quality and management is complex; indeed, several books have been written in an effort to explain and interpret it. Deming summarized his philosophy in what he called "A System of Profound Knowledge," which consists of four parts: (1) appreciation for a system, (2) understanding process variation, (3) theory of knowledge, and (4) psychology.

Systems

A **system** is a set of functions or activities within an organization that work together to achieve organizational goals. A system must have an aim, a purpose to which it continually strives. Deming believed that the aim of any system is for everybody—stockholders, employees, customers, community, the environment—to gain over the long term. Stockholders can realize financial benefits, employees can have opportunities for training and education, customers can receive products and services that meet their needs and create satisfaction, the community can benefit from business leadership, and the environment can benefit from socially responsible management.

For example, a McDonald's restaurant can be viewed as a system. It consists of the order-taker/cashier subsystem, grill and food preparation subsystem, drive-through subsystem, and so on. The components of any system must work together for the system to be effective. If the order taker places the wrong order or the grill breaks down, customers will not get what they

FIGURE 1.1   THE DEMING CHAIN REACTION

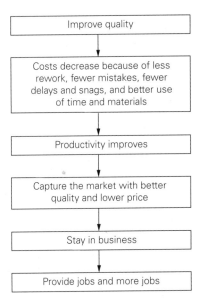

want. To run any system, managers must understand the interrelationships among all subsystems and the people that work in them (would a McDonald's operate successfully without a store manager?).

Deming emphasized that management's job is to optimize the system. By making decisions that are best for only a small part of the system (often encouraged by competition), we suboptimize. Suboptimization will prevent a system from achieving its goal. For example, a common practice is to purchase materials or services at the lowest bid. Inexpensive materials may be of such inferior quality that they will cause excessive costs in adjustment and repair during manufacture and assembly. Although the purchasing department's track record might look good, the overall system will suffer.

This concept applies to managing people also. Pitting individuals or departments against each other for resources is self-destructive. The individuals or departments will perform to maximize their expected gain, not that of the firm as a whole. Systems require cooperation.

Variation

Just as no two snowflakes are exactly alike, no two outputs from any production process are exactly alike. A production process contains many sources of variation. Different lots of material will vary in strength, thickness, or moisture content, for example. Cutting tools will have inherent variation in strength and composition. During manufacturing, tools will experience wear, machine vibrations will cause changes in settings, and electrical fluctuations will cause variations in power. Operators may not position parts on fixtures consistently. The complex interaction of all these variations in materials, tools, machines, operators, and the environment cannot be understood. Variation due to any individual source appears random; however, their combined effect is stable and can usually be predicted statistically. Factors that are present as a natural part of a process are called **common causes of variation**.

Common causes generally account for about 80 to 90 percent of the observed variation in a production process. The remaining 10 to 20 percent result from **special causes of variation**, often called **assignable causes**. Special causes arise from external sources that are not inherent in the process. A bad batch of material purchased from a supplier, a poorly trained operator, excessive tool wear, or miscalibration of measuring instruments are examples of special causes. Special causes result in unnatural variations that disrupt the random pattern of common causes. Hence, they are generally easy to detect using statistical methods, and it is usually economical to remove them.

A system governed only by common causes is stable and its performance can be predicted. Special causes disrupt the predictable pattern. (Think of your commute to work or school—what happens when a snowstorm or accident occurs?) Unfortunately, managers either overreact to common cause variation or ignore special causes when they do occur. If they try to "fix" a common cause, they will actually increase the variation in the system. If they ignore special causes, they miss the opportunity to improve.

In Deming's view, variation is the chief culprit of poor quality. In mechanical assemblies, for example, variations from specifications for part dimensions lead to inconsistent performance and premature wear and failure. Likewise, inconsistencies in service frustrate customers and damage a firm's image.

Variation also increases the cost of doing business. An example was published in the Japanese newspaper *Asahi* comparing the cost and quality of Sony televisions at plants in Japan and San Diego.[23] The color density of all the units produced at the San Diego plant was within specifications, although the density of some of those shipped from the Japanese plant was not (see Figure 1.2). However, the average loss per unit at the San Diego plant was $0.89 greater than that of the Japanese plant. This was because units out of specification at the San Diego plant were adjusted within the plant, adding cost to the process. Furthermore, a unit adjusted to just within specifications was more likely to generate customer complaints than a unit that was closer to the original target value, therefore incurring higher field service costs. Figure 1.2 shows that fewer U.S.-produced sets met the target value for color density. The distribution of quality in the Japanese plant was more uniform around the target value, and even though some units were out of specification, the total cost was less.

By minimizing variation, everyone benefits. The producer benefits by having less need for inspection, less scrap and rework, and higher productivity. The consumer is assured that all products have similar quality characteristics; this is especially important when the consumer is another firm using large quantities of the product in its own manufacturing or service operations. The only way to reduce common cause variation is to change the technology of the process—the machines, people, materials, methods, or measurement system. Only management can make these decisions; pressuring workers to perform at higher quality levels will only result in frustration. However, special cause variation can be identified by workers through the use of control charts, which are introduced in Chapter 7. This requires training and management support.

FIGURE 1.2   VARIATION IN U.S.-MADE VERSUS JAPANESE-MADE TELEVISION COMPONENTS

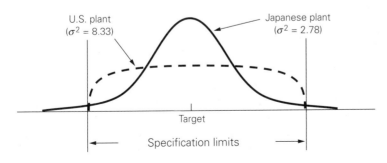

U.S. plant
($\sigma^2 = 8.33$)

Japanese plant
($\sigma^2 = 2.78$)

Target

Specification limits

Theory of Knowledge

The third part of Profound Knowledge is called the "theory of knowledge," which is a branch of philosophy concerned with the nature and scope of knowledge, its presuppositions and bases, and the general reliability of claims to knowledge. Deming was influenced greatly by Clarence Irving Lewis, author of *Mind and the World*.[24] Lewis stated, "There is no knowledge without interpretation. If interpretation, which represents an activity of the mind, is always subject to the check of further experience, how is knowledge possible at all? . . . An argument from past to future at best is probable only, and even this probability must rest upon principles which are themselves more than probable."

What this basically means is that management decisions should be driven by facts, data, and justifiable theories, not solely by opinions. Experience cannot be tested or validated, but good theories supported by data can establish a cause-and-effect relationship that can be used for prediction. Theory explains why things happen. For example, many companies have jumped on the latest fads advocated by popular business consultants, only to find that they result in failure. This often happens because they simply did not understand the context and assumptions required to make them work successfully.

Psychology

People design products and processes, serve customers, and achieve results. Psychology helps us to understand people, interactions between people and circumstances, interactions between leaders and employees, and the drivers of behavior. No leader can manage well without understanding these factors and incorporating them in key decisions. More important, people inherit the right to enjoy work. Psychology helps us to nurture and preserve people's positive innate attributes.

Little in Deming's system of Profound Knowledge is original. The concept of common and special causes of variation was developed by Walter Shewhart in the 1920s; behavioral theories to which Deming subscribes were developed in the 1960s; systems theory was refined by management scientists from the 1950s through the 1970s; and scientists in all fields have long understood the relationships among prediction, observation, and theory. Deming's contribution was in tying together some basic concepts. He recognized the synergy among these diverse subjects and developed them into a theory of management.

Peter Scholtes, a noted consultant, makes some salient observations about the failure to understand the components of Profound Knowledge:[25]

1. When people don't understand systems:
   - they see events as individual incidents rather than the net result of many interactions and interdependent forces;
   - they see the symptoms but not the deep causes of problems;

- they don't understand how an intervention in one part of [an organization] can cause havoc in another place or at another time;
- they blame individuals for problems even when those individuals have little or no ability to control the events around them; and
- they don't understand the ancient African saying, "It takes a whole village to raise a child."

2. When people don't understand variation:
   - they don't see trends that are occurring;
   - they see trends where there are none;
   - they don't know when expectations are realistic;
   - they don't understand past performance so they can't predict future performance;
   - they don't know the difference between prediction, forecasting, and guesswork;
   - they give others credit or blame when those people are simply either lucky or unlucky. This usually occurs because people tend to attribute everything to human effort, heroics, frailty, error, or deliberate sabotage, no matter what the systemic cause; and they are less likely to distinguish between fact and opinion.

3. When people don't understand psychology:
   - they don't understand motivation or why people do what they do;
   - they resort to carrots and sticks and other forms of induced motivation that have no positive effect and impair the relationship between the motivator and the one being motivated;
   - they don't understand the process of change and the resistance to it;
   - they revert to coercive and paternalistic approaches when dealing with people; and
   - they create cynicism, demoralization, demotivation, guilt, resentment, burnout, craziness, and turnover.

4. When people don't understand the theory of knowledge:
   - they don't know how to plan and accomplish learning and improvement;
   - they don't understand the difference between improvement and change; and
   - problems will remain unsolved, despite their best efforts.

Deming espoused a transformation in management with his "14 Points for Management," listed in Table 1.1. It is important to realize that the 14 Points date back several decades to when many organizations were ruled by autocratic managers who were driven by short-term profits and who had little regard for engaging the workforce or interest in quality improvement. Although management practices today are vastly different from when Deming first began to preach his philosophy, the 14 Points still convey important insights for managers. Failure to heed them might only lead to repeating the mistakes of the past.

TABLE 1.1   DEMING'S 14 POINTS FOR MANAGEMENT[26]

1. Create and publish to all employees a statement of the aims and purposes of the company or other organization. The management must demonstrate constantly their commitment to this statement.
2. Learn the new philosophy, top management and everybody.
3. Understand the purpose of inspection, for improvement of processes and reduction of cost.
4. End the practice of awarding business on the basis of price tag alone.
5. Improve constantly and forever the system of production and service.
6. Institute training.
7. Teach and institute leadership.
8. Drive out fear. Create trust. Create a climate for innovation.
9. Optimize toward the aims and purposes of the company the efforts of teams, groups, staff areas.
10. Eliminate exhortations for the workforce.
11. (a) Eliminate numerical quotas for production. Instead, learn and institute methods for improvement.
    (b) Eliminate MBO (Management by Objective). Instead, learn the capabilities of processes and how to improve them.
12. Remove barriers that rob people of pride of workmanship.
13. Encourage education and self-improvement for everyone.
14. Take action to accomplish the transformation.

1. *Management Commitment*—Making a commitment to drive improvement within an organization is still difficult for managers. Even when managers have conducted a thorough assessment of their organization and know what they need to change, many do not effectively follow up on opportunities.[27] Reasons range from denial ("We can't be that bad!") to excuses ("We have a lot of irons on the fire right now."). Effective leadership begins with commitment, and we will revisit this issue in Part IV of this book.

2. *Learn the New Philosophy*—Deming recognized that historical methods of management built on early twentieth-century principles of Frederick Taylor, such as quota-driven production, work measurement, and adversarial work relationships, simply don't work. Although leadership begins with commitment, it also requires new ways of thinking. Today, many companies have adopted the principles of total quality that we will study as an essential part of their business strategy (see Chapter 3). However, people change jobs and organizations generally have a short memory—both need to continually renew themselves to learn new approaches and relearn many older ones. Today's "new philosophies" include the Baldrige framework and Six Sigma, which will be studied in Chapter 2.

3. *Understand Inspection*—In the mid-twentieth century, inspection had been the principal means for quality control; companies employed dozens or even hundreds of people who inspected for quality on a full-time basis and added little value to the product. Deming suggested that inspection should be used judiciously as an information-gathering tool for improvement. Today, this new role of inspection has been integrated into the quality management practices of most companies. However, few managers truly know how variation affects their processes and inspection practices. Through better understanding, managers can eliminate unnecessary inspection, thus reducing non–value-added costs, or perform critical inspection tasks that avoid more expensive downstream repairs.

4. *End Price Tag Decisions*—Purchasing decisions traditionally have been driven by cost through competitive bidding, not by quality. Costs due to inferior materials and components increase costs in later stages of production and can far exceed the "savings" realized through competitive bidding. Deming promoted the recognition of purchasing departments as "internal suppliers" to production, and urged businesses to establish long-term relationships with a few suppliers, leading to loyalty and enhanced opportunities for improvement. Today's emphasis on supply chain management (SCM) reflects the achievement of Point 4. SCM focuses heavily on a system's view of the supply chain with the objective of minimizing total supply chain costs and developing stronger partnerships with suppliers. These ideas will be addressed in Chapter 4.

5. *Improve Constantly*—Traditionally, continuous improvement was not a common business practice; today it is recognized as a necessary means for survival in a highly competitive and global business environment. Improvements are necessary in both design and operations. Improved design of goods and services comes from understanding customer needs and continual market surveys and other sources of feedback, and from understanding the manufacturing and service delivery process. Improvements in operations are achieved by reducing the causes and impacts of variation, and engaging all employees to innovate and seek ways of doing their jobs more efficiently and effectively. The tools for improvement are constantly evolving, and organizations need to ensure that their employees understand and apply them effectively, which requires training, the focus of the next Point. Improvement will be studied further in Chapters 6 and 7.

6. *Institute Training*—People are an organization's most valuable resource; they want to do a good job, but they often do not know how. Not only does training result in improvements in product and service quality and organizational performance, but it adds to worker morale, and demonstrates to workers that the company is dedicated to helping them and investing in their future. Training must transcend such basic job skills as running a machine or following the script when talking to customers.

Training should include tools for identifying, diagnosing, analyzing, and solving quality and performance problems. Today, many companies have excellent training programs for technology related to direct production but still fail to enrich the ancillary skills of their workforce. Here is where some of the most lucrative opportunities exist to make an impact on key business results.

7. *Institute Leadership*—The job of management is leadership and guidance, not supervision and work direction. Supervisors should be coaches, not policemen, and supervision should provide the link between management and the workforce. Leadership can help to eliminate fear and encourage teamwork. Leadership was, is, and will continue to be a challenging issue in every organization, particularly as new generations of managers replace those who have learned to lead. Thus, this Point of Deming's will always be relevant to organizations.

8. *Drive Out Fear*—Fear in work manifests in many ways: fear of reprisal, fear of failure, fear of the unknown, fear of change. Fear encourages short-term, selfish thinking, not long-term improvement for the benefit of all. Fear is a cultural issue for all organizations. Creating a culture without fear is a slow process but can be destroyed in an instant with a transition of leadership and a change in corporate policies. Therefore, today's managers need to continue to be sensitive to the impact that fear can have on their organizations. Positive motivation will be studied in Chapter 9.

9. *Optimize Team Efforts*—Barriers between individuals and departments lead to poor quality, because "customers" do not receive what they need from their "suppliers." This is often the result of internal competition for raises or performance ratings. Teamwork helps to break down barriers between internal customers and suppliers. The focus should be on meeting customer needs and improving processes. Teamwork is an important means of achieving a company's goals, and we discuss this further in Chapter 8.

10. *Eliminate Exhortations*—Motivation can be better achieved through trust and leadership than slogans. Slogans calling for improved quality usually assume that poor quality results from a lack of motivation. Workers cannot improve solely through motivational methods when the system in which they work constrains their performance. On the contrary, they will become frustrated and their performance will decrease further. Improvement stems from better organizational design and use of data-driven processes (see Chapters 5 through 7).

11. *Eliminate Quotas and MBO (Management by Objective)*—Numerical quotas encourage short- rather than long-term behavior, particularly if rewards or performance appraisals are tied to meeting quotas. Deming acknowledged that goals are useful, but numerical goals set for others without incorporating a method to reach the goal generate frustration and resentment. Furthermore, variation in the system year-to-year or

quarter-to-quarter—a 5 percent increase or a 6 percent decrease, for example—makes comparisons meaningless. Management must understand the reasons for variation or poor performance and provide the means to improve, rather than focus on short-term goals.

12. *Remove Barriers to Pride in Workmanship*—Some organizations view workers as a "commodity." Factory workers are given monotonous tasks; provided with inferior machines, tools, or materials; told to run defective items to meet sales pressures; and report to supervisors who know nothing about the job. This attitude has given way to increased levels of empowerment, providing workers with a sense of ownership of their work processes and higher self-esteem. This will be explored further in Chapter 9.

13. *Institute Education*—"Training" in Point 6 refers to job skills; education refers to self-development. Firms have a responsibility to develop the value and self-worth of the individual. Investing in people is a powerful motivation method. Today, many companies understand that elevating the general knowledge base of their workforce—outside of specific job skills—returns many benefits. However, others still view this task as a cost that can be easily cut when financial tradeoffs must be made.

14. *Take Action*—Any cultural change begins with top management and includes everyone. Changing an organizational culture generally meets with skepticism and resistance that many firms find difficult to deal with, particularly when many of the traditional management practices Deming felt must be eliminated are deeply ingrained in the organization's culture. We address this further in Chapter 11.

Deming's principles continue to live in many organizations today (see the box on Louisville Slugger).

The Juran Philosophy

Joseph M. Juran joined Western Electric in the 1920s during its pioneering days in the development of statistical methods for quality. He spent much of his time as a corporate industrial engineer. In 1951 Juran wrote, edited, and published one of the most comprehensive books on quality, the *Quality Control Handbook*, which has been revised many times. Juran taught quality principles to the Japanese in the 1950s just after Deming and was a principal force in their quality reorganization.

Juran took a more pragmatic approach to change than Deming, advocating approaches that are designed to fit into a company's current strategic business planning with minimal risk of rejection. Juran views the pursuit of quality on two levels: (1) the mission of the firm as a whole is to achieve high product quality; and (2) the mission of each individual department in the firm is to achieve high production quality. Senior management must play an active and enthusiastic leadership role in the quality management process.

Louisville Slugger Hits a Home Run with Deming[28]

Hillerich & Bradsby Co. (H&B) has been making the Louisville Slugger brand of baseball bat for more than 115 years. In the mid-1980s, the company faced significant challenges from market changes and competition. CEO Jack Hillerich attended a four-day Deming seminar, which provided the basis for the company's current quality efforts. Returning from the seminar, Hillerich decided to see what changes that Deming advocated were possible in an old company with an old union and a history of labor-management problems. Hillerich persuaded union officials to attend another Deming seminar with five senior managers.

Following the seminar, a core group of union and management people developed a strategy to change the company. They talked about building trust and changing the system "to make it something you want to work in." Employees were interested, but skeptical. To demonstrate their commitment, managers examined Deming's 14 Points, and picked several they believed they could make progress on through actions that would demonstrate a serious intention to change. One of the first changes was the elimination of work quotas that were tied to hourly salaries and a schedule of warnings and penalties for failures to meet quotas. Instead, a team-based approach was initiated. Although a few workers took advantage of the change, overall productivity actually improved as rework decreased because workers were taking pride in their work to produce things the right way first. H&B also eliminated performance appraisals and commission-based pay in sales. The company also has focused its efforts on training and education, resulting in an openness for change and capacity for teamwork. Today, the Deming philosophy is still the core of H&B's guiding principles.

Juran contends that employees at different levels of an organization speak in different "languages." (Deming believes statistics should be the common language.) Top management speaks in the language of dollars, workers speak in the language of things, and middle management must be able to speak both languages and translate between dollars and things. Thus, to get top management's attention, quality issues must be cast in the language they understand—dollars. Juran advocates the accounting and analysis of quality costs to focus attention on quality problems.

At the operational level, Juran focuses on increasing conformance to specifications through elimination of defects, supported extensively by statistical tools for analysis. Juran defines quality as "fitness for use." This is broken down into four categories: quality of design, quality of conformance, availability, and field service. Quality of design focuses on market research, the product concept, and design specifications. Quality of conformance includes technology, manpower, and management. Availability focuses on reliability, maintainability, and logistical support. Field service quality comprises promptness, competence, and integrity.

Juran's prescriptions focus on three major aspects of quality called the Quality Trilogy (a registered trademark of the Juran Institute): quality planning: the process for preparing to meet quality goals; quality control: the process for meeting quality goals during operations; and quality improvement: the process for breaking through to unprecedented levels of performance.

Quality planning begins with identifying customers, both external and internal, determining their needs, and developing product features that respond to customer needs. Quality control involves determining what to control, establishing units of measurement so that data may be objectively evaluated, establishing standards of performance, measuring actual performance, interpreting the difference between actual performance and the standard, and taking action on the difference. Quality improvement is best achieved by identifying specific projects for improvement, getting the right people involved, diagnosing causes of poor performance, developing remedies for the causes, proving that the remedies will be effective, and providing control to hold improvements.

The Crosby Philosophy

Philip B. Crosby, who passed away in 2001, was corporate vice president for quality at International Telephone and Telegraph (ITT) for 14 years after working his way up from line inspector. After leaving ITT, he established Philip Crosby Associates in 1979 to develop and offer training programs. He also was the author of several popular books. His first book, *Quality Is Free*, sold about one million copies, and is credited with bringing quality to the attention of top American executives.

The essence of Crosby's quality philosophy is embodied in what he calls the Absolutes of Quality Management and the Basic Elements of Improvement.

Crosby's Absolutes of Quality Management are as follows:

- *Quality means conformance to requirements not elegance.* Crosby dispels the myth that quality is simply a feeling of "excellence." Requirements must be clearly stated so that they cannot be misunderstood. Requirements are communication devices and are ironclad. Once a task is done, one can take measurements to determine conformance to requirements. The nonconformance detected is the absence of quality. Quality problems become nonconformance problems—that is, variation in output. Setting requirements is the responsibility of management.
- *There is no such thing as a quality problem.* Problems must be identified by the individuals or departments that cause them. There are accounting problems, manufacturing problems, design problems, front-desk problems, and so on. Quality originates in functional departments, not in the quality

department, and the burden of responsibility for such problems lies with the functional departments. The quality department should measure conformance, report results, and lead the drive to develop a positive attitude toward quality improvement. This is similar to Deming's Point 3.

- *There is no such thing as the economics of quality: it is always cheaper to do the job right the first time.* Crosby supports the premise that "economics of quality" has no meaning. Quality is free. What costs money are all the actions that involve not doing jobs right the first time. The Deming Chain Reaction provides a similar message.

- *The only performance measurement is the cost of quality.* The cost of quality is the expense of nonconformance. Crosby notes that most companies spend 15 to 20 percent of their sales dollars on quality costs. A company with a well-run quality management program can achieve a cost of quality that is less than 2.5 percent of sales, primarily in the prevention and appraisal categories. Crosby's program calls for measuring and publicizing the cost of poor quality. Quality cost data are useful in calling problems to management's attention, selecting opportunities for corrective action, and tracking quality improvement over time. Such data provide visible proof of improvement and recognition of achievement. Juran also supports this theme.

- *The only performance standard is Zero Defects.* According to Crosby:

> Zero Defects is a performance standard. It is the standard of the craftsperson regardless of his or her assignment. . . . The theme of ZD is do it right the first time. That means concentrating on preventing defects rather than just finding and fixing them.
>
> People are conditioned to believe that error is inevitable; thus they not only accept error, they anticipate it. It does not bother us to make a few errors in our work . . . To err is human. We all have our own standards in business or academic life— our own points at which errors begin to bother us. It is good to get an A in school, but it may be OK to pass with a C.
>
> We do not maintain these standards, however, when it comes to our personal life. If we did, we should expect to be shortchanged every now and then when we cash our paycheck; we should expect hospital nurses to drop a constant percentage of newborn babies . . . We as individuals do not tolerate these things. We have a dual standard: one for ourselves and one for our work.
>
> Most human error is caused by lack of attention rather than lack of knowledge. Lack of attention is created when we assume that error is inevitable. If we consider this condition carefully and pledge ourselves to make a constant conscious effort to do our jobs right the first time, we will take a giant step toward eliminating the waste of rework, scrap, and repair that increases cost and reduces individual opportunity.[29]

Juran and Deming, by contrast, would argue that it is pointless, if not hypocritical, to exhort a line worker to produce perfection, because the overwhelming majority of imperfections are due to poorly designed manufacturing systems beyond the worker's control.

Crosby's Basic Elements of Improvement included *determination*—commitment by the organizational leadership, *education*, and *implementation*. Unlike Juran and Deming, Crosby's program was primarily behavioral. He placed more emphasis on management and organizational processes for changing corporate culture and attitudes than on the use of statistical techniques. Like Juran and unlike Deming, his approach fits well within existing organizational structures.

PRINCIPLES OF TOTAL QUALITY

The philosophies of Deming, Juran, and Crosby addresssed management deficiencies of the times and laid the foundation for the principles of modern quality management that have transcended time. A definition of *total quality* was endorsed in 1992 by the chairs and CEOs of nine major U.S. corporations in cooperation with deans of business and engineering departments of major universities, and recognized consultants:

> Total Quality (TQ) is a people-focused management system that aims at continual increase in customer satisfaction at continually lower real cost. TQ is a total system approach (not a separate area or program) and an integral part of high-level strategy; it works horizontally across functions and departments, involves all employees, top to bottom, and extends backward and forward to include the supply chain and the customer chain. TQ stresses learning and adaptation to continual change as keys to organizational success.[30]

Adopting a TQ philosophy requires significant changes in organization design, work processes, and culture. Organizations use a variety of approaches. Some emphasize the use of quality tools, such as Six Sigma, but have not made the necessary fundamental changes in their processes and culture. It is easy to focus on tools and techniques but very hard to understand and achieve the necessary changes in human attitudes and behavior. Others have adopted a behavioral focus in which the organization's people are indoctrinated in a customer-focused culture but fail to incorporate error prevention and design quality or continuous improvement efforts. Still other companies focus on operational improvement efforts but fail to focus on what is truly important to the customer. One-dimensional approaches can have some short-term success but do not seem to work well over time. Total quality requires a comprehensive effort that encompasses a total change in thinking, not a new collection of tools.

The philosophy of TQ involves some very basic management concepts: (1) customer and stakeholder focus; (2) a process orientation; (3) continuous improvement and learning; (4) empowerment and teamwork; (5) management by fact; and (6) visionary leadership that views TQ as a strategic organizational asset.

Customer and Stakeholder Focus

The customer is the judge of quality. Understanding customer needs, both current and future, and keeping pace with changing markets requires effective strategies for listening to and learning from customers, measuring their satisfaction relative to competitors, and building relationships. Customer needs—particularly differences among key customer groups—must be linked closely to an organization's strategic planning, product design, process improvement, and workforce training activities. Satisfaction and dissatisfaction information are important because understanding them leads to the right improvements that can create satisfied customers who reward the company with loyalty, repeat business, and positive referrals. Creating satisfied customers includes prompt and effective response and solutions to their needs and desires as well as building and maintaining good relationships. A business can achieve success only by understanding and fulfilling the needs of customers. From a total quality perspective, all strategic decisions a company makes are "customer-driven." In other words, the company shows constant sensitivity to emerging customer and market requirements. This requires an awareness of developments in technology and rapid and flexible response to customer and market needs.

Customer-driven firms measure the factors that drive customer satisfaction. A company close to its customer knows what the customer wants, how the customer uses its products, and anticipates the needs that the customer may not even be able to express. It also continually develops new techniques to obtain customer feedback. Customer opinion surveys and focus groups can help companies understand customer requirements and values. Some companies require their sales and marketing executives to meet with random groups of key customers on a regular basis. Other companies bring customers and suppliers into internal product design and development meetings. Banks, which traditionally have been rather customer-unfriendly—charging customers to speak to real people, for checking accounts, and for ATM access—have made some dramatic changes (see box "Banks Are Discovering that Customers Are People").

TQ views everyone inside the enterprise as a customer of an internal or external supplier, and a supplier of an external or internal customer. Internal customers—the recipients of any work output, such as the next department in a manufacturing process or the order-picker who receives instructions from an order entry clerk—are as important in assuring quality as are external customers who purchase the product. Failure to meet the needs of internal

---

Banks Are Discovering that Customers Are People[31]

Washington Mutual, known as "WaMu," is leading the charge (no pun intended) and changing traditional banking practices to become more customer-focused. In doing so, it has vaulted to become the seventh-largest financial institution in the U.S. and the number 2 home loan lender, increasing its assets by 18,000 percent since 1990. Being located in the same city as the Starbucks chain (Seattle), WaMu has drawn upon Starbucks' customer-friendly practices to make its operations more attuned to today's customer, for example, by hiring khaki-clad employees with retail experience and playing hip music in its "stores"—its term for branches. Everyone works on commission, from the branch manager on down; a beginning teller can earn up to $50,000 in his or her first year. WaMu was named one of Fortune's best places to work. Other banks are following suit; Bank One sent hundreds of employees out into the streets of Chicago to invite potential customers to visit the bank.

---

customers will likely affect external customers. Employees must view themselves as customers of some employees and suppliers to others. Employees who view themselves as both customers of and suppliers to other employees understand how their work links to the final product. After all, the responsibility of any supplier is to understand and meet customer requirements in the most efficient and effective manner possible.

Customer focus extends beyond the consumer and internal relationships, however. Society represents an important customer of every organization. A world-class company, by definition, is an exemplary corporate citizen. Business ethics, public health and safety measures, concern for the environment, and sharing quality-related information in the company's business and geographic communities are required. In addition, company support—within reasonable limits of its resources—of national, industry, trade, and community activities and the sharing of nonproprietary quality-related information demonstrate far-reaching benefits.

Process Orientation

The traditional way of viewing an organization is by surveying the vertical dimension—by keeping an eye on an organization chart. However, work gets done (or fails to get done) horizontally or cross-functionally, not hierarchically. One can no longer view an enterprise as a collection of separate, highly specialized individual performers and units, loosely linked by a functional hierarchy.

A **process** is a sequence of activities that is intended to achieve some result. According to AT&T, a process is how work creates value for customers.[32] We typically think of processes in the context of production: the collection of activities and operations involved in transforming *inputs* (physical facilities, materials, capital, equipment, people, and energy) into *outputs* (products and services). Common types of production processes include machining, mixing, assembly, filling orders, or approving loans. However, nearly every major activity within an organization involves a process that crosses traditional organizational boundaries. For example, an order fulfillment process might involve a salesperson placing the order; a marketing representative entering it on the company's computer system; a credit check by finance; picking, packaging, and shipping by distribution and logistics personnel; invoicing by finance; and installation by field service engineers. This is illustrated in Figure 1.3.

TQ views the enterprise as a system of interdependent processes, linked laterally over time through a network of collaborating (internal and external) suppliers and customers. Each process is connected to the enterprise's mission and purpose through a hierarchy of micro- and macro-processes. Every process contains sub-processes and is also contained within a higher process. This structure of processes is repeated throughout the hierarchy. A process perspective links all necessary activities together and increases one's understanding of the entire system, rather than focusing on only a small part (see box "Better Processes, Better Software"). Many of the greatest opportunities for improving organizational performance lie in the organizational interfaces—those spaces between the boxes on an organization chart.

FIGURE 1.3   PROCESS VERSUS FUNCTION

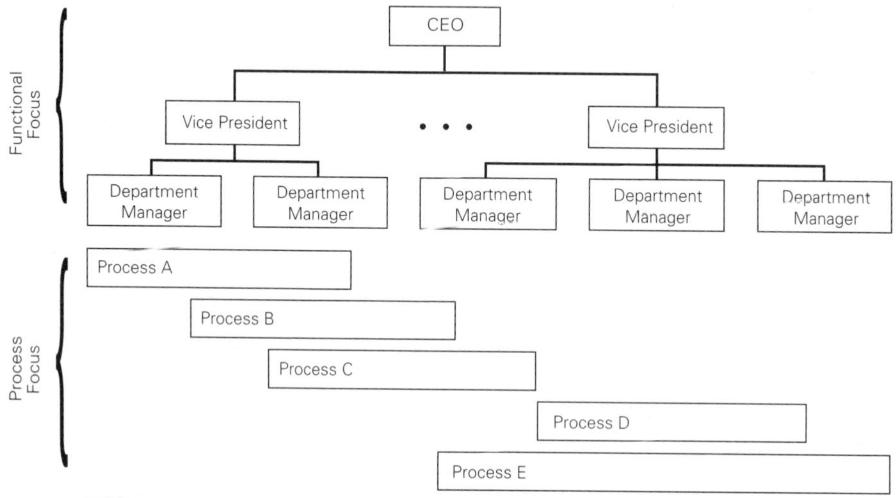

Source: James R. Evans and William M. Lindsay, *The Management and Control of Quality*, 6th ed., South-Western Thomson Learning, 2002.

Better Processes, Better Software[33]

Software crashes and bugs can be irritating at best, and fatal at worst. For example, thousands of trucks and school busses were recalled in 2000 because of faulty software in antilock brakes, and flaws in an altitude warning system were partially responsible for the crash of a Korean Air jet in 1997 that killed 228 people. Experts note that most software is thrown together without adequate testing or a focus on the process of software creation. Defects stem from the complexity of today's software requirements, pressure to bring out products quickly, lack of liability, and poor work methods. Most programs in testing have 5 to 10 defects per 1,000 lines of code, and it would take 50 person-years to find all of them. In response, Microsoft's Trustworthy Computing initiative taught programmers to spend more time in planning and thinking about quality, even delaying product launch of Windows Server 2003 software by a year. The Sustainable Computing Consortium stated that engineers and programmers have no way to measure the reliability of their designs, and is trying to create automated tools to analyze software for reliability. Taking a better process-focused approach to software design and development might prevent the "blue screens of death" and, more important, save lives.

Continuous Improvement and Learning

In TQ, the environment in which the enterprise interacts is changing constantly. If the enterprise continues to do what it has done in the past, its future performance relative to the competition will deteriorate. Management's job, therefore, is to provide the leadership for continual improvement and innovation in processes and systems, products, and services.

Continuous improvement is part of the management of all systems and processes. Achieving the highest levels of performance requires a well-defined and well-executed approach to continuous improvement and learning. "Continuous improvement" refers to both incremental and "breakthrough" improvement. Improvement and learning need to be embedded in the way an organization operates. This means they should be a regular part of daily work, seek to eliminate problems at their source, and be driven by opportunities to do better as well as by problems that need to be corrected.

Improvements may be of several types:

- enhancing value to the customer through new and improved products and services;
- improving productivity and operational performance through better work processes and reductions in errors, defects, and waste;

- improving flexibility, responsiveness, and cycle time performance; and
- improving organizational management processes through learning.

Improving Products and Services

Careful research is required to determine the needs of customers, and those needs must be reflected in the design of products and services. A Japanese professor, Noriaki Kano, suggests that three classes of customer needs exist:

- *Dissatisfiers*—those needs that are expected in a product or service, such as a radio, heater, and required safety features in an automobile. Such items generally are not stated by customers but are assumed as given. If they are not present, the customer is dissatisfied.
- *Satisfiers*—needs that customers say they want, such as air-conditioning or a compact disc player in a car. Fulfilling these needs creates satisfaction.
- *Delighters/exciters*—new or innovative features that customers do not expect. When first introduced, antilock brakes and air bags were examples of exciters. Newer concepts still under development, such as collision avoidance systems, offer other examples. The presence of such unexpected features, if valued, leads to high perceptions of quality.

The importance of this classification is realizing that although satisfiers are relatively easy to determine through routine marketing research, special effort is required to elicit customer perceptions about dissatisfiers and delighters/exciters. Over time, delighters/exciters become satisfiers as customers become used to them (as is the case today with antilock brakes and air bags), and eventually satisfiers become dissatisfiers (customers are dissatisfied if they are not provided). Therefore, companies must innovate continually and study customer perceptions to ensure that their needs are being met.

Improving Work Processes

Quality excellence derives from well-designed and well-executed work processes and administrative systems that stress prevention. Improvements in the work processes may lead to major reductions in scrap and defects and, hence, to lower costs, as the example about Dell Computer Corporation shows (see box "Michael Dell's Touch for Quality").

Improving Flexibility, Responsiveness, and Cycle Time

Success in globally competitive markets requires a capacity for rapid change and flexibility. Electronic commerce, for instance, requires more rapid, flexible, and customized responses than traditional market outlets. **Flexibility** refers to the ability to adapt quickly and effectively to changing requirements. This might mean rapid changeover from one product to another, rapid response to changing demands, or the ability to produce a wide range of customized services. Flexibility might demand special strategies such as modular designs, sharing components, sharing manufacturing lines, and specialized training for employees. It also involves outsourcing decisions, agreements with key suppliers, and innovative partnering arrangements.

Michael Dell's Touch for Quality[34]

Although Dell Computer Corporation's PCs have had some of the highest quality ratings in the industry, CEO Michael Dell became obsessed with finding a way to reduce their failure rates. The key, he believed, was to reduce the number of times that each hard drive—the most sensitive part of a PC—was handled during assembly. Production lines were revamped, and the number of "touches" were reduced from over 30 to less than 15. Soon after, the rate of rejected hard drives fell by 40 percent, and the overall failure rate for the company PCs dropped by 20 percent.

One important business metric that complements flexibility is cycle time. **Cycle time** refers to the time it takes to accomplish one cycle of a process—for instance, the time a customer orders a product to the time that it is delivered, or the time to introduce a new product. Reductions in cycle time serve two purposes. First, they speed up work processes so that customer response is improved. Second, reductions in cycle time can only be accomplished by streamlining and simplifying processes to eliminate non–value-added steps such as rework. This forces improvements in quality by reducing the potential for mistakes and errors. By reducing non–value-added steps, costs are reduced as well. Thus, cycle time reductions often drive simultaneous improvements in organization, quality, cost, and productivity. Significant reductions in cycle time cannot be achieved simply by focusing on individual subprocesses; cross-functional processes must be examined all across the organization. This forces the company to understand work at the organizational level and to engage in cooperative behaviors.

Agility is a term that is commonly used to characterize flexibility and short cycle times. Agility is crucial to such customer-focused strategies as mass customization, which requires rapid response and flexibility to changing consumer demand. Enablers of agility include close relationships with customers to understand their emerging needs and requirements, empowering employees as decision makers, effective manufacturing and information technology, close supplier and partner relationships, and breakthrough improvement.

Learning

"Learning" refers to understanding why changes are successful through feedback between practices and results, and leads to new goals and approaches. A learning cycle has four stages:

1. planning,
2. execution of plans,
3. assessment of progress, and
4. revision of plans based upon assessment findings.

Measurements provide critical data and information about key processes, outputs, and results. When supported by sound analytical approaches that project trends and infer cause-and-effect relationships, measurements provide an objective foundation for learning, leading to better customer, operational, and financial performance.

Empowerment and Teamwork

A company's success depends increasingly on the knowledge, skills, and motivation of its workforce. Employee motivation and success depend increasingly on having opportunities to learn and to practice new skills. These can be fostered by empowerment and teamwork. The traditional view of motivation is often summarized by McGregor's Theory X model of motivation: workers dislike work and require close supervision and control. TQ organizations support the premise of Theory Y: workers are self-motivated, seek responsibility, and exhibit a high degree of imagination and creativity at work. TQ managers provide leadership rather than overt intervention in the processes of their subordinates, who are viewed as process managers rather than functional specialists.

Much evidence supports the role of good human resource practices in organizational performance. For example, one study of call centers found that quit rates were lower and sales growth was higher in firms that emphasized high skills, employee participation in decision making and in teams, and human resource incentives such as better pay and job security.[35]

Empowerment simply means giving people authority—to make decisions based on what they feel is right, have control over their work, take risks and learn from mistakes, and promote change; for example, employees can make decisions that satisfy customers without a lot of bureaucratic hassles, and barriers between levels are removed. Empowerment requires, as the management philosophy of Wainwright Industries states, *a sincere belief and trust in people*. A survey by Annandale, Virginia-based Mastery-Works Inc. concluded that employees leave their organizations because of trust, observing that "Lack of trust was an issue with almost every person who had left an organization."[36]

In TQ formal and informal mechanisms encourage and facilitate teamwork and team development across the entire enterprise. Competitive behavior—one person against another or one group against another—is not a natural state in TQ. TQ reward systems recognize individual as well as team contributions and reinforce cooperation. The areas for teamwork and collaboration are broad, particularly in education, training, and meaningful involvement of employees in the improvement of processes that they affect and that affect their work. Teamwork can be viewed in three ways:

1. *Vertical*—teamwork between top management and lower-level employees.
2. *Horizontal*—teamwork within work groups and across functional lines (often called cross-functional teams).
3. *Interorganizational*—partnerships with suppliers and customers.

Vertical Teamwork

Everyone must participate in quality improvement efforts. The person in any organization who best understands his or her job and how it can be improved is the one performing it. Vertical teamwork is the sharing of responsibility among organizational levels through empowerment. This often represents a profound shift in the philosophy of senior management, as the traditional philosophy is that the workforce should be "managed" to conform to existing business systems. Dana Commercial Credit Corporation has a "just do it" policy to empower its people to act on ideas for improvement without prior approval.

Companies can encourage participation by recognizing team and individual accomplishments, sharing success stories throughout the organization, encouraging risk taking by removing the fear of failure, encouraging the formation of employee involvement teams, implementing suggestion systems that act rapidly, provide feedback, and reward implemented suggestions, and providing financial and technical support to employees to develop their ideas.

Employees need training in skills related to performing their work and to understanding and solving quality-related problems. Frontline workers need the skills to listen to customers; manufacturing workers need specific skills in developing technologies; and all employees need to understand how to use measurements to drive continuous improvement. Training brings all employees to a common understanding of goals and objectives and the means to attain them. Training usually begins with awareness of quality management principles and is followed by specific skills in quality improvement. Training should be reinforced through on-the-job applications of learning, involvement, and empowerment.

Horizontal Teamwork

Problem solving and process improvement are best performed by cross-functional work teams. For example, a product development team might consist of designers, manufacturing personnel, suppliers, salespeople, and customers. Texas Instruments Defense Systems & Electronics Group (since acquired by Raytheon) employs corporation teams to work on corporate-level goals, employee effectiveness teams to prevent potential problems in specific work areas, and department action teams to solve departmental problems. Granite Rock Company, with fewer than 400 employees, has about 100 functioning teams, ranging from 10 corporate quality teams to project teams, purchasing teams, task forces, and function teams composed of people who do the same job at different locations.

Interorganizational Partnerships

Partnerships must be created both internally and externally. Companies should seek to build partnerships that serve mutual and larger community interests. Partnerships might include those that promote labor-management cooperation such as agreements with unions that entail employee development, cross-training, or new work organizations. Rather than dictating specifications for purchased parts, a company might develop specifications jointly with suppliers to take advantage of the suppliers' manufacturing capabilities. Internal partnerships might also involve creating network relationships among company units to improve flexibility, responsiveness, and knowledge sharing. External partnerships might be with suppliers, customers, or educational organizations. Partnerships permit the blending of a company's core competencies with complementary strengths and capabilities of partners.

Suppliers, in particular, are important partners who need vital information, product designs, performance feedback and assistance, and so on. The aim of the partnership is innovation, reduction in variation of critical characteristics of supplied materials, lower costs, and better quality. The aim may be enhanced by reducing the number of suppliers and establishing long-term relationships.

One example of supplier partnerships involves local telephone companies who provide AT&T access to their customers. Following divestiture, AT&T established a Financial Assurance Organization to check the accuracy of access charges and to correct errors. By 1989, AT&T employed 1,100 people working to duplicate the supplier's access-billing system, anticipate charges, and resolve problems. In 1990, AT&T began a joint effort with Pacific Bell to design a single access billing verification process—involving both supplier and customer—that shifted focus from correction to prevention, moved accountability for accuracy to the supplier, and replaced post-bill resolution with pre-bill certification. As a result, the time needed in the validation process declined from three months to 24 hours, accuracy went up, and costs came down.

Management by Fact

Organizations need good performance measures for three reasons:

- to lead the entire organization in a particular direction; that is, to drive strategies and organizational change;
- to manage the resources needed to travel in this direction by evaluating the effectiveness of action plans; and
- to operate the processes that make the organization work and continuously improve.[37]

Data and information support analysis at all organizational levels. The types of information and how it is disseminated and aligned with organizational levels are equally vital to success. At the work level, data provide real-time information to identify assignable reasons for variation, determine root causes, and take corrective action as needed. This might require lean communication channels consisting of bulletins, computerized quality reports, and digital readouts of part dimensions to provide immediate information on what is happening and how things are progressing.

At the process level, operational performance data such as yields, cycle times, and productivity measures help managers determine whether they are doing the right job, whether they are using resources effectively, and whether they are improving. Information at this level generally is aggregated; for example, daily or weekly scrap reports, customer complaint data obtained from customer service representatives, or monthly sales and cost figures faxed in from field offices.

At the organization level, quality and operational performance data from all areas of the firm, along with relevant financial, market, human resource, and supplier data, form the basis for strategic planning and decision making. Such information is highly aggregated and obtained from many different sources throughout the organization.

A company should select performance measures and indicators that best represent the factors that lead to improved customer, operational, and financial performance. These typically include:

- customer satisfaction,
- product and service performance,
- market assessments,
- competitive comparisons,
- supplier performance,
- employee performance, and
- cost and financial performance.

A comprehensive set of measures and indicators tied to customer and company performance requirements provides a clear basis for aligning all activities of the company with its goals.

Visionary Leadership and a Strategic Orientation

Leadership for quality is the responsibility of top management. Senior leadership must set directions; create a customer orientation, clear quality values, and high expectations that address the needs of all stakeholders; and build them into the way the company operates. Senior leaders need to commit to the development of the entire workforce and should encourage participation, learning, innovation, and creativity throughout the organization. Reinforcement of the values and expectations requires the substantial personal commitment and involvement of senior management. Through their personal roles in planning, reviewing company quality performance, and recognizing employees for quality achievement, the senior leaders serve as role models, reinforcing the values and encouraging leadership throughout the organization.

If commitment to quality is not a priority, any initiative is doomed to failure. Lip service to quality improvement is the kiss of death. The CEO of Motorola, one of the first Baldrige winners, had quality as the first agenda item at every top management meeting. He frequently left after quality was discussed, sending the message that once quality was taken care of, financial and other matters would take care of themselves. When The Ritz-Carlton Hotel Company opens a new facility, the CEO works alongside the house-keeping and kitchen staffs making beds and washing dishes. Imagine the message these actions send to the workers! Many companies have a corporate quality council made up of top executives and managers, which sets quality policy and reviews performance goals within the company. Quality should be a major factor in strategic planning and competitive analysis processes.

Many of the management principles and practices required in a TQ environment may be contrary to long-standing practice. Top managers, ideally starting with the CEO, must be the organization's TQ leaders. The CEO should be the focal point providing broad perspectives and vision, encouragement, and recognition. The leader must be determined to establish TQ initiatives and committed to sustain TQ activities through daily actions in order to overcome employees' inevitable resistance to change.

Unfortunately, many organizations do not have the commitment and leadership of their top managers. This does not mean that these organizations cannot develop a quality focus. Improved quality can be fostered through the strong leadership of middle managers and the workforce. In many cases, this is where quality begins. Leadership provides people with opportunities for personal growth and development. People are able to take pride and joy in learning and accomplishment, and the ability of the enterprise to succeed is enhanced. People are active contributors, valued for their creativity and intelligence. Every person is a process manager presiding over the transformation of inputs to outputs of greater value to the enterprise and to the ultimate customer. In the long run, however, an organization cannot sustain quality initiatives without strong leadership at the top.

Achieving quality and market leadership requires a strong future orientation and a willingness to make long-term commitments to key stakeholders—customers, employees, suppliers, stockholders, the public, and the community. A focus on quality as a driver of strategic business planning is characteristic of TQ organizations; in others we usually see an emphasis on finance and marketing. Strategic business planning should be the driver for quality excellence throughout the organization and needs to anticipate many changes, such as customers' expectations, new business and partnering opportunities, the global and electronic marketplace, technological developments, new customer segments, evolving regulatory requirements, community/societal expectations, and strategic changes by competitors. Quality goals are the cornerstone of the business plan. Measures such as customer satisfaction, defect rates, and process cycle times receive as much attention in the strategic plan as financial and marketing objectives. Plans, strategies, and resource allocations need to reflect these influences. Improvements do not happen overnight. The success of market penetration by Japanese manufacturers evolved over several decades.

The principles of TQ are embodied in the business philosophy of many leading companies (see the box on KARLEE for an example of a company that exemplifies these principles). Our purpose in this book is to provide a solid link between concepts of total quality and the traditional management areas of organization theory, organizational behavior, and strategy. When any company begins to think of how to improve, it will be led to the various approaches that are united under the TQ concept. Today, total quality is a matter of survival.

TQ AND AGENCY THEORY[38]

One model in organizational theory that has received considerable attention is agency theory. Agency theory is based on the concept of an agency relationship, in which one party (the principal) engages another party (the agent) to perform work. Agency theory makes the assumption that individuals in agency relationships are utility maximizers and will always take actions to enhance their self-interests. As a consequence, when authority is delegated to agents on behalf of the principal, agents may use this power to promote their own well-being, at the expense of the principal. Monitoring is a central issue in agency theory, because it is a primary mechanism used by both parties to maintain and govern the relationship.

Agency theory provides a stark contrast to TQ. TQ views the management system as one based on social and human values, whereas agency theory is based on an economic perspective that removes people from the equation. Whereas agency theory propounds the belief that people are self-interested and opportunistic and that their rights are conditional and proportional to the value they add to the organization, TQ suggests that people are also motivated by interests other than self, and that people have an innate right to be respected. Agency theory assumes an inherent conflict of goals between agents and principals, and that agent goals are aligned with principal goals through formal contracts. In TQ, everyone in the organization shares common goals and a continuous improvement philosophy, and goals are aligned through adoption of TQ practices and culture. Sharing information to achieve these goals is fundamental to TQ, whereas agency theory suggests that information may be concealed to advance self-interests. TQ takes a long-term perspective based on continuous improvement, whereas agency theory focuses on short-term achievement of the contract between the principal and agent. In TQ, risk taking is necessary in order to innovate, whereas agency theory assumes that risks are to be minimized and shared between the two parties.

Finally, TQ leaders provide a quality vision and play a strategic role in the organization; leaders in agency theory develop control mechanisms and engage in monitoring. TQ proponents argue that it is a superior strategy because a quality culture can be sustained and is less costly in the long term.

Bringing TQ to Life at KARLEE[39]

KARLEE is a contract manufacturer of precision sheet metal and machined components for telecommunications, semiconductor, and medical equipment industries, located in Garland, Texas. Some of the ways it exemplifies the principles of TQ are described below.

Customer Focus. KARLEE made a strategic decision to carefully select customers that support its values—particularly a systematic approach to business and performance management, desire for long-term partnerships, and global leadership. Management and Team Leaders work with each customer to establish current requirements and future needs, and each customer is assigned a three-person Customer Service team that is on call 24 hours a day for day-to-day production issues.

Process Orientation. Processes such as prototype development, scheduling, production setup, fabrication, assembly, and delivery have process owners responsible for maintaining the process to customer requirements. A Quality Assurance team member works with manufacturing teams to create process documentation.

Continuous Improvement and Learning. Teams use a structured approach to evaluate and improve their processes, documenting them, and presenting a status report of improvements to senior leaders and the KARLEE Steering Committee. Teams benchmark competitors, "best practice" companies, and customers to learn from others.

Empowerment and Teamwork. Production and delivery processes are designed around cell manufacturing. Teams are responsible for knowing their customer's requirements and producing according to those requirements.

Teams are empowered to change targets recommended during strategic planning if they believe it will help them achieve higher performance, as well as to schedule work, manage inventory, and design the layout of their work areas.

Management by Fact. Teams analyze defect data, customer-reported problems, and control charts generated during production to identify problems and opportunities for improvement. Every business goal and project has defined methods for measurement, and senior leaders meet weekly to review company performance and ensure alignment with directions and plans.

Leadership and Strategic Planning. Senior Executive Leaders (SELs) and the KARLEE Leadership Committee (KLC) set the strategic direction of the company, and communicate and reinforce values and expectations through performance reviews, participation in improvement or strategic projects, regular interactions with customers and team members, and recognition of team member achievements.

All this has contributed to an annual average increase in sales growth of 35 percent from 1995 to 2000, and high levels of customer and employee satisfaction, and quality and operational performance.

Agency theory advocates suggest that high performance may be achieved by appropriately structuring agents' contracts and aligning their interests. As we shall see in Chapter 3, some elements of agency theory are evident in strategy implementation approaches within a TQ environment. Both theories have shaped the activities of scholars and practitioners, and research has yet to arrive at a definitive conclusion. However, it is difficult to argue with the results that firms choosing a clear TQ path have achieved.

TQ AND ORGANIZATIONAL MODELS[40]

Although TQ is a new way of thinking about the management of organizations, it is not a totally new paradigm. When compared with well-known organizational models, it can be seen as capturing many aspects of these established models and amplifying them by providing a useful methodology. Three major organizational models that management theorists have studied are the mechanistic, organismic, and cultural models of organizations. Contrasts between TQ and these models are summarized in Table 1.2. The mechanistic model, described by classical management theorists, views an organization as a tool or a machine designed solely to create profits for its owners. Work is reduced to elementary tasks with a focus on efficiency, conformity, and compliance. Although both the mechanistic model and TQ assume that the organization exists to achieve a specific performance goal, TQ has a broader definition of quality. It takes more of an open-systems perspective, which views managers as leaders and visionaries rather than as individuals who plan, organize, direct, and control. It broadens employees' roles; uses a horizontal, rather than vertical, work organization; and focuses on continuous improvement rather than stability. Narrow-minded managers and those who criticize TQ often view it in a mechanistic sense and do not see the broader implications.

The organismic model views organizational systems as living organisms that depend on their environments for resources and adjust the behavior of their parts to maintain the properties of the whole within acceptable limits. This model assumes that systems goals, such as the need to survive, displace performance goals, such as profit. TQ is similar in that survival in competitive environments is often the primary motivation for adopting it. Customer satisfaction as a definition of quality is compatible with this notion. In the organismic model, organizations are not autonomous entities. This is consistent with the notion of partnership development espoused by TQ: vision replaces fear as a motivator and driver of management actions; employees work for shared beliefs and values; horizontal communication becomes as important as vertical communication and direction in stressing coordination and organizational rationality; and the organization must adapt to a broad array of external forces. It is evident that TQ shares many similarities with this organizational model. This helps explain why many practitioners have

TABLE 1.2 SUMMARY OF TQ AND ORGANIZATIONAL MODELS (ADAPTED FROM SPENCER, 1994)

Dimension	TQ Paradigm	Mechanistic Model	Organismic Model	Cultural Model
Goal	Long-term survival	Organizational efficiency and performance	Organizational survival	Meet individual needs; human development
Definition of quality	Satisfying or delighting the customer	Conformance to standards	Customer satisfaction	Constituent satisfaction
Role/nature of environment	Blurred organization and environmental boundaries	Objective; outside boundary	Objective; inside boundary	Enacted/ boundaries defined through relationships
Role of management	Focus on improvement and creating a system that can produce quality outcomes	Coordinate and provide visible control	Coordinate and provide invisible control by creating vision and system	Coordinate and mediate negotiations regarding vision, system, rewards
Role of employees	Employees are empowered; training and education provide needed skills	Passive; follow orders	Reactive/self-control within system parameters	Active/self-control; participate in creation of vision, system
Structural rationality	Horizontal processes beginning with suppliers and ending with customers and supported by teams	Chain of command (vertical)	Process flow (horizontal and vertical)	Mutual adjustment in any direction
		Technical rationality	Organizational rationality	Political rationality
Philosophy toward change	Change, continuous improvement, and learning are encouraged	Stability is valued; learning arises from specialization	Change and learning assist adaptation	Change and learning are valued in themselves

viewed TQ as something new, whereas many academics recognize its roots in systems theory that was popular decades ago.

The cultural model views an organization as a collection of cooperative agreements entered into by individuals with free will. The organization's culture and social environment are enacted or socially constructed by organization members. From the perspective of this model, the goal of an organization is to serve the diverse needs of all whom it affects—its stakeholders—a view often expressed by TQ philosophers. Because of the multiplicity of stakeholders, quality has many meanings, although some degree of consensus regarding the organization's values and purposes is needed. Although TQ generally assumes that organizations must adapt to the expectations of customers, more recent views of building partnerships and sharing of best practices (even with competitors) is consistent with the cultural model. In the cultural model, managers take on a more distinctive leadership role, relinquishing control and sharing power in order to meet the needs of the many individuals in the organization; employees have greater voice in establishing organizational goals; all structural decisions are value-based and have clear implications with regard to individual autonomy (political rationality); and learning needs are driven not by adaptation to environmental forces but in response to individual needs. Many of these attributes are characteristic of recent trends in the evolution of TQ themes in high-performing organizations.

In summary, TQ appears to have evolved from reactionary influences against the mechanistic model of management and embraced many of the characteristics of the organismic model. Recent trends, however, suggest that ideas from the cultural model are influencing the maturity of TQ in modern organizations. This will become more evident as we discuss the Malcolm Baldrige Criteria for Performance Excellence in the next chapter.

REVIEW AND DISCUSSION QUESTIONS

1. Explain why quality became the most important issue facing American business in the 1980s. In addition to economic competition from Japan, what other factors may have contributed to the importance that quality has assumed?
2. Cite several examples in your own experience in which your expectations were met, exceeded, or not met in purchasing goods or services. How did you regard the company after your experience?
3. How might the definition of quality apply to your college or university? Provide examples of who some customers are and how their expectations can be met or exceeded.
4. Think of a product with which you are familiar. Describe the eight "multiple quality dimensions" for this product that are listed in this chapter.
5. What might the eight "multiple quality dimensions" mean for a college or university? For a classroom?
6. Explain the differences between manufacturing and service organizations and their implications for quality.
7. Summarize the Deming management philosophy. Why has it been controversial?
8. Explain the 14 Points in the context of the four categories of Profound Knowledge.
9. How might Deming's concepts of variation be applied to the classroom?

10. Why doesn't the Deming Chain Reaction terminate with "Increased Profits"? Would this contradict the basis of Deming's philosophy?

11. Provide an example of a system with which you are familiar and define its purpose. Examine the interactions within the system and whether the system is managed for optimization.

12. Describe a process with which you are familiar. List some factors that contribute to common cause variation. Cite some examples of special causes of variation in this process.

13. How does the theory of knowledge apply to education? What might this mean for improving the quality of education?

14. Explain the implications of not understanding the components of Profound Knowledge as suggested by Peter Scholtes.

15. Extract three or four key themes in Deming's 14 Points. How might the 14 Points be grouped in a logical fashion?

16. What implications might the 14 Points have for college education? What specific proposals might you suggest as a means of implementing the 14 Points at your school?

17. Discuss the interrelationships among Deming's 14 Points. How do they support each other? Why must they be viewed as a whole rather than separately?

18. The following themes form the basis for Deming's philosophy. Classify the 14 Points into these categories and discuss the commonalities within each category.
    a. Organizational purpose and mission
    b. Quantitative goals
    c. Revolution of management philosophy
    d. Elimination of seat-of-the-pants decisions
    e. Cooperation building
    f. Improvement of manager-worker relations

19. Summarize Juran's philosophy. How is it similar to and different from Deming's?

20. What is Juran's Quality Trilogy? Is it any different from management approaches in other functional areas of business, such as finance?

21. What implications might Juran's Quality Trilogy have for colleges and universities? Would most faculty and administrators agree that the emphasis has been on quality control rather than planning and improvement?

22. How could you apply Juran's Quality Trilogy to improve your personal approach to study and learning?

23. Summarize the Crosby philosophy. How does it differ from Deming and Juran?

24. Which quality philosophy—Deming, Juran, or Crosby—do you personally feel more comfortable with? Why?

25. Describe the key elements of total quality.

26. Why is a customer focus a critical element of TQ?
27. How might you apply the concepts of total quality to your personal life? Consider your relations with others and your daily activities such as being a student, belonging to a fraternity or professional organization, and so on.
28. Make a list of your personal "customers." What steps might you take to understand their needs and remain "close" to them?
29. Cite an example in which you did not purchase a product or service because it lacked "dissatisfiers" as defined in the chapter. Cite another example in which you received some "exciters/delighters" that you did not expect.
30. In what ways might the lack of top management leadership in a quality effort hinder or destroy it?
31. Explain the various areas within an organization in which continuous improvement and learning may take place.
32. Why is measurement important in a TQ effort?
33. Examine some process with which you are familiar. Make a list of ways that the process can be measured and improved. What difficulties might you face in implementing these ideas?
34. Describe the three ways of viewing teamwork.
35. Describe some possible ways in which vertical, horizontal, and inter-organizational teamwork can be applied at a college or university.
36. What does empowerment mean? How might an employee really know that he or she is truly empowered?
37. Have you ever felt restricted in your work because of a lack of empowerment? Can you cite any experiences in which you noticed a lack of empowerment in a person who was serving you? Why is this such a difficult concept to implement in organizations?
38. Explain the key differences between "traditional" management practices and those in a TQ environment.
39. Prepare a self-assessment questionnaire designed to determine whether an organization follows traditional management practices or a TQ approach. You might consider applying it to some organization.
40. How does TQ differ from agency theory?
41. Explain the mechanistic, organismic, and cultural models of organizations, and how TQ is similar to or different from them.
42. Investigate recent quality initiatives in either health care or education. What have these organizations learned from business? What unique issues do they face with respect to quality? How are they trying to overcome them?
43. Discuss the implications of the following statements with respect to introducing TQ principles in a college classroom.[41] Do you agree with them? How do they reflect TQ principles? What changes in traditional learning approaches would they require for both students and instructors?

    a. Embracing a customer focus doesn't mean giving students all As and abandoning standards.

    b. If students fail, the system has failed.

    c. Faculty members are customers of those who teach prerequisites.

    d. Treating students as customers means allowing students to choose not to come to class.

    e. Completing the syllabus is not a measure of success.

    f. New and tenured instructors should visit each other's classrooms.

    g. Eliminate performance appraisals based on classroom evaluations.

    h. No matter how good the test, luck will be involved.

44. For each of the principles of TQ (customer focus, process orientation, etc.) describe what you might see if you spent time in each of the following types of organizations:

    a. one with primarily traditional management practices;

    b. one that has a beginning awareness of the importance of TQ;

    c. one that has developed an effective system for TQ;

    d. one that has outstanding, world-class management practices.

CASES

Building Trust through Quality at Gerber[42]

Gerber is the leader in the development, manufacturing, and marketing of foods and products for children from birth through age three. The Gerber baby picture—which accompanies everything from strained carrots and banana cookies to teething rings and diapers—has developed into one of the most recognizable brand images in the world. The Gerber company has long been a leader in using TQ approaches to uphold its reputation. Although Gerber's quality programs have gone through various stages over the years, its goal has remained the same: to make sure consumers continue to see the Gerber baby, which has gone through periodic updatings of its own, as an emblem of excellence.

    The company began in the Gerber family kitchen in 1927. After watching her husband's messy attempt at straining peas for their daughter, Dorothy Gerber suggested that the task would be better accomplished at the family-owned canning plant. Daniel Gerber agreed and was so taken by the idea that within a year he had manufactured enough of five baby food flavors to begin national distribution. Understanding the concern parents have for what their babies consume, Gerber paid close attention to what went into the food and the processes involved in manufacturing it. This was one of the company's first steps toward committing to quality.

    While Gerber's quality systems have undergone several improvements over the years, teamwork was "one of the biggest things to hit quality at Gerber," says George Sheffier, a retired, 35-year Gerber veteran. He believes that fostering a team atmosphere taught Gerber how to help employees adjust to change, gave the company a head start on the diversity issues of the 1990s, and was critical when Gerber began spreading quality techniques throughout its plants.

Gerber experimented with teams in the 1970s but by the end of the decade the company still lacked the benefits a solid team atmosphere provided. An attempt to implement the concept to a more intense degree in 1983 was met by employee skepticism. Realizing that management and supervisors were themselves having a difficult time adjusting to the team methodology, Gerber hired consultants to teach facilitation skills. Soon supervisors were holding meetings not only to familiarize workers with the team concept but to discuss change—how employees felt about it and what the company could do to help make it easier. As employees began feeling more comfortable working in teams, they voiced concerns about trouble spots in systems and processes. Gerber also learned that the team atmosphere was a necessity in linking quality to every process in the company.

Once employees recognized the value of teamwork, the company began taking quality functions out of the quality department and spreading them throughout the plant. The goal of integrating quality into manufacturing was to build quality into the product on a more consistent basis. By expanding quality responsibilities to frontline operations, Gerber hoped to increase process control and reduce line inspections. To accomplish this purpose, Gerber teamed quality assurance (QA) staff with frontline operators in 1988 to establish procedures for each process. While hesitant at first, frontline employees liked the fact that they were involved in the process from the start and were able to determine their own auditing criteria. Within 18 months, Gerber was able to cut its number of line inspectors and increase its quality auditing functions.

As quality became widespread through the organization, Gerber needed to teach basic quality tools to its frontline operators. As with the team concept, however, employees accepted the new responsibilities once they realized the values of the tools. Employees came to prefer the use of these techniques, which enabled them to become more directly involved with the quality of the final product. The company also established management incentives for integrating quality into its manufacturing process. Many senior managers, for example, began to be compensated for maintaining a high level of consumer trust through the quality of the final product. Today, the company continues to improve the quality techniques it applies to each part of the manufacturing process. Its most recent project has been to install new software from SAS Institute Inc. The software gives employees instant access to data regarding the impact on the final product of each station in each process.

Although Gerber has always tried to create systems that meet the expectations of parents, the company didn't always utilize feedback from its customers. It wasn't until the company faced its largest crisis to date that Gerber realized the need to link the customer's voice with the quality system. This period, in the 1980s, was a defining point for Gerber, according to Gerber senior QA manager Jim Fisher. The company lost some trust in the eyes of the consumer, stemming from an instance of consumer tampering that brought Gerber unwanted national attention. Before the company had the opportunity to prove itself, the case snowballed into a media frenzy, leaving consumers questioning Gerber's quality. Gerber's history of continuous improvement and its well-documented manufacturing processes paid off, however. The investigation put the company under a microscope, with Fisher flying across the country to inspect jars of food and the Food and Drug Administration (FDA) spending three weeks reviewing Gerber's systems and records. In the end, the FDA gave the company a clean bill of health, and any claims against Gerber dissipated once the FDA's report became available to the public.

What Gerber found was that it needed a system allowing consumers to contact it directly with suggestions, complaints, and questions pertaining to Gerber products or infant care in general. Gerber's consumer relations department, established and operated by Dorothy Gerber in 1938, continued to receive a steady flow of letters, but the system wasn't timely and the feedback wasn't closely tied to either the quality or the safety department. Consequently, Gerber opened its telephone information service (800-4-GERBER) in 1986. The system provided a notable change for the company's quality discipline as it allowed telephone operators to log customer information into a database. In turn, trend analysis could be conducted and consumer demands could be integrated into the product development process. Because parents are up with their infants throughout the night, the company extended the department's operating hours in 1991, capturing information 24 hours a day. Gerber takes a daily average of 2,400 calls, accommodating all languages, and employs a team of letter correspondents to answer the 45,000 letters it receives yearly.

In 1947 Gerber management came to believe that the best way to ensure the safety of its product was to control as much of the food-making process as possible. At that time the company began forming alliances with its growers, giving Gerber better control of produce cultivation and allowing it to keep track of the pesticides growers used. By the 1950s, Gerber had implemented a proactive approach to controlling its manufacturing processes. The Gerber product analysis laboratories were formed in 1963 to provide data on the composition of ingredients, monitor the quality of internal and external water sources, and provide the analytical information needed to establish food formulations.

The company also created procedures to monitor potential hazards and ensured correctly functioning processes by employing a thermal processing staff. The staff was to determine the amount of time a product needs to be cooked to become commercially sterile, conduct audits of production facilities to ensure that processing equipment was operating correctly, and review and improve thermal processing systems. The thermal processing staff grew so large that it became its own department in 1994, and it continues to work closely with Gerber's quality and safety departments today.

Gerber's dedication to performance excellence continues to serve the company well. Thinking beyond quality trends in pesticide control continues to put the company ahead of others as Gerber investigates what it calls environmental quality—examining environmental factors not traditionally considered, such as pollutants carried into the plant by a supplier. This enabled Gerber to introduce sugarless and starch-free formulations less than a year after a 1995 report criticized the baby food industry for its use of fillers. By linking quality practices throughout its processes and making statistical information available to all employees, Gerber continues to enhance its quality.

Discussion Questions
1. From what definitional perspective does Gerber view quality?
2. How does Gerber exhibit the fundamental principles of total quality described in this chapter?

The Reservation Clerk

Mary Matthews works for an airline as a reservation clerk. Her duties include answering the telephone, making reservations, and providing information to customers. Her supervisor told her to be courteous and not to rush callers. However, the supervisor also told her that she must answer 25 calls per hour so that the department's account manager can prepare an adequate budget. Mary comes home each day frustrated because the computer is slow in delivering information that she needs, and sometimes reports no information. Without information from the computer, she is forced to use printed directories and guides.

Discussion Questions
1. What is Mary's job? What might Deming have said about this situation?
2. Drawing upon Deming's principles, outline a plan to improve this situation.

The Reservation Nightmare[43]

H. James Harrington, a noted quality consultant, related the following story in *Quality Digest* magazine: I called to make a flight reservation just an hour ago. The telephone rang five times before a recorded voice answered. "Thank you for calling ABC Travel Services," it said. "To ensure the highest level of customer service, this call may be recorded for future analysis." Next, I was asked to select from one of the following three choices: "If the trip is related to company business, press 1. Personal business, press 2. Group travel, press 3." I pressed 1.

I was then asked to select from the following four choices: "If this is a trip within the United States, press 1. International, press 2. Scheduled training, press 3. Related to a conference, press 4." Because I was going to Canada, I pressed 2.

Now two minutes into my telephone call, I was instructed to be sure that I had my customer identification card available. A few seconds passed and a very sweet voice came on, saying, "All international operators are busy, but please hold because you are a very important customer." The voice was then replaced by music. About two minutes later, another recorded message said, "Our operators are still busy, but please hold and the first available operator will take care of you." More music. Then yet another message: "Our operators are still busy, but please hold. Your business is important to us." More bad music. Finally the sweet voice returned, stating, "To speed up your service, enter your 19-digit customer service number." I frantically searched for their card, hoping that I could find it before I was cut off. I was lucky; I found it and entered the number in time. The same sweet voice came back to me, saying, "To confirm your customer service number, enter the last four digits of your social security number." I pushed the four numbers on the keypad.

The voice said: "Thank you. An operator will be with you shortly. If your call is an emergency, you can call 1-800-CAL-HELP, or push all of the buttons on the telephone at the same time. Otherwise, please hold, as you are a very important customer." This time, in place of music, I heard a commercial about the service that the company provides.

At last, a real person answered the telephone and asked, "Can I help you?" I replied, "Yes, oh yes." He answered, "Please give me your 19-digit customer service number, followed by the last four digits of your social security number so I can verify who you are." (I thought I gave these numbers in the first place to speed up service. Why do I have to rattle them off again?)

I was now convinced that he would call me Mr. 5523-3675-0714-1313-040. But, to my surprise, he said: "Yes, Mr. Harrington. Where do you want to go and when?" I explained that I wanted to go to Montreal the following Monday morning. He replied: "I only handle domestic reservations. Our international desk has a new telephone number: 1-800-1WE-GOTU. I'll transfer you." A few clicks later a message came on, saying: "All of our international operators are busy. Please hold and your call will be answered in the order it was received. Do not hang up or redial, as it will only delay our response to your call. Please continue to hold, as your business is important to us."

Discussion Questions

1. Summarize the service failures associated with this experience.
2. What might the travel agency have done to guarantee a better service experience for Mr. Harrington? How do your suggestions relate to the TQ principles?

Skilled Care Pharmacy[44]

Skilled Care Pharmacy, located in Mason, Ohio, is a $25 million privately held regional provider of pharmaceutical products delivered within the long-term care, assisted living, hospice, and group home environments. The following products are included within this service:

- medications and related billing services;
- medical records;
- information systems;
- continuing education; and
- consulting services to include pharmacy, nursing, dietary, and social services.

The key customer groups that Skilled Care provides services to include the senior population housed within the extended and long-term care environments. Customers within this sector depend on Skilled Care to provide their daily pharmaceutical needs at a competitive rate. Because of the high risk factor of its business, these needs require that the right drug be delivered to the right patient at the right time. Moreover, depending on the environment being served, different medication dispensing methods may be used such as vials, multidose packaging, or unit dose boxes. Also, depending on the customer type, specific delivery requirements may be implemented to better serve the end user.

Skilled Care's dedication and commitment to continuous quality improvement is evident throughout its internal and external operations. By reflecting on the principles needed to attain quality success across all levels of customers, Skilled Care adopted the quality policy statement shown in Figure 1.4. Skilled Care's employee population includes 176 culturally diverse associates committed to a substance-free workplace. The team

FIGURE 1.4   SKILLED CARE PHARMACY'S QUALITY POLICY

Our Quality Policy	
S	Services and products that meet or exceed both our internal and external customers' expectations
C	**Leading to** Complete customer satisfaction
P	**Resulting in** People working together to enchance the lives of those served

includes associates with all levels of educational training representing many of the following disciplines: pharmacists, pharmacy technicians, medical data entry, accountants, billing specialists, nurses, human resources, sales/marketing, purchasing, administrative and administrative assistance, delivery, customer service representatives, and IT certified personnel. At times, multifaceted work teams are formed through cross-functional approaches to complete the task(s) at hand. Skilled Care's deliverables are generated from its sole 24,000-square foot location in Mason, Ohio. The pharmacy, which is open 24 hours a day, 365 days a year, is secured by a Honeywell alarm system. The company's primary technology rests within its pharmacy software, Rescot. This system enables Skilled Care to process, bill, and generate pertinent data critical to the overall operations of the company. Other partnerships have also been established within Skilled Care's multidosed packaging capabilities and wholesaler purchasing interface.

SCP utilizes the Internet for publishing pertinent information and news as well as hosts a Web-enabled customer service application called Track-It to report specific information about customer issues for company-wide resolution. Advantages of e-commerce include quicker customer service response time for all areas of service including placing the order, pharmacist's review, delivery, and billing of the product.

Skilled Care Pharmacy faces key strategic challenges from the rapidly evolving financial structure of health care, a shortage of licensed pharmacist personnel, the constant evolution of medical practice, and employee retention at all levels. These as well as future challenges are always balanced with the responsibility to the stakeholders.

Discussion Questions

1. How might different definitions of quality apply to Skilled Care?
2. How are the principles of total quality reflected in Skilled Care's policy and operations?
3. Given the nature of Skilled Care's operations and the challenges it faces, discuss how a total quality approach can help the company meet these challenges and improve its ability to provide the services its customers need.

ENDNOTES

1. Thomas A. Stewart, "A Conversation with Joseph Juran," *Fortune*, January 11, 1999, 168–169.
2. Alex Taylor III, "Mercedes Hits a Pothole," *Fortune*, October 27, 2003, 140–146.
3. Jeffrey E. Garten, "The War for Better Quality Is Far From Won," *Business Week* editorial, December 18, 2000.
4. Kevin B. Hendricks and Vinod R. Singhal, "Does Implementing an Effective TQM Program Actually Improve Operating Performance? Empirical Evidence from Firms that Have Won Quality Awards," *Management Science*, Vol. 43, No. 9, September 1997.
5. Malcolm Baldrige National Quality Award Profiles of Winners, U.S. Department of Commerce, National Institute of Standards and Technology, and Trident Precision Manufacturing Award Application Summary.

6. "The Push for Quality," *Business Week*, June 8, 1987, p. 131.

7. "Reinventing Health Care," *Fortune,* July 12, 1993, advertisement section.

8. Lori L. Silverman with Annabeth L. Propst, "Quality Today: Recognizing the Critical SHIFT," *Quality Progress*, February 1999, pp. 53–60.

9. Nabil Tamimi and Rose Sebastianelli, "How Firms Define and Measure Quality," *Production and Inventory Management Journal,* Vol. 37, No. 3, Third Quarter 1996, pp. 34–39.

10. Courtesy of Deer Valley Resort.

11. David A. Garvin, "What Does 'Product Quality' Really Mean?", *Sloan Management Review*, Vol. 26, No. 1, 1984, pp. 25–43.

12. "A New Era for Auto Quality," *Business Week*, October 2, 1990, pp. 84–96.

13. D.A Collier, "The Customer Service and Quality Challenge," *The Service Industries Journal,*Vol. 7, No. 1, January 1987, p. 79.

14. Karl Albrecht and Ronald E. Zemke, *Service America*, Homewood, Ill.: Dow Jones-Irwin, 1985.

15. A. Parasuraman, V. A. Zeithaml, and L. L. Berry, "SERVQUAL: A Multiple-Item Scale for Measuring Consumer Perceptions of Service Quality," *Journal of Retailing*, Vol. 64, No. 1, Spring 1988, pp. 12–40.

16. Eryn Brown, "Heartbreak Hotel?", *Fortune,* November 26, 2001, pp. 161–165.

17. Carol A. King, "Service Quality Assurance Is Different," *Quality Progress*, Vol. 18, No. 6, June 1985, pp. 14–18.

18. For example, see Tony Dawe, "Human Interaction to Keep the Customer Satisfied," *The Times* (London), May 15, 2000, p. 7; and Anne R. Carey and Gary Visgaitis, "Pulling the Online Banking Plug," *USA Today*, citing *Cyber Dialogue*, February 12, 2000.

19. Larry English, "In E-Commerce, It's E-Quality or E-Bust," Column published in DM Review Magazine, August 2000.

20. W. Edwards Deming, *Out of the Crisis,* Cambridge, Mass.: MIT Center for Advanced Engineering Study, 1986.

21. John Hillkirk, "World-Famous Quality Expert Dead at 93," *USA Today*, December 21, 1993.

22. W. Edwards Deming, *The New Economics for Industry, Government, Education*, Cambridge, Mass.: MIT Center for Advanced Engineering Study, 1993.

23. April 17, 1979; cited in L. P. Sullivan, "Reducing Variability: A New Approach to Quality," *Quality Progress,* Vol. 17, No. 7, July 1984, pp. 15–21.

24. Mineola, N.Y.: Dover, 1929.

25. Peter R. Scholtes, "Communities as Systems," *Quality Progress*, July 1997, pp. 49–53.

26. Reprinted from *Out of the Crisis* by W. Edwards Deming by permission of MIT and W. Edwards Deming. Published by MIT, Center for Advanced Engineering Study, Cambridge, MA 02139. Copyright © 1986 by W. Edwards Deming.

27. Matthew W. Ford and James R. Evans, "Managing Organizational Self-Assessment: Follow-Up and Its Influence Factors," working paper, Department of Management & Marketing, Northern Kentucky University, 2003.

28. Adapted from March Laree Jacques, "Big League Quality," *Quality Progress*, August 2001, pp. 27–34.

29. Philip B. Crosby, *Quality Is Free*, New York: McGraw-Hill, 1979, pp. 200–201.

30. Procter & Gamble, "Report to the Total Quality Leadership Steering Committee and Working Councils," Cincinnati, Ohio, 1992.

31. Based on Scott M. Paton, "A Change for the Better," First Word Editorial, Quality Digest, December 2003, p. 4.

32. AT&T Corporate Quality Office, *"AT&T's Total Quality Approach,"* 1992, p. 6.

33. Based on Peter Svensson, "It's not just computers: Gadgets crash," The Cincinnati Enquirer, April 28, 2003, p. A3.

34. Andrew E. Serwer, "Michael Dell Turns the PC World Inside Out," *Fortune*, September 8, 1997, pp. 76–86.

35. Rosemary Batt, "Managing Customer Services: Human Resource Practice, Quit Rates, and Sales Growth," Academy of Management Journal, 45, 3, 587–597, 2002.

36. "It's My Manager, Stupid," *Across the Board*, January 2000, p. 9.

37. Kicab Casteñeda-Mendez, "Performance Measurement in Health Care," *Quality Digest*, May 1999, pp. 33–36.

38. See S. S. Masterson, J. D. Olian, and E. R. Schnell, "Belief versus practice in management theory: Total quality management and Agency Theory," in D. Fedor and S. Ghosh (eds.), *Advances in the Management of Organizational Quality* (Vol. 2), Greenwich, Conn.: JAI Press, 1997, pp. 169–209.

39. Adapted from KARLEE 2000 Malcolm Baldrige Application Summary, National Institute of Standards and Technology, U.S. Department of Commerce.

40. Based on Barbara A. Spencer, "Models of Organization and Total Quality Management: A Comparison and Critical Evaluation," *Academy of Management Review,* Vol. 19, No. 3, 1994, pp. 446–471.

41. Adapted from Ronald E. Turner, "TQM in the College Classroom," *Quality Progress,* Vol. 28, No.10, October 1995, pp. 105–108.

42. Adapted from Mark R. Hagen, "Quality for the Long Haul at Gerber," *Quality Progress*, Vol. 33, No. 2, February 2000, pp. 29–34. © 2000 American Society for Quality. Reprinted with permission.

43. Dr. H. James Harrington, CEO, Harrington Institute "Looking for a Little Service," *Quality Digest*, May 2000.

44. Appreciation for materials in this case is expressed to Nancy Mlinarik, VP of Quality, Skilled Care, Inc.

CHAPTER 2

Frameworks for Organizational Quality

The philosophies of Deming, Juran, Crosby, and others provide much guidance and wisdom in the form of "best practices" to managers around the world, leading to the development of numerous awards and certifications for recognizing effective application of TQ principles. Although awards justifiably recognize only a select few, the award or certification criteria provide frameworks for managing from which every organization can benefit. The two frameworks that have had the most impact on quality management practices worldwide are the U.S. Malcolm Baldrige National Quality Award and international ISO 9000 certification process. Recently, the concept of Six Sigma has evolved into a unique framework for managing quality.

This chapter introduces you to these three frameworks for managing and improving quality in organizations: The objectives of this chapter are

➤ to provide an overview of the Malcolm Baldrige National Quality Award and other related award programs, ISO 9000, and Six Sigma as frameworks for total quality.
➤ understand the differences in scope, purpose, and philosophy of these different frameworks, so as to make informed choices when deciding to pursue an approach to organizational excellence.

THE MALCOLM BALDRIGE NATIONAL QUALITY AWARD

The Malcolm Baldrige National Quality Award (MBNQA) has been one of the most powerful catalysts of total quality in the United States and, indeed, throughout the world. More important, the award's *Criteria for Performance Excellence* establish a framework for integrating total quality principles and practices in any organization. In this section we present an overview of the MBNQA, its criteria, and the award process.

History and Purpose

Recognizing that U.S. productivity was declining, President Reagan signed legislation mandating a national study/conference on productivity in October 1982. The American Productivity and Quality Center (formerly the American Productivity Center) sponsored seven computer networking conferences in 1983 to prepare for an upcoming White House Conference on Productivity. The final report on these conferences recommended that "a National Quality Award, similar to the Deming Prize in Japan, be awarded annually to those firms that successfully challenge and meet the award requirements. These requirements and the accompanying examination process should be very similar to the Deming Prize system to be effective." The Baldrige Award was signed into law (Public Law 100-107) on August 20, 1987. The award is named after President Reagan's Secretary of Commerce who was killed in an accident shortly before the Senate acted on the legislation. Malcolm Baldrige was highly regarded by world leaders, having played a major role in carrying out the administration's trade policy, resolving technology transfer differences with China and India, and holding the first Cabinet-level talks with the Soviet Union in seven years, which paved the way for increased access for U.S. firms in the Soviet market.

The purposes of the award are to

- help stimulate American companies to improve quality and productivity for the pride of recognition while obtaining a competitive edge through increased profits;
- recognize the achievements of those companies that improve the quality of their goods and services and provide an example to others;
- establish guidelines and criteria that can be used by business, industrial, governmental, and other enterprises in evaluating their own quality improvement efforts; and
- provide specific guidance for other American enterprises that wish to learn how to manage for high quality by making available detailed information on how winning enterprises were able to change their cultures and achieve eminence.

The Baldrige Award recognizes U.S. companies that excel in quality management practice and performance. The Baldrige Award does not exist simply to recognize product excellence, nor does it exist for the purpose of "winning." Its principal focus is on promoting high-performance management practices that lead to customer satisfaction and business results. Up to three companies can receive an award in each of the categories of manufacturing, small business, service, nonprofit health care, and nonprofit education. Health care and education award categories were established in 1999.

Table 2.1 shows the recipients through 2003.

TABLE 2.1   MALCOLM BALDRIGE AWARD RECIPIENTS THROUGH 2003

Year	Manufacturing	Small Business	Service
1988	Motorola, Inc. Westinghouse Commercial Nuclear Fuel Division	Globe Metallurgical, Inc.	
1989	Xerox Corp. Business Products and Systems Milliken & Co.		
1990	Cadillac Motor Car Division IBM Rochester	Wallace Co., Inc.	Federal Express (FedEx)
1991	Solectron Corp. Zytec Corp. (now part of Artesyn Technologies)	Marlow Industries	
1992	AT&T Network Systems (now Lucent Technologies, Inc., Optical Networking Group) Texas Instruments Defense Systems & Electronics Group (now part of Raytheon Systems Co.)	Granite Rock Co.	AT&T Universal Card Services (now part of Citigroup) The Ritz-Carlton Hotel Co. (now part of Marriott International)
1993	Eastman Chemical Co.	Ames Rubber Corp.	
1994		Wainwright Industries, Inc.	AT&T Consumer Communication Services (now the Consumer Markets Division of AT&T) Verizon Information Services (formerly GTE Directories, Inc.)
1995	Armstrong World Industries Building Products Operations Corning Telecommunications Products Division		
1996	ADAC Laboratories	Custom Research Inc. Trident Precision Manufacturing, Inc.	Dana Commercial Credit Corp.
1997	3M Dental Products Division Solectron Corp.		Merrill Lynch Credit Corp. Xerox Business Services

Continued

TABLE 2.1 MALCOLM BALDRIGE AWARD RECIPIENTS THROUGH 2003 *CONTINUED*

Year	Manufacturing	Small Business	Service
1998	Boeing Airlift and Tanker Programs Solar Turbines, Inc.	Texas Nameplate Company, Inc.	
1999	STMicroelectronics, Inc.–Region Americas	Sunny Fresh Foods	BI The Ritz-Carlton Hotel Company, L.L.C.
2000	Dana Corporation–Spicer Driveshaft Division (now Torque Traction Technologies, Inc.) KARLEE Company	Los Alamos National Bank	Operations Management International, Inc.
2001	Clarke American Checks, Inc.		Pal's Sudden Service
2002	Motorola, Inc. Commercial, Government and Industrial Solutions Sector		Branch-Smith Printing Division
2003	Medrad, Inc.	Stoner, Inc.	Boeing Aerospace Support Caterpillar Financial Services Corp. (U.S.)

Year	Healthcare	Education
2001		Chugach School District Pearl River School District University of Wisconsin–Stout
2002	SSM Health Care	
2003	Baptist Hospital, Inc. Pensacola, FL Saint Luke's Hospital of Kansas City	Community Consolidated School District #15, Palatine, IL

The award has evolved into a comprehensive National Quality Program, administered through the National Institute of Standards and Technology in Gaithersburg, Maryland, of which the Baldrige Award is only one part. The National Quality Program is a public-private partnership, funded primarily through a private foundation. The program's Web site at http://www.quality.

nist.gov provides current information about the award, the performance criteria, award winners, and a variety of other information.

The Criteria for Performance Excellence

The award examination is based upon a rigorous set of criteria, called the *Criteria for Performance Excellence*, designed to encourage companies to enhance their competitiveness through an aligned approach to organizational performance management that results in:

1. Delivery of ever-improving value to customers, contributing to market-place success
2. Improvement of overall company performance and capabilities
3. Organizational and personal learning

The criteria consist of a hierarchical set of *categories, items,* and *areas to address.* The seven categories are:

1. *Leadership:* This category examines how an organization's senior leaders address values, directions, and performance expectations, as well as a focus on customers and other stakeholders, empowerment, innovation, and learning. Also examined are an organization's governance and how the organization addresses its public and community responsibilities.
2. *Strategic Planning:* This category examines how an organization develops strategic objectives and action plans. Also examined is how the chosen objectives and plans are deployed and how progress is measured.
3. *Customer and Market Focus:* This category examines how an organization determines requirements, expectations, and preferences of customers and markets. Also examined is how the organization builds relationships with customers and determines the key factors that lead to customer acquisition, satisfaction, loyalty and retention, and to business expansion.
4. *Measurement, Analysis, and Knowledge Management:* This category examines how an organization selects, gathers, analyzes, manages, and improves its data, information, and knowledge assets.
5. *Human Resource Focus:* This category examines how an organization's work systems and employee learning and motivation enable employees to develop and utilize their full potential in alignment with the organization's overall objectives and action plans. Also examined are the organization's efforts to build and maintain a work environment and employee support climate conducive to performance excellence and to personal and organizational growth.
6. *Process Management:* This category examines the key aspects of an organization's process management, including key product, service, and

business processes for creating customer and organizational value, and key support processes involving all work units.

7. *Business Results:* This category examines an organization's performance and improvement in key business areas—customer satisfaction, product and service performance, financial and marketplace performance, human resource results, operational performance, and governance and social responsibility. Also examined are performance levels relative to competitors.

We encourage you to read the entire document for clarifying notes and explanations. Also, slightly different versions of the criteria are written for education and health care, primarily to conform to unique language and practices in these sectors. Because the criteria are updated each year, we suggest that you obtain the current version. A single free copy of the criteria can be obtained from the National Institute of Standards and Technology. Write to the Baldrige National Quality Program, National Institute of Standards and Technology (NIST), Administration Building, Room A600, 100 Bureau Drive, Stop 1020, Gaithersburg, Md. 20899-1020; call 301-975-2036; send a fax to 301-948-3716; e-mail nqp@nist.gov; or download the criteria from the Web site http://www.baldrige.org.

The seven categories form an *integrated management system* as illustrated in Figure 2.1. The umbrella over the seven categories reflects the focus that organizations must have on customers through their strategy and action plans for all key decisions. Leadership, Strategic Planning, and Customer

FIGURE 2.1   MALCOLM BALDRIGE NATIONAL QUALITY AWARD CRITERIA FRAMEWORK

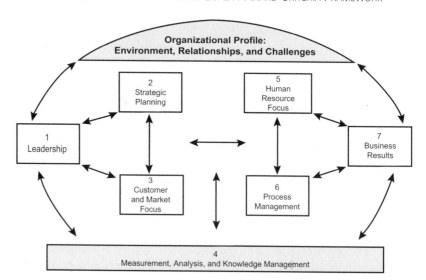

and Market Focus represent the "leadership triad," and suggest the importance of integrating these three functions. Human Resource Focus and
Process Management represent how the work in an organization is accomplished and leads to Business Results. These functions are linked to the leadership triad. Finally, Measurement, Analysis, and Knowledge Management
supports the entire framework by providing the foundation for a fact-based
system for improvement.

Each category consists of several *items* (numbered 1.1, 1.2, 2.1, etc.) or
major requirements on which businesses should focus. Each item, in turn,
consists of a small number of *areas to address* (e.g., 6.1a, 6.1b) that seek specific information on *approaches* used to ensure and improve competitive
performance, the *deployment* of these approaches, or *results* obtained from
such deployment. For example, the Leadership Category consists of the
following items and areas to address:

1. Organizational Leadership
   a. Senior Leadership Direction
   b. Organizational Governance
   c. Organizational Performance Review
2. Social Responsibility
   a. Responsibilities to the Public
   b. Ethical Behavior
   c. Support of Key Communities

The Senior Leadership Direction area asks organizations to answer the
following questions:

- How do senior leaders set and deploy organizational values, short- and
  longer-term directions, and performance expectations? How do senior
  leaders include a focus on creating and balancing value for customers
  and other stakeholders in their performance expectations? How do senior
  leaders communicate organizational values, directions, and expectations
  through your leadership system, to all employees, and to key suppliers
  and partners? How do senior leaders ensure two-way communication on
  these topics?
- How do senior leaders create an environment for empowerment, innovation, and organizational agility? How do they create an environment
  for organizational and employee learning? How do they create an environment that fosters and requires legal and ethical behavior?

Areas to address that request information on approach or deployment
begin with the word "how"; that is, they define a set of actionable management practices. Thus, the criteria define both an integrated infrastructure and
a set of fundamental practices for a high-performance management system.
These practices represent the collective wisdom of the nation's leading

business experts and reflect what a truly world-class high-performance organization must do to succeed.

One thing the criteria do not do is prescribe specific quality tools, techniques, technologies, systems, or starting points. Companies are encouraged to develop and demonstrate creative, adaptive, and flexible approaches to meeting basic requirements (see the box on The Ritz-Carlton Hotel Company). Many innovative approaches have been developed by Baldrige winners and are now commonly used by many other companies.

The Baldrige Award Evaluation Process

The Baldrige evaluation process is rigorous. In the first stage, each application is thoroughly reviewed by up to 10 or more examiners chosen from among leading quality professionals in business, academia, health care, and government (all of whom are volunteers). Examiners evaluate the applicant's response to each examination item, listing major "strengths" and "opportunities for improvement" relative to the criteria. Strengths demonstrate an effective and positive response to the criteria. Opportunities for improvement do not prescribe specific practices or examiners' opinions on what the company should be doing but, rather, deficiencies in responding to the criteria. To help examiners understand the context of the organization, applicants are required to provide an *Organizational Profile*, which is basically a snapshot of the organization that describes the organizational environment; key relationships with customers, suppliers, and other partners; types of employees and technologies used; the competitive environment; key strategic challenges it faces; and its system for performance improvement. The Organizational Profile helps the organization focus on key performance requirements and results, and helps examiners to understand the organization and what it considers important.

Based on the comments, a percentage score from 0 to 100 in increments of 10 is given to each item. Detailed scoring guidelines can be found in the criteria document. Each examination item is evaluated on approach/deployment or results. *Approach* refers to the methods the company uses to achieve the requirements addressed in each category. The factors used to evaluate approaches include:

- the appropriateness of the methods to the requirements;
- the effectiveness of methods, namely, the degree to which the approach is systematic, integrated, and consistently applied; the degree to which the approach embodies effective evaluation/improvement cycles; and the degree to which the approach is based upon reliable information and data;
- alignment with organizational needs; and
- evidence of innovation.

Baldrige Leadership Practices at The Ritz-Carlton Hotel Company, L.L.C.[1]

When Horst Schulze (who retired in 2001) became president in 1988, he and his leadership team personally took charge of managing for quality because they realized that managing for quality could not be delegated. They personally established the Gold Standards, which are the foundation of The Ritz-Carlton quality philosophy.

The Gold Standards, in their simplicity, represent an easy-to-understand definition of service quality, and are aggressively communicated and internalized at all levels of the organization. The constant and continuous reinforcement techniques of the Gold Standards, led by senior leaders, include lectures at new employee orientation, developmental training, daily lineup meetings, administration of both positive and negative reinforcement, mission statements displayed, distribution of Credo cards, The Credo as first topic of internal meetings, and peer pressure. As a result, employees have an exceptional understanding and devotion to the company's vision, values, quality goals, and methods.

Since 1984, all members of senior leadership have personally ensured that each new hotel's goods and services are characteristic of The Ritz-Carlton on opening day. An important aspect of this quality practice takes place during the concentrated and intense "seven-day countdown" when senior leaders work side by side with new employees using a combination of hands-on behavior modeling and reinforcement. During these formative sessions, which all new employees must attend, the president and COO personally interacts with every new employee, both individually and in a group setting. The president personally creates the employee-guest interface image and facilitates each department's first vision statement.

Throughout the entire process, the senior leaders monitor work areas for "start-up," instill Gold Standards, model the company's relationship management, insist upon 100 percent compliance to customers' requirements, and recognize outstanding achievement. Senior leaders set direction through seven specific approaches:

10-Year Vision: To Be The Premier Worldwide Provider of Luxury Travel and Hospitality Products and Services
5-Year Mission: Product and Profit Dominance
3-Year Objectives: The Vital Few Objectives
1-Year Tactics: Key Production and Business Processes
Strategy: Customer and Market Focus Strategy with Action Plans
Methods: TQM—Application of Quality Sciences; Malcolm Baldrige National Quality Award Criteria; The Greenbook, 2nd edition (the company's handbook of quality processes and tools)

Continued

> *Foundation*: Values and Philosophy—The Gold Standards, Credo, Motto, Three Steps of Service, Basics, Employee Promise
>
> Leadership effectiveness is evaluated on key questions of a semiannual employee satisfaction survey and through audits on public responsibility. Gaps in leadership effectiveness are addressed with development and training plans and extensive use of developmental job assignments.

Deployment refers to the extent to which the approaches are applied to all requirements of the item. The factors used to evaluate deployment include:

- use of the approach in addressing item requirements relevant to the organization, and
- use of the approach by all appropriate work units.

Results refers to the outcomes and effects in achieving the purposes given in the item. The factors used to evaluate results include:

- current performance levels,
- performance relative to appropriate comparisons and/or benchmarks,
- rate, breadth, and importance of performance improvements, and
- linkage of results measures to important customer, market, process, and action plan performance requirements identified in the approach/deployment items and the organizational profile.

Scores for each examination item are computed by multiplying the examiner's score by the maximum point value that can be earned, with a total possible score of 1,000. The scores are reviewed by a panel of nine judges without knowledge of the specific companies. The higher-scoring applications enter a *consensus stage* in which a selected group of examiners discuss variations in individual scores and arrive at consensus scores for each item. The panel of judges then reviews the scores and selects the highest-scoring applicants for site visits.

At this point, six or seven examiners visit the company for up to a week to verify information contained in the written application and resolve issues that are unclear. The judges use the site visit reports to recommend award recipients. All information is kept strictly confidential, and examiners are bound by conflict-of-interest rules and a code of conduct.

All applicants receive a feedback report that critically evaluates the company's strengths and areas for improvement relative to the award criteria. The feedback report, frequently 30 or more pages in length, contains the evaluation team's response to the written application. It includes a distribution of numerical scores of all applicants and a scoring summary of the individual applicant. This feedback is one of the most valuable aspects of applying for the award. We should note that the typical score for winners is in the 650–750 range. This indicates that although their practices and results are indeed outstanding, they still have opportunities for improvement. As a former Xerox CEO once said, quality is a race without a finish line.

Criteria Evolution

As the important management practices of any organization should be, the specific award criteria are evaluated and improved each year. Over the years, the criteria have been streamlined and simplified to make them more relevant and useful to organizations of all types and size, improve the linkage between process and results, and make the criteria more generic and user-friendly. Most significantly, the word *quality* was judiciously dropped in the mid-1990s. For example, prior to 1994, the Strategic Planning category was titled "Strategic Quality Planning." The change to "Strategic Planning" signifies that quality should be a part of business planning, not a separate issue. Throughout the document, the term *performance* has been substituted for quality as a conscious attempt to recognize that the principles of total quality are the foundation for a company's entire management system, not just the quality system. As Dr. Curt Reimann, former director and architect of the Baldrige Award Program, noted, "The things you do to win a Baldrige Award are exactly the things you'd do to win in the marketplace. Our strategy is to have the Baldrige Award criteria be a useful daily tool that simulates real competition."

To this end, the most significant changes in the criteria reflect the maturity of business practices and total quality approaches. The criteria evolved from a primary emphasis on product and service quality assurance in the late 1980s, to a broad focus on performance excellence in a global marketplace by the late 1990s. The improvements include the following shifts in emphasis:

- from quality assurance and strategic quality planning to a focus on process management and overall strategic planning;
- from a focus on current customers to a focus on current and future customers and markets;
- from human resource utilization to human resource development and management;
- from supplier quality to supplier partnerships;
- from individual quality improvement activities to cycles of evaluation and improvement in all key areas;
- from data analysis of quality efforts to an aggregate, integrated organizational level review of key company data; and
- from results that focus on limited financial performance to a focus on a composite of business results, including customer satisfaction and financial, product, service, and strategic performance.

In addition, criteria updates are designed to address, emerging and relevant issues facing business. In 2003, for example, the criteria strengthened its emphasis on organizational governance and ethics in the wake of the Enron, WorldCom, and Arthur Andersen fiascos that occurred the year before.

Using the Baldrige Criteria

The Baldrige Award criteria form a model for business excellence in any organization—manufacturing or service, large or small (see the box on Texas Instruments). Many small businesses (defined as those with 500 or fewer employees) believe that the Baldrige criteria are too difficult to apply to their organizations because they cannot afford to implement the same types of practices as large companies.

However, an organization's practices need not be formal or complex. For example, the ability to obtain customer and market knowledge through independent third-party surveys, extensive interviews, and focus groups, which are common practices among large companies, may be limited by the resources of a small business. What is important, however, is whether the company is using appropriate mechanisms to gather information and use it to improve customer focus and satisfaction. Similarly, large corporations frequently have sophisticated computer/information systems for data management, whereas small businesses may perform data and information management with a combination of manual methods and personal computers.

Also, systems for employee involvement and process management may rely heavily on informal verbal communication and less on formal written documentation. Thus, the size or nature of a business does not affect the appropriateness of the criteria but, rather, the context in which the criteria are applied.

Many organizations are using the award criteria to evaluate their own quality programs, set up and implement quality initiatives, communicate better with suppliers and partners, and for education and training, even if they have no intention to apply for the award. For example, although the legal profession in general has not adopted quality management practices, the Trial Division of Nationwide Insurance, which operates 56 law offices in 20 states, uses the Baldrige model as a key component of its business plan. Senior leaders introduced it to the company's managing trial attorneys and encouraged individual offices to apply for local or state Baldrige-based awards.

The incorporation of education and health care as categories in the award program in 1999 was a reflection of the growing interest in these sectors. Many school districts are now using the criteria. One large Chicago-area hospital applied for the Baldrige-based Lincoln Award for Excellence and prepared for its accreditation visit by the Joint Commission on Accreditation of Healthcare Organizations (JCAHO) at the same time, recognizing the synergy and overlap of Baldrige principles and JCAHO standards.

Baldrige Pays Off for Texas Instruments[2]

Texas Instruments (TI) Defense Systems & Electronics Group (acquired by Raytheon Corporation in 1997) faced a critical issue that many businesses struggle with: Is the payoff of greater competitive advantage worth the effort of achieving total quality, specifically competing for the Baldrige Award? Their answer is a definite yes.

TI understands firsthand that the real benefit of applying for the Baldrige Award lies in adopting its quality criteria. The application itself is the single most powerful catalyst for the kinds of organizational and cultural changes that companies must make to compete.

TI's commitment to quality and productivity improvement dates back to the 1950s. But, like most corporations, most of its efforts were aimed at improving manufacturing and product quality. In the early 1980s, a total quality initiative was formalized across the entire corporation. Some business units made tremendous progress; the semiconductor operation in Japan won the Deming Prize in 1985.

When the Baldrige Award criteria appeared, TI used them to provide focus and coherence to the activities across the corporation. Using the criteria, they were able to tackle a part of total quality that previously had been unreachable: implementing quality efforts in staff, support, and nonmanufacturing areas. In 1989, TI asked every business unit to prepare a mock award application as a way of measuring its progress. This task represented a radical change for some operations because, until that time, most staff functions were not required to measure their processes or their results.

The Defense Systems & Electronics Group's self-assessment revealed that they were a long way from applying for and winning the Baldrige Award. But the group aggressively adopted the criteria as a blueprint for improving its business.

Many executives did not believe that the criteria could be applied to defense contractors. Similarly, many executives today question whether small businesses can realistically meet the Baldrige Award criteria. TI discovered that all companies have one thing in common: customers. Focusing on customers to make the company more competitive gives meaning to the award.

The Baldrige Award application process changed almost everything within the Defense Systems & Electronics Group. Before applying, the group had no way of systematically measuring how well it understood its customers' concerns, captured customers' feedback, or made improvements in interacting with customers. Mountains of data were being collected, but most of the data measured internal criteria, not customer satisfaction. The structured, hierarchical management environment made it difficult to adopt ideas from outside sources.

Continued

The Baldrige Award process provided a way to make the customer the centerpiece of daily activities. It led to much better communication with customers and employees and accelerated progress toward less hierarchical, more functional work teams. It changed the management process from an individual activity to a team effort, leading to better decisions. Finally, it introduced two radical new ideas: benchmarking and stretch goals. Changing the culture was not easy and did not happen quickly. It took teamwork, consensus building, and buy-in. At TI, it took about five years of dedicated pulling in the same direction to begin seeing measurable results.

Most states have developed award programs similar to the Baldrige Award. State award programs generally are designed to promote an awareness of productivity and quality, foster an information exchange, encourage firms to adopt quality and productivity improvement strategies, recognize firms that have instituted successful strategies, provide role models for other businesses in the state, encourage new industry to locate in the state, and establish a quality-of-life culture that will benefit all residents of the state.[3] Each state is unique, however, and thus the specific objectives will vary. For instance, the primary objectives of Minnesota's quality award are to encourage all Minnesota organizations to examine their current state of quality and to become more involved in the movement toward continuous quality improvement, as well as to recognize outstanding quality achievements in the state. Missouri, by contrast, has as its objectives to educate all Missourians in quality improvement, to foster the pursuit of quality in all aspects of Missouri life, and to recognize quality leadership. Ohio's program is focused on developing organizations early in their performance excellence journey as well as recognizing outstanding organizations. Information about state award programs can be found at the Baldrige Web site cited earlier in this section.

The Baldrige Criteria and the Deming Philosophy

It is no secret that W. Edwards Deming was not an advocate of the Baldrige Award.[4] (Joseph Juran, however, was highly influential in its development.) The competitive nature of the award is fundamentally at odds with Deming's teachings. However, many of Deming's principles are reflected directly or in spirit within the criteria. In fact, one firm, Zytec, implemented its total quality system around Deming's 14 Points and received a Baldrige Award. Specific portions of the Baldrige criteria that support each of Deming's 14 Points are summarized here.

1. *Statement of Purpose.* Strategy development requires a mission and vision. Commitment to aims and purposes by senior leaders is specifically

addressed in the Leadership category and in enhancing customer satisfaction and relationships.

2. *Learn the New Philosophy.* Communication of values, expectations, customer focus, and learning is a key area of the Organizational Leadership item.

3. *Understand Inspection.* The Process Management category addresses the development of appropriate measurement plans. The Criteria also seek evidence of how a company aims to minimize the costs associated with inspection.

4. *End Price Tag Decisions.* This is implicitly addressed throughout the Process Management category and in the Criteria's emphasis on overall performance and linkages among processes and results.

5. *Improve Constantly.* Continuous improvement and learning is a core value of Baldrige. The Criteria specifically ask how the company evaluates and improves its processes.

6. *Institute Training.* The Human Resource Focus category recognizes the importance of training and employee development in meeting performance objectives.

7. *Teach and Institute Leadership.* Category 1 is devoted exclusively to leadership, and it is recognized as the principal driver of the management system in Figure 2.1.

8. *Drive Out Fear and Innovate.* The Human Resource Focus, Customer and Market Focus, and Strategic Planning categories focus on work design, empowerment, and implementation issues that support this point.

9. *Optimize the Efforts of Teams and Staff.* The Criteria have a significant focus on teamwork and customer knowledge in product/process design and process management, as well as in the Human Resource Focus category.

10. *Eliminate Exhortations.* While not directly addressed, the focus on work and job design as the driver of high performance makes this a moot point.

11. *Eliminate Quotas and MBO; Institute Improvement; and Understand Processes.* The Organizational Leadership and Strategy Deployment items, as well as the Measurement, Analysis and Knowledge Management and Process Management categories deal with fact-based management and understanding processes.

12. *Remove Barriers.* The Leadership and Human Resource Focus categories, as well as the Customer Satisfaction and Relationships item support this goal.

13. *Encourage Education.* This is addressed directly in the Human Resource Focus category.

14. *Take Action.* This role of leadership is addressed directly in the Leadership category.

The consistencies among Deming's 14 Points and the Baldrige criteria attest to the universal nature of quality management principles.

INTERNATIONAL QUALITY AWARD PROGRAMS

Numerous countries and regions of the world have established awards and award criteria. Many other award programs are similar in nature to the Baldrige criteria.

The Deming Prize

The Deming Application Prize was instituted in 1951 by the Union of Japanese Scientists and Engineers (JUSE) in recognition and appreciation of W. Edwards Deming's achievements in statistical quality control and his friendship with the Japanese people. The Deming Prize has several categories, including prizes for individuals, factories, and small companies, and the Deming application prize, which is an annual award presented to a company or a division of a company that has achieved distinctive performance improvements through the application of Companywide Quality Control (CWQC). As defined by JUSE, CWQC is a system of activities to assure that quality products and services required by customers are economically designed, produced and supplied while respecting the principle of customer-orientation and the overall public well-being. These quality assurance activities involve market research, research and development, design, purchasing, production, inspection and sales, as well as all other related activities inside and outside the company. Through everyone in the company understanding both statistical concepts and methods, through their application to all the aspects of quality assurance, and through repeating the cycle of rational planning, implementation, evaluation, and action, CWQC aims to accomplish business objectives.[5]

The judging criteria consist of a checklist of 10 major categories: policies, the organization and its operations, education and dissemination, information gathering, communication and its utilization, analysis, standardization, control/management, quality assurance, effects, and future plans. Each major category is divided into subcategories, or "checking points." For example, the policy category includes policies pursued for management, quality, and quality control; methods for establishing policies; appropriateness and consistency of policies; utilization of statistical methods; communication and dissemination of policies; checks of policies and the status of their achievement; and the relationship between policies and long- and short-term plans. Each category is weighted equally.

Hundreds of companies apply for the award each year. After an initial application is accepted as eligible for the process, the company must submit a detailed description of its quality practices. Based on review of the written descriptions, only a few companies believed to be successful in CWQC are selected for a site visit. The site visit consists of a company presentation, in-depth questioning by examiners, and an executive session with top managers. Examiners visit plants and are free to ask any worker any question.

For example, at Florida Power and Light (see box "Electric Quality"), examiners asked questions of specific individuals such as "What are your main accountabilities?" "What are the important priority issues for the corporation?" "What indicators do you have for your performance? For your target?" "How are you doing today compared to your target?" They request examples of inadequate performance. Documentation must be made available immediately. The preparation is extensive and sometimes frustrating.

Electric Quality[6]

Florida Power and Light (FPL) is one of the largest electric utilities in the United States. During the 1970s the company was forced to increase utility rates repeatedly because of increasing costs, slower sales growth, and stricter federal and state regulations. The company had become bureaucratic and inflexible. In 1981 Marshall McDonald, then chairman of the board, realized that the company had been concerned with keeping defects under control rather than improving quality. Because of his concern for quality, McDonald introduced quality improvement teams at FPL. Management knew this was a step in the right direction, but such teams alone would not bring about the change needed for the company to survive. McDonald tried to convince other executives that a total quality improvement process was needed, but all the experts that FPL talked to were in manufacturing, while FPL was primarily a service company. In 1983, while in Japan, McDonald met a president of Kansai Electric Power Company, a Deming Prize winner, who told him about their total quality efforts. Company officials began to visit Kansai regularly, and with their help, FPL began its quality improvement program (QIP) in 1983.

Its quality efforts included empowering each department to develop improvement plans, standardizing work routines, removing waste from them, promoting the concept of internal customers, and enabling better practice to be replicated from one location to another. FPL revamped a centralized suggestion system it had been using for many years. Only about 600 suggestions had been submitted annually and it usually took six months for evaluation. A new decentralized system was proposed with simplified procedures to improve the response time. Employees participated in the implementation of their own suggestions. In 1988, 9,000 suggestions were submitted; in 1989 this number increased to 25,000. As a result of these efforts, the average length of service interruptions dropped from about 75 minutes in 1983 to about 47 minutes in 1989; the number of complaints per 1,000 customers fell to one third of the 1983 level; safety has improved; and the price of electricity has stabilized. In 1989, FPL became the first non-Japanese company to win the Deming Prize.

Continued

> Five years after winning the Deming Prize, FPL still had an unwavering commitment to quality initiatives, which was noted by Dr. Noriaki Kano of the Union of Japanese Scientists and Engineers, after observing presentations from 11 FPL business units. Dr. Kano, who had served as a counselor to FPL since 1986, was "pleasantly surprised" that FPL had simultaneously reduced costs and improved quality. Kano noted that recent improvements were based on skills developed through QIP practices.
>
> For example, one team improved service reliability by reducing transformer failures due to lightning. Before, an average of 23 transformers out of 761 on their worst-performing feeder failed each year. This number was reduced to zero failures, even though lightning strikes had increased 250 percent. Newly installed transformers incorporate the team's recommended changes, and existing transformers are modified as needed. The team leader stated that they found creative ways to use quality improvement tools and techniques to their best advantage without getting caught up in excessive paperwork or attending compulsory meetings. "Like most employees, we're so familiar with the quality processes that it's almost second nature."

The Deming Prize is awarded to all companies that meet the prescribed standard. However, the small number of awards given each year is an indication of the difficulty of achieving the standard. The objectives are to ensure that a company has so thoroughly deployed a quality process that it will continue to improve long after a prize is awarded. The application process has no "losers." For companies that do not qualify, the examination process is automatically extended up to two times over three years.

European Quality Award

In October 1991, the European Foundation for Quality Management (EFQM) in partnership with the European Commission and the European Organization for Quality announced the creation of the European Quality Award. The award was designed to increase awareness throughout the European Community, and businesses in particular, of the growing importance of quality to their competitiveness in the increasingly global market and to their standards of life. The European Quality Award consists of two parts: the European Quality Prize, given to companies that demonstrate excellence in quality management practice by meeting the award criteria, and the European Quality Award, awarded to the most successful applicant. In 1992, four prizes and one award were granted for the first time.

The award process is similar to the Deming Prize and Baldrige Award. The assessment is based on customer satisfaction, business results, processes, leadership, people satisfaction, resources, people management, policy and strategy, and impact on society. Like Baldrige, results—including customer satisfaction, people (employee) satisfaction, and impact on society—constitute a high percentage of the total score. These are driven by "enablers"—the means by which an organization approaches its business responsibilities.

The categories are roughly equivalent to those in Baldrige. However, the results criteria of people satisfaction, customer satisfaction, impact on society, and business results are somewhat different.[7] The impact on society results category focuses on the perceptions of the company by the community at large and the company's approach to the quality of life, the environment, and the preservation of global resources. The European Quality Award criteria places greater emphasis on this category than is placed on the public responsibility item in the Baldrige Award criteria.

Canadian Awards for Business Excellence

Canada's National Quality Institute (NQI) recognizes Canada's foremost achievers of excellence through the prestigious Canada Awards for Excellence. NQI is a nonprofit organization designed to stimulate and support quality-driven innovation within all Canadian enterprises and institutions, including business, government, education, and health care. The Canadian Awards for Business Excellence quality criteria are similar in structure to the Baldrige Award criteria, with some key differences. The major categories and items within each category are:

1. *Leadership*: strategic direction, leadership involvement, and outcomes.
2. *Customer focus*: voice of the customer, management of customer relationships, measurement, and outcomes.
3. *Planning for improvement*: development and content of improvement plan, assessment, and outcomes.
4. *People focus*: human resource planning, participatory environment, continuous learning environment, employee satisfaction, and outcomes.
5. *Process optimization*: process definition, process control, process improvement, and outcomes.
6. *Supplier focus*: partnering and outcomes.

These categories seek similar information as the Baldrige Award criteria. For example, the People focus category examines the development of human resource planning and implementation and operation of a strategy for achieving excellence through people. It also examines the organization's efforts to foster and support an environment that encourages and enables people to reach their full potential.

Australian Business Excellence Awards

The Australian Business Excellence Awards were developed independently from the Baldrige Awards in 1988. The awards are administered by the Australian Quality Awards Foundation, a subsidiary of the Australian Quality Council. Four levels of awards are given.

1. *The Business Improvement Level*: encouragement recognition for "Progress Toward Business Excellence" or "Foundation in Business Excellence";
2. *The Award Level*: representing Australian best practices; recognition as a winner or finalist;
3. *The Award Gold Level*: open only to former award winners; represents a revalidation and ongoing improvement;
4. *The Australian Business Excellence Prize*: open only to former award winners; represents international best practices evident throughout the organization.

The assessment criteria address leadership, strategy and planning, information and knowledge, people, customer focus, processes, products and services, and business results. In this model, leadership and customer focus are the drivers of the management system and enablers of performance. Strategy, policy and planning, information and analysis, and people are the key internal components of the management system. Quality of process, product, and service is focused on how work is done to achieve the required results and obtain improvement. Business results are the outcome of the management system—a results category.

As with Baldrige, the framework emphasizes the holistic and interconnected nature of the management process. The criteria are benchmarked with the Baldrige criteria and the European Business Excellence Model. One of the distinctive aspects of Australia's program is solid union support.

ISO 9000:2000

As quality became a major focus of businesses throughout the world, various organizations developed standards and guidelines. Terms such as *quality management, quality control, quality system*, and *quality assurance* acquired different, and sometimes conflicting, meanings from country to country, within a country, and even within an industry.[8] As the European Community moved toward the European free trade agreement, which went into effect at the end of 1992, quality management became a key strategic objective.

To standardize quality requirements for European countries within the common market and those wishing to do business with those countries, a specialized agency for standardization, the International Organization for Standardization, founded in 1946 and composed of representatives from the national standards bodies of 91 nations, adopted a series of written quality standards in 1987, which were revised in 1994, and again (significantly) in 2000. The most recent version is called the *ISO 9000:2000* family of standards.

The standards have been adopted in the United States by ANSI with the endorsement and cooperation of ASQ. The standards are recognized by about 100 countries, including Japan. In some foreign markets, companies will not buy from noncertified suppliers. Thus, meeting these standards is becoming a requirement for international competitiveness. The standards are intended to apply to all types of businesses, including electronics and chemicals, and to services such as health care, banking, and transportation.

ISO 9000 defines *quality system standards*, based on the premise that certain generic characteristics of management practices can be standardized, and that a well-designed, well-implemented, and carefully managed quality system provides confidence that the outputs will meet customer expectations and requirements. The standards were created to meet five objectives:

1. Achieve, maintain, and seek to continuously improve product quality (including services) in relationship to requirements.
2. Improve the quality of operations to continually meet customers' and stakeholders' stated and implied needs.
3. Provide confidence to internal management and other employees that quality requirements are being fulfilled and that improvement is taking place.
4. Provide confidence to customers and other stakeholders that quality requirements are being achieved in the delivered product.
5. Provide confidence that quality system requirements are fulfilled.

Structure of the ISO 9000 Standards

The ISO 9000:2000 standards focus on developing, documenting, and implementing procedures to ensure consistency of operations and performance in production and service delivery processes, with the aim of continual improvement, and supported by fundamental principles of total quality. The standards consist of three documents:

- ISO 9000—Fundamentals and vocabulary
- ISO 9001—Requirements
- ISO 9004—Guidance for performance improvement

ISO 9000 provides definitions of key terms. ISO 9001 provides a set of minimum requirements for a quality management system, and is intended to demonstrate compliance with recognized quality principles to customers and for third-party certification. An example of one of the requirements is, "The supplier's management with executive responsibility shall define and document its policy for quality, including objectives for quality and commitment to quality. The quality policy shall be relevant to the supplier's organizational goals and the expectations and needs of its customers. The supplier shall ensure that this policy is understood, implemented, and maintained at all levels of the organization." Thus, the requirements state precisely what the organization needs to do. The requirements are organized into four major sections: Management Responsibility; Resource Management; Product Realization; and Measurement, Analysis, and Improvement.[9] Finally, ISO 9004 focuses on improving the quality management system beyond these minimum requirements.

The standards are intended to apply to all types of businesses, including electronics and chemicals, and to services such as health care, banking, and transportation. For example, in July 2000, the B2B (business-to-business) firm, bestroute.com, became the first e-commerce distributorship to achieve ISO registration. Interpreting the standards to e-business required some unique strategies to ensure compliance. The company focused on the key concept of the standard that is common to any industry: customer service. The company developed and documented processes for all aspects of bestroute.com's customer service—from call routing to return processing to phone etiquette. As the customer service manager observed, "In the end, the processes we established, implemented and are keeping on top of in order to comply with the standard are the very same things we needed to do to keep customers happy."[10]

Factors Leading to ISO 9000:2000

The original ISO 9000:1994 series standards consisted of 20 fundamental elements of a basic quality system that included such things as management responsibility, design control, purchasing, product identification and traceability, process control, inspection and testing, corrective and preventive action, internal quality audits, training, and statistical techniques.

The original standards and the 1994 revision met with considerable controversy.[11] The standards required only that the organization have a documented, verifiable process in place to ensure that it consistently produces what it says it will produce. A company could comply with the standards and still produce a poor-quality product—as long as it does so consistently! Dissatisfaction with ISO 9000 resulted in the European Union calling for deemphasizing ISO 9000 registration, citing the fact that companies are more concerned with "passing a test" than on focusing their energies on quality processes.

The deficiencies in the old ISO 9000 standards led to a joint effort in 1994 by the big three automobile manufacturers—Ford, Chrysler, and General Motors—as well as several truck manufacturers, to develop QS-9000, an interpretation and extension of ISO 9000 for automotive suppliers. The goal was to develop fundamental quality systems that provide for continuous improvement, emphasizing defect prevention and the reduction of variation and waste in the supply chain. QS-9000 is based on ISO 9000 and includes all ISO requirements. However, QS-9000 went well beyond ISO 9000 standards by including additional requirements such as continuous improvement, manufacturing capability, and production part approval processes.

ISO 9000:2000 is a response to the widespread dissatisfaction that resulted from the old standards. The new standards have a completely new structure, based on eight principles—"comprehensive and fundamental rules or beliefs for leading and operating an organization" that reflect the basic principles of Total Quality that we introduced in Chapter 1. These eight principles, shown in Table 2.2, were voted on, and overwhelmingly approved, at a conference in 1997 attended by 36 representatives of countries that have delegates in the TC 176 technical committee, charged with the responsibility of revising the ISO 9000 standards.[12]

With this underlying philosophy, the ISO 9000:2000 revision aligns much closer to the spirit of TQ. For example,

- Organizations now need a process to determine customer needs and expectations, translate them into internal requirements, and measure customer satisfaction and dissatisfaction.

TABLE 2.2   ISO 9000:2000 QUALITY MANAGEMENT PRINCIPLES

Principle 1: Customer Focus
Organizations depend on their customers and therefore should understand current and future customer needs, should meet customer requirements, and strive to exceed customer expectations.

Principle 2: Leadership
Leaders establish unity of purpose and direction of the organization. They should create and maintain the internal environment in which people can become fully involved in achieving the organization's objectives.

Principle 3: Involvement of People
People at all levels are the essence of an organization and their full involvement enables their abilities to be used for the organization's benefit.

Principle 4: Process Approach
A desired result is achieved more efficiently when activities and related resources are managed as a process.

Principle 5: System Approach to Management
Identifying, understanding, and managing interrelated processes as a system contributes to the organization's effectiveness and efficiency in achieving its objectives.

Principle 6: Continual Improvement
Continual improvement of the organization's overall performance should be a permanent objective of the organization.

Principle 7: Factual Approach to Decision Making
Effective decisions are based on the analysis of data and information.

Principle 8: Mutually Beneficial Supplier Relationships
An organization and its suppliers are interdependent and a mutually beneficial relationship enhances the ability of both to create value.

Source: The terms and definitions taken from the quality management principles of ISO 9000 are reproduced with the permission of the International Organization for Standardization, ISO. They can be obtained from any ISO member and from the Web site of the ISO Central Secretariat at the following address: http://www.iso.org. Copyright remains with ISO.

- Managers must communicate the importance of meeting customer and regulatory requirements, integrate ISO 9000 into business plans, set measurable objectives, and conduct management reviews. No longer can top management delegate the program to people lower in the organization.
- Organizations now must view work as a process and manage a system of interrelated processes. This is significantly different from the "document what you do" requirements of earlier versions.
- Analysis now needs to be done to provide information about customer satisfaction and dissatisfaction, products, and processes with the focus on improvement.
- Training effectiveness must be evaluated and personnel made aware of the importance of their activities in meeting quality objectives.
- In the previous standards, organizations were required to perform corrective and preventive action, but now must have a planned process for improvement.

Implementation and Registration

Implementing ISO 9000 is not an easy task.[13] The ISO 9000 standards originally were intended to be advisory in nature and to be used for two-party contractual situations (between a customer and supplier) and for internal auditing. However, they quickly evolved into criteria for companies who wished to "certify" their quality management or achieve "registration" through a third-party auditor, usually a laboratory or some other accreditation agency (called a registrar). This process began in the United Kingdom. Rather than a supplier being audited for compliance to the standards by each customer, the registrar certifies the company, and this certification is accepted by all of the supplier's customers.

The registration process includes document review by the registrar of the quality system documents or quality manual; preassessment, which identifies potential noncompliance in the quality system or in the documentation; assessment by a team of two or three auditors of the quality system and its documentation; and surveillance, or periodic reaudits to verify conformity with the practices and systems registered. During the assessment, auditors might ask such questions as (using *management responsibility* as an example): Does a documented policy on quality exist? Have management objectives for quality been defined? Have the policy and objectives been transmitted and explained to all levels of the organization? Have job descriptions for people who manage or perform work effecting quality been documented? Are descriptions of functions that affect quality available? Has management designated a person or group with the authority to prevent nonconformities in products, identify and record quality problems, and recommend solutions? What means are used to verify the solutions?[14]

Recertification is required every three years. Individual sites—not entire companies—must achieve registration individually. All costs are borne by the applicant, so the process can be quite expensive. A registration audit may cost anywhere from $10,000 to over $40,000, whereas the internal cost for documentation and training may exceed $100,000. As of December 1, 2000, over 400,000 organizations around the world have received registration.

Benefits of ISO 9000:2000

ISO 9000 provides a set of good basic practices for initiating a quality system, and is an excellent starting point for companies with no formal quality assurance program. In fact, it provides detailed guidance on process and product control. Thus, for companies in the early stages of developing a quality program, the standards enforce the discipline of control that is necessary before they can seriously pursue continuous improvement. The requirements of periodic audits reinforce the stated quality system until it becomes ingrained in the company.

Many diverse organizations have realized significant benefits from ISO 9000 (see box "Some Unusual ISO 9000 Approaches"). At DuPont, for example, ISO 9000 has been credited with increasing on-time delivery from 70 to 90 percent, decreasing cycle time from 15 days to 1.5 days, increasing first-pass yields from 72 to 92 percent, and reducing the number of test procedures by one third. Sun Microsystems' Milpitas plant was certified in 1992, and managers believe that it has helped deliver improved quality and service to customers.[15] In Canada, Toronto Plastics, Ltd. reduced defects from 150,000 per million to 15,000 per million after one year of ISO implementation.[16] The first home builder to achieve registration, Michigan-based Delcor Homes, reduced its rate for correctable defects from 27.4 to 1.7 in two years and improved its building experience approval rating from the mid-60s to the mid-90s on a 100-point scale.[17] Thus, using ISO 9000 as a basis for a quality system can improve productivity, decrease costs, and increase customer satisfaction.

SIX SIGMA

Six Sigma can best be described as a business improvement approach that seeks to find and eliminate causes of defects and errors in manufacturing and service processes by focusing on outputs that are critical to customers and a clear financial return for the organization. Six Sigma has garnered a significant amount of credibility over the last decade because of its acceptance at such major firms as Allied Signal (now part of Honeywell) and General Electric; however, is not as new a concept as it seems. This concept is facilitated through use of basic and advanced quality improvement and control tools by teams whose members are trained to provide fact-based decision-making information.

Some Unusual ISO 9000 Approaches[18]

The Rosemount Measurement Division of the Fisher-Rosemount Group of the Emerson Electric Company was named one of the "Best Plants in America" by Industry Week in 1993. Since achieving ISO certification that year, every department is audited internally at least once each year for conformance to the standards. Discrepancies found during an audit are fed back to the area on a corrective action form. Every corrective action is verified within about a month of a stated completion date. In most ISO 9000 systems, the quality department tends not to hold specific people responsible for system deficiencies. But if a Rosemount department head is tardy resolving a discrepancy, his or her name is found blinking in red letters on the computer monitor.

In other words, the person is held responsible for the lateness of the solution, not the actual problem. All discrepancies are therefore resolved in a timely manner As the audit teams visit all areas in the organization, they get very good at understanding which departments are best in class for certain process control features. Although most auditors tend to be neutral, the Rosemount system gives complete feedback of information. At postaudit meetings, the positive discoveries are shared first, and the department may be judged best in class in some process categories. In other categories, where some improvement is needed, the auditors may suggest that the audited department visit other departments that are best in class in those categories.

The auditors try to let the departments learn from one another rather than reinvent the wheel. The external auditors told the quality group that Rosemount has made great improvements in the two years that the best-in-class feedback method has been used.

The origin of the term *six sigma* is a statistical measure that equates to 3.4 or fewer errors or defects per million opportunities. *Six Sigma* relates to the broader philosophy and improvement approach. An ultimate "stretch" goal of all organizations that adopt a Six Sigma philosophy is to have all critical processes, regardless of functional area, at a Six Sigma level of capability.

Evolution of Six Sigma

Motorola pioneered the concept of Six Sigma as an approach to measuring product and service quality. The late Bill Smith, a reliability engineer at Motorola, is credited with originating the concept during the mid-1980s and selling it to Motorola's CEO, Robert Galvin. Smith noted that system failure rates were substantially higher than predicted by final product test and suggested several causes, including higher system complexity that resulted in more opportunities for failure and a fundamental flaw in traditional quality thinking. He concluded that a much higher level of internal quality was required and convinced Galvin of its importance.[19] As a result, Motorola set the following goals in 1987:

- Improve product and services quality 10 times by 1989, and at least 100-fold by 1991.
- Achieve Six Sigma capability by 1992.
- With a deep sense of urgency, spread dedication to quality to every facet of the corporation, and achieve a culture of continual improvement to assure total customer satisfaction. There is only one ultimate goal: zero defects—in everything we do.

The core philosophy of Six Sigma is based on some key concepts:[20]

1. Think in terms of key business processes and customer requirements with a clear focus on overall strategic objectives.
2. Focus on corporate sponsors responsible for championing projects, support team activities, help to overcome resistance to change, and obtain resources.
3. Emphasize such quantifiable measures as defects per million opportunities (dpmo) that can be applied to all parts of an organization: manufacturing, engineering, administrative, software, and so on.
4. Ensure that appropriate metrics are identified early in the process and that they focus on business results, thereby providing incentives and accountability.
5. Provide extensive training followed by project team deployment to improve profitability, reduce non–value-added activities, and achieve cycle time reduction.
6. Create highly qualified process improvement experts ("green belts," "black belts," and "master black belts") who can apply improvement tools and lead teams.
7. Set stretch objectives for improvement.

The recognized benchmark for Six Sigma implementation is General Electric (GE). The efforts by General Electric in particular, driven by former CEO Jack Welch, brought significant media attention to the concept and made Six Sigma a popular approach to quality improvement. In the mid-1990s, quality emerged as a concern of many employees at GE. Jack Welch invited Larry Bossidy, then CEO of Allied Signal, who had phenomenal success with Six Sigma, to talk about it at a Corporate Executive Council meeting. The meeting caught the attention of GE managers and, as Welch stated, "I went nuts about Six Sigma and launched it," calling it the most ambitious task the company had ever taken on.[21] To ensure success, GE changed its incentive compensation plan so that 60 percent of the bonus was based on financials and 40 percent on Six Sigma, and provided stock option grants to employees in Six Sigma training. In their first year, they trained 30,000 employees at a cost of $200 million and got back about $150 million in savings. From 1996 to 1997, GE increased the number of Six Sigma projects from 3,000 to 6,000 and achieved $320 million in productivity gains and profits. By 1998, the company had generated $750 million in Six Sigma savings over and above their investment, and would receive $1.5 billion in savings the next year.

GE had many early success stories. GE Capital, for example, fielded about 300,000 calls each year from mortgage customers who had to use voice mail or call back 24 percent of the time because employees were busy or unavailable. A Six Sigma team analyzed one branch that had a near perfect percentage of answered calls and applied their best practices to the other 41 branches, resulting in a 99.9 percent chance of customers' getting a representative on the first try. A team at GE Plastics improved the quality of a product used in CD-ROMs and audio CDs from a 3.8 sigma level to 5.7 level and captured a significant amount of new business from Sony.[22] GE credits Six Sigma with a 10-fold increase in the life of CT scanner X-ray tubes, a 400 percent improvement in return on investment in its industrial diamond business, a 62 percent reduction in turnaround time at railcar repair shops, and $400 million in savings in its plastics business.[23]

One of the key learnings GE discovered was that Six Sigma is not only for engineers. Welch observed the following:[24]

- Plant managers can use Six Sigma to reduce waste, improve product consistency, solve equipment problems, or create capacity.
- Human resource managers need it to reduce the cycle time for hiring employees.
- Regional sales managers can use it to improve forecast reliability, pricing strategies, or pricing variation.
- For that matter, plumbers, car mechanics, and gardeners can use it to better understand their customers' needs and tailor their service offerings to meet customers' wants.

After many years of implementation, Six Sigma has become a vital part of GE's company culture. In fact, as GE continues to acquire new companies, integrating Six Sigma into different business cultures is a significant challenge. Six Sigma is a priority in acquisitions and addressed early in the acquisition process.

Many other organizations such as Texas Instruments, Allied Signal (which merged with Honeywell), Boeing, 3M, Home Depot, Caterpillar, IBM, Xerox, Citibank, Raytheon, and the U.S. Air Force Air Combat Command have developed quality improvement approaches designed around the Six Sigma concept and also report significant results. Between 1995 and the first quarter of 1997, Allied Signal reported cost savings exceeding $800 million from its Six Sigma initiative. Citibank groups reduced internal callbacks by 80 percent, credit processing time by 50 percent, and cycle times of processing statements from 28 days to 15 days.[25]

Six Sigma as a Quality Framework

Six Sigma provides a blueprint for implementation of a total quality system (see the box on Samsung). In many ways, Six Sigma is the realization of many fundamental concepts of "total quality management," notably, the integration of human and process elements of improvement.[26] Human issues include management leadership, a sense of urgency, focus on results and customers, team processes, and culture change; process issues include the use of process management techniques, analysis of variation and statistical methods, a disciplined problem-solving approach, and management by fact. However, it is more than simply a repackaging of older quality approaches and traditional concepts of "total quality." Some of the contrasting features include:

- TQ is based largely on worker empowerment and teams; Six Sigma is owned by business leader champions.
- TQ activities generally occur within a function, process, or individual workplace; Six Sigma projects are truly cross-functional.
- TQ training is generally limited to simple improvement tools and concepts; Six Sigma focuses on a more rigorous and advanced set of statistical methods and a structured problem-solving methodology DMAIC—define, measure, analyze, improve, and control—which will be discussed in detail in Chapter 6.
- TQ is focused on improvement with little financial accountability; Six Sigma requires a verifiable return on investment and focus on the bottom line.

In addition, Six Sigma has elevated the importance of statistics and statistical thinking in quality improvement. Six Sigma's focus on measurable bottom-line results, a disciplined statistical approach to problem solving, rapid project completion, and organizational infrastructure make it a powerful methodology for improvement.

Six Sigma in Service Organizations

Because Six Sigma was developed in the manufacturing sector, and most publicity has revolved around companies such as Motorola and GE, many people in the service sector think that Six Sigma does not apply to their organizations. Nothing can be further from the truth.[27] All Six Sigma projects have three key characteristics:

1. a problem to be solved;
2. a process in which the problem exists; and
3. one or more measures that quantify the gap to be closed and can be used to monitor progress.

These characteristics are present in all business processes; thus, Six Sigma can easily be applied to a wide variety of transactional, administrative, and

---

Six Sigma Integration at Samsung[28]

Samsung Electronics Co. (SEC) of Seoul, Korea, was founded in 1969 and sold its first product, a television receiver, in 1971. Today Samsung is well known in the home, mobile, office networks, and core components businesses. Since its inception, SEC has used a variety of quality tools and approaches, but Six Sigma was added to upgrade its approaches and improve SEC's competitive position in world markets, specifically by optimizing the supply chain to make operations as efficient and timely as possible.

As a foundation for its Six Sigma thrust, SEC began by pursuing a goal of developing its internal resources, especially people, to put innovation first in the development and design of products, in manufacturing and marketing, and in the growth of employees. The Six Sigma process began in late 1999 and early 2000 with training for SEC's management, champions, and other employees responsible for planning and deployment. Within three years, about one third of its 49,000 employees received formal training. In 2000, manufacturing began to use Six Sigma improvement processes, and then expanded its scope to include "Design for Six Sigma" in designing new products. Next, Six Sigma was applied to business and internal support processes where customer needs and interactions have become increasingly critical. These processes include transactional activities such as completing an invoice, designing procedures to improve cycle time, and improving processes in human resources, accounting, business planning, sales, call centers, and customer service. All business processes are candidates for Six Sigma improvement. In 2000 and 2001, SEC completed 3,290 Six Sigma projects, which contributed to a 50 percent (an average) reduction in defects. No thought is given to improvement in quality and productivity without Six Sigma.

---

service areas. In fact, it is generally agreed that 50 percent or more of the total savings opportunity in an organization lies outside of manufacturing. Within the service sector, Six Sigma is beginning to be called *transactional Six Sigma*. Although Six Sigma applies equally well in service areas, it is true that services have some unique characteristics relative to manufacturing processes. First, the culture is usually less scientific and service employees typically do not think in terms of processes, measurements, and data. The processes are often invisible, complex, and not well defined or well documented. In addition, the work typically requires considerable human intervention, such as customer interaction, underwriting or approval decisions, or manual report generation. These differences make opportunities difficult to identify, and projects difficult to define. Finally, similar service activities are often done in different ways. If you have three people doing the same job, perhaps in three different locations, it is unlikely that they will do the job in the same way.

Because service processes are largely people-driven, measurements are often nonexistent or ill-defined, because many believe that defects cannot be measured. Therefore, one must create measurement systems before collecting any data. Applying Six Sigma to services requires examination of four key measures of the performance:

1. *Accuracy,* as measured by correct financial figures, completeness of information, or freedom from data errors
2. *Cycle time,* which is a measure of how long it takes to do something, such as pay an invoice
3. *Cost,* that is, the internal cost of process activities (in many cases, cost is largely determined by the accuracy and/or cycle time of the process; the longer it takes, and the more mistakes that have to be fixed, the higher the cost)
4. *Customer satisfaction,* which is typically the primary measure of success

Fortunately, important similarities can be shown between manufacturing and nonmanufacturing processes. First, both types of processes have "hidden factories," those places where the defective "product" is sent to be reworked or scrapped (revised, corrected, or discarded in nonmanufacturing terms). Find the hidden factory and you also find opportunities to improve the process. Performing manual account reconciliation in accounting, revising budgets repeatedly until management will accept them, and making repeat sales calls to customers because all the information requested by the customer was not available are all examples of the hidden factory.

Consider how a janitorial service company might use DMAIC. In the Define stage, a key question would be to define what a defect represents. One might first create a flowchart of the cleaning process, specifying what activities are performed. One example of a defect might be leaving streaks on windows, because it is a source of customer dissatisfaction, which is CTQ (critical to quality). In the Measure stage, not only would the firm want to collect data on the frequency of defects, but also information about what products and tools employees use. The Analyze stage might include evaluating differences among employees to determine why some appear better at cleaning than others. Developing a standard operating procedure might be the focus of the Improve stage. Finally, Control might entail teaching employees the correct technique and measuring improvement over time.

In one application at CNH Capital, Six Sigma tools were applied to decrease asset management cycle time in posting repossessions to a bid list and remarketing Web site.[29] Cycle time was reduced 75 percent, from 40 days to 10 days, resulting in significant ongoing dollar savings. A facility management company had a high level of "days sales outstanding." Initially, they tried to fix this issue by reducing the term of days in its billing cycle, which, however, upset customers. Using Six Sigma, they found that a large percentage of accounts with high days sales outstanding received invoices having numerous errors. After understanding the source of the errors and making process changes, the invoice process improved and days sales outstanding were reduced. At DuPont, a Six Sigma project was applied to improve cycle time for an employee's application for long-term disability benefits.[30] Some examples of financial applications of Six Sigma include the following:[31]

- Reduce the average and variation of days outstanding of accounts receivable.
- Close the books faster.
- Improve the accuracy and speed of the audit process.
- Reduce variation in cash flow.
- Improve the accuracy of journal entries (most businesses have a 3–4 percent error rate).
- Improve accuracy and cycle time of standard financial reports.

Other applications of Six Sigma in service organizations include a large insurance company that reduced its defect rate by more than 70 percent, increasing customer satisfaction dramatically, and saving over $250,000 in the first five months of the project; a financial services company that reconfigured its Web site that better reflected the questions being asked at its call center, reducing costs and improving the quality of customer service as customers were more easily able to access account information on the Web; and a facility management company that discovered that a large percentage of accounts with high days sales outstanding received error-ridden invoices from the company – by preventing these errors, days sales outstanding were reduced.[32]

COMPARING BALDRIGE, ISO 9000, AND SIX SIGMA

We examined three major frameworks for quality management systems: the Baldrige Criteria for Performance Excellence, ISO 9000, and Six Sigma. Although each of these frameworks are process-focused, data-based, and management-led, each offers a different emphasis in helping organizations improve performance and increase customer satisfaction. For example, Baldrige focuses on performance excellence for the entire organization in an overall management framework, identifying and tracking important organizational results; ISO focuses on product and service conformity for guaranteeing equity in the marketplace and concentrates on fixing quality system problems and product and service nonconformities; and Six Sigma concentrates on measuring product quality and driving process improvement and cost savings throughout the organization.

Although the 2000 revision of ISO 9000 incorporated many of the Baldrige criteria's original principles, it still is not a comprehensive business performance framework. Nevertheless, it is an excellent way to begin a quality journey. ISO 9000 provides a set of good basic practices for initiating a quality system, and is an excellent starting point for companies with no formal quality assurance program. In fact, it provides more detailed guidance on process and product control than Baldrige, and provides systematic approaches to many of the Baldrige criteria requirements in the Process Management category. Thus, for companies in the early stages of developing a quality program, the standards enforce the discipline of control that is necessary before they can seriously pursue continuous improvement. The requirements of periodic audits reinforce the stated quality system until it becomes ingrained in the company.

Implementing Six Sigma fulfills in part many of the elements of ISO 9000:2000, including the Quality Management System, Resource Management, Product Realization, and Measurement, Analysis, and Improvement sections of the standards.[33] For instance, Six Sigma helps to demonstrate management commitment through periodic review of Six Sigma plans and projects, providing champions to sponsor projects, providing training resources, and communicating progress and achievements.

A critical question is whether an organization using Baldrige will be more successful if it also uses Six Sigma, and vice versa. If one views Six Sigma as only a small part of the Process Management category, one might believe that the impact would be marginal. However, let us examine the role of Six Sigma in each of the seven Baldrige categories. Six Sigma enhances the ability of leadership to focus on the critical factors that make a business successful and select appropriate strategies and action plans. Therefore, Six Sigma can strengthen management practices in Leadership and Strategic Planning. Understanding customer requirements and linking them to processes and delivery systems is a principal focus of Baldrige. By focusing on critical to quality (CTQ) customer requirements—one of the important concepts in Six Sigma, organizations gain better knowledge about customer requirements, a key component of the Customer Focus category.

Six Sigma methodology is driven by a management-by-fact methodology. This basis can improve an organization's ability to meet the requirements in the Measurement, Analysis, and Knowledge Management category. The role of people in championing projects and providing the technical and application-specific knowledge is vital. Six Sigma can improve work systems, training, and the work environment—all critical components of the Human Resource Focus Baldrige category. With Six Sigma, process management is not a by-product, but it is one of the primary organizational goals. The DMAIC methodology provides a structured approach to Category 6, Process Management. Finally, Six Sigma's focus on business results leads organizations to track and monitor appropriate metrics.

REVIEW AND DISCUSSION QUESTIONS

1. Summarize the framework of the Baldrige Award. What are its key philosophical underpinnings?
2. Describe the key issues addressed in each of the seven categories of the Criteria for Performance Excellence.

3. How do the Baldrige criteria support Deming's 14 Points?

4. Explain the differences among the Baldrige, European, Canadian, and Australian Quality Awards.

5. Prepare a list of specific actions that a high-scoring company in the Baldrige Award process might take in each of the seven categories. How difficult do you think it is for a company to score well in all the categories?

6. Create a matrix diagram in which each row is a category of the Baldrige Award criteria and four columns correspond to a level of organizational maturity with respect to quality:
   • traditional management practices;
   • growing awareness of the importance of quality;
   • development of a solid quality management system;
   • outstanding, world-class management practice.
   In each cell of the matrix, list two to five characteristics that you would expect to see for a company in each of the four situations above for that criteria category. How might this matrix be used as a self-assessment tool to provide directions for improvement?

7. Discuss the implications of the Baldrige criteria for e-commerce. What are the specific challenges that e-commerce companies face within each category of the criteria?

8. Explain the benefits of and controversy surrounding ISO 9000. Can ISO 9000 lead an organization to world-class quality?

9. Map the elements of ISO 9000:2000 against the Baldrige criteria. How are they similar? How are they different?

10. Search the Web for detailed information about ISO 9000 requirements. Although the language of the standard appears to be primarily for manufacturing, try to rewrite some of the requirements in language that would provide a framework for a typical public school system to use the standard.

11. Describe the evolution of Six Sigma. What impact has it had on General Electric? What differences must be addressed in applying Six Sigma in service organizations?

12. What are the similarities and differences among Six Sigma, ISO 9000, and the Baldrige approaches?

13. What philosophical changes might be required to implement a Six Sigma process in a hospital, government agency, or not-for-profit organization? Are they likely to be easy or difficult?

14. How might the principles of Six Sigma be used to improve a quality process in a school or university? What elements of the Six Sigma philosophy might be difficult to obtain support for in the educational environment? Why?

15. Find a company that has implemented a Six Sigma process. What changes have they made in the organization in order to develop their Six Sigma approach?

CASES

Modern Steel Technology, Inc.

Modern Steel Technology, Inc. (MST) is a supplier of custom-designed, hardened steel components and replacement parts to heavy industry worldwide. Steel mills and mining companies account for 75 percent of sales, while aluminum, paper, chemical, and cement industries account for the remaining 25 percent. The main product groups are gears, couplings, wheels, and rolls.

MST operates three plants—two in Pennsylvania and one in Canada—and employs 374 people. The MST mission is to "serve our customers by producing and delivering products of superior quality and value; maintain a commitment to continuous improvement, and provide long-term value to our shareholders." Each year the president and his staff meet off-site to develop and refine a plan for the next year, discuss goals, strategies, and objectives, and make capacity, personnel, and quality decisions. This plan is then passed down to middle management for review and suggestions. Middle management takes the yearly plan and determines monthly goals for sales, production, inventory, backlog, expenses, and revenues. All employees have access to these plans. Every three months, managers review their department's progress against the plan and present the results to the president. If the plan is not being met, suggestions for improvement are discussed.

MST is conscious of its community responsibilities at its Pennsylvania headquarters. The CEO is a board member of the United Way, the Fine Arts Council, and other local community efforts. Annually, MST employees are encouraged to contribute to these causes. MST complies with all Environmental Protection Agency (EPA) and Occupational Safety and Health Act (OSHA) regulations, and offers flu shots and other health-related seminars to its employees.

MST understands its customer requirements. In a highly competitive industry, failure to meet a customer need usually results in a lost customer. For example, European Community customers required ISO 9000 certification, which MST was able to obtain in June of 1995. Customer satisfaction is determined by on-time delivery and quality results. Each year, the roll product managers visit all customers and conduct a survey on product performance. Often, a latent customer need is determined, and MST seeks ways to fulfill this need.

MST uses a mainframe computer-based information system to track quotes, orders, inventory, schedules, and purchasing activities. Networked PCs within the company allow different departments to access the same information. Departments have access only to those databases they use. For example, the Quality Department monitors on-time delivery, cycle time, and cost. Several improvements have been made. For example, roll heat treat recipes were kept in duplicate books by both the Metallurgy and Heat Treat departments, resulting in errors if only one book was updated. These are now maintained in a common database, accessible to both departments.

MST compares its performance to competitors by examining product performance of rolls at steel mills. In addition, the company uses annual surveys of the gear industry published by a manufacturing association to compare its gears against others based on performance and production cost. The company also uses cost-of-quality indicators to measure performance. An external measure is defined as the cost to repair or replace a product after it fails, and an internal measure is the cost of rework and scrap. Each internal incident is traced back and charged to the budget of the responsible department. These are analyzed in total to determine possible corrective actions.

Employee excellence is recognized through the use of annual employee appraisals. The employee and his or her immediate supervisor sit down and discuss the appraisal and the employee's score. Merit raises are based on the appraisal. The discussion also identifies any weaknesses the employee may have, and additional training may be suggested to strengthen the weak areas.

Promotions generally occur when vacancies are established. Consequently, turnover of salaried employees is relatively high. MST has an employee stock ownership plan. In 1997, the last of the company stock was distributed, and new employees contribute to a base retirement plan and are unable to participate in company ownership. Customer requirements are transmitted through blueprints. Blueprints are generated by the Engineering Department and contain product dimensions, specified hardness requirements, and other information necessary to manufacture the product.

Quality control measurement techniques are defined and vary by product. Key product characteristics, such as gear tooth thickness, are measured against tolerances. Inspection personnel are trained and certified in applicable testing techniques. If a dimension is out of tolerance, the inspector must call a technician who will decide whether immediate corrective action should be taken. A department manager makes the decision to take preventive action to stop an undesirable condition from recurring. MST maintains an informal partnership with a supplier of forgings. MST meets periodically to convey its requirements.

Currently, on-time delivery is above 90 percent for all product groups except gears, which is at a 60 percent level. Delivery dates for gears are difficult to determine because the product mix is constantly changing, cycle times vary, and machines used for production are common to several products, creating a challenge for capacity planners.

Assignment

Using the Baldrige criteria, identify any key strengths relating to MST's approach and deployment of its practices, and any major weaknesses or gaps. How well does the company address the three core principles of total quality?

TecSmart Electronics

TecSmart Electronics designs, manufactures, and repairs electronic power supplies for a variety of original equipment manufacturers in the computer, medical, and office products fields. The company's focus is summed up by three simple words: quality, service, and value. The top management team started its quality journey in the mid-1980s, basing it on Deming's 14 Points. They established a Deming Steering Committee to guide the process and champion each of the 14 Points, and trained most of the employees by sending them to Deming seminars. Although the Deming philosophy provided the foundation to carry the company into the twenty-first century, the current CEO decided to pursue a Baldrige focus and began a process of self-assessment against the criteria to identify opportunities for improvement.

As a first preparatory step, the executive team spent a day off site to think about its management practices and create an initial list of its strengths, which are summarized here.

- Senior leaders set company objectives and guide cross-functional teams to review and develop individual plans for presentation to employees. Each department manager develops a supporting objective for each company objective, and nearly every employee works on a team to support these objectives.
- Senior leaders participate in quarterly communication meetings with all employees to discuss company issues and answer questions. All employees receive full financial information from their managers each month.
- Senior leaders teach courses in TecSmart University on change management, customer service, quality, and leadership; meet with customers, suppliers, and benchmarking partners; and are actively engaged in professional and community organizations.
- The company collects operational data in every department and evaluates its information requirements in monthly senior staff meetings and cross-functional task team meetings.
- TecSmart sets Six Sigma goals for most of its processes and converted process measurements to parts per million on all product lines.
- All employees are trained in a five-step problem-solving process based on defining problems, collecting data, analyzing the cause of the problem, developing a solution, and implementing change.
- Inputs to the strategic planning process include customer feedback, market research, and benchmarking information from customers, suppliers, competitors, and industry leaders. Team analyses are evaluated at an off-site planning meeting by all managers, resulting in long-range strategic planning documents, which are discussed with the rest of the workforce as well as major suppliers for feasibility. Once agreed upon, department teams develop detailed action plans with measurable goals. The CEO reviews progress every month.

- TecSmart uses more than a dozen different processes to gather customer information, and validates the information by consolidation and cross-referencing.
- All employees receive customer relationship training. Customer service employees help define service standards, which are tracked on a routine basis.
- All complaints are handled by the vice president of sales and resolved within two days. The vice president is responsible for ensuring that any process that generated a complaint is improved.
- Customer satisfaction data is acquired from sales representatives, executive phone calls and visits, and satisfaction surveys. These data are reviewed and compared by the executive team during the strategic planning process.
- TecSmart uses self-managed work groups in which employees make most day-to-day decisions while managers focus on coaching and process improvement. Hourly workers can make process changes with the agreement of only one other person, and salespeople are authorized to travel whenever they feel it necessary for customer service.
- The average employee receives 72 hours of internal quality/service-related training, and quality training is mandatory for all salespeople, engineers, office staff, and managers.
- Employees are surveyed each year to gauge how effectively the company implemented Deming's 14 Points, rating each on a scale of 1 to 10.
- Cross-functional teams guide product development, which includes four interim reviews by executive management. Meetings are held with customers to identify needs and requirements and to review progress at the end of each phase of the development process.
- New product introduction teams work with design engineers and customers to ensure that design requirements are met during manufacturing and testing. All processes are formally documented, using statistical process control to monitor variation and provide a basis for corrective action. Statistical methods are used to optimize processes.
- Quality is assessed through internal audits, employee opinion surveys, and customer feedback.
- Suppliers are involved in early stages of a product development program. Quality requirements for suppliers have been identified, and certified suppliers' materials are exempt from incoming inspection.

Discussion Questions

1. Discuss how the practices that TecSmart identified support Deming's 14 Points.
2. How do these practices support the Baldrige criteria? Specifically, identify which of the questions in the criteria each of these practices address.

3. What are some of the obvious opportunities for improvement relative to the Baldrige criteria? What actions would you recommend that TecSmart do to improve its pursuit of performance excellence using the Baldrige criteria?

Can Six Sigma Work in Health Care?

Colin David is the CEO of Southwest Louisiana Regional Medical Center (SLRMC), a small nonprofit hospital with 150 beds and 825 employees, offering a wide range of outpatient and inpatient services. Colin had just returned from a health care conference during which one of the keynote speakers—from the financial services industry—discussed the philosophy and benefits of Six Sigma and urged health care organizations to consider moving toward a Six Sigma framework. Colin was quite excited. However, he knew that changing the culture in a hospital was indeed difficult. He felt that if he could accomplish that, SLRMC could truly become a nationally recognized leader in the industry. In discussing the concept, the executive management team was also excited at the possibilities. They identified four key areas where they thought that Six Sigma could lead to significant benefits: patient services, quality assessment, financial management, and human resources. As time was running short for the meeting, the team concluded with one major action item: the directors in charge of each of these four areas were to develop a set of strategic Six Sigma projects that would form the basis for the initiative. However, after the meeting broke up, Colin realized that in their initial euphoria over the potential of Six Sigma, they had not thought of how to introduce it to the hospital staff and physicians, or how to manage the initiative. Colin decided that it would be best to call in a consultant to help. Because *you* were highly recommended, you have a meeting scheduled with Colin in one week. What would be your agenda for this meeting? What questions would you need answered before proposing a Six Sigma implementation plan? How would you design an infrastructure to support Six Sigma at SLRMC?

ENDNOTES

1. Adapted from The Ritz-Carlton Hotel Co., 1992 and 1999 Malcolm Baldrige National Quality Award application summaries.

2. Adapted from Jerry R. Junkins, "Insights of a Baldrige Award Winner," *Quality Progress*, Vol. 27, No. 3, March 1994, pp. 57–58.

3. Paul M. Bobrowski and John H. Bantham, "State Quality Initiatives: Mini-Baldrige to Baldrige Plus," *National Productivity Review*, Vol. 13, No. 3, Summer 1994, pp. 423–438.

4. Letter from W. Edwards Deming, *Harvard Business Review*, January–February 1992, p. 134.

5. JUSE, The Deming Prize Guide for Oversea Companies, TOKYO, 1992, p. 5.

6. Brad Stratton, "A Beacon for the World," *Quality Progress*, May 1990, pp. 60–65; Al Henderson and Target Staff, "For Florida Power and Light After the Deming Prize: The Music Builds . . . and Builds . . . and Builds," *Target*, Summer 1990, pp. 10–21.

7. B. Nakkai and J. Neves, "The Deming, Baldrige, and European Quality Awards," *Quality Progress,* April 1994, pp. 24–29.

8. Michael J. Timbers, "ISO 9000 and Europe's Attempts to Mandate Quality," *Journal of European Business,* March/April 1992, pp. 14–25.

9. http://www.bsi.org.uk/iso-tc176-sc2/. "Transition Planning Guidance for *ISO/DIS 9001:2000,"* ISO/TC 176/SC 2/N 474, December 1999.

10. Richard C. Randall, "Quality in the Dot.Com World," *Quality Progress,* February 2001, 86–87.

11. Amy Zuckerman, "ISO/QS-9000 Registration Issues Heating Up Worldwide," *The Quality Observer,* June 1997, pp. 21–23.

12. Amy Zuckerman and Rosalind McClymont, "Tracking the Ongoing ISO 9000 Revisions," *Business Standards,* Vol. 2, No. 2, March/April 2000, pp. 13–15. Jack West with Charles A. Cianfrani and Joseph J. Tsiakals, "A Breeze or a Breakthough? Conforming to ISO 9000:2000," *Quality Progress,* March 2000, pp. 41–44. See also by West et al., "Quality Management Principles: Foundation of ISO 9000:2000 Family, Part 5," *Quality Progress,* February 2000, pp. 113–116; and "Quality Management Principles: Foundation of ISO 9000:2000 Family, Part 6," *Quality Progress,* March 2000, pp. 79–81.

13. Implementation guidelines are suggested by the case study by Steven E. Webster, "ISO 9000 Certification, A Success Story at Nu Visions Manufacturing," *IIE Solutions,* April 1997, pp. 18–21.

14. AT&T Corporate Quality Office, *Using ISO 9000 to Improve Business Processes,* July 1994.

15. ISO 9000 Update, *Fortune,* September 30, 1996, p. 134[J].

16. Astrid L. H. Eckstein and Jaydeep Balakrishnan, "The ISO 9000 Series: Quality Management Systems for the Global Economy," *Production and Inventory Management Journal,* Vol. 34, No. 4, Fourth Quarter 1993, pp. 66–71.

17. "Home Builder Constructs Quality with ISO 9000," *Quality Digest,* February 2000, p. 13.

18. Hank Rogers, "Benchmarking Your Plant against TQM Best-Practices Plants, Part 2," *Quality Progress,* April 1998, pp. 60–64.

19. "Origin of Six Sigma: Designing for Performance Excellence," *Quality Digest,* May 2000, 30; and Mikel Harry and Richard Schroeder, *Six Sigma,* New York: Currency, 2000, 9–11.

20. A composite of ideas suggested by Stanley A. Marash, "Six Sigma: Business Results Through Innovation," *ASQ's 54th Annual Quality Congress Proceedings,* 2000, 627–630; and Dick Smith and Jerry Blakeslee, *Strategic Six Sigma: Best Practices from the Executive Suite,* New York: Wiley, 2002.

21. Jack Welch, *Jack: Straight from the Gut,* New York: Warner Books, 2001, 329–330.

22. Welch, *Jack,* 333–334.

23. "GE Reports Record Earnings with Six Sigma," *Quality Digest,* December 1999, 14.

24. See note 21.

25. Rochelle Rucker, "Six Sigma at Citibank," *Quality Digest,* December 1999, 28–32.

26. Ronald D. Snee, "Guest Editorial: Impact of Six Sigma on Quality Engineering," *Quality Engineering,* 12, No. 3, 2000, ix–xiv.

27. This discussion of the adaptability of Six Sigma to services is adapted from Soren Bisgaard, Roger W. Hoerl, and Ronald D. Snee, "Improving Business Processes With Six Sigma," *Proceedings of ASQ's 56th Annual Quality Congress,* 2002 (CD-ROM), and Kennedy Smith, "Six Sigma for the Service Sector," *Quality Digest,* May 2003, 23–28.

28. Jong-Yong Yun and Richard C.H. Chua, "Samsung Uses Six Sigma to Change its Image," *Six Sigma Forum Magazine,* 2, No. 1, November 2002, 13–16.

29. Adapted from Elizabeth Keim, LouAnn Fox, and Julie S. Mazza, "Service Quality Six Sigma Case Studies," *Proceedings of the 54th Annual Quality Congress of the American Society for Quality,* 2000 (CD-ROM).

30. Lisa Palser, "Cycle Time Improvement for a Human Resources Process," *ASQ's 54th Annual Quality Congress Proceedings,* 2000 (CD-ROM).

31. Roger Hoerl, "An Inside Look at Six Sigma at GE," *Six Sigma Forum Magazine,* 1, No. 3, May 2002, 35–44.

32. Kennedy Smith, "Six Sigma for the Service Sector," *Quality Digest,* May 2003, 23–27.

33. Ronald D. Snee and Roger W. Hoerl, *Leading Six Sigma,* Upper Saddle River, N.J.: Prentice Hall, 2002.

CHAPTER 3

Total Quality, Competitive Advantage, and Strategic Management

Competitive advantage denotes a firm's ability to achieve market superiority over its competitors. In the long run, a sustainable competitive advantage provides above-average performance. A firm has many options in defining its long-term goals and objectives, the customers it wants to serve, the products and services it produces and delivers, and the design of the production and service system to meet these objectives. Creating a sustainable competitive advantage depends on developing and executing a good strategy. **Strategy** is the pattern of decisions that determines and reveals a company's goals, policies, and plans to meet the needs of its stakeholders. **Strategic planning** is the process by which the members of an organization envision its future and develop the necessary procedures and operations to carry out that vision.

This chapter focuses on how total quality contributes to competitive advantage and discusses the role of quality in an organization's business strategy. This chapter will

➤ examine the relationship between quality and profitability;
➤ discuss cost leadership, differentiation, and people as principal sources of competitive advantage, and their relationship to quality;
➤ describe the importance of quality in meeting customer expectations in product design, service, flexibility and variety, innovation, and rapid response;
➤ discuss the role of information in strategic planning and quality-focused decisions; and
➤ describe the role of quality in strategy formulation and implementation.

QUALITY AND COMPETITIVE ADVANTAGE

A strong competitive advantage has six characteristics,[1] each of which relates closely to, and is supported by, a total quality focus.

1. A strong competitive advantage is driven by customer wants and needs. A company provides value to its customers that competitors do not. Customer wants and needs form the basis for all quality initiatives. Six Sigma projects, for example, revolve around improving CTQs—"critical to quality" characteristics that are vital to customers.

2. A strong competitive advantage makes a significant contribution to the success of the business. There is considerable evidence that a TQ focus positively affects the bottom line. Baldrige winners have typically outperformed the industry as a whole, and Six Sigma projects must be justified financially.

3. A strong competitive advantage matches the organization's unique resources with the opportunities in the environment. No two companies have the same resources; a good strategy uses them effectively. TQ pays particular attention to an organization's human resources and process designs in executing a business strategy.

4. A strong competitive advantage is durable and lasting and difficult for competitors to copy. A superior research and development department, for example, can consistently develop new products or processes to remain ahead of competitors. A TQ culture takes years to develop but, once in place, is difficult to diffuse because it has become so ingrained in the attitudes and thinking processes of all employees—workers and managers alike.

5. A strong competitive advantage provides a basis for further improvement. A TQ culture is constantly focusing on improvement and learning, and exploits the myriad of tools and techniques available to implement improvements. Six Sigma projects are vital for continually improving designs and processes.

6. A strong competitive advantage provides direction and motivation to the entire organization. TQ initiatives marshal the collective talents of everyone. The GE experience in deploying Six Sigma throughout the company, for example, focuses everyone on working toward common goals. When supported by incentives and rewards, TQ initiatives can motivate everyone.

We may conclude that a total quality focus can be an important means of developing, gaining, and sustaining competitive advantage.

The role of quality in achieving competitive advantage was demonstrated by several research studies during the 1980s. PIMS Associates, Inc., a subsidiary of the Strategic Planning Institute, maintains a database of 1,200 companies and studies the impact of product quality on corporate perform-ance.[2] PIMS researchers have found that

- Product quality is the most important determinant of business profitability.
- Businesses offering premium quality products and services usually have large market shares and were early entrants into their markets.
- Quality is positively and significantly related to a higher return on investment for almost all kinds of products and market situations. PIMS studies have shown that firms with products of superior quality can more than triple return on sales over products perceived as having infe-rior quality.
- A strategy of quality improvement usually leads to increased market share but at a cost in terms of reduced short-run profitability.
- High-quality producers can usually charge premium prices.

General Systems Company, a prominent quality management consult-ing firm, has found that firms with TQ systems in place consistently exceed industry norms for return on investment. This is attributed to three factors:

1. TQ reduces the direct costs associated with poor quality.
2. Improvements in quality tend to lead to increases in productivity.
3. The combination of improved quality and increased productivity leads to an increase in market share.

These findings are summarized in Figure 3.1. The value of a product in the marketplace is influenced by the quality of its design. Improvements in performance, features, and reliability will differentiate the product from its competitors, improve a firm's quality reputation, and improve the perceived value of the product. This allows the company to command higher prices and achieve an increased market share. This, in turn, leads to increased revenues that offset the added costs of improved design.

FIGURE 3.1   QUALITY AND PROFITABILITY

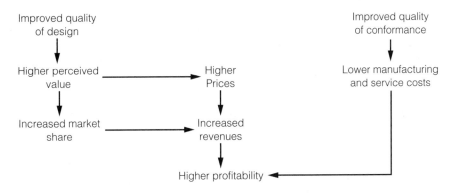

Improved conformance in production leads to lower manufacturing and service costs through savings in rework, scrap, and warranty expenses. This viewpoint was popularized by Philip Crosby in his book *Quality Is Free*.[3] As Crosby states:

> Quality is not only free, it is an honest-to-everything profit maker. Every penny you don't spend on doing things wrong, over, or instead of, becomes half a penny right on the bottom line. In these days of "who knows what is going to happen to our business tomorrow," there aren't many ways left to make a profit improvement. If you concentrate on making quality certain, you can probably increase your profit by an amount equal to 5 percent to 10 percent of your sales. That is a lot of money for free.

The net effect of improved quality of design and conformance is increased profits. Today, many consumers are basing their purchasing decisions on *value*. Value can be defined as quality relative to price. When organizations provide less perceived value than their competitors, they lose market share.

Flawless Isn't Enough[4]

According to *Consumer Reports*, one of the most reliable midsize cars in America is the Buick Regal. General Motors has been steadily improving its quality to the point where it has narrowed the gap compared with the best Japanese models, such as the Toyota Camry and Honda Accord. Domestic defect rates have fallen more than 80 percent since 1980. Despite its high level of conformance quality, the Regal did not receive a *Consumer Reports* recommendation, citing "ungainly handling . . . and front seats that become less comfortable the longer you sit in them." Increasing consumer demands on dimensions of quality beyond low levels of manufacturing defects has raised the bar for all automobile manufacturers. Many of today's complaints revolve around things that a carmaker builds flawlessly but aren't quite what a consumer wants. Technical failures have given way to failures to satisfy the customer. Even Toyota, whose conformance quality is near perfection, has been criticized for mundane styling. One review of the Lexus IS 300 suggested: "Spend less time 'passionately pursuing perfection' and spend more time pumping up the power and spicing up the sport." U.S. companies have been aggressively pursuing new and innovative model designs, even recruiting European designers. Chrysler's chief executive noted "We've changed the mindset of our employees to recognize that 'relatively good' is not good enough."

This is what happened to U.S. automakers in the 1970s and 1980s. Thus, firms must focus their efforts at both improving the quality of design and service as well as reducing costs.

One might think that simply providing high conformance quality would be enough to capture customers and markets. Thirty years ago it would have; today it is simply the "entry into the game" (see the box "Flawless Isn't Enough"). No longer can firms focus their quality efforts solely on defect elimination. Both Deming and Juran stressed the need for never-ending cycles of market research, improved product development and design, production, and sales.

Baldrige Award finalists and winners have demonstrated that quality leads to competitive advantage and improved business performance. A 1991 General Accounting Office study of Baldrige finalists explored four measurable areas of a company's operations that could demonstrate the impact of TQ practices on corporate performance:[5]

1. employee relations,
2. operating procedures,
3. customer satisfaction, and
4. financial performance.

In employee relations, significant improvements were realized in employee satisfaction, attendance, turnover, safety and health, and suggestions received. In operating procedures, favorable results were realized in reliability, timeliness of delivery, order-processing times, errors and defects, product lead time, inventory turnover, cost of quality, and overall cost savings. Overall customer satisfaction also improved, as customer complaints fell and customer retention rose. In the financial performance area, market share, sales per employee, return on assets, and return on sales all showed positive improvement for most companies.

The GAO developed a general framework for describing Total Quality Management and its effect on competitiveness (see Figure 3.2.). The solid line shows how TQ processes lead to improved competitiveness, beginning with leadership dedicated to improving products and services, as well as quality systems. Improvements in these areas lead to customer satisfaction and benefits to the organization, both of which improve competitiveness. The dotted lines show the information feedback necessary for continuous improvement. The arrows in the boxes show the expected direction of the performance indicators.

Although the GAO study is somewhat dated, the conclusions remain valid today. A more recent survey of almost 1,000 executives conducted by Zenger Miller Achieve noted similar benefits from quality initiatives, including increased employee participation, improved product and service quality, improved customer satisfaction, improved productivity, and improved employee skills.[6]

FIGURE 3.2   GENERAL ACCOUNTING OFFICE FRAMEWORK

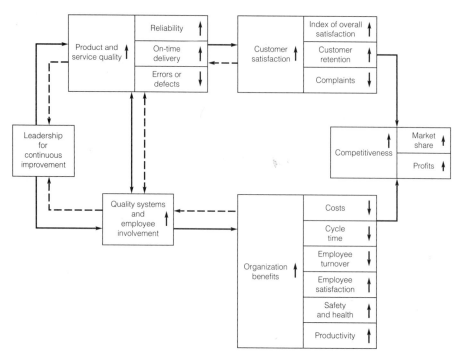

Perhaps the most comprehensive study to date, which has garnered a lot of attention in the business press, is that of Hendricks and Singhal.[7] Based on objective data and rigorous statistical analysis, the study showed that, when implemented effectively, total quality management approaches improve financial performance dramatically. Using a sample of about 600 publicly traded companies that have won quality awards either from their customers (such as automotive manufacturers) or through Baldrige and state and local quality award programs, Hendricks and Singhal examined performance results from six years before to four years after winning their first quality award.

The primary performance measure tracked was the percentage change in operating income and a variety of measures that might affect operating income: percentage change in sales, total assets, number of employees, return on sales, and return on assets. These results were compared to a set of control firms that were similar in size to the award winners and in the same industry. The analysis revealed significant differences between the sample and the control groups. Specifically, the growth in operating income of winners averaged 91 percent versus 43 percent for the control group. Winners also experienced a 69 percent jump in sales (compared to 32 percent for the control group), a 79 percent increase in total assets (compared to 37 percent), a 23 percent increase in the number of employees (compared to 7 percent), an 8 percent improvement on return on sales (compared to 0 percent), and a 9 percent improvement on return on assets (compared to 6 percent). Small companies actually outperformed large companies, and over a five-year period, the portfolio of winners beat the S&P 500 index by 34 percent.

SOURCES OF COMPETITIVE ADVANTAGE

The classic literature on competitive strategy suggests that a firm can possess two basic types of competitive advantage: low cost and differentiation.[8] For example, Marriott's Fairfield Inn was designed to appeal to business travelers who wanted clean, comfortable rooms at inexpensive prices. Within this market, they are focused on cost leadership. By contrast, The Ritz-Carlton hotels focus on differentiation (exceptional personal attention, twice-a-day housekeeping service, and special amenities such as bathrobes and rooms with bay windows) and can command premium prices. Figure 3.1 supports this premise by showing how cost reduction and improved design affect profitability. Modern thinking has added a third source of competitive advantage—an organization's people.[9]

Cost Leadership

Many firms gain competitive advantage by establishing themselves as the low cost leader in an industry. These firms produce high volumes of mature products and achieve their competitive advantage through low prices. Such firms often enter markets that were established by other firms. They emphasize achieving economies of scale and finding cost advantages from all sources.

A cost leader can achieve above-average performance if it can command prices at or near the industry average. However, it cannot do so with an inferior product (see the box about Schlitz Brewing Company). The product must be perceived as comparable with competitors or the firm will be forced to discount prices well below competitors' prices to gain sales. This can cancel any benefits that result from cost advantage.

Low cost can result from high productivity and high capacity utilization. More important, improvements in quality lead to improvements in productivity, which in turn lead to lower costs. Lower costs result from innovations in product design and process technology that reduce the costs of production and from efficiencies gained through meticulous attention to operations. This approach has been exploited by many Japanese firms. Japanese companies adopted many product innovations and process technologies that were developed in the United States. They refined the designs and manufacturing processes to produce high-quality products at low costs, resulting in higher market shares. Thus, a strategy of continuous improvement is essential to achieve a low-cost competitive advantage.

To achieve cost leadership for high-volume products, companies use a variety of approaches:[10]

- Early manufacturing involvement in the design of the product both for make-versus-buy decisions and for assurance that the production processes can achieve required tolerances.
- Product design to take advantage of automated equipment by minimizing the number of parts, eliminating fasteners, making parts symmetric whenever possible, avoiding rigid and stiff parts, and using one-sided assembly designs.
- Limited product models and customization in distribution centers rather than in the factory.
- A manufacturing system designed for a fixed sequence of operations. Every effort is made to ensure zero defects at the time of shipment. Work-in-process inventory is reduced as much as possible, and multiskilled, focused teams of employees are used.

Six Sigma can be an important way for organizations to build and sustain low-cost leadership, because they identify sources of problems and opportunities for process and design improvements that have clear financial justifications and impact on the bottom line. Moreover, Six Sigma creates the organizational infrastructure for continually focusing on cost reduction in all manufacturing and service operations.

You Can't Fool All of the People All of the Time

The problems with focusing on costs at the expense of quality are illustrated by the case of the Schlitz Brewing Company.[11] In the early 1970s, Schlitz, the second largest brewer in the United States, began a cost-cutting campaign. It included reducing the quality of ingredients in their beers by switching to corn syrup and hop pellets and shortening the brewing cycle by 50 percent.

In the short term, it achieved higher returns on sales and assets than Anheuser-Bush (and the acclaim of Wall Street analysts). *Forbes* magazine stated, "Does it pay to build quality into a product if most customers don't notice? Schlitz seems to have a more successful answer." But customers do recognize inferior products. Soon after, market share and profits fell rapidly.

By 1980 Schlitz's sales had declined 40 percent, the stock price fell from $69 to $5, and the company was eventually sold.

Differentiation

To achieve differentiation, a firm must be unique in its industry along some dimensions that are widely valued by customers. It selects one or more attributes that customers perceive as important and positions itself uniquely to meet those needs. For instance, Dell's direct business model was the first of its kind in the computer industry and continues to be a principal source of the company's success.

Often, a firm with a differentiation strategy can command premium prices and achieve higher profits. Juran cites an example of a power tool manufacturer that improved reliability well beyond that of competitors.[12] Field data showing that the differences in reliability resulted in significantly lower operating costs were publicized, and the company was able to secure a premium price.

However, a firm that uses differentiation as its source of competitive advantage must make its products or systems difficult to copy. Often this involves culture, habits, and sunk costs. For example, why doesn't every company copy Dell's superior direct business model? Dell's approaches are hardly a secret; even Michael Dell has written a book about it. Competitors have copied its Web site with stunning precision, but they face far greater difficulty copying the supporting activities—purchasing, scheduling, and logistics—that Dell has built around its direct model over several decades. Competitors are burdened by long-standing relationships with suppliers and distributors and by a different culture. [13]

People

The importance of people in building and sustaining a TQ organization is illustrated by the following anecdote about Toyota. Toyota's Georgetown, Kentucky, plant has been a three-time winner of the J. D. Power Gold Plant Quality Award. When asked about the "secret" behind the superior Toyota paint finishes, one manager replied, "We've got nothing, technology-wise, that anyone else can't have. There's no secret Toyota Quality Machine out there. The quality machine is the workforce—the team members on the paint line, the suppliers, the engineers—everybody who has a hand in production here takes the attitude that we're making world-class vehicles."[14] The human resource is the *only* one that competitors cannot copy, and the *only* one that can synergize—that is, produce output whose value is greater than the sum of its parts.

The competitive advantage resulting from an organization's people can drive low cost and differentiation. For example, over several decades, Southwest Airlines has been the most profitable U.S. carrier. It has fewer employees per aircraft and flies more passengers per employee. Much of its cost advantage comes from its very productive, motivated, and unionized workforce.[15]

Is its competitive advantage low cost, or is it the people? Southwest Airlines has one of the most distinct competitive advantages in the airline industry. Herb Kelleher, former CEO, once stated, "It's the intangibles that are the hardest things for competitors to imitate. You can get on an airplane. You can get ticket-counter space, you can get baggage conveyors. But it is our esprit de corps—the culture, the spirit—that is truly our most valuable competitive asset." Similar comments can be made about The Ritz-Carlton Hotel Company, a two-time Baldrige winner. One of the author's personal observations about Baldrige winners is the fact that employees genuinely like to work for their organizations and are highly satisfied with their jobs.

Providing a work environment that fosters cooperation, initiative, and innovation; educating and training the workforce; and enhancing the factors that affect well-being, satisfaction, and motivation are very difficult for competitors to copy. This is a significantly different philosophy from the work environment that came into being during the Industrial Revolution.

Prior to the Industrial Revolution, skilled craftspeople had a major stake in the quality of their products because their families' livelihoods depended on the sale of those products. The departure from the craftsmanship concept was promulgated by Frederick W. Taylor. Taylor concluded that a factory should be managed on a scientific basis. So he focused on work methods design, the establishment of standards for daily work, selection and training of workers, and piecework incentives. Taylor separated planning from execution, concluding that foremen and workers of those days lacked the education necessary to plan their work. The foreman's role was to ensure that the workforce met productivity standards. Other pioneers of scientific management, such as Frank and Lillian Gilbreth and Henry Gantt, further refined the Taylor system through motion study, methods improvement, ergonomics, scheduling, and wage incentive systems.

The Taylor system dramatically improved productivity and was principally responsible for the industrial growth of the twentieth century. However, it also changed many manufacturing jobs into a series of mundane and mindless tasks. Without a systems perspective and a focus on the customer, the responsibility for quality shifted from workers to inspectors, and as a result, quality eroded. The Taylor philosophy also contributed to the development of labor unions and established an adversarial relationship between labor and management that has yet to be completely overcome. Perhaps the most significant failure of the Taylor system was that it failed to make use of an organization's most important asset—the knowledge and creativity of the workforce. As executives at The Ritz-Carlton Hotel Company have stated, human beings don't serve a function, they have a purpose, and the role of the human resources function is to unleash the power of the workforce to achieve the goals of the organization.[16]

QUALITY AND DIFFERENTIATION STRATEGIES

Competitive advantage is gained from meeting or exceeding customer expectations—the fundamental definition of quality. A business may concentrate on any of several quality-related dimensions in order to differentiate itself from its competition. These key dimensions are:

- superior product and service design,
- outstanding service,
- high agility,
- continuous innovation, and
- rapid response.

Traditional management strategists advocated focusing on a single dimension. However, as consumers become more demanding, firms can no longer compete along only one dimension. Pursuing a strategy of total quality helps improve all of these dimensions. The following sections discuss these approaches to differentiation and the role of quality in each.

Competing on Superior Product Design

Among the most important strategic decisions a firm makes are the selection and development of new products (we focus on manufactured goods in this section). These decisions determine the growth, profitability, and future direction of the firm. Significant competitive advantage can be achieved by having products of superior design. In addition, products that are appealing, reliable, easy to operate, and economical to service give the consumer a perception of quality. One need only look at the evolution of computers and the continual change that is occurring in this industry to appreciate the value of good design.

The quality of a product's design is influenced by several dimensions, which we first introduced in Chapter 1:[17]

- *Performance*—the primary operating characteristics of the product: the horsepower of an engine or the sound quality of a stereo amplifier.
- *Features*—the "bells and whistles" of a product: antilock brakes or a CD player in an automobile or surround-sound options in an amplifier.
- *Reliability*—the probability of a product's surviving over a specified period of time under stated conditions of use: the ability of a car to start consistently in all types of weather and the lack of failure of electronic components.
- *Durability*—the amount of use one gets from a product before it physically deteriorates or until replacement is preferable: the number of miles one would expect from an automobile with normal maintenance.

- *Aesthetics*—how a product looks, feels, sounds, tastes, or smells: the sleekness of an automobile's exterior and the black "high-tech" look of modern stereo components, for example.

The product design function that traditionally was concerned solely with technical aspects of the product must now be concerned with manufacturing and marketing issues. Product designers must match the right products with the continually changing variety of customer needs. This requires great flexibility. At the same time, costs must be minimized, which demands attention to the manufacturing process during the design stage.

The Role of Total Quality in Product Design

A firm must focus on the key product dimensions that reflect specific customer needs. If these expectations are not identified correctly or are misinterpreted, the final product will not be perceived to be of high quality by customers. Innovative marketing efforts are needed to ensure that the needs are properly identified (see the box about the Honda Element).

The Malcolm Baldrige Award criteria emphasize the importance of systematic processes to design and improve products and the processes that create them. For example, the award application requires evidence of how customer requirements are identified and used for purposes of product planning. For many firms, product design is regarded as a key value creation process. From this perspective, these firms need good processes to translate customer needs into product requirements; select key process performance characteristics based on customer requirements; address quality requirements early in the design process; and coordinate and integrate designs with production and delivery systems.

A total quality focus in product design requires significant investment in engineering to ensure that designs meet customer expectations. Quality engineering is concerned with the plans, procedures, and methods for the design and evaluation of quality in goods and services. Useful techniques of quality engineering include:

- *concurrent engineering*, in which engineering and production personnel jointly develop product designs that are both functional and easy to manufacture, thus reducing opportunities for poor quality;
- *value analysis*, in which the function of every component of a product is analyzed to determine how it might be accomplished in the most economical fashion;
- *design reviews*, in which managers assess how well the design relates to customer requirements and how it might be improved prior to releasing it to production; and
- *experimental design*, in which formal statistical experiments are applied to determine the best combinations of product and process parameters for high quality and low cost.

All of these efforts involve a high level of teamwork.

Quirky, Funky, Independent, Maverick[18]

That's how the designers of the Honda Element describe it, meeting the challenge to design a totally new product that could coexist with both the current Civic model and appeal to both young gen-Y males and the new gen-X family that did not want to buy into mainstream vehicles or sell out to convention. Executives gave the design team carte blanche to understand how these potential customers were using their cars. The design team engaged in "immersion research," going to fraternity houses and hanging out with surfers and mountain bikers to understand their lifestyles. Honda designers incorporated several themes into the car—"hobby space," "campground friendly," and "road-trip friendly." The car was designed to fit two mountain bikes or a 10-foot surfboard. It can sleep two people comfortably. The car has spillproof material on seats and a wipeable flat floor.

Competing on Service

Until rather recently, companies viewed service as secondary in importance to manufacturing. However, next to the quality of the product itself, service is perhaps the greatest key to achieving competitive success (see the box on US Airways). This may be because, as the average level of product quality increases, consumers turn to service as the primary means of differentiating among competing firms. For example, one of the biggest sources of dissatisfaction for computer manufacturers is the lack of adequate service after the sale.

The importance of service was recognized in the early 1980s because of the book *In Search of Excellence* by Tom Peters and Bob Waterman.[19] One of their key themes was that excellent companies share an obsession with service. How important is it? A 1985 Gallup poll on the quality of American products and services found that the vast majority of consumers believe that quality is determined by employee behavior, attitudes, and competence. They also believe—to an even greater degree—that poor service quality is due to the same set of factors. These attitudes hold true even today.

Good service translates into dollars. Banking studies have found that 10 percent of customers leave each year,[20] and 21 percent of those leave because of poor service. Each customer contributes $121 per year in profit, and the cost to acquire a new customer is $150. If a bank has a base of 200,000 customers, this means that 4,200 will leave because of poor service. The arithmetic shows that the combined lost profit and replacement effort costs are more than $1 million per year. Similar studies in other industries have found a high correlation between customer retention and profitability.

Leveraging Service Improvement at US Airways

US Airways placed first in a 1999 survey of U.S. airline quality as measured by such attributes as on-time performance, as well as occurrences of denied boardings, mishandled luggage, and passenger complaints—one year after it finished dead last.[21] The airline launched a 12-point Customer Commitment program that, as described by the president and CEO, ". . . is to ensure that we offer, and our customers receive, the service level that they are entitled to on a consistent basis—the highest level of service possible." This included offering the lowest fares, providing timely information on flight delays or cancellations, providing on-time baggage delivery, giving customers 24 hours to cancel a purchased ticket without penalty, and responding promptly to complaints and requests for information. The airline devoted thousands of hours to developing procedures, refining programs, and implementing training plans.[22]

We discussed many aspects of services and how they differ from manufacturing in Chapter 1. However, managing intangible quality characteristics is more difficult, as they usually depend on employee behavior and system performance. Thus, two key components of service system quality are *employees* and *information technology*. Customers evaluate a service primarily by the quality of the human contact. A *Wall Street Journal* survey found that Americans' biggest complaints about service employees are of delivery people or salespeople who fail to show up when you have stayed home at a scheduled time waiting for them; salespeople who are poorly informed; and salesclerks who talk on the phone when waiting on you, who say "It's not my department," who talk down to you, or who cannot describe how a product works.

Researchers repeatedly have demonstrated that when service employee job satisfaction is high, customer satisfaction is high, and that when job satisfaction is low, customer satisfaction is low.[23] Many service companies act on the motto, "If we take care of our employees, they will take care of our customers." At FedEx, for instance, the company credo is stated simply as People, Service, Profits. All potential decisions in the company are evaluated on their effects on the employees (people), on their customers (service), and the company's financial performance (profits), in that order. In many companies, unfortunately, the frontline employees—salesclerks, receptionists, delivery personnel, and so on, who have the most contact with customers—receive the lowest pay, minimal training, little decision-making authority, and little responsibility (empowerment).

Information technology is essential in modern service organizations because of the high volumes of information they must process and because customers demand service at ever-increasing speeds. Intelligent use of information technology not only leads to improved quality and productivity but also to competitive advantage. This is particularly true when technology is used to better serve the customer and to make it easier for customers to do business with the company. Every service industry is exploiting information technology to improve customer service. Restaurants, for example, use handheld order-entry computer terminals to speed up the ordering process. An order is instantaneously transmitted to the kitchen or bar, where it is displayed and the guest check is printed. In addition to saving time, such systems improve accuracy by standardizing the order-taking, billing, and inventory procedures and reducing the need for handwriting. Credit authorizations, which once took several minutes by telephone, are now accomplished in seconds through computerized authorization systems.

Another important aspect of service is complaint resolution (an important criterion in the Baldrige Award). Research has shown that about 80 to 95 percent of unhappy customers (depending on the amount of loss) will purchase from a company again if their complaints are resolved quickly. This drops to around 20 to 45 percent if complaints are not resolved. Furthermore, of the majority of unhappy customers that do not complain at all, only about 10 to 40 percent will become repeat customers.

The Role of Total Quality in Service

For services, research shows that five key dimensions of service quality contribute to customer perceptions:

- *Reliability*—The ability to provide what was promised, dependably and accurately. Examples include customer service representatives responding in the promised time, following customer instructions, providing error-free invoices and statements, and making repairs correctly the first time.
- *Assurance*—The knowledge and courtesy of employees, and their ability to convey trust and confidence. Examples include the ability to answer questions, having the capabilities to do the necessary work, monitoring credit card transactions to avoid possible fraud, and being polite and pleasant during customer transactions.
- *Tangibles*—The physical facilities and equipment, and the appearance of personnel. Tangibles include attractive facilities, appropriately dressed employees, and well-designed forms that are easy to read and interpret.
- *Empathy*—The degree of caring and individual attention provided to customers. Some examples might be the willingness to schedule deliveries at the customer's convenience, explaining technical jargon in a layperson's language, and recognizing regular customers by name.
- *Responsiveness*—The willingness to help customers and provide prompt service. Examples include acting quickly to resolve problems, promptly crediting returned merchandise, and rapidly replacing defective products.

Understanding these features and proactively designing them into services and service delivery processes is an important aspect of a TQ organization.

Companies that have consistently provided superior service—such as IBM, Federal Express, Nordstrom, and many others—have certain elements in common:[24] They establish service goals that support business and product-line objectives.

1. They identify and define customer expectations for service quality and responsiveness.
2. They translate customer expectations into clear, deliverable, service features.
3. They set up efficient, responsive, and integrated service delivery systems and organizations.
4. They monitor and control service quality and performance.
5. They provide quick but cost-effective response to customers' needs.

These ideas are embodied in the Malcolm Baldrige Award criteria in the Customer and Market Focus category. The criteria look at how an organization builds relationships to acquire and satisfy customers and to develop repeat business and positive referrals. Included in the criteria requirements are how organizations determine key customer contact requirements, what access mechanisms are available for customers to seek information, conduct business, and make complaints, and how customer contact requirements are deployed along the entire response chain. The criteria also address an organization's complaint management process, and how it ensures prompt and effective problem resolution.

Competing on Agility

Success in globally competitive markets requires a capacity for flexibility and rapid change of product variety; this is called **agility**. **Flexibility** means adapting successfully to changing environmental conditions and process requirements. Flexibility might demand special strategies such as modular designs, sharing components, sharing manufacturing lines, and specialized training for employees. It also involves outsourcing decisions, agreements with key suppliers, and innovative partnering arrangements. **Variety** refers to the ability to produce a wide range of products and options. Companies that can change product lines more rapidly in the face of changing consumer demands and exploit new technologies can gain a competitive advantage in certain markets. E-business, for example, requires and enables more rapid, flexible, and customized responses.

To better understand these issues, we review some key concepts. Basically, there are three types of products: custom products, option-oriented products, and standard products.[25] Custom products, generally made in small quantities, are designed to meet customers' specifications precisely.

Two examples are a wedding gown or a machine tool designed to perform a specific, complex task. The production cost is relatively high and the assurance of quality requires careful attention at every step in the manufacturing process. Because custom products can only be produced on demand, the customer must wait for the product to be made.

Option-oriented products are unique configurations of subassemblies that are designed to fit together. The customer participates in choosing the options to be assembled. A good example is a personal computer system in which the customer defines the types of disk drives, modem, memory configurations, and so forth. The subassemblies are made in relatively large quantities; therefore, costs are reduced, and quality is easier to achieve because of repetition. Because the manufacturer cannot anticipate all of the configurations a customer may desire, the customer sometimes must wait while the product is assembled to the desired configuration.

Standard products are made in larger quantities. Examples include radios, TVs, appliances, and most consumer goods found in department stores. The customer has no options to choose from, and quality is easiest to achieve because the product is made the same way every time. Because the manufacturer makes standard products in anticipation of customer demands, the customer will not have to wait for the product unless it is out of stock.

Standard products offer many advantages in terms of manufacturing efficiency, quality, and dependability. Mass production on fixed assembly lines yields high levels of productivity. Thus, standard products are the basis for cost leadership. With fewer different parts to purchase, make, and assemble, quality is generally improved because there is less chance for error. Schedules are more predictable, so dependability is improved. Standard products also simplify purchasing and customer service. Orders of components are more consistent, and shipments can be scheduled more frequently, resulting in lower inventories.

Marketing personnel are concerned with sales and how to respond correctly and successfully in the market. They prefer products to be customized to the individual needs of customers. Custom and option-oriented products can be produced to meet customer expectations, whereas standard products offer little flexibility in meeting changing customer needs. Customer expectations can be incorporated only in the design stages. However, this leads to manufacturing efficiencies. This inherent conflict between manufacturing and marketing must be addressed from a strategic perspective.

In the quick-service restaurant industry, similar strategic choices are made. McDonald's, for example, produces a standard product and achieves an advantage in terms of service delivery. Burger King and Wendy's, by contrast, produce option-oriented products. Although their selection may be greater, these companies sacrifice speed of service. Neither the standard nor the option-oriented approach is necessarily better; each firm must decide what tradeoffs must be made with each approach and select the approach that best provides competitive advantage.

Many products begin as custom products and, over time, become standard products. For instance, Henry Ford was one of the first to standardize production of the automobile. Later, however, consumers demanded more variety of options, and the American automobile evolved into the classic option-oriented product. Customers can now choose from dozens of colors, seat types, engines, transmissions, tires, and other options. Many German and Japanese automobile manufacturers have chosen a strategy that limits the number of options. Few options exist, and some are installed by the dealer rather than the manufacturer. This strategy provides a distinct cost advantage and enables the factory to achieve higher levels of productivity. Flexibility is achieved by offering several model variations of the same car and frequent design changes. The Japanese can produce as many as seven models on a single production line. (Most U.S. manufacturers' production lines are dedicated to a single model.)

Many firms use flexibility and variety as a competitive weapon. Many firms are focusing their strategies on flexibility and variety—more and better product features, factories that can change product lines quickly, expanded customer service, and continually improving new products. For instance, Toshiba's computer factory assembles 9 different word processors on the same production line and 20 varieties of laptop computers on another.[26] The flexible lines guard against running short of a hot model or overproducing one whose sales have slowed. Nissan describes its strategy as "five anys": to make anything in any volume anywhere at any time by anybody. Nissan's high-tech Intelligent Body Assembly System can weld and inspect body parts for any kind of car, all in 46 seconds. As U.S. automakers think about dropping entire car lines, Nissan is gearing up to fill market niches with more models.

From the perspective of gaining competitive advantage, the value of flexibility and variety was illustrated by the "Honda-Yamaha war" in 1981. Honda, whose supremacy in motorcycles was being challenged by Yamaha, responded by introducing 113 new or revamped models in 18 months. Yamaha could only manage 37 model changes and finally announced that it was content to be number two.

The Role of Total Quality in Agility

To be agile, an organization needs both effective processes and the ability to modify those processes as business conditions change. For example, it requires the ability to continually monitor and sense changing customer needs and expectations, change designs as necessary, and rapidly roll out new processes and products. Drawing on the principles of TQ, a customer-focused organization and a process orientation are necessary prerequisites for agility.

Equally important is the ability of different functions and groups of employees to work together as teams in designing and operating the type of production systems that require continuous change and improvement. In fact, the Baldrige criteria seek evidence on how companies organize and manage work and jobs to achieve "the agility to keep current with business needs" in the Human Resource Focus category. Good supplier relations, a key issue in total quality, are also critical as designs and volumes change.

Competing on Innovation

Many firms focus on research and development as a core component of their strategy. Such firms are on the leading edge of product technology, and their ability to innovate and introduce new products is a critical success factor. Product performance, not price, is the major selling feature. When competition enters the market and profit margins fall, these companies often drop out of the market while continuing to introduce innovative new products. These companies focus on outstanding product research, design, and development; high product quality; and the ability to modify production facilities to produce new products frequently.

As global competition increases, the ability to innovate has become almost essential for remaining competitive. National Cash Register (NCR), for example, clung to outdated mechanical technologies for years, while competitors developed innovative new electronic systems. The lack of innovation nearly destroyed the company.

Today leading companies do not wait for customers to change; they use innovation to create new customer needs and desires. At 3M, for example, every division is expected to derive 25 percent of its sales each year from products that did not exist five years earlier. This forces managers to think seriously about innovation. Being innovative also requires being close to customers. As 3M's CEO, Jim McNerny, stated:

> We're fighting hard to get our customers into our hallways and our customers into our labs. With some customers, we've loaned them a full-time employee for a couple of years to help them use Six Sigma tools to improve their operations. This is not about getting a fast sale, but we do get something valuable: a much better understanding of our customer's needs.[27]

Such a spirit not only will result in new products but also will help managers to create better processes that improve quality.

The Role of Total Quality in Innovation

Managing for Innovation is one of the Core Values and Concepts in the Malcolm Baldrige Award criteria. The criteria state that Innovation should lead an organization to new dimensions of performance.

Innovation is no longer strictly the purview of research and development departments; innovation is important for all aspects of a business and all processes. Organizations should be led and managed so that innovation becomes part of the culture and is integrated into daily work.

The award criteria encourage innovation through several means:

- The criteria are nonprescriptive. They encourage creativity and breakthrough thinking because they channel activities toward the organization's purpose and are not focused on following specific procedures.
- Customer-driven quality emphasizes the "positive side of quality"—enhancement, new services, and customer relationship management. Success with the positive side of quality depends heavily on creativity, more so than on steps to reduce errors and defects that rely on well-defined techniques.
- Human resource focus stresses employee involvement, development, and recognition, and encourages creative approaches to improving employee effectiveness, empowerment, and contributions.
- Continuous improvement and learning are integral parts of the activities of all workgroups. This requires analysis and problem solving everywhere within the company. Emphasis on continuous improvement encourages change, innovation, and creative thinking in how work is organized and conducted.
- The focus on future requirements of customers encourages companies to seek innovative and creative ways to serve their patrons.

Competing on Time

In today's fast-paced society, people hate to wait. Time has come to be recognized as one of the most important sources of competitive advantage. **Cycle time** refers to the time it takes to accomplish one cycle of a process (e.g., the time from when a customer orders a product to the time that it is delivered, or the time to introduce a new product). Reductions in cycle time serve two purposes. First, they speed up work processes so that customer response is improved. Second, reductions in cycle time can only be accomplished by streamlining and simplifying processes to eliminate non–value-added steps such as rework. This approach forces improvements in quality by reducing the potential for mistakes and errors. By reducing non–value-added steps, costs are reduced as well. Thus, cycle time reductions often drive simultaneous improvements in organization, quality, cost, and productivity.

The total time required by a company to deliver a finished product that satisfies customers' needs is referred to as the product lead time. This includes time spent on design, engineering, purchasing, manufacturing, testing, packaging, and shipping. Short product lead times offer many advantages. First, they allow companies to introduce new products and penetrate new markets more rapidly (see the box on Moen). Being the first to market a new product allows a firm to charge a higher price, at least until competitive products are offered. For example, when first introduced, Kodak's Ektar film sold for 10 to 15 percent more than conventional film; Motorola's pocket-sized cellular telephone was 50 percent smaller than any competing Japanese product and sold for twice the price; and the Mazda Miata sold for up to $5,000 above sticker price. Second, every month saved in development time can save a large company millions of dollars in expenses. Third, short lead times reduce the need to forecast long-term sales, allow more accurate production plans to be developed, and reduce inventory. Short lead times increase the flexibility of a company to respond to changing customer needs.

The Role of Total Quality in Time Competitiveness

The Malcolm Baldrige Award criteria emphasize the importance of reducing cycle times in all business processes, particularly the design-to-introduction or innovation cycle time. Success in competitive markets increasingly demands shorter cycles for new or improved product and service introduction. Also, faster and more flexible response to customers is a more critical requirement of business management (see the box on Domino's).

Sending Old Designs Down the Drain[28]

Moen Inc. makes faucets for bathrooms and kitchens. In the mid-1990s, as plumbing fixtures became fashion necessities of new homes and remodeling projects, the company needed to provide a much larger set of styles in silver, platinum, and copper, instead of its current product line designed in the 1960s and 1970s. Moen revitalized its product design approach using the Web, collaborating with suppliers in the design process. Previously, engineers would spend six to eight weeks coming up with a new design, burning it onto CDs, and mailing them to suppliers in 14 countries that make the hundreds of parts that go into a faucet. The suppliers would return the CDs with changes and suggestions that needed to be reconciled with each other. Redesign activities and tool design and production might extend this process to up to 24 weeks.

With the Web-based approach, a new faucet goes from drawing board to store shelf in 16 months, down from an average of two years. The time savings allowed Moen's engineers to work on three times as many projects, and introduce from 5 to 15 new faucet lines each year. This helped boost sales by 17 percent from 1998 to 2001, higher than the industry average of 9 percent over the same period, and moved Moen from number 12 in market share to a tie for number three with rival Delta Faucet Co.

Domino's Pizza Changed the Rules[29]

Tom Monaghan, founder of Domino's Pizza, determined that customers ordering home-delivered pizza wanted their pizzas quickly because they were usually hungry when they ordered. He also understood that people anticipated having their pizzas delivered anywhere from 20 minutes to 2 hours after placing their orders. This wide variation in delivery was acceptable because people had been conditioned to accept that there were no other options available. Because fast, consistent delivery was not an option, customers placed their pizza orders based only on taste and price.

Monaghan changed all that by promising fast and consistent delivery—30 minutes or less—or it's free. Domino's exceeded customers' expectations. Today, this "delighter/exciter" has become a satisfier, and consistently fast delivery is often the first criterion in the pizza-ordering decision process.

Significant reductions in cycle time cannot be achieved simply by focusing on individual subprocesses; cross-functional processes must be examined all across the organization. Through these activities, the company comes to understand work at the organizational level and to engage in cooperative behaviors. Major improvements in response time often require work organizations, processes, and paths to be simplified and shortened. To accomplish this, more attention needs to be paid to time performance. This can be done by making response time a key indicator for work unit improvement processes. Simplified processes reduce opportunities for errors, leading to improved quality. Improvements in response time often result from increased understanding of internal customer-supplier relationships and teamwork. Cutting response time requires a significant commitment from all employees and leadership from top management. Such efforts must involve the entire organization and often require organizational redesign.

INFORMATION AND KNOWLEDGE FOR COMPETITIVE ADVANTAGE

Managing information and knowledge can require a significant commitment of resources as the sources of information grow dramatically each year. Information from internal operations, from the Internet, and from business-to-business (B2B) and business-to-consumer (B2C) communications challenges organizational abilities to provide the information that people need to do their work, keep current, and improve.

Understanding the impact of business decisions on results and benchmarking results against competitors and industry leaders has taken on

> ## "The Data Will Set You Free"[30]
>
> In the early 1990s, Boeing's assembly lines were morasses of inefficiency. A manual numbering system dating back to World War II bomber days was used to keep track of an airplane's four million parts and 170 miles of wiring; changing a part on a 737's landing gear meant renumbering 464 pages of drawings. Factory floors were covered with huge tubs of spare parts worth millions of dollars. In an attempt to grab market share from rival Airbus, the company discounted planes deeply and was buried by an onslaught of orders. The attempt to double production rates, coupled with implementation of a new production control system, resulted in Boeing being forced to shut down its 737 and 747 lines for 27 days in October 1997, leading to a $178 million loss and a shakeup of top management. Much of the blame was focused on Boeing's financial practices and lack of real-time data. With a new CFO and finance team, the company created a "control panel" of vital measures such as material costs, inventory turns, overtime, and defects using a color-coded spreadsheet. For the first time, Boeing was able to generate a series of bar charts showing which of its programs were creating value and which were destroying it. The results were eye-opening; not only did they help improve operations, but they also helped formulate a growth plan. As one manager noted, "The data will set you free."

increased importance in recent years. A supply of consistent, accurate, and timely information across all functional areas of business provides real-time information for evaluation and improvement of processes, products, and services to meet business objectives and rapidly changing customer needs— in short, to create and sustain a competitive advantage (see the box on Boeing). This requires a systematic and effective system for measuring performance and managing knowledge assets.

Organizations need performance measures for three reasons:

- to lead the entire organization in a particular direction; that is, to drive strategies and organizational change;
- to manage the resources needed to travel in this direction by evaluating the effectiveness of action plans; and
- to operate the processes that make the organization work and continuously improve.[31]

A survey conducted by William Schiemann & Associates found that measurement-managed companies are more likely to be in the top third of their industry financially, complete organizational changes more successfully, reach clear agreement on strategy among senior managers, enjoy favorable levels of cooperation and teamwork among management, undertake greater self-monitoring of performance by employees, and have a greater willingness by employees to take risks.[32]

Many managers and quality professionals view measurement activities only in terms of outputs from the production system. This is a mistake because a broad base of measurements, tied together by strong information systems, can help to align a company's operations with its strategic directions.

Most businesses have traditionally relied on organizational performance data based almost solely on financial or factory productivity considerations, such as return on investment, earnings per share, direct labor efficiency, and machine utilization.[33] Unfortunately, many of these indicators are inaccurate and stress quantity over quality.[34] They reward the wrong behavior; lack predictive power; do not capture key business changes until it is too late; reflect functions, not cross-functional processes; and give inadequate consideration to difficult-to-quantify resources such as intellectual capital.[35] Today, many organizations create a "balanced scorecard" of measures that provide a comprehensive view of business performance.

The term **balanced scorecard** was coined by Robert Kaplan and David Norton of the Harvard Business School in response to the limitations of traditional accounting measures. Its purpose is "to translate strategy into measures that uniquely communicate your vision to the organization." Their version of the balanced scorecard consists of four perspectives:

- *Financial Perspective*: Measures the ultimate results that the business provides to its shareholders. This includes profitability, revenue growth, return on investment, economic value added (EVA), and shareholder value.
- *Internal Perspective*: Focuses attention on the performance of the key internal processes that drive the business. This includes such measures as quality levels, productivity, cycle time, and cost.
- *Customer Perspective*: Focuses on customer needs and satisfaction as well as market share. This includes service levels, satisfaction ratings, and repeat business.
- *Innovation and Learning Perspective*: Directs attention to the basis of a future success—the organization's people and infrastructure. Key measures might include intellectual assets, employee satisfaction, market innovation, and skills development.

A good balanced scorecard contains both leading and lagging measures and indicators. *Lagging measures* (outcomes) tell what has happened; *leading measures* (performance drivers) predict what will happen. For example, customer survey results about recent transactions might be a leading indicator for customer retention (a lagging indicator); employee satisfaction might be a leading indicator for turnover, and so on. These measures and indicators should also establish cause-and-effect relationships across perspectives.

Kaplan and Norton's balanced scorecard is only one version of performance measurement systems that have emerged as companies recognize the need for a broad set of performance measures that provide a comprehensive view of business performance. Raytheon's version defines Customer, Shareholder, Process, and People perspectives. The Malcolm Baldrige Criteria for Performance Excellence Results category groups performance measures into six sets:

- Customer
- Product and service
- Financial and market
- Human resource
- Organizational effectiveness
- Governance and social responsibility

These performance indicators span the entire business operation, from suppliers to customers, and from frontline workers to top levels of management.

Wainwright Industries, for example, aligns the company's business objectives with customers' critical success factors: price, minimal line defects, delivery, and partnership. This alignment process prompted the development of five key strategic indicator categories: safety, internal customer satisfaction, external customer satisfaction, defect rate, and business performance. Within each category, Wainwright developed specific indicators and goals. For instance, for external customer satisfaction, they measure a satisfaction index and monthly complaints; for business performance, they track sales, capital expenditure, and market share for drawn housings.

Comparative information includes comparisons relative to direct competitors as well as best-practices benchmarking, either inside or outside of one's industry. Such information allows organizations to know where they stand relative to competitors and other leading companies, provides the impetus for breakthrough improvement, and helps them understand their own processes before they compare performance levels. For example, Corning Telecommunications Products Division (TPD) uses a Competitive Analysis Process to gather publicly available data to analyze competitors' intentions and capabilities, including manufacturing capacity, cost, and cost of incremental capacity, and determines product capability and quality through direct evaluation of competitors' products.

Companies need to ask the key question: How do overall improvements in product and service quality and operational performance relate to changes in company financial performance and customer satisfaction? Leading companies employ a variety of statistical tools and structured approaches for analyzing data and turning it into useful information. Fuji-Xerox, a Japanese subsidiary of Xerox, uses a variety of statistical techniques such as regression and analysis of variance to develop mathematical models relating such factors as copy quality, machine malfunctions, and maintenance time to

> ### Understanding the Drivers of Business Success[36]
>
> IBM's AS/400 Division in Rochester, Minnesota, winner of the 1990 Malcolm Baldrige National Quality Award, initiated a study to determine whether any relationships existed among a variety of measurements, such as market share, overall customer satisfaction, employee morale, job satisfaction, warranty costs, inventory costs, product scrap, and productivity. Using 10 years of data, the researchers identified a strong correlation among market share, customer satisfaction, productivity, warranty cost, and employee satisfaction. By developing a statistical model relating these variables, IBM learned that to improve employee satisfaction, a manager must focus on improving job satisfaction, satisfaction with management, and satisfaction with having the right skills for the job. This will positively impact productivity, market share, and customer satisfaction. Improving employee satisfaction will also directly impact productivity and customer satisfaction and will decrease warranty costs. Decreasing warranty costs will directly impact customer satisfaction and market share. Improving customer satisfaction also will directly impact market share.
>
> These relationships provide empirical evidence to support the conventional wisdom of TQ that we noted in many chapters of this book: that improving the human element in organizations positively impacts customers as well as business success.

customer satisfaction results. Such approaches can provide an indication of important cause-and-effect relationships (for another perspective, see the box on IBM).

TQ and Strategic Planning

The role of total quality in strategic planning can be viewed in two ways: first, how quality is reflected in an organization's strategy, and, second, how TQ concepts and practices can improve the strategic planning process.

Quality as a Strategic Focus

Effective strategies develop around a few key concepts and thrusts that provide focus. The essence of strategy is to build a posture that is so strong in selective ways that the organization can achieve its goals despite unforeseeable external forces that may arise. The traditional focus of business strategies has been finance and marketing, which parallel two of the principal sources of competitive advantage—cost and differentiation—discussed earlier in this chapter. Total quality leads to improvements in both areas.

Therefore, TQ can be viewed as a strategy in itself, particularly when one considers the importance of quality in meeting customer wants and needs. Many firms have recognized that a strategy driven by quality can lead to significant market advantages. However, the lines between a pure "quality strategy" and generic business strategies have become blurred to the point at which TQ principles are integrated into most businesses' normal business planning; that is, TQ is a basic operating philosophy that provides the foundation for effective management.

For most companies, integration of TQ into strategic business planning is the result of a natural evolution. For most new companies—or those that have enjoyed a reasonable measure of success—quality often takes a back seat to increasing sales, expanding capacity, or boosting production, and strategic planning usually focuses exclusively on financial and marketing strategies. As a company begins to face increasing competition, cost-cutting objectives take precedence. Some departments or individuals may champion quality initiatives, but quality is not integrated in the company's strategic business plan. However, in the face of market crises and rising consumer expectations, quality begins to take on increasing importance and becomes an integral part of the overall strategic plan and is viewed as a central operating strategy.

Quality in the Process of Strategic Planning

Strategic planning helps leadership mold an organization's future and manage change by focusing on an ideal vision of what the organization should and could be 10 to 20 years in the future and developing objectives and action plans both in the short and longer term to achieve that vision.

Many organizations do a poor job of strategic planning simply because they do not view it as a business process. This is where TQ principles can have a significant impact. The role of strategic planning, in addition to creating viable directions and specific objectives, is to align work processes with the company strategic directions, thereby ensuring that improvement and learning reinforce company priorities. Using a systematic process helps to optimize the use of resources, ensure the availability of trained employees, and ensure bridging between short-term and longer-term requirements that may entail capital expenditures or supplier development, for example.

In viewing strategic planning as a process, an organization needs to:

- plan for the long term, and understand the key influences, risks, challenges, and other requirements that might affect the organization's future opportunities and directions. This is to help ensure that short-term action plans are aligned with the organization's longer-term strategic directions.
- project the future competitive environment to help detect and reduce competitive threats, shorten reaction time, and identify opportunities.

- develop action plans and deploy resources—particularly human resources—to achieve alignment and consistency, and provide a basis for setting and communicating priorities for ongoing improvement activities.
- ensure that deployment will be effective—that a measurement system enables tracking of action plan achievement in all areas.

Strategic planning consists of two principal activities: *development* and *implementation.* Strategy development consists of defining the mission of the organization—the concept of the business and the vision of where it is headed; setting objectives—translating the mission into specific performance objectives; and defining a strategy—determining specific actions to achieve the performance objectives. Implementation focuses on executing the strategy effectively and efficiently, as well as on evaluating performance and making corrective adjustments when necessary.

Strategy Development

The organization's leaders first must explore and agree upon the mission, vision, and guiding principles of the organization; these form the foundation for the strategic plan. The **mission** of a firm defines its reason for existence. For example, Procter & Gamble states its mission ("purpose") as, "We will provide products of superior quality and value that improve the lives of the world's consumers." A firm's mission guides the development of strategies by different groups within the firm. It establishes the context within which daily operating decisions are made, and it sets limits on available strategic options. In addition, it helps to make tradeoffs among the various performance measures and between short- and long-term goals.

The **vision** describes where the organization is headed and what it intends to be. (See Chapter 9 for a discussion of vision from a leadership perspective.) Solectron's vision is simple: "Be the best and continuously improve." It is brief and memorable, inspiring and challenging, appeals to all stakeholders, and describes an ideal state.

The **values**, or **guiding principles** direct the journey to a vision by defining attitudes and policies for all employees that are reinforced through conscious and subconscious behavior at all levels of the organization. Federal Express states that, "We will be helpful, courteous, and professional to each other and the public. We will strive to have a completely satisfied customer at the end of each transaction." Not all companies clearly separate their mission, vision, and values.

The mission, vision, and guiding principles serve as the foundation for strategic planning. Top management and others who lead, especially the CEO, must articulate them. They also have to be transmitted, practiced, and reinforced through symbolic and real action before they become "real" to the employees and the people, groups, and organizations in the external environment that do business with the firm. It does not matter what you call them; what is important is that a company can articulate them and more importantly, commit to them.

Although an organization's mission, vision, and values rarely change, the environment in which the organization exists usually does. Thus, strategy development requires an environmental assessment of such key factors as customer and market requirements, expectations, and opportunities; technological and other innovations that might affect products or operations; organizational strengths and weaknesses, including human and other resources; financial, societal and ethical, regulatory, and other potential risks; changes in the global or national economy; and factors unique to the organization, such as partner and supply chain needs, strengths, and weaknesses. This information is usually gathered and maintained as inputs to the planning process. Such environmental assessments are often accompanied by SWOT (strengths, weaknesses, opportunities, threats) analyses, and help identify critical success factors on which a strategy must focus.

Strategy development leads to clear definitions of strategies, objectives, and action plans. **Strategies** are broad statements that set the direction for the organization to take in realizing its mission and vision. A strategy might be directed toward becoming a preferred supplier, a low-cost producer, a market innovator, or a high-end or customized service provider. **Strategic objectives** are what an organization must change or improve to remain or become competitive. They are typically focused externally and relate to customer, market, product, service, or technological opportunities and challenges. Strategic objectives set an organization's long-term direction and guide resource allocation decisions. For example, a strategic objective for a supplier in a highly competitive industry might be to develop and maintain a price leadership position. Specific **action plans** derive from strategy and clearly describe the things that need to be done, human resource plans and support, performance measures and indicators, and resource deployment. This process is summarized in Figure 3.3.

TQ and Strategy Development

The principles of TQ can help improve an organization's strategic planning process and therefore lead to better strategies. Effective strategic planning depends upon a clear understanding of customer and market needs and expectations, as well as the competitive environment and internal capabilities. The Ritz-Carlton, for instance, evaluates all action plans on how effectively they address customer requirements. A key goal is to become the first hospitality company with 100 percent customer retention; all plans must address this goal.

The focus on teamwork creates an expectation that everyone in the organization play a role in the formulation of the strategy. Top management, employees, and even customers or suppliers actively participate in the planning process in many organizations. At Solar Turbines, Inc., for example, the strategy development process involves people from all parts of its worldwide

FIGURE 3.3   STRATEGIC PLANNING PROCESS

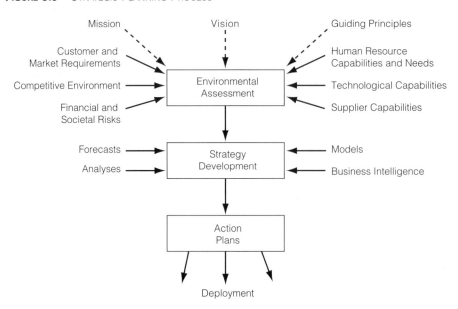

organization, customers, and suppliers. Sales, marketing, service, engineering, and manufacturing people in functional and cross-functional teams perform information gathering, analysis, and conclusions. This information is carried forward to the leadership system committees and the Operations Council where it is integrated and synthesized into strategies and critical success factor goals. It is not unusual for customers and suppliers to be involved in strategic planning efforts because of their importance in the supply chain. Customers and suppliers may offer vital advice to an organization as it plans for the future.

The focus on measurement and objective reasoning introduces a reality check in determining the effectiveness of strategy and performance in meeting goals and objectives. The notion of continuous improvement leads organizations to understand how to improve their strategic planning process (see the box on the Search Conference). The aspects of this process that could be improved are the forecasting of future demand, assessment of internal capabilities, and integration of internal and external perspectives into the planning process. One way of doing this is by studying effective processes used by others and adapting new ideas into their own organizations.

Strategy Implementation

Top management requires a method to ensure that their plans and strategies are successfully executed (the term "deployed" is frequently used) within the organization. The Japanese deploy strategy through a process known as

---

Searching for Strategy[37]

Xerox, Ford, Microsoft, Motorola, Hewlett-Packard, and other companies have used an approach called the Search Conference method to facilitate their strategic planning processes. A Search Conference is a participative event that enables a large group to collectively create a plan that its members will implement. Typically, 20 to 40 people from an organization work progressively for two or three days on planning tasks in large group plenary sessions.

They develop long-term strategic visions, achievable goals, and concrete action plans. All of the work is conducted in self-managed teams that are responsible for the entire planning process. Even after the conference, those who created the plan are responsible for its implementation. This democratic approach gives those employees most affected by the change more control over direction setting and policy deployment.

Senior management cannot manipulate a Search Conference agenda to steer participants in some predetermined direction. Furthermore, everything that is discussed is public information. The intended result is to produce a committed group of knowledgeable people who have a deep understanding of the challenges confronting their organization, agreement about the ideals the strategy is supposed to serve, action plans that are aligned with those ideals, a social mechanism for participation, and a process for engaging the whole system in the strategy implementation. As one Xerox vice president reflected, "We used the output from the Search Conference teams in our annual planning process to develop our business strategy for the next three years. Our culture has engineered a big shift; we've moved the [unit's] members from being highly dependent on top-down planning to acting like entrepreneurs."

---

hoshin planning, or policy deployment. **Hoshin** means policy or policy deployment. Policy deployment is a systems approach to managing change in critical business processes. It emphasizes organization-wide planning and setting of priorities, providing resources to meet objectives, and measuring performance as a basis for improving performance. Policy deployment is essentially a TQ-based approach to executing a strategy. King describes it eloquently:[38]

Imagine an organization that knows what customers will want five to ten years from now and exactly what they will do to meet and exceed all expectations. Imagine a planning system that has integrated [Plan, Do, Study, Act] language and activity based on clear, long-term thinking, a realistic measurement system with a focus on process and results, identification of what's important, alignment of groups, decisions by people who have the necessary information, planning integrated with daily activity, good vertical communication, cross-functional communication, and everyone planning for himself or herself, and the buy-in that results. That is hoshin planning.

With policy deployment, top management is responsible for developing and communicating a vision, then building organization-wide commitment to its achievement.[39] This vision is deployed through the development and execution of annual policy statements (plans). All levels of employees actively participate in generating a strategy and action plans to attain the vision.

At each level, progressively more detailed and concrete means to accomplish the annual plans are determined. The plans are hierarchical, cascading downward from top management's plans. There should be a clear link to common goals and activities throughout the organizational hierarchy. Policy deployment provides frequent evaluation and modification based on feedback from regularly scheduled audits of the process. Plans and actions are developed based on analysis of the root causes of a problem, rather than only on the symptoms.

Planning has a high degree of detail, including the anticipation of possible problems during implementation. The emphasis is on the improvement of the process, as opposed to a results-only orientation. An example of policy deployment is provided by Imai:[40]

> To illustrate the need for policy deployment, let us consider the following case: The president of an airline company proclaims that he believes in safety and that his corporate goal is to make sure that safety is maintained throughout the company. This proclamation is prominently featured in the company's quarterly report and its advertising.
>
> Let us further suppose that the department managers also swear a firm belief in safety. The catering manager says he believes in safety. The pilots say they believe in safety. The flight crews say they believe in safety. Everyone in the company practices safety. True? Or might everyone simply be paying lip service to the idea of safety?
>
> On the other hand, if the president states that safety is company policy and works with his division managers to develop a plan for safety that defines their responsibilities, everyone will have a very specific subject to discuss. Safety will become a real concern. For the manager in charge of catering services, safety might mean maintaining the quality of food to avoid customer dissatisfaction or illness.
>
> In that case, how does he ensure that the food is of top quality? What sorts of control points and checkpoints does he establish?

How does he ensure that there is no deterioration of food quality in flight? Who checks the temperature of the refrigerators or the condition of the oven while the plane is in the air?

Only when safety is translated into specific actions with specific control and checkpoints established for each employee's job may safety be said to have been truly deployed as a policy. Policy deployment calls for everyone to interpret policy in light of their own responsibilities and for everyone to work out criteria to check their success in carrying out the policy.

Figure 3.4 shows the general hoshin planning process. Policy deployment starts with the senior managers of the company. The senior managers establish the vision and core objectives of the company. An example of an objective might be "to improve delivery," which supports the long-term

FIGURE 3.4   HOSHIN PLANNING PROCESS

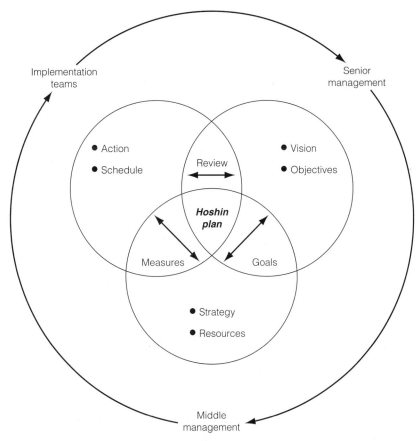

vision of "to be the industry leader in customer satisfaction." Middle management negotiates with senior management regarding the goals that will achieve the objectives. Goals specify numerically the degree of change that is expected. These should be challenging, but people should feel that they are attainable.

Strategies specify the means to achieve the goals. They include more specific actions to be taken. Middle managers are responsible for managing the resources to accomplish the goals. Middle management then negotiates with the implementation teams regarding the performance measures that are used to indicate progress toward accomplishing the strategies.

Measures are specific checkpoints to ensure the effectiveness of individual elements of the strategy. The implementation teams are empowered to manage the actions and schedule their activities. Senior management then uses a review process to understand both the progress of the implementation teams and the success of their planning system. The Seven Management and Planning Tools described in Chapter 7 are used extensively in the process.

Linking Human Resource Plans and Business Strategy

Prior to developing a TQ focus, most organizations neglected the strategic importance of human resource management. Now TQ-focused firms, such as Armstrong Building Products Operations (BPO), recognize that human resource management plays a key role in overall strategic planning. BPO's overall HR strategy is as follows:

- to provide the opportunity for employees to reach their full potential by developing a high performance organization which supports the operation's Vision, Mission, and Goal. The behavior in deploying the strategy will be consistent with our corporate Operating Principles;
- to attract, develop, challenge and retain a diverse workforce to assure we have the skills and organization to build our business;
- to involve and empower employees to improve processes and participate in decisions that affect the business;
- to recognize and reward performance that contributes to the business strategy and goals; and
- to continuously improve those elements of the work environment that enhance employees' well-being, satisfaction, and productivity.[41]

At Armstrong BPO, the translation of business needs to HR plans is performed by the same team that is accountable for business results, thus helping to ensure focus, alignment, and proper allocation of resources. Strategic human resource plans often include one or more of the following:

- redesign of the work organization to increase empowerment and decision making or team-based participation;
- initiatives for promoting greater labor/management cooperation, such as union partnerships;

- initiatives to foster knowledge sharing and organizational learning; and
- partnerships with educational institutions to help ensure the future supply of well-prepared employees.

Whatever the choices, it is vital that they support the organization's overall strategy. Without proper alignment, the work that people do can be focused in an entirely different direction than the organization intends to go.

TQ and Strategic Planning in Action

In this section we provide some examples that illustrate the themes we have discussed about strategic planning and its link to total quality.

Mission, Vision, and Values for the Stroh Brewery Company[42]

The Total Quality Management approach at the Stroh Brewery Company is based on the belief that employees hold the key to achieving a comprehensive focus on Service-Quality—an organized concerted effort to add value to products, including those processes through which services are delivered—that will enable Stroh to meet and exceed the expectations of its customers.

Service-Quality means more than a quality product. It is defined through customers' perception of value. The customer judges Stroh not just by the reliability of their basic product but also by the total experience of doing business with them. Every encounter with a company system or a company employee is a "moment of truth" when the customer will judge the Service-Quality efforts of Stroh. This philosophy is reflected in the company's strategic plan:

Vision
Our vision of The Stroh Brewery Company is one of a growing and prospering company with a dynamic and motivated organization providing our shareholders with reasonable return on their investment.

Mission
To achieve this vision, our mission is to produce, distribute, and market a variety of high-quality beers in a manner that meets or exceeds the expectations of our customers.

Values
Our company values provide a constant point of reference for all of our efforts and confirm our commitment to Stroh employees and to all of our customers. The core values of Quality, Integrity, and Teamwork will serve as the foundation upon which we will build success.

Quality. We seek to continuously improve the level of quality in all that we do. We pursue having the finest products, efficient production and distribution facilities, innovative marketing and sales programs, and totally supportive administrative policies and procedures. These efforts are directed at meeting or exceeding our customers' expectations—both inside and outside the company.

Integrity. We conduct all of our activities with integrity. We believe that the Stroh name stands for honesty and trust. We apply this belief to our relationship with all employees, our suppliers, wholesalers, and all others with whom we have business relationships. Our business activities will model our values, demonstrating that we are a responsible corporate citizen with a firm resolve to live up to our social and environmental responsibilities.

Teamwork. Teamwork is essential to our mutual success. Stroh employees are a valuable asset. Every employee is given respect and trust, regardless of position in the organization. All employees are encouraged to share their views and suggestions. It is through mutual respect, cooperation, and sharing of ideas with employees, suppliers, wholesalers, and retailers that the full potential of the company will be realized. We will fully support the submission and discussion of new ideas from all of our associates (employees, wholesalers, and suppliers). Commitment and innovation will be viewed as actions worthy of praise and recognition.

Strategic Planning at Branch-Smith Printing Division[43]

Branch-Smith, Inc., is a fourth-generation, family business founded by Aaron Smith in 1910. The Branch-Smith Printing Division in Ft. Worth, Texas, has only 70 full-time employees and specializes in creating multipage, bound materials with services ranging from design to mailing for specialty customers. The company produces publications, magazines, catalogs, directories, and books, as well as some general commercial printing, typically in quantities generally less than 20,000. It offers a complete array of turnkey services to customers, including design, image scanning, electronic and conventional prepress work, printing, binding, and mailing/delivery.

Within the Printing Division, the context of the business is set through their Vision Statement: "Market Leading Business Results through an Expert Team providing Turnkey Solutions to Customer Partners." This vision expresses the desire to produce strong and sustainable results through balanced performance improvement. It creates success for long-term customers and rewards for their employees who bring solutions to bear on our opportunities. The mission is stated as: "The mission of the Branch-Smith Printing Division is to provide expert solutions for publishers." This purpose guides Branch-Smith Printing in meeting customers' needs on its own terms.

Publishers work with them because Branch-Smith focuses on serving publishers' niche requirements for printing as well as offering the vertically integrated value-added services that result in lower costs, reduced cycle times, and on-time delivery. An important component of the solution is easy accessibility for the customer, and timely and appropriate information. It is also expressed in its Quality Policy, which states: "Branch-Smith Printing will seek to continuously improve results for all stakeholders through the application of its Innovating Excellence Process."

The printing industry is very competitive with numerous companies seeking market share. Branch-Smith Printing stands out among competitors based on its approach for identifying and serving a specific niche, focusing on development of long-term relationships, partnering with suppliers, and involvement in standard defining industry associations. To ensure a competitive position, it focuses on serving a select market niche that most other printers have difficulty serving well. Many competitors focus on attracting jobs with greater quantity outputs because of the limitations of their equipment. They charge much higher prices for the shorter runs, thus giving Branch-Smith an advantage in this market. Its equipment and technologies are directed to cost-effectively serve this niche through sheet-fed press versus the popular web printing. This technology allows for faster changeovers from one type of print to another and process automation offers cost savings.

Although Branch-Smith is a small family business, they engage in a formal planning process annually with monthly updates during management reviews. The process is built around a continuous learning cycle that begins with lessons learned from previous years to determine and implement improvements. The strategic planning process (SPP) is a key tool the company uses to visualize the ideal future and create strategies and plans to achieve it, and to incorporate improvement opportunities into prioritized action plans. Strategic planning occurs formally each year with updates and tracking conducted monthly during management reviews. Ongoing updates throughout the year allow the company to correct direction or to proactively respond to risks and opportunities.

Figure 3.5 represents the full strategic planning, deployment, and review process. A month prior to strategic planning, assignments are made to PLT members to research information needed for strategic decision making. The assignment list includes 28 specific areas for understanding organizational and supplier/partner capabilities, market conditions, stakeholder input and requirements, competitive information, industry issues, and risks. Branch-Smith gathers information through a customer survey, lost revenues, and complaints to identify customer needs and their importance, trends and directions of the printing industry, and market requirements from industry association networking.

Involvement in professional associations provides industry knowledge and benchmarks concerning customer needs and competitor actions, including emerging tools and competitors. Trade magazines and discussions with key suppliers provide additional input about customer needs, competitor directions, and supplier capabilities. Trends and directions in technology and other environmental changes are also identified through involvement with trade associations and external benchmarking groups, and through general understanding of the business climate gained through newspapers, journals, and periodicals.

One important source of information for strategic planning regarding human resource needs and capability is an annual employee survey. Human resource and operational capabilities are identified through review of aggregate measures of performance and productivity, which are enhanced with feedback from scheduled ISO audits that identify processes in need of improvement. Primary inputs on process efficiency and capability come from in-process productivity measures, revenue lost due to complaints, and other measures, which include spoilage cost, frequency, and reason. These measures are recorded daily through electronic, shop-floor data collection.

Strategic partnerships with key suppliers help to gather information about availability of materials and supplier growth plans to help determine their capability to meet Branch-Smith's changing needs. Finally, part of the annual operational review involves understanding suppliers' current financial position and trends in profitability and utilization, which is compared to external economic conditions to identify areas of potential risk and opportunity over the short and longer term.

The formal planning activity is conducted during the fall of each year by the Print Leadership Team (PLT) through a series of meetings on and off site. Step 1 of Figure 3.5 ensures that lessons learned and improvement cycles are built into the SPP. The PLT analyzes the effectiveness of the overall planning and deployment process to determine and implement improvements. The effectiveness of the leadership system is also evaluated and areas for improvement for the coming year are determined. These improvements are documented as potential actions for the strategic plan. In Step 2, the company reviews its vision, mission, and values to ensure they still reflect the current environment. Next, management reviews and revises objectives, which are intended to communicate to employees and all stakeholders what the company expects to accomplish in the next three to five years.

In Step 3, the company conducts an operational review to analyze the results of the organization's key performance measures for the prior year. They then review and incorporate information into the plan from annual Baldrige-based self-evaluation or from external review feedback. This analysis provides an understanding of key strengths and weaknesses for the SWOT (strengths, weaknesses, opportunities, and threats) analysis in Step 5. Step 4 involves a business analysis to evaluate the external environment to forecast changing trends and gain market requirements. PLT members bring forward defined inputs, including literature and studies for scanning the environment and identifying new opportunities for products, services, com-

FIGURE 3.5   STRATEGIC PLANNING PROCESS AT BRANCH-SMITH

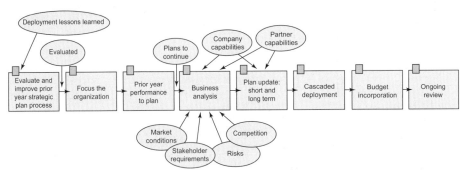

Source: Used with permission of AIM, Inc.

petitive advantage, marketing, and technology approaches. From the review of this information, the PLT develops a list of potential opportunities and threats for each environmental element. In Step 5, a SWOT analysis is conducted based upon the issues identified in Steps 1, 3, and 4. SWOT elements are used to identify and prioritize key areas to address.

Based upon the SWOT review, the PLT develops short- and longer-term strategies and actions to move the company toward its vision and objectives. They add in action plans that are still in process from the prior year to allow them to also be prioritized, set appropriate measures and goals for objectives and strategies, and sort and prioritize the action plans. Action plans are assigned to PLT members to develop (or update) steps, timelines, resources, costs, and measures of success. These plans are then entered into the Quality Improvement Database (QID) for review and tracking. A final balancing meeting is held to review the plan as a whole and make needed adjustments to timing of plans and financial and human resource requirements to balance the plan to resource constraints. In Step 6, the company creates documents and methods to support deployment of the plan.

Results of strategic planning are first communicated to employees through a deployment meeting. Leaders, with their departmental teams or other appropriate members, then discuss the plans during follow-up sessions. Teams and individuals update goals and mission statements for their departments that support the division plans, thus aligning actions, measures, and goals throughout the organization. Other stakeholders receive a variety of communications to detail plans and strategies for informational and planning purposes. For example, a supplier appreciation luncheon is held to provide a more direct opportunity to present plans to key supplier partners and receive feedback on plans and needs. In Step 7, financial resource requirements to accomplish the action plans are rationalized into short- and longer-term budget projections. Then, in Step 8, ongoing tracking of action plans is conducted through monthly management review of overall progress to plans and key measures. Throughout the year as needed, the strategic plan is updated with new or modified action plans to reflect the changes to the environment.

Hoshin Planning at Solectron[44]

Figure 3.6 shows Solectron's annual strategic planning process. The output of this process is an updated, three-year, long-range plan, annual operating plan, and annual improvement plan. In developing market projections, regional and site leaders and corporate staff develop their visions, business projections, and capability requirements. Account plans are developed for all customers. The corporate marketing group uses market and competitor information to assess risks. Information sources include industry tracking organizations, Solectron management and staff, and the 10-K reports of publicly held competitors. The marketing group also distills competitor data into a quarterly report to senior management to fine-tune projections for local markets. This process is followed by development of strategies, market targets, and financial targets for regions and sites. The plans for all regions are reviewed for alignment with the corporation as a whole. Next, one-year action plans are developed based on the three-year plan. Figure 3.7 shows the Hoshin Planning process that ties these plans together.

FIGURE 3.6   SOLECTRON CORPORATION'S STRATEGIC PLANNING PROCESS

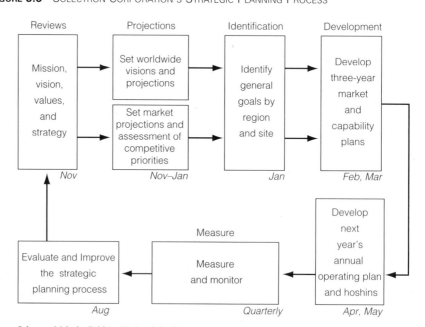

Source: Solectron Malcolm Baldrige National Quality Award Application Summary, 1997.

FIGURE 3.7 SOLECTRON CORPORATION'S HOSHIN PLANNING PROCESS

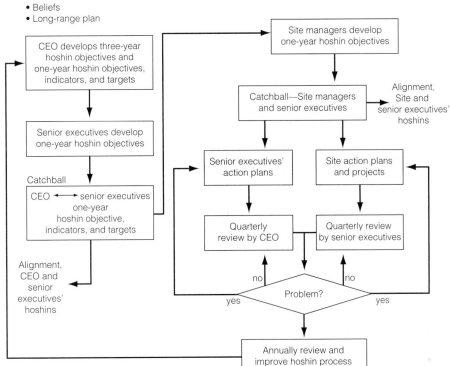

- Vision
- Mission
- Beliefs
- Long-range plan

Source: Solectron Malcolm Baldrige National Quality Award Application Summary, 1997.

TQ AND STRATEGIC MANAGEMENT THEORY[45]

The TQ perspective, as reflected in the Baldrige criteria, suggest several requirements for effective strategic planning:

- A definable approach for developing company strategy. The approach should consider factors related to the market environment, the competitive environment, risk, human resource capabilities, company capabilities, and supplier/partner capabilities.
- A clear company strategy with action plans derived from it, and human resource plans related to the action plans. Differences between short- and longer-range plans should be recognized and understood.
- An approach for implementing action plans. The approach should consider how the critical requirements for implementing action plans— including human resource plans, key processes, performance measures, and resources—will be aligned and deployed.

- An approach for monitoring company performance relative to the strategic plan.
- Projections of strategy-related changes in key indicators of company performance.

These projections should include relevant comparisons to competitors or other benchmarks, and the assumptions used in the projections.

Strategic planning and deployment have been issues of management research for many years, and the conceptual literature in strategic management generally supports these requirements. For example, strategy as a deliberate, definable undertaking has constituted an essential element of classical strategic management frameworks developed by strategy scholars. These classic frameworks portray the strategist as scanning the external environment for opportunities and threats, assessing the firm's internal resources and capabilities for strengths and weaknesses, and determining a strategic plan that exploits external-internal matches in the context of the firm's objectives. However, the general usefulness of strategy making to enhance performance has not been rigorously affirmed. Henry Mintzberg, for instance, suggests that an organization's realized strategy is a product of its planned, intended strategies and unplanned, emergent strategies, which are not a result of formal, top-down planning mechanisms. Many successful strategies can emerge without prior planning, often in response to unseen circumstances.

Three of the six factors that TQ perspectives suggest should comprise strategy development—market environment, competitive environment, and company capabilities—pervade most classic work in strategy formulation. However, the other three factors—financial and societal risk, human resource capabilities, and supplier/partner capabilities—gain only indirect support from the strategy literature. The criteria's specification of human resource capabilities and supplier/partner capabilities appears somewhat redundant, as these factors are asset classes that can be appropriately filed under the "internal capabilities" factor. The strategy literature sometimes refers to strategic plans as *strategic content*.

The Baldrige criteria provide little detail as to what a strategy or an action plan should contain, or the form it should take. Such a nonprescriptive stance fits the literature robustly, because strategy scholars have proposed many purposes and forms of strategy. A common notion among organization and strategy theorists has been that strategy must be broken down into plans for action for effective implementation. The specification for differentiating between short- and longer-term plans garners little direct literature support, although the notion can be indirectly linked to the general concept of dividing strategic goals into doable pieces.

Structure for implementing strategy, in the form of human resource plans, key processes, performance measures, and resources, must be aligned and deployed. Alignment, which was defined by the Baldrige criteria as "consistency of plans, processes, information, resource decisions, actions, results, analysis, and learning to support key organization-wide goals," requires a common understanding of purposes and goals and use of complementary measures and information for planning, tracking, analysis, and improvement at three levels: the organizational level, the key process level, and the work unit level. Aligning strategies to competitive challenges, resources to action plans, and action plans to measurements constitutes some of the most important activities that an organization must address. A well-aligned organization has its processes focused on achieving a shared vision and strategy.

Aligning the organization is a challenging task that is accomplished through a sound strategy and effective deployment. The most damaging alignment problem to which many TQ failures have been attributed is the lack of alignment between expectations that arise from TQ change processes and reward systems. In one survey, an overwhelming percentage (65.8 percent) of managers surveyed ranked the number one barrier to TQ as "Management's compensation is not linked to achieving quality goals."[46] The role of managerial systems, particularly those connected to middle management, in strategy implementation has been examined by several strategy researchers.

Although the TQ perspective requires only specification of how performance will be tracked, it addresses only indirectly the issue of control. Nevertheless, control has been a fundamental concept in management, dating back to Anthony's classic framework, and the literature is replete with studies on managerial control systems. The most compelling support of employing performance measures in strategic management, perhaps, relates to the managerial control notion that measurements provide objective information for managers to judge how well the organization is performing in comparison to strategic targets, and to signal the need for corrective action.

Stating the assumptions behind strategic projections has some grounding in systems theory and some strategy development literature. Inclusion of competitive comparisons and other benchmarks in performance projections can be indirectly related to the requirement for industry and competitive scanning as part of strategy.

REVIEW AND DISCUSSION QUESTIONS

1. Explain how a total quality perspective can support the six characteristics of competitive advantage introduced at the beginning of the chapter.
2. Discuss the three basic types of competitive advantage. Can a company achieve all of them?

3. List 10 firms or businesses that you have read about or have personal experience with. Describe their sources of competitive advantage and how you believe that quality supports (or does not support) their strategy.

4. Prepare a report (using sources such as business periodicals, personal interviews, and so on) profiling a company that competes on each of the major dimensions of differentiation discussed in the chapter. What aspects of their total quality approach support their strategic focus?

5. Think of a product or service you have purchased recently. What aspects of the product or service design made it attractive?

6. What is the importance of total quality to achieving competitive advantage?

7. Explain how quality affects profitability.

8. Discuss the key quality dimensions of differentiation strategies.

9. Explain the differences among custom, option-oriented, and standard products.

10. How might the dimensions of product design (performance, features, reliability, durability, and aesthetics) discussed in this chapter be applied to services?

11. Describe one good and one bad service experience that you encountered. How did this change your perceptions of the company?

12. How is agility a source of competitive advantage? What relationships does agility have with quality?

13. What is the role of quality in innovation?

14. How might the principles of competitive advantage that we discussed be applied to the management of your college or university? How about a fraternity or student professional organization? What types of results measurements would be appropriate?

15. What is a strategy? What elements does a formal strategy contain?

16. What factors have led companies to pursue a strategy based on quality?

17. Research some of the background of recent Baldrige winners. How do they integrate quality into their business strategies? Discuss different approaches that these firms use.

18. Discuss the process of strategy formulation. How can TQ improve this process?

19. Interview managers at some local companies to determine whether their businesses have well-defined missions, visions, and guiding principles. If they do, how are these translated into strategy? If not, what steps should they take?

20. What is hoshin planning, or policy deployment? Explain how this approach is used in organizations.

21. What are the differences between policy deployment and management by objectives?

22. Does your university or college have a mission and strategy? How might policy deployment be used in a university setting?

 **CASES**

Case of the Rotary Compressor[47]

In 1981 market share and profits in General Electric's appliance division were falling. The company's technology was antiquated compared to foreign competitors. For example, making refrigerator compressors required 65 minutes of labor in comparison to 25 minutes for competitors in Japan and Italy. Moreover, GE's labor costs were higher. The alternatives were obvious: either purchase compressors from Japan or Italy or design and build a better model.

By 1983 the decision to build a new rotary compressor in-house was made, along with a commitment for a new $120 million factory. GE was not a novice in rotary compressor technology; they had invented it and had been using it in air conditioners for many years. A rotary compressor weighed less, had one third fewer parts, and was more energy efficient than the current reciprocating compressors. The rotary compressor took up less space, thus providing more room inside the refrigerator and better meeting customer requirements.

Some engineers argued to the contrary, citing the fact that rotary compressors run hotter. This is not a problem in most air conditioners, because the coolant cools the compressor. In a refrigerator, however, the coolant flows only one tenth as fast, and the unit runs about four times longer in one year than an air conditioner. GE had problems with the early rotary compressors in air conditioners. Although the bugs had been eliminated in smaller units, GE quit using rotaries in larger units due to frequent breakdowns in hot climates.

GE managers and design engineers were concerned about other issues. Rotary compressors make a high-pitched whine, and managers were afraid that this would adversely affect consumer acceptance. Managers and consumer test panels spent many hours on this issue. The new design also required key parts to work together with a tolerance of only 50 millionths of an inch. Nothing had been mass-produced with such precision before, but manufacturing engineers felt sure they could do it.

The compressor they finally designed was nearly identical to that used in air conditioners, with one change. Two small parts inside the compressor were made out of powdered metal, rather than the hardened steel and cast iron used in air conditioners. This material was chosen because it could be machined to much closer tolerances, and it reduced machining costs. Powdered metal had been tried a decade earlier on air conditioners but did not work. The design engineers who were new to designing compressors did not consider the earlier failure important.

A consultant suggested that GE consider a joint venture with a Japanese company that had a rotary refrigerator compressor already on the market. The idea was rejected by management. The original designer of the air conditioner rotary compressor, who had left GE, offered his services as a consultant. GE declined his offer, writing him that they had sufficient technical expertise.

About 600 compressors were tested in 1983 without a single failure. They were run continuously for two months under elevated temperatures and pressures that were supposed to simulate five years' operation. GE normally conducts extensive field testing of new products; their original plan to test models in the field for two years was reduced to nine months because of time pressure to complete the project.

The technician who disassembled and inspected the parts thought they did not look right. Parts of the motor were discolored, a sign of excessive heat. Bearings were worn, and it appeared that high heat was breaking down the lubricating oil. The technician's supervisors discounted these findings and did not relay them to upper levels of management. Another consultant who evaluated the test results believed that something was wrong because only one failure was found in two years and recommended that test conditions be intensified. This suggestion was also rejected by management.

By 1986, only two and a half years after board approval, the new factory was producing compressors at a rate of 10 per minute. By the end of the year, more than one million had been produced. Market share rose and the new refrigerator appeared to be a success. But in July 1987 the first compressor failed. Soon after, reports of other failures in Puerto Rico arrived. By September the appliance division knew it had a major problem. In December the plant stopped making the compressor. Not until 1988 was the problem diagnosed as excessive wear in the two powdered-metal parts that burned up the oil. The cost in 1989 alone was $450 million. By mid-1990, GE had voluntarily replaced nearly 1.1 million compressors with ones purchased from six suppliers, five of them foreign.

Discussion Questions

1. What factors in the product development process caused this disaster? What individuals were responsible?
2. How might this disaster have been prevented? What lessons do you think GE learned for the future?
3. On what basis was GE attempting to achieve a competitive advantage? How did they fail?

Stroh Brewery's Strategy[48]

The strategy of the Stroh Brewery Company (whose vision, mission, and values were introduced in this chapter) follows.

Strategy

In support of our vision and mission, the following strategies will be employed to achieve our Service-Quality goal. WE WILL:

Maintain a competitive brand portfolio that allows us to capture unique market opportunities and strive to realize the potential of our present brands and new product introductions. Our goal is to increase unit volume. This does not mean, however, that every brand will experience unit growth every year. We will manage each brand based on its long-term growth potential, its strategic relevance, and its relationship to the company's overall business strategy.

Invest heavily in the development of our human resources through orientation and training, which will enable our employees to make better decisions and to improve processes. We will hire individuals who have the job-related skills and abilities that support Stroh's Service-Quality mode of operation.

Develop and introduce line extensions, new brands, and new packages, seeking to create innovative breakthroughs. New products are a critical element to Stroh's overall success. We will develop new products with a sense of urgency while maintaining a commitment to sound product concepts, excellent sales execution, and appropriate marketing support.

Maintain a flexible approach in the balance between national and regional marketing and sales efforts. Although there are aspects of marketing our products that have relevance to all markets (e.g., national advertising), we will always try to find ways to capitalize on regional strengths and opportunities.

Pursue opportunities to develop international markets. Our focus for the future extends to international markets where we believe there are significant opportunities to market our products both directly and in partnership with others.

Commit to maintaining the best distribution network in the industry along with our full support of the three-tier system. Our distribution system will function around the guiding principles of Service-Quality.

Strive to control production and administrative expenses, which allows us to provide the maximum funds to market our products. We will do this by constantly seeking ways to improve our method of completing tasks necessary to our business.

Consider acquiring assets to build synergies and to reduce production costs. The acquisition of additional brands, manufacturing facilities, and other businesses that will improve the company's overall strategic position is viewed as highly desirable.

Invest in plant equipment and new technologies to produce new products and to maintain our production facilities to remain competitive.

Be comfortable with change. We will pursue change as a strategic weapon. There is no safety in standing still, nor is there any advantage in abiding by the rules set by our competitors. Change will not be pursued for its own sake, but neither will change be avoided because it is uncomfortable or because of the risks associated with change.

Be market- and service-driven. We will develop systems and processes to facilitate this strategy.

Questions for Discussion
1. Who are the customers of Stroh's?
2. What aspects of Stroh's vision, mission, values, and strategy support the fundamental principles of TQ described in Chapter 1?

A Strategic Bottleneck[49]

An international bottle manufacturer produces glass containers for customers that include condiment producers, breweries, and wineries. The growing demand for plastic containers, and a history of higher production costs because of high scrap and return rates drove the business to focus its improvement efforts on cost and customer performance. However, the unique characteristics of the bottle manufacturing process and the way in which the company measured and motivated its workforce's performance made these improvements difficult to accomplish.

Bottle plants are traditionally organized around two primary functions: forming and selecting. Forming is where raw materials are melted in furnaces and molten glass is cut and formed by fast-moving, noisy, and dangerous machines that turn out thousands of bottles each minute. The workforce is primarily older males. In the selecting department, the work is relatively quiet and clean. The majority of workers are female, and the work is focused on spotting and removing bottles that fail to meet height, weight, dimension, centricity, and thickness specifications. The principal performance measure in the forming department is the pack-to-melt ratio, calculated by dividing the total weight of bottles shipped by the total weight of the raw materials used. Individual and team performance goals are typically tied to this measure. The focus is on throughput and getting the highest percentage of produced bottles packed and shipped to customers.

In the selecting department, customer satisfaction is the key measure of work performance, and compensation is based on how much product is accepted by the customer. As you can imagine, relations between the two departments were quite strained. To achieve its strategic goals of lower cost and improved customer performance, what could this company do to align the goals of the forming and selecting departments?

Corryville Foundry Company

Corryville Foundry Company (CFC) was founded in the mid-1940s in a 3,000-square-foot building with nine people as a small family business to produce castings. In the 1960s, as business grew, the company expanded its facilities and its capability to develop its own tooling patterns, eventually moving into a 40,000-square-foot building. Over this time period, the foundry industry declined from more than 12,000 companies to about 4,000.

With such a shrinking market, CFC began to listen more to its customers. They discovered that customers were not happy with the quality of the products they had been receiving. In 1989 CFC made a commitment to quality by hiring a quality assurance manager, Ronald Chalmer. Chalmer felt that upper management was committed to quality and saw an opportunity to change the company's culture. He also firmly believed in Deming's philosophy. One of the first things he did was to work with upper management in developing a mission statement:

> Our mission at CFC is to improve the return on investment. We can accomplish this by changing attitudes and incorporating a quality/team environment. This will improve the quality of our products, enhance our productivity (which in turn will allow us to quote competitive prices), and elevate our service and response level to our customers. There are several factors which make positive change imperative. The standards for competitive levels of quality and service are becoming more demanding. The emergence of the "World Market" has brought on new challenges. We are in a low-growth, mature market. In order for CFC to improve return on investment, we must develop a strategy to improve quality and responsiveness in all areas of the company. We need to have all employees recognize the importance of product quality and service and move toward more favorable pricing. We need to change thinking throughout the organization to get employees involved, to encourage teamwork, to develop a more flexible workforce and adaptable organization. We need to instill pride in the workplace and the product. We believe that we can best achieve the desired future state by study of and adherence to the teachings of W. Edwards Deming.

Under Chalmer's direction, CFC made some substantial improvements in the quality of castings, particularly reducing scrap and reject rates. He worked closely with the factory workers directly responsible for the products, asking them what they needed to get the job done and ensuring management commitment to provide the necessary resources. For example, CFC invested in a new controller for the furnaces that provided a digital readout of temperature. With this technology, workers were able to categorize the metal temperatures needed for each casting type and were able to adjust the process as needed. The success of this project led the company to empower employees to control many other aspects of the system.

Three years later, the president and CEO retired. The new CEO, who had been a vice president of a major manufacturing company, did not feel that the mission statement provided a clear and vivid direction. Consequently, he set up a planning retreat for senior management (including Chalmer) to develop a new strategic vision.

Discussion Questions

1. Comment on the current mission statement. Does it provide the strategic direction necessary for success for this company?
2. How can the mission statement be improved? Suggest a better statement of mission, vision, and guiding principles.

ENDNOTES

1. S. C. Wheelwright, "Competing through Manufacturing," in Ray Wild (ed.), *International Handbook of Production and Operations Management*, London: Cassell Educational, Ltd., 1989, pp. 15–32.
2. *The PIMS Letter on Business Strategy*, The Strategic Planning Institute, No. 4, Cambridge, Mass., 1986.
3. Philip Crosby, *Quality Is Free*, New York: McGraw-Hill, 1979.
4. Kathleen Kerwin, "When Flawless Isn't Enough," *Business Week*, December 8, 2003, pp. 80–82. The quote on Lexus appeared in a column by Carol Traeger, "Lexus IS 300 loses luster," Cincinnati Enquirer, July 31, 2004, pp. G1, G2.
5. U.S. General Accounting Office, "Management Practices: U.S. Companies Improve Performance through Quality Effort," GA/NSIAD-91-190, May 1991.
6. "Progress on the Quality Road,"*Incentive*, April 1995, p. 7.
7. Kevin B. Hendricks and Vinod R. Singhal, "Does Implementing an Effective TQM Program Actually Improve Operating Performance? Empirical Evidence from Firms That Have Won Quality Awards," *Management Science*, Vol. 43, No. 9, September 1997, pp. 1258–1274.
8. Michael E. Porter, *Competitive Advantage: Creating and Sustaining Superior Performance*, New York: Free Press, 1985.
9. See, for example, J. Pfeffer and J. F. Veiga, "Putting People First for Organizational Success," *Academy of Management Executive*, Vol. 13, No. 2, 1999, p. 37; J. Pfeffer, *Competitive Advantage through People*, Cambridge: MA: Harvard Business School Press, 1994; C. A. O'Reilly III and J. Pfeffer, *Hidden Value: How Great Companies Achieve Extraordinary Results with Ordinary People*, Cambridge, MA: Harvard Business School Press, 2000.
10. H. Lee Hales, "Time Has Come for Long-Range Planning of Facilities Strategies in Electronic Industries," *Industrial Engineering*, April 1985.
11. Bradley T. Gale, "Quality Comes First When Hatching Power Brands," *Planning Review*, July/August 1992, pp. 4–9, 48.
12. J. M. Juran, *Juran on Quality by Design*, New York: The Free Press, 1992, p. 181.
13. Larry Selden and Geoffrey Colvin, "Will Your E-Business Leave You Quick or Dead?" *Fortune*, May 28, 2001, pp. 112–124.
14. Robin Yale Bergstrom, "People, Process, Paint," *Production*, April 1995, pp. 48–51.
15. Jeffrey Pfeffer, *Competitive Advantage through People*, Boston: Harvard Business School Press, 1994.
16. Town Hall discussion at the Quest for Excellence Conference, Washington, D.C., March 2000.
17. David A. Garvin, "What Does Product Quality Really Mean?" *Sloan Management Review*, Vol. 26, No. 1, 1984, pp. 25–43.
18. "Fast Talk: Hard Drive," Profile of Tim Benner, Honda Motor Company, Co-designer, Honda Element, *Fast Company*, May 2003, p. 62.

19. Tom Peters and Bob Waterman, *In Search of Excellence*, New York: Harper & Row, 1982.

20. F. F. Reichheld and W. E. Sasser, Jr. "Zero Defections: Quality Comes to Services," *Harvard Business Review*, September–October, 1990.

21. The Associated Press, "US Airways Makes Quality Turnaround," *Cincinnati Enquirer*, April 20, 1999, p. B7.

22. http://www.usair.com/company/news/nw_99_1214b.htm

23. Ron Zemke, "Auditing Customer Service: Look Inside as Well as Out," *Employee Relations Today*, Vol. 16, Autumn 1989, pp. 197–203.

24. Jeffrey Margolies, "When Good Service Isn't Good Enough," *The Price Waterhouse Review*, Vol. 32, No. 3, New York: Price Waterhouse, 1988, pp. 22–31.

25. Charles A. Horne, "Product Strategy and Competitive Advantage," *P&IM Review with APICS News*, Vol. 7, No. 12, December 1987, pp. 38–41.

26. Thomas A. Stewart, "Brace for Japan's Hot New Strategy," *Fortune*, September 21, 1992, pp. 62–73.

27. *Fortune* magazine special insert: CEOs on Innovation (undated).

28. Faith Keenan, "Opening the Spigot," *BusinessWeek* e.biz, June 4, 2001, pp. EB17–20.

29. Joan Uhlenberg, "Redefining Customer Expectations," *Quality*, September 1992, pp. 34–35.

30. Jerry Useem, "Boeing Versus Boeing," *Fortune*, October 2, 2000, 148–160.

31. Kicab Casteñeda-Méndez, "Performance Measurement in Health Care," *Quality Digest*, May 1999, pp. 33–36.

32. Laura Struebing, "Measuring for Excellence," *Quality Progress*, December 1996, 25–28.

33. Robert S. Kaplan and David P. Norton, "The Balanced Scorecard—Measures That Drive Performance," *Harvard Business Review*, January/February 1992, pp. 71–79.

34. Ernest C. Huge, "Measuring and Rewarding Performance," in Ernst & Young Quality Consulting Group, *Total Quality: An Executive's Guide for the 1990s*, Homewood, Ill.: Irwin, 1990.

35. New Corporate Performance Measures, A Research Report, Report Number 1118-95-RR, New York: The Conference Board, 1995.

36. Steven H. Hoisington and Tse-Hsi Huang, "Customer Satisfaction and Market Share: An Empirical Case Study of IBM's AS/400 Division," in Earl Naumann and Steven H. Hoisington, *Customer Centered Six Sigma*, Milwaukee, Wisc.: ASQ Quality Press, 2001.

37. Ronald E. Purser and Steven Cabana, "Involve Employees at Every Level of Strategic Planning," *Quality Progress*, May 1997, pp. 66–71.

38. Bob King, *Hoshin Planning: The Developmental Approach*, Methuen, Mass.: GOAL/QPC, 1989, pp. 2–3.

39. The Ernst & Young Quality Improvement Consulting Group, *Total Quality: An Executive's Guide for the 1990s*, Homewood, Ill.: Dow Jones-Irwin, 1990.

40. M. Imai, *Kaizen: The Key to Japan's Competitive Success*, New York: McGraw-Hill, 1986, pp. 144–145. Reproduced with permission of McGraw-Hill.

41. Armstrong Building Products Operations Malcolm Baldrige National Quality Award Application Summary, 1995.

42. Adapted with permission from "TQM," the Stroh Brewery Company.

43. Branch-Smith Printing, Application Summary, 2002. Courtesy of David Branch, President.

44. Solectron Malcolm Baldrige National Quality Award Application Summary, 1997.

45. Based on Ford and Evans, op. cit.

46. Nabil Tamimi and Rose Sebastianelli, "The Barriers to Total Quality Management," *Quality Progress*, June 1998, pp. 57–60.

47. Reprinted by permission of *The Wall Street Journal*, © 1990 Dow Jones & Company, Inc. All rights reserved worldwide.

48. "TQM," the Stroh Brewery Company.

49. Adapted from Victor Cvascella, "Effective Strategic Planning," *Quality Progress*, November 2002, pp. 62–67. Copyright © 2002, American Society for Quality. Reprinted with permission.

PART 2

Total Quality and Organization Theory

CHAPTER 4

Quality in Customer-Supplier Relationships

Businesses have recognized that supply chain management is crucial for effective operations and meeting customer needs. A supply chain includes the materials and other inputs purchased from suppliers, their use in the production of goods and services, and distribution and service to customers. Quality should start with the customer, and extend back through the supply chain to the sources of procurement.

The customer is the ultimate judge of quality. In Japanese the same word—*okyakusama*—means both "customer" and "honorable guest." World-class organizations are obsessed with meeting and exceeding customer expectations. Many companies such as Disney and Nissan Motor Co.'s Infiniti division were built on the notion of satisfying the customer. The service philosophy of Home Depot, cited by Wal-Mart's CEO as the best retail organization in the United States, is "Every customer has to be treated like your mother, your father, your sister, or your brother."

Many businesses traditionally have kept suppliers at arm's length, but the quality of output can be no better than the quality of the input. In 1982 IBM purchased some parts from a Japanese manufacturer. According to the specifications, IBM would accept 300 defective parts per million of the product. The response from Japan raised a lot of questions and gave IBM the opportunity to change its perspective on quality and relationships with suppliers. The Japanese commented, "We have a hard time understanding North American business practices. But the 3 defective parts per 10,000 have been included and are wrapped separately. Hope this pleases."[1]

Developing strong and positive relationships with customers and suppliers within the supply chain is a basic principle of total quality. This chapter will

> demonstrate the importance of customer-supplier relationships to achieving total quality;
> identify the principles and practices of quality customer-supplier relationships;

➤ give examples of effective partnerships between customers and suppliers; and

➤ compare the TQ approach to customers and suppliers to conventional organizational theories.

CUSTOMER-SUPPLIER RELATIONSHIPS AND TOTAL QUALITY

From the TQ perspective, every company is part of a long chain (actually many long chains) of customers and suppliers.[2] Each company is a customer to its suppliers and a supplier to its customers, so it does not make sense to think of a company as only one or the other (Figure 4.1). One implication of this concept is that your customer's customers are, in a sense, your customers as well. Sometimes a company must focus on both their immediate customers and those next in the chain. Procter & Gamble, for example, works hard to satisfy the needs of both the people who use their products and the retail establishments that sell them. Companies should try to establish the same kinds of productive relationships with their suppliers that they have with their customers.

Many companies work closely with suppliers that share common values. This close relationship improves supplier capabilities by teaching them quality-related tools and approaches. Although many companies have formal supplier certification programs in which they rate their suppliers, some companies ask suppliers to rate them as customers. Motorola uses a 15-member council of suppliers that rates Motorola's practices and offers suggestions for improving, for example, the accuracy of production schedules or design layouts that Motorola provides.[3] Some typical questions that companies might ask of their suppliers might be:[4]

- What expectations do you have that are not being met?
- What type of technical assistance would you like from us?
- What type of feedback would you like from us?
- What benefits are you looking for in a partnership?

Better two-way communication can improve both products and relationships. By developing partnerships, customers and suppliers can build

FIGURE 4.1   THE CUSTOMER-SUPPLIER CHAIN

relationships that will help them satisfy their shared customers further along the customer-supplier chain.

This is why we have written one chapter on customer-supplier relationships, rather than separate chapters on customers and suppliers. The idea of creating mutually beneficial relationships with both customers and suppliers is a major departure from the traditional approach to customer and supplier relationships (CSRs). As one book on quality recently put it, "The historical picture of customer-supplier relationships has been one of self-interested adversaries negotiating against each other to maximize their slice of the pie at the expense of the other."[5] The authors go on to say that the focus of CSRs under TQ is on expanding the pie rather than on arguing over its division.

The Importance of Customers

The importance of customers has evolved over the years, from a view of the customer as a buyer to increase profitability, to a view of the customer as an active partner and the focus of all quality activities. Customer satisfaction translates directly into increased profits. However, while satisfaction is important, modern firms need to look further. Achieving strong profitability and market share requires *loyal* customers—those who stay with a company and make positive referrals. Satisfaction and loyalty are very different concepts.

To quote Patrick Mehne, the chief quality officer at The Ritz-Carlton Hotel Company: "Satisfaction is an attitude; loyalty is a behavior." Customers who are merely satisfied may often purchase from competitors because of convenience, promotions, or other factors. Loyal customers place a priority on doing business with a particular organization, and will often go out of their way or pay a premium to stay with the company. Loyal customers spend more, are willing to pay higher prices, refer new clients, and are less costly to do business with. For instance, although Home Depot customers spend only about $38 each visit, they shop 30 times annually and spend more than $25,000 throughout a lifetime.[6] Carl Sewell, owner of Sewell Cadillac in Dallas, calculated that the average lifetime value of a loyal customer for his dealership was $332,000.[7] Statistics also show that the typical company gets 65 percent of its business from existing customers, and it costs at least five times more to find a new customer than to keep an existing one happy.[8]

Poor-quality products and services, by contrast, lead to customer dissatisfaction in the form of complaints, returns, and unfavorable word-of-mouth publicity (see the box on "The Insolent Night Clerk"). Dissatisfied customers purchase from competitors. One study found that customers are five times more likely to switch because of perceived service problems than for price concerns or product quality issues.[9] Studies have also shown that dissatisfied customers tell at least twice as many friends about bad experiences than they tell about good ones.

For many companies, "The Customer Comes First" is a guiding principle (see the box about Southwest Airlines). It is impossible to overstate the importance of customers to TQ. Customers are at the very center of every TQ activity, and devotion to satisfying them is the first principle of TQ. Customers are recognized as the guarantee of the organization's continued existence.

Therefore, a focus on customers, rather than internal issues, is the foundation of the TQ approach to management. Customer-driven quality is recognized as a core value of the Malcolm Baldrige National Quality Award. The award guidelines state:[10]

> Quality is judged by customers. Thus, quality must take into account all product and service features and characteristics that contribute

---

The Insolent Night Clerk[11]

Two business travelers held guaranteed, confirmed reservations at a hotel (part of a national chain) in a southern U.S. city. The rooms were held for late arrival with a major credit card. They arrived at 2:00 A.M. Here are some of the things that occurred:

- "Mike," the night clerk, said the only rooms left were off-limits because their plumbing and air-conditioning had broken.
- He was unapologetic and did nothing to find alternative accommodations, noting, "Most of our guests don't arrive at two o'clock in the morning" while explaining why it was the travelers' fault that the hotel could not honor the reservation.
- When they suggested that the least he should have done was line up other rooms in advance, Mike bristled and said, "I have nothing to apologize to you for."
- Eventually Mike started checking other hotels and found only smoking rooms in (as the travelers observed) a "dump" six miles farther from downtown.
- To make matters worse, a colleague was arriving first thing in the morning. The travelers left him a note in care of Mike. The clerk on duty the next morning never got the note.

As the travelers pointed out in a follow-up PowerPoint presentation sent to the hotel managers and their bosses:

- chance of winning the UK Lottery: 1 in 13,983,816;
- chance of us returning to this hotel: worse than this.

Then they proceeded to e-mail their story to a few friends with a request to share it with *their* friends! Within a short time, thousands of people had heard their story through the Internet.

value to customers and lead to customer satisfaction, preference, and retention. Value and satisfaction may be influenced by many factors throughout the customer's overall purchase, ownership, and service experiences. These factors include the company's relationship with customers that helps build trust, confidence, and loyalty.

The Importance of Suppliers

The quality of goods and services received from suppliers, the upstream portion of the supply chain, has a significant effect on the quality of goods and services that downstream customers receive. Suppliers are those companies that provide the organization with goods and services that help them to satisfy the needs of their own customers. A manufacturing company assembling parts made by suppliers illustrates this point: the final product cannot be any better than the parts that comprise it. For example, the U.S. Federal Aviation Administration (FAA), after a widespread and comprehensive review of Boeing's commercial jet unit, concluded that the company failed to maintain adequate control over its supplier base. In one instance, several suppliers provided aluminum parts that were defective and prone to cracking after the parts were installed. Aircraft already in service have had to undergo extensive testing and inspection to eliminate the possibility of catastrophic failure.[12]

If a supplier's performance is of consistently high quality, its customer can decrease or eliminate costly incoming inspections that add no value to the product. For these reasons, many organizations have increasingly demanded tangible progress in quality from all their suppliers. Companies that do not accept this requirement are dropped from supplier lists. The importance of suppliers is at least as great when they provide training, software, or other goods or services that do not physically become part of the final product; they will influence its quality nevertheless by shaping the quality of the processes used to produce it.

However, as Terry A. Carlson, corporate vice president of purchasing for Maytag, stated, "Superior quality, consistent service, and competitive pricing are just the price of entry to get into the game." What sets world-class suppliers apart from the rest are a formal company-wide effort to continually improve their products and services, the ability and willingness to align products, processes, and business strategies with customers for mutual success, and a proven ability to be an industry leader in developing new technologies and products.[13]

In business today, operations are often highly decentralized and dispersed around the world. Consequently, managing a complex network of suppliers becomes a critical interorganizational issue. Suppliers play a vital role throughout the product development process, from design through distribution. Suppliers can provide technology or production processes not internally available, early design advice, and increased capacity, which can

---

Flying the Customer-Friendly Skies[14]

Southwest Airlines began service on June 18, 1971, with flights to Houston, Dallas, and San Antonio, and has grown to become the fifth largest U.S. airline in terms of domestic customers carried. The airline operates more than 2,150 flights daily with more than 23,000 employees. Known for its legendary service, the Southwest culture ensures that it serves the needs of its Customers (with a capital *C*) in a friendly, caring, and enthusiastic manner. Kevin and Jackie Freiberg, authors of *NUTS! Southwest Airlines' Crazy Recipe for Business and Personal Success*, note that legendary service is a key component of Southwest's culture.

Southwest wants its customers to experience service that makes a lasting impression, service that is kind and loving, service that is fun and makes them laugh. . . . Thus, Southwest will go a long way to defend and support an employee who may violate a company policy to bend toward the customer. The company instills in every employee the idea that happy, satisfied customers who return again and again create job security.

Every one of the approximately 1,000 customers who write to the airline get a personal response (not a form letter) within four weeks, and frequent fliers even get birthday cards. The airline even moved a flight up a quarter-hour when five medical students who commuted weekly to an out-of-state medical school complained that the flight got them to class 15 minutes late. Customer focus applies to internal customers also; each operating division identifies an internal customer. Mechanics who service planes target the pilots who fly them, and marketers treat reservation agents as customers. It is not unusual to find pilots helping ground crews unload baggage. As Executive VP Colleen Barrett stated: "We are not an airline with great customer service. We are a great customer service organization that happens to be in the airline business." Southwest has been one of the most profitable airlines in the United States.

In many years, the airline has been recognized for best baggage handling, fewest customer complaints, and best on-time performance, and has been recognized with numerous honors, including one of America's Most Admired Corporations by *Fortune* magazine for many years.

---

result in lower costs, faster time-to-market, and improved quality for their customers. In turn, they are assured of stable and long-term business. At Daimler-Chrysler, for example, suppliers are involved early in the design process.[15] As a result, Daimler-Chrysler often finds out about new materials, parts, and technologies before other automakers.

Increasingly, suppliers are viewed as *partners* with customers, because there usually is a codependent relationship. A powerful example of supplier partnerships is the response that occurred when a fire destroyed the main source of a crucial $5 brake valve for Toyota.[16] Without it, Toyota had to shut down its 20 plants in Japan. Within hours of the disaster, other suppliers began taking blueprints, improvising tooling systems, and setting up makeshift production lines. Within days, the 36 suppliers, aided by more than 150 other subcontractors, had almost 50 production lines making small batches of the valve. Even a sewing-machine company that had never made car parts spent 500 person-hours refitting a milling machine to make just 40 valves a day. Toyota promised the suppliers a bonus of about $100 million "as a token of our appreciation."

PRINCIPLES FOR CUSTOMER-SUPPLIER RELATIONSHIPS

Three governing principles describe CSRs under total quality:

- recognition of the strategic importance of customers and suppliers,
- development of win-win relationships between customers and suppliers, and
- establishing relationships based on trust.

First, every organization must recognize that its customers and suppliers are absolutely crucial to its success (see the box "Customers in the Fine Arts"). Although this may sound obvious, many organizations seem to be driven by the need to observe standard operating procedures and maintain rigid boundaries between jobs, rather than trying to meet customer expectations.

Many employees don't think that it's their "job" to serve customers beyond their job descriptions. For example, a hotel desk clerk's formal job description might be to greet and register guests and process bills. Does this mean that they should not respond to special requests like bringing extra pillows to a room (housekeeping's "job"), or make a restaurant reservation (the "job" of the concierge)? As the first and last contact a guest makes with the hotel, front-desk personnel probably have the largest impact on guest satisfaction of anyone. It is frightening to imagine how much damage that a poor attitude from a desk clerk might have on his or her organization. Of course, the responsibility for this attitude may ultimately rest with the hotel organization that apparently has created a system in which people are more interested in maintaining boundaries than in serving customers.[17]

Customers must be at the center of the organizational universe (see the box "The Boomerang Principle"). Satisfying their needs leads to repeat business and positive referrals, as opposed to one-shot business and negative referrals. Suppliers also must be considered crucial to organizational success, because they make it possible to create customer satisfaction. Neither the quality nor the cost of the organization's product can be brought to competitive levels and continuously improved without the contributions of suppliers.

Customers in the Fine Arts[18]

Car dealers have customers, bookstores have customers, but how about symphony orchestras and art museums? Traditionally, such organizations have acted as if they were your customer. But fine arts organizations in Cincinnati, spurred both by economic necessity and the proximity and influence of several quality-conscious corporations, have begun to think hard about satisfying customers. Some of the results:

- The Cincinnati Symphony Orchestra initiated a series of concerts on Thursday nights. Dress is more casual for these concerts, and tickets can be easily exchanged.
- The Taft Museum doubled the number of events it holds—from 20 to 40 per season.
- The Cincinnati Opera scheduled a series of operas linked by a popular theme. For example, "Pretty Women" included *Carmen* and *The Barber of Seville*.

The increased focus on satisfying customers, which has begun to pay off economically, is reflected by statements from leaders in these organizations. Paul A. Stuhireyer III, managing director of the opera, believes that "the goal should not be an international reputation while losing sight of what [local customers] want. . . . I want to make sure we're still putting 3,000 people into Music Hall for each performance. Then I know we're taking care of the citizens of Cincinnati." Gretchen Mehring, Cincinnati Art Museum director of public service, puts it: "Our primary focus is the family, especially the children. We're not operating a museum or creating exhibitions to appeal to art experts."

The second principle of customer-supplier relationships is the need to develop mutually beneficial (often called win-win) relationships between customers and suppliers. This was discussed previously as working together to increase the size of the pie, rather than competing over how to divide it.

The goal of building partnerships with customers and suppliers can be seen as an extension of the teamwork principle that applies to all TQ activities and as a recognition that the needs of both partners must be satisfied if productive long-term relationships are to be created. W. Edwards Deming advocated these principles for decades, as is evident in his 14 Points (Chapter 2). Joseph Juran developed a useful framework to distinguish between adversarial and teamwork relationships with suppliers.[19] Traditionally, customers have used many different suppliers for the same purchased item, and they typically have been awarded short-term (annual) contracts. This practice fosters a competitive situation in which suppliers

The Boomerang Principle[20]

Feargal Quinn is the executive chairman of Superquinn, a 5,600-person, 19-store chain of supermarkets in Ireland. In every deed, the focus is on persuading the customer to return. Quinn calls it the "boomerang principle." His tireless and inventive exploration of this principle earned him a reputation as Ireland's "pope of customer service." Superquinn inspires such intense devotion that many customers say that they drive out of their way—and past several of its biggest competitors—to shop there. At Superquinn, you don't have to pay for broccoli stalks and carrot tops you never use; the store provides scissors to cut off what you don't want. The checkout technology provides a running tab on a screen that faces the customer, and then organizes the final receipt by product category, rather than the order in which products were scanned. Every store features a professionally staffed playhouse where mothers can leave young children while they shop. The program costs the company a bundle, but it has earned even more in loyal customers and reputation.

Kindergarten teachers around the country (Ireland doesn't have preschool) recognize "Superquinn kids" as the most socialized and school-ready of each new class. Each month, Superquinn managers are required to spend time in customers' shoes, shopping, asking questions, lodging complaints, waiting in line. Superquinn's fresh produce, butchers, and fishmongers are mixed in with futuristic flat screen displays, digital shelf labels, and kiosks that link customers to their bank, their SuperClub account, as well as to wine recommendations and interactive recipe planners. Quinn notes that, "What seems reasonable or even valuable from the perspective of the company is often glaringly wrong from the point of view of the customer."

strive to outbid each other and may sacrifice quality for cost. A teamwork relationship results in the need for fewer suppliers, with many items being single-sourced. With few suppliers, companies do not have to rely on annual bidding, and can award longer-term contracts. This enhances the motivation to work together for mutual benefits. For instance, quality planning, problem solving activities, and efforts to adjust to market changes are performed jointly, rather than independently. This helps both the customer and supplier focus on "fitness for use" to meet customer needs rather than simply trying to conform to specifications. It also fosters a spirit of continuous improvement, in which larger customers often help smaller suppliers develop their quality management systems and process capabilities. Similar ideas were also advocated by Deming in his 14 Points.

The third principle of effective CSRs is that they must be based on trust rather than suspicion. This point is described by Juran as the "pattern of collaboration." The costs of mistrust are staggering: witness the tremendous number, detail, and rigidity of rules that characterize the U.S. Department of Defense's contracts with its suppliers. The suppliers often incur substantial costs in terms of both money and time because of multiple levels of review and inspection. Although a certain level of rigidity is to be expected in the acquisition of weapons, it is harder to understand when applied to more ordinary items.

Aside from the obvious teamwork implications for relationships based on trust versus suspicion, monitoring supplier or customer behavior does not add any value to the product. If a trusting relationship between customers and suppliers can be developed so that neither must check up on the behavior of the other, the costs of monitoring, such as inspection and auditing, can be avoided. Many Japanese firms do not inspect items purchased from other companies in Japan; they do, however, often inspect those purchased from America. Trust is not a blind leap into the unknown; it is developed over time "through a pattern of success by all parties to fully and faithfully deliver that which was promised."[21] In other words, trust depends upon trustworthy behavior by both parties in a CSR.

PRACTICES FOR DEALING WITH CUSTOMERS

How can these principles be translated into specific practices? The most basic practices for dealing with customers are: (1) to collect information constantly on customer expectations; (2) to disseminate this information widely within the organization; and (3) to use this information to design, produce, and deliver the organization's products and services.

Collect Customer Information

Acquiring customer information is critical to understanding customer needs and identifying opportunities for improvement. The Japanese auto industry is known for trying to understand customer needs so thoroughly that it can incorporate design features that customers would never have asked for but love once they experience them. Teams of automobile designers visit people at home and observe how they live in order to anticipate their automotive needs. Hideo Sugiura, executive vice president of Honda, comments on his company's efforts to anticipate customer needs: "We should not try to sell things just because the market is there, but rather we should seek to create a new market by accurately understanding the potential needs of customers and society."[22] Lexus, Toyota's luxury car line, has succeeded dramatically in this manner and is consistently at the top of owner satisfaction surveys.

Perhaps one of the best examples of understanding customer needs and using this information to improve competitiveness is Frank Perdue's chicken business.[23] Perdue learned what customers' key purchase criteria were; these included a yellow bird, high meat-to-bone ratio, no pinfeathers, freshness, availability, and brand image. He also determined the relative importance of each criterion, and how well the company and its competitors were meeting each of them. By systematically improving his ability to exceed customers' expectations relative to the competition, Perdue gained market share even though his chickens were premium-priced. Among Perdue's innovations was a used jet engine that dried the chickens, allowing the pinfeathers to be singed off.

In Chapter 1, we cited the model of customer requirements:

- Dissatisfiers
- Satisfiers
- Exciters/delighters

In trying to understand customer needs, it is important to go beyond what customers say they need and anticipate what will really excite them. It is a well-known principle of innovation that customers will seldom express enthusiasm for a product that is different from anything they have experienced. Thus, the original market survey for computers suggested that only a few would be sold, and it took years for 3M to become convinced that Post-It notes would actually be valuable to people in offices. As Kozo Ohsone of Sony puts it, "When you introduce products that have never been invented before, what good is market research?"[24]

Some of the most popular ways to collect information about customers are surveys, service evaluation cards, focus groups, and listening to what customers say during business transactions, especially when they complain. Some companies, such as Marriott Hotels, have developed elaborate methods for keeping abreast of customer needs. This is not a low-profile activity at Marriott: Chairman Bill Marriott, Jr., himself reads approximately 800 letters from customers and 15,000 guest questionnaires every month![25] The rewards of taking customer information seriously are also apparent at Marriott, where occupancy rates are consistently 10 percent above the industry average.

Getting employees involved in collecting customer information improves worker skills and learning, makes work more meaningful, and enhances motivation (see the discussion of job characteristics theory in Chapter 8). For example, employees at Saturn conduct customer surveys themselves—this makes them more accountable for quality while building relationships with customers.[26] In a similar vein, sending employees into customer facilities, another popular practice, provides not only feedback from customers, but also valuable information to employees about the importance of what they do. A manager in a foundry that follows this practice commented: "We take shop floor people and take them out to the customer's plant. We want them to see the final product in place. It gets our employees out in the world to meet the customers. They get to know the customers better and really by doing that, the employees get to have a better, more caring attitude. Because they know more about what's going on."

Having top managers of the company act as customers of their own organizations—renting a room in their own hotel or buying a suit from a retail outlet—is another way to better understand customer needs. This not only gives them a sense of the quality of service but also makes them more sensitive to how the organizational policies they have created actually affect customers.[27]

A more recent approach to collecting customer information is to monitor the Internet.[28] In recent years, the growth of the Internet is offering companies a fertile arena for finding out what consumers think of their products. Internet users frequently seek advice from other users on strengths and weaknesses of products, share experiences on service quality, or pose specific problems they need to resolve. By monitoring the conversations on Usenet discussion groups, managers can obtain valuable insights on customer perceptions and product or service quality problems. In open forums, customer comments can often be translated into creative product improvements. In addition, the Internet can be a good source of information about competitors' products.

The cost of monitoring Internet conversations is minimal compared to the costs of other types of survey approaches, and customers are not biased by any questions that may be asked. However, the conversations may be considerably less structured and unfocused, and thus may contain less usable information. Also, unlike a focus group or telephone interview, inaccurate perceptions or factual errors cannot be corrected.

Beyond getting a thorough understanding of customer needs, companies also need to assess how well their products and services are meeting customer needs. A simple approach is to ask them directly, using a process called the **voice of the customer** (see the box "The Good, the Bad, and the Ugly"). Some companies have developed unconventional and innovative ways of understanding customers. British Airways (BA) has installed video kiosks at Heathrow Airport outside London and Kennedy Airport in New York. When upset, customers can enter the booth and create a video message for BA's management. The videos have proven so informative that, although they were initially viewed only by executives, frontline employees demanded and were given access to them. One important aspect of this method is that it gives people a sense of the emotion associated with customer response to the quality of service ("you lost my *&%$# baggage!"), which cannot easily be conveyed by checking a number from one through five on a customer satisfaction survey, especially when done weeks later. Texas Instruments created a simulated classroom to understand how mathematics teachers use calculators, and a manager at Levi Strauss used to talk with teens who were lined up to buy rock concert tickets.

A more formal approach to getting into customers' minds is called **imprint analysis**.[29] "Imprint" refers to the collection of associations and emotions unconsciously linked to a word, concept, or experience. The stronger the emotion, the stronger the imprint. Events and experiences imprinted with strong emotions at an early age usually last just below the level of consciousness for a person's entire life. By looking deeply into

The Good, the Bad, and the Ugly

One regional chain of restaurants realized that customers know what they want, but have a difficult time expressing their needs in ways that are meaningful to managers. This means that the company must be able to effectively translate customers' language into actionable business terms. Here are some real examples during voice of the customer research in cities in which the chain was considering expanding:

- "So there I was, like herded cattle, standing on the hard concrete floor, cold wind blasting my ankles every time the door opened, waiting and waiting for our name to be called."
- "And then I saw a dirty rag being slopped around a dirty table."
- "This is a great place because you can just come in and plop in a booth, just like at Mom's house."
- "The manager said, 'That's not a gnat—that's black pepper,' so I said, 'I know the difference between black pepper and a gnat—black pepper doesn't have little wings on it!'"
- "I swear! The salad looked like the server ran down to the river bank and picked weeds and grass—I'm never going back!"
- "When they're that age, going to the bathroom is a full-contact sport—they're reaching and grabbing at everything, and you're trying to keep them from touching anything because the bathroom is so dirty. And, by the way, isn't the kitchen just a few steps away?"
- "The server just stood there staring at me, chomping his gum like a cow chewing its cud."

In the first example, what the customer really was saying is, "Make me comfortable!" What do you think they were really saying in the others?

people's past experiences, imprint analysis can help companies understand what drives today's behavior. Also, imprints of current experiences reveal emerging needs; thus, imprint analysis can actually forecast customer behavior. One ice cream company, faced with responding to a shift to healthier eating, needed to understand whether they should develop a nonfat product or reduce the sugar content. An imprint analysis uncovered a surprising new customer segment whose eating habits defied common sense. During the week, these customers would consume low-fat foods and deprive themselves of desserts. But on weekends, they wanted a super-rich ice cream, acting as a reward for eating healthy during the week! Another paradox the analysis uncovered was that although customers said they wanted many different flavors, they tended to buy those that were fundamentally vanilla. The analysis revealed two senses of taste: one in the body and one in the mind. By creating vanilla variations with exciting names (and premium priced extra-creamy ice cream), the company created loyalty among existing customers while also attracting new customers.

The principles of TQ can help organizations to collect customer information by engaging the participation of everyone who encounters customers in their jobs; focusing on the processes used to collect information, such as segmenting customer groups and prioritizing customer requirements; and continually improving those processes.

Disseminate Customer Information

After people in the organization have gathered information about customer needs, the next step is to broadcast this information within the organization. After all, if the people in the firm are going to work as a team to meet customer expectations, they must all be "singing from the same hymnbook," as the saying goes. Information does little good if it stays with the person or department that brought it into the organization. Wainwright Industries has a unique approach. A room at the headquarters building, named Mission Control (by one of the managers who is a Star Trek fan), serves as the company's key information center. Not only are customer report cards displayed on a wall (along with other key quality and business information), but green and red flags are used to designate customers for whom everything is going well or a problem has arisen. Red flags signal the convening of a customer team to address the problem.

AT&T, whose divisions have won several Baldrige Awards, is one organization trying to maintain a constant customer focus. Jerre Stead, president of Global Business Communications Systems, tells people in his unit: "I say if you're in a meeting, any meeting, for 15 minutes and we're not talking about customers or competitors, raise your hand and ask why. If it goes on for half an hour, leave! Leave the meeting!"[30]

Customer information must be translated into the features of the organization's products and services. This is the bottom line of quality customer-supplier relations from the supplier's point of view: giving the customers what they want. Translating customer needs into product features can be done in a structured manner using quality function deployment (QFD), a technique discussed in Chapter 3. QFD allows people to see how aspects of their products and services relate to customer satisfaction, and to make informed decisions about how their products should be improved. The overall process of using information from customers to provide quality products is summarized in Figure 4.2.

Use Customer Information

Customer information is worthless unless it is used. Customer feedback should be integrated into continuous improvement activities. For example, by listening to customers, Bank One opened nearly 60 percent of its 1,377

FIGURE 4.2   THE CUSTOMER-DRIVEN QUALITY CYCLE

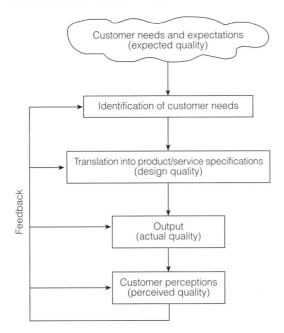

branches in Ohio and Texas on Saturdays, and 20 percent on Sundays. A 24-hour customer hotline is also available.

Binney & Smith, the company that produces Crayola™ crayons and markers, makes it a point to improve its products by taking advantage of customer feedback. Many of the letters the company receives from parents laud the role that crayons play in the artistic development of their children. Some letters complained that the markers created permanent stains in children's clothes. After two years of research, Binney & Smith responded by developing a new line of washable markers. Marker sales doubled, demonstrating the company's ability to learn and provide what customers are looking for.[31] Binney & Smith also sponsored a contest in which customers could name one of 16 new crayon colors the company created for its Big Box. "Part of our reason for introducing new colors came from consumer suggestions. More than 50 percent said they wanted us to expand and add new colors," according to Brad Dexler, a company spokesman.

Perhaps the most important use of customer information is in developing business strategies and in designing goods and services (see the box on Harrah's). In the Malcolm Baldrige criteria, for example, one of the key questions is how a company collects and analyzes customer and market needs, expectations, and opportunities, and relates them to the development of strategies. Analyzing customer information can uncover a myriad of opportunities for new and improved goods and services.

Gambling for Customers[32]

Dr. Gary Loveman, a Harvard Business School professor who was instrumental in introducing the "Service-Profit Chain" to the business literature, has been chief operating officer and CEO of Harrah's Entertainment, owner of casinos in Las Vegas and other locations. The service-profit chain argues that a direct correlation exists between profitability and a focus on customer loyalty and rewards to front-line employees who have the most contact with customers. Recognizing that gambling is fundamentally entertainment, he focused Harrah's strategy on the casino floor, rather than peripheral entertainment activities that are characteristic of other casino enterprises. He also directed more attention to the large numbers of loyal customers who could not be classified as "high rollers." For example, he helped devise a three-tiered loyalty card system that encouraged people to spend more to get perks like discounted rooms, no-line check-in, and separate buffet seating. The cards also collect reams of useful customer data. Harrah's also launched a program that gave these customers free or deeply discounted flights on chartered planes, shuttle service to the casino, and even blue margaritas. Of course, customers were expected to return the favor!

Manage Customer Relationships

A company builds customer loyalty by developing trust and effectively managing the interactions and relationships with customers through customer-contact employees. Truly excellent companies foster close and total relationships with customers. These companies also provide easy access to their employees. Customers of Ames Rubber Corporation have immediate access to top division management, manufacturing personnel, quality engineers, sales and service representatives, and technical support staff.

In services, customer satisfaction or dissatisfaction takes place during *moments of truth*—every instance in which a customer comes in contact with an employee of the company. Moments of truth may be direct contacts with customer representatives or service personnel, or when customers read letters, invoices, or other company correspondence. In leading fundamental change at Procter & Gamble (P&G), CEO A. G. Lafley felt that P&G was letting technology rather than consumer needs dictate new products, and that the company was not working closely enough with retailers, where consumers first see the product on the shelf—the "first moment of truth," as he called it—and that the company wasn't concerned enough with the consumer's experience at home—the "second moment of truth." Lafley summed up his strategy for P&G simply: "The consumer is boss."[33]

One study concluded that 70 percent of customers leave a supplier because of poor-quality service, not problems with products per se, and many companies are struggling to bring their service up to the level of their products.[34] One of the main areas on which companies have focused is telephone service, especially how long it takes to get someone on the phone, and to get one's question answered or order taken. Many companies have worked to make sure that phone calls are answered on the third ring, but to AMP, Inc., the world's largest manufacturer of electronic interconnection systems, three rings is an eternity. Customer calls to AMP are answered within six seconds—that is, on the first ring. Why such an ambitious goal? AMP found that 8 percent of their customers were hanging up before their calls were answered under the three-ring standard. They don't lose many calls now.[35] TQ principles help to view customer service as a process, and focus on improving service delivery and reducing points of failure that can result in dissatisfaction. Well-designed processes for building customer relationships can help to identify early signal of customer dissatisfaction or defection.

Customer-contact employees are particularly important. They are the people whose main responsibilities bring them into regular contact with customers—in person, by telephone, or through other means. Companies must carefully select these employees who are then extensively trained and empowered to meet and exceed customer expectations. Job applicants often go through rigorous screening processes and extensive training. LeBoeuf, Lamb, Greene, & MacRae, LLP, one of the world's leading law firms, created an in-house curriculum with such workshops as "Care and Feeding of the Customer," which reinforces the idea that no matter where people are in the firm, they are customer service employees first, and what they do not only reflects on the firm but also on themselves as individuals. The course presents real work situations, and the discussion relates to "How do you think you are perceived when certain situations happen?" and "Do you realize you might be perceived as . . . ?" with a focus on improvement activities.[36]

Service standards are measurable performance levels or expectations that define the quality of customer contact. Service standards might include technical standards such as response time (answering the telephone within two rings), or behavioral standards (using a customer's name whenever possible). Companies need to communicate and continually reinforce their service standards. Finally, a company should implement a process for tracking adherence to the standards and providing feedback to the employees to improve their performance. Information technology supplies the data for effectively tracking conformance to customer service standards.

Despite all efforts to satisfy customers, every business experiences unhappy customers. Complaints can adversely affect business if not dealt with effectively. Many customers do not complain because they feel it wouldn't do any good or they are uncomfortable with the process. World-class organizations make it easy for customers to complain. Besides providing easy access to the company using toll-free telephone numbers (which should be adequately staffed and supported), many firms actively solicit complaints. Nissan, for instance, telephones each person who buys a new car or brings one in for significant warranty work. Its objective is to resolve all dissatisfaction within 24 hours.[37] Effective resolution of complaints increases customer loyalty and retention. At The Ritz-Carlton Hotel Company, for example, employees can spend up to $2,000 to resolve complaints with no questions asked.

Exploit CRM Technology

Customer relationship management (CRM) software is designed to help companies increase customer loyalty, target their most profitable customers, and streamline customer communication processes. More than $11 billion was spent on CRM-related U.S. sales at the turn of the century and is growing significantly.[38] A typical CRM system includes market segmentation and analysis, customer service and relationship building, effective complaint resolution, cross-selling goods and services, order processing, and field service. CRM helps firms gain and maintain competitive advantage by:

- Segmenting markets based on demographic and behavioral characteristics.
- Tracking sales trends and advertising effectiveness by customer and market segment.
- Identifying and eliminated non–value-adding products that would waste resources as well as those products that better meet customers' needs and provide increased value.
- Identifying which customers should be the focus of targeted marketing initiatives with predicted high customer response rates.
- Forecasting customer retention (and defection) rates and providing feedback as to why customers leave a company.
- Studying which goods and services are purchased together, leading to good ways to bundle them.
- Studying and predicting which Web characteristics are most attractive to customers and how the Web site might be improved.
- Streamlining processes around customers rather than traditional functions, resulting in improved flow of information and cycle times.

Technology is a key enabler of CRM (see the box on Tsutaya). CRM systems provide a variety of useful operational data to managers, including the average time spent responding to customer questions, comments, and concerns, average order tracking (flow) time, total revenue generated by each customer (and sometimes their family or business) from all goods and services bought by the customer—the total picture of economic value of the customer to the firm, cost per marketing campaign, and price discrepancies.

It is important to realize that although CRM can provide many benefits, it is not a solution to customer relationship problems. CRM can help an organization use data wisely to customize its product to better serve its markets, but it first requires an understanding of customer needs. In addition,

---

Tsutaya Online: Building Personal Customer Relationships[39]

One company that exploits technology in developing customer relationships is Tsutaya, Japan's largest video, book, and CD chain. Using a point-of-sale system that facilitates real-time inventory tracking between headquarters and franchises and a Web and wireless site called Tsutaya Online (TOL), Tsutaya tracks purchases, demographic data, spending behavior, and by implication, lifestyles and interests. This system enables them to offer personalized product recommendations. For example, if you bought a CD by a certain artist, TOL will e-mail a digital music clip when the next album debuts. Tsutaya also developed a sophisticated recommendation engine to match a customer's video rental history and mood to the ideal movie selection. Many other companies, such as Amazon.com and BMG Music Service, use technology in similar ways.

---

one can easily capture a lot of useless information simply because it is easy to do. This makes analysis difficult, and can frustrate users.

Don't Ignore Internal Customers

Individual departments and key cross-functional processes within a company have **internal customers** who contribute to the company's mission and depend on the department's or function's products or services to ultimately serve consumers and external customers. For instance, manufacturing is a customer of purchasing, a nursing unit is a customer of the hospital laundry, and reservations is a customer of the information systems department for an airline or hotel. In addition, each employee receives inputs from others and produces some output to internal customers. A customer may be the assembly-line worker at the next station, an executive's secretary, the order taker who passes along orders to the food preparer at McDonald's, or an X-ray technician who must meet a physician's request. The linkages among internal customers build up the "chain of customers and suppliers" throughout the company that connect every individual and function to the external customers and consumers.

The principle of mutually beneficial relationships also applies to internal customer-supplier relationships (see box "Partnering with Internal Customers").

PRACTICES FOR DEALING WITH SUPPLIERS[40]

In business today, operations are often highly decentralized and dispersed around the world. Consequently, managing a complex network of suppliers becomes a critical interorganizational issue. Suppliers play a vital role throughout the product development process, from design through distribution.

Partnering with Internal Customers[41]

GTE Supply negotiates contracts, purchases products, and distributes a vast array of goods needed for telephone operations, from office supplies to telecommunications equipment. Its major customers are internal network, business, and telephone operations customer groups at each GTE local telephone company. The company created a systematic, highly effective process of obtaining and using information from internal customers, making partners of previous adversarial groups, reducing costs, and improving customer satisfaction.

This was based on systematically surveying internal customers and using the results as a basis for quality improvement. Respondents rate GTE Supply on how well it

- provides complete information,
- understands customers' needs,
- does the job right the first time,
- provides timely responses to questions and requests,
- makes it easy to do business with,
- follows up on services,
- provides clear communication, and
- various other attributes.

Other questions seek information about overall satisfaction, quality, and value, as well as open-ended questions about improvement opportunities. Detailed reports and analyses are provided to managers who use the information to set objectives, develop action plans, and implement them.

The survey and quality improvement process has transformed the organization from one of the worst-regarded to one of the best-regarded organizations in the company. They learned that extensive, focused communication with internal customers can produce spectacular increases in satisfaction levels and decrease costs and cycle times.

Suppliers can provide technology or production processes not internally available, early design advice, and increased capacity, which can result in lower costs, faster time-to-market, and improved quality for their customers. In turn, they are assured of stable and long-term business.

Successful suppliers have a culture where employees and managers share in customers' goals, commitments, and risks to promote such long-term relationships (recall one of Deming's 14 Points about supplier relationships—not purchasing solely on the basis of price). Strong customer-supplier relationships are based on three guiding principles:

1. recognizing the strategic importance of suppliers in accomplishing business objectives, particularly minimizing the total cost of ownership,

2. developing win-win relationships through partnerships rather than as adversaries, and
3. establishing trust through openness and honesty, thus leading to mutual advantages.

Although the principles of CSRs are the same in dealing with suppliers as they are with customers, the practices are somewhat different. In many companies, suppliers are treated as if they were actually a part of the organization. For example, functions such as cafeteria service, mailroom operations, and information processing are being performed by suppliers at their customers' facilities. As more and more of this type of outsourcing is done, the lines between the customer and the supplier become increasingly blurred.

To ensure that suppliers can provide high quality and reduce costs associated with incoming inspection or testing, many companies provide many types of assistance to their suppliers in developing quality assurance programs or solving quality problems. Joint conferences, training, incentives, recognition, and long-term agreements help to improve suppliers' abilities to meet key quality requirements. The Delco Moraine Division, a manufacturer of automotive brake controls, uses an awareness program that includes a videotape presentation emphasizing quality shown at supplier plants. After viewing the tape, supplier employees were better able to relate their work to Delco.

Base Purchasing Decisions on Quality and Cost

The first and most obvious practice is that purchasing decisions should be based on the quality of the product and not just its cost.[42] This, however, goes against the grain in most organizations. Generally speaking, the technical people will determine the specifications for a product to be purchased, and then the purchasing department will solicit bids or check prices with several suppliers and negotiate the contract with the one that fills the order. Purchasing personnel traditionally have been rewarded primarily for negotiating low prices, and thus this has been their focus. Supplier firms have often responded to this situation in the obvious way: by doing whatever they need to do (including sacrificing quality) to maintain low prices.

Beyond the compromises this creates for the quality of the final product, there are two other problems with this approach. First, low purchase cost often does not equal low overall cost. If a cheap (in both senses of the word) part causes a large amount of scrap or leads to high warranty costs, it may end up with a higher overall cost, often referred to as life-cycle cost. Second, pressing suppliers for ever-lower prices will minimize their profits. Although this benefits the customer in the short run, in the long run it keeps suppliers operating so close to the bone that they forgo capital investments, maintenance, and other expenses necessary to improve or even maintain their quality.[43]

Reduce the Number of Suppliers

Firms pursuing TQ also reduce the number of suppliers they work with to the point of having only one supplier for some components. Xerox reduced its suppliers by about 90 percent—from more than 4,000 to about 450 in 1990.[44] In the automotive industry, General Motors cut domestic suppliers by 45 percent, from 10,000 down to 5,500, by 1991. Ford Motor Co. likewise reduced its number of suppliers from 1,800 down to 1,000.[45] This also goes against the grain of conventional purchasing practices, as it increases the dependence of the organization on the supplier, thus weakening its bargaining position and exposing it to the possibility of an interruption in supply in the case of a labor stoppage or similar problem with the supplier.

Several advantages offset these disadvantages. For one thing, administrative costs are greatly reduced.[46] (Imagine the time to be saved by eliminating the paperwork associated with 90 percent of suppliers!) Also, cutting the number of suppliers reduces the variability in the incoming products, making it much easier to control the quality of outgoing products. This is because there are fewer "special causes" of variation, to use Deming's term.

The type of intensive CSRs that characterize TQ simply cannot be maintained with a large number of suppliers. The significance of partners (like friends or vice presidents) is lost if you have too many of them. For these reasons, many organizations continue to reduce the number of suppliers with which they do business.

Establish Long-Term Contracts

Related to the idea of fewer suppliers is the practice of establishing long-term contracts with suppliers. Establishing long-term contracts allows suppliers to make greater commitments to improving the quality of products and provides greater opportunity for joint improvement efforts and the development of teamwork across organizational boundaries.

Measure and Certify Supplier Performance

Texas Instruments measures suppliers' quality performance by parts per million defective, percentage of on-time deliveries, and cost of ownership.[47] An electronic requisitioning system allows a paperless procurement process. More than 800 suppliers are linked to Texas Instruments through an information exchange system. Integrated data systems track the incoming quality and timeliness of deliveries as materials are received. Analytical reports and online data are used to identify material defect trends. Performance reports are sent each month to key suppliers. Joint customer-supplier teams are formed to communicate and improve performance. A supplier management task force of top managers directs current and strategic approaches to improving supplier management practices.

Supplier certification is used by many companies as the focal point of their supplier management system. Formal programs typically are established to rate and certify suppliers who provide quality materials in a cost-effective and timely manner. At the Gillette Company, the supplier certification program begins with Gillette identifying those suppliers with a proven ability to meet its specifications.[48] Once a supplier is selected to participate, Gillette expects them to establish a preproduction planning system to assess the capability of their process to meet Gillette's specifications. Feedback is offered in the form of recommended changes that will improve quality, reduce cost, or facilitate ease of manufacture.

Some companies, such as Motorola, have suppliers rate them as customers. Motorola uses a 15-member council of suppliers that rates Motorola's practices and offers suggestions for improving, for example, the accuracy of production schedules or design layouts that Motorola provides.[49]

At Dana Commercial Credit, strategic suppliers include financial institutions and law firms. Legal requirements are communicated at the early stages of a relationship; feedback from customers determines whether requirements are being met. Corning TPD classifies its suppliers in a hierarchy: Level 1 suppliers have a direct impact on customer satisfaction; Level 2 suppliers are important, but do not have direct linkage to customer satisfaction; Level 3 suppliers provide commodity-like products. Level 1 suppliers are supported by cross-functional teams and integrated into development activities. Armstrong conducts site visits and has a 5-level scale to help suppliers understand where they stand in meeting the company's expectations. STMicroelectronics developed an annual Supplier Quality & Service Plan, which sets goals for suppliers and specifies how ST will review performance, share data, and carry out other responsibilities in the relationship. Long-term partnerships with quality-minded suppliers enabled Texas Nameplate Company to nearly eliminate inspections of incoming materials. These "ship-direct-to-stock" suppliers are required to be defect-free for at least two years and meet all requirements specified on purchase orders.

Develop Cooperative Relationships and Strategic Alliances

Increasingly, suppliers are viewed as partners with customers, because there usually is a codependent relationship. Thus, the cornerstone of TQ-style customer-supplier relationships is cooperation. In a sense, practices such as long-term contracts and fewer suppliers create an environment in which cooperation can flourish. Similar to the operation of teamwork within an organization (see Chapter 7), quality customer-supplier relations help both parties to achieve their goals.

One common form that cooperation takes is the early involvement of suppliers in the design of new products.[50] Early involvement allows suppliers to make cost-cutting and quality-improving suggestions about the design while changes are relatively easy and inexpensive to make. When the product design is not revealed to suppliers until late in the process, often out of concern that it will be leaked to competitors, such opportunities are lost.

Security concerns can be dealt with through nondisclosure agreements.[51] Another indication of cooperation is the effort of customers to help suppliers improve quality, which can take many forms. Many TQ-oriented corporations present quality-improvement seminars for their suppliers.[52] Juran recommends joint quality planning between customers and suppliers, featuring the exchange of quality-related information.[53] Although customers traditionally have hammered suppliers to lower their prices, in a cooperative relationship the focus is on helping suppliers to lower their costs, which will ultimately benefit both parties.[54]

Today, suppliers are being asked to take on greater responsibilities to help their customers. As companies focus more on their core competencies—the things they do best—they are looking outside their organizations for assistance with noncritical support processes. Customer-supplier partnerships represent an important strategic alliance in achieving excellence and business success. For example, partnerships with suppliers have helped Dell drive down parts inventories from 25 hours to 3 hours. Benefits of such partnerships include access to technology or distribution channels not available internally, shared risks in new investments and product development, improved products through early design recommendations based on supplier capabilities, and reduced operations costs through better communications. For example, FedEx and Jostens formed a strategic partnership that enabled both to benefit from new sales of scholastic jewelry and yearbooks.[55] They took advantage of each other's strengths: Josten provided a high-quality product with superior service, and FedEx provided reliable high-volume, short-interval delivery for these time-critical products.

Quality Customer-Supplier Relationships in Action

Many of the aspects of quality CSRs we have been discussing are illustrated by the relationship between GE Appliance and D.J. Inc., both of Louisville, Kentucky.[56] In nine years, D.J. went from being one of 100 G.E. suppliers of plastic parts to being its sole source. D.J. improved its quality by taking advantage of GE's supplier seminars in statistical process control (SPC).

The company must have studied hard, as it has not had a single lot of parts rejected by GE since 1978. Early involvement in product design is commonplace for these two companies. In one typical case, D.J. recommended a minor change in product design that reduced the cost of a part by more than 5 percent and increased its expected life by 16 percent. This example typifies the advantages enjoyed by companies with quality customer-supplier relationships.

Granite Rock Company of Watsonville, California, a 1992 Malcolm Baldrige Award winner, has also devoted itself to absorbing and making use of information from customers.[57] Bruce Woolpert, who shares with his brother Steve the CEO title at Granite Rock, believes that the role of manager is "to make sure there's a flood of information coming into the company." Where does the flood come from? Granite Rock has its customers rate its performance against its competitors in "report cards," longer surveys, quick-response cards, and focus groups. Information on what customers need and what is being done to satisfy them is distributed throughout the company via team meetings, an annual recognition day, and the appropriately titled company newsletter, *Rock Talk*.

Granite Rock learned that quarry customers wanted to pick up rock very quickly at any time of the day or night. To satisfy this need, the company invested a great deal of money in Granite Xpress, a system that allows customers to pull up to the quarry, check the computer for their order, and insert a magnetic card to load their own orders. Not only does this system operate 24 hours a day, but it has reduced the time at the quarry for truckers from 30 minutes to 10.

Granite Rock personnel also frequently make trips to benchmark other companies, both in their industry (aggregate and concrete producers) and out of their industry (a gold mine). Perhaps the furthest afield they have roamed is to Domino's Pizza, another company that is concerned about on-time delivery. Domino's told Granite Rock where to get better maps and suggested that they adopt Domino's practice of writing house numbers on maps.

A third example is EMC Corporation, a manufacturer of data storage systems.[58] In the winter of 1999, a bank in Wisconsin suddenly lost access to its data-storage facility. In quick succession, the screens in the bank's computer center started flashing "data unavailable"—a message that might as well have read "Closed for business." Within minutes, customer service engineers at EMC headquarters had retrieved, remotely, the logs of EMC's storage systems at the bank and had begun to examine them, but the cause of the problem was not readily evident. Four hours later, the engineers who designed the machine joined the effort. They recreated the bank's setup in a $1 billion facility that EMC created for such simulations, including a double of the EMC machine that was faulty. Only then did they find the problem, and they created a patch that they immediately sent to Wisconsin. But this was just the beginning; the VP of global technical support jumped on a plane to Wisconsin, and walked into the bank's boardroom to help restore faith in the company by answering the questions: "What happened?"; "Why did it happen?"; and "How do we make sure it doesn't happen again?" By the end of the meeting, the VP had sold the bank on a new EMC system that builds a mirror copy of data, which is always available.

CUSTOMER-SUPPLIER RELATIONS IN ORGANIZATION THEORY

Much of the organization literature has argued that firms should consider customers as partners for success.[59] As far back as 1973, Gersuny and

Rosengren argued that diverse customer roles require new bonds of interdependence and an increasingly complex social network that crosses traditional organizational boundaries.[60] They identified four distinct roles for customers:

1. resource,
2. worker (or coworker),
3. buyer, and
4. beneficiary (or user).

A fifth role has emerged from work in the human service area: customers can be a key outcome, or product, of value-creating transformation activities, such as education and health delivery. In the first two roles, customers act as inputs to the transformation process, while in the last three, they act as outputs. Each of these roles is instrumental in creating competitive quality within a firm.

In reviewing the organizational literature for these roles, Lengnick-Hall suggests that the following organizational practices are positively related to the competitive quality of production processes and outcomes:

- practices that deliberately select and carefully manage customer resources, foster an effective alliance between the firm and its customer resources, and improve the quality of its customer resources;
- practices that provide clear opportunities for co-production, enhance customer abilities as co-producers, and increase customer motivation toward co-production;
- activities that foster trust, develop interdependence, share information, and initiate friendly, mutually beneficial customer-organization bonds;
- activities that foster unambiguous communication with users, focus on meeting customer needs, offer realistic previews, achieve dimensions of quality that customers truly care about, and ensure that actual use is consistent with intended use; and
- activities that create opportunities for direct communication and interaction between users and production/core service personnel.

Thus, firms should design systems that involve and empower customers throughout the input-transformation-output system, rather than merely rely on customers to define their preferences and evaluate the products and services provided to them. This conclusion is certainly the foundation of modern TQ approaches and is reflected in the Baldrige Award criteria. One example of this in practice is ADAC Laboratories, a manufacturer of high-technology health care equipment and a 1996 Baldrige winner. Not only does ADAC survey customers and potential customers and measure satisfaction, they invite customers to participate in strategic planning meetings, have lunch with customers attending new equipment training sessions, and host formal user group meetings to help prioritize product enhancements, share tips on new uses, and provide other information.

Total quality also can be related to a number of traditional organizational theories. The following sections discuss TQ's relationship with the resource dependence perspective and the theory of integrative bargaining.

The Resource Dependence Perspective

The organizational theory most directly comparable to the TQ view of customer-supplier relations is the Resource Dependence Perspective (RDP) developed by Jeffrey Pfeffer and Gerald Salancik.[61] This perspective—which deals with how organizations manage to get the resources they need from their environment—resembles TQ in some ways, yet differs in others.

The most important similarity between the two perspectives is their mutual emphasis on the idea that the sources of an organization's success lie outside its boundaries. Although the idea that customers ultimately grant the organization its continued existence has become familiar as a fundamental principle of TQ, Pfeffer and Salancik point out that much organization theory focuses on the internal operations of organizations, giving less emphasis to the organization's environment:

> Most current writers give only token consideration to the environmental context of organizations. The environment is there, somewhere outside the organization, and the idea is mentioned that environments constrain or affect organizations. . . . After this, the task of management is considered. Somehow, the things to be managed are usually within the organization, assumed to be under its control, and often have to do with the direction of low-level hired personnel. When authors get down to the task of describing the running of the organization, the relevance of the environment fades.[62]

According to the RDP, the effectiveness of an organization should be understood in terms of how well it meets the demands of external groups and organizations that are concerned with its actions and products. This is similar to the TQ conception of quality as meeting or exceeding customer expectations. There is an interesting difference, however, between the RDP concept of effectiveness and the TQ concept of quality.

TQ has traditionally focused almost exclusively on the organization's customers—that is, those who purchase the organization's products and provide the wherewithal for the organization's continued survival. The RDP, however, recognizes that organizations must satisfy the demands of not only customers, but also other entities in the environment including various government agencies, interest groups, shareholders, and—to some extent—society as a whole.

A government regulatory agency can make life miserable for an organization it does not believe is following government regulations—for example, a coal mine with inadequate safety procedures or a restaurant with unsanitary practices. In the extreme case, the government can even shut them down. Interest groups can influence customers to boycott a product for reasons unrelated to the quality of the product itself. Certain brands of California wine were boycotted for years because of the alleged mistreatment of the migrant farm workers who picked their grapes.

Shareholders of public corporations in recent years have become a constituency to be reckoned with. They are making increasing demands on how corporations operate, including not only economic but also social and environmental aspects of performance such as minority hiring and use of recyclable materials.

From this perspective it is clear that although customers are important, groups and organizations other than customers can play a major role in determining an organization's success. TQ advocates can take two avenues in dealing with this issue. The first would be to enlarge the concept of customers to include all those who have a stake in the organization. Following this logic, an organization would not be seen as practicing TQ unless it met the expectations of all of its constituencies, not just its customers in the traditional sense. However, different groups are apt to have very different expectations for the behavior of an organization, thus making it quite difficult to satisfy all parties.

The other avenue would be for TQ advocates to recognize that although providing quality to customers is the overriding focus of an organization's activities, satisfying customers alone will not necessarily guarantee continued success, due to the potential influence of other constituencies. Interestingly, this perspective has been incorporated into the Baldrige Award criteria through its core value of Social Responsibility.

> An organization's leaders should stress responsibilities to the public, ethical behavior, and the need to practice good citizenship. Leaders should be role models for your organization in focusing on business ethics and protection of public health, safety, and the environment. . . . Planning should anticipate adverse impacts from production, distribution, transportation, use, and disposal of your products. Effective planning should prevent problems, provide for a forthright response if problems occur, and make available information and support needed to maintain public awareness, safety, and confidence. . . . Organizations should not only meet all local, state, and federal laws and regulatory requirements, but they should treat these and related requirements as opportunities for improvement "beyond mere compliance." . . . Highly ethical conduct should be a requirement of and should be monitored by the organization's governance body. (2004 Baldrige National Quality Program Criteria for Performance Excellence, pp. 3–4)

Another similarity between TQ and the RDP is in their recognition of interdependence between organizations as a fact of organizational life that must be managed effectively.

In the current dense environment ... interdependencies are the problem. The dominant problems of the organization have become managing its exchanges and its relationships with the diverse interests affected by its actions. ... The increasing density of relationships among diverse interests has led to less willingness to rely on unconstrained market forces. Negotiation, political strategies, the management of the organization's institutional relationships—these have all become more important.[63]

Thus, the RDP shares with TQ the idea that managing interdependencies with other organizations is a key to success. The two perspectives diverge again, however, when it comes to how such interdependencies should be managed. Quality customer-supplier relationships are seen from the TQ perspective as consisting of mutually beneficial partnerships. Such an option, however, is not anticipated in the RDP. From this perspective, interdependence should be managed by some combination of gaining as much control as possible over the other organization, minimizing the other party's control over one's own organization, making it difficult for the other organization to monitor and influence one's behavior, and so on.

When compared to the protection of self-interest inherent in the recommendations of the RDP, the TQ win-win doctrine sounds somewhat naive. Yet most organizations practicing TQ and building partnerships with their customers and suppliers have traditionally managed customer-supplier relationships in the manner suggested by the RDP and have been dissatisfied with the results. The partnership efforts are mostly in their early stages, and there is no guarantee that they will ultimately succeed. As of now, however, they are the preferred method of many firms for managing interdependence.

Integrative Bargaining

The idea of building cooperative relationships that benefit both parties to a negotiation is not something that was created by writers or practitioners of TQ. The idea of mutually beneficial relationships and win-win bargaining comes from a long tradition of research and writing on conflict management and negotiation.[64]

The idea behind this research tradition is that both parties will benefit more in the long run if they work together to help each other, rather than each one striving to win each round of negotiation. This tradition has been appropriated by writers on TQ, perhaps because it is consistent with the idea of customer orientation and teamwork. This is another area where TQ doctrine derives in a straightforward manner from existing organizational theory.

The key ideas of integrative bargaining (or principled negotiation) are

1. separate the people from the problem;
2. focus on interests, not positions;

3. invent options for mutual gain; and
4. insist on using objective criteria.

These principles have significant implications for CSRs in total quality. The first point deals with eliminating emotions from issues, forcing participants to work together to attack the problem and not each other. For example, focus on interests, not positions, means that it is important to search for ways to meet each party's needs, not necessarily the way they have been met in the past. Rather than focusing on the position (I want air-conditioning in the car), one searches for the underlying interest (I spend a lot of time in the car, so it is important to be comfortable), and then finds a way to meet that interest. The second point results from the fact that a negotiating position often obscures what the bargainers really want. Compromising on positions, as is often done in union agreements, may not take care of the true needs that led people to adopt the positions in the first place. For the third point, it is difficult to make decisions in the presence of an adversary. Creatively identifying options without the pressure of adversarial negotiation can reconcile differing interests and "expand the pie." Finally, fair solutions result from deciding on the criteria on which to evaluate the result, not the personalities of the negotiators.

REVIEW AND DISCUSSION QUESTIONS

1. What can be learned about customer-supplier relationships from the story about IBM and its Japanese supplier?
2. What is the difference between customer satisfaction and customer loyalty?
   Why is it important to distinguish between these two concepts?
3. Draw a diagram of a customer-supplier chain that includes at least four organizations. What attributes of quality are required at each link in the chain? How does quality at the beginning of the chain influence quality at the end?
4. Why are suppliers important to a company's quality efforts?
5. Identify three practices through which companies can better understand their customers' needs.
6. Prepare a list of moments of truth that you encounter during a typical quarter or semester at your college or university.
7. Analyze the remaining voice of the customer statements in the example box "The Good, the Bad, and the Ugly," and try to determine what the customers are saying in actionable terms that are meaningful to the managers of the restaurant.
8. Think of a type of customer that you know reasonably well. Try to identify some unmet needs of this type of customer and to think of some new features of the products and/or services they purchase that would excite them. Why do you think these features are not being offered?

9. Consider the following customer expectations for a fast-food (quick service) restaurant. Would you classify them as dissatisfiers, satisfiers, or exciters/delighters?
    a. special prices on certain days
    b. food that is safe to eat
    c. hot food that is served hot
    d. service that is friendly
    e. background music
    f. playland for children
    g. a clean environment
    h. food that is fresh
    i. a "one-bite" money-back guarantee
    j. phoning in orders for pickup at a separate window
10. Identify a customer-supplier relationship in which you are involved. How does it compare to the principles and practices of TQ relationships? In what specific ways could adopting some of the principles and practices discussed in this chapter improve this relationship?
11. Consider the following customer experiences.[65] What would your reaction be to each of them?
    a. Looking for a cell phone, I met a saleswoman who introduced herself, asked my name, went through the features related to my needs, and didn't try to sell me the most expensive phone.
    b. I was shopping in a home-improvement store and encountered a salesman who remarked "Oh, shopping for your husband?"
    c. At one restaurant, we were stranded in a booth without silverware or a waiter. We finally made contact with a waitress who said "Your waiter is late, and I can't take your order because this isn't my station."
    d. I was shopping for a TV antenna, and asked the salesman the difference between the models. He replied "They're all pretty much the same. Some cost more because they look better."
12. How do the terms used for customers in different industries and occupations (e.g., patients, clients, passengers, students) influence how people in these industries think about their customers?
13. Think about a prescription that a doctor may write. Describe the different types of customers involved in the process of filling the prescription.
14. How would TQ and the resource dependence perspective differ in describing the quality and effectiveness of a state university?
15. Can you think of a situation in which customers are not important to the success of an organization?
16. How should an organization go about deciding who its customers are? Identify the customers of a university, a government agency, and a movie producer.
17. Below are listed the key principles of TQ. Describe what steps a company could take upstream in the supply chain to practice these principles.
    a. customer-driven quality

     b. built-in quality at the source

     c. management by fact

     d. a focus on prevention rather than detection

     e. process focus

     f. striving for zero defects

     g. continuous improvement

     h. making quality everyone's responsibility

18. Customer satisfaction is generally discussed from the consumer viewpoint. However, it is equally important from a business-to-business transaction perspective. Discuss what suppliers to other businesses can do to improve satisfaction.

CASES

The Case of the Missing Reservation

Mark, Donna, and their children, along with another family, traditionally attend Easter brunch at a large downtown hotel. This year, as in the past, Donna called and made a reservation about three weeks prior to Easter.

Because half the party consisted of small children, they arrived 20 minutes prior to the 11:30 reservation to assure being seated early. When they arrived, however, the hostess said that they did not have a reservation. The hostess explained that guests sometimes fail to show and that she would probably have a table available for them before long. Mark and Donna were quite upset and insisted that they had made a reservation and expected to be seated promptly. The hostess told them, "I believe that you made a reservation, but I can't seat you until all the people on the reservation list are seated. You are welcome to go to the lounge for complimentary coffee and punch while you wait." When Mark asked to see the manager, the hostess replied, "I am the manager," and turned to other duties. The party was eventually seated at 11:45, but was not at all happy with the experience.

The next day, Mark wrote a letter to the hotel manager explaining the entire incident. Mark was in the MBA program at the local university and was taking a course on total quality management. In the class, they had just studied issues of customer focus and some of the approaches used at The Ritz-Carlton Hotel, a two-time Baldrige Award winner. Mark concluded his letter with the statement, "I doubt that we would have experienced this situation at a hotel that truly believes in quality." About a week later, he received the following letter:

> We enjoy hearing from our valued guests, but wish you had experienced the level of service and accommodations that we strive to achieve here at our hotel. Our restaurant manager received your letter and asked me to respond as Total Quality Lead.

Looking back at our records we did not show a reservation on the books for your family. I have addressed your comments with the appropriate department head so that others will not have to experience the same inconveniences that you did.

Thank you once again for sharing your thoughts with us. We believe in a philosophy of "continuous improvement," and it is through feedback such as yours that we can continue to improve the service to our guests.

Discussion Questions

1. Were the hostess's actions consistent with a customer-focused quality philosophy? What might she have done differently?
2. How would you have reacted to the letter that Mark received? Could the Total Quality Lead have responded differently? What does the fact that the hotel manager did not personally respond to the customer tell you?

Pauli's Restaurant and Microbrewery

You have been appointed General Manager of Pauli's Restaurant and Microbrewery, a popular downtown pub in a major city after working there for several years as a waiter and recently a shift manager. Pauli's has locations in six regional cities and operates a corporate Web site. One of the features of the Web site is a customer feedback section that is sent directly to the corporate VP and to the appropriate General Manager. After your first weekend on the job, you received the following comment:

> We had a lousy service experience last Saturday at your restaurant. We eat there several times a year before the theater and had 6:15 reservations, with which we are usually done eating—including dessert—by 7:30 or 7:40 the latest to get to the theater in time. Service was ridiculously slow. We finally ordered dessert around 7:20–7:25 and it took at least 10 min for the waitress to come back and tell us they didn't have the coconut key lime pie that was listed on special; we ordered something else and waited and waited. Eventually we had to find the waitress and tell her to forget it because we didn't have time. My wife couldn't even flag her down to get her coffee refilled in a half an hour. To top it off, we didn't even receive an apology; the only thing she did quickly was to process the check. She was clearly over-committed to too many tables to provide us with adequate service. Very disappointing for what we considered one of our favorite places, and bringing friends with us who had never been there before.

Draft a response to this customer. Analyze the responses of your classmates. What makes a good "service recovery" response? Develop some general guidelines.

Lands' End: The Secrets of Success

Lands' End, a popular and very successful catalog company, recently shared with customers the secrets of its success. The following are some of the things they had to say:[66]

> Here at Lands' End, in the heartland of America, we still believe the customer comes first. . . . There are four basic ways we put the customer first. We hope you'll take a few minutes to read about them. Then decide if you'd like to be treated that way yourself.

1. **Make your merchandise as good as you can.** Our goal has always been to make our clothing and accessories as good as they could possibly be. By adding back features others have taken out over the years. By using the finest fabrics available. By inspecting the finished goods by eye to make sure they measure up.
2. **Always, always price it fairly.** It's our policy to mark up products modestly, just enough to give us a fair profit and to give you a terrific value. Admittedly, we have a few advantages. We're direct merchants with no middlemen taking a bite out of the profits. We don't spring for glitzy, budget-busting advertising. Our main headquarters is in Dodgeville, Wisconsin, surrounded by cornfields (no kidding).
3. **Make it a snap to shop, 24 hours a day.** Our store never closes. We're open around the clock every day of the week to accommodate the varied schedules and different time zones of our customers. . . . Should you have detailed questions, we'll hook you up with one of our Specialty Shopper operators. They're our elite corps—the best of the best—able to answer any questions you might have about styling, fit, color matching, and more.
4. **Guarantee it. Period.** We strive for perfection, but sometimes a flawed product slips through. The color may be a shade too dark. A button may break. A seam may unravel. In those cases, we beg your tolerance and offer you one final protection. If at any time you are not completely satisfied, return the item for a full refund or exchange. And please, never feel bad about sending something back. We'd rather have a truckload of returns than one dissatisfied customer.

Discussion Questions

1. How is Lands' End practicing total quality in its products and services?
2. How would the experience of purchasing a shirt through a catalog company differ from purchasing the same shirt from a department store? Could they both represent high quality?

Gold Star Chili

Gold Star Chili, Inc., based in Cincinnati, Ohio, was founded in 1965 as a family-owned system of franchised and company-owned restaurants. Gold Star currently operates 118 regional locations (99 of which are franchised; the remaining are company restaurants or are co-owned). The Gold Star menu is based on a unique, "Cincinnati-style" chili recipe, flavored with a proprietary blend of spices from around the world. Chili is prepared in a central commissary, which reduces equipment needs at individual restaurants, promotes consistency, and reduces labor costs.

Gold Star operates in a highly competitive market against other multilocation chili firms and traditional fast-food competitors such as McDonald's, Taco Bell, and Kentucky Fried Chicken. Gold Star Chili defines two key customer groups: direct customers who use its products and services, and indirect customers with whom Gold Star has other relationships. Direct customers are broken down into six customer segments, determined by product use: restaurant customers, franchisees, franchise applicants, retail customers, retail wholesalers, and mail-order customers. Indirect customers include product suppliers, service suppliers, copackers, brokers/consultants, shareholders, and regulatory agencies.

Franchisees are attracted by the relatively low investment required to join the Gold Star family of restaurants, the opportunity to operate a profitable business, and to profit from the strong brand equity built into the Gold Star name. They expect consistency in chili product, effective corporate direction in the form of advice, market feedback, and promotional activities. Prior to the addition of a new restaurant, a geodemographic analysis of potential locations is performed to ensure that any new facility will not take more than 10 percent of its business from another Gold Star location. Gold Star's Franchisee Service Representatives (FSRs) take product orders from individual franchisees by telephone on a daily/weekly basis. These frequent interactions create a continuous dialog between the franchisee and the FSR as well as the delivery person who delivers product.

Numerous opportunities are created to listen to and learn from franchisees, including a Franchise Advisory Council consisting of elected owners that meet monthly to review and determine business decisions that affect the chain. The council members are also assigned to committee groups that meet with department heads to review business practices in areas of marketing, purchasing, menu pricing, operational costs, and gross profit analysis. Gold Star also conducts quarterly business meetings with restaurant owners and key managers. These meetings cover operations issues affecting the chain; outside suppliers are welcome to attend the meetings also.

Discussion Questions

1. Describe the rather complex supply chain that Gold Star manages. What quality issues does it face?
2. Although consumers eat chili produced by the Gold Star Chili, franchise owners are independent businesses that are not owned by the company. What challenges does this present to Gold Star and its ability to meet the needs of consumers? What approaches can it take to ensure consistent performance and a quality experience for consumers?

ENDNOTES

1. Reported in "Total Quality Management and Competitiveness" by G. Pouskouleli, *Engineering Digest,* December 1991, pp. 14–17. The Japanese response is based on a story in the *Toronto Sun* by S. Ford, April 25, 1983, p. 6.

2. This idea has been promoted by Richard J. Schonberger in his book, *Building a Chain of Customers.* New York: Free Press, 1990.

3. Myron Magnet, "The New Golden Rule of Business," *Fortune,* February 21, 1994, 60–64.

4. Patricia C. La Londe, "Surveys As Supplier Relationship Tool" ASQ's 54th Annual Quality Congress proceedings, Indianapolis, IN, 2000, 684–686.

5. Arthur R. Tenner and Irving J. DeToro, *Total Quality Management: Three Steps to Continuous Improvement.* Reading, Mass.: Addison-Wesley, 1992, p. 197.

6. Patricia Sellers, "Companies That Serve You Best," *Fortune* May 31, 1993, pp. 74–88.

7. Carl Sewell and Paul B. Brown, *Customers for Life.* New York: Doubleday-Currency, 1990.

8. Jane Norman, "Royal Treatment Keeps Customers Loyal," *Cincinnati Enquirer,* May 31, 1998, E3, E5.

9. The Forum Corporation, *Customer Focus Research,* Executive Briefing, Boston 1988.

10. 2004 Criteria for Performance Excellence, Malcolm Baldrige National Quality Award. Gaithersburg, Md.: National Institute of Standards and Technology, United States Department of Commerce.

11. Based on a "graphic complaint" that has been extensively distributed and shared over the Internet. The names of the actual hotel and participants have been disguised.

12. Robert J. Trent, "Applying TQM to SCM," *Supply Chain Management Review*, May/June 2001, pp. 70–78.

13. Tim Minahan, "What Makes a Supplier World-Class?" *Purchasing,* Vol. 125, No. 2, August 13, 1998, pp. 50–61.

14. Sources: Southwest Airlines home page, http://iflyswa.com; Richard S. Teitelbaum, "Where Service Flies Right," *Fortune,* August 24, 1992, pp. 117–118; and Kevin Freiberg and Jackie Freiberg, *NUTS! Southwest Airlines' Crazy Recipe for Business and Personal Success.* Austin, Tex.: Bard Press, 1996.

15. Justin Martin, "Are You as Good as You Think You Are?" *Fortune,* September 30, 1996, pp. 142–152.

16. Valerie Reitman, "Toyota's Fast Rebound after Fire at Supplier Shows Why It's Tough," *Wall Street Journal,* May 8, 1997, p. 1.

17. We are indebted to David Waldman for this insight.

18. Based on "Arts Groups Try to Keep the Customer Satisfied" by Owen Findsen and Cliff Radel, *Cincinnati Enquirer,* February 7, 1993.

19. J. M. Juran, *Juran on Leadership for Quality: An Executive Handbook.* New York: Free Press, 1989.

20. Adapted from the article on Feargal Quinn by Polly Labarre in "Who's Fast in 2002," *Fast Company,* November 2001, pp. 88–94.

21. John Carlisle, quoted in Tenner and DeToro, *Total Quality Management.*

22. Richard C. Whiteley, *The Customer-Driven Company, Moving from Talk to Action.* Reading, Mass.: Addison-Wesley, 1991, p. 7.

23. Robert D. Buzzell and Bradley T. Gale, *The PIMS Principles: Linking Strategy to Performance.* New York: Free Press, 1987.

24. Quoted in "When Customer Research Is a Lousy Idea" by Willard I. Zangwill, *Wall Street Journal,* March 8, 1993.

25. Marriott's approach to gathering information from customers is discussed in detail in Whiteley, *The Customer-Driven Company.*

26. Mark Graham Brown, "And the Survey Says . . . Customer Behavior Can't Always Be Predicted," *The Journal for Quality and Participation*, Vol. 23, No. 2, March/April 2000, pp. 30–32.

27. See Benson P. Shapiro, V. Kasturi Rangan, and John J. Sviokla, "Staple Yourself to an Order," *Harvard Business Review,* July-August 1992, pp. 113–122.

28. Byron J. Finch, "A New Way to Listen to the Customer," *Quality Progress,* Vol. 30, No. 5, May 1997, pp. 73–76.

29. Cristina Afors and Marilyn Zuckerman Michaels, "A Quick, Accurate Way to Determine Customer Needs," *Quality Progress,* July 2001, pp. 82–87.

30. Quoted in "Could AT&T Rule the World?" by David Kirkpatrick, *Fortune,* May 17, 1993.

31. Whiteley, *The Customer-Driven Company.*

32. Julie Schlosser, "Teacher's Bet," *Fortune,* March 8, 2004, pp. 158–164.

33. Robert Berner, "P&G, New and Improved," *Business Week,* July 7, 2003, pp. 52–63.

34. Whiteley, *The Customer-Driven Company.*

35. "Complex Quality: AMP Rings up Service Success," by Dick Schaaf, *The Quality Imperative,* September 1992, pp. 16–26.

36. Ron Zemke, "The Best Customer to Have Is the One You've Already Got," *The Journal for Quality and Participation,* March/April 2000, pp. 33–35.

37. "Focusing on the Customer, " *Fortune,* June 5, 1989, p. 226.

38. See "Behind the Numbers," *CIO Magazine,* November 2, 2000, available at http://www2.cio.com.

39. Eric Almquist and Carla Heaton, "Customers Are Disappearing," *Across the Board,* July–August 2002, 61–63.

40. These practices are based on *The Deming Route to Quality and Productivity* by William W. Scherkenbach (Rockville, Md.: Mercury Press, 1988) and on *Juran on Leadership for Quality* by Joseph M. Juran (New York: Free Press, 1989).

41. James H. Drew and Tye R. Fussell, "Becoming Partners with Internal Customers," *Quality Progress,* Vol. 29, No.10, October 1996, pp. 51–54.

42. This idea has long been championed by Deming. See the discussion of his 14 Points in Chapter 2.

43. For a discussion of these two points, see David N. Burt, "Managing Suppliers Up to Speed," *Harvard Business Review,* July-August 1989, pp. 127–135.

44. Tenner and DeToro, *Total Quality Management.*

45. John R. Emshwiller, "Suppliers Struggle to Improve Quality as Big Firms Slash Their Vendor Rolls," *Wall Street Journal,* August 16, 1991, B2.

46. Patrick J. McMahon, "Supplier Involvement," Chapter 9 in *The Improvement Process* by H. James Harrington (New York: McGraw-Hill, 1987).

47. Texas Instruments Defense Systems & Electronics Group, Malcolm Baldrige Application Summary (1992).

48. Mike Lovitt, "Responsive Suppliers Are Smart Suppliers," *Quality Progress,* June 1989, pp. 50–53.

49. McMahon, op. cit.

50. This point is discussed by Randall S. Schuler and Drew L. Harris in *Managing Quality: The Primer for Middle Managers.* Reading, Mass.: Addison-Wesley, 1992.

51. McMahon, op. cit.

52. McMahon, op. cit.

53. Juran, *Juran on Leadership for Quality.*

54. Schuler and Harris, *Managing Quality.*

55. AT&T Corporate Quality Office, *Supplier Quality Management: Foundations,* 1994, p. 52.

56. This example is discussed by David N. Burt in "Managing Suppliers up to Speed," *Harvard Business Review,* July-August 1989, pp. 127–135.

57. The section on Granite Rock is based on "The Changemasters" by John Case, *INC.,* March 1992, pp. 58–70.

58. Mike Ruettgers, "When a Customer Believes in You . . . They'll Stick with You Almost No Matter What," *Fast Company,* June 2001, pp. 138–145.

59. Cynthia A. Lengnick-Hall, "Customer Contributions to Quality: A Different View of the Customer-Oriented Firm," *Academy of Management Review,* Vol. 21, No. 3, 1996, pp. 791–824.

60. C. Gersuny and W. R. Rosengren, *The Service Society*, Cambridge, Mass.: Schenkman Press, 1973.

61. Jeffrey Pfeffer and Gerald R. Salancik. *The External Control of Organizations: A Resource Dependence Perspective*. New York: Harper & Row, 1978.

62. Ibid., pp. 257–258.

63. Pfeffer and Salancik, *The External Control of Organizations*, p. 94.

64. See, for example, David W. Johnson and Frank P. Johnson, *Joining Together: Group Theory and Group Skills*. Englewood Cliffs, N.J.: Prentice Hall, 1975; Max H. Bazerman and Roy J. Lewicki (eds.), *Negotiating in Organizations*. Beverly Hills, Calif.: Sage Publications, 1983; M. Afzalur Rahim, "A Strategy for Managing Conflict in Complex Organizations," *Human Relations*, Vol. 38, No. 1, 1985, pp. 81–89. From a popular standpoint, the book *Getting to Yes* by Roger Fisher and William Ury (New York: Penguin Books USA, 1981) addresses the principles described in this section in more detail.

65. "Getting to Very Satisfied," *Fast Company*, February 2004, p. 32.

66. Lands' End Direct Merchants. Reprinted with permission.

CHAPTER 5

Designing Organizations for Quality

In 1950 Deming drew the following picture on a blackboard for a handful of Japanese executives:

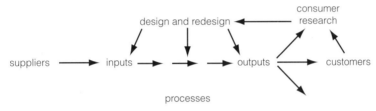

Reprinted from *Out of the Crisis* by W. Edwards Deming by permission of MIT and the W. Edwards Deming Institute. Published by MIT, Center for Advanced Educational Services, Cambridge, MA 02139. © 1986 by The W. Edwards Deming Institute.

Many people see this as simply a diagram of a typical production system that is linked to customers and suppliers. Visionaries in the practice of TQ see this as a better model of an organization chart.

Many organizations implementing total quality have found it necessary to reconfigure the structures of their organizations. This chapter discusses the changes in organization design necessary to achieve total quality. The chapter will

> describe the functional structure, the most common structure used at the plant or business unit level;
> show how many aspects of the functional structure stand in the way of quality and what changes are necessary to create organization structures that support TQ;
> provide several examples of how firms are making substantial changes in their organizations in order to implement TQ; and
> compare organizational design from a TQ point of view to more conventional perspectives.

THE FUNCTIONAL STRUCTURE

In the functional structure shown in Figure 5.1, the organization is divided into functions such as operations and maintenance, each of which is headed by a manager. The title of such managers is often "director" in small organizations and "vice president" in larger ones. In such organizations, communication occurs vertically up or down the chain of command, rather than horizontally across functions.

Functional structures provide organizations with a clear chain of command and allow people to specialize in the aspect of the work for which they are best suited. They also make it easy to evaluate people based on a narrow but clear set of responsibilities. For these reasons, functional structures are common in both manufacturing and service organizations at plant and business unit levels.

Problems with the Functional Structure

Despite its popularity, the functional structure is designed primarily for the administrative convenience of the organization, rather than for providing high-quality service to customers. From a TQ point of view, the functional structure has several inadequacies.

The Functional Structure Separates Employees from Customers

Few employees in the functional organization have direct contact with customers or even a clear idea of how their work combines with the work of others to satisfy customers. The functional structure tends to insulate

FIGURE 5.1   FUNCTIONAL STRUCTURE FOR A MANUFACTURING COMPANY

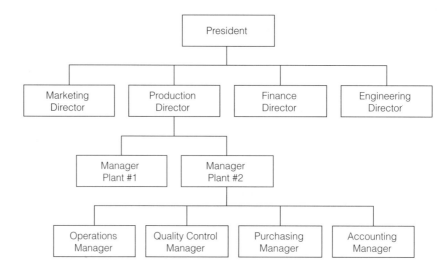

employees from learning about customer expectations and their degree of satisfaction with the service or product the firm is providing. Being insulated from customers encourages in workers a narrow conception of their responsibilities. This is often expressed in statements such as "It's not my job" or "I just work here." Even when such employees want to help customers, they often have such a limited understanding of how their organizational system works that they are unable to do so. This often results in demotivated workers and poor quality work.

Most of us have experienced this phenomenon when we call a large organization trying to get help and get switched to several different people before (if we're lucky) finding someone willing and able to help us. If our needs as customers relate to the product or service as a whole, but the knowledge and responsibilities of anyone with whom we deal relate only to their function, we are doomed to disappointment.[1] More seriously, the functional structure promotes the idea that one's boss is the customer whom the employee must satisfy. Of course, this manager is trying to satisfy the next-level manager, and so on. If the chain ended at the customer, the structure might work, but this is generally not the case. Managers in functional organizations are usually rewarded for satisfying functional goals, such as meeting design deadlines and limiting manufacturing costs, rather than for providing value to customers.

The focus on vertical reporting relationships to the exclusion of horizontal coordination has led many observers to refer to departments in functional organizations as "chimneys" or "silos." As Myron Tribus describes it, "The enterprise is viewed as a collection of separate, highly specialized individual performers and units. . . . Lateral connections are made by intermediaries close to the top of the provinces."[2]

Paul Allaire, former Xerox chairman and CEO, presided over a massive restructuring of the corporation. He described the company's problems with the functional organization and its new approach as follows:

> We were an extremely functional organization. If you were in manufacturing, you strived to make manufacturing as good as possible— and only secondarily to make the businesses that manufacturing affected work well. The same was true for sales, R&D, or any other function. . . .We [now] want people who can hold two things in their heads at the same time, who can think in terms of their individual organizations but also in terms of the company as a whole. Our architecture won't work if people take a narrow view of their jobs and don't work together.[3]

The Functional Structure Inhibits Process Improvement

No organizational unit has control over a whole process, although most processes involve a large number of functions. This is because the breakup of the organization into functions is usually unrelated to the processes used to deliver a product to the customer. This structure is likely to create complex, wasteful processes, as people do things in one area that must be redone or undone in another. For example, some organizations maintain a group of engineers whose sole responsibility is to redesign products so that they can be manufactured effectively. The engineers who design the products in the first place worry only about product performance, not manufacturability. (For another example of problems in coordinating design and manufacturing, see the case "Barriers? What Barriers?" at the end of this chapter.) Worse yet, if one function tries to improve its part, it may well make things worse (more wasted time and effort, more cost) for another part of the process. In this environment, continuous process improvement doesn't stand a chance.

Richard Palermo, who was a vice president for quality and transition at Xerox, explains the problems with functional structures in terms of "Palermo's law," which states: "If a problem has been bothering your company and your customers for years and won't yield, that problem is the result of a cross-functional dispute, where nobody has total control of the whole process." The corollary to Palermo's law? "People who work in different functions hate each other."[4]

Functional Organizations Often Have a Separate Function for Quality, Called Quality Control or Quality Assurance

This may send a message to the rest of the organization that there is a group dedicated to quality, so it's not their responsibility. Furthermore, it breaks the feedback loop that informs employees that their work needs to be improved. The QC department is generally responsible for collecting and maintaining quality statistics, which may not seem as valid to the departments actually doing the work.[5] This arrangement obviously stands in the way of continuous process improvement. Organizations pursuing TQ often retain their quality assurance departments, but these units act more as coaches or facilitators to employees, rather than as the group with primary responsibility for quality.

In summary, the functional organization compromises total quality in several ways: It distances people from customers and insulates them from customer expectations. It promotes complex and wasteful processes and inhibits process improvement. It separates the quality function from the rest of the organization, providing people with an excuse for not worrying about quality. The next section discusses some remedies for the quality problems caused by the functional structure.

Redesigning Organizations for Quality

Poor organization design can be devastating to a company (see the box "Wired for Failure"). One of Deming's 14 Points is to "break down barriers between departments" because "people in various departments must work as a team."[6] This slogan captures in a nutshell what the TQ philosophy entails for organizational design. People cannot contribute to customer

---

Wired for Failure

The "New Economy," as many call it, was supposed to revolutionize business. For example, between Thanksgiving and Christmas, 1999, some 22 million shoppers spent more than $5 billion shopping online.[7] Traffic on sites like Yahoo and Kbkids.com grew by 500 percent. Outpost.com, a computer and electronics retailer, sold $2 million of merchandise in one day. However, it wasn't long before Internet message boards were filled with comments such as, "I doubt I will ever shop again online for Christmas." and other comments unfit to print here. As *Fortune* magazine noted ". . . it takes much more than a logo and a Website to run an e-tailing operation. Online retailers aren't so different from brick and mortar stores. They run out of stock, sell damaged merchandise, and hire rude sales help. . . . Hordes of companies flooded the market. Trouble is, many of them spent heavily to market and promote their brands but scrimped on infrastructure—the unglamorous side of the business, which focuses on delivering products to customers. The results were often disastrous." Amazon.com, for example, initially tried to have suppliers maintain inventory but found that it needed to build traditional distribution centers around the country to improve customer service and control over the product.[8]

A. Blanton Godfrey, former CEO of the Juran Institute, notes that many organizations are "wired for failure"—that is, their processes are not designed effectively or aligned with each other.[9] He cites other examples in addition to the problems that confronted e-retailers. One example is over-scheduling at airports. During the 4:15 to 4:30 P.M. time slot, 35 arrivals are scheduled in Atlanta, even though in optimal weather conditions the airport can handle only 25 in 15 minutes; with bad weather, this drops to 17. Another company celebrated its largest sales contract in history only to discover that all qualified suppliers for critical materials were at capacity. A third example is the unwillingness of departments to work together. For example, when products fail in the plant or in service, it isn't because designers choose components they know will fail; they often have insufficient information about the problems that result from their choices.

---

satisfaction and continuous improvement if they are confined to functional prisons where they cannot see customers or hear their voices. Some of the more effective ways to break down these barriers are to focus on processes, recognize internal customers, create a team-based organization, reduce hierarchy, and use steering committees.

Focus on Processes

According to AT&T, a **process** is how work creates value for customers.[10] Common business processes include acquiring customer and market knowledge, fulfilling customer orders, purchasing, developing new products or services, strategic planning, production or service delivery, distribution, research and development, information management, performance measurement, and training, to name just a few. Individuals or groups, known as **process owners**, are accountable for process performance and have the authority to manage and improve their process. Process owners may range from high-level executives who manage cross-functional processes to workers who run machinery on the shop floor. Assigning process owners ensures that someone is responsible to manage the process and optimize its effectiveness.

Processes that drive the creation of products and services, are critical to customer satisfaction, and have a large impact on the strategic goals of an organization are generally considered **value-creation**, or **core processes** of a business. Value-creation processes are those most important to "running the business" and maintaining or achieving a sustainable competitive advantage. Value-creation processes typically include design, production/delivery, and other critical business processes. Design processes involve all activities that are performed to incorporate customer requirements, new technology, and past learning into the functional specifications

---

Chili, Spaghetti, and Cheese: It's the Process That Counts

You probably would not expect that a regional chain of small chili restaurants takes a formal view of process management, but Gold Star Chili, Inc., based in Cincinnati, Ohio, does just that. The company operates over 100 regional locations (most of which are franchised; the remaining are company restaurants or are co-owned). The Gold Star menu is based on a unique, "Cincinnati-style" chili recipe—the basic "3-way" is a plate of spaghetti, topped with chili that is flavored with a proprietary blend of spices from around the world, followed by finely shredded cheese. (Visit the company's Web site: http://www.goldstarchili.com.)

Figure 5.2 shows a process-based organization of the company. Three major core processes link the operation of the company to its customers and other stakeholders: (1) franchising, (2) restaurant, and (3) manufacturing/distribution.

Sustaining these core processes are various support processes, such as research and development, human resources, accounting, purchasing, operations, training, marketing, and customer satisfaction. Even restaurant operations are viewed from a process focus. Key processes such as Cash Register, Steam Table, Drive-Thru, Tables, Bussers, and Management are designed to ensure that customer needs are served in a timely manner. Prior to opening each restaurant, training sessions ensure that these processes are performed correctly and according to company standards.

FIGURE 5.2   GOLD STAR CHILI, INC., ORGANIZATION

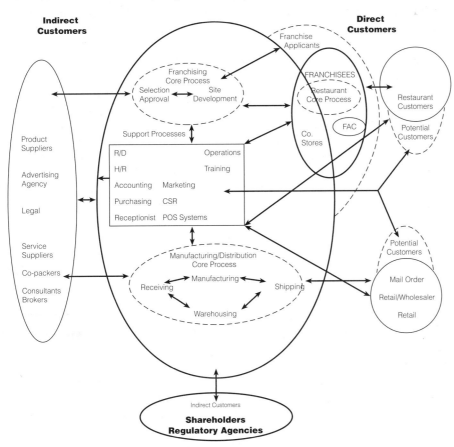

of a manufactured good or service, and thus define its fitness for use. Production/delivery processes create or deliver the actual product; examples are manufacturing, assembly, dispensing medications, teaching a class, and so on. These processes must be designed to ensure that the product will conform to specifications (the manufacturing definition of quality) and also be produced economically and efficiently. Because product design greatly influences the efficiency of manufacture as well as the flexibility of service strategies, it must be coordinated with production/delivery processes. The ultimate value of the product and, hence, the perceived quality to the consumer, depend on both these types of processes.

Support processes are those that are most important to an organization's value creation processes, employees, and daily operations, but generally do not add value directly to the product or service. AT&T Consumer Communication Services, for example, defines its core processes as the network servicing process that addresses engineering, provisioning, and maintenance of the AT&T Worldwide Intelligent Network; the customer servicing process that guides customers to CCS employees for operator call completion, sales inquiries and assistance, billing inquiries, and account inquiries or billing adjustments; and the account management and billing process that manages the systems and interfaces for over 85 million customer accounts. Support processes include information and software services, human resources, public relations, law, regulatory, finance, marketing, and network security. A process such as order entry that might be considered a core process for one company (e.g., a direct mail distributor) might be considered as a support process for another (e.g., a custom manufacturer). In general, core processes are driven by *external* customer needs while support processes are driven by *internal* customer needs. A process focus is not just for large companies like AT&T (see the box on Gold Star Chili).

Table 5.1 shows the value creation processes and their requirements defined by Pal's Sudden Service. Their support processes include accounting/finance, human resources, maintenance, management information systems, ordering, and stocking. Other critical support processes that lead to business success and growth might be research and development, technology acquisition, supply chain management and supplier partnering, mergers and acquisitions, project management, or sales and marketing. These processes will differ greatly among organizations, depending on the nature

TABLE 5.1   VALUE CREATION PROCESSES FOR PAL'S SUDDEN SERVICE

Process	Principal Requirements
Order Taking	Accurate, fast, friendly
Cooking	Proper temperature
Product Assembly	Proper sequence, sanitary, correct ingredients and amounts, speed, proper temperature, neat
Cash Collection	Accurate, fast, friendly
Slicing	Cut/size, freshness/color
Chili preparation	Proper temperature, quantity, freshness
Ham/chicken preparation	Proper temperature, quantity, freshness
Supply chain management	Price/cost, order accuracy
Property acquisition	Sales potential, adherence to budget
Construction	On time, within budget
Marketing & advertising	Clear message, brand recognition

Source: Courtesy of Pal's Sudden Service.

of products and services, customer and market requirements, global focus, and other factors.

As discussed in Chapter 1, a process focus, as opposed to the functional structure, involves some form of cross-functional cooperation (see Figure 1.3). A process perspective helps managers to recognize that problems arise from processes, not people. By aligning the structure of an organization with the actual work processes that the organization performs, customers may be served more effectively. We will address further details of designing and managing processes in the next chapter.

Recognize Internal Customers

We discussed the concept of internal customers in Chapter 4. An internal customer is another person or group within the organization who depends on one's work to get their work done. For example, machine operators in a manufacturing plant are customers of maintenance; if maintenance does not do its job well, the machines will not produce quality products (or perhaps not any products at all). In a university, professors and students are customers of the audiovisual staff, who provide and maintain overhead projectors and VCRs.

In a restaurant, the servers are internal customers of the kitchen staff, because the servers' ability to serve appetizing food in a timely manner to customers depends on the kitchen. In Figure 5.3, product design is the internal customer of both research and development and marketing, manufacturing is the customer of product design and purchasing, and sales is the customer of manufacturing. Although not shown in the diagram, all of these departments are customers of staff groups such as human resources and finance.

One way that organizations can promote quality and teamwork is to recognize the existence of internal customers. However, Richard Schonberger, a noted consultant and writer on manufacturing and quality, has taken the internal customer idea one step further by arguing that organizations should be designed as "chains of customers." That is, customer-supplier links should be forged, one at a time, from the organization's

FIGURE 5.3   INTERNAL CUSTOMERS IN A MANUFACTURING COMPANY

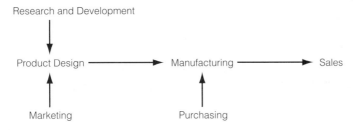

suppliers all the way to its external (real) customers.[11] Motorola has used this idea in its approach to designing and managing processes:

1. *Identify the product or service:* What work do I do?
2. *Identify the customer:* Who is the work for?
3. *Identify the supplier:* What do I need and from whom do I get it?
4. *Identify the process:* What steps or tasks are performed? What are the inputs and outputs for each step?
5. *Mistake-proof the process:* How can I eliminate or simplify tasks? What poka-yoke (a Japanese term for mistake-proofing) devices can I use?
6. *Develop measurements and controls, and improvement goals:* How do I evaluate the process? How can I improve further?

By linking customers and suppliers together at the individual level, the nature of cross-functional processes becomes clearer. Eventually, everyone can better understand their role in satisfying not only their internal customers, but also the external customers.

An effective way to understand internal customer-supplier relationships and improve processes is through **process mapping**. Flowcharts (see Chapter 3) provide one means of describing a process as a sequence of steps (Step 4 in the Motorola approach). A process map can then be analyzed to reduce complexity and improve quality.

A rather new approach to process mapping developed by Fernando Flores is gaining popularity.[12] Termed "coordination mapping," this approach is based on the premise that each process activity includes two players, a customer and a provider. Each coordinating conversation between these agents moves through four phases: (1) preparation and the making of a request or offer, (2) negotiation and agreement (or failure to reach agreement), (3) performance and a report that the work is complete, and (4) assessment of the work and a declaration of satisfaction or dissatisfaction.

This cyclic process is represented graphically by a loop. The mapping process involves identifying each conversation, its customer and provider, the customers' conditions of satisfaction, and how each of the moves is taken, as well as interdependencies among conversations. Working through and analyzing the interactions one by one often reveals hidden or implicit assumptions and discoveries of breakdowns in the process. Figure 5.4 shows an example of a university residence hall check-in process developed using this approach by a Cincinnati-based consulting firm, Workflow Dynamics, Inc.[13] What on the surface is a seemingly simple process can indeed be quite complex, resulting in numerous process failures (the "cloudbursts" in the figure). Such maps can provide the basis for reengineering or other types of process improvement efforts.

Promoting the idea of internal customers does not change the organization's structure as much as it changes the way that people think about the

FIGURE 5.4   COORDINATION MAP FOR RESIDENCE HALL CHECK-IN PROCESS

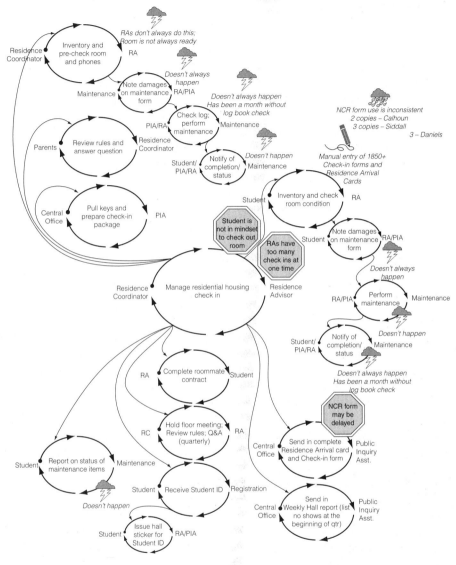

Project: U.C. residence hall as is workflow map. Prepared by: Workflow Dynamics, Inc.

structure. Rather than focusing on satisfying their immediate supervisor (vertical), people begin to think about satisfying the next person in the process (horizontal), who is one step closer to the ultimate customer. In a pizza delivery business, the people who deliver the pizzas are internal customers of the people who make them, who in turn are customers of the order-takers. Satisfying internal customers first is the best way to satisfy the external customer. An unusual customer-supplier relationship was uncovered at Oregon State University (see box "Where's the Paperwork?").

Some managers resist the idea of internal customers, arguing that the only customers people should worry about are the ones who pay the bills. But for those employees who never come near a "real" customer, a focus on internal customers helps them to help those who do. Of course, this only works if the needs expressed by internal customers are in fact closely related to their ability to satisfy actual customers. A certain amount of trust that this is the case is necessary for the system to work.

A good example of creating links between internal customers and their suppliers is provided by an event at AMP Incorporated, a global electronic connector company. Sales engineers visited two of AMP's manufacturing plants and cooked a barbecue lunch for production workers. After lunch, the sales engineers introduced themselves, talked about their customers, and displayed some of the end products, such as power tools, into which the connectors made at the plant are placed. One production associate's reaction was, "I sometimes felt that we made millions of these parts and they simply dumped them in the ocean after we shipped them out. Now I know where most of them go."[14]

Create a Team-Based Organization

As more and more companies accept the process view of organizations, they are structuring the quality organization around functional or cross-functional teams, each of which has the responsibility to carry out and improve one of the organization's core processes.[15] Teams encourage free-flowing participation and interaction among its members. FedEx has more than 4,000 Quality Action teams; Boeing Airlift and Tanker Division has more than 100 integrated product teams (IPTs) that are typically made up of engineering, work-team, customer, and supplier representatives. AT&T established nine expert breakthrough teams—called Achieving Process Excellence Teams—that identify process improvements for developing and deploying products faster in the market. Granite Rock, with fewer than 400 employees, has about 100 functioning teams, ranging from 10 corporate quality teams to project teams, purchasing teams, task forces, and function teams composed of people who do the same job at different locations. Special efforts keep the teams relevant and make sure that no teams exist just for the sake of having them. Texas Nameplate Company builds its leadership system upon a team framework that includes a Business Excellence Leadership Team, a Daily Operations & Innovation Team, teams within each production and support service department for daily work activities, corrective action teams, and various other teams such as the Recognition Committee.

Mark Kelly provides an example of an organizational structure based on teams in *The Adventures of a Self-Managing Team*.[16] The building blocks

Where's the Paperwork? Quality Improvement at Oregon State[17]

Oregon State University was among the first universities to embrace TQM. In 1990, faced with state budget cuts and trying to improve the quality of its operation, Oregon State began the process of quality improvement. Like many schools, it focused first on improving administrative areas.

The physical plant was among the first areas singled out for quality improvement. Specifically, the group that did repair and remodeling at the university tackled the time it took to complete a work order, which its internal customers identified as the number one problem with the service they were receiving. When the group began to address the problem, they found that the average time to complete a job was 195 days, just over six months.

None of the people who actually did the work could believe the entire process took so long, as individually each knew that their work lasted only a few days or weeks. In attempting to understand why it took so long, the group set up a flowchart of the process they used in their work.

They discovered that a woman in another group received their work orders first, and it took 10 days for the paperwork to make its way to the repair and remodeling group. Group members approached the woman and asked what she did with the paperwork during the time she kept it. She did her job and she did it well, exactly as she had been instructed, she told them.

What exactly had she been told to do? When the paperwork arrives, put it aside and after 10 days, send it on to the repair and remodeling group! As it turned out, there had been a time when the group had had trouble getting the material they needed for jobs delivered. Having no success in expediting the flow of material, they simply slowed down the flow of paperwork, so that they would have a head start on the job when the paperwork arrived. Eventually the problems with material delivery were resolved, but no one had remembered to undo the 10-day waiting period. Because the paperwork was held by another functional group, no one in repair and remodeling had a broad enough view of the process to see what was going on. Sometimes process improvement is hard work. But, in this case, the repair and remodeling group could get off to a fast start by immediately knocking 10 days off of their time!

of the "Clear Lake Plant" organization are process-based teams. Tasks that transcend processes (such as innovation and safety) are handled in task teams made up of members drawn from each of the process teams. This organization is depicted in Figure 5.5. (Compare this to the functional organization in Figure 5.1 to get an idea of the size of the changes we are talking about.)

FIGURE 5.5   ORGANIZATIONAL STRUCTURE OF THE CLEAR LAKE PLANT

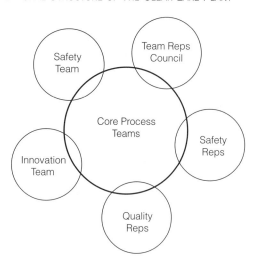

Other team-based organizations revolve around customers, as shown in Figure 5.6. Another example is that of GTE Directories, shown in Figure 5.7. In this organizational structure, the management board leads the quality effort, meeting twice each month to discuss and review management and quality issues. Quality is implemented through various teams: core process business team, cross-functional coordinating committee, regional management councils, major business process management teams (PMTs), Malcolm Baldrige National Quality Award (MBNQA) teams, and quality improvement teams. The regional management councils identify and address key regional issues; the cross-functional coordinating committee reviews major proposals for consistency with the strategic plan and business priorities. Such team-based organization structures spread the ownership, and the accountability, for quality throughout the organization. The "quality department" serves as an internal consulting group, providing advice, training, and organizational development to the teams. Clearly, each organization needs to create a structure that meets its own unique needs.

Depending on the size of the organization and the nature of the processes, teams may include everyone who contributes to a given process or only a representative subset. Similarly, the teams may meet continuously on a crash basis until their new process design is complete, after which they may meet periodically or on an ad hoc basis whenever necessary. For example, Solectron Corporation, a two-time Baldrige recipient, has a customer focus team for each customer that includes personnel from quality, manufacturing management, project engineering, sales, production control, test engineering, and a project buyer and program manager.

This approach eliminates many of the problems with the functional structure. By bringing together everyone associated with a process, practices

FIGURE 5.6   TEAM-BASED ORGANIZATIONAL CHART

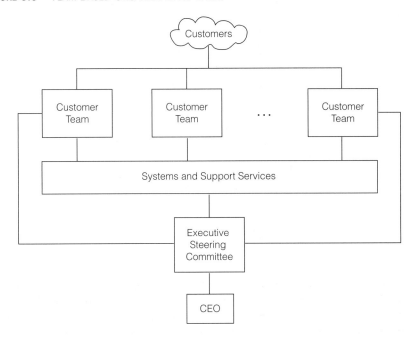

that are wasteful or compromise quality become much easier to identify and eliminate. If a team has responsibility for an entire process, they don't have to worry that their improvement efforts will be undermined—intentionally or unintentionally—by the actions of another group.

FIGURE 5.7   GTE DIRECTORIES MANAGEMENT STRUCTURE

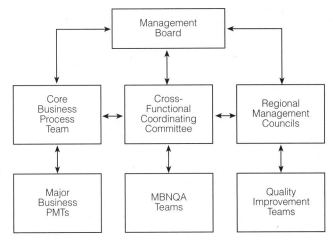

Courtesy of Verizon Information Services.

Using processes as a grouping method can create substantial improvement in organizations by allowing people to see and change procedures they couldn't see or change in the functional structure. As Robert Brookhouse, member of a process organization at Xerox, puts it, "When you create a flow [Xerox's term for process organization], you find where you're wasting time, doing things twice. And because we own the entire process, we can change it."[18]

This is not to suggest that changing to a process-based organization is simple or easy. On the contrary, it takes a lot of thought, because it means essentially taking the organization apart and putting it back together again. As Robert Knorr and Edward Thiede describe it: "The restructuring should begin by defining each process in terms of its operations, information, and skill needs. . . . Process definition also answers key questions about the lines of integration needed among processes and functions, such as who must interact and when? What changes are needed in upstream processes to accommodate the needs of those downstream, and vice versa?"[19]

Project teams are fundamental to Six Sigma. Six Sigma projects require a diversity of skills that range from technical analysis, creative solution development, and implementation. Thus, Six Sigma teams not only address immediate problems but also provide an environment for individual learning, management development, and career advancement. Six Sigma teams will be discussed further in Chapter 8.

Reduce Hierarchy

A third type of structural change that often results from a focus on internal customers and the creation of process teams is a reduction in the number of hierarchical layers in the organization. Several levels of middle management are often eliminated. (Of course, if an organization is designed for quality from its inception, those levels are not there in the first place.) This reduction in middle management is also facilitated by advances in information systems that have taken over many of the information summarization and transmission roles formerly played by middle managers.

With the elimination of non–value-added activities and the empowerment of frontline workers to improve processes, there is also less supervision and coordination for managers to do. An additional benefit of such "flatter" organizations is improved communication between top managers and frontline employees, as well as between customers and the decision makers.

This is not to say that the flattening of organizational structures is without its drawbacks. People—sometimes many people—lose their jobs. This is not only a significant disruption in the lives of the individuals affected, but also a loss of their experience to the organization. Furthermore, the morale of the people who remain in the organization may suffer. For all of these reasons, organizations should approach flattening with an attitude of caution and concern.

Use Steering Committees

A fourth type of structural change associated with TQ is the creation of a high-level planning group invested with the responsibility for guiding the organization's quality efforts. Such groups—called *steering committees*, *quality councils*, or *quality improvement teams*—are a key part of many firms' quality improvement efforts and an important part of the quality recommendations of both Juran and Crosby.

At Custom Research Inc., for example, a four-person steering committee is the center of the leadership system (see Figure 5.8). The steering committee sets the company directions, integrates performance excellence goals, and promotes the development of all employees. Steering committee members have frequent interaction with associates, and review overall company performance daily. They meet formally each month to evaluate performance and identify areas for improvement. The AT&T Network Operations Group has several quality councils: an executive quality council, vice president quality councils, director quality councils, and division/district manager quality councils, all of which are networked together. Quality councils assume many responsibilities such as incorporating total quality principles into the company's strategic planning process and coordinating the overall effort.

At AT&T, the quality council is characterized by four essential elements:[20]

- *Leadership*: promoting and articulating the quality vision, communicating responsibilities and expectations for management action, aligning the

FIGURE 5.8   CUSTOM RESEARCH INC. LEADERSHIP SYSTEM

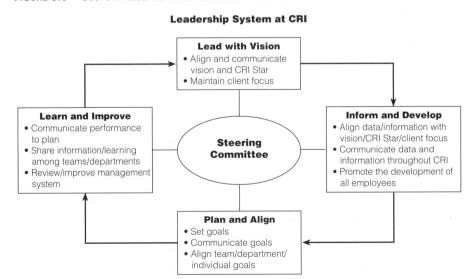

business management process with the quality approach, maintaining high visibility for commitment and involvement, and ensuring that business-wide support is available in the form of education, consulting, methods, and tools.

- *Planning*: planning strategic quality goals, understanding basic customer needs and business capabilities, developing long-term goals and near-term priorities, formulating human resource goals and policies, understanding employees' perceptions about quality and work, ensuring that all employees have the opportunity and skills to participate, and aligning reward and recognition systems to support the quality approach.
- *Implementation*: forming key business process teams, chartering teams to manage and improve these processes, reviewing improvement plans, providing resources for improvement, enlisting all managers in the process, reviewing quality plans of major organizational units, and working with suppliers and business partners in joint quality planning.
- *Review*: tracking progress through customer satisfaction and internal measures of quality, monitoring progress in attaining improvement objectives, celebrating successes, improving the quality system through auditing and identifying improvement opportunities, planning improvements, and validating the impact of improvements.

Although many firms use only top managers in such groups, Portman Equipment Company—an industrial equipment sales, service, and rental company—uses people from all types of jobs. Richard Buck, Portman's vice president for quality, argues that the presence of frontline associates in the committee has made a big difference in the decisions the group has made:

> We have general managers, we have some supervisory people, and we have some hourly people. It was our decision in forming a steering committee to break precedence from every company we've studied that used only executives on the steering committee. We opted to break that pattern and listen to the voices of all of our people as we formulate our plans. I think it's one of the better decisions we've made. And looking back on decisions we have made in the steering committee, I think there's good evidence that some of our decisions would not have been the same if we did not have representation from hourly people. I think as managers we tend to learn to think the way managers think . . . having hourly people gives us a different perspective. We see a broader picture and it's been good for our quality initiative.[21]

Develop an Agile Organization

Agility, which we introduced in Chapter 3, is an important characteristic for any organization that wishes to develop and maintain a focus on the customer and react to competitive challenges, particularly as e-commerce grows and requires more rapid, flexible, and customized responses. Businesses face ever shorter cycles for the introduction of new or improved products and services. These often require simplification of work processes and rapid changeover from one process to another.

In the early days of the quality movement, it was the large companies that received the glory. Motorola, Xerox, and AT&T were among the large companies that received Baldrige awards, some having multiple winners across divisions. Large companies were early adopters of quality tools and processes, and had the resources to implement them. Although some large organizations such as Dana Corporation continue to excel in performance excellence, many smaller companies, for example, Trident Precision Manufacturing with under 200 employees, Custom Research Incorporated with about 100 employees, and Texas Nameplate with only 66 employees, have received Baldrige awards and have outstanding quality systems and business results. Small organizations are often more agile, meaning that they can adapt quickly and flexibly to changing customer requirements and demand, a key characteristic in today's globally competitive markets. Small organizations also often have simple leadership systems, highly motivated employees, and are closer to customers. In addition, small organizations avoid bureaucratic barriers that stifle innovation and lead to complex processes, and thus they can implement changes more effectively and smoothly.

In recent years, evidence suggests that many large companies, including Johnson & Johnson, AT&T, IBM, and Microsoft, are undergoing massive reorganizations by forming groups of small companies or divisions. The reorganization is aimed at embracing a large company/small company hybrid that combines a large company's resources, market share, and capital with a small company's mindset of simplicity, flexibility, and ability to get closer to the customer.

Research has suggested that organization size can have a significant effect on employee job satisfaction and customer satisfaction; thus, organizations that are attempting to make a transformation to a large company/small company hybrid should pay close attention to employee satisfaction.[22]

Redesign Work Systems

It's difficult to make any fundamental changes in organizational structure or strategic direction without considering their impacts on work systems. TQ organizations design work systems to achieve high performance (see the box "No Egg on Their Faces"). **Performance** simply means the extent to which an individual contributes to achieving the goals and objectives of an organization. **High-performance work** is characterized by flexibility, innovation, knowledge and skill sharing, alignment with organizational directions, customer focus, and rapid response to changing business needs and marketplace

No Egg on Their Faces[23]

Sunny Fresh Foods (SFF) manufactures and distributes more than 160 different types of egg-based food products to more than 12,000 U.S. food service operations, such as quick service restaurants, schools, hospitals, convenience stores, and food processors. A subsidiary of Cargill, Inc., SFF operates three manufacturing facilities with a total of 380 employees. At SFF, a satisfied, motivated workforce is a vital ingredient of the company's successful operational and business performance.

SFF refers to its workers as "stakeholders" and ensures that they share in the benefits of continuous improvement. For example, although the base pay is set slightly below the industry midpoint for salaried workers, incentives can increase earnings above the 75th percentile. In addition, extensive reward and recognition systems, including monetary rewards for exemplary safety performance to extra vacation days for quality achievements, also help to motivate employees to contribute to the company's progress toward its improvement goals.

Sunny Fresh Foods designs its work systems to emphasize safety, quality, compensation and recognition, and employee development in support of individual development and SFF's long-term goals. Many of its work systems are unique to the industry. Examples are a "ramp-in" schedule in which new employees are allowed to work for only a specified number of hours to learn their jobs and minimize the potential for repetitive stress injuries; and a rotation system by which employees rotate to another workstation every 20 minutes. This format ensures that workers can understand and respond to product quality issues at any stage of the process and understand their internal customers; it also fights boredom, reduces repetitive stress injuries, and promotes learning. In addition, SFF uses a "buddy" system in which new employees are matched with high-performing experienced employees who serve as role models for operational excellence and behavioral competencies.

requirements. Teams, as we have already suggested, often provide the infrastructure for high performance work systems.

Organizations may be viewed at three levels: the individual job level, the process level, and the organizational level (think of front-line or shop floor workers, middle managers, and senior executives). The design of high-performance work systems can be addressed using this framework. At the individual level, work systems should enable effective accomplishment of work activities and promote flexibility and individual initiative in managing and improving work processes. Empowering employees and using work teams are ways to achieve these objectives. At the process level, work systems must promote cooperation, cross-functional teamwork, and communication. This often is done through project teams and other forms of cross-functional communication (such as product design teams). At the organizational level, senior managers must design a supportive work environment through compensation and recognition policies, and health, safety, and support services.

Several common approaches to work design—job enlargement, job rotation, and job enrichment—support TQ-based work systems. IBM was apparently the first user of **job enlargement**, in which workers' jobs were expanded to include several tasks rather than one single, low-level task. This approach reduced fragmentation of jobs and generally resulted in lower production costs, greater worker satisfaction, and higher quality, but it required higher wage rates and the purchase of more inspection equipment. **Job rotation** is a technique by which individual workers learn several tasks by rotating from one to another. The purpose of job rotation is to renew interest or motivation of the individual and to increase his or her complement of skills. However, several studies showed that the main benefit was to increase workers' skills but that little, if any, motivational benefit could be expected.[24] Finally, **job enrichment** entails "vertical job loading" in which workers are given more authority, responsibility, and autonomy rather than simply more or different work to do.

Garvin presents an interesting example of how Japanese managers in the air-conditioning industry view job enrichment as important to quality.[25] In Japan, newly hired workers are trained so that they can do every job on the line before eventually being assigned to only one job. Training frequently requires 6–12 months, in contrast to the standard training time of one to two days for newly hired production workers in U.S. air-conditioning companies. The advantage of this "enriched" training is that workers are better able to track a defect to its source and can frequently suggest remedies to problems because they understand the entire process from start to finish. Job enrichment has been used successfully in a number of firms, notably AT&T, which experienced better employee attitudes and performance, as well as Texas Instruments, IBM, and General Foods.

ORGANIZATIONAL DESIGN FOR QUALITY IN ACTION

Promoting the concept of internal customers, forming process teams, reducing hierarchy, and creating steering committees all facilitate quality. This section presents examples of organizations that use these ideas to ensure or improve quality in their operations.

Boeing Airlift and Tanker Programs[26]

Boeing Airlift and Tanker (A&T) Programs designs, develops, and produces the C-17 airlifter used by the U.S. Air Force to transport large, heavy cargo to sites around the world. In 1996, A&T signed a $14.2 billion agreement to deliver 80 C-17s to the Air Force. A few years earlier, the Defense Department had threatened to cancel the C-17 program because of technical problems, cost overruns, and late deliveries. The organization, then a unit of McDonnell Douglas Corp., responded with a complete overhaul of its business, aiming to become "process-focused and customer-driven." It initiated partnerships with customers, unions, and suppliers and replaced manager-controlled teams with empowered teams that now function like small businesses motivated by common, systematically developed goals. A&T directly involved its 7,000 Air Force customers and suppliers in planning and decision making at all organizational levels.

Interdependence and integration characterize A&T's organizational structure and its approaches to performance improvement. A high-level "enterprise process model" defines the entire business as eight interconnected process "families." These major groupings range from enterprise leadership and new business development to production and postdelivery product support.

Each family encompasses up to 10 major processes, which, in turn, are made up of several tiers of supporting subprocesses. The result is a coherent framework for process management. The model provides a direct line-of-sight from A&T-wide initiatives to the work plans and goals of teams and workers. It also helps to identify apparent operational dependencies that link subsets of process families. A&T manages these cross-cutting relationships as "megaprocesses" that typically extend to suppliers and customers.

Solar Turbines, Inc.[27]

Solar Turbines, Inc., is a wholly owned subsidiary of Caterpillar, and one of the world's largest supplier of midrange industrial gas turbine systems. Solar Turbines combines both a traditional functional organizational structure with team-based approaches. First, through a functional organizational structure led by the president's staff, Solar maintains a focus on functional excellence through recruitment, hiring, development of critical skills, and the application of tools and common processes to continuously improve functional effectiveness. Second, three cross-functional leadership structures, comprised of managers and technical experts selected from multiple levels of the organization, facilitate company-wide teamwork and decision making.

This Expanded Leadership Team, consisting of the Operations Council (74 leaders from across the business) and the Expanded Leadership Group (more than 400 managers and supervisors), enable Solar to develop the next generation of business leaders. It also promotes rapid, effective communication among employees with cross-functional teams at all levels of the organization.

The third organizational structure is the set of 10 interlocking committees that coordinate and integrate all business areas. These committees, which include sales and operations planning, products committee, ERP/IT committee, and ethics and compliance committee, provide a mechanism to strengthen organizational learning through cross-functional sharing, company-wide communication, and strategic direction setting. Members of the president's staff chair key committees and, along with other senior business leaders, actively participate to provide guidance, learn, share, and support each other's decisions.

Texas Nameplate Company, Inc.[28]

Founded in 1946, Texas Nameplate Company, Inc. (TNC) manufactures and sells identification and information labels that are affixed to refrigerators, oil-field equipment, computers, and other products. TNC, with only 66 employees, has honed the raw attributes inherent to its small size—from streamlined communications and rapid decision making to shared goals and accessible leaders—into competitive advantages. The result is a closely knit organization that is finely tuned to the requirements of its customers. TNC aims to create a continuous learning environment that enables teams of workers to take charge of processes and deliver products and services with high quality. Long-term partnerships with customers and suppliers are the rule. Sustained relationships with quality-minded suppliers have enabled TNC to nearly eliminate inspections of incoming materials.

Company President and CEO Dale Crownover and his seven top managers make up the Business Excellence Leadership Team, which aligns the focus and direction of all employees with the company's vision to "become the recognized supplier of commercial nameplates in the United States." Primary responsibility for accomplishing company goals rests with work teams—so much that the company disbanded its Quality Control Department in 1998. Because teaming has become so engrained into its culture, TNC no longer needs formal procedures for rotating employee participation. Processes and jobs are designed to allow flexibility so that employees can respond quickly to customer requirements and changing business needs. Production workers are responsible for tailoring processes to optimize contributions to company goals and to meet team-set standards.

General Electric Bayamon[29]

Located near San Juan, Puerto Rico, GE Bayamon produces surge protectors that keep power stations and electric lines from being zapped by lightning. Bayamon is the newest high performance workplace designed by Philip Jarrosiak, human resources manager for capacitor and power protection operations at GE. Bayamon's approximately 190 employees are structured into three levels: the plant manager, fifteen "advisers," and the hourly workers. According to Jarrosiak, a traditionally structured plant would have twice as many managers. The hourly workers are divided into teams of about 10 people, each of which has responsibility for a process such as shipping and receiving.

Team members represent all parts of a process, so that team decisions take into consideration a wide variety of views and needs. The advisers act as resources for the teams, becoming active only when a team needs help. To prepare them for such extensive responsibility, workers at Bayamon are given a great deal of training in such areas as machine maintenance, quality control, business practices, and English. The more workers learn, the more they are paid. Workers rotate through the plant's four work areas every six months, so that they bring a broad vision of how the factory operates to their teams.

The design for quality at Bayamon seems to be paying off. In just one year, the plant exceeded the productivity of similar plants by 20 percent and its productivity continues to increase.

The San Diego Zoo[30]

With $75 million in revenues, 1,200 employees, and 5 million visitors annually, the Zoological Society of San Diego (a.k.a. the San Diego Zoo) is a force to be reckoned with in the animal world. Even during the recession of the early 1990s, the zoo (and its Wild Animal Park) managed to increase attendance. Its overall objectives include recreation, education, and conservation.

One of the reasons for the zoo's success may be its reorganization. In the old system, the animals were organized by species (e.g., *phascolarctos cinereus*) and the humans by functions (e.g., *homo sapiensbeancounterus*). In fact, the humans were divided into 50 different departments, each of which played a role in the care and feeding of either animals, customers, or both.

This led to a somewhat sterile and unrealistic environment for everyone involved. For example, a groundskeeper confessed to occasionally sweeping a cigarette butt from the path under a bush, so it would become the gardener's responsibility instead of his own. In the new organization, the animals are grouped into bioclimatic zones that mirror their natural habitats. Gorilla Tropics groups the animals normally found in an African rain forest, while Tiger River recreates the environment of a jungle in Asia.

The humans haven't been forgotten in the new zoo design. They are now organized into teams, each of which has responsibility for one of the bioclimatic zones. The team that runs Tiger River includes specialists in mammals and birds, as well as maintenance and construction personnel. Although turf was jealously guarded in the old organization, team members are now learning one another's skills and cooperate in making improvements that transcend the old functional boundaries. As the teams have taken over responsibility for activities that were previously the prerogatives of management, managers have been freed up to find ways to bring more people to the zoo. (As in any organization with a high level of fixed costs, maintaining a consistently high level of revenues is crucial to its survival.)

COMPARISON TO ORGANIZATIONAL DESIGN THEORY

This section compares the total quality view of organizational design to the viewpoint from organization theory. Topics discussed are structural contingency theory and the institutional theory of organization structure.

Structural Contingency Theory

The structural contingency model, which originated in the 1960s, is the dominant view of organizational design in the management literature. According to this view, the two principal types of organization structures are mechanistic (centralized, many rules, strict division of labor, formal coordination across departments) and organic (decentralized, few rules, loose division of labor, informal coordination across departments).[31] These structures are described in detail in most management and organizational theory textbooks. The structural contingency model holds that there is no "one best way" to organize and that the choice between mechanistic and organic structures should be a function of certain contingencies, most often characteristics of the organization's environment and technology.

The choice between mechanistic and organic structures is usually seen as a function of uncertainty. Organizations face a great deal of uncertainty if their environments are complex and changing and if the technology they use in creating their products is not well understood. The microcomputer industry is a good example of this type of industry. The contingency model says that organizations facing uncertainty should adopt an organic structure. By contrast, organizations that experience little uncertainty—their environments are simple and stable, and their technology is well understood—are seen as needing a mechanistic structure.

The rationale for these recommendations is that organic organizations are better able to process the information necessary to deal with a complex environment and uncertain technology. They also are more flexible and can adapt to the changing circumstances associated with an unstable environment.

However, this information processing and adaptive capacity comes at the expense of efficiency and control. Although mechanistic organizations may not be able to accomplish uncertain tasks or to change rapidly, they are better suited for accomplishing straightforward tasks in a predictable environment. The mechanistic organization will accomplish such tasks quite reliably, with little danger of employees engaging in costly experiments to see whether there is a better way to do the job. The organic organization sacrifices reliability for flexibility.

Clearly a quality-oriented organization practicing continuous improvement cannot afford to freeze its processes by using a mechanistic structure, although some do. Some organizations view quality as a set of rigid procedures and formal coordination activities among groups. These organizations often plateau or eventually disband their quality efforts. Most organizations practicing total quality move in the direction of organic structures. The number of levels in their hierarchy decreases, teams are created, and employees are given the authority (and even the responsibility) to develop new and better ways of accomplishing their tasks. Coordination also tends toward the informal, as people who are interdependent are able to coordinate their work on a personal basis without the interference of a bureaucratic hierarchy. The relatively broader jobs in a TQ company give employees a better sense of how their work contributes to customer satisfaction, whether their customers are internal or external.

John Akers, the former CEO of IBM who presided over a substantial reorganization of his company, stated that "Every reorganization solves some problems and creates some problems."[32] Are problems created by the adoption of organic-type TQ organizational designs? It is too early to tell. Few organizations are more than a few years into TQ, so there is not enough of a track record on which to judge. Even fewer, however, have reverted from a TQ-type design to a more mechanistic design, and more organizations all the time are adopting a design that features internal customers, process teams, broad employee responsibilities, and quality steering committees. This indicates that such structures are seen as viable and necessary by an increasing number of managers and organizations.

How can the "one best way" approach of the quality movement be justified in light of organization theory's historical endorsement of a contingency approach to design? It may be that few industries and technologies are simple and stable enough for a mechanistic design to operate effectively.

A second possibility is that TQ designs have capacities for producing efficiencies unanticipated in the old mechanistic-organic distinction. Once the improvement of a particular process has reached the point where it is impractical to search for further gains, teams may establish the process as their standard and attempt to recreate it perfectly each time without the involvement of their managers. In other words, efficiencies would be created through different methods than those used in mechanistic firms.

A third possibility is that TQ-oriented firms pay a price in efficiency for their organizational structures, but that the superior quality of their products more than makes up for the higher prices that a lack of efficiency entails. Such firms would be unlikely to compete effectively in markets, such as textiles, where price is the overriding competitive factor.

A final possibility is that firms structured to achieve quality are paying a price for inefficiency that is not offset by their advantages. In this case such structures are not viable in the long run. This possibility does not seem to be the case, based on the limited information currently available.

Institutional Theory

Structural contingency theory, like most organizational design theories, is based on the assumption that organizations choose structures to help them perform better—provide high quality, low costs, and so forth. Institutional theory, by contrast, holds that organizations try to succeed by creating structures that will be seen as appropriate by important external constituencies—customers, other organizations in the industry, government agencies, and so on.[33]

According to institutional theory, an aspect of organizational structure need not contribute to organizational performance to be worthwhile. If the adoption of a certain structure helps the organization to be seen as legitimate in the eyes of those who have power to determine the organization's fate, then it is worthwhile. For example, many businesses have departments devoted to achieving environmental goals. Whether these departments help achieve these goals is debatable, but the existence of such departments helps to promote the legitimacy of these organizations as being concerned about the environment.

From an institutional theory standpoint, it is important to ask whether quality-oriented organization designs that include steering committees and extensive use of teams are actually intended to promote quality or are merely a means of legitimizing the organization as a progressive, quality-conscious organization. Little evidence has been generated to suggest that such structures demonstrably improve performance, yet they continue to be adopted in huge numbers by organizations in all sectors of the economy. Some writers describe these structures as "fads" or "fashions."[34] A fad is something that is normally a new idea, developed in a vague and previously undefined area, and about which users are initially enthusiastic, but can quickly lose interest. A fashion has been defined as the pursuit of novelty for its own sake. Both are temporary phases in an organization, and unless they become entrenched in the organization, they will never achieve their purpose or endure for the long haul.

In some settings, the adoption of quality-oriented structures is motivated primarily by institution concerns. For example, any company that wishes to compete in Europe must be certified as complying with the ISO 9000 quality standards. Suppliers to American automobile producers must also have elaborate quality programs in place. Many organizations have adopted a Six Sigma approach, primarily because of the publicity surrounding the use of Six Sigma by Jack Welch at General Electric. Thus, institutional theory provides another way of thinking about the rapid proliferation of quality-oriented structures in organizations. Although some organizations may be primarily seeking higher performance through the adoption of teams and steering committees, others may be primarily seeking the approval of important constituencies.

 REVIEW AND DISCUSSION QUESTIONS

1. What are the advantages and disadvantages of the functional structure? How does a process focus overcome some of the disadvantages?
2. What are the major types of structural change exhibited by organizations pursuing total quality?
3. Think back to an experience you have had with poor customer service from an organization. Whom did you blame for it? Do you know anything about the design of the organization involved? Do you think it was the fault of the individual(s) involved or could the problem have resulted from a poorly designed system? Would what you have learned in this chapter change your reaction to receiving poor quality service? How?
4. What are the core processes in a restaurant? A video rental store? A department store? How could these organizations be redesigned around these processes? What barriers would need to be overcome to accomplish this?
5. Find an organizational chart for your college or university. Is it primarily functional or process-focused? What advantages or problems do you see with this organizational structure? How might the structure be redesigned to better meet the needs of students and other stakeholders?
6. How does the organizational structure of Gold Star Chili reflect Deming's view of a production system?
7. Explain how a focus on internal customers and a team-based organization supports the process view of organizations.
8. How do teams support organizational design for TQ?
9. What is high-performance work? What types of HR practices contribute to a high performance work environment?
10. Explain the differences between job enlargement, job enrichment, and job rotation. Provide some examples from your experience.
11. Discuss how each of the organizations described in the section "Organizational Design for Quality in Action" addresses the issues presented in the section on "Redesigning Organizations for Quality."
12. Richard Palermo of Xerox was quoted in *Fortune* as saying that "people in different functions hate each other." Allowing for some exaggeration because of dramatic license, do you find this to be true? Talk to several people in a functional organization, and ask them about their feelings for people in other functions. How would you explain the variation in attitudes? If you were assigned to try to solve the problem of bad feelings between departments, how would you begin?
13. Could total quality be effective in a company with a mechanistic structure? How would it work?

14. Do you feel that the institutional theory of structure is a good description of why organizations choose quality-oriented organization designs? Why or why not?

 CASES

The State University Experience

Wow! That State University video was really cool. It has lots of majors; it's close to home so I can keep my job; and Mom and Dad loved it when they visited. I wish I could know what it's really like to be a student at State. Hmmm, I think I'll ask Mom and Dad to take a campus tour with me. . . .

I'm sure that we took our tour on the hottest day of the summer. The campus is huge—it took us about two hours to complete the tour and we didn't even see everything! I wasn't sure that the tour guide knew what he was doing. We went into a gigantic lecture hall and the lights weren't even on. Our tour guide couldn't find them so we had to hold the doors open so the sunlight could come in. About three-fourths of the way through the tour, our guide said, "State University isn't really a bad place to go to school; you just have to learn the system." I wonder what he meant by that? . . .

This application is really confusing. How do I let the admissions office know that I am interested in physics, mechanical engineering, and industrial design? Even my parents can't figure it out. I guess I'll call the admissions office for some help. . . .

I'm so excited! Mom just handed me a letter from State! Maybe they've already accepted me. What? What's this? They say I need to send my transcript. I did that when I mailed in my application two weeks ago. What's going on? I hope it won't affect my application. I'd better check with Admissions. . . .

You can't find my file? I thought you were missing only my transcript. I asked my counselor if she had sent it in yet. She told me that she sent it last week. Oh, you'll call me back when you locate my file? OK. . . .

Finally, I've been accepted! Wait a minute. I didn't apply to University College; that's a two-year program. I wanted physics, M.E., or industrial design. Well, since my only choice is U. College and I really want to go to State, I guess I'll send in the confirmation form. It really looks a lot like the application. In fact, I know I gave them a lot of the same information. I wonder why they need it again? Seems like a waste of time. . . .

Orientation was a lot of fun. I'm glad they straightened out my acceptance at U. College. I think I will enjoy State after all. I met lots of other students. I saw my advisor and I signed up for classes. All I have left to do is pay my tuition bill. Whoops. None of my financial aid is on this bill. I know I filled out all of the forms because I got an award letter from State.

There is no way my parents and I can pay for this without financial aid. It says at the bottom, I'll lose all of my classes if I don't pay the bill on time. . . .

I'm not confirmed on the computer? I sent in my form and the fee a long time ago. What am I going to do? I don't want to lose all of my classes. I have to go to the admissions office or my college office and get a letter that says I am a confirmed student. OK. If I do that tomorrow, will I still have all of my classes? . . . I can't sleep; I'm so nervous about my first day. . . .

Discussion Questionss

1. What breakdowns in service processes has this student experienced? How might these be a function of organizational design?
2. What types of process management activities should State University administrators undertake?

Barriers? What Barriers?

The general manager of an elevator company had a common problem: He was utterly frustrated with the lack of cooperation between the mechanical engineers who designed new elevators, and the manufacturing engineers who determined how to produce them in the factory. The mechanical engineers would often completely design a new elevator without any consultation from the manufacturing engineers, and then expect the factory to somehow figure out how to build it. (This is known as "throwing it over the wall" to manufacturing.)

Often the new products were difficult or nearly impossible to build, and their quality and cost suffered as a result. The designs were usually sent back to the mechanical engineers (often more than once) for engineering changes to improve their manufacturability. While designers and manufacturers played volleyball with the design, customers were forced to wait—often for months—for deliveries.

The general manager knew that if the two sets of engineers would simply communicate early in the design process, many of these problems could be eliminated before they occurred. At his wits' end, he found a large empty room in the facility and had the mechanical and manufacturing engineers working on the next product moved into the room, one group on one side and one on the other. Certainly if all they had to do to communicate was to walk from one side of the room to the other, communication would improve.

The manager relaxed somewhat, feeling that his problem had finally been solved. Upon returning to the new home of the engineers a few weeks later, he was in for a big surprise. The two sets of engineers had finally learned to cooperate! They had cooperated in building a wall of bookcases and file cabinets right down the middle of the room, effectively separating the large room into two separate offices, so they could continue as before.

Discussion Questions

1. What principles of total quality are illustrated or violated in this case?
2. Why do people feel such strong allegiance to their functional departments?
3. What could the general manager have done to improve the communication and the quality of the designs?

The British Post Office

The post office in Britain has undertaken a restructuring to improve the quality of service it provides.[35] Under the old organization, delivery of the mail and counter services were both handled through functional departments. At the local level, it was found that head postmasters were giving a great deal more attention to delivery, given its day-to-day urgency, than to counter service.

Upon reorganization, three new divisions were created: Royal Mail Letters, Royal Mail Parcels, and Post Office Counters, Ltd. By undertaking a focused set of customers and processes, each of these organizations has been able to reduce overhead and shorten the chain of command. In addition, responsibility for decision making has been placed much closer to the customer, and customers of each of the various post office services have an organization specifically charged with responding to their needs.

The corporate functional departments that remain, such as information technology, charge the divisions for their work. Periodic checks are made to ensure that the quality and costs of their service are comparable to what could be obtained outside the organization. Eventually these departments are expected to become full-fledged profit centers, so that the divisions are not burdened with subpar in-house suppliers.

Discussion Questions

1. Should the application of total quality be any different in a government agency than in a private organization?
2. What internal customer relationships have been created in the new organization?
3. Do you feel that the new organization will promote improved quality?

Child Focus, Inc.[36]

Child Focus, Inc. (CFI), whose mission is to join with communities in strengthening families and improving the quality of life for children, offers a wide variety of programs in Clermont, Hamilton, and Brown counties in Ohio. With an agency budget in excess of $11 million dollars, the spectrum of services includes Head Start programs for children ages 0–5, parenting education, family literacy, GED test preparation, substance abuse prevention, partial hospitalization, mental health prevention and counseling services in schools, foster care, independent living, case management, outpatient individual, family, and group therapy, diagnostic testing, psychiatric services, and professional training. CFI's 240 employees have a broad range of professional education, including high school, associate's, bachelor's, master's, Ph.D., R.N., and M.D. degrees. All staff share the authority, dedication, and commitment to promote the mission of serving children and families.

Facilities include intranet, Internet, a Web site (http://www.child-focus. org), specifically designed management information systems with necessary office equipment, 22 vehicles to provide client transportation, and two commercial kitchens that serve more than 800 meals a day. Facilities and programs are supervised by a volunteer Board of Trustees and by the accreditation standards of the National Association for the Education of the Young Child, Day Care Licensing Regulations, Head Start Performance Standards, and Ohio Departments of Education, Mental Health, Alcohol and Drug Addiction Services, and Job and Family Services.

As CFI continues to expand its programs through new and larger contracts, the biggest challenge is to provide quality services. Personnel and human resources issues are another challenge. They continually strive to find qualified staff who are willing to work with some of the most challenging children and dysfunctional families. Although their turnover rate is approximately 15 percent, most of it is in less-skilled positions. Consequently, this loss of staff increases training costs. Training existing staff to meet higher educational standards and continuing to find office and service space to meet growing needs is also a challenge.

CFI's diversity of programming, reporting, and funding to multiple agencies and organizations requires continuous management at all levels within the agency. The governing Board of Trustees for Child Focus is a diverse group of volunteers that have experience as attorneys, teachers, homemakers, and CFI consumers. Federal, state, and county legislative and regulatory changes can affect programming or present financial challenges. These entities, in turn, may have competing philosophies, which complicate administration or delay program implementation.

CFI management has several procedures in place to identify and manage these organizational challenges. Customer, staff, and collaborators' recommendations and complaints are identified through evaluation and administrative programs in both the Early Childhood and Behavioral Health divisions and are continuously monitored by staff, management, and the Board of Trustees. Through a continuous strategic planning process, CFI identifies ways in which to improve and expand its services through program modification or development.

The CEO is committed to building a total quality organization. If you were asked to help in this quality journey, what questions would you want answered? What advice concerning organizational design would you provide?

ENDNOTES

1. An interesting perspective on this problem is provided by Benson P. Shapiro, V. Kasturi Rangan, and John J. Sviokla, in "Staple Yourself to an Order," *Harvard Business Review*, July–August 1992, pp. 113–122.

2. Myron Tribus, "Total Quality in Education," unpublished manuscript. Hayward, Calif.: Exergy, Inc.

3. Quoted from "The CEO as Organizational Architect: An Interview with Xerox's Paul Allaire" by Robert Howard, in *Harvard Business Review*, September–October 1992, pp. l06–121.

4. Thomas A. Stewart, "The Search for the Organization of Tomorrow," *Fortune*, May 18, 1992.

5. J. M. Juran, *Juran on Leadership for Quality: An Executive Handbook.* New York: Free Press, 1989.

6. W. E. Deming, *Out of the Crisis.* Cambridge, Mass.: MIT Center for Advanced Engineering Study, 1986.

7. Adapted from Katrina Brooker, "The Nightmare before Christmas," *Fortune*, January 24, 2000, pp. 24–25.

8. Robert Hof, Debra Sparks, Ellen Neuborne, and Wendy Zellner. "Can Amazon Make It?" *Business Week*, July 10, 2000, pp. 38–43.

9. A. Blanton Godfrey, "Planned Failures," *Quality Digest*, March 2000, p. 16.

10. *AT&T's Total Quality Approach*, AT&T Corporate Quality Office, 1992, p. 6.

11. R. J. Schonberger, *Building a Chain of Customers.* New York: Free Press, 1990.

12. See Jack Reilly, "Using the Methods of Fernando Flores," *Center for Quality of Management Journal*, Vol. 6, No. 1, Spring 1997, and Grant Harris and Steve Taylor, "Escaping from the Box: Using a New Process Model to Support Participation and Improve Coordination," *Center for Quality of Management Journal*, Vol. 6, No. 3, Winter 1997.

13. We are indebted to Jackie Messerschmidt of Workflow Dynamics for graciously providing this example.

14. Jerry G. Bowles, "Leading the World-Class Company," *Fortune*, September 21, 1992.

15. Jeannie Coyle, "Aligning Human Resource Processes with Total Quality," *Employment Relations Today*, Vol. 18, No. 3, Fall 1991.

16. Mark Kelly, *The Adventures of a Self-Managing Team.* Raleigh, N.C.: Mark Kelly Books, 1990.

17. Based on "TQM-Quality with Reduced Resources," a talk given by Dr. Edwin Coate, vice president for finance and administration, Oregon State University, presented via teleconference by Cuyahoga Community College, September 9, 1992.

18. Stewart, "The Search for the Organization of Tomorrow."

19. Robert O. Knorr and Edward F. Thiede, Jr., "Making New Technologies Work," *The Journal of Business Strategy*, Vol. 12, No. 1, pp. 46–49.

20. AT&T Quality Steering Committee, *Leading the Quality Initiative*, AT&T Bell Laboratories, 1990, pp.13–14.

21. Interview with Richard Buck.

22. Nadav Goldschmidt and Beth G. Chung, "Size Does Matter: The Effect of Organizational Size on Customer Satisfaction," *Journal of Quality Management*, Vol. 6, 2001, pp. 47–60.

23. *Source:* Malcolm Baldrige National Quality Award, Profiles of Winners, National Institute of Standards and Technology, Department of Commerce.

24. J. R. Hackman and G. R. Oldham, *Work Redesign.* Reading, Mass.: Addison-Wesley, 1980.

25. David A Garvin, *Managing Quality.* New York: Free Press, 1988, pp. 202–203.

26. Adapted from Boeing Airlift and Tanker Programs 1998 Award Winner Profile, Baldrige National Quality Program. U.S. Department of Commerce.

27. Solar Turbines, Inc. Malcolm Baldrige National Quality Award Application Summary, 1999, p. 4.

28. Adapted from Texas Nameplate Company, Inc. 1998 Award Winner Profile, Baldrige National Quality Program. U.S. Department of Commerce.

29. Based on Stewart, "The Search for the Organization of Tomorrow."

30. Based on Stewart, "The Search for the Organization of Tomorrow."

31. This version of the contingency model comes from T. Burns and G. M. Stalker, *The Management of Innovation*. London: Tavistock, 1961.

32. Quoted in D. Hellriegel, J. W. Slocum and R. W. Woodman, *Organizational Behavior (Fifth Edition)*. St. Paul, Minn.: West Publishing Company.

33. See J. W. Meyer and B. Rowan, "Institutionalized Organizations: Formal Structure as Myth and Ceremony," *American Journal of Sociology*, Vol. 83, 1977, pp. 340–363, and W. R. Scott, "The Adolescence of Institutional Theory," *Administrative Science Quarterly*, Vol. 32, 1987, pp. 493–511.

34. R. E. Cole, *Managing Quality Fads*, Oxford University Press, New York, 1999; B. G. Dale, M. B. F. Elkjaer, A. van der Wiele, and A. R. T. Williams, "Fad, Fashion, and Fit: An Examination of Quality Circles, Business Process Re-engineering and Statistical Process Control," *International Journal of Production Economics*, Vol. 73, 2001, pp. 137–152; Gerald Zeitz, Vikas Mittal, and Brian McAulay, "Distinguishing Adoption and Entrenchment of Management Practices: A Framework for Analysis," *Organization Studies*, Vol. 20, No. 5, 1999, pp. 741–776.

35. Based on R. M. Tabor, "Planning for Postal Services," *Long Range Planning*, Vol. 23, No. 5, 1990, pp. 91–96.

36. Child Focus, Inc., 2003 Greater Cincinnati Chamber of Commerce Small Business Awards Application. Thanks go to Tara Dawson for providing this information.

CHAPTER 6

Designing, Controlling, and Improving Organizational Processes

Joseph Juran describes quality management as the "Quality Trilogy": *planning*, *control*, and *improvement*. He says that most managers devote too much attention to control, and too little to planning and improvement—which may be the most important activities for meeting and exceeding customer expectations and gaining competitive advantage. All three of these activities characterize the concept of process management. **Process management** involves design, control, and improvement—the key activities necessary to achieve a high level of performance in key value creation and support processes, and identifying opportunities for improving quality and operational performance, and ultimately, customer satisfaction. Good process management helps to prevent defects and errors, eliminate waste and redundancy, and thereby lead to better quality and improved company performance through shorter cycle times, improved flexibility, and faster customer response.

Nearly every leading company views process management as a fundamental business activity. AT&T, for example, bases its process management philosophy on the following principles:

- Process quality improvement focuses on the end-to-end process.
- The mind-set of quality is one of prevention and continuous improvement.
- Everyone manages a process at some level and is simultaneously a customer and a supplier.
- Customer needs drive process quality improvement.
- Corrective action focuses on removing the root cause of the problem rather than on treating its symptoms.
- Process simplification reduces opportunities for errors and rework.
- Process quality improvement results from a disciplined and structured application of the quality management principles.[1]

A wide variety of tools and techniques are used in process management; these will be addressed in the next chapter. In this chapter we will

➤ discuss general concepts of designing, controlling, and improving processes;
➤ identify the types of changes necessary for a high performance organization—specifically, continuous improvement, breakthrough improvement, and organizational learning; and
➤ provide examples of firms undertaking these changes.

PROCESS DESIGN

Good process management begins with good process design. The design of the processes that produce and deliver goods and services—to both external and internal customers—can have a significant impact on cost (and hence profitability), flexibility (the ability to produce the right types and amounts of products as customer demand or preferences change), and quality. See the box on Netflix for an example of an innovative process design that centers on efficiency and rapid customer service.

The design of a process begins with the process owner. A process owner might be an individual, a team, a department, or some cross-

---

90,000 DVDs and No Shelves[2]

Netflix turned the DVD rental industry on its ear by offering an all-DVD library of more than 15,000 titles sent through the mail, with no due dates and no late fees. In 2003, Netflix had over one million customers. Netflix's Worcester, Massachusetts, hub is a former shoe warehouse that stocks around 90,000 DVDs, and yet has no shelves. Each morning at 8:00, the U.S. Postal Service (cheaper and quicker than the alternatives, incredibly) drops off "pumpkin carts," orange bins with thousands of returned DVDs from all over New England. Instead of cataloging titles at fixed shelf locations and retrieving them to satisfy a customer order, operators scan the returned discs, collecting data, which computers at Netflix's San Jose headquarters match to new orders. After lunch, the Worcester operators rescan every disc in their inventory; with each scan, they act on instructions from San Jose to "Ship Disc," if a customer wants the film, or "Scan Tomorrow," if not. The Scan Tomorrows move faster, set aside by the handful. Ship Discs get an envelope and a pair of stickers. Outgoing discs pass through the Omega, a 40-foot-long machine that can organize more than 20,000 outgoing rentals an hour into bins specified by zip codes. Presorting saves Netflix six to seven cents per DVD, as well as providing faster shipping times to customers.

functional group. A basic approach to process design is suggested by Motorola:

1. *Identify the product or service:* What work do I do?
2. *Identify the customer:* Who is the work for?
3. *Identify the supplier:* What do I need and from whom do I get it?
4. *Identify the process:* What steps or tasks are performed? What are the inputs and outputs for each step?
5. *Mistake-proof the process:* How can I eliminate or simplify tasks and prevent defects and errors?
6. *Develop measurements and controls, and improvement goals:* How do I evaluate the process? How can I improve further?

Steps 1 through 3 address such questions as "What is the purpose of the process?" "How does the process create customer satisfaction?" and "What are the essential inputs and outputs of the process?" Step 4 focuses on the actual process design by defining the specific tasks performed in transforming the inputs to outputs. Step 5 focuses on making the process efficient and capable of delivering high quality. Step 6 ensures that the process will be monitored and controlled to the level of required performance. This monitoring involves gathering in-process measurements and/or customer feedback on a regular basis and using this information to control and improve the process.

A good process design focuses on the prevention of poor quality by ensuring that goods and services meet both external and internal customer requirements, and that the process is capable of achieving the requisite level of performance. Standardized processes establish consistency of output. For example, in producing a new, very small CD player, Sony had to develop entirely new manufacturing processes, because no process in existence was able to make this product as small and as accurate as the design required. FedEx developed a wireless data collection system that employs laser scanners to manage millions of packages daily through its six main hubs, improving not only customer service, but saving labor costs as well.[3] However, standardized processes may not be able to meet the needs of different customer segments. Today, many companies such as Dell use a strategy of **mass customization**— providing personalized, custom-designed products to meet individual customer preferences at prices comparable to mass-produced items. Mass customization requires significant changes to traditional processes that focus on either customized, crafted products, or mass-produced, standardized products.[4] These include flexible manufacturing technologies, just-in-time systems, information technology, and an emphasis on cycle time reduction.

A process design should include a step-by-step process map, or flowchart (see the next chapter for details about developing and using flowcharts), along with standard operating procedures and work instructions. Many companies use ISO 9000 as a basis for defining and documenting key processes. Branch-Smith Printing, for example, created more than 40 process maps as part of the process of converting to ISO 9000. Corning Telecommunications Products Division (TPD) has identified and documented more than 800 processes in all areas of its business, of which 50 are designated as "core business processes" that merit special emphasis in continuous improvement efforts. Each core process is owned and managed by a key business leader.

Design for Quality in Service Processes

The fundamental differences between manufacturing and service processes deserve special attention in process design. This aspect is especially important because support processes are basically services. Some common examples of service processes are preparing an invoice, taking a telephone order, processing a credit card, and checking out of a hotel. First, the outputs of service processes are not as well defined, as are manufactured products. For example, even though all banks offer similar tangible goods such as checking, loans, automatic tellers, and so forth, the real differentiating factor among banks is the service they provide. Second, most service processes involve a greater interaction with the customer, often making it easier to identify needs and expectations. By contrast, customers often cannot define their needs for service until after they have some point of reference or comparison. Fast-food restaurants, for example, have carefully designed (or have redesigned) their processes to improve quality of service and speed.[5] New hands-free intercom systems, better microphones that reduce ambient kitchen noise, and screens that display a customer's order are all focused on these requirements. Timers at Wendy's count every segment of the order completion process to help managers identify problem areas. Kitchen workers wear headsets to hear orders as they are placed. McDonald's eliminated many items from its menu to simplify kitchen operations, and developed new menu boards showing more pictures to keep ordering simple. It also reduced the number of possible keypad options on registers and installed newly automated drink dispensers and French fry bins.

Service processes often involve both internal and external activities, a factor that complicates quality design. In a bank, for example, poor service can result from the way that tellers treat customers and also from poor quality of computers and communications equipment beyond the control of the tellers. Internal activities are primarily concerned with efficiency (quality of conformance), whereas external activities—with direct customer interaction—require attention to effectiveness (quality of design). All too often, workers involved in internal operations do not understand how their performance affects the customers they do not see. The success of the process depends on everyone—workers involved in internal as well as external activities—understanding that they add value to the customer.

Services have three basic components: physical facilities, processes, and procedures; employees' behavior; and employees' professional judgment.[6] Designing a service essentially involves determining an effective balance of these components. The goal is to provide a service whose elements are internally consistent and directed at meeting the needs of a specific target market segment. Too much or too little emphasis on one component will lead to problems and poor customer perceptions. For example, too much emphasis on procedures might result in timely and efficient service, but might also suggest insensitivity and apathy toward the customer. Too much emphasis on behavior might provide a friendly and personable environment at the expense of slow, inconsistent, or chaotic service. Too much emphasis on professional judgment might lead to good solutions to customer problems but also to slow, inconsistent, or insensitive service.

A useful approach to designing effective services is first to recognize that services differ in the degree of customer contact and interaction, the degree of labor intensity, and the degree of customization. For example, a railroad is low in all three dimensions. On the other hand, an interior design service would be high in all three dimensions. A fast-food restaurant would be high in customer contact and labor intensity, but low in customization. Services low in all three dimensions of this classification are more similar to manufacturing organizations. The emphasis on quality should be focused on the physical facilities and procedures; behavior and professional judgment are relatively unimportant.

As contact and interaction between the customer and the service system increases, two factors must be taken into account. In services low in labor intensity, the customer's impression of physical facilities, processes, and procedures is important. Service organizations must exercise special care in choosing and maintaining reliable and easy-to-use equipment. With higher levels of contact and interaction, appropriate staff behavior becomes increasingly important. As labor intensity increases, variations between individuals become more important; however, the elements of personal behavior and professional judgment will remain relatively unimportant as long as the degrees of customization and contact and interaction remain low. As customization increases, professional judgment becomes a bigger factor in the customer's perception of service quality. In services that are high in all three dimensions, facilities, behavior, and professional judgment must be equally balanced.

PROCESS CONTROL

Control is the activity of ensuring conformance to the requirements and taking corrective action when necessary to correct problems and maintain stable performance. Lack of control can not only cause customer dissatisfaction, but can result in serious consequences, not only for the business, but for customers as well (see the box on Coca-Cola). Not recognizing when contamination occurs in a bottling process, for instance, signifies a lack of control.

Any control system has three components: (1) a standard or goal, (2) a means of measuring accomplishment, and (3) comparison of actual results

Poor Control Can Leave a Bitter Taste

An international study by Landor & Associates, an independent design and image firm, showed conclusively that Coca-Cola is the number one brand in the minds of soft-drink consumers around the world, and affirmed that the company is totally committed to quality. Coca Cola has stated, "Our commitment to quality is something for which we will never lose our taste."[7] However, in early June, 1999, quite a few people in Europe did when almost 100 Belgian children fell ill after drinking Coca-Cola. This incident caused the Belgian Health Ministry to require Coca-Cola to recall millions of cans of product in Belgium and to cease product distribution. Later, France and the Netherlands also halted distribution of Coke products as the contamination scare spread. It was quickly determined that contaminated carbon dioxide had been used during the carbonation process at the Antwerp bottling facility. According to the official statement from Coca-Cola, "Independent laboratory testing showed that the cause of the off-taste in the bottled products was carbon dioxide. That carbon dioxide was replaced and all bottles with off-taste have been removed from the market. The issue affects the taste of the soft drinks only. . . . The second issue involves an external odor on some canned products. In the case of the Belgian distribution system, a substance used in wood treatment has caused an offensive odor on the outside bottom of the can. Independent analysis determined that the product is safe. The Company, in conjunction with its bottling partner in Belgium, is taking all necessary steps to eliminate this offensive odor."[8] After two weeks, the company was allowed to begin producing and distributing products in the three countries.

with the standard, along with feedback to form the basis for corrective action. Goals and standards are defined during planning and design processes. They establish what is supposed to be accomplished. These goals and standards are reflected by measurable quality characteristics, such as dimensions of machined parts, numbers of defectives, customer complaints, or waiting times. For example, golf balls must meet five standards to be considered as conforming to the Rules of Golf: minimum size, maximum weight, spherical symmetry, maximum initial velocity, and overall distance.[9] Methods for measuring these quality characteristics may be automated or performed manually by the workforce. Golf balls are measured for size by trying to drop them through a metal ring—a conforming ball sticks to the ring while a nonconforming ball falls through; digital scales measure weight to one-thousandth of a gram; and initial velocity is measured in a special machine by finding the time it takes a ball struck at 98 mph to break a ballistic screen at the end of a tube exactly 6.28 feet away.

Short-term corrective action generally should be taken by process owners who are responsible for doing the work. In many organizations, such as The Ritz-Carlton Hotel Company, this extends to everyone. The company has a policy by which the first person who detects a problem is empowered to break away from routine duties, investigate and correct the problem immediately, document the incident, and then return to their routine. Long-term corrective action is the responsibility of management.

The responsibility for control can be determined by checking the three components of control systems. A process owner must have the means of knowing what is expected (the standard or goal) through clear instructions and specifications; they must have the means of determining their actual performance, typically through inspection and measurement; and they must have a means of making corrections if they discover a variance between what is expected of them and their actual performance. If any of these criteria is not met, then the process is the responsibility of management, not the process owner. Both Juran and Deming made this important distinction. If process owners are held accountable for or expected to act on problems beyond their control, they become frustrated and end up playing games with management. Juran and Deming stated that the majority of quality problems are management-controllable.

Process control requires a good measurement system to track quality and operational performance. Measurement provides the ability to capture important quality and performance indicators to reveal patterns about process performance. Each measurement should aim for a standard or target that is driven by customer requirements. Meeting these two conditions ensures that sufficient data can be collected to reveal useful information for evaluation and control, as well as learning that leads to improvement and maturity. For example, the key measures used by SSM Health Care to monitor their processes are shown in Table 6.1. Daily, weekly, monthly, and quarterly performance assessments provide the opportunity to review and manage these measures and identify ways of preventing potential errors before they affect the patient.

Many companies use statistical process control, which is based on analyzing data patterns statistically; this will be described further in the next chapter. Granite Rock, for instance, was the first in the construction materials industry to apply statistical process control in the management of production of aggregates, concrete, and asphalt products. Others use various automated and visual control systems. For example, DaimlerChrysler manufactures the PT Cruiser at the company's Toluca Assembly Plant in Mexico. To ensure quality, the Toluca plant verifies parts, processes, fit, and finish every step of the way, from stamping and body to paint and final assembly. The control practices include visual management through quality alert systems, which are designed to call immediate attention to abnormal conditions. The system provides visual and audible signals for each station for tooling, production, maintenance, and material flow.[10]

TABLE 6.1   PROCESSES, REQUIREMENTS, AND MEASURES USED BY SSM HEALTH CARE

Process	Key Requirements	Key Measures
Admit		
Admitting/ Registration	Timeliness	• Time to admit patients to the setting of care • Timeliness in admitting/registration rate on patient satisfaction survey questions
Assess		
Patient Assessment	Timeliness	• % of histories and physicals charted within 24 hrs or prior to surgery • Pain assessed at appropriate intervals, per hospital policy
Clinical laboratory and radiology services	Accuracy & Timeliness	• Quality control results/Repeat rates • Turnaround time • Response rate on medical staff satisfaction survey
Care Delivery/Treatment		
Provision of clinical care	Nurse responsiveness Pain management Successful clinical outcomes	• Response rate on patient satisfaction and medical staff survey questions • Wait time for pain medications • % CHF patients received med instructions/weighing • % Ischemic heart patients discharged on proven therapies • Unplanned readmits/Returns to ER or Operating Room • Mortality
Pharmacy/ Medication use	Accuracy	• Use of dangerous abbreviations in medication orders • Med error rate or adverse drug events resulting from med errors
Surgical services/ Anesthesia	Professional skill, competence/ communication	• Clear documentation of informed surgical and anesthesia consent • Perioperative mortality • Surgical site infection rates
Discharge		
Case management	Appropriate utilization	• Average length of stay (ALOS) • Payment denials • Unplanned readmits
Discharge from setting of care	Assistance and clear directions	• Discharge instructions documented and provided to patient • Response rate on patient satisfaction survey

Source: Courtesy of SSM Health Care.

Process Control in Services

Many people think that process control applies only to manufacturing. This assumption could not be further from the truth. The approach used by The Ritz-Carlton Hotel Company to control quality is proactive because of their intensive personalized service environment.[11] Systems for collecting and using quality-related measures are widely deployed and used extensively throughout the organization. Each hotel tracks service quality indicators on a daily basis. The Ritz-Carlton recognizes that many customer requirements are sensory, and thus, difficult to measure. However, by selecting, training, and certifying employees in their knowledge of The Ritz-Carlton Gold Standards of service, they are able to assess their work through appropriate sensory measurements—taste, sight, smell, sound, and touch—and take appropriate actions.

The company uses three types of control processes to deliver quality:

1. Self-control of the individual employee based on their spontaneous and learned behavior.
2. Basic control mechanism, which is carried out by every member of the workforce.
3. Critical success factor control for critical processes. Process teams use customer and organizational requirement measurements to determine quality, speed, and cost performance. These measurements are compared against benchmarks and customer satisfaction data to determine corrective action and resource allocation.

In addition, The Ritz-Carlton conducts both self-audits and outside audits. Self-audits are carried out internally at all levels, from one individual or function to an entire hotel. Process walk-throughs occur daily in hotels while senior leaders assess field operations during formal reviews at various intervals. Outside audits are performed by independent travel and hospitality rating organizations. All audits must be documented, and any findings must be submitted to the senior leader of the unit being audited. They are responsible for action and for assessing the implementation and effectiveness of recommended corrective actions.

PROCESS IMPROVEMENT

The distinction between control and improvement is illustrated in Figure 6.1. Any process performance measure naturally fluctuates around some average level. Abnormal conditions cause an unusual deviation from this pattern. Removing the causes of such abnormal conditions and maintaining level performance is the essence of control. Improvement means changing the performance to a new level. Organizations use formal problem-solving methodologies such as the Deming Cycle or Six Sigma DMAIC (described later in this chapter) to identify potential improvements, analyze data, and implement solutions. See the box for a discussion of how The Ritz-Carlton addresses improvement.

To be able to improve a process, it must be (1) repeatable, and (2) measurable. Repeatability means that the process must recur over time. The cycle

FIGURE 6.1   CONTROL VERSUS IMPROVEMENT

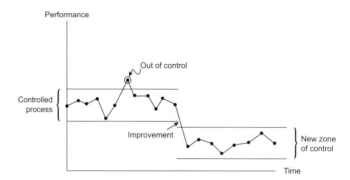

may be long, as with product development processes or patent applications; or it may be short, as with a manufacturing operation or an order entry process. In other words, you need the ability to learn from both successes and failures.

Keeping That Touch of Elegance

The Ritz-Carlton has eight mechanisms devoted solely to the improvement of process, product, and service quality:

1. New hotel startup improvement process: a cross-functional team from the entire company that works together to identify and correct problem areas.
2. Comprehensive performance evaluation process: the work area team mechanism that empowers people who perform a job to develop the job procedures and performance standards.
3. Quality network: a mechanism of peer approval through which an individual employee can advance a good idea.
4. Standing problem-solving team: a standing work area team that addresses any problem it chooses.
5. Quality improvement team: special teams assembled to solve an assigned problem identified by an individual employee or leaders.
6. Strategic quality planning: annual work area teams that identify their missions, primary supplier objectives and action plans, internal objectives and action plans, and progress reviews.
7. Streamlining process: the annual hotel evaluation of processes, products, or services that are no longer valuable to the customer.
8. Process improvement: the team mechanism for corporate leaders, managers, and employees to improve the most critical processes.

Continuous Improvement and Kaizen

Continuous improvement to provide quality to customers is essential to total quality. The TQ ideal is *not* to make a big splash by improving a system, only to mindlessly operate in the same "new and improved" manner for years to come. TQ-oriented organizations relentlessly improve their processes, products, and services, as well as their people (through training) day-by-day and month-by-month, over years and even decades. A good illustration is Dell. Although it has had some of the highest quality ratings in the PC industry, CEO Michael Dell became obsessed with finding ways to reduce machine failure rates. He concluded that failures were related to the number of times a hard drive was handled during assembly, and insisted that the number of "touches" be reduced from an existing level of more than 30 per drive. Production lines were revamped and the number was reduced to fewer than 15. Soon after, the reject rate of hard drives fell by 40 percent and the overall failure rated dropped by 20 percent.[12]

The concept of continuous improvement dates back many years. One of the earliest examples in the United States was at National Cash Register Company (NCR). After a shipment of defective cash registers was returned in 1894, the company's founder discovered unpleasant and unsafe working conditions. He made many changes, including better lighting, new safety devices, ventilation, lounges, and lockers. The company offered extensive evening classes to improve employees' education and skills, and instituted a program for soliciting suggestions from factory workers. Workers received cash prizes and other recognitions for their best ideas; by the 1940s the company was receiving an average of 3,000 suggestions each year. Over the years, many other companies such as Lincoln Electric and Procter & Gamble developed innovative and effective improvement approaches. However, many of these focused almost exclusively on productivity and cost. A focus on quality improvement, by contrast, is relatively recent, stimulated by the success of the Japanese. Toshiba in 1946, Matsushita Electric in 1950, and Toyota in 1951 initiated some of the earliest formal continuous improvement programs. Toyota, in particular, pioneered just-in-time (JIT), which showed that companies could make products efficiently with virtually zero defects. JIT established a philosophy of continuous improvement, which the Japanese call **kaizen** (pronounced ki- zen).

Kaizen strategy has been called "the single most important concept in Japanese management—the key to Japanese competitive success." It is the cumulative effect of hundreds or thousands of small improvements that creates dramatic change in performance. In the kaizen approach as practiced in Japan, financial investment is minimal; everyone participates in the process; and improvements result from the know-how and experience of workers. At Nissan Motor Co., Ltd., for instance, any suggestion that saves at least 0.6 seconds in a production process is seriously considered by management. This is not to say that large improvement breakthroughs do not occur; they certainly do, especially in the early phases of TQ. To use football as a metaphor, the successful practice of TQ is not reflected in the glamour of the occasional "long bomb," it consists of grinding out improvements "one yard at a time."

Consider the chart in Figure 6.2, which shows the result of attempts by a foundry to reduce its production of scrap (products rejected because of poor quality) over three years. Several points about continuous improvement are illustrated by this chart.

- The average amount of scrap declined each year, from approximately 9.5 in the first year to 6.5 in the second year and to 3.5 in the third year.
- Not only the level but also the variation from month to month declined each year. Compare the wild variation in the first year to the relative stability of the third.
- Even when quality efforts had not been undertaken, the company occasionally got lucky and produced good quality. It took the foundry two years to produce a month as good as the first month of the first year.

Obviously, the first-year first-month was a fluke, as scrap was 50 percent higher the next month! The philosophy of continuous improvement was captured very well by the quality manager who said, "We're nowhere near where we ought to be, but we're getting better. And we're going to be better tomorrow."

FIGURE 6.2   SCRAP REDUCTIONS IN A FOUNDRY OVER THREE YEARS

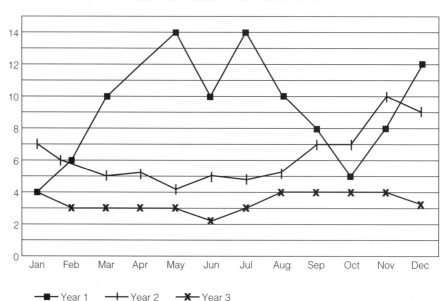

The kaizen philosophy has been widely adopted and is used by many firms in the United States and around the world. For example, at ENBI Corporation, a New York manufacturer of precision metal shafts and roller assemblies for the printer, copier, and fax machine markets, kaizen projects have resulted in a 48 percent increase in productivity, a 30 percent reduction in cycle time, and a 73 percent reduction in inventory.[13] Kaizen has been successfully applied in the Mercedes-Benz truck factory in Brazil, resulting in reductions of 30 percent in manufacturing space, 45 percent in inventory, 70 percent in lead time, and 70 percent in setup time over a three-year period. Sixteen employees have full-time responsibility for kaizen activities.[14]

Continuous improvement efforts can be directed at a number of different types of improvement. For example, changes could result in work being done more easily, more accurately, faster, at lower cost, more safely, and in a way that provides greater customer satisfaction.[15] Thinking about continuous improvement in this way makes it clear how many opportunities for improvement exist in almost any system. How many operations are there that couldn't be improved on even one of these dimensions? Persistence is important in pursuing continuous improvement. Not only will small changes in operations take some time to add up to any serious improvement but also they are often disruptive when first implemented.

According to the late Japanese manufacturing expert, Shigeo Shingo:[16]

> Since improvement . . . demands new procedures, a certain amount of difficulty will be encountered. . . . Initially, new methods will be difficult. Old procedures, however, are easy just because they are familiar. . . . As long as it is unfamiliar, even an improved procedure will be more difficult and will take more time than the old procedure. . . . Thus, no improvement shows its true worth right away . . . 99 percent of all improvement plans would vanish without a trace if they were to be abandoned after only a brief trial.

Like the cultural change that motivates it, continuous improvement is difficult to sustain. Perhaps the "if it's not broke, don't fix it" mentality is too deeply embedded our culture. In any case, many organizations that wish to embrace continuous improvement have not been able to do so successfully.

The most important ingredient for continuous improvement is one we have already discussed: an appropriate organizational culture (see the box "The Law of Quality"). If everyone in the organization understands and believes in the importance of continuous improvement, the rest is a question of technique. If not, no techniques will do the job.

Given the large number of possible areas in an organization that could be improved, setting priorities is crucial, and there are several ways to do this. Many organizations rely on customer input and feedback to help set their priorities.[17] For example, if late deliveries are the most common customer complaint, continuous improvement efforts should be directed at

---

The Law of Quality[18]

Implementing a continuous improvement process in most law firm cultures can be difficult. This is partly because lawyers' compensation is directly linked to the number of hours they bill; many don't see themselves being able to devote time to a quality initiative, even though, in the long run, such a program would likely streamline their processes and give them more time. In a culture with many individual habits and idiosyncrasies, standardizing processes and procedures can be difficult, if not impossible.

Nevertheless, some firms have made remarkable progress. The 130-lawyer firm of Mays & Valentine in Richmond, Virginia, set up quality improvement teams. A short survey was mailed to clients to find out where the firm stood with its external customers. At the same time, an internal survey was administered to the entire firm to determine whether the firm's culture was receptive to the TQ philosophy. The firm's executive committee carefully selected the mission and objectives for each team. Based on the survey results, they chose areas for improvement of attorney responsiveness and accessibility to clients, the firm's copying operations, and the use of alternative billing methods. Some of the changes that resulted included new standards for responsiveness to clients, which were made firm policy; a new branch office telephone system; outsourcing copy center operations to Xerox; and new measurements for administrative systems such as computer performance, turnover rate, central fax operations, speed of billing, complaints, and collection rates.

Not only has service improved, but employees are more satisfied because they are asked for their input and encouraged to suggest ways to improve effectiveness.

---

reducing delivery times. Often customers cannot see inside the organization to identify the root causes of problems, so some additional sorting out is generally necessary.

The time-honored tradition of the suggestion system has taken on a new life under TQ to serve this purpose. At Portman Equipment Company, an employee who sees an improvement opportunity fills out a Proposal for Change form, which initiates the formation of a team to attack the issue.[19] At Wainwright Industries, employees fill out a short form describing their idea (which may be as simple as repairing a frayed extension cord before an accident occurs), and obtain a supervisor's approval. The employee's name is entered in a weekly drawing (a safety idea counts as three entries, and all members of a team idea receive an entry); the winner receives a gift certificate for whatever they want. The process is run entirely by employees without management involvement; they even set the program's annual budget.

IMPROVEMENT PROCESSES

Managers need systematic approaches to drive continuous improvement programs. Some organizations follow some standard and popular approaches, while others develop unique approaches to meet their own needs and cultures. For example, Eastman Chemical uses seven steps for accelerated continuous improvement.

1. *Focus and pinpoint.* "Focus" is about getting everyone on the same page with regard to goals; "pinpoint" is about specifying in measurable terms what is expected.
2. *Communicate.* Communication is done company-wide by publicizing key result areas, the vision, and the mission statement so that employees can answer the questions: What is being improved? Why is it important to the customer, to the company, and to me? What has the management team committed to do to help? And what, specifically, is the company asking me to do?
3. *Translate and link.* Teams translate the company-wide objectives into their own language and environment.
4. *Create a management action plan.* Management creates a plan with specific actions to reach a goal, including metrics to measure success. Each team member is asked to know what tasks need to be done, why they are important, and what the team's role is in getting them done.
5. *Improve processes.* Teams use a six-step problem-solving process.
6. *Measure progress and provide feedback.* Eastman is adamant about the importance of unambiguous, visual feedback to employees and appropriate measures of performance. Eastman's rules include:
   - Feedback should be visual, frequent, simple, and specific.
   - The baseline performance should be shown for comparison.
   - The past, current period, and goals should be posted.
   - The best-ever score should be posted.
   - A chart should be immediately understandable.
   - A good scorecard allows comments and annotations.
7. *Reinforce behaviors and celebrate results.* Eastman reinforces that learning leads to positive results by encouraging teams at celebrations to answer the questions: What did you do? Why did it work? Why is it important for the customer, the company, and the team? How did the team accomplish its achievement?

Much of Eastman's approach deals with organizational and cultural issues. Eastman points out that its formula cannot be blindly followed by others but must be adapted to the specific corporate culture. Nevertheless, the human principles are universal.

The real work is done in Step 5. Most organizations use some type of structured problem solving approach, which describes a logical, data-driven process for solving problems. These approaches are routinely taught in employee training programs and form the basis for disciplined problem-solving efforts. They generally include four key steps:

1. redefining and analyzing the perceived problem,
2. generating ideas,
3. evaluating ideas and selecting a workable solution, and
4. implementing the solution.

In redefining and analyzing a problem, information is collected and organized, the data and underlying assumptions are analyzed, and the problem is reexamined from new perspectives. At this stage, the goal of the problem solver is to collect facts and achieve a useful problem definition. The purpose of generating ideas is to develop novel solutions. After ideas have been generated, they are evaluated and the best one is identified and selected. Finally, the solution must be put to work, for example, by making changes to processes or procedures. We discuss some of the more popular approaches.

The Deming Cycle

One of the earliest approaches focused on quality improvement that can be learned and applied by everyone in an organization is the Deming Cycle. The **Deming Cycle** is a methodology for improvement, based on the premise that improvement comes from the application of knowledge.[20] Knowledge of engineering, management, or operations may make a process easier, more accurate, faster, less costly, safer, or better suited to customer needs. Three fundamental questions to consider are

1. What are we trying to accomplish?
2. What changes can we make that will result in improvement?
3. How will we know that a change is an improvement?

This methodology was originally called the Shewhart Cycle after Walter Shewhart, its founder, but was renamed for Deming by the Japanese in 1950.

The Deming Cycle is composed of four stages: Plan, Do, Study, Act (Figure 6.3). Sometimes it is called the PDSA cycle. The Plan stage consists of studying the current situation, gathering data, and planning for improvement. In the Do stage, the plan is implemented on a trial basis in a laboratory, pilot production process, or with a small group of customers. The Study stage is designed to determine whether the trial plan is working correctly and to see whether any further problems or opportunities can be found. The last stage, Act, is the implementation of the final plan to ensure that the improvements will be standardized and practiced continuously. This leads back to the Plan stage for further diagnosis and improvement (see box "Crying Out for the Deming Cycle" on page 242).

FIGURE 6.3   THE DEMING CYCLE

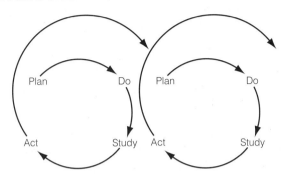

As Figure 6.3 suggests, this cycle is never ending. That is, it is focused on continuous improvement, so the improved standards serve as a springboard for further improvements. This distinguishes it from more traditional problem-solving approaches and is one of the essential elements of the Deming philosophy.

Six Sigma DMAIC Methodology

The standard problem-solving approach used in Six Sigma is known as DMAIC—Define, Measure, Analyze, Improve, and Control.

1. Define

After a Six Sigma project is selected, the first step is to clearly define the problem. This activity is significantly different from project selection. Project selection generally responds to symptoms of a problem and usually results in a rather vague problem statement. One must describe the problem in operational terms that facilitate further analysis. For example, a firm might have a history of poor reliability of electric motors it manufactures, resulting in a Six Sigma project to improve motor reliability. A preliminary investigation of warranty and field service repair data might suggest that the source of most problems was brush wear, and more specifically, suggest a problem with brush hardness variability. Thus, the problem might be defined as "reduce the variability of brush hardness." This process of drilling down to a more specific problem statement is sometimes called **project scoping.**

A good problem statement also should identify customers and the CTQs that have the most impact on product or service performance, describe the current level of performance or the nature of errors or customer complaints, identify the relevant performance metrics, benchmark best performance standards, calculate the cost/ revenue implications of the project, and quantify the expected level of performance from a successful Six Sigma effort. The Define phase should also address such project management issues as what will need to be done, by whom, and when.

Crying Out for the Deming Cycle[21]

Kevin Dooley and his wife applied the Deming Cycle and various quality tools to help stop their infant daughter from crying whenever her diaper was changed, which as any new parent or older sibling knows, can break your heart or drive you crazy.

Their first cycle involved creating an experiment to determine the percentage of time crying while on the diaper changing table (Plan); collecting data on 15 diaper changes and plotting them on a run chart (Do); observing that the data appeared to be random (Study); and focusing on the steps involved in the changing process (Act). The second cycle involved developing a flowchart to document the steps in changing a diaper (Plan); constructing the chart (Do); studying the process (which did not appear complex or incorrect—Study); and deciding to seek other causes (Act).

Cycles 3, 4, and 5 involved developing a cause-and-effect diagram, collecting data to test the hypothesis that the type of outfit worn caused her to cry more (studied with a Pareto diagram), and looking for correlations between the time crying and the time since last changing. In cycle 6, the Dooleys collected data to determine whether she cried less when being changed by her mother. Histograms confirmed a difference between the parents! Cycle 7 was to observe what Kevin's wife did differently (Plan); make a list of key differences (Do); study the differences—his wife had captured the baby's attention better—and develop some attention-getting strategies (Act).

The last cycle implemented these, and data indeed confirmed an improvement! We're sure the Dooleys can't wait to apply the Deming Cycle to their daughter's driving . . .

2. Measure

This phase of the DMAIC process focuses on how to measure the internal processes that impact CTQs. It requires an understanding of the causal relationships between process performance and customer value. However, once they are understood, procedures for gathering facts—collecting good data, observation, and careful listening—must be defined and implemented. Data from existing production processes and practices often provide important information, as does feedback from supervisors, workers, customers, and field service employees.

3. Analyze

A major flaw in many problem-solving approaches is a lack of emphasis on rigorous analysis. Too often, we want to jump to a solution without fully understanding the nature of the problem and identifying the source of the problem. The Analyze phase of DMAIC focuses on *why* defects, errors, or excessive variation occur.

After potential variables are identified, experiments are conducted to verify them. These experiments generally consist of formulating some hypothesis to investigate, collecting data, analyzing the data, and reaching a reasonable and statistically supportable conclusion. Statistical thinking and analysis plays a critical role in this phase. It is one of the reasons why statistics is an important part of Six Sigma training (and one that engineering and many business curricula often ignore). Other experiments might employ computer simulation techniques.

4. Improve

Once the root cause of a problem is understood, the analyst or team needs to generate ideas for removing or resolving the problem and improve the performance measures and CTQs. This idea-gathering phase is a highly creative activity, because many solutions are not obvious. One of the difficulties in this task is the natural instinct to prejudge ideas before thoroughly evaluating them. Most people have a natural fear of proposing a "silly" idea or looking foolish. However, such ideas may actually form the basis for a creative and useful solution. Effective problem solvers must learn to defer judgment and develop the ability to generate a large number of ideas at this stage of the process, whether practical or not.

After a set of ideas have been proposed, it is necessary to evaluate them and select the most promising. This process includes confirming that the proposed solution will positively impact the key process variables and the CTQs, and identifying the maximum acceptable ranges of these variables.

Problem solutions often entail technical or organizational changes. Often some sort of decision or scoring model is used to assess possible solutions against important criteria such as cost, time, quality improvement potential, resources required, effects on supervisors and workers, and barriers to implementation such as resistance to change or organizational culture. To implement a solution effectively, responsibility must be assigned to a person or a group who will follow through on what must be done, where it will be done, when it will be done, and how it will be done.

5. Control

The Control phase focuses on how to maintain the improvements, which includes putting tools in place to ensure that the key variables remain within the maximum acceptable ranges under the modified process. These improvements might include establishing the new standards and procedures, training the workforce, and instituting controls to make sure that improvements do not die over time. Controls might be as simple as using checklists or periodic status reviews to ensure that proper procedures are followed, or employing statistical process control charts to monitor the performance of key measures. These topics are discussed in Chapter 7.

The box on American Express shows an example of the DMAIC process.

Using DMAIC at American Express[22]

American Express used Six Sigma to improve the number of customers who received renewal cards. (In this example, data have been masked to protect confidentiality.) A brief description of how DMAIC was applied follows.

Define and Measure: On average in 1999, American Express received 1,000 returned renewal cards each month. Of these renewals, 65 percent are due to the fact that the card members changed their addresses and did not tell the company. The U.S. Post Office calls these forwardable addresses. American Express does not currently notify a card member when they receive a returned plastic card.

Analyze: Analysis of the data noted significant differences in the causes of returned plastics between product types. Optima, the revolving card product, had the highest incidence of defects, but was not significantly different from other card types in the percentage of defects. Renewals had by far the highest defect rate among the three areas of replacement, renewal, and new accounts. After additional testing, returns with forwardable addresses were overwhelmingly the largest percentage and quantity of returns.

Improve: An experimental pilot study was run on all renewal files issued, comparing records against the National Change of Address database. As a result, they were able to reduce the dpmo (defects per million opportunities) rate by 44.5 percent, from 13,500 to 6,036 defects per million opportunities. This action enabled over 1,200 card members who would not have automatically received their credit cards to receive them, increasing revenue and customer satisfaction.

Control: American Express began tracking the proportion of returns over time as a means of monitoring the new process to ensure that it remains in control.

Lean Thinking

Lean production refers to approaches initially developed by the Toyota Motor Corporation that focus on the elimination of waste in all forms, including defects requiring rework, unnecessary processing steps, unnecessary movement of materials or people, waiting time, excess inventory, and overproduction. A simple way of defining it is "getting more done with less."[23] It involves identifying and eliminating non–value-added activities throughout the entire value chain to achieve faster customer response, reduced inventories, higher quality, and better human resources. As one article about Toyota observed, to see the Toyota production system in action is to "behold a thing of beauty."

Lean production is facilitated by a focus on measurement and continuous improvement, cross-trained workers, flexible and increasingly automated equipment, efficient machine layout, rapid setup and changeover, just-in-time delivery and scheduling, realistic work standards, worker empowerment to perform inspections and take corrective action, supplier partnerships, and preventive maintenance. Some of the benefits claimed by proponents of lean production include the following:

- At least 60 percent reduction in cycle times
- 40 percent improvement in space utilization
- 25 percent greater throughput
- 50 percent reduction in work-in-process and finished goods inventories
- 50 percent improvement in quality
- 20 percent improvements in working capital and worker productivity

However, as one industry expert observed, it takes "an incredible amount of detailed planning, discipline, hard work, and painstaking attention to detail." Surveys have noted that mid-sized and large companies are likely to be familiar with lean principles and have systems in place; however, few small manufacturing shops have much familiarity with the principles. Thus, considerable opportunity exists for this important economic sector.

Some of the key tools used in lean production include:

- *The 5S's.* The 5S's are derived from Japanese terms: *seiri* (sort), *seiton* (set in order), *seiso* (shine), *seiketsu* (standardize), and *shitsuke* (sustain). They define a system for workplace organization and standardization. Sort refers to ensuring that each item in a workplace is in its proper place or identified as unnecessary and removed. Set in order means to arrange materials and equipment so that they are easy to find and use. Shine refers to a clean work area. Not only is this important for safety but, as a work area is cleaned, maintenance problems such as oil leaks can be identified before they cause problems. Standardize means to formalize procedures and practices to create consistency and ensure that all steps are performed correctly. Finally, sustain means to keep the process going through training, communication, and organizational structures.
- *Visual controls.* Visual controls are indicators for tools, parts, and production activities that are placed in plain sight of all workers so that everyone can understand the status of the system at a glance. Thus, if a machine goes down, or a part is defective or delayed, immediate action can be taken.
- *Efficient layout and standardized work.* The layout of equipment and processes is designed according to the best operational sequence, by physically linking and arranging machines and process steps most efficiently, often in a cellular arrangement. Standardizing the individual tasks by clearly specifying the proper method reduces wasted human movement and energy.
- *Pull production.* In this system (also described as *kanban* or *just-in-time*), upstream suppliers do not produce until the downstream customer signals a need for parts.

- *Single minute exchange of dies (SMED).* SMED refers to rapid changeover of tooling and fixtures in machine shops so that multiple products in smaller batches can be run on the same equipment. Reducing setup time adds value to the operation and facilitates smoother production flow.
- *Total productive maintenance.* Total productive maintenance is designed to ensure that equipment is operational and available when needed.
- *Source inspection.* Inspection and control by process operators guarantees that product passed on to the next production stage conforms to specifications.
- *Continuous improvement.* Continuous improvement provides the link to Six Sigma. In order to make lean production work, one must get to the root causes of problems and permanently remove them. Teamwork is an integral part of continuous improvement in lean environments. Many techniques that we discuss in subsequent chapters are used.

One example of the application of lean concepts is found at Sunset Manufacturing, Inc., of Tualatin, Oregon, a 35-person, family-owned machine shop.[24] Because of competitive pressures and a business downturn, Sunset began to look for ways to simplify operations and cut costs. They established a lean steering committee to coordinate and drive the process. The committee chartered a kaizen team to reduce setup time on vertical milling machines by 50 percent. The team used SMED and the 5S's approach as their basic tools. Several actions were taken, including: (1) standardizing parts across milling machines; (2) reorganizing the tool room; (3) incorporating the SMED approach in machine setups; and (4) and implementing what was termed "dance cards," which gave operators the specific steps required for the SMED of various machines and products. The results were impressive. Tool preparation time dropped from an average of 30 minutes to less than 10 minutes, isolation and identification of worn tools was improved, improved safety and appearance in the tool room due to 5S's application was apparent, machine setup time was reduced from an average of 216 minutes to 36 minutes (an 86 percent improvement). Estimated savings were $33,000 per year, with an implementation cost of less than half of that amount. The net impact was to allow smaller lots to be run, a 75 percent reduction in setup scrap, emergence of a more competitive organization, and a morale boost for team members.

Lean production can easily be applied to nonmanufacturing environments. Pure service firms such as banks, hospitals, and restaurants have benefited from lean principles. In these contexts, lean production is often called **lean enterprise.** For example, banks require quick response and efficiency to operate on low margins, making many of their processes, such as check sorting and mortgage approval, natural candidates for lean enterprise solutions.[25] Handling of paper checks and credit card slips, for instance, involves a physical process not unlike an assembly line. The faster a bank moves checks through its system, the sooner it can collect its funds and the better its returns on invested capital.

Six Sigma is a useful and complementary approach to lean production. For example, a cycle time reduction project might involve aspects of both. Lean tools might be applied to streamline an order entry process. This application leads to the discovery that significant rework occurs because of incorrect addresses, customer numbers, or shipping charges and results in high variation of processing time. Six Sigma tools might then be used to drill down to the root cause of the problems and identify a solution. Because of these similarities, many industry training programs and consultants have begun to focus on "Lean Six Sigma," drawing upon the best practices of both approaches. Both are driven by customer requirements, focus on real dollar savings, have the ability to make significant financial impacts on the organization, and can be used in non-manufacturing environments.

However, some differences clearly exist between lean production and Six Sigma. First, they attack different types of problems. Lean production addresses visible problems in processes, for example, inventory, material flow, and safety. Six Sigma is more concerned with less visible problems, for example, variation in performance. Another difference is that lean tools are more intuitive and easier to apply by anybody in the workplace, whereas many Six Sigma tools require advanced training and expertise of Black Belt or Master Black Belt specialists, or consultant equivalents. For example, the concept of the 5S's is easier to grasp than statistical methods. Thus, organizations might be well advised to start with basic lean principles and evolve toward more sophisticated Six Sigma approaches.

BREAKTHROUGH IMPROVEMENT

Breakthrough improvement refers to discontinuous change, as opposed to the gradual, continuous improvement philosophy of kaizen. Breakthrough improvements result from innovative and creative thinking; often these are motivated by **stretch goals**, or **breakthrough objectives**. Stretch goals force an organization to think in a radically different way, and to encourage major improvements as well as incremental ones. When a goal of 10 percent improvement is set, managers or engineers can usually meet it with some minor improvements. However, when the goal is 1,000 percent improvement, employees must be creative and think "out of the box." The seemingly impossible is often achieved, yielding dramatic improvements and boosting morale.

Two approaches for breakthrough improvement that help companies achieve breakthrough improvement are benchmarking and reengineering.

Benchmarking

Benchmarking is the search for best practices that will lead to superior performance. Benchmarking helps a company learn its strengths and weaknesses—and those of other leading organizations—and incorporate the best practices into its own operations. The term **best practices** refers to approaches that produce exceptional results, are usually innovative in terms of the use of technology or human resources, and are recognized by customers or industry experts. Through benchmarking, a company discovers its strengths and weaknesses and those of other industrial leaders and learns how to incorporate the best practices into its own operations. Benchmarking can provide motivation by helping employees to see what others can accomplish. For example, to meet a stretch target of reducing the time to build new 747 and 767 airplanes at Boeing from 18 months (in 1992) to 8 months, teams studied the world's best producers of everything from computers to ships. By 1996 the time had been reduced to 10 months.[26]

Modern benchmarking was initiated by Xerox, an eventual winner of the Malcolm Baldrige National Quality Award. Xerox initially studied its direct competitors and discovered that

- its unit manufacturing cost equaled the Japanese selling price in the United States,
- the number of production suppliers was nine times that of the best companies,
- assembly-line rejects were ten times higher,
- product lead times were twice as long, and
- defects per hundred machines were seven times higher.

These results helped Xerox to understand the amount of change that would be required and to set realistic targets to guide its planning efforts.

Two major types of benchmarking are competitive and generic. *Competitive benchmarking* usually focuses on the products and manufacturing of a company's competitors, as Xerox initially did. *Generic benchmarking* evaluates processes or business functions against the best companies, regardless of their industry. Xerox recognized the potential for improving all business processes and realized that better practices in service companies and other types of manufacturing firms could be adapted to its operations. For example, the warehousing and distribution practices of L.L. Bean were adopted by Xerox. Thus, benchmarking should not be aimed solely at direct competitors (see box "Smart Bombs and Pink Cadillacs" on page 250).

In order to be effective, benchmarking must be applied to all facets of a business. For example, Motorola encourages everyone in the organization to ask "Who is the best person in my own field and how might I use some of their techniques and characteristics to improve my own performance in order to be the best (executive, machine operator, chef, purchasing agent, and so on) in my 'class'"?

The benchmarking process can be described as follows:

1. *Determine which functions to benchmark.* These should have a significant impact on business performance and key dimensions of competitiveness. If fast response is an important dimension of competitive advantage,

then processes that might be benchmarked would include order processing, purchasing, production planning, and product distribution. There also should be an indication that the potential for improvement exists.

2. *Identify key performance indicators to measure.* These should have a direct link to customer needs and expectations. Typical performance indicators are quality, performance, and delivery.

3. *Identify the best-in-class companies.* For specific business functions, benchmarking might be limited to the same industry: a bank in one state might benchmark the check-processing operations of a bank in another state. For generic business functions, it is best to look outside one's own industry: a university financial aid office might benchmark a bank's loan operation, for example. Selecting companies requires knowledge of which firms are superior performers in the key areas. Such information can be obtained from published reports and articles, industry experts, trade magazines, professional associations, former employees, or customers and suppliers.

4. *Measure the performance of the best-in-class companies and compare the results to your own performance.* Such information might be found in published sources or might require site visits and in-depth interviews.

5. *Define and take actions to meet or exceed the best performance.* This usually requires changing organizational systems. Simply trying to emulate the best is like shooting at a moving target—their processes will continually improve. Therefore, attempts should be made to exceed the performance of the best.

Briefly, benchmarking is the search for best practices in any company, in any industry, anywhere in the world, and reengineering is the radical redesign of business processes to achieve significant improvements in performance. As an example of benchmarking, when Granite Rock could not find any company that was measuring on-time delivery of concrete, it talked with Domino's Pizza, a worldwide leader in on-time delivery of a rapidly perishable product (a characteristic shared with freshly mixed concrete) to acquire new ideas for measuring and improving its processes. By observing how a NASCAR pit crew worked, General Mills was able to cut the time it took workers to change a production line from one Betty Crocker product to another from 4.5 hours to 12 minutes. It also looked at how Stealth bomber pilots and maintenance crews cooperated and improved its own teamwork, cutting production costs by 25 percent at one plant.[27]

To illustrate the concept of reengineering, Intel Corporation previously used a 91-step process costing thousands of dollars to purchase ballpoint pens—the same process used to purchase forklift trucks! The improved process was reduced to eight steps. In rethinking its purpose as a customer-driven, retail service company rather than a manufacturing company, Taco Bell eliminated the kitchen from its restaurants. Meat and beans are cooked outside the restaurant at central commissaries and reheated. Other food

Smart Bombs and Pink Cadillacs

Although Xerox is credited with developing modern approaches to bench-marking, the concept of benchmarking is not new.[28] In the early 1800s, Francis Lowell, a New England industrialist, traveled to England to study manufacturing techniques of the best British mill factories. Henry Ford created the assembly line after taking a tour of a Chicago slaughterhouse and watching carcasses, hung on hooks mounted on a monorail, move from one work station to another. Toyota's just-in-time production system was influenced by replenishment practices of U.S. supermarkets. Convex Computer Corporation sent its facilities manager to Disney World to see what they could learn about facilities management. And Texas Instrument's former Defense Systems and Electronics Group, makers of "smart bombs" and other advanced weapon systems, studied the kitting (order preparation) practices of six companies, including Mary Kay Cosmetics (the pink Cadillac being a reward to their top salespeople), and designed a process that captured the best practices of each of them, cutting kitting cycle time in half.

items such as diced tomatoes, onions, and olives are prepared off-site. This innovation saved about 11 million hours of work and $7 million per year over the entire chain.

Reengineering

Reengineering (also known as process redesign) is focused on "break-through" improvement to dramatically improve the quality and speed of work and to reduce its cost by fundamentally changing the processes by which work gets done (see the box on Procter & Gamble).

Reengineering involves asking basic questions about business processes: Why do we do it? and Why is it done this way? Such questioning often uncovers obsolete, erroneous, or inappropriate assumptions. Reengineering is often used when the improvements needed are so great that incremental changes to operations will not get the job done. Ten percent improvements can be created by tinkering, but 50 percent improvements call for process redesign. The goal is to achieve quantum leaps in performance. For example, IBM Credit Corporation cut the process of financing IBM computers, software, and services from seven days to four hours by rethinking the process. Originally, the process was designed to handle difficult applications and required four highly trained specialists and a series of handoffs. The actual work took only about 1.5 hours; the rest of the time was spent in transit or delay. By questioning the assumption that every application was unique and difficult to process, IBM Credit Corporation was able to replace the specialists

---

Reengineering for Cycle Time Reduction at Procter & Gamble

One example of a reengineering effort to reduce cycle time was carried out by Procter & Gamble's over-the-counter (OTC) clinical division, which conducts clinical studies that involve testing drugs, health care products, or treatments in humans.[29] Such testing follows rigorous design, conduct, analysis, and summary of the data collected. P&G had at least four different ways to perform a clinical study and needed to find the best way to meet its research and development needs. They chose to focus on cycle time reduction. Their approach built on fundamental TQ principles: focusing on the customer, fact-based decisions, continual improvement, empowerment, the right leadership structure, and an understanding of work processes. An example is shown in Figure 6.4. The team found that final reports took months to prepare. Only by mapping the existing process did they fully understand the causes of long production times and the amount of rework and recycling during review and signoff. By restructuring the activities from sequential to parallel work and identifying critical measurements to monitor the process, they were able to reduce the time to less than four weeks.

---

by a single individual supported by a user-friendly computer system that provided access to all the data and tools that the specialists would use.

The irony of reengineering is that, once the new process is in place, people often feel that the new way of operating is so much better, they should have thought of it long ago. Another common reaction is "Why did we ever do it like that in the first place?" The answer is often, "That's the way we've always done it." GE Chairman Jack Welch has compared his company to a 100-year-old attic, which has collected a lot of useless junk over the years.

Process redesign (called *Work-Out* in GE jargon) is the process of cleaning all the junk out of the attic.[30] Often the old ways of doing things were a function of administrative, rather than customer-centered, thinking. In one plant, a product was boxed and wrapped to be sent from one side of the plant to the other, only to be unwrapped and unboxed. Why? Because the two parts of the plant were separate profit centers, and the first had to "sell" the product to the second!

If a process is driven by an administrative logic such as cost accounting or functional specialization, it is ripe for reengineering.[31] The importance of process redesign to quality improvement can be seen in Figure 6.5, based on the work of Professor Asbjorn Aune of Norway.[32] Process is what connects customer expectations to the products or services they receive. It is what ensures (or fails to ensure) that products meet or exceed customer expectations.

FIGURE **6.4**   FINAL REPORT "IS" AND "SHOULD" PROCESS DESIGN

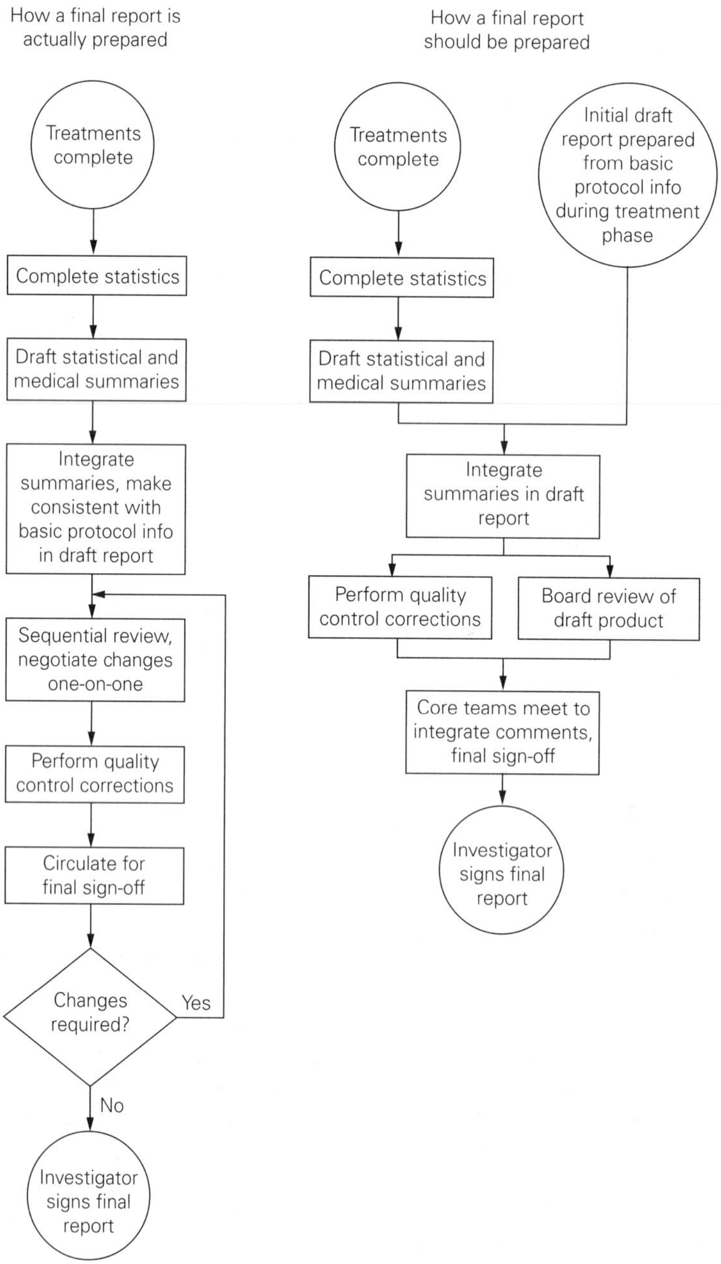

How a final report is
actually prepared

How a final report
should be prepared

Source: David A. McCamey, Robert W. Bogs, and Linda M. Bayuk, "More, Better, Faster from Total Quality Effort," *Quality Progress*, August 1999, pp. 43–50. © 1999 American Society for Quality. Reprinted with permission.

FIGURE 6.5   THE KEY ROLE OF PROCESS

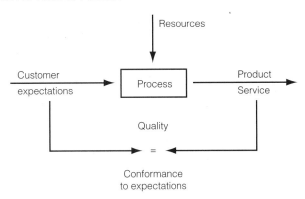

Principles of Process Redesign

Waste is the enemy of effective processes. Reducing waste of any kind encompasses both TQ and JIT practices and is a central theme in Japanese manufacturing management. Poor processes waste time, money, material, effort, and customer good will. Redesigning processes to reduce waste is, at this point at least, more an art than a science. Every process redesign is unique, but the general principles of redesign include:[33]

1. *Reduce handoffs*. Every time a process is handed from one person or group to another, errors can occur (think of passing the baton in a relay race). Time is often wasted as one group waits for the other to finish or needs to consult with the first group before continuing.
2. *Eliminate steps*. The best way to save time on a step is not to do it at all. If the step does not add value to the product or service or make the product more attractive to customers, stop doing it. In manufacturing organizations, moving, storing, and inspecting products rarely add value and should be eliminated wherever possible.
3. *Perform steps in parallel rather than in sequence*. Unless one operation cannot be done until another is finished, why not do them both at once? Many organizations operate like two people doing the dishes, where one washes all the dishes that will fit in the drainer, then calls the other to dry them. When the drying is done, the dryer calls the washer back in and leaves again. Stupid? Yes, but that's the way they've always done it.
4. *Involve key people early*. The point of this is to avoid doing things over when key people do not give their input until the process is under way. For years, manufacturing companies have had their engineers design entire products before consulting the manufacturing engineers who will have to build them. The manufacturing engineers would then suggest a number of changes that the designers would reluctantly incorporate into

their designs. Many firms recently have changed this process to allow early involvement of manufacturing.[34] This is one of the most common forms of process reengineering and is consistent with the TQ principle, "Do it right the first time!"

Organizational Issues in Process Design and Improvement[35]

Process design and improvement are difficult activities to accomplish in many organizations, yet represent one of the most common types of organizational change. Success rates, however, are far from satisfactory. The organizational literature addresses the factors that facilitate or inhibit successful implementation. For example, one research study identified two factors critical to the long-term success of reengineering initiatives:

1. *Breadth*: the extent to which the process maps onto the dimensions of the business, from a single activity in one function to spanning the entire business unit; and
2. *Depth*: how many of the "depth levers"—structure, skills, IT systems, roles, measurements/incentives, and shared values—are manipulated.

Others have investigated resistance to change, top management support, diversity of human resources involved, methodological rigor, and the pay-offs associated with these efforts. Interestingly, some data suggest that success is more likely when sponsorship is strong; when mid-level managers, rather than top executives, sponsor the projects; and when fact-based measurements drive the efforts (failed projects were often described qualitatively). In Chapter 11, we shall discuss organizational change further.

PROCESS MANAGEMENT IN ACTION

Many organizations have made substantial improvements by applying process management, continuous improvement, and organizational learning principles. This section highlights some of them.

Chugach School District[36]

The Chugach School District (CSD) is located in Southcentral Alaska and includes most of the Prince William Sound coastline and islands. With less than 20 full-time faculty, CSD serves students scattered throughout 22,000 square miles of isolated and remote area. Some village and school sites are 100% Aleut (Native Alaskan), while other sites include heterogeneous groups. The Chugach School District is fairly representative of "Bush Alaska" in regard to the obstacles standing in the way of educational excellence, including high unemployment and poverty, and various social problems in the communities served. Students receive educational services in one of three small villages, accessible by small aircraft, or from itinerant teachers who regularly visit wilderness homes in the Valdez and Fairbanks regions through the Extension School Program.

A comprehensive restructuring effort was initiated in 1994. Using input from schools, communities and businesses, CSD realigned its curriculum to create ten performance-based standards; mathematics, science, technology, reading, writing, social sciences, service learning, career development, cultural awareness and expression, and personal/ social/health development. Individual Learning Plans (ILP), Student Assessment Binders (SAB), Student Learning Profiles (SLP), and Student Lifeskills Portfolios support and document consistent progress toward proficiency in all standards. CSD developed performance standards continuums for all content areas.

The success of CSD's educational programs and services lies in the design and delivery of their educational processes and continuous improvement efforts as seen in Figure 6.6. The processes maintain a focus on students with student input garnered from beginning to end. The design process integrates customer requirements from all stakeholders to secure a powerful shared vision, which can be supported by all. Action plans drove the design of this process. The process is simple, efficient, effective and includes evaluation and refinement segments to continually improve each step of the process, as well as the process itself.

A key process is the Chugach Instructional Model (CIM), which has been continuously improved and now encompasses clear and effective teaching methods. The CIM is summarized in Figure 6.7. This instructional methodology aims to create real-life learning situations in all content areas. Chugach has developed a process for creating thematic units, which allow teachers to

FIGURE 6.6   CSD EDUCATIONAL DESIGN AND DELIVERY PROCESSES

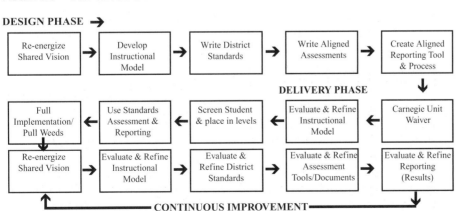

FIGURE 6.7   CHUGACH INSTRUCTIONAL MODEL

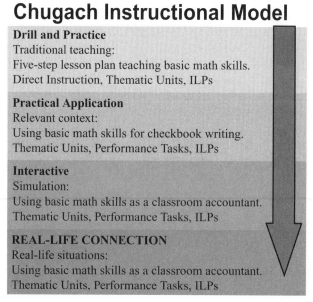

Chugach Instructional Model

Drill and Practice
Traditional teaching:
Five-step lesson plan teaching basic math skills.
Direct Instruction, Thematic Units, ILPs

Practical Application
Relevant context:
Using basic math skills for checkbook writing.
Thematic Units, Performance Tasks, ILPs

Interactive
Simulation:
Using basic math skills as a classroom accountant.
Thematic Units, Performance Tasks, ILPs

REAL-LIFE CONNECTION
Real-life situations:
Using basic math skills as a classroom accountant.
Thematic Units, Performance Tasks, ILPs

Source: Chugach School District.

design contextual units relevant to students. The Chugach staff participates in this process every April to plan for the following year. Thematic units directly support the purpose of the CIM, which is to help teachers make a connection with students' performance levels and the theme being developed. Thematic units teach relationships among disciplines. 1By its nature and definition it is expansive, respecting no walls with names like math, science, social studies, and art. Thematic units, put simply, take and nurture the natural propensity of humans to make connections between disciplines.

The Student Learning Profile has been developed to help teachers anticipate the whole child and facilitate learning, not just the intellectual system. It helps students to understand themselves as learners with unique patterns. CSD anticipated this revolutionary approach as a need by CSD after years of trial and error and stakeholder input. Each student's intellectual, emotional, and volitional development patterns are identified and used to better focus instruction for each student. Cognitive, emotional, and values information gained through testing is at the teachers' and students' fingertips to focus instruction and learning.

A unique feature of CSD is the lack of grade levels. One student may work in level V Math for a year while another student the same age masters the same level in four months and moves on to level VI. Developmental levels are the levels at which students are working, based on what is known about how children and youth develop, learn, and demonstrate their learning at various ages. The students' performance levels coincide with the developmental levels of the Chugach developmental report card. The levels permit students to work at their own rate continually. An Individual Learning Plan is a custom-designed document written and used by students, teachers, and parents to meet the educational needs of the individual student. Goals are identified and tied to standards focusing on student-driven performance, implementation, and accountability. The ILP anticipates individual differences and allows every child in the system to design their education by setting goals. Students create and achieve ILP goals throughout the year.

These processes have had remarkable results. National percentile scores on the California Achievement Test in reading increased from 28.44 to 71.1 between 1995 and 1999; in language from 26.46 to 71.9; in math from 53.6 to 78.1; and in spelling from 22 to 65. Chugach was the only school district in the United States to be awarded the New American High School Award, a national award earned by top performing high schools, and in addition, was one of the first education sector winners of the Malcolm Baldrige National Quality Award in 2001.

Froedtert Hospital[37]

Medication administration and laboratory processing/results reporting are examples of complex systems in health care that are known to be error prone. At Froedtert Hospital in Milwaukee, Wisconsin, errors with IV medication drips and laboratory processing and results reporting were well documented. Additionally, errors in ordering, transporting, analyzing, and reporting clinical laboratory tests were known to be a significant source of error at the hospital. A consortium was created by four Milwaukee-based organizations committed to the development of an approach to use Six Sigma to reduce errors and improve patient safety.

The design employed the classic Six Sigma DMAIC process. A multidisciplinary group of physicians, nurses, pharmacists, and administrators identified medication delivery by continuous IV infusions as a process subject to substantial error. Continuous IV infusions are used in many clinical settings and errors can severely impact patient well-being. Team members developed a process map (flowchart) to delineate each step in the procedure for continuous IV medication infusion: (1) physician order, (2) order review, (3) pharmacist order entry, (4) dose preparation, (5) dose dispensing, (6) infusion rate calculation, (7) IV pump setup, (8) pump programming, and (9) pump monitoring. Each of the steps was analyzed to identify possible points of failure and effects of failures based on frequency of occurrence, detectability, and severity. The analysis confirmed that IV rate calculations and IV pump setup were the two most error-prone steps in the IV infusion process, and initial efforts to determine the causes and reduce errors focused on these two steps. Specific interventions included implementation of standardized physician order sheets, a policy requiring preparation of all IV medications in a standard concentration, and use of color-coded labels when nonstandard concentrations were in use. Thirty days after implementation, measurable improvement was evident. Level 1 discrepancies fell from 47.4 percent to 14 percent. Level 2 discrepancies fell from 21.1 percent to 11.8 percent and level 3 discrepancies fell from 15.8 percent to 2.9 percent.

Using Six Sigma methods and statistical tools, the team also examined the hospital's clinical laboratory process. Key elements in the acquisition, laboratory analysis, and reporting of patient specimens were identified. The steps included (1) physician order, (2) order entry, (3) matching the order to the patient, (4) collecting the specimen, (5) labeling the specimen, (6) transporting the specimen, (7) analyzing the specimen, (8) reporting the results, and (9) entering the results into the patient's chart. Each of these steps is subject to error. Applying Six Sigma analysis, the most critical steps leading to errors were: order entry by the unit clerical staff, transportation of the specimens to the lab, and analysis of specimens in the lab. A laboratory error reduction task force was established that included members from administration, lab, nursing, clerical staff, information systems, and quality management. The task force used various Six Sigma tools to analyze the clinical laboratory problem in depth and prioritize the steps in the laboratory analysis in terms of their vulnerability to error.

The Walt Disney Company

One unusual example is provided by the Walt Disney Company.[38] The opening of Euro Disneyland in 1992 near Marne la Vallee, France, brought to four the number of parks operated around the world by the Walt Disney Company. Disneyland, the original, opened in 1955 in Anaheim, California. Disney World, in Orlando, Florida, opened in 1971 and was expanded in 1982 to include Epcot Center and later MGM Studios Theme Park. Tokyo Disneyland, Disney's first overseas park, opened in 1983.

Disney faced a difficult challenge in bringing its American style of fun to the French people, who are often ambivalent at best about American cultural imperialism. The opening of Euro Disney was not without problems, as Disney faced labor disputes over its personal appearance policies, such as no facial hair, and substantial difficulties with getting construction work done on time and under budget. The company anticipated and tried to defuse any cross-cultural difficulties through an exchange of hundreds of European and American managers.

One major advantage possessed by Disney in establishing its European park was its ability to learn from its past successes, as well as its past mistakes. When the original park was opened in Anaheim, it was quickly surrounded by hotels and restaurants that competed with Disney's own. This mistake was not repeated either in Orlando, where Disney bought 28,000 acres (much of which is still unused), or in France.

Disney built six hotels for the opening of Euro Disney, far more than would be immediately needed. Why? The company had dragged its heels in building hotels in Florida, allowing competitors to become established.

Almost unbelievably, the plans for Euro Disney (to be completed in 2017) call for an additional 4,000 hotel rooms, a retail and industrial park, and even 8,000 private homes. When one thinks of continuous improvement, processes that are repeated every hour, day, or week come to mind. However, Disney has applied continuous improvement to the process of park design, which it has practiced only about every 10 years!

General Electric[39]

Jack Welch, former CEO of General Electric for over 20 years, has been recognized as one of the greatest corporate leaders of the twentieth century. In his first letter to GE shareholders in 1981, he noted that "This commitment to the utmost in quality and personal excellence is our surest path to continued business success. Quality is our best assurance of customer allegiance. It is our strongest defense against foreign competition and the only path to sustained growth and earnings." Mr. Welch's approach to business improvement has gone through three cycles of learning:

1. In the first cycle (early 1980s to late 1980s), he focused GE on the elimination of variety in its portfolio of businesses by reducing the nonperforming business units as judged by market performance. The elimination of unprofitable businesses permitted a better use of working capital. However, only so much gain can result from trimming the organization or eliminating bureaucracy. This led to the next phase of learning.
2. During the late 1980s to mid-1990s, he focused the company on simplifying and eliminating non–value-added activities through creative efforts of teams using Work-Outs and the Change Action Process (later renamed the Change Acceleration Process). Work-Out is a tool for involving all people from all ranks, levels, and functions of the organization for problem solving and improvement. Work-Out demolished the artificial barriers and walls within the organization and fostered the idea of "boundaryless learning."
3. Throughout his learning journey, Welch had challenged his people to keep looking for creative ways to apply new learning from any source to improve the business. In 1995, Welch discovered Six Sigma and studied its implementation at both Motorola and Allied Signal. This phase of discovery focused on the elimination of variation from already lean business operations to drive gains in productivity and financial performance with a better focus on the customer.

Welch's process for continuous learning led to the discovery that business must simplify first, then automate best practice that has been designed for robust performance in the face of variation in business conditions. As Welch noted, "It is this passion for learning and sharing that forms the basis for the unrelenting optimism with which we view the future, and for the conviction that our greatest days lie ahead."

REVIEW AND DISCUSSION QUESTIONS

1. Identify some of the key processes associated with the following business activities for a typical company: sales and marketing, supply chain management, managing information technology, and managing human resources.
2. What is process management? What are the three types of activities that it comprises?
3. Describe Motorola's approach to process design. How does this approach help to ensure high quality and performance?
4. How does service process design differ from manufacturing? What implications does it mean for both control and improvement?
5. Explain how a control system works. Provide some examples in your everyday life.
6. What is the difference between control and improvement?
7. Provide some examples of standardized processes with which you are familiar. How are they controlled? Can you identify any improvements?
8. Can you think of any company that has been successful for a long time without improving its product? What conditions have made this possible?
9. How could you apply continuous improvement methods to the job of being a student?
10. The kaizen philosophy seeks to encourage suggestions, not to find excuses for failing to improve. Typical excuses are "If it's not broken, don't fix it," "I'm too busy to work on it," and "It's not in the budget." Think of at least five other excuses why people don't try to improve.
11. How could you improve your process for studying for an exam? Getting to class on time? Cleaning your room or apartment?
12. What is the Deming Cycle? Explain the activities that comprise each step.
13. Identify a problem in your work or school activities. Outline a plan for using the Deming Cycle to improve it.
14. How might a professor use the Deming Cycle to improve his or her teaching performance?
15. Explain the Six Sigma DMAIC methodology. How is it similar to or different from the Deming Cycle?
16. What is lean thinking? Describe some of the popular tools used in lean production.
17. Explain how Six Sigma can complement lean thinking.

18. Give some examples of breakthrough improvement. How can the notion motivate workers? What must management do to ensure success?

19. Explain the concepts of benchmarking and best practices. How might these be used by students to improve learning?

20. Discuss how a college or university might apply benchmarking to improve its operations. You might solicit views from academic administrators and from business people. (You might find some differences of opinion!)

21. What is reengineering? How can benchmarking support reengineering efforts?

22. Identify a process in your school or work environment. Use the principles of process redesign to suggest improvements.

23. What might the "learning organization" concept mean to a college or university?

24. How might internal benchmarking be applied within your college? What types of activities would be appropriate?

25. Propose some reasons to support the findings that successful process improvement changes are more likely when sponsorship is strong; when mid-level managers, rather than top executives, sponsor the projects; and when fact-based measurements drive the efforts.

CASES

The Machine That Didn't Change the World[40]

Mike Weaver, president of Weaver Popcorn Company of Van Buren, Indiana, had always believed that if the customer was not happy with an order, the only thing to do was to take it back. "No sale is complete if the customer isn't satisfied," the Reverend Ira E. Weaver, company founder and Mike's grandfather, was fond of saying. What if the order was 280,000 pounds of popcorn (use your imagination), and what if it was in Tokyo, and what if it was worth $70,000? "Let's bring it back," Weaver told Pat Vogel, the company's export manager, when awakened with the bad news around midnight one evening in October 1985.

The refusal of the order by Shintoa Koeki Kaisha Ltd., on the basis of excess impurities, was a hard kernel to swallow for Weaver the man and Weaver the company. Both had regarded the order from Japan as an indication of the company's ability to sell popcorn to anybody, anywhere. How could the company recover its quality image in the face of such an embarrassment?

A few months later, trucks pulled up to the Weaver plant bearing $1 million worth of high-speed optical scanners. The new machines would subject anything passing beneath their electronic eyes to a coldhearted inspection, dooming to the trash heap any weed seeds, dirt clods, and soybeans trying to pass themselves off as popcorn. Goodbye foreign particles. Goodbye irate customers. Hello quality!

However, continuous improvement seldom occurs in big bangs and rarely can be accomplished simply by buying new technology. These were the quality lessons learned by Weaver in the months and years after the new equipment was installed. Although the machines couldn't solve Weaver's quality problems, they certainly made people more aware of them. Questions were raised about virtually every aspect of the operation, including the raw materials, the tools, and the people.

Things came to a head when, during a quality meeting, Marty Hall from processing informed the group that all the talk about quality was nonsense as long as Weaver was accepting popcorn that was way out of spec, for example in moisture content. Aware that the outgoing product cannot be good if the incoming raw materials are not, Hall believed that the quality efforts to date were useless.

This sparked dramatic changes in Weaver's operations. Mike Weaver began to give vastly increased responsibility for quality to people in the plant. The resigning plant manager was replaced by seven team leaders from the plant floor. Employees were brought into the process of hiring, even for managers. Hundreds of minor changes have been made by employees now sensitized to the importance of quality, which has been steadily improving. The lesson? According to Mike Weaver, "With the machines there, everybody began to see that it takes so much more than machines. Nothing has a greater impact on the quality of the corn than these people." As Mike's grandfather might have added, "Amen."

Discussion Questions

1. Would you have made the same decision as Mike Weaver to bring back the popcorn from Japan? Why or why not?
2. Did the optical scanners turn out to be a good idea?
3. Did the fact that Weaver is a family-owned business make a difference in how Mike Weaver thought about quality? Can the same attitude be created in shareholder-owned companies?
4. What elements of the company had to change for the quality of the popcorn to improve?
5. Can quality ever be completely automated so that people don't make any difference?

Metropolitan Water Works

The Metropolitan Water Works (MWW) serves approximately 1.5 million customers in a major city. Its billing system allows customer service representatives (CSRs) to retrieve information from customer accounts quickly using almost any piece of data such as customer name, address, phone number, social security number, and so on. Besides a customer's account history, the system contains everything that was said in a call, including documentation of past problems and their resolution. An integrated voice response system provides automated phone support for bill paying and account balances, tells customers of the approximate wait time to speak to a CSR, and allows the customers to leave a message for a CSR to return a call. An information board in the department shows the number of customers waiting, average length of time waiting, and the number of CSRs that are busy and doing postcall work. A pop-up screen provides CSRs with customer data before the phone rings so that he or she will have the customer's information before they even say hello. Work orders taken by CSRs, such as a broken water main or leaking meter, are routed automatically to a field service supervisor for immediate attention. This system is also used internally to allocate maintenance workers when a problem arises at a pumping station or treatment facility. A geographic information system is used for mapping the locations of water mains and fire hydrants, and provides field service employees, meter readers, and contractors exact information to accomplish their work. Handheld meter readers are used to locate meters and download data into computers. Touch pad devices provide exterior connections to inside meters, eliminating the necessity to enter a house or building. MWW is also investigating automated meter readers and radio frequency devices that simply require a company van to drive by the building to automatically obtain readings.

Discuss how technology has affected the processes of MWW. What specific types of improvements (quality, cycle time, etc.) were these applications designed to address? Can you think of similar uses of these technologies in other service applications?

Process Redesign at McDonald's[41]

McDonald's used to make food to stock, storing sandwiches in a large tray used to fulfill customer orders. When sales went flat in the mid-1990s and independent market testing showed a widening gap with competition in food quality, McDonald's recognized that the make-to-stock process was not meeting customer demands. After five years of lab and market testing, McDonald's rolled out the new "Just for You" system, which began in March 1998, to create a make-to-order environment. This shift required a massive change in technology with computers to coordinate orders; food production equipment using "rapid toasters" and temperature-controlled "launching zones" to replace the old heat lamps and holding bins; new food preparation tables, and retraining efforts for the entire domestic food production organization of more than 600,000 crew members. However, this system has apparently backfired. Sales did not improve as expected and customers complained about slow service. The new system increased the average service time two to three minutes per order, and 15-minute waits were not uncommon.

McDonald's stock price decreased, and rivals such as Wendy's captured additional market share.

What lessons does this experience suggest for process management? What might McDonald's have done differently?

ENDNOTES

1. AT&T Quality Steering Committee, Process Quality Management & Improvement Guidelines, AT&T Publication Center, AT&T Bell Laboratories (1987).
2. Lucas Conley, "90,000 DVDs. No Shelves," *Fast Company*, September 2003, p. 38.
3. Kelly Scott, "How Federal Express Delivers Customer Service," *APICS—The Performance Advantage*, November 1999, pp. 44–46.
4. Rebecca Duray and Glenn W. Milligan, "Improving Customer Satisfaction Through Mass Customization," *Quality Progress*, August 1999, pp. 60–66.
5. Sarah Anne Wright, "Putting Fast-Food to the Test," *Cincinnati Enquirer*, July 9, 2000, F1, 2; and David Grainger, "Can McDonald's Cook Again?" *Fortune*, April 14, 2003, pp. 120–129.
6. John Haywood-Farmer, "A Conceptual Model of Service Quality," *International Journal of Operations and Production Management* 8, No. 6 (1988), pp. 19–29.
7. "Coca-Cola: A Taste for Quality," The Coca-Cola Company, Atlanta, Georgia.
8. http://www.thecoca-colacompany.com/news/NewsDetail.asp?NewsDate=6/15/99.
9. "Testing for Conformity: An Inside Job," *Golf Journal*, May 1998, 20-25.
10. "DaimlerChrysler's Quality Practices Pay Off for PT Cruiser," News and Analysis, Metrologyworld.com (accessed March 23, 2000).
11. Adapted from The Ritz-Carlton Hotel Company, Application Summaries for the Malcolm Baldrige National Quality Award, 1992 and 1999.
12. Andrew E. Serwer, "Michael Dell Turns the PC World Inside Out," *Fortune*, September 8, 1997, pp. 76–86.
13. Lea A. P. Tonkin, "Kaizen Blitz[SM] 5: Bottleneck-Bashing Comes to Rochester, NY," *Target*, Vol. 12, No. 4, September/October 1996, pp. 41–43.
14. Mark Oakeson, "Makes Dollars & Sense for Mercedes-Benz in Brazil," *IIE Solutions*, April 1997, pp. 32–35.
15. Based on Chapter 14 in Alan Robinson (ed.), *Continuous Improvement in Operations: A Systematic Approach to Waste Reduction*. Cambridge, Mass.: Productivity Press, 1991.
16. S. Shingo, *The Sayings of Shigeo Shingo: Key Strategies for Plant Improvement*. Cambridge, Mass.: Productivity Press, 1987, p. 152.
17. See Chapter 4 for a discussion of various ways to get ideas from customers.
18. Adapted from Nancy Blodgett, "Law Firm Pioneers Explore New Territory," *Quality Progress*, April 1996, pp. 90–94.
19. Interview with Richard Buck, vice president for Quality, Portman Equipment.
20. Gerald Langley, Kevin Nolan, and Thomas Nolan, "The Foundation of Improvement," Sixth Annual International Deming User's Group Conference, Cincinnati, Ohio, August, 1992.
21. Adapted from Kevin Dooley, "Use PDSA for Crying Out Loud," *Quality Progress*, October 1997, pp. 60–63.
22. Chris Bott, Elizabeth Keim, Sai Kim, and Lisa Palser, "Service Quality Six Sigma Case Studies," ASQ's 54th Annual Congress Proceedings, 2000, 225–231.
23. Gary Conner, "Benefiting from Six Sigma," *Manufacturing Engineering* 130, No. 2, February 2003.
24. Gary Conner, "Benefiting from Six Sigma," *Manufacturing Engineering*, February 2003, pp. 53–59.
25. Anthony R. Goland, John Hall, and Devereaux A. Clifford, "First National Toyota," *The McKinsey Quarterly*, No. 4, 1998, pp. 58–66.

26. Shawn Tully, "Why to Go for Stretch Targets," *Fortune*, November 14, 1994, pp. 45–58.

27. Pallavi Gogoi, "Thinking Outside the Cereal Box," *Business Week*, July 28, 2003, pp. 74–75.

28. Christopher E. Bogan and Michael J. English, "Benchmarking for Best Practices: Winning Through Innovative Adaptation," *Quality Digest*, August 1994, pp. 52–62.

29. David A. McCamey, Robert W. Bogs, and Linda M. Bayuk, "More, Better, Faster From Total Quality Effort," *Quality Progress*, August 1999, pp. 43–50.

30. N. Tichy and R. Charan, "Speed, Simplicity, and Self-Confidence: An Interview with Jack Welch," in J. Gabarro (ed.), *Managing People and Organizations*. Boston, Mass.: Harvard Business School Publications, 1992.

31. Robinson, *Continuous Improvement*.

32. Reprinted from "Total Quality Management: Time for a Theory?" Paper presented at the EOQ Conference in Prague, 1991, by Asbjorn Aune.

33. These principles are based on Richard C. Whiteley, *The Customer-Driven Company: Moving from Talk to Action*. Reading, Mass.: Addison-Wesley, 1991.

34. See J. W. Dean, Jr., and G. I. Susman, "Organizing for Manufacturable Design," *Harvard Business Review*, January–February 1989.

35. Martin Smith, "Business Process Design: Correlates of Success and Failure," *Quality Management Journal*, 10, 2, 2003, pp. 38–49.

36. Chugach School District.

37. Adapted from Cathy Buck, "Application of Six Sigma to Reduce Medical Errors," Proceedings of the 55th Annual Quality Congress of the American Society for Quality, 2001 (CD-ROM). Reprinted with permission.

38. Based on Cheri Henderson, "Monsieur Mickey," *TQM Magazine*, September/October 1992, pp. 220–224.

39. Gregory H. Watson, "Cycles of Learning: Observations of Jack Welch," *Six Sigma Forum Magazine*, Vol. 1, No. 1, November 2001, pp. 13–17.

40. Reprinted with permission of *Inc. Magazine*, May 1990. Copyright 1990 by Goldhirsh Group, Inc., 38 Commercial Wharf, Boston, Mass. 02110.

41. John E. Ettlie, "What the Auto Industry Can Learn from McDonald's," *Automotive Manufacturing & Production*, October 1999, p. 42; David Stires, "Fallen Arches," *Fortune*, April 29, 2002, pp. 74–76.

CHAPTER 7

Tools and Techniques for Total Quality

Quality practitioners have adapted a variety of tools from other disciplines, such as statistics, operations research, and creative problem solving to help design, improve, and control processes. These tools provide a means by which problems and issues can be viewed objectively, data can be used as a basis for fact-driven decisions, and managers can deal with variation in a logical fashion. This chapter is intended to be only an elementary introduction and the list presented here is by no means exhaustive. The bibliography at the end of this book provides supplementary reading on these and other tools for quality improvement.

The objectives of this chapter are

- ➤ to describe how quality function deployment, concurrent engineering, concept engineering, and DFMEA can improve the process of designing products and services to achieve better customer satisfaction;
- ➤ to show how simple graphical tools can improve management planning;
- ➤ to illustrate the application of a variety of tools for process improvement;
- ➤ to discuss the importance of creativity and innovation for quality improvement and the management environment that fosters these characteristics; and
- ➤ to describe principles of statistical thinking as a basis for effective management and to introduce statistical process control.

TOOLS FOR QUALITY DESIGN

Customers' needs and expectations drive the planning process for products and the systems by which they are produced. Marketing plays a key role in identifying customer expectations. Once they are identified, managers must translate them into specific product and service specifications that manufacturing and service delivery processes must meet. In some cases the product or service that customers receive is quite different from what they expect. It is management's responsibility to minimize such gaps. Firms use several tools and approaches to help them focus on their external and internal customers.

Quality Function Deployment

Quality function deployment (QFD) is a methodology used to ensure that customers' requirements are met throughout the product design process and in the design and operation of production systems. QFD is both a philosophy and a set of planning and communication tools that focuses on customer requirements in coordinating the design, manufacturing, and marketing of goods. A major benefit of QFD is improved communications and teamwork among all constituencies in the production process—marketing and design, design and manufacturing, and purchasing and suppliers. QFD allows companies to simulate the effects of new design ideas and concepts. This allows them to bring new products into the market sooner and to gain competitive advantage.

QFD originated in 1972 at Mitsubishi's Kobe shipyard site. Toyota began to develop the concept shortly thereafter, and it has been used since 1977. The initial results were impressive: Between January 1977 and October 1979, for example, Toyota realized a 20 percent reduction in startup costs on the launch of a new van. By 1982 startup costs had fallen 38 percent from the 1977 baseline, and by 1984 they were reduced by 61 percent. In addition, development time fell by one third and quality improved.

In the United States, the 1992 Cadillac was planned and designed entirely with QFD. The concept has been publicized and developed in the United States by the American Supplier Institute, Inc., a nonprofit organization, and by GOAL/QPC, a consulting firm in Massachusetts. Today QFD is successfully used by manufacturers of electronics, appliances, clothing, and construction equipment, and by firms such as General Motors, Ford, Mazda, Motorola, Xerox, Kodak, IBM, Procter & Gamble, Hewlett-Packard, and AT&T.

The focus of QFD is translating customer requirements into the appropriate technical requirements for each stage of product development and production. The customers' requirements—expressed in their own terms— are appropriately called *the voice of the customer*. These are the collection of customer needs, including all satisfiers, delighters/exciters, and dissatisfiers —the "whats" that customers want from a product. For example, a consumer might ask that a dishwashing liquid be "long lasting" and "clean effectively" or that an MP3 player have "good sound quality." Sometimes these requirements are referred to as *customer attributes*. Under QFD, all operations of a company are driven by the voice of the customer, rather than by top management edicts or design engineers' opinions.

Technical features are the translation of the voice of the customer into technical language. They are the "hows" that determine the means by which customer attributes are met. For example, a dishwashing detergent loosens grease and soil from dishes. The soil becomes trapped in the suds so dishes can be removed from the water without picking up grease. Eventually the suds become saturated with soil and break down. Thus, a technical feature of a dishwashing liquid would be the weight of greasy soil that the suds generated by a fixed amount of dishwashing liquid can absorb before breaking down. Another might be the size of the soap bubble (which, incidentally, has been found to be a key attribute of customers' perception of cleaning effectiveness!).

A set of matrices is used to relate the voice of the customer to technical features and production planning and control requirements. The basic planning document is called the customer requirement planning matrix. Because of its structure (Figure 7.1), it is often referred to as the **House of Quality**. The House of Quality relates customer attributes to technical features to ensure that any engineering decision has a basis in meeting a customer need.

FIGURE 7.1   THE HOUSE OF QUALITY

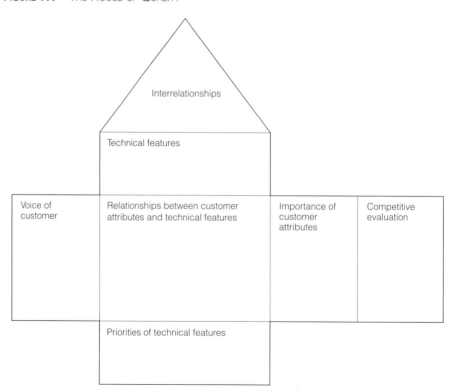

Building the House of Quality requires six basic steps:

1. Identify customer attributes.
2. Identify technical features.
3. Relate the customer attributes to the technical features.
4. Evaluate competing products.
5. Evaluate technical features and develop targets.
6. Determine which technical features to deploy in the production process.

The first step is identifying customer attributes. In applying QFD, it is important to use the customer's own words so as not to have customer needs misinterpreted by designers and engineers. Recall that not all customers are end users. For a manufacturer, customers might include government regulators, wholesalers, and retailers. Thus, many classes of customer needs may exist.

The second step is listing the technical features that are necessary to meet customer requirements. These technical features are design attributes expressed in the language of the designer and engineer. They form the basis for subsequent design, manufacturing, and service process activities. They must be measurable, because the output will be controlled and compared to objective targets.

The roof of the House of Quality shows the interrelationships between any pair of technical features. Various symbols are used to denote these relationships. A typical scheme is to use the symbol • to denote a very strong relationship, ○ for a strong relationship, and Δ to denote a weak relationship. These notations help determine the effects of changing one product characteristic and enable planners to assess the tradeoffs between characteristics. This process enables designers to focus on features collectively rather than individually.

Next, a relationship matrix between the customer attributes and the technical features is developed. Customer attributes are listed down the left column, and technical features are written across the top. In the matrix itself, a symbol is used to indicate the degree of relationship in a manner similar to that used in the roof of the house. The purpose of the relationship matrix is to show whether the final technical features adequately address the customer attributes. This assessment may be based on expert experience, customer responses, or controlled experiments.

Technical features can affect several customer attributes. The lack of a strong relationship between a customer attribute and any of the technical features suggests that the attributes are not being addressed and that the final product will have difficulty meeting customer needs. Similarly, if a technical feature does not affect any customer attribute, it may be redundant or the designers may have missed an important customer attribute.

The next step is adding market evaluation and key selling points. This step includes rating the importance of each customer attribute and evaluating existing products on each of the attributes. Customer importance ratings represent the areas of greatest interest and highest expectations to the customer.

Competitive evaluation helps highlight the absolute strengths and weaknesses of competing products. This step enables designers to seek opportunities for improvement. It also links QFD to a company's strategic vision and allows priorities to be set in the design process. For example, focusing on an attribute that receives a low evaluation on all competitors' products can help to gain a competitive advantage. Such attributes become key selling points and help establish promotion strategies.

Next comes the evaluation of the technical features of competitive products and the development of targets. This is usually accomplished through in-house testing and translated into measurable terms. These evaluations are compared with the competitive evaluation of customer attributes to find inconsistencies. If a competing product best satisfies a customer attribute, but the evaluation of the related technical feature indicates otherwise, then either the measures used are faulty or the product has an image difference (either positive toward the competitor or negative toward the product) that affects customer perceptions. Targets for each technical feature are set on the basis of customer importance ratings and existing product strengths and weaknesses.

The final step in building the House of Quality is selecting technical features to be deployed in the remainder of the process. This means identifying the characteristics that have a strong relationship to customer needs, have poor competitive performance, or are strong selling points. These characteristics need to be deployed—or translated into the language of each function—in the design and production process, so that proper actions and controls are taken to maintain the voice of the customer. Characteristics that are not identified as critical do not need such rigorous attention.

A simple example of a House of Quality is shown in Figure 7.2 for the hypothetical case of a quick-service franchise that wishes to improve its hamburger. The voice of the customer consists of four attributes. The hamburger should

- be tasty,
- be healthy,
- be visually appealing, and
- provide good value.

The technical features that can be designed into the product are price, size, calories, sodium content, and fat content. The symbols in the matrix show the relationships between each customer attribute and technical feature. For example, taste bears a strong relationship to sodium content, a moderate relationship to fat content, and a weak relationship to caloric content. In the roof of the house, price and size are seen to be strongly related (as size increases, the price must increase). The competitive evaluation shows that competitors are currently weak on nutrition and value; these can become key selling points in a marketing plan if the franchise can capitalize on them.

FIGURE 7.2 HOUSE OF QUALITY EXAMPLE

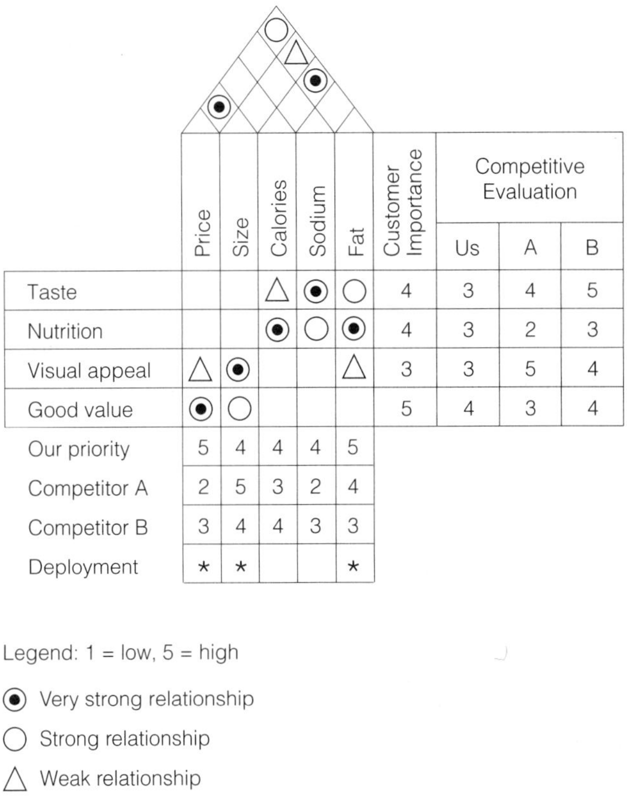

	Price	Size	Calories	Sodium	Fat	Customer Importance	Competitive Evaluation		
							Us	A	B
Taste			△	◉	○	4	3	4	5
Nutrition			◉	○	◉	4	3	2	3
Visual appeal	△	◉			△	3	3	5	4
Good value	◉	○				5	4	3	4
Our priority	5	4	4	4	5				
Competitor A	2	5	3	2	4				
Competitor B	3	4	4	3	3				
Deployment	★	★			★				

Legend: 1 = low, 5 = high

◉ Very strong relationship

○ Strong relationship

△ Weak relationship

Finally, at the bottom of the house, are targets for the technical features based on an analysis of customer importance ratings and competitive ratings. The features assigned asterisks will be deployed in subsequent design and production activities.

The House of Quality provides marketing with an important tool to understand customer needs and gives top management strategic direction. However, it is only the first stage in the QFD process. The voice of the customer must be carried throughout the production process. Three other houses of quality are used to deploy the voice of the customer to component parts characteristics, process planning, and production planning. These are

1. *technical features deployment matrix*, which translates technical features of the final product into design requirements for critical components;
2. *process plan and quality control charts*, which translate component features into critical process and product parameters and control points for each; and

3. *operating instructions,* which identify operations to be performed by plant personnel to assure that important process and product parameters are achieved.

Most of the QFD activities represented by the first two houses of quality are performed by people in the product development and engineering functions. At the next stage, the planning activities begin to involve supervisors and production-line operators. This represents the transition from planning to execution. If a product component parameter is critical and is created or affected during the process, it becomes a control point. This tells the company what to monitor and inspect and forms the basis for a quality control plan for achieving those critical characteristics that are crucial to achieving customer satisfaction. The last house relates the control points to specific requirements for quality assurance activity. This includes specifying control methods, sample sizes, and so on, to achieve the necessary level of quality.

The success of QFD depends on effective communication and cooperation among all major functions that contribute to getting a product to market. The designer's objective is to create a product that meets the desired functional requirements. The manufacturing engineer's objective is to produce the designed product efficiently. The salesperson's goal is to sell the product, and that of finance personnel is to make a profit. Purchasing must ensure that purchased parts meet quality requirements. Packaging and distribution personnel must ensure that the product reaches the customer in good operating condition. Because all these functions have a stake in the product, they must all work together. Building cross-functional teams to accomplish product development is often called **concurrent engineering**.

Concept Engineering

Concept engineering (CE) emerged from a consortium of companies that included Polaroid and Bose along with researchers at MIT, and is promoted and taught by the Center for Quality of Management (http://www.cqm.org). CE is a focused process for discovering customer requirements and using them to select superior product or service concepts that meet those requirements. Although similar to QFD in many respects, it puts the voice of the customer into a broader context and employs numerous other techniques to ensure effective processing of qualitative data.

Five major steps comprise the process:

1. *Understanding the customer's environment.* This step involves first project planning activities such as team selection, identifying fit with business strategy, and gaining team consensus on the project focus. It also includes collecting the voice of the customer to understand the customer's environment—physical, psychological, competitive, and so on.

2. *Converting understanding into requirements.* In this step, teams analyze the customer transcripts to translate the voice of the customer into more specific requirements. Essentially, this step focuses on identifying the technical requirements we discussed in the context of QFD, selecting the most significant requirements, and "scrubbing" the requirements to refine them into clear and insightful statements.

3. *Operationalizing what has been learned.* This step involves determining how to measure how well a customer requirement is met. For example, a requirement developed for a project at Polaroid was "Document photographer delivers document photo quickly while the customer waits." The principal requirement is about throughput time, so the concept of "quickly" needs to be operationalized and measured.[1] Once potential metrics are defined, they are evaluated to reduce the number of metrics that need to be used while ensuring that they cover all key requirements. This evaluation usually requires some sort of customer questionnaire to identify the importance of the requirements and prioritize them.

4. *Concept generation.* This step focuses on generating ideas for solutions that will potentially meet customers' needs. One unique approach is to brainstorm ideas that might resolve each individual customer requirement, select the best ones, and then classify them under the more traditional functional product characteristics. This approach helps to develop a "market in" rather than a "product out" orientation. Creative thinking techniques are applied here to increase the number and diversity of potential ideas.

5. *Concept selection.* Finally, the potential ideas are evaluated with respect to meeting requirements, tradeoffs are assessed, and prototyping may begin. The process ends with reflection on the final concept to test whether the decision "feels right" based on all the knowledge acquired.

Like QFD, concept engineering leaves a strong audit trail back to the voice of the customer. This evidence makes it difficult for skeptics to challenge the results and easier to convert them. The process helps to build consensus and gives the team confidence in selling the concept to management. It takes a lot of discipline and patience, but the end result is well worth the effort. See the box "The Perfect Supplier" for an example of CE in action.

Design Failure Mode and Effects Analysis

The purpose of **design failure mode and effects analysis (DFMEA)** is to identify all the ways in which a failure can occur, to estimate the effect and seriousness of the failure, and to recommend corrective design actions. A DFMEA usually consists of specifying the following information for each design element or function:

- *Failure modes*—ways in which each element or function can fail. This information generally takes some research and imagination. One way to

The Perfect Supplier

Bose Corporation, a leader in high-end audio products, used concept engineering to improve its European delivery system, at the same time decreasing overhead cost to the company.[2] The delivery system included every activity from the time a dealer realizes that he or she needs a product from Bose until the product is delivered. In personal visits to dealers in France, Germany, Holland, Spain, Belgium, and the United Kingdom, Bose developed an interview guide that addressed the following:

1. How do you describe the perfect supplier?
2. Please describe your process of ordering.
3. Where does customer service fit into your business?
4. General questions about your impressions of Bose.

In processing the qualitative data obtained from the interviews, Bose focused on the question, "What scenes or images come to mind when you visualize a supplier's delivery system?" From an analysis of more than 100 customer requirements, 24 were selected as key requirements for a world-class delivery system. This analysis led the team to the conclusion that supplier reliability and system efficiency build confidence and create trusting relationships. Next, these requirements were stated in measurable terms and questionnaires were developed to ensure that the requirements truly reflected the opinions of the dealers. For example, a requirement might be "Have a simple and swift return policy for faulty or damaged products." This requirement might then be measured by the amount of information required to process a product return.

The team spent nearly three days generating potential solutions for each customer requirement. As they discussed the strengths of each idea, new ideas often emerged, even from seemingly bizarre ideas. The four strongest ideas were chosen, and the team wrote a story or scenario with specific changes that needed to be made to the delivery system as a way of presenting the solution; this form of presentation would enable those outside of the team to understand how the new systems would work in delighting the customer. Although the process was quite tedious, the team members agreed that it was an excellent approach for arriving at an effective solution and turned them "into believers."

start is with known failures that have occurred in the past. Documents such as quality and reliability reports, test results, and warranty reports provide useful information.

- *Effect of the failure on the customer*—such as dissatisfaction, potential injury or other safety issues, downtime, repair requirements, and so on. Maintenance records, customer complaints, and warranty reports provide good sources of information. Consideration should be given to failures on the function of the end product, manufacturability in the next process, what the customer sees or experiences, and product safety.

- *Severity, likelihood of occurrence, and detection rating.* Severity might be measured on a scale of 1 to 10, where a "1" indicates that the failure is so minor that the customer probably would not notice it, and a "10" might mean that the customer might be endangered. The frequency of occurrence based on service history or field performance provides an indication of the significance of the failure. Based on severity and likelihood, a risk priority can be assigned to identify critical failure modes that must be addressed.
- *Potential causes of failure.* Often failure is the result of poor design. Design deficiencies can cause errors either in the field or in manufacturing and assembly. Identification of causes might require experimentation and rigorous analysis.
- *Corrective actions or controls.* These controls might include design changes, mistake proofing, better user instructions, management responsibilities, and target completion dates.

Using DFMEA will not only improve product functionality and safety but also reduce external failure costs—particularly warranty costs, as well as decrease manufacturing and service delivery problems. It also can provide a defense against frivolous lawsuits. DFMEA should be conducted early in the design process to save costs and reduce cycle times, and provide a knowledge base to improve subsequent design efforts. This approach also can be used for processes to identify hazardous conditions that may endanger a worker or operational problems that can disrupt a production process and result in scrap, downtime, or other non–value-added costs.

TOOLS FOR QUALITY PLANNING

Planning is one of the basic functions of every manager. Because of the complexity of today's business environment, planning is not always easy to do. However, various tools have been developed by several Japanese companies over the last half-century as part of their planning processes. These are described next.

The Seven Management and Planning Tools

The "seven management and planning tools" had their roots in post–World War II operations research developments in the United States, but were refined in Japan. They were popularized in the United States by the consulting firm GOAL/QPC and have been used by a number of firms since 1984 to improve their quality planning and improvement efforts. They are new only to managers who have not previously seen what powerful aids they can be in improvement processes.

These tools can be used to address problems typically faced by managers who are called upon to structure unstructured ideas, make strategic plans, and organize and control large, complex projects. Due to space limitations, only a brief discussion of each tool follows. (See books by Brossart, Brassard, and Mizuno[3] for further details and examples.)

Affinity Diagram/KJ Method

This is a technique for gathering and organizing a large number of ideas, opinions, and facts relating to a broad problem or subject area. It enables problem solvers to sift through large volumes of information efficiently and to identify natural patterns or groupings in the information. This method was developed in the 1960s by Kawakita Jiro, a Japanese anthropologist. "KJ" is a trademark registered by the Kawayoshida Research Center.

The technique requires that a group of six to eight people meet to consider a broad issue, such as identifying the elements of poor quality cost for their organization. Responses can be recorded on a flipchart or on small cards that can be posted and moved around on a board. For example, in determining the elements of quality cost, the group will probably list various elements in a random fashion. Once many ideas have been generated, they can be grouped according to their "affinity," or relationship, to each other. An example is shown in Figure 7.3. This technique helps managers focus on the key issues and their elements rather than an unorganized collection of information.

FIGURE 7.3   EXAMPLE OF AN AFFINITY DIAGRAM

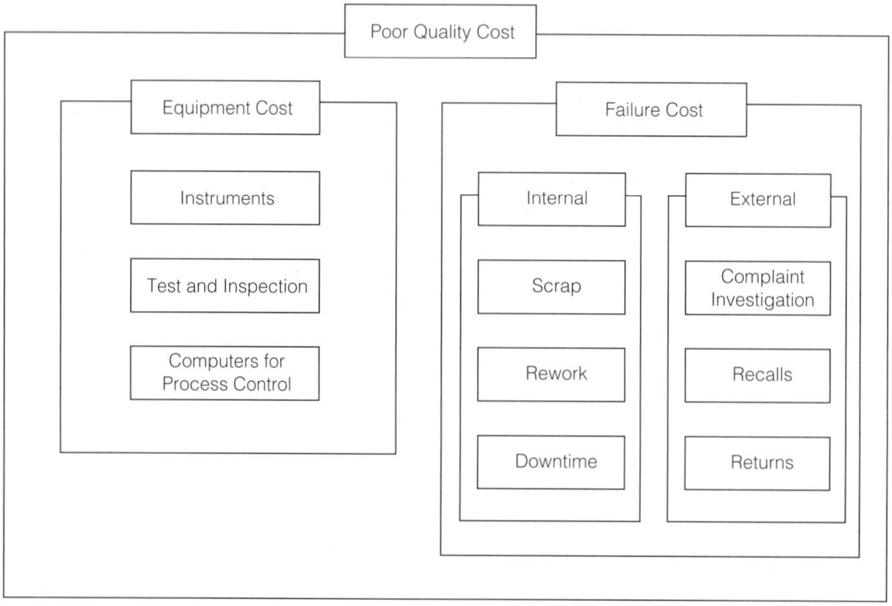

The Affinity Diagram/KJ Method is intended to be a creative, rather than a logical process. It resembles brainstorming and "story-boarding," a technique developed by Walt Disney to create cartoons and movies.

Interrelationship Digraphs

The purpose of an interrelationship digraph is to take a central idea and map out logical or sequential links among related categories. It shows that every idea can be logically linked with more than one idea at a time, and allows for "lateral" rather than "linear" thinking. This technique often is used after the affinity diagram has brought issues and problems into clearer focus. Figure 7.4 shows an example of how failure costs are influenced by other factors.

Like affinity diagrams, this technique also depends on getting together a team of people who own the problem. Some of the same cards or flipchart lists developed in the affinity diagram can be duplicated and used in this technique. New cards or lists of specific items must be added frequently as the issue becomes more focused.

Tree Diagram

A tree diagram maps out the paths and tasks that need to be accomplished to complete a specific project or to reach a specified goal. A planner uses this technique to seek answers to such questions as "What sequence of tasks needs to be completed to address the issue?" or "What are all of the factors that contribute to the existence of the key problem?" This technique brings the issues and problems disclosed by the affinity diagram and the interrelationship digraph down to the operational planning stage. A clear statement of the problem or process must be specified. From this general statement, a team can be established to recommend steps required to solve the problem

FIGURE 7.4   EXAMPLE OF AN INTERRELATIONSHIP DIGRAPH

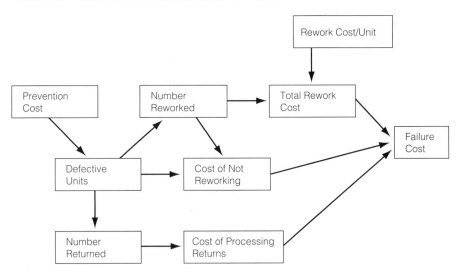

or implement the plan. The "product" produced by this group would be a tree diagram with activities and recommendations for timing the activities. Figure 7.5 shows an example of some of the key elements in establishing a quality cost system.

Matrix Diagrams

These are spreadsheets that graphically display relationships between characteristics, functions, and tasks in such a way as to provide logical connecting points between each item. The House of Quality is an example of one of the many matrix diagrams now used for planning and quality improvement.

Matrix Data Analysis

This process takes data from matrix diagrams and seeks to arrange it quantitatively to display the strength of relationships among variables so that they can be easily viewed and understood. Matrix data analysis is a rigorous, statistically based "factor analysis" technique. GOAL/QPC personnel feels that this method, although worthwhile for many applications, is too quantitative to be used on a daily basis and they have developed an alternative tool called a prioritization matrix that is easier to understand and implement.

This approach bears a lot of similarity to decision matrices that you may have studied in a quantitative methods course. Interested readers should consult Brassard's book for further details.

FIGURE 7.5   EXAMPLE OF A TREE DIAGRAM

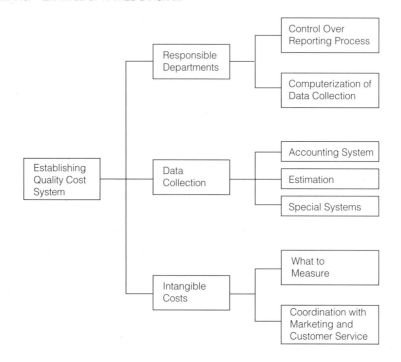

Process Decision Program Chart (PDPC)

This is a method for mapping out every conceivable event and contingency that can occur when moving from a problem statement to possible solutions. It is used to plan for each possible chain of events that could occur when a problem or goal is unfamiliar. A PDPC takes each branch of a tree diagram, anticipates possible problems, and provides countermeasures that will prevent the deviation from occurring or be in place if the deviation does occur. Figure 7.6 shows one example.

Arrow Diagrams

These have been used by construction planners for years in the form of CPM and PERT project planning techniques. Arrow diagramming has also been taught extensively in quantitative methods, operations management, and other business and engineering courses in the United States for a number of years. Unfortunately, its use has been confined to technical experts. By adding it to the "quality toolbox," it has become more widely available to general managers and other nontechnical personnel.

Implementation of process improvements is an essential, but frequently ignored, step. Process improvements often are not implemented because they are too complex to work in practice or are not accepted by those who

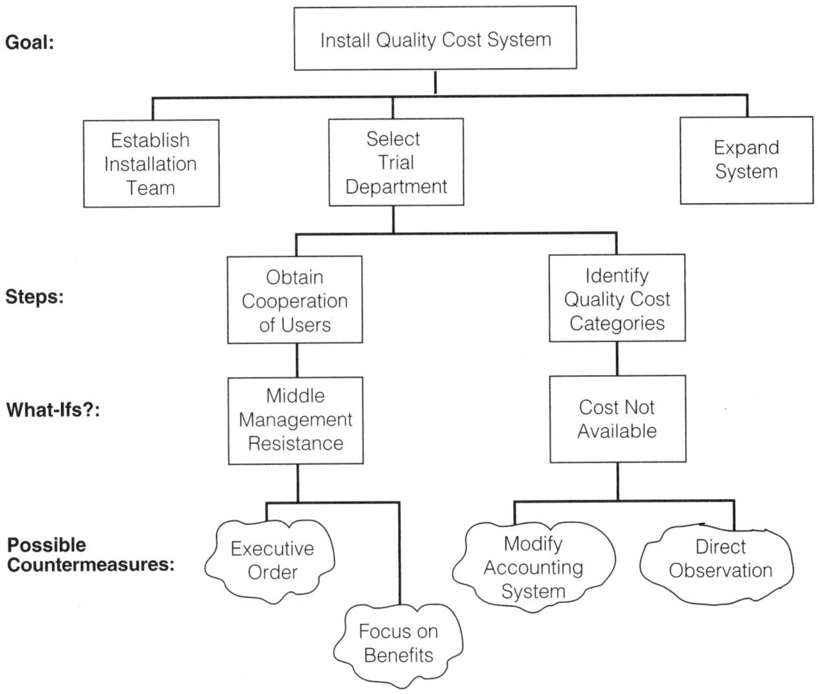

FIGURE 7.6   EXAMPLE OF A PROCESS DECISION PROGRAM CHART

have the responsibility to carry them out. These seven quality improvement tools assist managers in implementing improvements through active involvement.

Tools for Continuous Improvement

Many tools have been created or adapted from other disciplines (such as operations research and industrial engineering) to facilitate the process of continuous improvement. In this section, we describe the most common ones used in quality improvement applications.

Tools for Process Analysis

Seven simple statistically based tools are used extensively to gather and analyze data. Like the seven management and planning tools, these tools—flowcharts, check sheets, histograms, Pareto diagrams, cause-and-effect diagrams, scatter diagrams, and control charts—are visual in nature and simple enough for anyone to understand. Historically, these tools preceded the seven management and planning tools and often are called the "seven QC (quality control) tools," which is a bit of a misnomer as they deal primarily with improvement. The seven management and planning tools have been referred to as the "new seven."

Flowcharts

A flowchart (or **process map**) is a picture of a process that shows the sequence of steps performed. Figure 7.7 is an example. Flowcharts are best developed by the people involved in the process—employees, supervisors, managers, and customers. A facilitator often is used to provide objectivity, to ask the right questions, and to resolve conflicts. The facilitator can guide the discussion through questions such as "What happens next?," "Who makes the decision at this point?," and "What operation is performed here?" Often the group does not agree on the answers to these questions, due to misconceptions about the process or a lack of awareness of the "big picture."

Flowcharts help the people involved in the process to understand it better. For example, employees realize how they fit into a process—that is, who their suppliers and customers are. By helping to develop a flowchart, workers begin to feel a sense of ownership in the process and become more willing to work on improving it. Using flowcharts to train employees on standard procedures leads to more consistent performance.

Once a flowchart is constructed, it can be used to identify quality problems as well as areas for improvement. Questions such as "How does this operation affect the customer?," "Can we improve or eliminate this operation?," or "Should we control a critical quality characteristic at this point?" help to identify such opportunities. Flowcharts help people to visualize simple but important changes that could be made in a process.

FIGURE 7.7   EXAMPLE OF A FLOWCHART FOR TRAINING NEW PRINTING PRESS OPERATORS

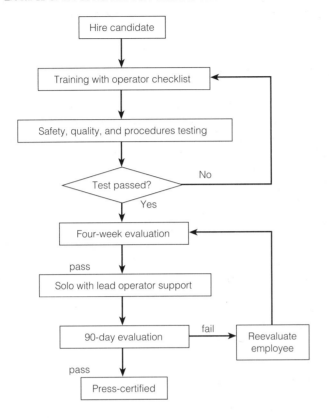

Check Sheets

These tools aid in data collection. When designing a process to collect data, one must first ask basic questions such as:

- What question are we trying to answer?
- What type of data will we need to answer the question?
- Where can we find the data?
- Who can provide the data?
- How can we collect the data with minimum effort and minimum chance of error?

Check sheets are data collection forms that facilitate the interpretation of data. Quality-related data are of two general types—attribute and variable. *Attribute data* are obtained by counting or from some type of visual inspection: the number of invoices that contain errors, the number of parts that conform to specifications, and the number of surface defects on an automobile panel, for example. *Variable data* are collected by numerical measurement on a continuous scale. Dimensional characteristics such as

FIGURE 7.8   EXAMPLE OF A CHECK SHEET FOR ATTRIBUTE DATA: AIRLINE COMPLAINTS

Type	Week 1	Week 2	Week 3	Week 4
Lost baggage	|		||	|
Baggage delay	ⅢⅡ |	||||	ⅢⅡ |||	ⅢⅡ
Missed connection	||	|	|||	|
Poor cabin service	|||	ⅢⅡ	|||	|||
Ticketing error	|			|

distance, weight, volume, and time are common examples. Figure 7.8 is an example of an attribute data check sheet, and Figure 7.9 shows a variable data check sheet.

Histograms

Variation in a process always exists and generally displays a pattern that can be captured in a histogram. A histogram is a graphical representation of the variation in a set of data. It shows the frequency or number of observations of a particular value or within a specified group.

FIGURE 7.9   EXAMPLE OF A CHECK SHEET FOR VARIABLE DATA

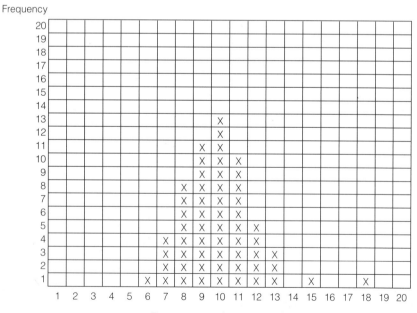

Frequency

Time to process loan request (days)

Histograms provide clues about the characteristics of the population from which a sample is taken. Using a histogram, the shape of the distribution can be seen clearly, and inferences can be made about the population. Patterns can be seen that would be difficult to see in an ordinary table of numbers. The check sheet in Figure 7.9 was designed to provide the visual appeal of a histogram as the data are tallied. It is easy to see how the output of the process varies and what proportion of output falls outside of any specification limits.

Pareto Diagrams

Pareto analysis is a technique for prioritizing types or sources of problems. Pareto analysis separates the "vital few" from the "trivial many" and provides help in selecting directions for improvement. It is often used to analyze the attribute data collected in check sheets. In a Pareto distribution the characteristics are ordered from largest frequency to smallest. For example, if the data in Figure 7.8 is placed in order of decreasing frequency, the result is:

1. Baggage delay
2. Poor cabin service
3. Missed connection
4. Lost baggage
5. Ticketing error

A Pareto diagram is a histogram of these data, as shown in Figure 7.10.

A cumulative frequency curve is usually drawn on the histogram, as shown. Such pictures clearly show the relative magnitude of defects and can be used to identify the most promising opportunities for improvement. They also can show the results of improvement projects over time.

Cause-and-Effect Diagrams

The most useful tool for identifying the causes of problems is a cause-and-effect diagram, also known as a fishbone or Ishikawa diagram, named after the Japanese quality expert who popularized the concept. A cause-and-effect diagram is simply a graphical representation of an outline that presents a chain of causes and effects.

An example is shown in Figure 7.11 on page 285. At the end of the horizontal line is the problem to be addressed. Each branch pointing into the main stem represents a possible cause. Branches pointing to the causes are contributors to these causes. The diagram is used to identify the most likely causes of a problem so that further data collection and analysis can be carried out.

Cause-and-effect diagrams are usually constructed in a brainstorming setting so that everyone can contribute their ideas. Usually small groups drawn from operations or management work with an experienced facilitator. The facilitator guides the discussion to focus attention on the problem and

FIGURE 7.10   EXAMPLE OF A PARETO DIAGRAM

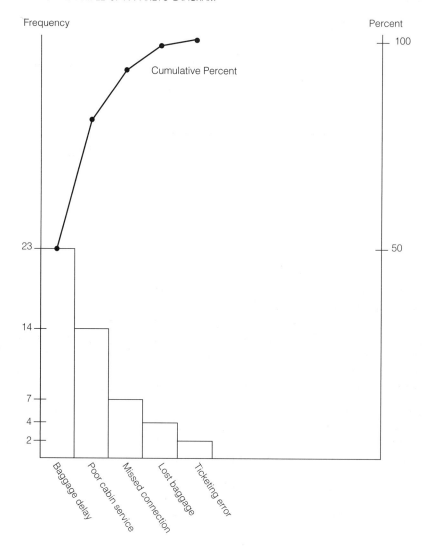

its causes, on facts, not opinions. This method requires significant interaction among group members. The facilitator must listen carefully to the participants and capture the important ideas.

Scatter Diagrams

Scatter diagrams illustrate relationships between variables, such as the percentage of an ingredient in an alloy and the hardness of the alloy, or the number of employee errors and overtime worked (Figure 7.12). Typically the variables represent possible causes and effects obtained from cause-and-effect diagrams.

FIGURE 7.11   EXAMPLE OF A CAUSE-AND-EFFECT DIAGRAM

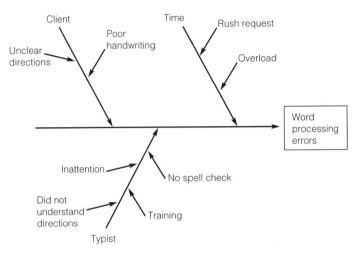

A general trend of the points going up and to the right indicates that an increase in one variable corresponds to an increase in the other. If the trend is down and to the right, an increase in one variable corresponds to a decrease in the other. If no trend can be seen, then it would appear that the variables are not related. Of course, any correspondence does not necessarily imply that a change in one variable causes a change in the other. Both may be the result of something else. However, if there is reason to believe causation, the scatter diagram may provide clues on how to improve the process.

Control Chart

These tools are the backbone of statistical process control (SPC), and were first proposed by Walter Shewhart in 1924. We will defer discussion of this tool until later in the chapter when we discuss statistical thinking.

FIGURE 7.12   EXAMPLE OF A SCATTER DIAGRAM

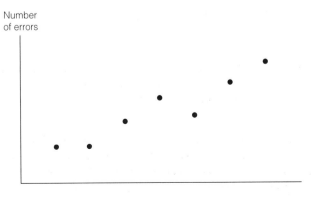

The seven QC tools provide excellent communication vehicles both vertically and horizontally across organizational boundaries (see box "Shooting for Quality").

Poka-Yoke (Mistake-Proofing)

Poka-yoke is an approach for mistake-proofing processes using automatic devices or methods to avoid simple human error. The poka-yoke concept was developed and refined by the late Shigeo Shingo, a Japanese manufacturing engineer who developed the Toyota production system. The idea is to avoid repetitive tasks or actions that depend on vigilance or memory in order to free workers' time and minds to pursue more creative and value-adding activities.

Poka-yoke is focused on two aspects: prediction, or recognizing that a defect is about to occur and providing a warning, and detection, or recognizing that a defect has occurred and stopping the process. Many applications of poka-yoke are deceptively simple, yet creative. Usually, they are inexpensive to implement. Some examples:

- Many machines have limit switches connected to warning lights that tell the operator when parts are positioned improperly on the machine.

Shooting for Quality[4]

Timothy Clark observed that in basketball games, his son Andrew's free-throw percentage averaged between 45 and 50 percent. Andrew's process was simple: Go to the free throw line, bounce the ball four times, aim, and shoot. To confirm these observations, Andrew shot five sets of 10 free throws with an average of 42 percent, showing little variation among the five sets. Timothy developed a cause-and-effect diagram (Figure 7.13) to identify the principal causes. After analyzing the diagram and observing his son's process, he believed that the main causes were not standing in the same place on the free-throw line every time and having an inconsistent focal point.

They developed a new process in which Andrew stood at the center of the line and focused on the middle of the front part of the rim. The new process resulted in a 36 percent improvement in practice (Figure 7.14). Toward the end of the 1994 season, he improved his average to 69 percent in the last three games.

During the 1995 season, Andrew averaged 60 percent. A control chart (Figure 7.15) showed that the process was quite stable. In the summer of 1995, Andrew attended a basketball camp where he was advised to change his shooting technique. This process reduced his shooting percentage during the 1996 season to 50 percent. However, his father helped him to reinstall his old process, and his percentage returned to its former level, also improving his confidence.

FIGURE 7.13   FREE-THROWING CAUSE-AND-EFFECT DIAGRAM

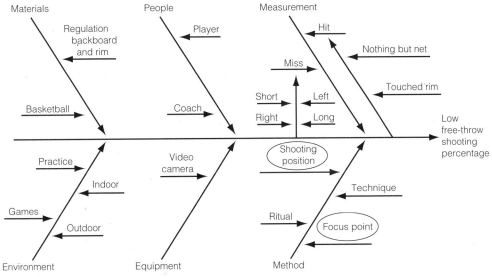

© 1997 American Society for Quality. Reprinted with permission.

FIGURE 7.14   FREE-THROWING SHOTS MADE BEFORE AND AFTER IMPLEMENTING THE IMPROVEMENT (3/17/94–11/23/94)

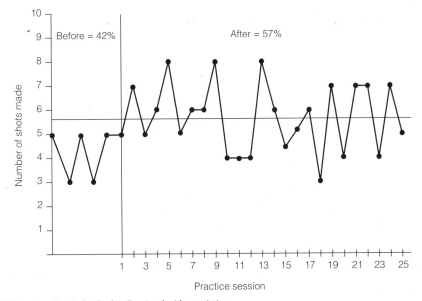

© 1997 American Society for Quality. Reprinted with permission.

FIGURE 7.15   DETERMINING WHETHER THE FREE-THROW PROCESS IS STABLE (3/17/94–1/18/96)

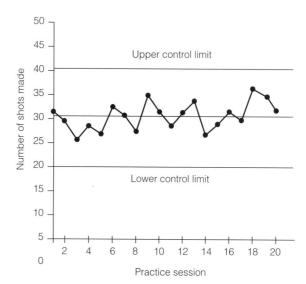

- A device on a drill counts the number of holes drilled in a workpiece; a buzzer sounds if the workpiece is removed before the correct number of holes has been drilled.
- Passwords or email addresses are often required to be entered twice for verification.
- Pills roll down an incline; broken ones can't and are easily eliminated.

Poka-yoke techniques are also applied to the design of consumer products to prevent inadvertent user errors or safety hazards. For example, a 3.5-inch diskette is designed so that it cannot be inserted unless the disk is oriented correctly (try it!). These disks are not perfectly square, and the beveled right corner of the disk allows a stop in the disk drive to be pushed away if it is inserted correctly. Power lawn mowers now have a safety bar on the handle that must be engaged in order to start the engine. Computer software such as Microsoft Word will automatically check for any unsaved files before closing down. A proxy ballot for an investment fund will not fit into the return envelope unless a small strip is detached. The strip asks the respondent to check whether the ballot is signed and dated.

Richard B. Chase and Douglas M. Stewart suggest that the same concepts can be applied to services.[5] The major differences are that service mistake-proofing must account for the customers' activities as well as those of the producer, and mistake-proof methods must be set up for interactions conducted directly or by phone, mail, or other technologies, such as ATM. Chase and Stewart classify service poka-yokes by the type of error they are designed to prevent: server errors and customer errors. Server errors result from the *task, treatment,* or *tangibles* of the service. Customer errors occur during *preparation, the service encounter,* or during *resolution.*

Task errors include doing work incorrectly, in the wrong order, or too slowly, as well as doing work not requested. Some examples of poka-yoke devices for task errors are computer prompts, color-coded cash register keys, measuring tools such as McDonald's French fry scoop, and signaling devices. Hospitals use trays for surgical instruments that have indentations for each instrument, preventing the surgeon from leaving one of them in the patient.

Treatment errors arise in the contact between the server and the customer, such as lack of courteous behavior, and failure to acknowledge, listen, or react appropriately to the customer. A bank encourages eye contact by requiring tellers to record the customer's eye color on a checklist as they start the transaction. To promote friendliness at a fast-food restaurant, trainers provide the four specific cues for when to smile: when greeting the customer, when taking the order, when telling about the dessert special, and when giving the customer change. They encourage employees to observe whether the customer smiled back, a natural reinforcer for smiling.

Tangible errors are those in physical elements of the service, such as unclean facilities, dirty uniforms, inappropriate temperature, and document errors. Hotels wrap paper strips around towels to help the housekeeping staff identify clean linen and show which ones should be replaced. Spell checkers in word processing software help eliminate misspellings (provided they are used!).

Customer errors in preparation arise when customers do not bring necessary materials to the encounter, do not understand their role in the service transaction, or do not engage the correct service. Digital Equipment provides a flowchart to specify how to place a service call. By guiding the customers through three yes-or-no questions, the flowchart prompts them to have the necessary information before calling.

Customer errors during an encounter can be because of inattention, misunderstanding, or simply a memory lapse, and include failure to remember steps in the process or to follow instructions. Poka-yoke examples include height bars at amusement rides that indicate rider size requirements, beepers that signal customers to remove cards from ATM machines, and airplane lavatory doors that must be locked to turn on the lights. Some cashiers at restaurants fold back the top edge of credit card receipts, holding together the restaurant's copies while revealing the customer's copy.

Customer errors at the resolution stage of a service encounter include failure to signal service inadequacies, learn from experience, adjust expectations, and execute appropriate postencounter actions. Hotels might enclose a small gift certificate to encourage guests to provide feedback. Strategically placed tray-return stands and trash receptacles remind customers to return trays in fast-food facilities.

Mistake-proofing a service process requires identifying when and where failures generally occur (see box about the election process). Once a failure is

---

Mistake-Proofing the U.S. Election Process?[6]

The controversy surrounding the 2000 U.S. presidential election is well known. A difference of roughly 500 votes out of 5.8 million cast in Florida is smaller than the predictable number of errors for miscounted votes, miscast votes, incorrectly rejected ballots, and other vote-casting and vote-counting errors caused by systems and processes (people, equipment, methods, materials, and environment). Several issues affect the quality of the results.

- The prescored punch cards commonly used for ballots require that voters punch the cards in a way that meets machine specifications. The stylus used to punch out the chad (the little piece that gets punched out of the ballot card) could be inadequate in terms of shape or sharpness. The die that prescores the cards during manufacturing wears down over time. Cards may be too thick or thin. Cards exposed to too much humidity may not be counted properly in machines.
- Process errors can occur in several places. The voter may not have actually cast a vote, or the voter may not have been able to vote for the candidate of choice because of confusing ballot design. The ballot may not have been counted correctly. Manual recounts may not record the voter's intent correctly.
- Lack of uniform standards among voting jurisdictions make it difficult to predict process error rates accurately.

Reducing such errors will require a systematic approach to problem solving built on quality principles and mistake-proofing ideas. Although such thinking has been successful in many organizations, it has not become a part of the public policy dialog nor has it been institutionalized as part of any national debate.

---

identified, the source must be found. The final step is to prevent the mistake from occurring through source inspection, self-inspection, or sequential checks.

Kaizen Blitz

A **kaizen blitz** is an intense and rapid improvement process in which a team or a department throws all its resources into an improvement project over a short time period, as opposed to traditional kaizen applications, which are performed on a part-time basis. Blitz teams are generally comprised of employees from all areas involved in the process who understand it and can implement changes on the spot. Improvement is immediate, exciting, and satisfying for all those involved in the process. Some examples of using kaizen blitz at Magnivision include the following:[7]

- The molded lens department ran two shifts per day, using 13 employees, and after 40 percent rework, yielded 1,300 pieces per day. The production line was unbalanced and work piled up between stations, which added to quality problems as the work-in-process was often damaged. After a three-day blitz, the team reduced the production to one shift of six employees and a balanced line, reducing rework to 10 percent and increasing yield to 3,500 per day, saving more than $179,000.

- In Retail Services, a blitz team investigated problems that continually plagued employees, and discovered that many were related to the software system. Some of the same customer information had to be entered in multiple screens, sometimes the system took a long time to process information, and sometimes it was difficult to find specific information quickly. Neither the programmers nor the engineers were aware of these problems. By getting everyone together, some solutions were easily determined. Estimated savings were $125,000.

CREATIVITY AND INNOVATION

Creativity is the ability to discover useful new relationships or ideas; *innovation* refers to the practical implementation of such ideas. Research studies have suggested that the achievement of business excellence requires a change-oriented environment where creativity of employees is nurtured, developed, and sustained.[8] Thus, creativity and innovation are instrumental in achieving the principles of total quality discussed in the first chapter.

From the perspective of total quality, creativity and innovation are needed to better respond to customer needs, particularly the "exciters/delighters" that customers cannot articulate, and to develop the products and services that will position an organization strategically ahead of its competitors. They also are needed to support continuous improvement efforts, for example the poka-yoke devices and methods discussed in this chapter. Finally, an environment that fosters creativity and innovation can motivate employees more than any extrinsic reward—"joy in work" as Deming used to say (see box "Creativity in the Heartland").

In Japanese, the word *creativity* has a literal translation as *dangerous opportunity*. In the Toyota production system, which has become the benchmark for world-class efficiency, a key concept is *soikufu*—creative thinking or inventive ideas, which means capitalizing on worker suggestions. The chairman of Toyota once observed: "One of the features of Japanese workers is that they use their brains as well as their hands. Our workers provide 1.5 million suggestions a year, and 95 percent of them are put to practical use. There is an almost tangible concern for improvement in the air at Toyota."[9]

Creativity is often motivated by an individual's or group's need to invent solutions from limited resources. The Japanese have shown remarkable creativity in developing solutions to manufacturing quality problems. This is no wonder, given the limited natural resources in Japan and the Japanese culture focused on eliminating waste and conserving every

Creativity in the Heartland

In 1994, three companies received the Malcolm Baldrige National Quality Award: AT&T Consumer Communications Services (CCS), GTE Directories Corporation, and Wainwright Industries. AT&T CCS (the long-distance provider) and GTE Directories (which publishes and sells advertising for telephone directories) are large, innovative firms, with sophisticated technologies and human resource development activities that support empowered teams and foster an atmosphere of creativity throughout their organizations. Both companies also offer a wide variety of training and education courses, including courses devoted specifically to creativity and innovation. It is not surprising that they have achieved remarkable results in product and service quality, customer satisfaction, and in various operational and financial measures.

Wainwright Industries, headquartered in rural St. Peters, Missouri, is considerably different from CCS and GTE. Wainwright is a small, family-owned business that manufactures stamped and machined parts for the automotive and other industries. Since initiating continuous improvement processes in 1991, Wainwright has seen continual, and sometimes dramatic, improvements in customer satisfaction, defect and scrap rates, work-related accidents, manufacturing cycle times, and quality costs. At the same time, market share, productivity gains, and profit margins have all increased.

Innovation is a way of life at Wainwright. Each associate averages more than one *implemented improvement* per week! That's over 50 each year, in an industry that averages at most one *suggestion* per employee per year in the United States. Wainwright does not have the comparable resources available to large corporations like AT&T or GTE. The company spends a relatively high proportion of its budget on training, some of which is outsourced, yet no formal creativity training is offered. What the company does have is a *culture* that exudes a spirit of creativity and innovation. The plant has a folksy, Midwestern atmosphere.

Everyone—up to the chairman of the board—wears a company uniform with his or her first name stitched on it. The human resources function is called "The People Zone." The training director is known simply as "The Training Guy." And a stuffed duck is the company's mascot and symbol of quality leadership.

Wainwright is an excellent example of how creativity, integrated within a traditional American company, can lead to exceptional improvements in quality and business performance. More important, when visitors tour the plant, they see clearly the spirit and enthusiasm exuded by Wainwright associates. The associates are having *fun*! Improving quality—and work itself—*should* be fun, and people have fun when they are creative.

precious resource available. The largest source of creativity in any organization is the frontline employee. They gather a wealth of data and information about their work every day. To tap into their knowledge, companies must make creativity a key part of their culture and think of improvement as everybody's job. This requires companies to empower their employees to allow them to put their ideas to work. We will address this further in Chapter 9.

Innovation and creativity are important aspects of the Malcolm Baldrige National Quality Award Criteria for Performance Excellence. Mechanisms used to encourage innovation and creativity include:

1. The nonprescriptive nature of the criteria, which encourages innovative approaches and breakthrough thinking toward meeting the purpose of the specific items in the criteria. This channels activities toward purpose, not toward following procedures.
2. Customer-driven quality, which places major emphasis on the positive side of quality, and stresses enhancement, new services, and customer relationship management. Enhancing the positive side of quality relies heavily on creativity, usually more so than steps to reduce errors and defects, which tend to rely more on well-defined techniques.
3. Continuous improvement and cycles of learning, which are stressed as integral parts of the activities of all work units. This encourages analysis and problem solving everywhere within the company.
4. Strong emphasis on cycle time reduction in all company operations, which encourages companies to analyze work processes, work organizations, and the value-added contributions of all process steps. This fosters change, innovation, and creative thinking in how work is organized and conducted.
5. Focus on future requirements of customers, which encourages companies to seek innovative and creative ways to serve needs.

Many examples of creativity and innovation are seen in firms that have received the Baldrige Award. Among the many examples are:

- The benchmarking process, pioneered by Xerox.
- Granite Xpress, an automatic loading system for rock, sand, aggregates, and other construction materials, developed by Granite Rock. The system is similar to an automatic teller machine and allows customers to rapidly, accurately, and automatically order, load, and invoice materials 24 hours a day, seven days a week.
- Wainwright Industries' practice of reenacting and videotaping workplace accidents for study and prevention.

Research has shown that people can be taught and learn to be more creative. Organizations need to understand how creative thinking tools can help to improve organizational performance and quality.

Creativity and Organizational Systems

Warren Bennis, a recognized expert on leadership, noted: "There are two ways of being creative. One can sing and dance. Or one can create an environment in which singers and dancers flourish." While the tools discussed in this chapter all help to promote creative thinking, they cannot be applied effectively in a noncreative environment. Because management designs the organizational systems, management is responsible for developing a climate conducive to creativity and innovation. The organizational literature contains many different recommendations for fostering creativity. Some of these are:[10]

- *Remove or reduce obstacles to creativity within an organization.* These obstacles include the various environmental blocks such as autocratic bosses, distractions (constant meetings or phone calls), and lack of management support. In addition, creative people should be relieved of routine duties and administrative chores.
- *Match jobs to individuals' creative abilities.* Some people work best alone; others work better in groups. Some work well in 9-to-5 time frames; others require flex time. Managers need to be tolerant of individual idiosyncrasies, nonconformity of dress codes, frequent coffee breaks, and so on.
- *Tolerate failures and establish direction.* Creative people need an atmosphere that allows radical ideas without being harshly judged. Seemingly silly ideas often turn into the best products. However, appropriate direction must be given, and realistic goals and objectives must be set to maintain a sense of urgency.
- *Improve motivation to increase productivity and solve problems creatively.* Creative accomplishments should be recognized publicly, to peers, superiors, and upper management. Such recognition increases both self-esteem and motivation.
- *Enhance the self-esteem and build the confidence of organization members.* Creative individuals are at their best when their minds are challenged—not their security or ego. Job security, adequate wages, and job satisfaction enhance an individual's self-confidence and security.
- *Improve communication so that ideas can be better shared.* This is certainly true within an organization. Creative individuals also have the need to communicate with peers outside the organization; such activities should be encouraged. Creative people need a sounding board for their ideas and continuous feedback from their efforts.
- *Place highly creative people in special jobs and provide training to take advantage of their creativity.* Establish career paths and financial rewards so as not to disadvantage creative people who are not part of the line organization.

If you examine carefully the underlying principles of Deming's 14 Points, you see many similarities with attitudes and organizational structures that support creativity. This is particularly true in the elimination of fear, the removal of barriers that inhibit joy in work, elimination of numbers driven and short-term goal-driven management, a focus on continuous improvement, leadership, and continual training and education. Fear, in particular, is a creativity killer. The head of a corporate legal office commented that "when someone tries to use fear to motivate me, I get all tied up. I get less creative and less willing to take chances, and you've got to take risks to do good work." A midlevel manager observed, "Where there is a lot of fear of screwing up, people don't change behaviors or work systems. Creativity is inhibited. People work one day at a time, rather than looking to the future."[11] Generally, the cultures of most organizations do not support the conditions that lead to creative behavior. Cultural change, education, and training are necessary to develop a creative climate.

Leadership, in particular, can have a significant influence on creativity.[12] Researchers have noted that personality, cognitive style orientation, and level of intrinsic motivation are core characteristics for employee creativity. Cognitive style is the natural orientation or preferred means of problem solving. An individual with an innovative cognitive style will seek and integrate diverse information, redefine posed problems, and generate novel ideas. Those with adaptive cognitive styles will tend to use data within a well-established domain, accept problems as defined, and generate ideas consistent with accepted convention. When people enjoy creativity-related tasks, their level of creative output is high. Researchers have discovered that creativity does not appear to be enhanced for employees working with supervisors having similar cognitive styles. In particular, those with innovative cognitive styles receive little benefit from working with supervisors who also exhibit creative tendencies, probably because they already possess the skills, confidence, and values to be creative. However, it appears that when employees work with supervisors who possess a similar intrinsic motivation, creative performance is enhanced.

Researchers also have found that when employees with a low intrinsic motivation for creativity are assigned to high intrinsic motivation supervisors, they produced lower creative output, perhaps because such supervisors may unintentionally intimidate or suppress creativity of these employees.

These findings have practical implications for selecting, assigning, and training employees. Managers must consider individuals' motivation to be creative. Identifying and assigning employees with the appropriate motivational orientation for jobs involving creative tasks is likely to enhance innovation.

Placing a supervisor with a true appreciation for creative work among employees with the motivation to create is also useful. The ability and willingness of supervisors to create positive experiences conducive to creativity may provide a powerful and effective means by which organizational creativity can be enhanced. We will discuss issues of leadership and motivation further in later chapters.

STATISTICAL THINKING AND PROCESS CONTROL TOOLS

Statistical thinking is at the heart of the Deming philosophy and is the basis for good management. **Statistical thinking** is a philosophy of learning and action based on the principles that:

1. all work occurs in a system of interconnected processes,
2. variation exists in all processes, and
3. understanding and reducing variation are keys to success.[13]

Statistical thinking is more than simply applying statistical methods. Statistical thinking focuses on understanding and reducing variation, not merely quantifying it. Nevertheless, statistical methods are important to be a good statistical thinker.

A sign that the president of the former Texas Instruments Defense Systems and Electronics Group (now Raytheon Systems Company) had in his office said: "Unless you change the process, why would you expect the results to change?" By viewing work as a process, we can apply management-by-fact and various quality tools to establish consistent, predictable processes, study them, and improve them. By viewing processes as interconnected components of a system, we avoid suboptimization—one of the key principles of Deming's Profound Knowledge. When managers make decisions in isolation, they often fail to see chains of events that might occur throughout the company because of their decisions. A typical example is designing a product without consideration of the capability of processes to manufacture it or the support systems required to service it in the field.

Recognizing and understanding variation is the essence of statistical thinking. We discussed principles of variation within the context of Deming's Profound Knowledge in Chapter 1, particularly the differences between common and special causes of variation. Although variation exists everywhere, many business decisions do not often account for it. How often do managers make decisions based on a single data point or two, seeing trends when they don't exist, or manipulating financial figures they cannot truly control (see box "The VP's Dilemma")?

The lack of broad and sustained use of statistical thinking in many organizations is due to two reasons.[14] First, statisticians historically have functioned as problem solvers in manufacturing, research, and development, and thereby focused on individual clients rather than on organizations. Second, statisticians have focused primarily on technical aspects of statistics rather than emphasizing the focus on process variation that will lead to bottom-line results. Process management—category 6 in the Baldrige criteria—includes process definition, measurement, control, and improvement. Each of these are fundamental to statistical thinking.

The VP's Dilemma[15]

Brian Joiner, a noted quality management consultant, relates the following case:

Ed was a regional VP for a service company that had facilities around the world. He was determined that the facilities in his region would get the highest customer satisfaction ratings in the company. If he noticed that a facility had a major drop in satisfaction ratings in one month or had "below average" ratings for three months in a row, he would call the manager and ask what had happened—and make it clear that next month's rating had better improve. And most of the time, it did!

As the average satisfaction score dropped from 65 to 60 between February and March, Ed's memo to his managers read:

Bad news! We dropped five points! We should all focus on improving these scores right away! I realize that our usage rates have increased faster than anticipated, so you've really got to hustle to give our customers great service. I know you can do it!

As Joiner observed, Do you look at data this way? This month versus last month? This month versus the same month last year? Do you sometimes look at the latest data point? The last two data points? I couldn't understand why people would only want to look at two data points. Finally, it became clear to me. With any two data points, it's easy to compute a trend: "Things are down 2 percent this month from last month. This month is 30 percent above the same month last year." Unfortunately, *we learn nothing of importance by comparing two results when they both come from a stable process . . . and most data of importance to management are from stable processes."*

Understanding processes provides the context for determining the effects of variation and the proper type of managerial action to be taken. This variation is quantified through statistical analysis of process data, and requires understanding the sources, magnitude, and nature of the variation.

Senior management needs to champion the use of statistical thinking by defining the strategy and goals of the approach, clearly and consistently communicating the benefits and results, providing the necessary resources, coaching others, and recognizing and rewarding the desired behavior. To help managers work in this fashion, many organizations are using Six Sigma initiatives to create core groups of highly trained professionals who are skilled in statistical thinking and can help others to use it effectively. This requires an environment conducive to learning new behaviors and concepts.

Statistical Process Control

Statistical process control (SPC) is a methodology for monitoring a process to identify special causes of variation and signaling the need to take corrective action when it is appropriate. As such, it provides a rational basis for applying statistical thinking to controlling processes. When special causes are present, the process is deemed to be *out of control*. If the variation in the process is due to common causes alone, the process is said to be *in statistical control*. Basically, statistical control means that both the process average and variance are constant over time.

SPC is a proven technique for improving quality and productivity. Many customers require their suppliers to provide evidence of statistical process control. Thus, SPC provides a means by which a firm may demonstrate its quality capability, an activity necessary for survival in today's highly competitive markets. Because SPC requires processes to show measurable variation, it is ineffective for quality levels approaching Six Sigma. However, SPC is quite effective for companies in the early stages of quality efforts.

Walter Shewhart was the first to distinguish between common causes and special causes in process variation. He developed the control chart to identify the effects of special causes. A control chart displays the state of control of a process (Figure 7.16). Time is measured on the horizontal axis, and the value of a variable on the vertical axis. A central horizontal line usually corresponds to the average value of the quality characteristic being measured. Two other horizontal lines represent the upper (UCL) and lower (LCL) control limits, chosen so that there is a high probability that sample values

FIGURE 7.16   EXAMPLE OF A CONTROL CHART

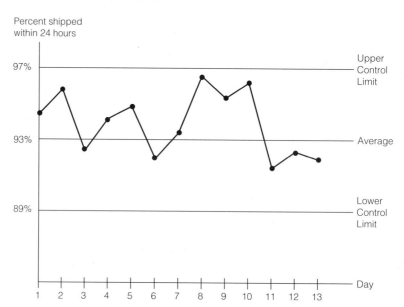

will fall within these limits if the process is under control—that is, affected only by common causes of variation. If points fall outside of the control limits or if unusual patterns such as shifts up or down, trends up or down, cycles, and so forth exist, special causes may be present.

Although control charts were first developed and used in a manufacturing context, they are easily applied to service organizations. Table 7.1 lists just a few of the many potential applications of control charts for services. The key is in defining the appropriate quality measures to monitor. Most service processes can be improved through the appropriate application of control charts.

Consider the following example. The Joint Commission Accreditation of Health Care Organizations (JCAHO) monitors and evaluates health care providers according to strict standards and guidelines. Improvement in the quality of care is a principal concern. Hospitals are required to identify and monitor important quality indicators that affect patient care and establish "thresholds for evaluation" (TFEs), which are levels at which special investigation of problems should occur. TFEs provide a means of focusing attention on nonrandom errors (that is, special causes of variation). A logical way to set TFEs is through control charts. For instance, a hospital collects monthly data on the number of infections after surgeries. These data are shown in Table 7.2.

TABLE 7.1 APPLICATIONS OF CONTROL CHARTS IN SERVICE ORGANIZATIONS

Organization	Quality Measure
Hospital	Lab test accuracy
	Insurance claim accuracy
	On-time delivery of meals and medication
Bank	Check-processing accuracy
Insurance company	Claims-processing response time
	Billing accuracy
Post Office	Sorting accuracy
	Time of delivery
	Percentage of express mail delivered on time
Ambulance	Response time
Police Department	Incidence of crime in a precinct
	Number of traffic citations
Hotel	Proportion of rooms satisfactorily cleaned
	Checkout time
	Number of complaints received
Transportation	Proportion of freight cars correctly routed
	Dollar amount of damage per claim
Auto service	Percentage of time work completed as promised
	Number of parts out of stock

TABLE 7.2   MONTHLY DATA ON INFECTIONS AFTER SURGERY

Month	Surgeries	Infections	Percent
1	208	1	0.48
2	225	3	1.33
3	201	3	1.49
4	236	1	0.42
5	220	3	1.36
6	244	1	0.41
7	247	1	0.40
8	245	1	0.41
9	250	1	0.40
10	227	0	0.00
11	234	2	0.85
12	227	4	1.76
13	213	2	0.94
14	212	1	0.47
15	193	2	1.04
16	182	0	0.00
17	140	1	0.71
18	230	1	0.43
19	187	1	0.53
20	252	2	0.79
21	201	1	0.50
22	226	0	0.00
23	222	2	0.90
24	212	2	0.94
25	219	1	0.46
26	223	2	0.90
27	191	1	0.52
28	222	0	0.00
29	231	3	1.30
30	239	1	0.42
31	217	2	0.92
32	241	1	0.41
33	220	3	1.36
34	278	1	0.36
35	255	3	1.18
36	225	1	0.44
	7,995	55	

FIGURE 7.17 CONTROL CHART FOR SURGERY INFECTIONS

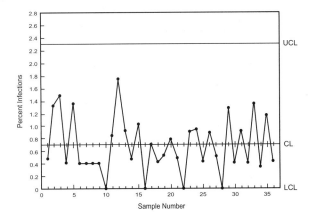

Hospital administrators are concerned about whether the high percentages of infections (such as 1.76 percent in month 12) are caused by factors other than randomness. A control chart constructed from these data is shown in Figure 7.17. (Note that if the control limits are removed, it becomes a simple run chart.) The average percentage of infections is $55/7995 = 0.688$ percent.

Using formulas described in more advanced books, the upper control limit is computed to be 2.35 percent. None of the data points fall above the upper control limit, indicating that the variation each month is due purely to chance and that the process is stable. To reduce the infection rate, management would have to attack the common causes in the process. The upper control limit would be a logical TFE to use, because any value beyond this limit is unlikely to occur by chance. Management can continue to use this chart to monitor future data.

REVIEW AND DISCUSSION QUESTIONS

1. Why is good planning important to achieving high quality? Why should managers invest in the time to learn many of the tools presented in this chapter?
2. Explain the benefits of the quality function deployment approach. How does it help organizations to design better products and services?
3. Using whatever "market research" techniques you feel are appropriate, define a set of customer attributes for (a) purchasing books at your college bookstore, (b) a hotel room used for business, and (c) a college registration process. How might QFD be used to improve these processes? Define a set of "hows" and try to construct the relationship matrix for the House of Quality for each of these examples.

4. Most organizations have well-defined mission statements that include a set of goals for the firm and actions that the firm can take. How might QFD be used to ensure that the actions are consistent with the goals? Find some company's mission statement to illustrate this.

5. What is concurrent engineering? What type of organizational culture would be required to make concurrent engineering successful?

6. Explain concept engineering. Why is it an important tool for assuring quality in product and process design activities?

7. What is design failure mode and effects analysis (DFMEA)? Provide a simple example illustrating the concept.

8. Explain the purpose of the seven management and planning tools.

9. How might you use the seven management and planning tools in your daily activities (schoolwork, fraternity or honor society operations, and so on)? Provide specific examples.

10. Explain the purpose and uses of each of the "seven QC tools."

11. Select a process that you do routinely (for example, washing your car, preparing for an exam, preparing a meal) and draw a flowchart of it. Explain how the flowchart helps you to understand and improve the process.

12. A flowchart for a fast-food drive-through window is shown in Figure 7.18. Discuss the important quality characteristics inherent in this process and suggest possible improvements.

13. Design a check sheet to help a high school student who is getting poor grades on a math quiz determine the source of his or her difficulty.

14. Develop cause-and-effect diagrams for (a) a poor exam grade; (b) no job offers; (c) too many speeding tickets; (d) being late for work or school.

15. Identify several sources of errors in your personal life. Develop some mistake-proofing approaches that might prevent them.

16. How might poka-yoke be applied to the U.S. election system based on the information described in the example in this chapter? You might wish to do some additional research on the subject or find out how your local election process is performed.

17. Search the Internet for John Grout's Poka-Yoke Web site. Read several of the interesting articles available there and write a report on the information you discover.

18. At a university library, many activities take place. Some of these are:
    - processing request forms from patrons for copying of journal articles;
    - reshelving books that readers have left on desks (books are picked up, placed on carts, sorted, and reshelved); and
    - locating missing books.

    For these activities, identify potential problems that might arise and what the library might do to "mistake-proof" its activities to provide better service.

19. What is a kaizen blitz? How does it differ from the original notion of kaizen described in the previous chapter?

20. What is statistical thinking?

FIGURE 7.18   FLOWCHART OF A FAST-FOOD DRIVE-THROUGH PROCESS

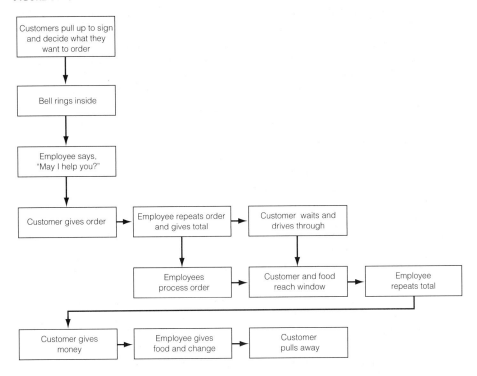

21. Explain how creativity is embodied in the various tools and approaches described in this chapter.

22. In a book, *Weird Ideas That Work* (New York: Free Press, 2002), Robert I. Sutton suggests 11 1/2 practices for promoting, managing, and sustaining innovation. These include:
    - hiring "slow learners" (of the organizational code);
    - hiring people who make you uncomfortable, even those you dislike;
    - encouraging people to ignore and defy superiors and peers;
    - finding some happy people, and get them to fight;
    - thinking of some ridiculous or impractical things to do, then planning to do them; and
    - forgetting the past, especially your company's successes.

    Why do you think these practices work? If you have few ideas, you should probably read the book!

23. What is statistical thinking? How might the traditional teaching of statistics be improved by incorporating this notion? Draw your response from your own experiences in learning statistics.

24. Explain the concept of statistical process control. How does it support the Deming philosophy discussed in Chapter 1?

CASES

Scott's Fitness Center

Figure 7.19 shows a partially completed House of Quality for a proposed fitness center.

1. Examine the relationships in the roof of the House of Quality. Explain why they make sense (or if you think they do not, explain why). How would this assessment help in the design activity?

FIGURE 7.19   HOUSE OF QUALITY FOR SCOTT'S FITNESS CENTER

		Program offerings	Program times	Maint. schedule	Maint. staff	Fitness staff	Training	Facility size	Instructions	Aml./types equip.	Staff schedule	Facility hours	Access control	Fee structure	Lighting	Internet access
Programs and Activities	Has programs I want															
	Programs are convenient															
	Family activities available															
Facilities	Clean locker rooms															
	Well-maintained equipment															
Atmosphere	Safe place to be															
	Equipment available when desired															
	Wide variety of equipment															
	Adequate parking															
Staff	Friendly and courteous															
	Knowledgeable and professional															
	Available when needed															
	Respond quickly to problems															
Other	Easy to sign up for programs															
	Value for your money															

◉ Very strong relationship
○ Strong relationship
△ Weak relationship

2. Complete the matrix in the body of the House of Quality. That is, examine each pair of customer and technical requirements and determine whether there is a very strong relationship, strong relationship, weak relationship, or no relationship, and fill in the appropriate symbols in the matrix.

3. Suppose that the most important customer requirements identified through surveys and focus groups are "Has programs I want," "Family activities available," "Equipment available when desired," "Easy to sign up for programs," and "Value for your money." "Staff available when needed" was ranked low, while the remaining were ranked moderate in importance.

Based on this information, identify the most important technical requirements that should be addressed in subsequent design activities.

Welz Business Machines[16]

Welz Business Machines sells and services a variety of copiers, computers, and other office equipment. The company receives many calls daily for service, sales, accounting, and other departments. All calls are handled centrally by customer service representatives and routed to other individuals as appropriate.

A number of customers had complained about long waits when calling for service. A market research study found that customers became irritated if the call was not answered within five rings. Scott Welz, the company president, authorized the customer service department manager, Tim, to study this problem and find a method to shorten the call-waiting time. Tim met with the service representatives who answered the calls to attempt to determine the reasons for long waiting times. The following conversation ensued:

Tim: This is a serious problem. How a customer phone inquiry is answered is the first impression the customer receives from us. As you know, this company was founded on efficient and friendly service to all our customers. It's obvious why customers have to wait: You're on the phone with another customer. Can you think of any reasons that might keep you on the phone for an unnecessarily long time?

Robin: I've noticed quite often that the person to whom I need to route the call is not present. It takes time to transfer the call and to see whether it is answered. If the person is not there, I end up apologizing and transferring the call to another extension.

Tim: You're right, Robin. Sales personnel often are out of the office on sales calls, away on trips to preview new products, or away from their desks for a variety of reasons. What else might cause this problem?

Ravi: I get irritated at customers who spend a great deal of time complaining about a problem that I cannot do anything about except refer to someone else. Of course, I listen and sympathize with them, but this eats up a lot of time.

Lamarr: Some customers call so often, they think we're long-lost friends and strike up a personal conversation.

Tim: That's not always a bad thing, you realize.

Lamarr: Sure, but it delays my answering other calls.

Nancy: It's not always the customer's fault. During lunch, we're not all available to answer the phone.

Ravi: Right after we open at 9 a.m., we get a rush of calls. I think that many of the delays are caused by these peak periods.

Robin: I've noticed the same thing between 4 and 5 p.m.

Tim: I've had a few comments from department managers who received calls that didn't fall in their areas of responsibility and had to be transferred again.

Mark: But that doesn't cause delays at our end.

Nancy: That's right, Mark, but I just realized that sometimes I simply don't understand what the customer's problem really is. I spend a lot of time trying to get him or her to explain it better. Often, I have to route it to someone because other calls are waiting.

Ravi: Perhaps we need to have more knowledge of our products.

Tim: Well, I think we've covered most of the major reasons why many customers have to wait. It seems to me that we have four major reasons: the phones are short-staffed, the receiving party is not present, the customer dominates the conversation, and you may not understand the customer's problem. Next we need to collect some information about these possible causes. I will set up a data collection sheet that you can use to track some of these things. Mark, would you help me on this?

Over the next two weeks, the staff collected data on the frequency of reasons why some callers had to wait. The results are summarized as follows:

Reason	Total number
Operators short-staffed	172
Receiving party not present	73
Customer dominates conversation	19
Lack of operator understanding	61
Other reasons	10

Discussion Questions

1. From the conversation between Tim and his staff, draw a cause-and-effect diagram.
2. Perform a Pareto analysis of the data collected.
3. What actions might the company take to improve the situation?

Southwest Regional Hospital

Stuart Kendall just returned from an annual medical conference. Stuart is director of Southwest Regional Hospital. At the conference, he heard that over 50,000 people die each year from medical errors, and of those, medication errors account for about 7,000 deaths a year. Medication errors can also lead to disabilities, lawsuits, and millions of dollars spent on longer hospital stays and medical treatments. Dr. Kendall knew that SWRH had to be more proactive in preventing medication errors. After pulling together a team to map the process, shown in Figure 7.20, he hired you to analyze it and make some recommendations to help prevent errors and mistakes. Discuss possible sources of errors, the types of individuals responsible (e.g., physicians, nurses, pharmacists, other), and poka-yokes that might be used to mitigate these errors.

The Quarterly Sales Report[17]

Suppose that Ron Hagler, the vice president of sales for Selit Corp., had just gotten a report on the past five years of quarterly sales data for the regions under his authority (see Figure 7.21 on page 308). Not happy with the results, he got on the phone to his secretary. "Marsha, tell the regional managers I need to speak with them this afternoon. Everyone must attend." Marsha had been Hagler's secretary for almost a decade. She knew by the tone in his voice that he meant business, so she contacted the regional managers about the impromptu meeting at 2 P.M. At 1:55 P.M., the regional managers filed into the room. The only time they were called into a meeting together was when Hagler was unhappy.

FIGURE 7.20 Medical Administration Process at Southwest Regional Hospital

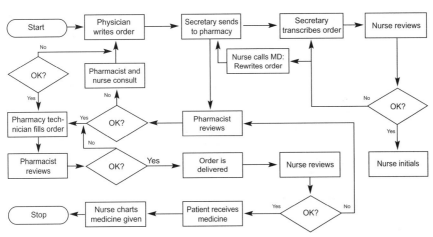

Source: Ellen Williams and Ray Tailey, "The use of Failure Mode Effect and Criticality Analysis in a Medication Error Subcommittee," *ASQC Health Care Division Newsletter*, Winter 1996, 4. © 1996 American Society for Quality. Reprinted with permission.

FIGURE 7.21   SALES BY REGION FOR SELIT CORP., 1998–2002

1998 Sales (in thousands)

Region	First Quarter	Second Quarter	Third Quarter	Fourth Quarter
Northeast	$924	$928	$956	$1,222
Southwest	$1,056	$1,048	$1,129	$1,073
Northwest	$1,412	$1,280	$1,129	$1,181
North Central	$431	$470	$439	$431
Mid-Atlantic	$539	$558	$591	$556
South Central	$397	$391	$414	$407

1999 Sales (in thousands)

Region	First Quarter	Second Quarter	Third Quarter	Fourth Quarter
Northeast	$748	$962	$983	$1,024
Southwest	$1,157	$1,146	$1,064	$1,213
Northwest	$1,149	$1,248	$1,103	$1,021
North Central	$471	$496	$506	$573
Mid-Atlantic	$540	$590	$606	$643
South Central	$415	$442	$384	$448

2000 Sales (in thousands)

Region	First Quarter	Second Quarter	Third Quarter	Fourth Quarter
Northeast	$991	$978	$1,040	$1,295
Southwest	$1,088	$4,322	$1,256	$1,132
Northwest	$1,085	$1,125	$910	$999
North Central	$403	$440	$371	$405
Mid-Atlantic	$657	$602	$596	$640
South Central	$441	$366	$470	$426

2001 Sales (in thousands)

Region	First Quarter	Second Quarter	Third Quarter	Fourth Quarter
Northeast	$756	$1,008	$1,038	$952
Southwest	$4,352	$1,353	$1,466	$1,196
Northwest	$883	$851	$997	$878
North Central	$466	$536	$551	$670
Mid-Atlantic	$691	$723	$701	$802
South Central	$445	$455	$363	$462

2002 Sales (in thousands)

Region	First Quarter	Second Quarter	Third Quarter	Fourth Quarter
Northeast	$1,041	$1,020	$976	$1,148
Southwest	$1,330	$1,003	$1,197	$1,337
Northwest	$939	$834	$688	$806
North Central	$588	$699	$743	$702
Mid-Atlantic	$749	$762	$807	$781
South Central	$420	$454	$447	$359

Hagler wasted no time. "I just received the quarterly sales report. Northeast sales were fantastic. Steve, you not only improved 17.6 percent in the fourth quarter, but you also increased sales a whopping 20.6 percent over the previous year. I don't know how you do it!" Steve smiled. His philosophy to end the year with a bang by getting customers to stockpile units paid off again. Hagler had failed to notice that Steve's first quarter sales were always sluggish.

Hagler continued: "Terry, Southwest sales were also superb. You showed an 11.7 percent increase in the fourth quarter and an 11.8 percent increase over the previous year." Terry also smiled. She wasn't sure how she did so well, but she sure wasn't going to change anything. "Jan, Northwest sales were up 17.2 percent in the fourth quarter, but down 8.2 percent from the previous year," said Hagler. "You need to find out what you did previously to make your sales go through the roof. Even so, your performance in the fourth quarter was good." Jan tried to hide his puzzlement. Although he had received a big order in November, it was the first big order he had received in a long time. Overall, sales for the Northwest were declining.

Hagler was now ready to deal with the "problem" regions. "Leslie, North Central sales were down 5.5 percent in the fourth quarter, but up 4.7 percent from the previous year. I don't understand how your sales vary so much. Do you need more incentive?" Leslie looked down. She had been working very hard the past five years and had acquired numerous new accounts. In fact, she received a bonus for acquiring the most new business in 1998.

"Kim, Mid-Atlantic sales were down 3.2 percent in the fourth quarter and down 2.6 percent from the previous year. I'm very disappointed in your performance. You were once my best sales representative. I had high expectations for you. Now, I can only hope that your first quarter results show some sign of life." Kim felt her face get red. She knew she sold more units in 2000 than in 1999. "What does Hagler know anyway," she thought to herself. "He's just an empty suit."

Hagler turned to Dave, who felt a surge of adrenaline. "Dave, South Central sales were the worst of all! Sales were down 19.7 percent in the fourth quarter and down 22.3 percent from the previous year. How can you explain this? Do you value your job? I want to see a dramatic improvement in this quarter's results or else!" Dave felt numb. This was a tough region, with a lot of competition. Sure, accounts were lost over the years, but those lost were always replaced with new ones. How could he be doing so badly?

Discussion Question

1. How can Hagler improve his approach by applying principles of statistical thinking? Use any analyses of the data that you feel are appropriate to fully explain your thinking and help him.

The HMO Pharmacy Crisis[18]

John Dover just completed an intensive course, "Statistical Thinking for Continuous Improvement," that was offered to all employees of a large health maintenance organization (HMO). There was no time to celebrate, however, because he was already under a lot of pressure. Dover worked as a pharmacy assistant in the HMO's pharmacy, and his manager, Juan de Pacotilla, was about to be fired. Pacotilla's dismissal appeared imminent because of numerous complaints—and even a few lawsuits—over inaccurate prescriptions.

Pacotilla now was asking Dover for his assistance in trying to resolve the problem. "John, I really need your help," said Pacotilla. "If I can't show some major improvement or at least a solid plan by next month, I'm history." "I'll be glad to help," replied Dover, "but what can I do? I'm just a pharmacy assistant." "Your job title isn't important. I think you're just the person who can get this done," said Pacotilla. "I realize that I've been too far removed from day-to-day operations in the pharmacy, but you work there every day. You're in a much better position to find out how to fix the problem. Just tell me what to do, and I'll do it." "But what about the statistical consultant you hired to analyze the data on inaccurate prescriptions?" asked Dover.

"To be honest, I'm really disappointed with that guy. He has spent two weeks trying to come up with a new modeling approach to predict weekly inaccurate prescriptions. I tried to explain to him that I don't want to predict the mistakes, I want to eliminate them. I don't think I got through, however, because he said we need a month of additional data to verify the model before he can apply a new method he just read about in a journal to identify 'change points in the time series,' whatever that means. But get this, he will only identify the change points and send me a list. He says it's my job to figure out what they mean and how to respond. I don't know much about statistics.

The only thing I remember from my course in college is that it was the worst course I ever took. I'm becoming convinced that statistics really doesn't have much to offer in solving real problems. Since you've just gone through the statistical thinking course, maybe you can see something I can't. I realize it's a long shot, but I was hoping you could use this as the project you need to officially complete the course."

"I used to feel the same way about statistics, too," replied Dover. "But the statistical thinking course was interesting because it didn't focus on crunching numbers. I have some ideas about how we can approach making improvements in prescription accuracy. I think it would be a great project. But we might not be able to solve this problem ourselves. As you know, there is a lot of finger pointing going on. Pharmacists blame the doctors' sloppy handwriting and incomplete instructions for the problem. Doctors blame the pharmacy assistants, who do most of the computer entry of the prescriptions, claiming that they are incompetent. Pharmacy assistants blame the pharmacists for assuming too much about their knowledge of medical terminology, brand names, known drug interactions, and so on."

"It sounds like there's no hope," said Pacotilla. "I wouldn't say that at all," replied Dover. "It's just that there might be no quick fix we can do by ourselves in the pharmacy. Let me explain what I'm thinking about doing and how I would propose attacking the problem using what I just learned in the statistical thinking course."

Discussion Question

1. How do you think John should approach this problem, using what he has just learned? Assume that he really did pick up a solid understanding of the concepts and tools of statistical thinking in the course.

ENDNOTES

1. Christina Hepner Brodie, "A Polaroid Notebook: Concept Engineering," *Center for Quality of Management Journal* 3, No. 2 (1994), pp. 7–14.

2. Laura Horton and David Boger, "How Bose Corporation Applied Concept Engineering to a Service," *Center for Quality of Management Journal* 3, No. 2 (1994), pp. 52–59.

3. Michael Brassard, *The Memory Jogger Plus +*, Meuthen, Mass.: GOAL/QPC, 1989; James L. Brossert, *Quality Function Deployment*, Milwaukee, WI: ASQ Quality Press, 1990; Shigeru Mizuno, *Management for Quality Improvement: The 7 New QC Tools*, Cambridge, Mass.: Productivity Press, 1988.

4. Timothy Clark and Andrew Clark, "Continuous Improvement on the Free Throw Line," *Quality Progress*, October 1997, pp. 78–80.

5. Excerpts reprinted from Richard B. Chase and Douglas M. Stewart, "Make Your Service Fail-Safe," *Sloan Management Review*, Vol. 35, No. 3, Spring 1994. Copyright 1994 by the Sloan Management Review Association. All rights reserved.

6. Howard R. Schussler, "Can Quality Concepts and Tools Fix the U.S. Election Process?" *Quality Progress*, April 2001, pp. 46–50.

7. Eleanor Chilson, "Kaizen Blitzes at Magnivision: $809,270 Cost Savings," *Quality Management Forum* 29, No. 1 (Winter 2003).

8. See, for example, Jacob Eskildsen, Jens Dahlgaard, and Anders Norgaard, "The Impact of Creativity and Learning on Business Excellence," *Total Quality Management*, Vol. 10, Issue 4/5, July 1999, S523–S530.

9. Masaaki Imai, *Kaizen: The Key to Japan's Competitive Success*, New York: McGraw-Hill, 1986, p. 15.

10. Mark R. Edwards and J. Ruth Sproull, "Creativity: Productivity Gold Mine?" *Journal of Creative Behavior*, Vol. 18, No. 3, 1984, pp. 175–184; and Michael K. Badawy, "How to Prevent Creativity Mismanagement," *Research Management*, Vol. 29, No. 4, 1986, p. 28.

11. Kathleen D. Ryan and Daniel K. Oestreich, *Driving Fear Out of the Workplace*, San Francisco: Jossey-Bass, Inc., 1991, pp. 63, 64.

12. Pamela Tierney, Steven Farmer, and George Graen, "An Examination of Leadership and Employee Creativity: The Relevance of Traits and Relationships," *Personnel Psychology*, Vol. 52, No. 3, Autumn 1999, pp. 591–620.

13. Adapted from Galen Britz, Don Emerling, Lynne Hare, Roger Hoerl, and Janice Shade, "How to Teach Others to Apply Statistical Thinking," *Quality Progress*, June 1997, pp. 67–79. © 1997 American Society for Quality. Reprinted with permission.

14. Ronald D. Snee, "Getting Better Business Results: Using Statistical Thinking and Methods to Shape the Bottom Line," *Quality Progress*, June 1998, pp. 102–106.

15. Adapted from Brian L. Joiner, *Fourth Generation Management*, New York: McGraw-Hill, 1994, p. 129.

16. This problem was developed from a classic example published in "The Quest for Higher Quality: The Deming Prize and Quality Control" by RICOH of America, Inc.

17. Adapted from Britz, et al. See Note 13.

18. Adapted from Britz, et al. See Note 13.

PART 3

Total Quality and Organizational Behavior

CHAPTER 8

Quality Teamwork

Deming urged leaders to abandon competition and to seek cooperation. Teams provide a way of doing this, as well as enhancing Deming's concept of "pride and joy in work." A **team** is a small number of people with complementary skills who are committed to a common purpose, a set of performance goals, and an approach for which they hold themselves mutually accountable.[1] Teams are ubiquitous in our world—the Denver Broncos, Navy SEALS, the Tokyo String Quartet, the cast of *ER*, and Jeff Gordon's pit crew, to name just a few. Teams also are a central facet of Total Quality.

Although many types of teams exist in organizations pursuing TQ, the concept of teamwork is widespread and is a key contributor to TQ success in just about any setting. This chapter will

➤ explain the importance of teams in TQM,
➤ identify the different types of teams used in TQM,
➤ explain some of the factors associated with the successful use of teams,
➤ give examples of effective teams in action, and
➤ relate the use of teams in TQM to organizational behavior theories.

THE IMPORTANCE OF TEAMS IN TQ

Teams are everywhere in TQ organizations: at the top and bottom and in every function and department in between. For instance, Corning Telecommunications Product's Division, a former Baldrige recipient, has employee-designed work teams, customer account teams, market teams, new product development teams, and manufacturing operation teams. FedEx has more than 4,000 Quality Action teams; Boeing Airlift and Tanker Division has more than 100 integrated product teams (IPTs) that are typically made up of engineering, work-team, customer, and supplier representatives. Granite Rock, with fewer than 400 employees, has about 100 functioning teams, ranging from 10 corporate quality teams to project teams, purchasing teams, task forces, and function teams composed of people who do the same job at different locations.

Teamwork for Fun and Profit at Motorola[2]

Dina Trinidad is a mold operator at a Motorola semiconductor plant in Manila, Philippines. She had worked for Motorola for over 17 years and had never left her native country. Then the company sent her and 11 of her coworkers to a posh resort in Scottsdale, Arizona, for five days to make a presentation to top executives and be treated like royalty as part of Motorola's Total Customer Satisfaction (TCS) team competition. This competition helps to renew emphasis on team processes, recognize and reward outstanding team performance, reaffirm the environment for continuous improvement, demonstrate the power of focused team effort, and communicate the best team achievements throughout the company.

Some 5,000 teams take part in preliminary contests in each of Motorola's business units, and one to five teams from each region move forward to the worldwide finals. With names such as the Green Tray Packers, Document Doctors, and Irish Risky, teams are awarded points in seven categories: project selection (tied to Motorola's key initiatives), teamwork (participation and contributions), analysis (analytical tools leading to root causes and solution identification), remedies (consistent with analysis), results, institutionalization (sustainable improvement over time), and presentation (clear and concise). One team saved $1.8 million in 1996 by reducing polyimide delamination for electronic circuits by 85 percent, another increased production capacity for cellular phone production by 50 percent in just eight weeks; and the winning team's efforts were expected to save over $6 million in one year.

For Dina Trinidad, the competition only reinforced the feeling that Motorola values its employees. She, like others, says she will treasure every one of her TCS memories: "The experience emphasized even more the value of each individual in the company. It's worth remembering time and again—even forever."

Why are there so many teams? The TQ philosophy recognizes the interdependence of various parts of the organization and uses teams as a way to coordinate work. Teamwork enables various parts of the organization to work together in meeting customer needs that can seldom be fulfilled by employees limited to one specialty. Teams promote equality among individuals, encouraging a positive attitude and trust. The diversity inherent in teams often provides unique perspectives on work, spontaneous thought, and creativity. In addition, teams develop a greater sense of responsibility for achieving goals and performing tasks. In short, teams provide a variety of benefits that are not derived from individuals working alone.

TQ organizations recognize that the potential contributions of employees are much greater than in the traditional organization, and teams are an attempt to take advantage of this potential. Furthermore, the competitive environment of modern business requires flexible, fast reaction to changes in customer demands or technological capacity. Teams can provide the capacity for rapid response. During the past few years, many companies have gone public with stories of their successful teams as well as sharing their recognition efforts (see the box on Motorola). Managers are always looking for ideas that produce results, and teams certainly fall squarely within this category.

TYPES OF TQ TEAMS

TQ uses so many different types of teams that sometimes it is difficult to tell one from another. Some common types of teams include:

- *Steering committees (or quality councils)*—management teams that lead an organization and provide direction and focus.
- *Problem-solving teams*—teams of workers and supervisors that meet to address workplace problems involving quality and productivity, or ad-hoc teams with a specific mission such as organizational design teams that act as architects of change as discussed in the previous chapter.
- *Natural work teams*—people who work together every day to perform a complete unit of work.
- *Self-managed teams*—Work teams that are empowered to make and control their own decisions.
- *Virtual teams*—teams whose members communicate by computer, take turns as leaders, and jump in and out as necessary. Virtual teams are beginning to play an increasingly important role because of the Internet and electronic communication.
- *Project teams*—teams with a specific mission to develop something new or to accomplish a complex task. Project teams have recently gained a new measure of importance and respect in the context of Six Sigma.

Management teams, natural work teams, self-managed teams, and virtual teams typically work on routine business activities—managing an organization, building a product, or designing an electronic system—and are an integral part of how work is organized and designed. Quality circles, problem-solving teams, and project teams, by contrast, work more on an ad-hoc basis to address specific tasks or issues, often relating to quality improvement. Also, natural work teams, self-managed teams, and quality circles typically are intraorganizational; that is, members usually come from the same department or function. Management teams, problem-solving teams, virtual teams, and project teams are usually cross-functional; they work on specific tasks or processes that cut across boundaries of several different departments regardless of their organizational home.

An example of the cross-functional nature of teams is the platform team approach to automotive vehicle development introduced by Chrysler.[3] This cross-functional team approach brings together professionals from engineering, design, quality, manufacturing, business planning, program management, purchasing, sales, marketing, and finance to work together to get a new vehicle to market. This idea, brought to Chrysler by its merger with smaller, more innovative AMC/Jeep was not accepted at Chrysler without significant upheaval and struggles. "You talk about internal strife," recalls one Chrysler loyalist, "This was war!"[4] Nevertheless, the concept was just what was needed to pull the company from bankruptcy and near collapse. The Dodge Viper, introduced in 1992, and the 1993 Jeep Grand Cherokee tested this approach, which led to the development of the Chrysler Concorde, Dodge Intrepid, and Eagle Vision in just 39 months, not only on time and under budget, but exceeding 230 product excellence targets. Today, all automobile manufacturers develop products using similar cross-functional team approaches.

Steering Committees

Most organizations practicing total quality have a steering committee, called a **quality council** by Juran[5] and a **quality improvement team** by Crosby.[6] Steering committees are responsible for establishing policy for TQ and for guiding the implementation and evolution of TQ throughout the organization.

The top manager of the organization is usually on the steering committee, as is the manager with overall responsibility for quality—for example, the Vice President/Director of Total Quality. The steering committee may meet fairly often when a TQ effort is getting started, but usually meets only monthly or quarterly once things are under way. This group makes key decisions about the quality process—how quality should be measured and what structures and approaches should be used to improve quality. The steering committee also periodically reviews the status of TQ and makes the adjustments necessary to ensure customer satisfaction and continuous improvement. In general, the steering committee has overall responsibility for the progress and success of the TQ effort.

As TQ is becoming more integrated within organizations, the notion of a separate steering committee dedicated to TQ is disappearing. TQ efforts often are led by the executive management team, which acts both as a quality council and a business leadership team. At Custom Research, Inc., for example, a four-person steering committee sets company directions, integrates performance excellence goals, and promotes the development of all employees. Committee members have frequent interaction with associates, review overall company performance daily, and meet formally each month to identify areas for improvement.

Problem-Solving Teams

The second, and probably most common, type of team used in TQ is the problem-solving team. As the name implies, problem-solving teams work to improve quality by identifying and solving specific quality-related problems facing the organization. Such teams are sometimes referred to as *corrective action teams*, or *quality circles* (see box on quality circles in Japan), although many organizations have created their own names for them. Two basic types of problem-solving teams are departmental and cross-functional.

Departmental Problem-Solving Teams

These teams are limited in membership to employees of a specific department and are limited in scope to problems within that department. Such groups typically meet once a week for one to two hours and progress through a standardized problem-solving methodology. First they identify a set of problems and select one to work on. Then they collect data about the causes of the problem and determine the best approach to solving it. (Often this will entail using many of the techniques described in Chapter 7.)

If the solution does not require any major changes in procedures or substantial resources, the group frequently can implement its own solution. If this is not the case, group members will make a presentation to some level of management, requesting approval for their solution and the resources to implement it. These teams typically remain relatively intact as they address a number of problems in succession.

The problems that such teams work on can be quite diverse. A team of hourly workers at a U.S. steel plant solved a number of crippling quality problems, helping to reduce the amount of steel rejected by automotive customers by 80 percent.[7] A team of service technicians at an equipment rental company simplified the form used to perform preventive maintenance, saving the company considerable time in the process. A team of people from the "re-sort" department at Federal Express improved the process of package sorting, which created savings in labor costs and helped to avoid the cost and embarrassment of having to send overnight packages via commercial airlines.[8] An information systems team for a manufacturing company addressed a serious problem with internal customer satisfaction about its response to requests for application changes and help with using new software.[9]

Cross-Functional Teams

Cross-functional teams are not unique to total quality—they are commonly used in new product development, for example—but are increasingly becoming a mainstay of quality programs. These teams are similar in many ways to the departmental teams just discussed: they receive training in problem solving, identify and solve problems, and either implement or recommend solutions.

The differences are that members of cross-functional teams come from several departments or functions, deal with problems that involve a variety of functions, and typically dissolve after the problem is solved. For example,

Quality Circles in Japan: Still Unbroken

Quality circles were among the first Japanese management practices used in the United States. When visiting Japan in the 1970s, American managers noticed groups of workers meeting to address quality problems. The managers recognized this as a practice that could easily be copied and returned home to institute it in their own companies. Quality circles (QCs) took off in the United States as the Japanese management mania peaked, and firms like Lockheed and Westinghouse reported early successes with QCs. The movement boomed in the early 1980s as most large American companies introduced the practice.

The bloom was soon off the rose, however, as firms found themselves devoting a lot of time and attention to QCs and receiving relatively little in return. There were a number of reasons for the lack of results. Employees were only encouraged to work on quality problems during their meetings (usually about an hour a week) and spent the rest of their week just "doing their job." Supervisors were often not involved in the program and were indifferent, if not downright hostile, to it. Perhaps the biggest problem was that QCs were "just a program," cut off from and often opposed to the way the organization usually worked. Managers preached about the importance of quality work during their QC events, but when crunch time came, their attitude was, in the words of one QC member, "If it doesn't smoke, ship it!" Not surprisingly, companies started to disband their QC programs, which were soon dismissed as just another passing fad. In the context of the current interest in total quality, many managers look back on QCs as essentially a false start on the road to quality. It is interesting in this light to note that many Japanese companies still operate QCs and that they are seen as a critical part of the total quality control (TQC) effort in these companies.[10]

According to the Union of Japanese Scientists and Engineers, 5.5 million workers take part in 750,000 circles. Managers as well as frontline employees are involved, and the circles are considered a normal part of working life, rather than a "program." In fact, QCs often work to achieve the objectives set in the *kaizen* process (see Chapter 6), which puts them in the mainstream of TQC activity. Some organizations provide monetary incentives for suggestions provided by circles, and employees in some firms make dozens of suggestions per year. It appears that the mistake made in the U.S. introduction of quality circles was not in introducing them, but in not taking them seriously.

a cross-functional team in a brokerage might deal with problems in handling questions from clients. The issues raised would not be limited to stocks, bonds, or mutual funds, so people from all of these areas would be involved.

Cross-functional teams make a great deal of sense in an organization devoted to process improvement, because most processes do not respect functional boundaries. If a process is to be comprehensively addressed, the team addressing it cannot be limited, by either membership or charter, to only one function. To be effective, cross-functional teams should include people from several departments: those who are feeling the effects of the problem, those who may be causing it, those who can provide remedies, and those who can furnish data.[11]

Cross-functional teams are often used for solving specific problems. For example, one cross-functional team made up of nurses, dieticians, and other nursing unit and food services staff addressed the problem of patients receiving their dinners late. This problem was quite aggravating to patients, but if it had been addressed by only the nursing unit, ignorance or apathy in the food services department would most likely have been blamed. Had the problem been addressed by food services, nursing would likely have been blamed. In either case, little would have been accomplished. A cross-functional team was required to unravel the complex scheduling and delivery issues associated with the problem. Similarly, a cross-functional team at New York Life Insurance Company addressed the problem of returned mail. This was crucial for the company, because if policyholders do not receive their premium notices, New York Life does not get paid (see box "Gravedigging in New York" on the next page).

Cross-functional teams are natural vehicles for implementing large-scale organizational changes. A large North American wholesale and retail grocery company had embarked on a major organizational transformation because of competitive threats. Several cross-functional teams were established to support the transformation effort. Some were leadership teams that focused on organizational change and improvement; others were more specific design and development teams.[12]

Natural Work Teams

Natural work teams are organized to perform a complete unit of work, such as assembling a motorcycle, creating circuit plans for a television set, or performing a market research study from beginning to end. The "unit of work" need not be the final product, but some intermediate component. Natural work teams replace rather than complement the traditional organization of work. What is different in this work design structure is that work tasks are not narrowly defined as they would be on an assembly line, for instance.

Team members share responsibility for completing the job and are usually cross-trained to perform all work tasks and often rotate among them. A team in an automotive manufacturing plant placed an advertisement in the classified section of their local newspaper that read in part:

> Our team is down one good player. Join our group of multiskilled Maintenance Associates who work together to support our assembly teams. . . . We are looking for a versatile person with . . . ability to set up and operate various welding machinery . . . willingness to

work on detailed projects for extended time periods, and general overall knowledge of the automobile manufacturing process. . . . You must be a real team player, have excellent interpersonal skills, and be motivated to work in a highly participative environment.[13]

This ad illustrates many of the differences between natural work teams and the traditional organization of work for non-managerial employees. For example, members of such teams are expected to actually work as a team, rather than just perform their own jobs capably. Their knowledge must be broad rather than narrow, their skills interpersonal as well as technical. Natural work teams lead to self-managed teams, which are discussed next.

Self-Managed Teams

Self-managed teams (SMTs), also known as self-directed teams or autonomous work groups, are natural work teams with broad responsibilities,

Gravedigging in New York[14]

Have you ever sent a letter only to have it returned as "undeliverable" by the post office? How about 7,000 undeliverable pieces of mail every week? This was the problem faced by New York Life Insurance Company. Most of the mail being returned was notices to people that their premiums were due, so a great deal of revenue was being lost. In fact, the company estimated the problem to be costing them as much as $80 million.

The team formed to attack this problem became known as the Gravediggers, because of their relentlessness in "digging up" addresses so that premium notices could be delivered. The 18-member team, whose members were drawn from around the nation, met via teleconference once or twice a week. Following total quality principles, the team began by looking for the root causes of undeliverable mail. Some of the most common were: (1) policyholders who forgot to notify New York Life when they moved, and (2) long addresses that did not fit into the window on the mailing envelope.

The Gravediggers instituted a number of corrective measures to deal with the problem. They created units in each of the company's service offices to find addresses and keep company records up to date, they worked out a deal with the post office to forward mail and provide the company with corrected addresses, and they used a more elaborate mail-sorting system with bar codes. Early results found that the volume of returned mail was reduced by more than 20 percent, and the postal service provided the company with 61,000 correct addresses in a nine-month period. In fact, the Gravediggers are already among the most successful teams in the history of New York Life's total quality effort.

including the responsibility to manage themselves. SMTs are empowered to take corrective action and resolve day-to-day problems; they also have direct access to information that allows them to plan, control, and improve their operations. Self-managed teams have been used for decades (the SMT concept was developed in Britain and Sweden in the 1950s, and one of the early companies to adopt it was Volvo, the Swedish auto manufacturer), and are common in TQ organizations.

In the absence of a supervisor, SMTs often handle budgeting, scheduling, setting goals, and ordering supplies. Some teams even evaluate one another's performance and hire replacements for departing team members. For example, the GE aircraft-engine plant in Durham, North Carolina is a totally self-managing facility. Workers manage everything from process-improvement and work schedules to overtime budgets. Each engine is built by a single group of people, and that group "owns" the engine—from initial assembly to the moment it's put on the truck. GE/Durham team members take such pride in the engines they make that they routinely take brooms in hand to sweep out the beds of the 18-wheelers that transport those engines—just to make sure that no damage occurs in transit. Equipment maintenance and the cleaning of areas like bathrooms are contracted out, but team members keep their own areas clean.[15] In short, members of such teams are more like managers than employees in the traditional sense, hence the term self-managed teams (see the box on the Radius restaurant).

SMTs have resulted in improved quality and customer service, greater flexibility, reduced costs, faster response, simpler job classifications, increased employee commitment to the organization, and the ability to attract and retain the best people.[16] Experts estimate that SMTs are 30 to 50 percent more productive than conventional teams. FedEx, for instance, reduced service errors by 13 percent; one 3M facility increased production by 300 percent; in a Mercedes-Benz plant, defects were reduced by 50 percent. A study of 22 manufacturing plants using SMTs found that more than half of them made improvements in quality and productivity, removed at least one layer of management or supervision, and decreased their levels of grievances, absenteeism, and turnover.[17]

Virtual Teams

Virtual teams are groups of people who work closely together despite being geographically separated. Virtual teams rarely meet face-to-face; their primary interaction is through technologies such as telephone, fax, shared databases and collaborative software systems, the Internet, e-mail, and video conferencing. In 1998, over eight million workers were members of such teams, and this number has undoubtedly grown as new technology has proliferated.

Virtual teams are becoming important because of increasing globalization, flatter organizational structures, an increasing shift to knowledge work,

A Little Spice and a Heaping Scoop of Teamwork[18]

A great restaurant has superb cuisine, a special ambience, and a chef with presence. Radius, a hot restaurant in Boston's Financial District, has another ingredient: a real commitment to teamwork. Great teamwork starts in the kitchen. The Radius kitchen is made up of stations: the meat station, the fish station, the garde-manger station, the pastry station. Two people work at each station, and they have full responsibility for their part of the meal. In other words, the team at the meat station not only cooks the meat but also butchers it and seasons it—a sharp departure from the standard procedure at most restaurants.

Radius has also developed a series of meetings in which both the spirit and the practice of teamwork get reinforced. One weekly meeting focuses on frontline service. The sous-chefs and the pastry chefs meet with the back waiters and the food runners (the waiters' support staff) to review dishes and procedures. Because servers at Radius announce each course, they need to know what is on each plate, how to put it down in front of a guest, and how to pronounce it.

A daily meeting (the kitchen-staff session) focuses on behind-the-scenes operations. About 30 staffers gather around Chef Michael Schlow to discuss plans for the evening. He reminds them about his obsession with using as much of every ingredient as possible. "Can we make a sauce with that extra crème fraîche?" he asks. Then there's the daily service meeting. This meeting includes all of the waitstaff, the floor managers, and the hosts and hostesses. The general manager begins by going over that night's reservations: who the customers are—their names, what they do, if they've been to Radius before. Then all eyes shift to a plate of food. The general manager calls on a server to describe the dish. She follows with a series of highly detailed questions. "What are the red beads around the plate?" she asks. "Spicy tomato oil," the server answers.

and the need to bring diverse talents and expertise to complex projects and customize solutions to meet market demands. For example, a product design team in the United States can hand off its work to another team in Asia or Australia, resulting in an almost continuous work effort that speeds up development time considerably.

Because of their physical separation, some have difficulty applying the team concept to virtual teams. Virtual teams can face some unique challenges including language, culture, style differences, and the lack of social relationships that can lessen team commitment.[19] These require special efforts to ensure that a team environment is truly realized, particularly paying attention to communication, strong interpersonal relationships, and formal structures

---

Whoever Gets the Call Owns the Problem[20]

A good example of an SMT in action is found at AT&T Credit Corporation. In most financial companies, the jobs in the back offices consist of processing applications, claims, and customer accounts—tasks that are similar to manufacturing assembly lines: dull and repetitive. The division of labor into small tasks and the organization of work by function are characteristic of many service organizations. At AT&T Credit Corporation, which was established in 1985 to provide financing for customers who lease equipment, one department handled applications and checked the customer's credit standing, a second drew up contracts, and a third collected payments. No one person had responsibility for providing full service to a customer. Recognizing these drawbacks, the company president decided to hire his own employees and give them ownership of the process and accountability for it. Although his first concern was to increase efficiency, his approach had the additional benefit of providing more rewarding jobs. In 1986 the company set up 11 teams of 10 to 15 newly hired workers in a high-volume division serving small businesses.

The three major lease-processing functions were combined in each team. The company also divided its national staff of field agents into seven regions and assigned two or three teams to handle business from each one. In this way, the same teams always worked with the same sales staff, establishing a personal relationship with both them and their customers. Above all, team members took responsibility for solving customers' problems. Their slogan became, "Whoever gets the call owns the problem." Members make most decisions on how to deal with customers, schedule their own time off, reassign work when people are absent, and interview prospective new employees. The teams process up to 800 lease applications daily versus half that amount under the old system, and they have reduced the time for final credit approvals from several days to 24 to 48 hours.

---

that support their work. For example, team member roles and objectives often must be made more explicit. All the issues that we describe in subsequent sections affect virtual teams in the same fashion as co-located teams, and should be incorporated into their design.

Six Sigma Project Teams

Project teams are fundamental to Six Sigma. Six Sigma projects require a diversity of skills that range from technical analysis, creative solution development, and implementation. Thus, Six Sigma teams not only address immediate problems, but also provide an environment for individual learning, management development, and career advancement. Six Sigma teams are comprised of several types of individuals:

- *Champions*: Senior-level managers who promote and lead the deployment of Six Sigma in a significant area of the business. Champions understand the philosophy and tools of Six Sigma, select projects, set objectives, allocate resources, and mentor teams. Champions own Six Sigma projects and are responsible for their completion and results; typically they also own the process that the project is focused on improving. They select teams, set strategic direction, create measurable objectives, provide resources, monitor performance, make key implementation decisions, and report results to top management. More importantly, champions work toward removing barriers—organizational, financial, personal—that might inhibit the successful implementation of a Six Sigma project.
- *Master Black Belts*: Full-time Six Sigma experts who are responsible for Six Sigma strategy, training, mentoring, deployment, and results. Master Black Belts are highly trained in how to use Six Sigma tools and methods and provide advanced technical expertise. They work across the organization to develop and coach teams, conduct training, and lead change, but are typically not members of Six Sigma project teams.
- *Black Belts*: Fully-trained Six Sigma experts with up to 160 hours of training who perform much of the technical analyses required of Six Sigma projects, usually on a full-time basis. They have advanced knowledge of tools and DMAIC methods, and can apply them either individually or as team leaders. They also mentor and develop Green Belts. Black Belts need good leadership and communication skills in addition to technical skills and process knowledge. They should be highly motivated, eager to gain new knowledge, and well-respected among their peers. As such, Black Belts are often targeted by the organization as future business leaders.
- *Green Belts*: Functional employees who are trained in introductory Six Sigma tools and methodology and work on projects on a part-time basis, assisting Black Belts while developing their own knowledge and expertise. Typically, one of the requirements for receiving a Green Belt designation is to successfully complete a Six Sigma project. Successful Green Belts are often promoted to Black Belts.
- *Team Members*: Individuals from various functional areas who support specific projects. The roles of the Six Sigma champion and the Master Black Belt leader are similar to those of the champion and sponsor. The role of a Black Belt is similar to a staff quality expert, while Green Belts are typically given the team leadership role.

EFFECTIVE TEAMWORK

Teams are the main structure of many TQ organizations.[21] Thus, effective teamwork is critical to a successful TQ effort. If teams are not effective, TQ processes will suffer. Steering committees will choose poor directions and policies for the organization; departmental and cross-functional problem-solving teams will choose inappropriate problems or won't be able to solve the problems they identify; and self-managed teams will not be able to fulfill the promise of an empowered, creative workforce.

This section explores what it takes for teams to be effective in a TQ environment. Although the relative importance of these factors will vary from one type of team to another, they generally apply to any type of team found in TQ organizations. As you read this section, consider the ideas in light of your own experiences, rewarding or otherwise, on teams. If you are currently on a team, you may identify some ideas for improvement.

Criteria for Team Effectiveness

There are several criteria for team effectiveness. First, the team must achieve its goals of quality improvement. For example, a steering committee must move the TQ effort ahead, a problem-solving team must identify and solve important problems, a self-managed team must operate and improve a set of production or service processes.

Second, teams that improve quality performance quickly are more effective than those that take a long period of time to do so. One of the strengths of teams is their potential for rapid adaptation to changing conditions. A team that takes a long time to accomplish anything is losing the potential benefits of having problems solved sooner and is consuming a greater-than-necessary amount of resources, including the time devoted to team meetings. In short, it is inefficient.

Third, the team must maintain or increase its strength as a unit. Think of the team as representing an asset—a quantity of human capital—beyond that represented by its individual members. This additional human capital is based on the ability to understand and adjust to one another's work styles, the development of an effective set of routines, the growth of trust among team members, and so on. A team that remains intact over a period of time preserves and enhances this human capital. A team that solves an important problem, but has such miserable relations that it dissolves, does not. It may make a contribution to the TQ effort, but it squanders a considerable amount of human capital in the process.

Fourth, the team must preserve or strengthen its relationship with the rest of the organization. With apologies to John Donne, "no team is an island," especially in the TQ environment. A team that accomplishes its goals at the cost of alienating others in the organization violates the TQ spirit of teamwork and compromises its ability to perform successfully in the future, when the collaboration of others may well be needed.

Peter Scholtes, a leading authority on teams for quality improvement, has suggested 10 ingredients for a successful team:

1. *Clarity in team goals.* As a sound basis, a team agrees on a mission, purpose, and goals.

2. *An improvement plan.* A plan guides the team in determining schedules and mileposts by helping the team decide what advice, assistance, training, materials, and other resources it may need.

3. *Clearly defined roles.* All members must understand their duties and know who is responsible for what issues and tasks.

4. *Clear communication.* Team members should speak with clarity, listen actively, and share information.

5. *Beneficial team behaviors.* Teams should encourage members to use effective skills and practices to facilitate discussions and meetings.

6. *Well-defined decision procedures.* Teams should use data as the basis for decisions and learn to reach consensus on important issues.

7. *Balanced participation.* Everyone should participate, contribute their talents, and share commitment to the team's success.

8. *Established ground rules.* The group outlines acceptable and unacceptable behaviors.

9. *Awareness of group process.* Team members exhibit sensitivity to nonverbal communication, understand group dynamics, and work on group process issues.

10. *Use of the scientific approach.* With structured problem-solving processes, teams can more easily find root causes of problems.[22]

Team Membership and Roles

Like any system, teams cannot function effectively without high-quality input. The most important elements of team processes are the team members themselves. Managers need to understand why people do and do not join teams. People participate on teams for many reasons:[23]

- They want to be progressive in making decisions that affect their work.
- They believe that being involved in teams will enhance their potential for promotion or other job opportunities.
- They believe that teams will be privy to information that typically is not available to individuals.
- They enjoy the feeling of accomplishment and believe that teams provide greater possibilities.
- They want to use team meetings to address personal agendas.
- They are genuinely concerned about the future of the organization and feel a sense of obligation to help improve it.
- They enjoy the recognition and rewards associated with team activity.
- They find teams to be a comfortable social environment.

Likewise, many people refuse to join teams for reasons such as outside commitments, fear or embarrassment, an overwhelming workload, mistrust of management, fear of failure or losing one's job, or simply an "I don't care" attitude. True leaders need to develop strategies for dealing with these issues.

To be effective, team members must be representative of the departments or functions related to the problem being addressed. For example, a steering committee made up of members from one part of the organization would be insufficiently representative of the organization to be effective. Representation is particularly important for cross-functional teams.

Team members assume a variety of roles in performing their duties. Some are task-oriented, for example, initiating projects, collecting information, analyzing data, using TQ tools (flowcharts, cause-and-effect diagrams, etc.), creating action plans, writing reports, and so on. Others are relationship-oriented, such as encouraging other team members, listening carefully, and respecting others' opinions. Both types of roles are necessary for teams to function effectively, and proper selection and training of team members is important to ensure that they possess both technical and interpersonal skills to perform these roles. In fact, one study of cross-functional organizational design teams suggests that team skills, as well as a clear purpose and expectations, are significant predictors of team performance.[24]

Team members must possess the necessary technical knowledge to solve the problem at hand. This may mean understanding metallurgy for a team in a steel mill or understanding credit approval for a team in a bank. All members need not share the same knowledge, and in fact team members are often selected on the basis of specialized knowledge, but all of the appropriate technical bases must be covered for the team to be effective.

The critical importance of interpersonal skills is demonstrated by the following passage from a book on self-managed teams: We often hear experienced team leaders and members make remarks like this one: "I'll take someone with a good attitude over someone with just technical skills any day. I can train technical skills." With further prodding, we usually discover that they are really talking about interpersonal skills. . . . Because these qualities can be difficult to detect in a casual selection process, they are often overlooked in the pursuit of apparent, more objectively measured technical skills.[25]

What is meant by interpersonal skills? Think of people who are easy to work with in a group. They are good listeners and do not ignore or downgrade someone else's ideas in order to promote their own. They try to understand other people's positions, even when they do not agree with them. They offer help to other group members, rather than waiting to be asked. They are willing and able to communicate their opinions, ideas, and any information that needs to be shared. They can deal with conflict without turning it into a personal issue. Finally, they are willing to share credit for accomplishments with other members of the group, rather than trying to keep the limelight for themselves.[26] If you have worked on a team with people who possess even most of these skills, you are lucky indeed!

Another important attribute of team membership is diversity. Many organizations have found that the best decisions stem from cross-fertilization of ideas from individuals with varied backgrounds, experiences, and interests; it has become a cliché that decisions emanating from groups of aging white males won't do.[27] Kraft Foods, for example, has developed a course for every new employee called The Power of Differences. The course focuses on the company's conviction that it is a team-based organization, that innovation and ideas are critical to its business, and that the diversity of thought gives the best solution. The course teaches that these solutions arise from the interactions of style and approach and personality types. It gets people thinking in terms of What's our skill set?, What's our match?, and How do we know when we've actually got a blind spot?

Team Processes

Many processes are undertaken within TQ teams, including quality planning, problem selection and diagnosis, communication, data collection, and implementation of solutions. Team processes are not fundamentally different from other processes, such as assembling an electronic device, taking a patient's vital signs, or preparing coq au vin. The customers of all these processes can be identified, their elements can be placed in a flowchart, steps that do not add value can be removed, and their quality can be improved continuously.

Most people, however, are not accustomed to thinking of group processes in this manner. This may be why group meetings are often long and boring and why so many people try to escape committee assignments and avoid committee meetings like the plague. A willingness to tolerate poor quality group processes has no place in organizations practicing total quality. This section identifies a few of the processes used in teams and provides some ideas about how teams can use them to operate effectively.

Problem Selection

One of the processes undertaken at least occasionally by most teams and frequently by problem-solving teams is the choice of problems or issues on which to work. This process can be particularly difficult for newly empowered employees, who are more accustomed to being told what to do than they are to establishing their own agenda. New teams are often tempted to select the biggest, most glaring problem in sight that has been haunting them for years. Selecting such problems—called "world hunger" problems in TQ jargon—is usually a mistake. New teams generally are not skilled enough to solve massive problems, and a failure to address such a visible problem successfully may be difficult for the team to overcome. It makes more sense for a team initially to select a problem of moderate importance and difficulty and to move on to more complex and difficult problems when the team is better established. This approach is more likely to lead to successful solutions, which will build momentum for each team and for the quality effort as a whole.

Another common problem among new teams is that they select problems that are not associated—at least in management's eyes—with important business or quality issues. When given a voice for the first time, many teams ask for things they have been denied in the past, such as a better lunch area or break room. Although managers often consider such behavior an indictment of quality teams, it is in fact an indictment of management itself. It is unrealistic to expect employees to focus on business issues when managers have not taken seriously employee requests for adequate facilities. In fact, it is better for issues such as these to be worked out prior to initiating a team-based quality effort, rather than allowing them to undermine such efforts.

The selection of "trivial" problems by teams may also indicate that management has not done an effective job of sharing information about the business with team members. If they truly understand the nature of the important problems faced by the organization, teams are much more likely to choose worthwhile issues on which to work.

Problem Diagnosis

After problems to be addressed are identified, their causes must be ascertained. Thus a second critical process in TQ groups is problem diagnosis, the process by which the team investigates potential causes of problems to identify potential solutions. Juran refers to this step as the "diagnostic journey" and explains that it consists of three parts:

1. understanding the symptoms (for example, a process out of control),
2. theorizing as to causes (for example, preventive maintenance neglected), and
3. testing the theories (for example, reviewing preventive maintenance records to see whether they relate to the problems experienced).

Many teams want to bypass problem diagnosis and begin problem solving as soon as possible, usually because they mistakenly believe that the problem's causes are obvious. Teams that spend more time diagnosing problems have been shown to be much more effective than those that proceed immediately to solutions. Spending time pinning down the sources of problems is consistent with the TQ principle of decision making based on facts and reduces the potential for what are sometimes called "type 3 errors"— solving the wrong problem. Training in methods of diagnosis and analysis is important for team effectiveness.

Work Allocation

Another important process is the allocation of work within the team. Many teams approach this process haphazardly, assigning tasks to the next in line or the first person who volunteers. Assigning tasks is one of the keys to team effectiveness and should not be taken so lightly.[28] Each team member has certain skills and will perform well on tasks that use those skills and not so well on tasks that use other skills. The team needs to assign people tasks that will utilize their skills to the greatest extent possible.

Imagine a women's college basketball team that consists of some tall women who are excellent rebounders and inside shooters and some shorter (vertically challenged?) women who are skilled ball handlers and outside shooters. This team will be much more successful if the coach takes the time to assess the skills of each player and assigns them to the position where they can best help the team.

When explained in this context, the point is obvious, but you would be amazed at how many teams have the tall members bring the ball down the floor and pass to the short members underneath the basket! Differences in status within the group can be a problem if team members in higher positions are assigned the more glamorous roles, even when others are more qualified to fulfill them.[29] The status problem is particularly acute in organizations that have very high- and very low-status members, especially when (as in medicine) these differences are institutionalized in society. The vice president of quality at one hospital described a team with this problem: We had an emergency room physician who was a disaster. He was very much the old school expert and he was not about to be egalitarian in his approach. This created a lot of problems for that team. In spite of that, we were able to achieve some success with that team but it was, I'm sure, limited. If there was one factor [that hurt us], it was probably his impact on the team.

Communication

Communication is a key process for any team attempting to improve quality. Steering committees communicate priorities to employees. Members of problem-solving teams communicate among themselves and to their internal and external customers. For example, problem-solving teams often have to present their recommendations to management. Self-managed teams have similar communication needs and often must communicate effectively across shifts.

Three times every day in thousands of hospitals, mines, and manufacturing plants, teams of nurses, miners, and machine operators explain to the next shift what has happened in the last eight hours and what needs to be done in the next. The quality of this communication can dramatically affect the performance of the team on the next shift.

The communication process can be improved by carefully assigning people to key communication tasks and by training people in communication. We spend so much time communicating in our daily lives that we sometimes forget that skills such as listening and asking questions are vital to effective communication. Communication within and across teams also can be enhanced by using a variety of media. Many TQ teams use e-mail and fax machines, but also benefit from such low-tech media as posters and graphs posted on the walls. As with many team processes, any specific recommendations are less important than the general idea of recognizing communication as a process that consists of a series of steps that can be improved.

Coordination

Another key process is coordinating the team's work with other teams and departments in the organization. Teams cannot work in isolation, and maintaining good relationships outside the team is one criterion of team effectiveness.

New product teams, for example, depend on other parts of the organization for resources, information, and support while also acting as primary internal suppliers. Coordination often involves resolving issues of interdependent schedules, but may also include some negotiation. Thus, teams often play a "boundary spanner" role.[30] The boundary-spanning literature shows positive relationships between communication and performance. However, researchers have often found a tendency among teams to turn inward, believing that their own needs, ideas, and plans are more valid than those of "outsiders." Ironically, the more cohesive the team becomes, the greater the likelihood of this occurring.[31]

Such a tendency is antithetical to TQ, but it is a danger faced by virtually all groups. Teams can try to overcome this problem by keeping their customers in mind and using customer satisfaction as the yardstick against which ideas and plans are measured. Remaining aware of the need to improve team processes should also guard against the tendency to downplay the potential contributions of non–team members, as outsiders are often the source of ideas for improvement that team members have overlooked.

Finally, good communication should also help to coordinate work with other teams and departments. The likelihood of following a path that works against the needs or plans of other groups will be diminished if teams communicate with other groups early and often. Tools such as quality function deployment and affinity diagrams, discussed in Chapter 3, can be used to enhance such communication.

In a sense, quality-oriented process improvement and problem solving are a minefield for the unsuspecting team. Whenever changes are made in an organization, vested interests are challenged. By carefully managing the coordination process, teams will reduce the potential for unnecessary conflict with groups outside the team and will greatly enhance their potential for long-term effectiveness.

In summary, team processes can be improved just like any other process. Several key processes that are candidates for improvement are problem identification and diagnosis, work allocation, communication, and coordination of work with other teams and departments.

Organizational Support

However skillful the team, they will find it hard to be successful unless their efforts are supported by the organization in general and by management in particular. Organizational support is the foundation for effective teamwork.

Management must provide the following if a TQ team is to be successful. First, management must issue a clear charge to the group; that is, a description of what the group is and is not expected to do. This is often called a *team charter*. Many teams have wasted a great deal of time and energy on issues that they later found they were not authorized to pursue.

Management's guidance as to the quality priorities of the organization is crucial, especially in the early stages of a team's work. Several organizational researchers have found that team performance improved for teams with charters and clear expectations.[32]

Second, human resource management (HRM) systems often must be adjusted. Conventional HRM systems may be barriers to effective teamwork that will undermine TQ if not changed.[33] The need for enhanced training is particularly acute, as team members must be brought up to speed on the various types of skills necessary for effective teamwork.

Performance appraisal and reward systems are also a concern. Many of these systems are designed to reward individual effort or the attainment of functional goals, rather than teamwork. Numerous research studies over the past several decades have pointed out the problems and pitfalls of performance appraisals.[34] Many legitimate objections can be made:[35]

- They tend to foster mediocrity and discourage risk taking.
- They focus on short-term and measurable results, thereby discouraging long-term planning or thinking and ignoring important behaviors that are more difficult to measure.
- They focus on the individual and therefore tend to discourage or destroy teamwork within and between departments.
- The process is detection-oriented rather than prevention-oriented.
- They are often unfair, since managers frequently do not possess observational accuracy.
- They fail to distinguish between factors that are within the employees' control and system-determined factors that are beyond their control.

These can greatly undermine teamwork and can be fatal to the team if not addressed.

Performance appraisals are most effective when they are based on the objectives of the work teams that support the organization.[36] In this respect, they act as a diagnostic tool and review process for individual, team, and organizational development and achievement. The performance appraisal can also be a motivator when it is developed and used by the work team itself. Team efforts are harnessed when team members are empowered to monitor their own workplace activities. In a TQ culture, quality improvement is one of the major dimensions on which employees are evaluated.

Xerox, for instance, changed its performance review criteria by replacing traditional measures such as "follows procedures" and "meets standards" to evaluating employees on the basis of quality improvement, problem solving, and team contributions. Many companies use peer review, customer evaluations, and self-assessments as a part of the appraisal process.

Selection processes may also be changed in conjunction with TQ implementation. Companies like Procter & Gamble seek entry-level college graduates who understand total quality principles. They specifically want their new employees to think in terms of creating quality and value for consumers, to understand their customers and needs, and to work toward results despite obstacles. The members of self-managed teams often take much of the responsibility for hiring people for their team. Human resource professionals should play a consultative role in such efforts, however, to make sure that selection is done in a fair and legal manner.

Third, management must provide the team with the resources necessary to be successful. These include a place and time to meet and the tools to get the job done. Human resources are also important: management should avoid moving people on and off teams frequently, as this can disrupt teamwork and send a message that quality and teamwork are really not a high priority for the organization.

Fourth, when teams make a proposal, management must respond swiftly and constructively. It is not realistic to expect that every quality improvement proposal made by a team will be implemented. For those proposals that cannot be implemented, management owes the team a reasonable explanation as to why it is not feasible and some guidance as to how the proposal might be modified so that it would be acceptable. Few experiences are as demoralizing to quality teams as making an elaborate, reasoned presentation, only to be met with deafening silence from management. This was one of the problems that undermined quality circle programs. It is less of a problem for self-managed teams that generally have broad authority to implement their own solutions.

For those proposals that are accepted, some form of recognition for the team is in order. At The Ritz-Carlton, team awards include bonus pools and sharing in the gratuity system. Many companies have formal corporate recognition programs, such as IBM's Market Driven Quality Award for outstanding individual and team achievements in quality improvement, or the Xerox President's Award and Team Excellence Award. Solectron rewards groups by buying entire divisions lunch and bringing in ice cream for the entire plant. Often the most effective forms of recognition are symbolic, such as a citation or picture in the company newspaper.

Many organizations view team development as an important business process and manage it accordingly. Figure 8.1 shows the approach used by Boeing Airlift & Tanker Programs to develop raw teams into self-managed teams, a result of an historic agreement between the company and union to support employee participation.

TEAMWORK IN ACTION

This section provides two examples of quality teamwork: one a problem-solving team in a general hospital (a winner of the RIT/USA Today Quality Cup Competition—see box on page 337), and a high tech team at Analog Devices. As you read these examples, reflect on whether the teams are effectively practicing the team processes we have discussed.

FIGURE 8.1   BOEING ARILIFT & TANKER TEAM DEVELOPMENT PROCESS

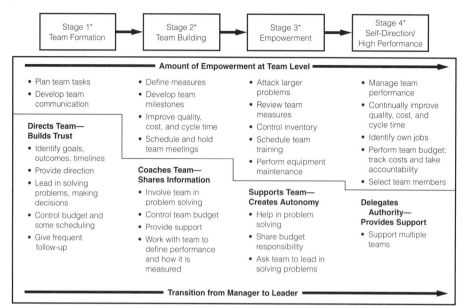

*Stages may overlap under certain conditions. Team maturity and level of process improvement already in place may impact stage application. **Source:** Courtesy of Boeing Airlift and Tanker Programs.

A Team with a Transparent Problem[37]

Have you ever had tests done in a hospital and wondered why it takes so long to get the results back? So did the employees and managers in the radiology department at Sentara Norfolk General Hospital in Norfolk, Virginia.

Although everyone associated with the process felt that they were working as fast as they could, performing and reporting the results of an X-ray or CAT scan was taking three days on average (72.5 hours, to be precise). A nine-person team was formed to address the problem, and they vowed to cut the time down to 24 hours.

The first step was to focus the team on the process, rather than on individual performance, and to create a sense of teamwork that would override the differences in status that sometimes hamper the work of medical professionals. Pat Curtis, head of cardiac nursing, was chosen as the team's facilitator, partially for her recognized skills but also because she was from outside radiology and had no formal authority over team members.

Although the team met infrequently, the members had plenty of work to do between meetings, mostly on collecting information. Using techniques associated with Norfolk General's CQI effort (Continuous Quality Improvement, as TQ is often known in health care), the team identified 40 steps in the X-ray process and 50 possible causes of delay, only a few of

The RIT/USA Today Quality Cup[38]

The RIT/USA Today Quality Cup Competition, established in 1991, recognizes teams that make significant contributions to the improvement of quality in their organization. The competition is conducted as a cooperative academic-industry effort between the College of Business at the Rochester Institute of Technology and *USA Today*. Team awards are presented in six categories:

- education,
- government,
- health care,
- manufacturing industry,
- service industry, and
- small businesses with fewer than 500 employees.

Each year, up to three teams are honored in each of the six categories. The winning team receives a hand-crafted pure silver Quality Cup, which sits atop a white marble cylinder with a sterling silver disk at its base. Quality Cup winners and finalists are recognized at a ceremony at *USA Today* Headquarters near Washington, D.C., and also receive recognition in special pages of *USA Today*.

One of the past winners was a team from Allied Signal Aerospace. They resolved a problem of unacceptable faults in a valve on the Airbus-300 aircraft. It was among the top 10 reasons for flight delays and cancellations. Valve manufacturer Allied Signal had tried nine times since 1974 to correct the problems when it decided to look at the entire system. The team spent days in the hangars where American Airlines performs its most comprehensive inspections, allowing the engineers to see what happens when a fault light comes on. One discovery was that in a typical fix, the existing valve would be replaced with a spare because it takes only minutes. But by tracking each $37,500 valve that had been removed, the team found that many of them didn't need to be replaced. Judge Chuck Blevins of Blevins Harding Group noted "This shows that a group, given the right environment, can become very creative and effective." More information can be found at the Web site, http://www.qualitycup.org.

which were causing most of the problems. Rather than waiting for a grand changeover at the culmination of their work, the team made improvements to the process as they discovered them. This was greatly facilitated by the cross-functional representation and the presence of managers on the team. As one member put it, "Folks who could effect change were part of the decision making." None of the changes the team made were particularly dramatic. Curtis helped the nursing department to reduce errors such as forgetting to note whether patients would need stretchers or oxygen. X-ray technologists began to deliver developed films to the next person in the process, rather than waiting for the internal mail service to move them. Fourteen of the 40 steps were redesigned out of the process.

The results were clearly dramatic. The average time to process an X-ray dropped to 13.8 hours, an 81 percent improvement! This achievement was impressive enough to win the team a Rochester Institute of Technology/USA Today Quality Cup for team accomplishment in the not-for-profit category.

Physicians in the hospital report that the faster availability of diagnostic information is helping them to improve their own processes, and other companies and government agencies in the Norfolk area are looking to the hospital for help with their own quality improvement challenges.

The team has responded to its success with a renewed commitment to continuous improvement. The introduction of a CD-based digital system to replace tapes for dictating physician comments is expected to cut the time down to 11 hours. The team's new goal? Eight hours.

Self-Managed Teams at Analog Devices[39]

In 1996 one unit of Analog Devices was under intense time pressure to get a new wafer fabrication plant up and running in an empty building in Cambridge, Massachusetts. The new "wafer fab" (as such plants are typically called in the semiconductor industry) was for a new division and would be relatively small, as wafer fabs go. At an early step of the process, it became clear they needed people who were very experienced, unusually flexible, and highly cross-trained, and who had unusually effective and efficient communication mechanisms available. The director of manufacturing saw this small-scale, clean-slate situation as an appropriate opportunity for him to deploy self-directed work teams (SDWT).

The Analog Devices Cambridge wafer fab runs 24 hours a day, seven days a week. Four separate teams handle a continuous operations schedule of shifts. During any one shift, the one team on duty for that shift runs the plant. Each team must cover the areas of chemical vapor deposition, trim, diffusion, etch, implant, photolithography, and thin film. Each area includes several relevant functions, and it is desirable for team members to become certified for all functions within multiple areas. These teams do not have supervisors on their shifts. In fact, all of the operators (called manufacturing technicians or MTs in the Cambridge operation) on all four teams report to the production manager. These supervisorless teams completely run the plant day by day, planning and deciding everything that must be done.

Because various aspects of operation require specific attention, each team rotates members through roles: production representative, yield representative, safety representative, continuous improvement representative, and training representative, to push cross-training. The people in some of these roles need to coordinate with engineering and with the senior managers of the plant, and appropriate meetings are held. The relevant representatives are expected to attend these meetings, which may be at times when the people are not on shift. Someone on each team is also designated "site manager": the person who is to speak for the plant in case of some sort of emergency.

In addition to getting the new plant up and running well with a small staff over a short time, the company found that in the long run, productivity has been higher than expected because the self-directed work teams run the plant very effectively and efficiently.

Some comments from team members show their perspectives on SDWTs:

> The biggest pro is that SDWT enables a group of people to manage themselves using a set of predetermined guidelines through constant communication and redefinition of these guidelines for the common goals of an organization. In addition, it provides a sense of worth that one usually doesn't feel in a normal work environment.
>
> Cons? It takes a strong amount of respect, both for yourself and for your teammates, to communicate on an even plane. Most people do not have it in them; and because of this a lot of issues arise and, many times, never go away.
>
> Trust is an important factor for the SDWT to succeed. When one member of the team loses trust, the team breaks down, causing animosity. Regaining the trust is essential. Maintaining a positive attitude and an open mind gives you flexibility and encourages participation from all members. Opinions shouldn't be taken personally but understood professionally and utilized in formulating decisions.

COMPARISON TO ORGANIZATIONAL BEHAVIOR THEORIES

Little conflict exists between the use of teams in TQ and theories of organizational behavior, but there are differences in emphasis. Along with social psychology and sociology, organizational behavior (OB) is the source of much of what is known about groups or teams. Since there is no separate tradition of research or thinking about groups within TQ, virtually all of the practices and recommendations ultimately derive from conventional (or unconventional) management theory.

The sociotechnical systems (STS) approach is devoted to the effective blending of both the technical (job requirements) and social aspects of the work environment. These two factors must be considered jointly, because work designs that optimize one factor may not be optimal for the other. The STS approach has been prevalent since the 1950s, and its principles were first developed in manufacturing by Eric Trist, its leading founder, who was guided by earlier systems thinking, research on participation, and the action research work of Kurt Lewin. More recently, this approach has been adapted and refined to nonmanufacturing organizations. The approach has more relevance today than ever before, as organizational personnel seek more fruitful means of empowerment and as their organizations strive for greater productivity and viability in increasingly turbulent environments.[40] Teams—particularly self-directed teams—support many of the benefits of STS approaches.

Research knowledge about groups is most heavily emphasized in organizational development (OD), the branch of the organizational sciences that deals with changing and improving organizations. Most team-based practices in TQ come from OD. Some of these practices, such as the nominal group technique, are based on research in organizational behavior or social psychology; others are not.

Teams are actually a subset of the organizational behavior/social psychology concept of groups. All teams are groups, but not all groups are teams. Compare our definition of a team as "people working together to achieve a goal" to the following definition of a group: "A number of persons who communicate with one another often over a span of time, and who are few enough in number that each person may communicate with all the others."[41]

Clearly we ask more of our teams than we do of our groups! Organizational behavior has traditionally focused on workgroups, people who work together in the same function. Theory has addressed why some groups are more cohesive or productive than others and whether groups are likely to support or undermine organizational goals.

The specific types of teams used in TQ efforts are also derived from OB research. Self-managed teams are a modern version of semiautonomous work groups, which were championed for use in underground coal mines by researchers from Britain's Tavistock Institute more than 40 years ago.[42] Similarly, cross-functional teams have been discussed within OB for many years as a way to integrate work across interdependent functions.[43]

Much of the knowledge from OB research on groups has not yet been absorbed into TQ thinking in a widespread manner, but it probably should be. This includes the research on the relative advantages of homogeneous and heterogeneous groups, which appears to be relevant to effective team building. Research has shown that homogenous groups (those in which members are similar in age, race, gender, experience, and so on) are better suited to well-defined, familiar tasks, where the emphasis is on efficient production.

Heterogeneous groups, on the other hand, are better at tasks that require creative thinking. This implies that teams used in TQ efforts generally should be quite diverse, due to the heavy emphasis on creativity and fresh thinking in the tasks they face. Based on this research, managers selecting people for teams should make heterogeneity their goal.

Research also suggests that cultural values play a role in an employee's support of, or resistance to, self-managed teams.[44] This is particularly important as companies expand globally. (Motorola and Eastman Kodak, for example, each have operations in more than 50 countries.) People from collectivistic cultures—those who value the welfare of the group more than the individual, such as South Korea, China, and Sweden—appear to have more of the skills and attitudes that lead to the acceptance of SMTs. In contrast, people in individualistic cultures like the United States have more of a tendency to resist SMTs. The success of SMTs is therefore related to the extent to which organizations manage culture-based resistance. Practitioners should consider using selection systems in each country to obtain employees having those values most compatible with SMT requirements and adopt SMTs that mesh with the cultural values of the country.

Recently, more research on the impacts of diversity is being conducted.[45] Although the anecdotal thinking promotes diversity as beneficial, research results suggest some contingencies. For instance, a multimethod field study of 92 workgroups explored the influence of three types of workgroup diversity (social category diversity, value diversity, and informational diversity) and two moderators (task type and task interdependence) on workgroup outcomes. Informational diversity positively influenced group performance, while social category diversity positively influenced group member morale.

However, value diversity decreased satisfaction, intent to remain, and commitment to the group. Another study found that social category diversity resulted in increased relationship conflict, even though group members reported increased morale, which runs counter to both conventional wisdom and past research. This study also shed light on patterns that practitioners can expect in diverse work groups. In particular, task conflict is likely in these teams and such conflict may enhance performance, something that managers and members of cross-functional teams can take comfort in. At the same time, race and tenure diversity may increase emotional conflict, especially in new groups with non-routine tasks. Anticipating such a possibility may be critical if organizations hope to manage employees' background differences successfully.

REVIEW AND DISCUSSION QUESTIONS

1. Donald Peterson, former CEO of Ford, said "No matter what you are trying to do, teams are the most effective way to get the job done." Do you agree? Why or why not?
2. Petronius, a Roman satirist, noted back in 66 A.D.: "We trained hard—but it seemed that every time we were beginning to form up into teams, we would be reorganized. I was to learn later in life we tend to meet any new situation by reorganizing, and a wonderful method it can be for creating the illusion of progress while producing confusion, inefficiency, and demoralization." What implications does this quote have for modern managers?

3. How might a jazz quartet be viewed as a metaphor for a team in a business situation? If possible, watch a jazz quartet in action in addition to simply listening.

4. What are the similarities and differences among the types of teams used in TQ?

5. Think of a team that you are on, or have been on recently. How does it stack up against the criteria for quality teamwork? What specific steps could be used to improve the performance of your team? How could TQ techniques be used to improve team processes?

6. How are Six Sigma project teams different from the other types of teams discussed in this chapter?

7. How did the team at Norfolk General Hospital illustrate the effective teamwork practices discussed in the text?

8. If self-managed teams can succeed without active intervention from managers, what—if anything—does this imply about the traditional roles of management (to plan, organize, and control) in organizations? Should a new set of roles be identified for such situations?

9. Do you think that the current popularity of teams in organizations is a fad or a fundamental change in the way we manage organizations? Why?

10. Are teams absolutely necessary for total quality to be successful? Sketch out a plan for a total quality effort that does not involve teams.

11. Discuss the conditions under which team incentives may work. When is it a poor idea to install such systems?

12. How might a team leader deal with "social loafing," when members of the team are freeloaders, willing to receive the benefits of teamwork without doing the work themselves? How would you deal with it if it occurred in a class project?

 Cases

Golden Plaza Hotel

Sandra Wilford was recently promoted to General Manager of the Golden Plaza Hotel, San Francisco. She had previously been an assistant manager at the corporation's hotel in Denver. The Denver hotel was truly a team-based organization. Sandra had seen the benefits from teamwork that propelled the hotel to the top of the corporation in customer satisfaction ratings. In fact, it was one of the reasons she was asked to take over the San Francisco property. The previous General Manager's policies had created large turnover among the staff and continuing loss of market share that led to his firing.

Sandra was reviewing her notes from a meeting with all the hotel's supervisors and assistant managers. The meeting tried to identify why many employees were reluctant to be "team players" or even to participate on teams that she was trying to initiate based on her experiences in Denver. Among the reasons that surfaced were the following:

- Child care obligations, classes, and other outside commitments made it difficult for some associates to meet before or after shifts.
- Many of the custodial workers who were functionally illiterate seemed to be uncomfortable in interaction with other associates.
- Several associates feel that their current jobs are simply too demanding to take on the additional meetings that would be necessary.
- One assistant manager felt that some of her people preferred to work alone and usually disrupted meetings in which they were involved.
- Because of the previous general manager, there was a lot of cynicism among the associates and many didn't trust management. They felt that teams were simply a political ploy to get support for unpopular decisions. He had established some teams that had failed miserably and many associates were bitter and had conflicts with other departments. There seemed to be a widespread attitude of "What's in it for me?"
- Some associates thought that the expectations of team processes would be overwhelming and were afraid if the team fails, they would be held personally responsible and their careers would be in jeopardy. Others thought that their jobs might be eliminated.

Sandra stared at this list and wondered what she got herself into. What recommendations would you make to her to address these issues?

A Self-Managed Cheese-Making Team[46]

Monday at 6 A.M., the Green team relieves the Silver team for a 12-hour shift at the R.G. Bush plant of Schreiber Foods. Schreiber is the second-largest producer of cheese in America, and the 53 employees at the Bush plant (near Tempe, Arizona) are responsible for making bulk cheese that is further processed into finished products by other plants. The Bush plant is extremely efficient, producing about a million pounds of cheese each week, due to both advanced production control technology and the use of self-managed teams. In addition to the Green and Silver teams, there are also Red, Blue, maintenance, support, and management teams.

The process that the six-member Green team has just assumed responsibility for includes condensing, evaporating, filling, packing, and palletizing operations. As the shift begins, the designated communicators from the two teams discuss a potential pH problem that was identified overnight. Two team members take their places in the process control room in front of a bank of computer screens, switches, and meters. They check the performance of the process over the past few hours and consult a schedule for preventive maintenance. The other three team members are in the barrel room today and will be performing manual labor: making cardboard barrels, filling them with cheese, and placing them on pallets. The team members rotate among these tasks, including the communicator job, which is the closest thing to a designated team leader at the plant.

Team members have taken over the functions of team advisers, non-team personnel who guided the teams until they were no longer needed. At this plant, the practice of job rotation is seen as more important than having the most qualified person in a job at all times: Larry is the most technically qualified person on the team, but today he is filling barrels with cheese.

The team addresses a number of problems during its shift. The computer screen alerts Tim in the control room to a problem with an evaporator. He calls Tony, who escapes from the barrels for a few minutes to find and clean out a clogged check valve. Later, the pH problem reappears; it is now so low that it is out of specification. To make matters worse some burned cheese has been detected. The evaporator must be shut down for cleaning, and the team takes the maintenance team's advice to perform a more extensive cleaning that has to be done soon anyway.

The team wants to get the process back on line as soon as possible because the evaporator shutdown costs the company money, and the out-of-spec cheese is reflected in the team's incentive payout. After a filter is replaced and the cleaning completed, the process is ready to roll.

While the team works, they are literally surrounded with information. A three-foot-long electronic sign updates them on various aspects of performance including conformance, production, and customer complaints. A bulletin board is crammed with information on raw material consumption, the incentive system, and so on. Wrapped around the control room is a banner that exhorts them to "Do it right the first time." Green team members communicate constantly. Beyond their daily job communication, they have a monthly team meeting to discuss goals, problems, schedules, and whatever else needs to be covered. There are also corrective action team meetings, communicators' meetings, and incentive meetings. Members understand all of the meetings as the price of empowerment and teamwork, but feel that the sacrifice is better than letting management make all the decisions.

The team recently had its first experience with firing a member, which was particularly hard because he was a friend and a teammate. They had hired him because of his technical ability, despite past problems with attendance. They did everything they could to keep him, but the attendance problems continued, and the team felt he was letting them down.

Ted, the newest member of the Green team, summarizes the team's feeling about self-management:

> When I got here, I knew that this was just up my alley. I don't need a boss looking over my shoulder, because I know how to do the work. It never made sense to me to see grown-ups standing around watching other grown-ups do their jobs. I could see it if you were 14 years old. But I'm an adult, and Schreiber respects that.

Discussion Questions

1. Outline what a day at work would be like in a cheese plant that utilized a more conventional organization—no teams, foremen, many job classifications. How would this differ from the day the Green team at Schreiber's Bush plant experienced? What are the advantages and disadvantages of the two arrangements?

2. In the text it was argued that team members should be assigned to the work that they do best. Yet in the Green team case, team members rotated through all jobs regardless of their skills. Do you think this is a good idea? Why or why not?

3. What would a manager's job be like in this kind of plant? Would you want to work as a manager there?

Can Teams Work in Sales?

A commercial supplier of electrical components for industrial and residential applications uses teams in its sales office. Budget and commission teams partner two salespeople together to achieve their budget and not duplicate the work available. They are responsible for helping one another to contract jobs and accomplish their work. However, the lead sales engineer noted that teams are hard to implement in the sales office. Employees seem to be focused on individual performance and are used to having to compete to gain recognition.

In contrast, a small radio station also uses sales teams. The sales team consists of five employees each responsible for several advertising accounts. The team is self-managed, setting monthly and yearly goals for themselves. Each week they meet to discuss progress and any problems they may be having with their accounts. No reports are required; they are empowered to make decisions to benefit the station. Only in matters that would greatly affect the business do they need a supervisor's approval. When the team reaches a goal, all employees in the office receive a bonus.

Discussion Questions

1. What are the advantages and disadvantages of using teams for sales?

2. What differences are apparent in how these two organizations approach teamwork? How would these differences impact team effectiveness?

ENDNOTES

1. Jon R. Katzenback and Douglas K. Smith, "The Discipline of Teams," *Harvard Business Review,* March/April 1993, pp. 111–120.

2. Adapted from Leigh Ann Klaus, "Motorola Brings Fairy Tales to Life," *Quality Progress,* June 1997, pp. 25–28.

3. "Platform Approach at Chrysler," *Quality '93:Empowering People with Technology, Fortune* Advertisement, September 20, 1993.

4. Brock Yates, *The Critical Path.* Boston: Little, Brown and Co., 1996, p. 76.

5. J. M. Juran, *Juran on Leadership for Quality: An Executive Handbook*. New York: Free Press, 1989.

6. P. B. Crosby, *Quality Is Free: The Art of Making Quality Certain*, New York: McGraw-Hill, 1979.

7. James R. Healey, "U.S. Steel Learns from Experience," *USA Today*, April 10, 1992.

8. Martha T. Moore, "Hourly Workers Apply Training in Problem Solving," *USA Today*, April 10, 1992.

9. Helene F. Uhlfelder, "It's All About Improving Performance," *Quality Progress*, February 2000, pp. 47–52.

10. The information on quality circles in Japan is from B. G. Dale and J. Tidd, "Japanese Total Quality Control: A Study of Best Practice," *Proceedings of the Institution of Mechanical Engineers*, Vol. 205, No. 4, pp. 221–232.

11. Juran, *Juran on Leadership for Quality*.

12. Eileen M. van Aken and Brian M. Kleiner, "Determinants of Effectiveness for Cross-Functional Organizational Design Teams," *Quality Management Journal*, Vol. 4, No. 2, 1997, pp. 51–79.

13. Richard S. Wellins, William C. Byham, and Jeanne M. Wilson, *Empowered Teams: Creating Self-Directed Work Groups That Improve Quality, Productivity, and Participation*, p. 21. San Francisco: Jossey-Bass, 1991.

14. Based on Jerry G. Bowles, "Leading the World-Class Company," *Fortune*, September 21, 1992.

15. Charles Fishman, "How Teamwork Took Flight," *Fast Company*, October 1999, p. 188.

16. Ron Williams, "Self-Directed Work Teams: A Competitive Advantage," *Quality Digest*, November 1995, pp. 50–52.

17. Peter Lazes and Marty Falkenberg, "Work Groups in America Today," *The Journal for Quality and Participation*, Vol. 14, No. 3, June 1991, pp. 58–69.

18. Gina Imperato, "Their Specialty? Teamwork," *Fast Company*, January 2000, p. 54.

19. Jane E. Henry, and Meg Hartzler, "Virtual Teams: Today's Reality, Today's Challenge," *Quality Progress*, May 1997, pp. 108–109.

20. Adapted from "Benefits for the Back Office, Too," *Business Week*, July 10, 1989, p. 59.

21. P. Alexander, M. Biro, E . G. Garry, D. Seamon, T. Slaughter, and D. Valerio, "New Organizational Structures and New Quality Systems," in J. P. Kern, J. J. Riley, and L. N. Jones (eds.), *Human Resources Management*. Milwaukee: ASQC Quality Press, 1987, pp. 203–268.

22. Peter R. Scholtes, et al., *The Team Handbook: How to Use Teams to Improve Quality*, Madison, Wisc.: Joiner Associates, Inc., 1988, pp. 6-10–6-22.

23. Michael Jaycox, "How to Get Nonbelievers to Participate in Teams," *Quality Progress*, March 1996, pp. 45–49.

24. Van Aken and Kleiner, op. cit.

25. Wellins et al., *Empowered Teams*, p. 147.

26. Partially based on Wellins et al., *Empowered Teams*, and H. J. Harrington, *The Improvement Process: How America's Leading Companies Improve Quality*. New York: McGraw-Hill, 1987.

27. Willard C. Rappleye, Jr., "Diversity in the Workforce," *Across the Board*, Vol. XXXVII, No. 10, Nov/Dec 2000 (special advertising section).

28. This point is based on a model developed by I. Steiner in his book *Group Process and Productivity*, New York: Academic Press, 1972.

29. The problems of differential status in groups are discussed by Alvin Zander in *Making Groups Effective*, San Francisco: Jossey-Bass, 1982.

30. Deborah G. Ancona and David F. Caldwell, "Bridging the Boundary: External Activity and Performance," *Administrative Science Quarterly*, Vol. 37, No. 4, December 1992, p. 634.

31. The classic statement of this problem is by Irving Janis in his book *Groupthink*, 2nd ed. Boston: Houghton-Mifflin, 1982.

32. Van Aken and Kleiner, op. cit.

33. Wellins et al., *Empowered Teams*. See also S. A. Snell and J. W. Dean, Jr., "Integrated Manufacturing and Human Resource Management: A Human Capital Perspective," *Academy of Management Journal*, August 1992, pp. 467–504.

34. Douglas McGregor, "An Uneasy Look at Performance Appraisal," *Harvard Business Review*, September/October 1972; Herbert H. Meyer, Emanuel Kay, and John R. P. French, Jr., "Split

Roles in Performance Appraisal," *Harvard Business Review*, January/February 1965; Harry Levinson, "Appraisal of What Performance?" *Harvard Business Review*, January/February 1965; A. M. Mohrman, *Deming versus Performance Appraisal: Is There a Resolution?* Los Angeles: Center for Effective Organizations, University of Southern California, 1989.

35. John F. Milliman and Fred R. McFadden, "Toward Changing Performance Appraisal to Address TQM Concerns: The 360-Degree Feedback Process," *Quality Management Journal*, Vol. 4, No. 3, 1997, pp. 44–64.

36. Stanley M. Moss, "Appraise Your Performance Appraisal Process," *Quality Progress*, November 1989, p. 60.

37. Based on Kevin Anderson, "X-Ray Processing Time Cut 81%," *USA Today*, April 10, 1992.

38. RIT/USA Today Quality Cup Web site, http://www.qualitycup.org; and Doug Levy, "Manufacturing Winners Teamed to Trouble-Shoot Valve Problem," *USA Today*, May 1, 1998, p. 4B.

39. Adapted from Ira Moskowitz and Ken Bethea, "Self-Directed Work Teams at Analog Devices," *Center for Quality of Management Journal*, Vol. 9, No. 1, Summer 2000, pp. 17–24.

40. William M. Fox, "Sociotechnical System Principles and Guidelines: Past and Present," *The Journal of Applied Behavioral Science*, Vol. 3, No. 1, March 1995.

41. G . C. Homans, *The Human Group*, New York: Harcourt, Brace, and World, 1959, p. 2.

42. E. Trist and K. W. Bamforth, "Some Social and Psychological Consequences of the Long Wall Method of Coal-Getting," *Human Relations*, Vol. 4, No. 1, 1952, pp. 3–38.

43. For example, J. E. McCann and J. R. Galbraith, "Interdepartmental Relations," in P. C. Nystrom and W.H. Starbuck (eds.) *Handbook of Organizational Design, Vol. 2. Remodeling Organizations and Their Environments*, New York: Oxford University Press, 1981.

44. Bradley L. Kirkman and Debra L. Shapiro, "The Impact of Cultural Values on Employee Resistance to Teams: Toward a Model of Globalized Self-Managing Work Team Effectiveness," *Academy of Management Review*, Vol. 22, No. 3, 1997, pp. 730–757.

45. This discussion stems from Karen A. Jehn, Gregory B. Northcraf, and Margaret A. Nealeand, "Why Differences Make a Difference: A Field Study of Diversity, Conflict, and Performance in Workgroups," *Administrative Science Quarterly*, Vol. 44, No. 4, December 1999, pp. 741–763; and Lisa Hope Pelled, Kathleen M. Eisenhardt, and Katherine R. Xin, "Exploring the Black Box: An Analysis of Work Group Diversity, Conflict, and Performance," *Administrative Science Quarterly*, Vol. 44, No. 1, March 1999, pp. 1–28.

46. Wellins et al., *Empowered Teams*, Chapter 4.

CHAPTER 9

Empowerment and Motivation

In 1988 Takeo Miura of Hitachi Corporation made the following statement to a group of senior U.S. business executives:

> We are going to win and the industrial West is going to lose out; there's nothing much you can do about it, because the reasons for your failure are within yourselves. . . . With your bosses doing the thinking while the workers wield the screwdrivers, you're convinced deep down that this is the right way to run a business. For you, the essence of management is getting the ideas out of the heads of the bosses and into the hands of labor. We are beyond the Taylor model: business, we know, is so complex and difficult that survival for firms . . . depends on the day-to-day mobilization of every ounce of intelligence.[1]

Miura threw down the gauntlet to American business: bring the brainpower of your entire organization to the competition, or prepare to lose permanently.

In the years since this challenge was issued, American firms have begun to undertake the process of employee empowerment. This chapter will

➤ explain what is meant by empowerment,
➤ explain the importance of empowerment to quality,
➤ identify the principles of successful empowerment,
➤ provide examples of firms practicing empowerment, and
➤ link empowerment to theories of motivation.

INTRODUCTION TO EMPOWERMENT

Empowerment means giving someone power—granting the authority to do whatever is necessary to satisfy customers, and trusting employees to make the right choices without waiting for management approval. In the quote that introduced this chapter, Takeo Miura took American managers to task for ignoring the creative and intellectual energies of the workforce. The objective of empowerment is "to tap the creative and intellectual energy of everybody in the company, not just those in the executive suite . . . to provide everyone with the responsibility and the resources to display real leadership within their own individual spheres of competence."[2] By empowering employees, organizations drive decision making down to its lowest possible level. Empowerment allows organizations to flatten their organizational structure because fewer managers are needed to "direct and control" employees. Many companies have found that giving people throughout the organization the power to make a difference contributes greatly to providing quality products and services to their customers.

Examples of empowerment abound. Self-managed teams discussed in the previous chapter are perfect examples. Workers in the Coors Brewery container operation give each other performance evaluations, and even screen, interview, and hire new people for the line. At Motorola, sales representatives have the authority to replace defective products up to six years after purchase, a decision that used to require top management approval. Hourly employees at GM's antilock brake system plant in Dayton, Ohio, can call in suppliers to help solve problems, and manage scrap, machine downtime, absences, and rework. See the box on UPS for a good example.

One survey found that more than 40 percent of the largest U.S. corporations are moderate to high users of employee involvement practices such as empowerment.[3] Manufacturing, especially in the chemical and electronics industries, has tended to empower employees more than service organizations, although the financial services industry has taken a leading role.

Empowerment has even played a role in such business successes as the Ford Taurus program.[4] Employee ideas were responsible for reducing the number of different welding guns on the assembly line from three to one and for developing a standard screw size for use in the car's interior plastic moldings. Although these changes may not sound very dramatic, a Ford executive estimated that such ideas often are worth more than $300,000 each.

The need to empower the entire workforce in order for quality to succeed has long been recognized, even if it is only recently coming into practice. Five of Deming's 14 Points relate directly to the notion of empowerment.

Point 6: Institute training.
Point 7: Teach and institute leadership.
Point 8: Drive out fear. Create trust. Create a climate for innovation.
Point 10: Eliminate exhortations for the workforce.
Point 13: Encourage education and self-improvement for everyone.[5]

Juran wrote that "ideally, quality control should be delegated to the workforce to the maximum extent possible."[6] Empowerment resembles

Juran's concept of "self-control." For employees to practice self-control, they must know their unit's goals and their actual performance and have a means for changing performance if the goals are not being met.[7] Although it is a difficult struggle, organizations are increasingly meeting these conditions.

Empowerment is a natural extension of employee involvement concepts such as worker participation in decision making. In some companies empowerment is used as the umbrella term for increasing employee involvement in decision making. Empowerment is more than another term for involvement, however. It represents a high degree of involvement in which employees make decisions themselves and are responsible for their outcomes. This is a more radical change than having employees merely participate in managers' decisions, even when they are given some influence (see Figure 9.1).

For empowerment to occur, managers must undertake two major initiatives:[8]

1. identify and change organizational conditions that make people powerless, and
2. increase people's confidence that their efforts to accomplish something important will be successful.

The need to do both of these implies that organizational systems often create powerless employees and that these systems must be changed first. Examples of systems in need of change are those that specify who can (and cannot) make certain types of decisions and systems of standard operating procedures (and who can override them). Even when systems are changed to permit empowerment, individuals who have lived under those systems are not readily able to operate in an empowered manner. The other need in empowering people is to deal with the psychological aftereffects of powerlessness by convincing people that they are in fact able to "make a difference." Empowerment is an application of the teamwork principle of total quality, embodying "vertical" teamwork between managerial and nonmanagerial personnel. If employees are given important responsibilities—and the authority that goes along with them—it is more realistic to describe their relationship with management as teamwork than it would be in a hierarchical system. After all, people can hardly be seen as team members if they only execute decisions made by others.

The traditional treatment of employees by American managers led W. Edwards Deming to plead with managers to drive out fear—defined as

FIGURE 9.1 CONTINUUM OF EMPLOYEE INVOLVEMENT PRACTICES

Participation		Empowerment
Low	Involvement	High
Small	Change from Traditional Organization	Large

Stuff Happens[9]

Jim Kelly, UPS chairman and CEO recounted an example of empowerment in a speech to Rutgers University:

> At UPS, we've got thousands of heroes every day. Not the kind that make headlines, but the kind that do make a difference.
>
> For instance, there's the story of an account executive who took responsibility for a damaged parcel that was packed incorrectly. This particular parcel was a rare numbered art print sent by an elderly home-bound couple in Florida to their son in Wisconsin.
>
> The print was valued at $350, but it had much greater emotional value. It was a beautiful limited edition of an elk in a forest, and the couple sent it as a best wishes offering to their son who raised elk on his farm. It arrived in Wisconsin badly damaged. The elderly couple was devastated.
>
> However, our account executive in Wisconsin wanted to help. A wildlife art collector himself, he knew that most artists keep a couple of extra unnumbered prints around for such misfortunes. He contacted the artist in Florida, had a new print renumbered and shipped back to Wisconsin. He then personally delivered it to the delighted son. The son was impressed. His parents were overjoyed. The point is, one of our people took a lot of initiative and responsibility for a problem he didn't even directly cause. He took a bad situation and turned it into a customer-for-life situation.

"feeling threatened by possible repercussions as a result of speaking up about work-related concerns."[10] Today managers in quality-oriented companies, hampered by decades of policies encouraging employees to keep their ideas to themselves, struggle to find ways to encourage employees to take responsibility for their work.

THE IMPORTANCE OF EMPOWERMENT

Businesses have learned that to satisfy customers, they must first satisfy employees. FedEx, for instance, has found direct statistical correlation between customer and employee satisfaction; a drop in employee satisfaction scores precedes a drop in customer satisfaction by about two months. Heskett, Sasser, and Schlesinger[11] of the Harvard Business School have conducted research in a number of service operations in industries ranging from communications to banking to fast food, and they observed similar relationships.

They found that as employee satisfaction increased, so did customer satisfaction and loyalty to the organization. If employees were satisfied with their working conditions and jobs, they stayed with the company, became familiar with customers and their needs, had the opportunity to correct errors because the customers knew and trusted them, and had outcomes of higher productivity and high service quality. Customers of these firms became more loyal, thus providing more repeat business, were willing to complain about service problems so that employees could fix them, and benefited from the relationship by seeing lower costs and better service, thus leading to a new cycle of increased customer satisfaction. Empowerment leads to greater levels of satisfaction among the workforce.[12] This is not much of a surprise, as we have all been victimized at some point by surly employees who decided to take their organizational powerlessness out on us.

Companies—for example, Disney—that excel at customer service have long been aware of this relationship. Disney cast members, as those who work at Disneyland and Disney World are called, are treated with special care. For example, before the opening of the Star Tours attraction, it was previewed by cast members and their families for four nights. The cast members who tried it received free dinners. Social events for cast members are also held, including Minnie's Moonlight Madness, an after-hours treasure hunt.[13]

It's not just "being nice" to employees that leads them to provide better customer service. The continuous improvement of organizational processes removes many hassles that produce disgruntled employees, who in turn produce dissatisfied customers. As Hal Rosenbluth, president of Rosenbluth Travel, puts it, "By maintaining an enjoyable, bureaucracy-free work environment, one that encourages innovative thinking . . . and honest communication, people are freed to concentrate solely on the needs of the clients."[14] (See the box on Pixar for another perspective.)

Empowerment is important primarily because it improves organizational performance. A survey of 55,000 workers by the Gallup Organization found that four employee attitudes, taken together, correlate strongly with higher profits:[15]

- Workers feel they are given the opportunity to do what they do best every day.
- They believe their opinions count.
- They sense their fellow workers are committed to quality.
- They've made a direct connection between their work and the company's mission.

Giving employees responsibility for their own work has led not only to improvements in motivation, customer service, and morale, but also to improvements in quality, productivity, and the speed of decision making.[16]

The benefits of empowerment have become obvious to many managers, such as Art Wegner, president of Pratt & Whitney, a producer of jet engines: "If I try to make a lot of decisions with the goal of reducing costs by 30

> ### Pixar's Fun House[17]
>
> Pixar Animation Studios, creators of such innovative feature films as *Toy Story* and *A Bug's Life*, clearly recognizes the Deming principle of bringing pride and joy to work in their workplace environment. *A Bug's Life* generated enough profits for Pixar to build a new studio in Emeryville, California. From the street, it looks like an early-twentieth-century factory, but inside it's literally a fun house. Animators whiz around on scooters down hallways that double as an employee art gallery. They watch dailies in the Bay Area's snazziest cinema and eat lunch in an atrium outfitted with a trattoria. Anything goes for office décor. One animator created a Hawaiian tiki lodge; another built a '60s style "love nest" complete with disco lights. As Steve Jobs stated, "[W]here you work defines you. Even though we use computers, our films are hand-made, and we wanted the building to reflect that."
>
> Everyone in an organization is an asset, albeit an asset whose value is not automatically realized. If money is put into a closet instead of a bank, it will not gain interest. Employees who are put into jobs that are like being in a closet (in the dark, isolated) similarly will not provide value to the organization.

percent, I'm not likely to understand all the issues very well. But if you get everybody—all those people in the organization—asking themselves, 'How am I going to get 30 percent of the costs out of there?' the power of that is unbelievable."[18]

Although empowerment is relevant for all aspects of organizational performance, it plays a special role in quality improvement. Total quality requires people to make real changes in the way work is done and relies on in-depth understanding of the current system. Only employees involved in the system day to day possess such an understanding, which is why so many managers see employee involvement as an integral part of total quality. As one survey concluded, "Employee involvement . . . may be viewed as creating the organizational context needed to support quality improvement processes."[19] The relationship between empowerment and quality is summarized in Figure 9.2.

PRINCIPLES OF EMPOWERMENT

Although many organizations have undertaken the journey toward empowerment, many have become lost along the way. Empowerment may sound easy, but there is a lot more to it than telling employees they are (poof!) empowered, like the Fairy Godmother's transformation of Cinderella before the ball. A number of principles are involved in successfully giving power to employees.

FIGURE 9.2   HOW EMPOWERMENT LEADS TO QUALITY

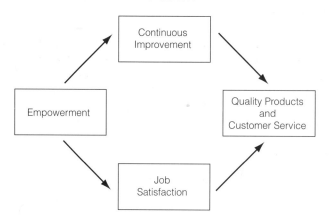

Empower Sincerely and Completely

It should go without saying that empowerment must be done sincerely. It cannot be done superficially. One executive observed that in many large companies, empowerment is 90 percent psychological and only fractionally real.[20] To gain its benefits, managers must empower for its improvement value, not for its public relations value. As Dan Ciampa, a consultant with expertise in empowerment, puts it:

> "Simply bringing employees together once a month and exhorting them to work harder to achieve the business's objectives is not enough." A process is needed that enables them to make significant improvements in their own work area that help meet the business imperatives in a way that will satisfy the needs of the individual employee.[21]

Furthermore, nothing could be worse for employees than to be told they are responsible for something, only to be jerked back at the first sign of trouble or uncertainty. Managers must think long and hard before making the commitment to empowerment—once done, it can't be done halfway. Semi-empowerment just doesn't work. Senior managers need to ask three critical questions:

1. How can I make fewer decisions, thereby letting others become more involved in managing the business?
2. How can I teach others how to make solid decisions once they're given the chance?
3. How can I recruit others to be more aware of changes that need to be made in order to keep our company competitive—and then help them

feel they can make these changes without begging for permission each and every time?[22]

This does not mean that there should be no limits. On the contrary, managers must be clear on exactly what responsibility and authority rests with employees. Questions such as "What procedures can we change?" and "How much money can we commit?" must be answered ahead of time. Finally, managers must be willing to wait for results, as miracles do not happen overnight.[23]

Establish Mutual Trust

As Juran has put it, "The managers must trust the workforce enough to be willing to make the delegation, and the workforce must have enough confidence in the managers to be willing to accept the responsibility."[24] Trust is not created just by saying you trust someone; it must be backed up by actions (see the box on Texas Nameplate).

In one plant utilizing self-managed teams, trust was symbolized by giving each new employee a key to the plant, a highly unusual practice.[25] The ultimate issue for many employees, however, is job security. They must trust that management will not take advantage of productivity increases to cut the workforce, in effect working themselves out of a job. Firms embarking on employee involvement activities often make explicit commitments to this effect to employees.[26] Southwest Airlines, for example, has never downsized a single employee, even through jet fuel spikes, recessions, and the Gulf War.

Even in the aftermath of the September 11, 2001, terrorist attacks, when competitors announced job cuts of 20 percent, Southwest managers schemed how to cut costs by delaying deliveries of new planes and scrapping plans to renovate headquarters. CEO James F. Parker noted, "We are willing to suffer some damage, even to our stock price, to protect the jobs of our people." Think employees are fiercely loyal? You bet. And empowerment is a major principle of the airline's philosophy, as the example in Chapter 4 illustrated.

Provide Employees with Business Information

For empowerment to succeed, it must focus on making the organization more competitive.[27] Empowerment can contribute to organizational performance only if employees have access to the necessary information about the business and its performance, such as their personnel files and resources such as the quality improvement budget.[28] Information about the employees' department or other subunit is particularly necessary, as this is the level of performance that they can affect. Sharing business information with employees relates directly to quality, customer service, and competitiveness.[29] At DuPont's Delaware River plant, for example, management shares

---

All You Need Is Trust[30]

Texas Nameplate Company (TNC), a small (fewer than 70 people), privately held firm founded in 1946, makes nameplates, the small metal tags with etched lettering that get riveted to refrigerators, computers, high-pressure valves, and military equipment. When serious work started on reducing non-conformances through statistical process control in 1992, total nonconformances amounted to about 15–18 percent of billing—a significant amount of lost profit. Improvement activities were able to drive that rate down to 3.7 percent by 1997, in an industry that averages around 10 percent. But Dale Crownover, the company president, wasn't happy.

TNC started a gainsharing plan that distributed bonuses equally to all employees, beginning with nonconformance rates of less than 5 percent. Results are posted daily. By the end of 1997, TNC employees whittled non-conformances down to 1 percent. In January 1998, in an attempt to further carve away at the problem, TNC did away with its quality control department. In the first month following that move, which Crownover said was part of the company's strategic plan, nonconformances were cut in half. Quality improvement now comes through DOIT—Daily Operation Innovation Team—consisting of supervisors who meet every other week to discuss accomplishments and opportunities for further improvements. They are charged with sharing information discussed at meetings with their employees.

"People on the floor can figure out what's happening and make adjustments the fastest," says Troy Knowlton, company operations manager. He added that they are quick to help out when one person is having a problem; they know what's at stake. "People listen to peers more than supervisors. We tried that for 45 years, and it didn't work. We have found the value of letting people do the work, with management providing the guidance." Not surprisingly, in 1998 TNC became the smallest company ever to win a Baldrige Award.

---

cost figures with all workers.[31] By sharing this information, management believes that workers will think more for themselves and identify with company goals. To help employees make decisions on issues affecting production, a department manager at Texas Eastman Chemicals Plant supplied operators with a daily financial report that showed how their decisions affected the bottom line. As a result, department profits doubled in four months and quality improved by 50 percent as employees began suggesting cost-saving improvements.[32]

In the absence of appropriate information, empowered employees may squander their power on problems that are not very important. As Peter

Senge has put it, "Empowering the individual where there is a relatively low level of alignment [between organizational and employee goals] worsens the chaos and makes managing . . . even more difficult."[33]

The criticism of misplaced goals was often leveled at earlier employee involvement efforts, such as quality circles. Although managers formerly blamed employees for having the wrong priorities, sophisticated managers today recognize that they are responsible for providing employees with the information necessary to develop educated priorities.

Ensure That Employees Are Capable

"You can't empower incompetence," says one manager. If employees are going to take on important organizational responsibilities, they must be prepared to do so. To operate in an empowered, TQ environment, employees must possess not only technical skills (including statistics) but also interpersonal and problem-solving skills (see the box on Starbucks). Unfortunately, many people entering the workforce today lack even the most basic skills in reading and math, let alone these relatively advanced skills.[34]

Employee capability can be ensured through selection and training processes. Unless the human resource processes are adapted to provide capable employees, empowerment cannot succeed, and management's worst nightmares will be realized. Unfortunately, many employees are not trained in these areas, which helps explain the mixed results many organizations have had with empowerment.[35] A Corning Glass plant in Erwin, New York, exemplifies this principle.[36] The union agreed to replace 21 different jobs with one "specialist" job. Employees were placed in teams and given broad authority over production scheduling and the division of labor. Did a bright new day dawn at Erwin? Not exactly. Conflict and confusion went up, and productivity went down. Plant manager Gary Vogt concluded: "We took steps to empower people, but the desired outcomes were not reached because we had not prepared them." An elaborate training program was created, and workers now become certified for the various tasks in the operation through testing. The promise of empowerment is now being fulfilled, and quality and productivity have increased.

Empowerment also requires that employees understand their appropriate limits of discretion. At The Ritz-Carlton Hotel Company, each employee can "Move heaven and earth" and spend up to $2,000 to satisfy a customer. However, whenever they apply this privilege, they must complete a report that explains the problem and actions taken, which is evaluated to determine why the problem occurred, take preventive measures, and ensure that the empowered action taken was appropriate.

Don't Ignore Middle Management

A well-known principle of organization theory popularized by Deming is that organizations are systems. When changing one part of an organization,

---

Spilling the Beans: Secrets of Starbucks' Success[37]

Starbucks Coffee, which grew from a small Seattle retailer to a national phenomenon, can be found in cities and airports across America, as well as up in the friendly skies. Its consistency and precision stem from its employee training program. All "partners," as employees are called, complete five classes during their first six weeks with the company, including "Brewing the Perfect Cup," "Coffee Knowledge," and "Customer Service." All partners have to memorize and practice the rules. Milk must be steamed to at least 150° F but never more than 170° F. Every espresso shot must be pulled within 23 seconds—or tossed. Trainers demonstrate how to wipe oil from the coffee bin, open a giant bag of beans ("In a sanitary manner! You never put your hand in there!"), and clean the milk wand on the espresso machine ("It's like blowing a little boy's nose"). They demonstrate how to fill sacks with coffee and affix a sticker exactly one-half inch over the Starbucks logo. Practicing on lattes, the trainer cries out, "Fabulous foam! It's okay to practice in your stores. Pull ten shots and dump 'em. And what does it taste like when the milk in your latte is 190° F? Be a mad scientist behind the bar . . . you'll understand why customers complain."

Three guidelines (Star Skills) govern interpersonal relations: maintain and enhance self-esteem, listen and acknowledge, and ask for help. Throughout the training, partners are encouraged to share their feelings about selling, about coffee, about working for the company. They also learn relaxation techniques so they can focus on the cappuccinos, to take personal responsibility for the cleanliness of the coffee bins—even when it's someone else's job—and to treat partners respectfully and do the right thing when one of them spills a gallon of milk.

---

it is necessary to consider the effects of the change on other parts of the system. Thus, managers must consider how empowering lower-level employees will affect middle managers. If the needs and expectations of middle managers are ignored, empowerment will be confusing at best and disastrous at worst. One manager described the situation with middle managers in his company like this:

> We pretty much promoted people because of their technical knowledge, not their management skills. Therefore we have a group of people in supervisory positions who aren't people-oriented; they don't know how to get the ideas and the solutions and better ways of doing things out of their people. And they are not receptive to employee-involvement programs, they are not receptive to too much change in their lives, they feel comfortable in this doing role

rather than a coaching or facilitator's role. So therefore we have to train these people to think differently and manage their departments from a management point of view rather than a doer's point of view. . . . It's the middle management transition from the old style of management to today's new style of management that's the problem, that stops companies from getting where they need to be as fast as they need to get there.

Among the roles for middle managers in organizations with empowered workforces are:[38]

- maintaining focus on the organization's values,
- managing solutions to system-level problems (those that involve many functions and departments), and
- acting as teachers and coaches.

It's tempting to think of middle managers faced with empowerment efforts as dinosaurs, rapidly becoming extinct because the world has changed too quickly for them. However, remember that most middle managers are a product of their organizations and have attained their level of success in an environment that rewarded different things than are needed from managers now. Given a new set of instructions from top management, backed up by new performance appraisal criteria, many (but far from all) managers will be able to make the necessary transition.

Change the Reward System

Rarely can substantial organizational change be created without changing the reward system. When organizations ask employees to assume new challenges and responsibilities, the question "What's in it for me?" ultimately gets asked. The reward system includes all of the rewards that employees receive, as well as the criteria for distributing these rewards. An organization is to its reward system like a boat is to its anchor: unless the reward system is changed, the organization may drift a little bit in one direction or another, but it won't get very far.

It is hard to specify exactly what kind of reward systems will be needed to complement empowerment. Some of the practices common to organizations utilizing employee involvement include pay-for-skills, in which employees' pay increases as they learn new job-relevant skills, and profit-sharing, in which employees receive bonuses related to the profits of their organization.[39] (The box on Texas Nameplate on page 356 described its gain-sharing plan.) Nor should intrinsic rewards be overlooked: simple but sincere expressions of appreciation by supervisors, a picture in the company newsletter, or an evening of celebration upon a major accomplishment may be of tremendous value to employees who have seldom received any recognition at all in the past (see the box on Yum Brands). In fact, a Conference

Board survey found that noncash recognition for hourly/production workers was found to be effective to "great/ some extent" by 84 percent of business units in contrast to only 63 percent for cash recognition.[40]

As one example, in October 1994, Continental Airlines' new CEO Gordon Bethune calculated that late and canceled flights were costing the company $6 million per month to put passengers on rival airlines or send them to hotels. He declared that if Continental ranked among the top three airlines for on-time performance in any month, he would split half the savings (about $65 per person) with all non-executive employees. Within two months, Continental was first. To ensure that the bonuses made a vivid impression, Bethune issued the checks separately and traveled around the country to distribute thousands of them personally. The behavioral changes are best illustrated by a story executives like to retell. A catering truck pulls up to a plane but is 10 meals short. In the old days, the flight attendant would have told the driver to get the extra meals while the plane sat at the gate for 40 minutes. The newly gung ho flight attendant, however, crisply tells the catering guy not to screw up again and shuts the cabin door. The plane pushes back on schedule, and she finds a bunch of investment bankers and offers them free liquor in place of the meal.[41]

Caught Doing Things Right[42]

When the chicken strips at a KFC sold out that day, a customer had to wait while employees cooked up a fresh batch. Gardner, working the lunch shift, apologized for the delay and offered the man a free side item so he wouldn't go hungry. She and her team members "were just so attentive to me," the customer recalls. It was no ordinary customer experience—and the man, it turned out, was no ordinary customer. As senior VP of public affairs at Yum Brands Inc. (formerly Tricon Global Restaurants), KFC's parent company, Jonathan Blum was in a position to recognize employees going the extra mile. Blum hurried back to nearby Yum headquarters, grabbed one of his signature awards—a seat belt on a plaque, symbolizing the "roller coaster" nature of the restaurant business—and returned to the KFC to fete Gardner. "In front of all her peers, I said, 'You didn't know that I work at Yum. I want you to know how proud I am of you.' " Today, a photo of a beaming Gardner hangs in Blum's office.

In Yum parlance, they call it "catching people doing things right"—taking time to notice and publicly reward employees who exceed expectations. "People innately want to be recognized for their hard work," says Yum chairman and CEO David Novak.

Empowerment in Action

The following three sections present three examples of how empowerment is practiced, followed by some observations as to its lack of universal appeal.

Semco

Semco is a machinery manufacturer in Brazil, with sales of over $30 million per year.[43] Semco's president, Ricardo Semler, practices three-pronged empowerment with his 800-person workforce: sharing power, sharing information, and sharing profits. Semler believes that empowerment saved the company from failure in the 1980s, so it is not surprising that he is a firm believer in the connection between empowerment and organizational performance.

The company is divided into units, called cells, of 150 people or less; when a unit reaches this size, it is subdivided. The 11 layers of management that the firm had in the 1970s have been reduced to three. Important decisions at Semco are made by self-managed cross-functional teams, which set their own working hours, strategies, and even salaries. Great care is taken to make sure that these decisions are based on the best information available, by making timely and accurate financial and performance data available to the teams at all times.

To reward its associates for the unusual amount of responsibility they assume for running the company, and to keep them focused on the overall performance of the firm, bonuses are distributed based on corporate profits. The teams have responsibility for allocating the bonuses, and they usually do it on an equal basis. In general, Semco appears to have firmly embraced the principles of empowerment.

The Ritz-Carlton Hotel Company

"Ladies and gentlemen serving ladies and gentlemen." That's how Horst Schulze, former president of The Ritz-Carlton, described customer service in his company.[44] Although in some companies the emphasis on customers might seem to diminish the importance of employees, The Ritz-Carlton has found a way to treat both groups with dignity and respect. Its efforts in this direction were rewarded with a Malcolm Baldrige National Quality Award.

Living out the ideal of respect for both customers and employees requires some subtle compromises. Many guests, whose schedules are very demanding, want breakfast delivered to their rooms within 30 minutes after it is ordered. However, chefs work at different paces, and not all menu items can be prepared within this time. The solution was to offer only certain items with a half-hour guarantee and to provide time ranges for others, so that different chefs can work in their preferred manner. In this way both customers and chefs are satisfied.

Schulze dramatizes the importance of employees when he introduces himself to them: "My name is Horst Schulze. I'm president of this company; I'm very important. [Pause.] But so are you. Absolutely. Equally important." Employees' feeling of importance may be responsible for a turnover rate that is less than half the industry average.

The Ritz-Carlton relies heavily on employees' suggestions for quality improvement. Their goal is to have twice as many employee complaints as customer complaints—the rationale being to resolve problems before customers experience them. Sometimes managers have to take a deep breath before implementing employee suggestions. Schulze himself received a proposal from a room service waiter to spend $50,000 to implement a recycling program.

The company's commitment to empowerment was sufficient to make the investment, which has really paid off: weekly garbage pickups have been reduced by two days, and The Ritz-Carlton now sells its cardboard and paper, rather than paying someone to take it away. The changes save $80,000 a year, so the initial investment was quickly paid back.

Los Alamos National Bank

Los Alamos National Bank (LANB) is the largest independent bank in New Mexico.[45] In the mid-1990s, employee survey results revealed that workers did not understand their role in the bank's strategic direction. Under the leadership of LANB's Quality Council, which has members from every area and level of the company, the performance appraisal system was redesigned to magnify the direct link between job performance and corporate performance.

The form used for this system lists corporate goals, departmental objectives, and the annual and long-term goals of the employee, which he or she writes in consultation with a supervisor. Employees also complete a personal self-assessment of their strengths and of opportunities to improve their customer-service skills and technical competence. Once they complete the annual appraisal process, employees have a complete snapshot of what they must do to perform at a high level and to earn the attendant incentives and rewards, which include profit sharing and employee stock ownership. Such incentive payouts average over 21 percent of an employee's annual salary.

Employee empowerment is vital to accomplishing LANB's goals for performance improvement and double-digit growth in annual income. Management consciously acts to distribute leadership responsibilities throughout the organization. In fact, over 90 percent of LANB's employees received leadership training in 1999 as compared to 8 percent of bank employees nationally.

Employees are expected to create value for customers, and they are given the authority and resources to act proactively and decisively. For example, all workers have the authority to resolve complaints on the spot. Also, high lending limits and flexible underwriting standards enable loan officers to respond innovatively to loan applicants with special circumstances. Yet,

LANB's charge-offs for loan losses (as a percentage of average assets) have been declining since 1997 to about one third the average percentage for local competitors. The bank's empowerment strategies were clearly evident during the 2000 Cerro Grande fire that ravaged over 48,000 acres and destroyed 280 homes, when employees set up shop without direct supervision in schools and other locations to keep the bank running and provide extraordinary measures to help the community overcome the crisis.

When Empowerment Doesn't Work

Beverly Reynolds thought she wanted to be an empowered worker.[46] After nine months at an Eaton Corporation plant, however, she left for another job. Although she liked the idea of being her own boss, she hated the headaches that came with it—fixing broken machines and having to learn a wide variety of jobs.

Many workers prefer the old-style approach with narrowly defined tasks and find that an empowered organizational culture is simply not for them. Saturn Corporation, for instance, found that many job candidates from old-style General Motors plants just couldn't adjust to a new style of work. This provides a big challenge to organizations to recruit the right people at the outset.

Other efforts at empowerment have failed because of the inability of management to understand and implement it properly. Among the reasons for failure are:[47]

- Management support and commitment is nonexistent or not sustained.
- Empowerment is used as a manipulative tool to ensure employees complete tasks and assignments without giving them any real responsibility or authority.
- Managers use empowerment to abdicate responsibility or task accountability, accepting accolades for successes and assigning fault to others for failure.
- Empowerment is deployed selectively, segmenting the workforce into those who are empowered and those who are not.
- Empowerment is used as an excuse to not invest in training or employee development.
- Managers fail to provide feedback and do not recognize achievements.

These problems can be avoided by applying the principles discussed earlier in this chapter.

MOTIVATION

Without willing, sustained, individual effort and coordinated teamwork focused on meeting organizational goals, TQ is an impossible dream. However, when organizations ask employees to assume new challenges and responsibilities, the question "What's in it for me?" ultimately gets asked.

Understanding human behavior and motivation are major elements of Deming's Profound Knowledge discussed in Chapter 1. Deming spoke of motivation as being primarily intrinsic (internal), and was suspicious of extrinsic (external) forms of motivation, such as incentives and bonuses, even though they are popular with business organizations and appear to positively reinforce employees.

Both extrinsic and intrinsic rewards are vital to sustained individual efforts. As managers in a TQ environment increasingly take on the roles of coaches and facilitators, their skills in motivating employees become even more crucial. There is no such thing as an unmotivated employee, but the system within which people work can either seriously impede motivation or enhance it. Compensation, recognition/reward systems, and the work environment must be carefully designed to motivate employees to achieve organizational as well as personal objectives.

Compensation

Compensation is always a sticky issue, closely tied to the subject of motivation and employee satisfaction. Although money can be a motivator, it often causes employees to believe they are being treated unfairly, and forces managers to deliver negative messages. Eventually, it diminishes intrinsic motivation and creates win-lose situations. The objectives of a good compensation system should be to attract, retain, and not demotivate employees. Other objectives include reducing unexplainable variation in pay (think about Deming's principles) and encouraging internal cooperation rather than competition. Most companies still use traditional financial measures, such as revenue growth, profitability, and cost management, as a basis for compensation; more progressive organizations use quality measures such as customer satisfaction, defect prevention, and cycle time reduction to make compensation decisions.

Many companies link compensation to company track records, unit performance, team success, or individual achievement (see the box on Nucor).[48] At Kaiser Aluminum, such performance-based compensation incentives led to an 80 percent improvement in productivity and 70 percent decrease in poor quality costs over five years.[49] Team-based pay and gainsharing, an approach in which all employees share savings equally, are gaining in popularity and importance. Compensation for individuals is sometimes tied to the acquisition of new skills, often within the context of a continuous improvement program in which all employees are given opportunities to broaden their work-related competencies.

Recognition and Rewards

Special recognition and rewards can be monetary or nonmonetary, formal or informal, individual or group. These rewards might include trips, promotional gifts, clothing, time off, or special company-sponsored awards and

Compensation for Motivation

Nucor Corporation, one of the nation's largest steel producers, is well-known for having succeeded in attacking quality, productivity, participation, and compensation issues.[50] Nucor has more than 6,000 employees in plants in the United States. All employees, from the president on down, have the same benefits; the only differences in individual pay are related to responsibilities. Workers at Nucor's five nonunion steel mills earn base hourly rates that are less than half of the going rate for unionized steelworkers. Nucor uses pay incentives designed around groups of 40 to 50 workers, including secretaries and senior managers. They offer four basic compensation plans:

1. *Production Incentive Plan.* Employees involved directly in manufacturing are paid weekly bonuses on the basis of production of their work groups, which range from 20 to 40 workers each, and can average 80–150 percent of the base wage. The bonuses are paid every week to reinforce motivation. The average worker at Nucor earns several thousand dollars per year more than the average worker in the industry, whereas the company is able to sell its steel at competitive worldwide market prices.

2. *Department Manager Incentive Plan.* Department managers earn incentive bonuses paid annually based primarily on the return on assets of their facility.

3. *Nonproduction and Nondepartment Manager Incentive Plan.* Participants include accountants, engineers, secretaries, and other employees. The bonus is based on the facility's return on assets. Each month every operation receives a report showing progress, which is posted in the employee cafeteria or break area to keep employees appraised of their expected bonus levels throughout the year.

4. *Senior Officers Incentive Plan.* Senior officers do not receive profit sharing, pension, discretionary bonuses, or retirement plans. A significant part of their compensation is based on Nucor's return on stockholder's equity above a certain minimum earnings. If Nucor does well, compensation is well above average, as much as several times base salary. If the company does poorly, compensation is limited to base salary, which is below the average pay at comparable companies.

During downturns, managers at Nucor frequently find that their bonuses are cut, even while hourly workers continue to receive theirs, based on production rates. However, even in tough times, Nucor maintained its policy of no layoffs as it had throughout the history of the current company. More about the Nucor story can be found on its Web site at http://www.nucor.com.

events. Most important, rewards should lead to behaviors that increase customer satisfaction. A Conference Board study found that a combination of cash and noncash recognition works better for clerical and hourly workers than for managers and professional/technical employees; for these groups, compensation-based incentives such as stock options are more successful.

Recognition provides a visible means of promoting quality efforts and telling employees that the organization values their efforts, which stimulates their motivation to improve. Employees should contribute to the company's performance and recognition approaches. L.L. Bean, for example, gives dinners or certificates exchangeable for merchandise. Winners of "Bean's Best Awards" are selected by cross-functional teams based on innovative ideas, exceptional customer service, role modeling, expertise at their jobs, and exceptional management ability.[51]

Work Environment

Working in an organization that cares for its employees is perhaps the best form of motivation (see the box on SAS Institute). Most companies provide many opportunities to enhance the quality of working life. They can provide personal and career counseling, career development and employability services, recreational or cultural activities, daycare, special leave for family responsibilities or for community services, flexible work hours, outplacement services, and extended health care for retirees. Johnson & Johnson's Ethicon Endosurgery Division, in Blue Ash, Ohio, has a Wellness Center with exercise rooms and equipment to support employees in their manufacturing and R&D facility. Employees can use the center before or after working hours or during their breaks. In addition, those workers who are assembling products get regular, programmed "ergonomic" breaks every few hours, where they

---

Working for the Best

SAS Institute, Inc., consistently one of *Fortune*'s "100 Best Companies to Work For," is a high-tech software development company based in Cary, North Carolina. SAS has a people-focused founder and CEO in the person of James Goodnight. Perhaps the most eye-opening policy of the firm is its mandated seven-hour workday. No "all-nighters" are expected of SAS employees. The multibillionaire Goodnight sets the example by leaving the office at 5 P.M., sharp. Many of the lavish employee perks at the sprawling corporate campus are family and lifestyle-oriented, from daycare centers, lactation rooms, a Montessori school, and a college prep private high school, to a 55,000-square-foot athletic facility, free massages, free car washes, and end-of-year bonuses. The payoff? SAS has about 4 percent turnover in an industry where 20 percent is the norm.[52]

are required to do exercises designed to prevent repetitive motion injuries. All of these opportunities contribute to creating a more productive, safer, and more enjoyable in work environment.

EMPOWERMENT AND THEORIES OF MOTIVATION

The TQ approach to the management of employees in general, and empowerment in particular, is quite consistent with organizational behavior (OB) theory. In fact, most of TQ thinking about empowerment and motivation is derived, directly or indirectly, from OB theory. Managers' willingness to accept these ideas and put them into practice, however, has been greatly increased by the incorporation of these ideas into the total quality package.

A few examples should serve to make our point. The idea that quality problems are usually attributable to management-created systems rather than employee motivation was proposed by organizational psychologist Chris Argyris.[53] Rensis Likert described an organizational system he called "System IV," which featured empowered workgroups and cross-functional teams. Douglas McGregor developed the well-known "Theory Y" approach to managing employees, which is based on the assumption that people wish to do a good job and emphasizes that people in organizations should make decisions for themselves. These are the fundamental principles of the TQ approach to managing people, but they were developed decades ago by theorists concerned with reconciling the psychological needs of people and the economic needs of businesses.

The TQ philosophy is also consistent with several more recent theories of work motivation. This means that implementing TQ should result in increased employee motivation, because the kinds of changes that TQ represents are among those that theories say will result in increased effort on the job. Specifically, the following sections discuss the TQ approach in terms of job characteristics theory, acquired need theory, and goal setting theory. The theories themselves are not described in detail, as they are covered in OB and management textbooks. Here they are compared to total quality practices.

Job Characteristics Theory

The job characteristics theory (JCT) states that people will be more motivated to work and more satisfied with their jobs to the extent that their jobs possess certain core characteristics: skill variety, task identity (doing a meaningful unit of work), task significance, autonomy, and feedback. If jobs do not have such characteristics—that is, involve few skills and give workers little control over what they do—most employees are likely to be unmotivated and dissatisfied.[54] This theory, developed by Hackman and Oldham, is described in Figure 9.3.

In general, we would expect TQ to increase the motivating potential of jobs through increases in the foregoing task characteristics. In fact, TQ

FIGURE 9.3   HACKMAN-OLDHAM JOB CHARACTERISTICS THEORY

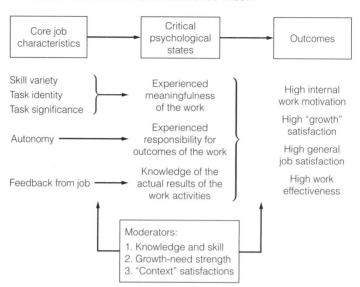

Source: WORK REDESIGN by Hackman/Oldham, © 1980. Reprinted by permission of Pearson Education, Inc., Upper Saddle River, NJ.

practices resemble some of the steps recommended by job design experts for making jobs more motivating. For example, getting people involved in problem solving and other quality improvement activities should increase both the variety of skills they use in their jobs and their perception of doing a meaningful unit of work. Empowerment should increase the degree of autonomy people feel they have in doing their work. Focusing their efforts on increasing customer satisfaction should increase people's perception of the significance of their roles in the organization.

Three factors have been identified that will influence the way people react to jobs that have high levels of the task characteristics: knowledge and skill, growth-need strength, and satisfaction with contextual factors.[55] Knowledge of how to do one's job should be enhanced by the training that often accompanies TQ and empowerment. Growth-need strength, by contrast, is rooted in people's personalities and is unlikely to be affected by TQ. Satisfaction with contextual factors (company policies, working conditions) may increase with implementation of TQ, as various groups in the organization make improvements to satisfy internal customers. This means that TQ is likely not only to increase the levels of task characteristics that people find motivating, but also to change two of the three factors that influence how people react to these characteristics, in such a way that they are more likely to find such jobs motivating. Such work design practices prevalent in TQ organizations as job enlargement, job rotation, and job enrichment are supported by this theory.

Acquired Needs Theory

Another perspective on employee motivation states that people are motivated by work that fulfills their needs. Specifically, the need for achievement, the need for affiliation, and the need for power have been the subjects of extensive research.[56] People who have a strong need for achievement will work hard to reach a high standard of excellence. The need for affiliation refers to the desire to have close relationships with other people, for example as part of a team. The need for power is the desire to have influence over one's environment and the people in it. How will the implementation of TQ, including empowerment practices, influence people who are motivated by these needs? As research has not addressed this question, we can only speculate. The need most likely to be fulfilled by participation in TQ is the need for affiliation. The most obvious way this would occur is through the formation of self-managed or cross-functional teams. TQ promotes close relationships between people in the same or different subunits, and even in different organizations in the customer-supplier chain.

The connection between TQ and the need for achievement is a bit murkier. Effective utilization of TQ should allow organizations to achieve higher levels of performance in such areas as quality and customer satisfaction, but these achievements are likely to come through team, rather than individual, efforts. Thus, the opportunity to participate in such efforts is likely to motivate people with high achievement motivation only if they can see the relationship between their own work and team performance and feel a sense of achievement on that basis. TQ and empowerment are likely to be motivating for employees with a high need for power. In fact, employees with a high need for power are likely to be quite frustrated with traditional organizations that give them little influence. Empowerment, if it follows the principles described in this chapter, should go a long way toward reducing this frustration and provide newfound motivation for individuals with a high need for power.

However, empowerment can be a double-edged sword. Middle managers whose subordinates are being empowered may feel that their own needs for power are less fulfilled under TQ. This need not occur, as empowerment of lower-level employees should be accompanied by finding new and fulfilling roles for middle managers. Many organizations will not be able to accomplish this, however, and even if they do, a certain number of middle managers with a high need for power will miss the old "command and control" type of organization.

Goal-Setting Theory

The central insight of goal-setting theory is that people whose goals are clear will work more quickly, perform better, and generally be more motivated than people who lack clear goals (you might look back on the Los Alamos

National Bank case as a practical example of this concept). A great deal of research has been performed on goal-setting theory and generally supports the theory's predictions. According to the theory, goals will be motivating to people when they are specific and difficult, and people accept them as their own.[57] However, goals should also be attainable; specific, challenging goals that seem impossible are demotivating.

How does goal-setting theory relate to total quality in general and empowerment in particular? This connection has not been the subject of research, but we can offer some conjecture about it. One likely link between empowerment and goal setting is the goal-acceptance aspect of the theory. Although there has been some debate about this among scholars, it seems that people who set their own goals (as in empowerment) are likely to be more motivated by them than are people whose goals are set by others (as in the traditional organization). People who set their own goals may also find that their goals are clearer (to them, at least).

The principle that goals should be specific and difficult can be related to total quality and empowerment. In general, the principle of breakthrough improvement leads to fairly difficult goals. In traditional management, when an acceptable level of performance is reached, people simply try to maintain it. Under TQ, an acceptable performance level would be a stepping-stone to further improvements. Therefore, the difficulty of goals would be enhanced by TQ. Goals need not be impossible; even incremental (and thus seemingly achievable) improvement goals supported by the kaizen philosophy fall into this realm. One wonders whether this compromises the long-run specificity of goals.

Continuous improvement is a noble ideal, likely to spur heroic efforts in many cases. When, if ever, is the goal reached? Can workers be motivated by a goal of eternal improvement or must milestones be placed along the way to maintain motivation and enthusiasm? Perhaps as organizations gain more experience with TQ, such questions will be answered. Given the increasing importance of continuous improvement for competitiveness, organizations will need to find ways to motivate employees for sustained improvement in order to be economically viable in the twenty-first century.

REVIEW AND DISCUSSION QUESTIONS

1. What is employee empowerment? What do you see as the most important barriers to employee empowerment?
2. How might the concept of empowerment be employed in a classroom?
3. Have you ever experienced fear in the workplace? What impact did it have on your performance? Is a little bit of fear a good thing for motivating performance?
4. Are there circumstances in which employee empowerment would hurt rather than improve quality? Why would this occur?

5. What risks does an organization face in empowering its employees?

6. How will employees know when they are empowered?

7. What sort of performance appraisal process would be appropriate for empowered workers in a total quality company?

8. Which of the principles of empowerment do you think is most important? Why?

9. Have you ever received exceptional service from an empowered employee? What happened? How did you react to it?

10. In what ways do Semco, The Ritz-Carlton, and LANB exemplify the principles of empowerment?

11. What can managers do to mitigate the risks of failure associated with empowerment?

12. Which theory of motivation do you see as most consistent with empowerment? Why?

13. Philip Atkinson tells the story of a government agency that fired up its employees to do great things with a wilderness training experience.[58] One young man, on his return to work, noticed some parking spaces owned by the organization in a busy part of the city. The spaces were always free and could be rented for a substantial sum. The young man made a proposal to do so, but it was rejected out of hand. Undeterred, he rented the spaces himself, only to find that there was no mechanism to deposit the checks into corporate accounts. Eventually, the young man left the company to work for one in which people's ideas were taken more seriously, and initiative was valued. How does this story illustrate the principles of empowerment discussed in this chapter?

14. Think of a job you have had. Apply the Hackman and Oldham model to evaluate how the job design impacted your motivation and satisfaction, as well as organizational effectiveness.

15. How does empowerment differ from such approaches as job enrichment and other forms of employee involvement?

CASES

The Case of the Stranded Traveler

One of the author's colleagues traveled to Texas to attend a meeting. Before leaving home, he made a reservation to be picked up by a shuttle company (one with operations in several cities) and taken to his hotel, about one half hour from the airport. The company's promotional materials strongly recommended securing reservations, as this would ensure "priority service." He was instructed to call the shuttle service once inside the terminal. He was told on the phone where to wait, what the sign on the van would say, and that it would pick him up within about 10 minutes. He was happy to hear that the van would be arriving soon, because it was raining and unseasonably cool, even for February, and it had been a long flight.

After 20 minutes, although many of the company's vans had passed by, the van with the correct destination sign still had not arrived. One of the company's drivers pulled over and asked the traveler which van he was waiting for. The driver radioed the dispatcher, who told him that the correct van would be there momentarily.

After another 15 minutes, another of the company's vans pulled over, but it was still not the right one. The woman driving this van asked the traveler which van he was waiting for and, after hearing the story, also radioed the dispatcher. She requested and received permission to change her route to take the traveler to his hotel.

The traveler relaxed in the back seat of the van, believing that his experience with "priority service" was almost over. As it became increasingly clear that the van was not leaving the airport, but was circulating among the terminals, the traveler asked the driver what was going on. She said that drivers were not allowed to leave the airport with fewer than three passengers.

She had requested permission to drive the traveler immediately to his hotel to make up for the inconvenience he had suffered, but the request was denied. The driver apologized and said she would take him directly to the hotel if it were up to her. After another 10 minutes or so cruising the terminals, a couple boarded the van. The driver requested permission to leave the airport, and this time permission was granted. Fortunately, one of the passengers knew a good route to the hotel, because the driver was not very familiar with this destination.

As the traveler got out of the van, the driver continued to apologize for the poor service he had received from the company and gave him the name of a manager to call to complain. Like most people in this situation, the traveler did not call the manager, but quietly resolved never to use this company's services when visiting this or any other airport.

Discussion Questions

1. In what ways did the shuttle company fail to provide quality service?
2. Were the dispatcher's decisions appropriate?
3. How would you change the company's policies to improve quality?
4. What are the lessons about empowerment from this case?

The Frustrated Manager

A professional colleague who teaches total quality concepts received the following e-mail from a former student: [59]

> I was wondering if you could offer me some thoughts on a particular situation that plagues the company I work for. Our workforce unionized and has a long history of anticompany sentiment. Upper

management has set up the assembly area as an example of employee involvement and the blossoming empowered workforce to show off to customers. They often bring in customers to help gain future contracts. That customer is very sensitive to cost, quality, and schedule, and has had some bad experiences with us in the past. The customer has clearly told us that it wants to see an empowered workforce making key decisions. If this does not happen, it will not award the contract. This information has been relayed to the work teams in the area, but several work teams, in their team meetings, tell us they don't want to be empowered. The attitude (as I see it) appears to be as follows: "We know how to build our products, the customer does not. So, get the customer out of our business and tell them to take the product when we're done with it regardless of how we choose to build it." As many times as I inform them that the customer will not buy our products in that manner, I am given the same answer back. How would you suggest I get these teams to take the gun away from their own heads? They have a management who is willing to hand over the power. They have the tools necessary to make informed decisions on the shop floor. They just don't have the inspiration to take the power and to run with it. My question is simple: Is it possible to create an empowered workforce in an old union environment?

How would you advise him?

The Insolent Night Clerk (Reprise)

Review the story of the Insolent Night Clerk in Chapter 4. Do you think his actions were the result of lack of empowerment or other factors? If he were truly empowered, how might he have acted? Write an alternative story of how the scenario might have occurred if the hotel were practicing TQ and empowered its employees.

The MBA Candidate[60]

Gretchen Faulkner was interviewing for an MBA program. She was a liberal arts major in college, and for the last several years had worked at the art museum in the city where she attended college. During the conversation, the MBA program director asked her why she decided to quit and pursue and MBA. "Actually I had been quite happy with the job," she said. "After I'd been there for three years, I was able to work more autonomously, troubleshooting problems, taking steps to resolve those problems and taking the initiative to improve my job. Guided by the museum's mission statement and my department's mission statement, I felt empowered to make changes or take steps to achieve the museum's strategic goals. After a while, I learned that my job wasn't entirely about following strict procedures. It was a real epiphany for me to figure out that I could make decisions and think on my feet to benefit a visitor, a volunteer, a co-worker, etc. For example, every year in May, the museum experiences a rush of school tours. It's the busiest time of year with school groups touring every day, Tuesday through Friday, on the hour or half-hour. The more years I worked through this crunch, the better equipped I was to promote positive changes for the 'spring rush.' Two years ago, the museum had a spring exhibit of Egyptian artifacts that was expected to attract many school tours. Working with many other departments like Security and Marketing, I was able to help implement school tours on Mondays when we were normally closed to the public and relieve some of the problems associated with the high demand. That said, though, I ended up leaving the museum because there was no place for me to go in my position."

How did Gretchen's job relate to the Hackman and Oldham job characteristics theory? What aspects motivated her? What positive outcomes in the model were evident? What aspects of the theory explain her decision to leave?

ENDNOTES

1. Quoted in David Ulrich and Dale Lake, "Organizational Capability: Creating Competitive Advantage," *Academy of Management Executive*, Vol. 5, No. 1, 1991, pp. 77–92.

2. M. J. Kiernan, "The New Strategic Architecture: Learning to Compete in the Twenty-First Century," *Academy of Management Executive*, Vol. 7, No. 1, 1993, p. 14.

3. E. E. Lawler, S. A. Mohrman, and G. E. Ledford, *Employee Involvement and Total Quality Management*, San Francisco: Jossey-Bass, 1992.

4. Richard C. Whiteley, *The Customer-Driven Company: Moving from Talk to Action*, Reading, Mass.: Addison-Wesley, 1991.

5. Phillip A. Smith, William D. Anderson, and Stanley A. Brooking, "Employee Empowerment: A Case Study," *Production and Inventory Management*, Vol. 34, No. 3, 1993, pp. 45–50.

6. J. M. Juran, *Juran on Leadership for Quality: An Executive Handbook*, New York: Free Press, 1989, p. 264.

7. Juran, *Juran on Leadership for Quality*, pp. 147–148.

8. J. A. Conger and R. N. Kanungo, "The Empowerment Process: Integrating Theory and Practice," *Academy of Management Review*, Vol. 13, No. 3, 1988, pp. 471–482.

9. Brad Stratton, "UPS: Its Long-Term Design Delivers Quality Millions of Times Each Day," *Quality Progress*, October 1998, pp. 37–38.

10. Kathleen D. Ryan and Daniel K. Oestreich, *Driving Fear Out of the Workplace*, San Francisco: Jossey-Bass, 1991.

11. James L. Heskett, W. Earl Sasser, Jr., and Leonard A. Schlesinger, *The Service Profit Chain*, New York: Free Press, 1997, p. 101.

12. Lawler, Mohrman, and Ledford, *Employee Involvement*, p. 60.

13. Brad Stratton, "How Disneyland Works," *Quality Progress*, July 1991, pp. 17–30.

14. Hal F. Rosenbluth, "Have Quality, Will Travel," *The TQM Magazine*, November/December 1992, pp. 267–270.

15. Linda Grant, "Happy Workers, High Returns," *Fortune*, January 12, 1998, p. 81.

16. Lawler, Mohrman, and Ledford, *Employee Involvement*; Dan Ciampa, *Total Quality: A User's Guide for Implementation*, Reading, Mass.: Addison-Wesley, 1992.

17. Brent Schlender, "Pixar's Fun House," *Fortune*, July 23, 2001, p. 266.

18. Quoted in Whiteley, *The Customer-Driven Company*, p. 180.

19. Lawler, Mohrman, and Ledford, *Employee Involvement*, p. 105.

20. Tom Brown, "The Empowerment Myth," *Across the Board*, March/April 2001, pp. 71–72.

21. Dan Ciampa, *Total Quality: A User's Guide for Implementation*, Reading, Mass: Addison-Wesley, 1991.

22. Brown, ibid.

23. Lawler, Mohrman, and Ledford, *Employee Involvement*, p. 51.

24. Juran, *Juran on Leadership for Quality*, p. 277.

25. Mark Kelly, *The Adventures of a Self-Managing Team*, Raleigh, N.C.: Mark Kelly Books, 1990.

26. Lawler, Mohrman, and Ledford, *Employee Involvement*, p. 47.

27. Ciampa, *Total Quality*.

28. A. R. Tenner and I. J. DeToro, *Total Quality Management: Three Steps to Continuous Improvement*, Reading, Mass.: Addison-Wesley, 1992.

29. Lawler, Mohrman, and Ledford, *Employee Involvement*, p. 60.

30. Adapted from Brad Stratton, "Texas Nameplate Company: All You Need Is Trust," *Quality Progress*, October 1998, pp. 29–32.

31. "Changing a Culture: DuPont Tries to Make Sure That Its Research Wizardry Serves the Bottom Line," *The Wall Street Journal*, March 27, 1992, p. A5.

32. Robert S. Kaplan, "Texas Eastman Company," Harvard Business School Case, No. 9-190-039.

33. Peter M. Senge, *The Fifth Discipline: The Art and Practice of the Learning Organization*, New York: Doubleday Currency, 1990.

34. See *America's Choice: High Skills or Low Wages!*, National Center on Education and the Economy's Commission on the Skills of the American Workforce, National Center on Education and the Economy, 1990.

35. Lawler, Mohrman, and Ledford, *Employee Involvement*, p. 16.

36. Based on Ronald Henkoff, "Companies That Train Best," *Fortune*, March 22, 1993, pp. 62–75.

37. Jennifer Reese, "Starbucks: Inside the Coffee Cult," *Fortune*, December 9, 1996, pp. 190–200.

38. Based on Jack Johnson and Jack T. Mollen, "Ten Tasks for Managers in the Empowered Workplace," *Journal for Quality and Participation*, December 1992, pp. 18–20.

39. Lawler, Mohrman, and Ledford, *Employee Involvement*, p. 20.

40. The Conference Board, "Innovative Reward and Recognition Strategies in TQM," Report Number 1051, 1993, p. 15.

41. Brian O'Reilly, "The Mechanic Who Fixed Continental," *Fortune*, December 20, 1999, pp. 176–186.

42. Curtis Sittenfeld, "Great Job! Here's a Seat Belt!" *Fast Company*, January 2004, p. 29.

43. The information on Semco is from Matthew J. Kiernan, "The New Strategic Architecture: Learning to Compete in the Twenty-First Century," *Academy of Management Executive*, Vol. 7, No. 1, pp. 7–21. See also R. Semler, "Managing Without Managers," J. J. Gabarro (ed.), *Managing People and Organizations*, Boston: Harvard Business School, 1992.

44. Based on Cheri Henderson, "Putting on the Ritz," *The TQM Magazine*, November/December 1992, pp. 292–296.

45. Los Alamos National Bank 2000 Award Winner Profile, Baldrige National Quality Program, U.S. Department of Commerce, and Los Alamos National Bank Baldrige National Quality Award Application Summary.

46. Timothy Aeppel, "Not All Workers Find Idea of Empowerment as Neat as It Sounds," *The Wall Street Journal*, September 8, 1998, pp. A1, A13.

47. Sharafat Khan, "The Key to Being a *Leader Company*: Empowerment," *Journal for Quality and Participation*, January/February 1997, pp. 44–50.

48. "Bonus Pay: Buzzword or Bonanza?" *Business Week*, November 14, 1994, 62–64.

49. Woodrumm Imberman, "Pay for Performance Boosts Quality Output," *IIE Solutions*, October 1996, 34–36.

50. Nancy J. Perry, "Here Come Richer, Riskier Pay Plans," *Fortune*, December 19, 1988, 50–58; "The Nucor Story," available at http://www.nucor.com.

51. Dawn Anfuso, "L.L. Bean's TQM Efforts Put People Before Processes," *Personnel Journal*, July 1994, 73–83.

52. Michelle Conlin and Kathy Moore, "Photo Essay—SAS," *Business Week*, June 19, 2000, 192–202.

53. This discussion of organizational behavior theory's contribution to TQ thinking is based on J. J. Riley, "Human Resource Development: An Overview," in J. P. Kern, J. J. Riley, and L. N. Jones (eds.), *Human Resources Management*, Milwaukee: ASQC Quality Press, 1987.

54. Job characteristics theory is described in J. R. Hackman and G. R. Oldham, *Work Redesign*, Reading, Mass.: Addison-Wesley Publishing Company, 1980.

55. Hackman and Oldham, *Work Redesign*.

56. D .C. McClelland, *Assessing Human Motivation*, Morristown, N.J.: General Learning Press, 1971. See also D. C. McClelland and R. E. Boyatzis, "Leadership Motive Pattern and Long-Term Success in Management," *Journal of Applied Psychology*, 1982, pp. 67, 737–743.

57. Edwin Locke, "Toward a Theory of Task Performance and Incentives," *Organizational Behavior and Human Performance*, Fall 1968, pp. 167–189. For a more recent treatment of goal-setting, see Mark E. Tubbs and Steven E. Ekeberg, "The Role of Intentions in Work Motivation: Implications for Goal-Setting Theory and Research," *Academy of Management Review*, January 1991, pp. 180–199.

58. Philip Atkinson, "Leadership, Total Quality, and Cultural Change," *Management Services*, Vol. 35, No. 6, 1991, pp. 16–19.

59. My thanks go to Professor James Thom of Purdue University for sharing this anecdote. The actual letter was edited to preserve the confidentiality of the company.

60. My thanks to Gretchen Faulkner for allowing me to develop a case based on comments and observations from her quality management class journal in the MBA program at the University of Cincinnati.

PART 4

Leadership and Implementation

CHAPTER 10

Quality Leadership

Motorola's former CEO, Bob Galvin, made a habit of making quality the first item on the agenda of executive staff meetings—and leaving the meeting before discussion of financials. His actions spoke louder than words: if quality was taken care of, financial performance would follow. His leadership guided Motorola to become one of the first winners of the Malcolm Baldrige National Quality Award.

Leadership is fundamental to management and organizational behavior and is on just about everyone's short list of prerequisites for organizational success. Thus, it is not surprising that leadership plays a crucial role in the total quality organization. Virtually every article and book written about quality emphasizes leadership. "Teach and institute leadership" is one of W. E. Deming's 14 Points. Leadership is the first category in the Malcolm Baldrige National Quality Award and is recognized as the "driver" of successful quality systems. Indeed, leadership is seen by many quality experts as the *sine qua non* (if you don't have it, you have nothing) of TQ. As two quality experts put it, "Without management leadership, quality and productivity will result only as fortunate accidents."[1] This chapter will

➢ discuss the importance of leadership for quality,
➢ describe the role of leaders in pursuing total quality,
➢ provide some examples of leaders who have inspired their organizations to attain very high quality in businesses as disparate as raising chickens in Maryland and making noodle soup in Japan, and
➢ compare the TQ view of leadership to several prominent leadership theories.

PERSPECTIVES ON LEADERSHIP

In practice, the notion of leadership can be as elusive as the notion of quality itself. Most definitions of leadership reflect an assortment of behaviors, for example:

• vision that stimulates hope and mission that transforms hope into reality;
• radical servanthood that saturates the organization;

- stewardship that shepherds its resources;
- integration that drives its economy;
- the courage to sacrifice personal or team goals for the greater community good;
- communication that coordinates its efforts;
- consensus that drives unity of purpose;
- empowerment that grants permission to make mistakes, encourages the honesty to admit them, and gives the opportunity to learn from them; and
- conviction that provides the stamina to continually strive toward business excellence.[2]

Although true leadership applies to everyone in an organization, we generally think of *executive leadership*, which focuses on the roles of senior managers in guiding an organization to fulfill its mission and meet its goals, when we use the term.

The many activities that senior executives perform include the following:

- defining and communicating business directions
- ensuring that goals and expectations are met
- reviewing business performance and taking appropriate action
- creating an enjoyable work environment that promotes creativity, innovation, and continual improvement
- soliciting input and feedback from customers
- ensuring that employees are effective contributors to the business
- motivating, inspiring, and energizing employees
- recognizing employee contributions
- providing honest feedback

Effective leaders empower employees to assume ownership of problems or opportunities, and to be proactive in implementing improvements and making decisions in the best interests of the organization. The philosophy at GTE Directories Corporation summarizes this facet of leadership nicely: *Put a stake in the ground, get out of the way, and stay the course.*

Why is leadership so important to quality? Leaders establish plans and goals for the organization. If the plans and goals do not include quality or, worse yet, are antithetical to quality, the quality effort will die. Leaders help to shape the culture of the organization through key decisions and symbolic actions. If they help to shape a culture that puts convenience or short-term benefits ahead of quality, it will die. Leaders distribute resources. If resources are showered on programs that cut short-term costs while quality is starved for resources, quality will die. This list could go on. Virtually everything that an organization needs to succeed in meeting its customers' expectations—goals, plans, culture, resources—can either be helped or hurt by leaders (see the box on Jack Welch). With this in mind, let us examine in more detail the roles that leaders play in a total quality company.

Many writers and managers have tried to define what a manager must do as an effective quality leader. Edwin L. Artzt was Chairman of Procter & Gamble, one of the nation's oldest and most successful companies and one of the earliest to emphasize quality. He believes: "To lead quality—and I'm talking about leaders at every level in an organization—means providing the clear strategic choices, the guiding principles, and the disciplined application to continually improve and reinvent ourselves . . . and to do that with a focus on the good of the whole."[3]

The criteria for the Malcolm Baldrige National Quality Award also dwell heavily on leadership. Here is the philosophy of leadership within the Baldrige criteria:

"An organization's senior leaders should set directions and create a customer focus, clear and visible values, and high expectations. . . . The directions, values, and expectations should balance the needs of all your stakeholders. Your leaders should ensure the creation of strategies, systems, and methods for achieving excellence, stimulating innovation, and building knowledge and capabilities. The

---

The Man Who Hated Quality[4]

Jack Welch, CEO of General Electric, is probably regarded as the most admired CEO of his generation. The following dialog about General Electric's Six Sigma quality initiative (see Chapter 3) took place between a *Fortune* magazine reporter and Welch in 1999 prior to his retirement from GE:

Fortune: Jack, you're doing a total-quality thing 10 or 15 years after the rest of corporate America did it. Why are you doing it, and why now?

Welch: There was only one guy in the whole country who hated quality more than me. I always believed quality would come from just operating well and fast, and all these slogans were nonsense. The guy who hated quality more was Larry Bossidy. He hated quality totally. Then he left GE and went to Allied Signal. In order to resurrect Allied Signal, Larry went out, saw Motorola, and did some stuff on Six Sigma. And he called me one day and he said, "Jack, this ain't b.s.—this is real stuff, this is really great stuff." We poll 10,000 employees every year. In '95 they came back and said, "We desperately need a quality issue." So Six Sigma was something we adopted then. The results are fantastic. We're going to get $1.2 billion of gain this year. For years our operating margin was never over 10. It's been improving, and it's going to be 16.7 this year. Our working-capital turns were four for 35 years. It will be nine this year.

Jack Welch showed that not only was he a strong leader but also he didn't have all the answers and needed to continually learn, one of the hallmarks of leadership for quality.

values and strategies should help guide all activities and decisions of your organization."

Senior leaders should inspire and motivate your entire workforce and should encourage all employees to contribute, to develop and learn, to be innovative, and to be creative. Senior leaders should serve as role models through their ethical behavior and their personal involvement in planning, communications, coaching, development of future leaders, review of organizational performance, and employee recognition. As role models, they can reinforce values and expectations when building leadership, commitment, and initiative throughout your organization.[5]

A final overview of the concept of quality leadership comes from Dan Ciampa, president and chief executive officer of Rath & Strong, a consulting group specializing in total quality: The mandate is to inspire, to invoke commitment, to enable employees to form a different concept of the organization in which they believe deeply, and to change without being threatened.[6]

THE ROLES OF A QUALITY LEADER

Underlying the concept of quality leadership are three clear imperatives for managers who aspire to quality leadership. First, they must establish a vision. Second, they must live the values. Third, they must lead the improvement efforts. Let's examine each of these in turn.

Establish a Vision

Leaders are visionaries; they manage for the future, not the past (think back to the first of Deming's 14 Points). Vision is crucial at every level during times of change. Leaders recognize the radical organizational changes taking place today as opportunities to move closer to total quality. Jack Welch, for example, pushed GE to become a leader among traditional Old Economy companies in embracing the Internet after noticing his wife Christmas shopping on the Web. "I realized that if I didn't watch it, I would retire as a Neanderthal," he was reported as saying, "So I just started reading everything I could about it." He began by pairing 1,000 Web-savvy mentors with senior people to get his top teams up to Internet speed quickly.[7] Visionary leaders create mental and verbal pictures of desirable future states and share these visions with their organizational partners, including customers, suppliers, and employees.

A **vision** is a vivid concept of what an organization could be. It is a striking depiction of possibilities, of potential. It is a dream, both in the sense of being desirable and in the sense of being a long way from the current reality, but it is not an "impossible dream." A vision should be clear and exciting to an organization's employees. It should be linked to customers' needs and convey a general strategy for achieving the mission. For example, PepsiCo states, "We will be an outstanding company by exceeding customer expectations through empowered people, guided by shared values." Alcoa's vision is stated as: "Alcoa is a growing worldwide company dedicated to excellence through quality—creating value for customers, employees, and shareholders through innovation, technology, and operational expertise. Alcoa will be the best aluminum company in the world, and a leader in other businesses in which we choose to compete." To be quality leaders, managers must establish a vision for and in their organization. "Establishing" a vision implies both the intellectual and emotional work of conceiving the vision and the interpersonal and managerial work of communicating the vision to the organization and leading employees to embrace it.

Quality-oriented visions have inspired some of the most dramatic corporate success stories in business history. IBM was founded on the idea of exceptional customer service and fair treatment of employees. Federal Express sought what at the time was seen as almost inconceivable speed and reliability in the package delivery market. Apple Computers wanted to make computing accessible to the masses.[8] These visions were creative, captivating, and most of all achievable. (For more examples, see the box "A World of Vision.")

Jane Carroll, president of The Forum Corporation, Europe/Asia, emphasizes the visionary role of leadership for quality, which she calls focus. She believes that most managers do not understand the need for a quality vision and their personal involvement in establishing it: "In our experience, very few CEOs have a real sense of what their role is in the quality improvement process. It goes far beyond simply being a cheerleader and handing out an occasional award. Top management has to provide the proper focus for the organization. This is not something that can be delegated."[9]

Putting together a vision is hard work, but quality leaders do not have to do it alone. They can draw on the talents and imagination of all the members of their organizations in developing their vision. In fact, in many organizations, people are walking around with "minivisions" of their own that sound like "if only we could [do something they have been told can't be done], things would be so much better around here." The raw material for a vision may be all around leaders in the organization. The first step may be simply listening for it. Leaders who are open to the ideas of people throughout the organization will be much better prepared to develop a vision that people will accept.

In the current competitive environment, if a given organization is not pursuing a customer-oriented vision, competing organizations probably are and are planning to use their vision to win over the competition's customers (or are already doing so). This is why a quality vision is such a crucial first step in quality leadership. An organization with no vision about how to create long-term customer loyalty has little chance of survival (unless, of course, it's a monopoly).

A World of Vision

Visit almost any major corporate Web site and you will find a vision statement. Some are short; some are long, but all focus on competitive leadership. Here is just a sampling:

State Farm Insurance Our vision for the future is to be the customer's first and best choice in the products and services we provide. We will continue to be the leader in the insurance industry and we will become a leader in the financial services arena. Our customers' needs will determine our path. Our values will guide us.

Bell Atlantic Our vision is to be the leading wireless provider in each market we serve. We use our domestic market presence to achieve maximum scale advantages and invest selectively in international properties where we can use our management expertise to create value.

CIGNA . . . we intend to be the best at helping our customers enhance and extend their lives and protect their financial security. Satisfying customers is the key to meeting employee needs and shareholder expectations, and will enable CIGNA to build on our reputation as a financially strong and highly respected company.

AMR We will be the global market leader in air transportation and related information services. That leadership will be attained by: Setting the industry standard for safety and security. Providing world-class customer service. Creating an open and participative work environment which seeks positive change, rewards innovation and provides growth, security and opportunity to all employees. Producing consistently superior financial returns for shareholders.

USWest We will be the leader in providing telecommunications solutions that make the lives of our customers better, easier, and hassle free. And deliver to them applications that communicate, educate, entertain and inform.

Goodyear Goodyear ranked by all measures as the best tire and rubber company in the world, and returning to our position as the industry's undisputed world leader by the end of the year 2000.

Texas Instruments . . . to become a premier electronics company providing world leadership in digital solutions for the networked society—a society transformed by personalized electronics, all speaking the same digital language, all able to communicate anytime, anywhere.

The second part of establishing a vision is instilling it in all the members of the organization. This will be a lot easier if many people were involved in the first part of the process, and the leader doesn't act like Moses coming down the mountain with the stone tablets. When Corning Glass instituted a quality vision, Chairman Jamie Houghton introduced it to employees at all levels in countries all over the world. Communication is vitally important.

A leader who is able to present the vision in an intriguing way has an advantage in trying to capture the imagination of the people in the organization, according to Francis Adamson, manager of quality engineering/TQM at Heinz U.S.A.: "The ability to fascinate is one of the most powerful tools of the charismatic leader. Leaders can use it to weave a fabric of commitment throughout the organization. This is the empowering function of the leader: allowing everyone to buy into the vision."[10]

Live the Values

Pursuing the quality vision commits the organization to living by a set of values such as devotion to customers, continuous improvement, and teamwork. A manager who hopes the organization will embrace and live by these values must live them to the utmost. As former Procter & Gamble Chairman and CEO Edwin Artzt puts it, "Leaders of the best companies profoundly believe in, and promote, the core values of customer-focused quality."[11] By "walking the talk," leaders serve as role models for the whole organization.

Many CEOs lead quality training sessions, serve on quality improvement teams, work on projects that do not usually require top-level input, and personally visit customers. For example, senior managers at Texas Instruments Defense Systems and Electronics Group (now part of Raytheon) led 150 of 1,900 cross-functional teams. At Custom Research, Inc., the top four senior leaders ensure that employees have the responsibility, training, and information they need to do their jobs through empowering everyone to do what it takes to serve clients, work with nine other senior people to set strategy, and make middle managers the real leaders.

When dramatic organizational changes are taking place, people in organizations are very sensitive to any sign of hypocrisy. A leader can undermine 100 hours of speeches with one decision that reveals his or her commitment to quality values to be superficial. This is not just a symbolic issue: Harvard's David Garvin found in a study of the air-conditioner industry that the quality of a firm's products was strongly related to the quality values expressed by management.[12]

Managers' actions can symbolize their commitment to quality-oriented values in many concrete ways. For example, they can attend training programs on various aspects of quality, instead of just sending others. They can practice continuous improvement in processes that they control, such as strategic planning and capital budgeting. Perhaps most importantly, they can provide adequate funding for quality efforts, so that TQ will not be the "poor cousin" to other business issues.[13]

Virtually every management team that has staged a major quality turnaround has recognized this need to "walk," not just "talk," quality. In looking back on the return to financial success from near-bankruptcy of his company, Harley-Davidson's Ron Hutchinson stated: "We realized that, if we really wanted to communicate to our people a change in the company's direction and approach, what we needed to do as senior managers was demonstrate that we were going to live by a new set of rules."

Lead Continuous Improvement

Beyond establishing a vision for the organization and expressing quality values through their decisions and actions, quality-oriented leaders must lead the continuous process improvement efforts that are the meat and potatoes of total quality management. All of the vision and values in the world are worthless if the organization is not continuously making strides to improve its performance in the eyes of customers. Visions of world-class quality and competitiveness can only be achieved if an organization keeps finding ways to do things a little better and a little faster. Leaders must be at the center of these efforts.

Managers are sometimes reluctant to take an active role in the organization's improvement efforts for fear of dominating or undercutting their newly empowered workers. Like many aspects of management, this is a question of balance, but it is a mistake for managers to remain uninvolved in process improvement efforts. Harry Levinson and Chuck DeHont, quality leaders at Sierra Semiconductor, have thought about this dilemma and concluded: "It is often perceived, incorrectly, that management should never specify how problems should be solved, that to do so would be considered improper delegation. What is actually true is that managers who set no rules for how problems should be solved have abdicated their leadership roles."[14]

There are a number of ways for managers to lead continuous improvement, and which ones make the most sense will depend on the specific organization. One option already mentioned is for leaders to lead by example, by working continuously to improve the processes that they control. For some of these processes, organizational members are among the customers, which gives management the opportunity to model for them the behaviors associated with obtaining and acting on customer input.[15] If management were to streamline the capital budgeting procedure by speeding up the process and eliminating non–value-added activities, it would provide a powerful example for people to emulate.

A second way that managers can lead process improvement is to help organization members prioritize processes to work on. Here managers can take advantage of their knowledge of the "big picture" and suggest avenues of improvement that are likely to have big payoffs in terms of quality improvement and customer satisfaction. This point was underscored by a recent statement by Gerhard Schulmeyer, president and CEO of Asea Brown Boveri, a multinational company headquartered in Germany: It doesn't help simply to encourage everybody to work harder. The issue is to take a fresh look at the problems and concentrate our efforts on core processes that have the largest leverage in improving our position in the market.[16]

A third way is to inspire people to do things they do not believe they can do. Motorola set aggressive goals of reducing defects per unit of output in every operation by 100-fold in four years and reducing cycle time by 50 percent each year. One of Hewlett-Packard's goals is to reduce the interval between product concept and investment payback by one half in five years. The 3M Company seeks to generate 25 percent of sales from products less than two years old. To promote such "stretch goals," leaders provide the resources and support necessary to meet them, especially training.

Of course, managers leading process improvement bear some responsibility for educating all their associates as to how the various processes within the company fit together. If this is done effectively, organization members will be able eventually to set their own priorities for process improvement.

Managers also can lead this effort by removing barriers to success in process improvement.[17] Barriers may consist of a nettlesome standard operating procedure or a recalcitrant manager in a key position. Without leadership

---

Tampopo: **The Quest for the Perfect Noodle Soup**[18]

Like many aspects of organizations, the nature of leadership is changed dramatically by TQ. Moving beyond a command-and-control mentality, leaders in a TQ organization help their associates to provide better products and services to customers. This style of leadership is personified by Goro, a truck driver and noodle expert who in the film *Tampopo* helps Tampopo in her quest to create the perfect noodle soup. An unlikely blend of western and samurai movie cliches, *Tampopo* is at the same time a parody and a virtual roadmap for continuous quality improvement.

Goro and his friend Guntu meet Tampopo when they stop in at the Lai Lai noodle stand for a quick bite. When Goro tells a drunken customer that Tampopo's noodles are mediocre, he gets taken outside and beaten up, a fate that (metaphorically at least) awaits many leaders who publicly state that the status quo is not good enough. But Tampopo is wise enough to accept Goro's judgment on the poor quality of her noodles and asks for his help.

One of Goro's first suggestions is to study her customers as they enter the shop, so that she can adjust her service to their needs. Tampopo soon begins to recognize that quality noodle soup involves a lot more than just cooking. She closes her shop until further notice and devotes herself to elevating the quality of her noodle business. In a scene reminiscent of Rocky, Tampopo (now in a sweat suit) runs through the park, with Goro following on a bicycle. She then practices lifting pots of boiling water, working to reduce her soup production time below three minutes.

The next step is to learn from the competition. The nearby shop Goro and Tampopo visit first is full, demonstrating that customers are there if only Tampopo is good enough. In the second shop, the cooks talk to each other too much and forget people's orders. In the third, the cook's motions are

Continued

elegant, with no wasted motion. In the fourth, a busy place by a rail station, the cook must keep track of many orders at once. Tampopo shows her progress by rattling off all the orders that have been given. At the fifth shop, the broth is so good that Goro and Tampopo stoop to spying to try to duplicate the recipe. At the sixth, the owners see what is going on and kick them out, but Tampopo tells them they have nothing worth stealing: their dough sat out too long, their pork is overcooked, and their soup tasteless.

Although this noodle benchmarking tour has greatly improved the quality of Tampopo's soup, she recognizes that it is not yet good enough. Help then comes from an unlikely source, an old friend of Goro's living in a hobo camp where everyone is a gastronome. He takes them to yet more restaurants, including one where they rescue a man from choking. The man lends them his chauffeur, who against all odds is also a noodle expert, and takes them to even more restaurants. (The quest for quality can be exhausting, and in this case pretty rough on the waistline.)

In the shop with the best-tasting noodles, Tampopo has to trick the proprietor into divulging his process: "These noodles are not as good as usual, perhaps you did not let them sit long enough." "I left them overnight, as usual," he growls, and so on until Tampopo has the entire recipe.

At this point, Goro and Tampopo's other advisors urge her to reopen her shop, now renamed after her. The drunken customer from her old shop turns out to be a contractor and decorator, who remodels the shop for efficiency and attractiveness. Tampopo herself also gets remodeled, as she drops her dumpy old outfit for a new chef's uniform. The transformation is remarkable.

Still the quest for improvement continues. The experts tell Tampopo that her soup "lacks profundity" and suggest adding spring onions. Although the other elements are nearly perfect, there is nothing to distinguish it, no unexpected element to delight customers and exceed their expectations. With the spring onions added, she tries again. The experts drink her soup to the bottom.

Success! Soon customers are swarming to her new shop, and Goro and the others drift away, as Tampopo no longer needs them. A cycle of quality leadership is complete, and Goro rides off into the sunset.

from management, such barriers may undermine efforts at process improvement. Of course, in dealing with such barriers managers must continue to operate in a manner consistent with quality values. For example, managers who balk at changes must be treated with respect and their reservations considered seriously, even if they are eventually overruled.

One final way for managers to lead process improvement is to keep track of improvement efforts, to encourage them, and to provide recognition when key milestones are reached. Solectron managers, for example, recognize and reward groups for exceptional performance. Besides monetary awards,

Solectron often buys lunch for an entire division or brings in ice cream for the whole corporation. One top manager of our acquaintance makes it a practice always to be present for such recognition ceremonies. If he cannot attend, the ceremony is rescheduled. By doing this, the manager is accomplishing several things at once: he is showing his sincere interest in the process, he is providing reinforcement for those people working to make key changes, and he is letting his subordinates know that it is not acceptable to make excuses for missing quality-related functions. (For an additional and unusual example of leadership for continuous improvement, see the box on *Tampopo*.)

QUALITY LEADERSHIP IN ACTION

Some of the best examples of leadership come from Baldrige Award winners. In this section we describe some of the leadership activities of two winning companies, Solectron Corporation (the first repeat winner) and Armstrong Building Products Operations.

Solectron Corporation[19]

Solectron was founded in 1977 in San Jose, California. Dr. Winston Chen, the first CEO, established the entrepreneurial foundation for the company's leadership system. He focused all employees on:

- the needs of the customer,
- the improvement of quality in manufacturing processes,
- the challenge of providing a reasonable return to shareholders, and
- the responsibility to do what it takes to satisfy the customer.

Dr. Chen also developed a set of basic values, the Solectron Beliefs, to use as the model for behavior for all employees. These are:

Customer First—The customer is our first priority and it is our constant objective to satisfy customer requirements on time with zero defects. We do this by strengthening partnership relationships and providing products and services of the greatest value through innovation and excellence.

Respect for the Individual—We recognize the importance of listening to every employee. We emphasize employee dignity, equality, and growth.

Quality—Customers are entitled to products and services that meet their expectations and specifications. It is our goal to execute with excellence and exceed customer expectations.

Supplier Partnership—We emphasize partnership, communication, and measurement.

Business Ethics—Honesty, integrity, and dependability are the cornerstones of all successful relationships. We believe we must conduct our business with uncompromising integrity.

Shareholder Value—We optimize business results through continuous improvement.

Social Responsibility—It is our objective to be an asset to our community.

In 1988, Dr. Koichi ("Ko") Nishimura joined Solectron as chief operating officer. Dr. Nishimura's objective was to develop and sustain an infrastructure and management system that would meet the challenge of a 30 percent annual growth rate, while maintaining profit levels, improving levels of customer satisfaction, and providing growth opportunities for employees.

Solectron's vision is to be the best electronics design and manufacturing service company in the world. In 1989, Dr. Nishimura adopted the Malcolm Baldrige National Quality Award criteria as the foundation and framework for Solectron's business and leadership system. In order to accelerate the compliance of Solectron's leadership system and company-wide processes to the Baldrige criteria, Ko suggested that Solectron should enter the award process in order to get examiner feedback on how they could improve. Since 1989, the company's leadership group under Dr. Nishimura, who is now Solectron's chairman, president, and CEO, has been using the Baldrige criteria, including both external and internal assessments, to drive business excellence.

The Baldrige road map has helped Solectron to grow and thrive, resulting in an average compound annual growth rate in excess of 50 percent. Ko taught the leadership team that their job is to manage the business to assure the needs of all stakeholders are addressed. Ko coaches the leadership team to live the Solectron Beliefs. The Solectron Beliefs have been in place for many years and have been reaffirmed year after year. Ko emphatically states that if behavior does not reflect the Solectron Beliefs, then they need to change behavior, not the beliefs.

Ko Nishimura and the senior leadership team drive the annual planning process for the corporation. The process includes developing the long-range plan (LRP), the annual operating plan (AOP), and the annual improvement plan (Hoshin). Senior leaders continuously review company performance. Key performance reviews include:

- Each site manager monitors operational, quality, business, supplier, and customer data daily.
- Performance to strategic and annual plans is reviewed by the CEO every month and then collectively reviewed at the bimonthly general managers' meeting. All region presidents, site general managers, and corporate vice presidents attend and present status and results.

- Z Ko Nishimura travels to each site every quarter to review performance in detail. These reviews allow various line managers and employees to make presentations to the CEO. Ko reinforces the company's commitment to customers, shareholders, and employees in these meetings. He also facilitates internal communication between sites.

- Site general managers conduct quarterly informational meetings for employees. They review quarterly business results, developments with key customers, and the status of important strategic initiatives. These meetings are also used to recognize contributions of employees and employee teams.

- The results of an annual customer executive survey are reviewed in detail at general managers' meetings. These data are analyzed for both near-term actions and longer-term capability enhancement. Critical issues are integrated into action plans and are reviewed during the CEO's site visits.

Solectron is focused on satisfying customers' requirements on a global basis, with facilities in North America, Europe, and Asia. The firm has grown both by setting up "greenfield" locations and by buying facilities from customers.

Ko Nishimura manages Solectron as an entrepreneurial company. Ko has set up a Business Conduct Guide that defines the individual responsibilities for conducting business in the highest ethical manner. This guide drives home the point that the Solectron Beliefs are the principles for running the company. Solectron is also proactively involved with various government and regulatory groups to help in shaping policy. Among various recognitions for its environmental approaches, Solectron California was awarded a "special recognition" by the San Francisco Bay Areas Peninsula Conservation Center Foundation for its environmental, pollution prevention, and recycling programs.

Armstrong Building Products Operation[20]

Reporting to the Executive Office of Armstrong World Industries, Inc., the Building Products Operation (BPO) Quality Leadership Team, consisting of the president and direct reports, leads and manages all aspects of Armstrong's U.S. ceilings business. In 1990, as a result of an internal self-assessment against the 1989 Baldrige criteria, BPO leaders reorganized to improve customer focus and satisfaction, forming the BPO General Management Team (GMT). The purpose of this reorganization was to more formally define and execute a leadership system within BPO. Its focus: improving customer satisfaction, financial performance, and capabilities across functional lines.

In January 1994, BPO aligned key support services into the operation to better communicate and integrate its values and expectations for employees, customers, and shareholders. Shortly thereafter, the BPO GMT reorganized into the BPO Quality Leadership Team (QLT), which now includes the key support staff leaders as well as the leaders of the five value-adding functions.

The purpose of the QLT is "to ensure that the values, goals, and systems are in place to guide the sustained pursuit of customer value and operational performance improvement." The leadership system that the QLT has developed and refined to drive for business excellence includes the following specific roles and responsibilities:

- The QLT creates quality values and sets rational stretch goal expectations for BPO.
- Management-led Quality Improvement Teams (QITs) extend the leadership system to each location and focus on customer requirements and continuous improvement.
- The QLT uses the Baldrige criteria to assess performance.
- Based on Baldrige feedback, QLT members are assigned specific areas to develop and implement action plans to capitalize on their strengths and address opportunities for improvement.
- The QLT keeps refining the BPO planning process to create an integrated strategic management process aimed at delivering value and satisfaction to customers, employees, and shareholders.
- QLT members and many other employees systematically participate in various customer advisory committee meetings, national customer conventions, and conversations with customers to communicate and reinforce BPO's quality values.
- The QLT refines relationships with BPO's channel customers.
- QLT members conduct and participate in a wide variety of education, training, benchmarking, and capability development.
- QLT members communicate and reinforce their values to a long list of stakeholders outside of Armstrong.

The foundation of BPO's values is Armstrong's operating principles; the ethics behind them date from the company's beginnings in 1860. The company's operating principles have been unchanged since they were first set to paper in 1960, on Armstrong's 100th anniversary. They are the roots of the firm's quality values and are discussed with all new employees on their first day. The operating principles are

- to respect the dignity and inherent rights of the individual human being in all dealings with people;
- to maintain high moral and ethical standards and to reflect honesty, integrity, reliability, and forthrightness in all relationships;
- to reflect the tenets of good taste and common courtesy in all attitudes, words, and deeds; and
- to serve fairly and in proper balance the interests of all groups associated with the business—customers, stockholders, employees, suppliers, community neighbors, government, and the general public.

The QLT (and the former GMT) has been very successful in leading changes in culture, organizational structure, and levels of performance. This has been achieved through an ever-improving understanding of the dynamics of markets, competitors' performance, and drivers of business results.

The QLT meets twice per month to review, evaluate, and manage performance against the strategic plan. All QLT members review their functional action plan performance a minimum of once per quarter and at the QLT semiannually. They manage performance daily. The president and other QLT members review plants' action plans with each manufacturing plant during semiannual plant quality and service review meetings and global plant managers meetings. Every year, the president and the quality manager meet with each plant's QIT solely to review the plans and progress of its quality improvement process. Each member of the QLT conducts individual employee performance reviews each year. Members of the QLT actively participate in BPO's annual quality council meetings, where QIT leaders come together to review their strengths and areas for improvement. The QLT reviews the company's strategic management process annually. QLT members use a variety of systematic approaches to evaluate and improve the effectiveness of their personal and collective leadership. These include employee feedback, performance reviews, Baldrige assessments, and benchmarking.

In 1990 Armstrong's quality managers developed Armstrong's 14 actions based on the quality philosophy of Philip Crosby. In 1994 the 14 actions were refined again to improve the company's approaches and bring in new methods and systems, such as capability development. The refined 14 actions are:

1. *Leadership.* Demonstrate understanding, commitment, and resolve to improve quality in all areas of the organization.
2. *Quality Improvement Teams.* Plan, implement, and evaluate the organization's quality improvement activities.
3. *Customer Satisfaction.* Assure that the systems to improve quality, and actions to change culture, focus on markets and customers.
4. *Planning and Goal-Setting.* Establish specific targets and assess progress.
5. *Awareness.* Increase awareness of the importance of quality improvement among all employees.
6. *Education and Training.* Provide employees with the education required to effectively participate in improvements.
7. *Measurement.* Know whether we are meeting our customers' requirements. Understand and communicate current performance.
8. *Process Improvement.* Identify all major business processes in the organization, establish ownership, and clarify improvement priorities.
9. *Opportunities for Improvement.* Provide a system for all employees that encourages, communicates, and recognizes improvement ideas.
10. *Supplier Quality Management.* Involve Armstrong suppliers in our efforts to improve quality and achieve customer satisfaction.
11. *Recognition.* Encourage, recognize, and reward participation in improvement activities.

12. *Quality Councils.* Periodically bring leaders together to share information and set direction.
13. *Benchmarking.* Provide a disciplined approach for comparing the performance of our processes against best-in-class criteria.
14. *Assessment.* Evaluate the organization's performance against recognized standards.

Principles, values, and plans are communicated and reinforced throughout the entire organization. They are communicated by BPO's senior management during presentations at management meetings, Team Expos, crew meetings, and talks with customers, suppliers, and community neighbors. Behavior is reinforced by linking variable compensation to these values through business strategies. Over 90 percent of all BPO manufacturing employees are part of the company's Gainsharing Plan, which compensates plant employees (hourly and salaried) for improvements in safety, quality, productivity, and customer service. All other BPO employees are rewarded through the Salaried Employees' Bonus Plan. In 1994, record results in sales and profitability resulted in Armstrong BPO's highest-ever payout in both plans.

TQ and Leadership Theory

There are a great number of theories of leadership, and we can discuss the relationship of TQ to only a few of them. This section outlines some theories that seem to relate most closely to TQ and compares them to the TQ view of leadership.

The Roles of Managers

One well-known model, advanced by Henry Mintzberg, categorizes the work of managers into 10 roles. Although this is a model of managerial roles, rather than leadership per se, it is useful to explore how roles may change as managers attempt to practice total quality leadership.

There are *interpersonal roles* (figurehead, leader, and liaison), *informational roles* (monitor, disseminator, spokesperson), and *decisional roles* (entrepreneur, disturbance handler, resource allocator, and negotiator).[21] Each of these roles is likely to be played by managers practicing total quality, although the relative importance of the roles, and the ways in which they are played, may differ from more traditional organizations.

Interpersonal Roles

The figurehead role, which involves the ceremonial or symbolic tasks of managers, is certainly played in TQ organizations. A manager presiding at a recognition ceremony for a team's quality accomplishments would be fulfilling this role. The leadership role would obviously be important for TQ-oriented managers, but the directing and controlling aspects of this role would be downplayed.

The liaison role—dealing with customers, suppliers, and others—would still be played, but also it would be fulfilled to an increasing extent by employees, as an outgrowth of their empowerment.

Informational Roles

The informational roles of management would continue to be played, but nonmanagerial personnel would be more involved in these activities, rather than looking to managers as the source of all information. Employees involved in benchmarking, for example, would play an important part in monitoring and disseminating information. Whereas top managers would retain an important role as spokespersons, this role also would be increasingly shared with people throughout the organization. By now, probably hundreds if not thousands of nonmanagerial personnel have stepped up to the microphone to share their teams' accomplishments with the world.

Decisional Roles

Many of the behaviors leaders use to initiate and support a TQ program are characterized by the entrepreneurial role, one of the decisional roles. In this role, managers try to improve their organization by identifying problems and instituting processes to solve them. The disturbance-handler role—in which leaders resolve conflicts among subunits—should be diminished, at least in the long run, as people take on a more holistic view of the organizational mission. The resource-allocator role continues to be key, as TQ will not succeed unless leaders are unswerving in their commitment of resources to continuous improvement and customer satisfaction. Finally, the negotiator role will still be played, but it will be different, as companies try to create long-term, win-win arrangements with suppliers, unions, and customers.

The Mintzberg model attempts to describe the behavior of managers, not to prescribe what they should do. It also attempts to capture the broad scope of managerial activities across many types of organizations. For this reason it is difficult to compare it directly to the more limited, but explicitly prescriptive, content of the TQ leadership model. Nevertheless, the comparison is instructive in linking this discussion to the mainstream management literature on leadership: Managers in TQ settings will play some roles (entrepreneurial) more than other managers, other roles (disturbance handler) less often, and others (leader) differently.

Consideration and Initiating Structure

In a series of studies done several decades ago at Ohio State University, researchers tried to identify the behaviors associated with effective leadership. These studies concluded that many of these behaviors could be captured by two dimensions: consideration and initiating structure.

Consideration (also known as socioemotional orientation) means taking care of subordinates, explaining things to them, being approachable, and generally being concerned about their welfare. **Initiating structure** (also known as task orientation) means getting people organized, including setting goals and instituting and enforcing deadlines and standard operating procedures. Research has indicated that, although different situations will require different leadership behaviors, most organizational units over a period of time will require both types of leadership in order to be successful.[22]

One apparent difference between this classic view of leadership and the TQ view is that the former emphasizes leadership at the workgroup level, whereas the latter deals with the more global level of organizations or major subunits. Writers on TQ leadership have focused less on lower-level leaders, due perhaps to the emphasis on self-management at those levels.

Despite these differences, consideration and initiating structure are not irrelevant for organizations pursuing TQ. Such organizations recognize the importance of employees for the success of their quality efforts and for their performance in general. Thus leaders will certainly need to be considerate of employee needs. The section on Rosenbluth in Chapter 8 illustrated how consideration of employees minimizes their frustration and allows them to focus on customer service and continuous improvement. In a TQ environment, consideration would not be done in a paternalistic manner, emphasizing the power of leaders over subordinates. On the contrary, people would be treated as respected associates.

Initiating structure also will be appropriate in the TQ environment but perhaps will be accomplished differently than in the traditional organizational setting. Traditionally, leaders were responsible for the whole gamut of activities associated with initiating structure-setting goals, establishing deadlines, enforcing rules, and so on. In organizations striving for empowerment, many of these activities will be taken over by employees.

The discussion of leadership for TQ suggests that quality leadership consists more of setting a direction for people through establishing a vision and identifying values. By leading continuous improvement efforts, leaders will establish priorities for activities throughout the organization. Such activities will provide the necessary context for employees to initiate structure for themselves.

Transformational Leadership Theory

Another model that can be compared to the TQ approach is Transformational Leadership Theory.[23] According to this model, leadership has four principal dimensions:

1. Inspirational motivation—providing followers with a sense of meaning and challenge in their work;
2. Intellectual stimulation—encouraging followers to question assumptions, explore new ideas and methods, and adopt new perspectives;

3. Idealized influence—behaviors that followers strive to emulate or mirror;
4. Individualized consideration—special attention to each follower's needs for achievement and growth.

Leaders who wish to have a major impact on their organizations must take a long-term perspective, work to stimulate their organizations intellectually, invest in training to develop individuals and groups, take some risks, promote a shared vision and values, and focus on customers and employees as individuals.

The transformational leadership model dovetails with leadership for TQ. Many of its aspects (emphasis on vision and focus on customers and employees as individuals) are right out of the TQ playbook, while others are generally consistent with TQ. For instance, Deming emphasized the necessity for managers to have "constancy of purpose"—to pursue diligently the long-term goal of remaining competitive through continuous improvement processes. They should also communicate an appealing vision emphasizing continuous improvement, teamwork, and customer service in order to inspire followers. Moreover, managers can act as role models by taking a personal interest in activities geared toward improving processes and customer relationships.[24]

It would be tempting to say that all managers in TQ organizations should be transformational leaders, but this is unrealistic and probably unwise. It is not realistic because few, if any, organizations have such a concentration of transformational leaders. It is not wise because such a concentration would likely breed more chaos than quality. An organization pursuing TQM needs both those who establish visions and those who are effective at the day-to-day tasks needed to achieve them.[25] These "transactional leaders" play an important role in promoting total quality.

Situational Leadership

Ken Blanchard and Paul Hersey concluded that no single theory of leadership works in every situation, and developed a simple model known as *situational leadership* in the late 1960s. This model suggests that the style of leadership that one should use depends on the maturity of those being led. The premise behind the situation leadership model is that leadership styles might vary from one person to another, depending on their "readiness," which is characterized by their skills and abilities to perform the work, and their confidence, commitment, and motivation to do it. The Situational Leadership model defines four levels of readiness:

1. Unable and unwilling
2. Unable but willing
3. Able but unwilling, and
4. Able and willing

Blanchard and Hersey defined four leadership styles that best address these four levels of readiness:

1. *Directing.* In this style of leadership, managers define tasks and roles, and closely supervise work. Communication is generally one way—top down. This style applies best to people who lack the skills and knowledge to perform a job and lack the confidence or commitment to their work (unable and unwilling).
2. *Coaching.* In this style, leaders set the overall approach and direction but work with subordinates and allow them to manage the details. Leaders might need to provide some experience or support to individuals having the drive and motivation to do a good job, but who might lack some experience or skills (unable but willing).
3. *Supporting.* Here, leaders allocate tasks and set direction, but the subordinate has full control over the performance of the work. These individuals do not need much supervision or direction, but may require motivation and confidence (able but unwilling), particularly if the task is new.
4. *Delegating.* In this style, subordinates can do their work with little supervision or support. Once the work is delegated, leaders take a hands-off approach, except when asked to provide assistance by the subordinate. They are both able and willing to work on a project by themselves with little supervision or support.

A leader also might apply different styles to the same person at different times. This can be difficult, as most people seem to be more comfortable in one style. However, the choice should not be driven by personal preference but, rather, the needs of the subordinates. In fully empowered TQ organizations and those with strong self-directed teams, you would probably find the delegating style to be most prevalent. However, when introducing new skills, such as Six Sigma, into an organization, it may be necessary to provide more direct control, coaching, or support when individuals are learning and practicing new skills or are transitioning into new job responsibilities. As managers work with different individuals in different stages of careers and maturity, it is his or her responsibility to adapt the leadership style to the individual and the situation.

The situational leadership model is directly reflected in the process model for creating self-directed teams at Boeing Airlift & Tanker that we illustrated in Chapter 8 (see Figure 8.1). Thus, it provides a structure for transitioning to an empowered organization. In fact, some research has suggested that the model provides a natural basis for leading organizational change processes as organizations pursue TQ.[26]

Management and Leadership

A recent treatment of leadership by John Kotter compares the concept of leadership to the concept of management.[27] According to this view, management is needed to create order amid complexity, and leadership is needed to stimulate the organizational change necessary to keep up with a changing environment. This view avoids the simplistic ideas that management is somehow trivial, generally unnecessary, and should be replaced by leadership, and that the same person cannot practice both management and leadership.

Kotter differentiates leadership from management by contrasting the activities central to each. Although management begins with planning and budgeting, leadership begins with setting a direction. Direction-setting involves creating a vision of the future, as well as a set of approaches for achieving the vision. To promote goal achievement, management practices organizing and staffing, whereas leadership works on aligning people—communicating the vision and developing commitment to it. Management achieves plans through controlling and problem solving, whereas leadership achieves its vision through motivating and inspiring.

Kotter's view of leadership—similar to transformational theory—dovetails with our depiction of quality leadership. Both focus on developing and communicating a vision. Kotter's view of inspiring resembles our discussion of giving people values to embrace and then making sure that the leader is practicing them. The idea of aligning people is consistent with the idea of empowerment, because it gives people a goal, then leaves them to move in that direction. Our description of the role of leaders in continuous improvement is more hands-on than Kotter's description, perhaps suggesting that some management behaviors will continue to be important to leaders in total quality organizations.

REVIEW AND DISCUSSION QUESTIONS

1. What three processes must leaders undertake to promote total quality in their organizations?
2. Joseph Conklin proposes 10 questions for self-examination to help you understand your capacity for leadership.[28] Answer the following questions, and discuss why they are important for leadership.
   a. How much do I like my job?
   b. How often do I have to repeat myself?
   c. How do I respond to failure?
   d. How well do I put up with second guessing?
   e. How early do I ask questions when making a decision?
   f. How often do I say "thank you"?
   g. Do I tend to favor a loose or strict interpretation of the rules?
   h. Can I tell an obstacle from an excuse?
   i. Is respect enough?
   j. Have I dispensed with feeling indispensable?

3. State some examples in which leaders you have worked for have exhibited leadership practices discussed in this chapter. Can you provide examples for which they have not? How did their behavior affect you and your co-workers?

4. Review Deming's 14 Points in Chapter 3. What aspects of leadership theories are evident in them, either individually or as a holistic philosophy?

5. Most of the talk on leadership for quality focuses on top managers. What can middle- and first-level managers do to promote quality in their organizations? How does this differ from the role of top management?

6. John Young, former president and CEO of Hewlett-Packard, has summarized the role of the CEO in quality improvement in the following recommendations.[29]

   a. Dramatize the importance of quality to the organization.
   b. Establish agreed-on measures of quality.
   c. Set challenging and motivating goals.
   d. Give people the resources and information needed to do the job.
   e. Reward results.
   f. Keep an attitude that high quality is not only desirable, but possible. How do these recommendations differ from those given in this chapter? Are they really different or do they capture the same ideas in different words?

7. The Baldrige criteria defined the *leadership system* as "how leadership is exercised, formally and informally, throughout the company—the basis for and the way that key decisions are made, communicated, and carried out. It includes structures and mechanisms for decision making, selection and development of leaders and managers, and reinforcing values, practices, and behaviors." What are some attributes of an effective leadership system? How would you design one for an organization?

8. William Scherkenbach, a quality expert and Deming disciple, states: "If management is to improve their organization, they must change the process. This means that they cannot accept conference room promises, but must work directly with their people on the process, the how and the why. During this period of transition, everyone must be willing to learn. . . . No one is too senior to be involved in the how."[30]
   Do you agree or disagree? Why?

9. What aspects of an organization's culture or structure could keep managers from leading effectively?

10. Sir John Harvey-Jones, head of Britain's Imperial Chemical Industries from 1982 to 1987, once commented, "The task of leadership is really to make the status quo more dangerous than launching into the unknown."[31] Do you think this statement represents a good approach to total quality leadership? Why or why not?

11. Compare the leadership practices of Solectron and Armstrong BPO. How do these practices relate to the concepts developed in this chapter? What differences and similarities can you point to?
12. Can leadership be viewed as a business process? If so, how? How might an organization quantify the performance of its leadership system?

 CASES

David Kearns and the Transformation of Xerox[32]

David Kearns, former chairman and CEO of Xerox, provides an excellent example of leadership for quality. Xerox's problems in the early 1980s were legion and typical of American manufacturers facing serious foreign competition for the first time. Xerox discovered to its horror that Japanese companies were able to sell copiers in the United States for roughly what it cost Xerox to build them. Its former lion's share of the copier market had dwindled to a paltry 8 percent. Even at the time, Xerox was hardly complacent: productivity was increasing by as much as 7 or 8 percent every year. Kearns calculated that gains closer to 18 percent a year were needed to catch Xerox's competitors.

About this time, Kearns read Philip Crosby's book, *Quality Is Free*, and invited Crosby to address Xerox's management. Kearns's pleas for change initially were resisted by a management team who said they were already doing everything they could. This led Kearns to tell his managers that trying to change Xerox was like "pushing a wet noodle." It was time for more drastic action.

In 1983 the top management team at Xerox designed a new approach to quality that was dubbed "Leadership through Quality." The central principle of the new approach was that quality would be defined as customer satisfaction, not internal standards. If customers were not satisfied, quality had not been attained. A second principle was to focus on processes, not just outcomes.

In the past, poor outcomes were an occasion to blame someone and to hammer into them the importance of doing better. This was replaced with an approach that focused on examining the process that had created the outcome and improving it.

In order to operate according to these principles, a number of specific practices were undertaken. Xerox is perhaps best known for its extensive use of benchmarking—a process of comparing your operations to the best practices of other companies. The company's approach is to benchmark against the best, in whatever industry it is found. Xerox has benchmarked its billing processes against American Express and its distribution processes against L.L. Bean.

To demonstrate their commitment to these principles, Kearns and his management team were the first to undergo the newly devised quality training. They then became the teachers for the next level of management, and training flowed throughout the organization in this manner. In a move that represented a major departure from tradition, each senior manager was made responsible for taking calls from customers one day a month. Xerox managers still interrupt their meetings to take such calls.

Although Kearns's efforts were crucial to this process, he believes that leadership must (and in this case did) come from other sources as well, including the Amalgamated Clothing & Textile Workers, the union representing Xerox's production employees:

> We've also learned that it's important to have union leaders as deeply committed to the quality process as management. A strong and enlightened union leadership shared management's vision and understood that changes had to be made if there was to be a future for all Xerox employees. We shared each other's trust.[33]

Xerox's competitive resurgence was dramatic. Market share, revenues, and profits all have recovered substantially. In 1989 Xerox became one of the first winners of both the American and Canadian National Quality Award.

Kearns believes that "Xerox is probably the first American company in an industry targeted by the Japanese to regain market share without the aid of tariffs or government help."[34] Despite the recovery and the awards, however, Kearns has not abandoned the principle of continuous improvement: "We take great satisfaction in winning these awards, but the fact is that we're far from finished with our drive to improve. We have learned that the pursuit of quality is a race with no finish line. We see an upward and never-ending spiral of increased competition and heightened customer expectations."[35]

David Kearns was succeeded as Xerox's chairman in 1991 by Paul Allaire. Kearns is now working within the U.S. Department of Education to bring the quality perspective to America's schools.

Discussion Questions

1. How did David Kearns fulfill the roles of a quality leader at Xerox?
2. Is Kearns's approach broadly applicable, or would different approaches be needed in other settings?
3. Kearns began a practice of having senior managers personally take phone calls from customers with problems. Call the president of an organization of which you are a customer and report a quality or service problem you are experiencing. Will the president take the call? Will the president or someone else return your call? (If you get to talk to someone, congratulate them on their responsiveness, and be as constructive as possible in describing your problem.)

4. Trace the issues that Xerox has confronted since Kearns stepped down (for example, check the archives of *Fortune* magazine and other business periodicals). What impact did leadership have on the company?

The Power of Leadership Teams[36]

When the top management group at Georgia Power Company's Plant Hammond decided to become a team, everyone was quite sure that they were already a team and worked pretty well together. The top leadership group in early 1995 was 10 people from three management levels and two individual contributors. The management style was much the same as they had been using for many years in the utility industry and was characterized by an emphasis on the chain of command for most decisions—with the important ones made by one or two people. Information and business results were communicated on a "need to know" basis. For the most part, each department operated and made decisions independently.

This management style served the utility business well, given its business requirements. The business was relatively predictable and structured with a regulated rate of return, regional market protection, and 100 percent control of access to its own distribution facilities. A watershed development, however, occurred in the early 1990s—a move toward deregulation. This demanded fundamental changes in the way Plant Hammond operated and managed its resources.

In the early 1990s, the plant had reduced the number of employees by about one third, resulting in fewer management levels and fewer managers in those levels. In early 1995, the parent organization, Southern Company, implemented a transformation process to improve the plant's ability to compete. This transformation process required an emphasis on business results at all levels and creation of an organization culture that could deal with uncertainty and competition.

As the plant manager considered the requirements for the future, he determined that the structure, processes, and culture of the plant would need to change. Therefore, top management must change how it operated, broadening capabilities at all levels. Processes were needed to manage decision-making risk and gain consensus on direction. A new organizational structure was one of the early steps in their transformation. The structure provided an "outside in" focus—identifying the operations function as the primary internal customer, and grouped plant activities into several functional areas.

However, plant management knew that simply changing the boxes on an organization chart was not sufficient for real change. In the summer of 1995, the plant manager and nine other employees took their first step toward becoming a team when they came together at a facilitated off-site meeting. They clarified individual roles and responsibilities on this new team and began developing team relationships. They agreed that the role of each leadership-team member should be one of "shared responsibilities with a functional focus." Top managers at the plant could no longer make decisions from only their own departments' view. In fact, managers were required to consider the impact of their decisions—not only on the total plant but also on the total operating system of the Southern Company.

Each member took on the responsibility to champion specific transformation activities for the leadership team. The team began to have regular one-day session meetings where they discussed and made decisions on strategic and operational issues. This management team took a key developmental step in 1996 by setting expectations for their behavior and presenting them to their organizations during reviews of the 1996 plant strategic plan. Putting these expectations "on the record" built incentives to act accordingly.

The team found several tools to be helpful in its operation and development. One was a *common work plan* that served multiple purposes: (1) to ensure integration of their efforts and to track team results; (2) to establish member accountability; (3) to facilitate the delegation of traditional plant manager tasks; and (4) as a catalyst to surface strategic issues. Each team member took responsibility for the accomplishment of particular parts of the work plan.

The team also used various *assessment instruments* to understand and deal with the different individual styles of team members. Each team member discussed his or her assessment in an open forum. As a result, members made commitments for change and support. Each team member also formulated his or her own development plan based on these and other assessments.

Because one of the plant's strategies was to improve the capabilities of the management team, the team worked with an outside consultant to identify strengths and weaknesses. The consultant observed each of the team members in work situations and provided specific personal feedback and suggestions over an extended period of time. Each team member reviewed his or her assessment with the group and asked for reactions and recommendations. The consultant also provided feedback on group processes and worked in concert with an internal consultant to improve teamwork processes.

Discussion Questions

1. What lessons do you think the company learned about transforming its leadership system to a team-based organization?
2. What conditions do you think are necessary for management teams to become "real teams" and not just a grouping of independent functional managers who cooperate with each other?
3. What challenges do leadership teams like these face?

Situational Leadership in Action[37]

A large pharmaceutical manufacturer was highly motivated to meet quality challenges. They implemented an ISO 9000–compatible quality system to ensure not only FDA compliance requirements, but also customer satisfaction.

As the manufacturing plants of the organization were audited by the internal audit division, it became apparent that some plants were meeting the challenge, while others continued to struggle in both the quality and the regulatory aspects of production. This fact was evident in the reports of internal findings and in FDA inspection reports.

For the most part, the manufacturing plants share consistent resources and face similar environments. All were issued the responsibility of meeting the expectations of the quality system through the same mechanism. All understood the consequence of not conforming, that is, jeopardizing their manufacturing license as bound by the consent decree. The issue then became why some plants could successfully design and implement the requirements of the quality system, whereas others could not and still cannot.

Although the plants were similar in many ways, they differed in terms of leadership, as each plant has its own CEO. The CEO, as the leader of his or her plant, has the responsibility of ensuring the successful implementation of a quality system. The plants also differ in their organizational members, those who are to be led by the CEO. The relationship between the leader and the organizational members is critical to a plant's ability to implement an effective quality system, with effectiveness being a measure of how successfully a plant can comply with FDA regulations and internal quality standards.

Both plants had a similar culture that could be best described as conserving, reflecting a level of rigidity in response to the external environment, but demonstrating organizational commitment. The strategy used by the leader in Plant A was a combination of moderate to high amounts of structuring actions, with high to moderate amounts of inspiring actions, whereas the strategy used by Plant B's CEO was a combination of moderate to low amounts of structuring actions, with moderate to high amounts of inspiring actions.

Discussion Questions

1. What type of situational leadership style did the CEO of each Plant A demonstrate?
2. Which of these styles was more appropriate in view of the Situational Leadership model? Why?
3. Would it be surprising to find out that Plant A was more successful in achieving the goals of the quality system?

Crosby's Quality Nightmare

An example of what is not needed in a quality leader is provided by Philip Crosby in *Quality Is Free*.[38] Crosby goes to visit his old pal Ernest Dinsmore, manager of the Flagship Hotel, to see how a real hotel is run "from the inside." Crosby's arrival at the hotel is a comedy of errors. He dashes inside through a cloudburst as the doorman watches safely from the door. He has to wait several hours for his room to be made up, then has to climb the stairs because the elevator is broken and, to top things off, his car is towed from the front of the hotel.

Dinsmore dismisses these problems as "growing pains" and takes Crosby on a tour of the guts of the hotel. The maids are gathered in one room arguing because, due to a shortage of vacuum cleaners, those on the upper floors cannot vacuum until those on the lower floors are finished. Dinsmore decrees, Solomon-like, that henceforth the rooms will be vacuumed only every other day, first the bottom floors, then the top. This way there will be enough vacuum cleaners to go around. Another dispute, this time among the bellmen, is also handled by Dinsmore. The tips, which seem to be getting lower all the time, will all be given to the bell captain, who will distribute them according to the effort he feels people are exerting. When Crosby remarks on the number of room service trays laying in the hallway, Dinsmore tells him that guests don't mind, because it reminds them that room service is available.

After this madness, the hotel restaurant appears to Crosby an oasis of quality and efficient service. They are promptly seated, drinks quickly appear, and the promises of an attractive menu are fulfilled as wonderful presentations emerge from the kitchen. This oasis turns out to be a mirage, because Dinsmore wants to "improve" the operation. Although most hotels lose money on their restaurants, this one was making about 10 percent net profit. It was obvious to Dinsmore that by raising prices and cutting back on the help, it could be turned into a real money machine.

At their farewell meeting, Dinsmore discusses the difficulty of finding people willing to do quality work and complains about the falling standards of today's workers. A few months later, Crosby learns that the Flagship has been closed and Dinsmore has been offered a position running a chain of motels. He hopes Crosby can be his guest at one of them sometime soon. Crosby says he "can hardly wait."

Discussion Questions

1. In what specific ways did Ernest Dinsmore fail to fulfill the roles of a quality leader?
2. What advice would you give him on how to start improving the quality of the service in his chain of motels?

 ENDNOTES

1. Harry J. Levinson and Chuck DeHont, "Leading to Quality," *Quality Progress*, May 1992, pp. 55–60.
2. Rick Edgeman, Su Mi Park Dahigaard, Jens J. Dalhgaard, and Franz Scherer, "On Leaders and Leadership," *Quality Progress*, October 1999, pp. 49–54.
3. Quoted in Jerry G. Bowles, "Leading the World-Class Company," *Fortune*, September 21, 1992.
4. Jack Welch, Herb Kelleher, Geoffrey Colvin, and John Huey, "How to Create Great Companies and Keep Them That Way," *Fortune*, Vol. 139, No. 1, January 11, 1999, p.163.

5. 2004 Criteria for Performance Excellence, Baldrige National Quality Program.

6. Dan Ciampa, *Total Quality: A User's Guide for Implementation,* Reading, Mass.: Addison-Wesley, 1992, p. 115.

7. Award, the Newsletter of Baldrigeplus, May 7, 2000. Available at http://www.baldrigeplus.com.

8. These examples are from A. R. Tenner and I. J. DeToro, *Total Quality Management,* Reading, Mass.: Addison-Wesley, 1992.

9. Quoted in Bowles, "Leading the World-Class Company."

10. F. B. Adamson, "Cultivating a Charismatic Quality Leader," *Quality Progress,* July 1989, pp. 56–57.

11. Quoted in Bowles, "Leading the World-Class Company."

12. D. Garvin, "Quality Problems, Policies, and Attitudes in the United States and Japan: An Exploratory Study," *Academy of Management Journal,* 1986, Vol. 29, No. 4, pp. 653–673.

13. These and other means of demonstrating commitment to TQ values were suggested by Tenner and DeToro, *Total Quality Management.*

14. Levinson and DeHont, "Leading to Quality," p. 56.

15. See P. Richards, "Right-Side-Up Organization," *Quality Progress,* October 1991, pp. 95–96.

16. Quoted in Bowles, "Leading the World-Class Company."

17. This idea is discussed in Howard S. Gitlow and Shelly J. Gitlow, *The Deming Guide to Quality and Competitive Position,* Englewood Cliffs, N.J.: Prentice Hall, 1987.

18. Based on James C. Spee, "What the Film *Tampopo* Teaches about Total Quality Management." *Tampopo* is directed by Juzo Itami and stars Nobuko Miyamoto and Tsutomu Yamazaki, 1987 Itami Productions. Available on Republic Pictures Home Video in Japanese with English subtitles.

19. Adapted from Solectron Malcolm Baldrige National Quality Award Application Summary, 1997.

20. Adapted from Armstrong Building Products Operations Malcolm Baldrige National Quality Award Application Summary, 1995.

21. Henry Mintzberg, *The Nature of Managerial Work,* New York: Harper & Row, 1973.

22. R. House and M. Baetz, "Leadership: Some Generalizations and New Research Directions," in B. M. Staw (ed.), *Research in Organizational Behavior,* Greenwich, Conn.: JAI Press, 1979, p. 359.

23. B. M. Bass, *Leadership and Performance Beyond Expectations,* New York: Free Press, 1985. This discussion is based on David A. Waldman, "A Theoretical Consideration of Leadership and Total Quality Management," *Leadership Quarterly,* 1993, Vol. 4, pp. 65–79. See also J. Conger and R. Kanungo, "Toward a Behavioral Theory of Charismatic Leadership in Organizational Settings," *Academy of Management Review,* October 1987, pp. 637–647.

24. David A. Waldman, "The Contributions of Total Quality Management to a Theory of Work Performance," *Academy of Management Review,* Vol. 19, No. 3, pp. 510–536.

25. Philip Atkinson, "Leadership, Total Quality and Cultural Change," *Management Services,* June 1991, pp. 16–19.

26. Richard A. Grover and H. Fred Walker, "Changing from Production to Quality: Application of the Situational Leadership and Transtheoretical Change Models," *Quality Management Journal,* 10, 3, 2003, pp. 8–24.

27. J. P. Kotter, "What Leaders Really Do," in J. J. Gabarro (ed.), *Managing People and Organizations,* Boston: Harvard Business School Press, 1992, pp. 102–114.

28. Joe Conklin, "What It Takes to Be a Leader," *Quality Progress,* November 2001, 83.

29. John A. Young, "The Quality Focus at Hewlett-Packard," *The Journal of Business Strategy,* Vol. 5, No. 3, 1985, pp. 6–9.

30. William W. Scherkenbach, *The Deming Route to Quality and Productivity,* Washington, D.C.: SPC Press Books, George Washington University, 1986, p. 139.

31. Quoted in Sir John Harvey-Jones, Harvard Business School Case 9-490013, p. 8.

32. This case is based on David Kearns, "Leadership through Quality," *Academy of Management Executive,* 1990, Vol. 4, No. 2, pp. 86–89; "A CEO's Odyssey Toward World-Class Manufacturing," *Chief Executive,* September 1990; and Alan C. Fenwick, "Five Easy Lessons," *Quality Progress,* December 1991.

33. Kearns, "Leadership through Quality," p. 88.

34. Ibid.

35. Ibid.

36. Adapted from Billie R. Day and Michael Moore, "Plugging Into the Power of Leadership Teams," *The Journal for Quality and Participation,* May/June 1998, pp. 21–24.

37. Adapted from Lisa Walters, "Leading for Quality: The Implications of Situational Leadership," *Quality Management Journal,* 8, 4, October 2001, pp. 48–63.

38. Philip B. Crosby, *Quality Is Free,* New York: McGraw-Hill, 1979.

CHAPTER 11

TQ and Organizational Change

Psychologists suggest that individuals go through four stages of learning:

1. Unconscious incompetence: You don't know that you don't know.
2. Conscious incompetence: You realize that you don't know.
3. Conscious competence: You learn to do, but with conscious effort.
4. Unconscious competence: Performance comes effortlessly.

Organizations seem to follow the same paradigm. Many companies in the United States languished in stage 1 until receiving a wake-up call in the 1980s with regard to quality. Many today are finding themselves in the same situation. Unfortunately, as many organizations move into stage 2, they tend to shoot the messenger and refuse to accept their state of "incompetence." To move from stage 2 to stages 3 and 4, organizations must change.

Lewis Lehr, former CEO of 3M Corporation, once observed, "Our successes of the past are no guarantee of the future. Perhaps our biggest need at 3M is for people who are uncomfortable without change."[1] Organizational change is fundamental to total quality; indeed, there can be no quality without it. Anyone concerned with managing an organization dedicated to quality must understand what types of change are necessary in such an organization, how to make them happen, and how to manage them. This chapter explores these issues. Specifically, we will

➤ explain the importance and scope of organizational change to TQ;
➤ explore how organizations build a TQ culture, sustain performance, and continually improve organizational effectiveness;
➤ provide some examples of firms undertaking these changes and the approaches they use; and
➤ explain how TQ perspectives on organizational change relate to organization theory.

THE IMPORTANCE OF CHANGE

For organizations committed to pursuing total quality, change is a way of life. Organizational change is needed in implementing TQ and constantly thereafter. In the initial stage, an effort must be mounted to begin to change the culture of the organization. Unless a culture based on customer satisfaction, continuous improvement, and teamwork is established, TQ will be little more than "just another one of management's programs." Indeed, this is often the cause of failure of TQ initiatives.

Once TQ is under way in an organization, continuous improvement efforts will relentlessly create changes in product designs, standard operating procedures, and virtually every other aspect of organizations. One important aspect of continuous improvement is reengineering, in which the processes by which the organization operates are reexamined and redesigned to provide higher quality at lower cost.

Why are these changes necessary? The major reason is that customer expectations continuously evolve. Features or services that delight customers one year may be taken for granted the next, and products that customers find acceptable one year may be perceived as substandard the next. Competition continues to raise the standard for quality, and organizations must keep up. (See the box "Quality Never Goes Out of Style.") When first published, *USA Today*'s use of color and graphics was exceptional. In short order, however, newspapers copied these features so widely that exclusive use of black and white on the front page began to look old-fashioned.

Any organization that focuses on meeting a fixed set of quality goals quickly will find itself trampled into the dust by competitors racing to keep up with customers. As one Xerox executive stated, "Quality is a race without a finish line." Change is also required because processes tend to become unnecessarily complicated over a period of time, even when they are initially designed in a sensible manner. Each new person working on a process adds a wrinkle or two until, eventually, a monster has been created.

Strategic Change versus Process Change[2]

It is important to differentiate between organizational changes resulting from strategy development and implementation (i.e., "strategic change"), and organizational changes resulting from operational assessment activities (i.e., "process change"). Strategic change stems from strategic objectives, which are generally externally focused and relate to significant customer, market, product/service, or technological opportunities and challenges. This is what an organization must change to remain or become competitive. Strategic change is broad in scope, is driven by environmental forces, and is tied

Quality Never Goes Out of Style[3]

In 1853 a young German immigrant named Strauss took a 17,000-mile trip on a clipper ship from New York around South America to San Francisco. He intended to set up shop selling dry goods to people lured to California by the gold rush. By the time he reached San Francisco, however, he had sold all the goods he brought except for some canvas for tents.

The miners told him he should have brought pants instead of canvas to sell, because most pants fell apart too quickly while they dug for gold. The enterprising young Strauss immediately took the heavy brown canvas to a tailor and created the world's first pair of jeans. Those "pants of Levi's" (Strauss's first name) were so popular that he quickly sold all of his canvas and switched to a heavy serge fabric made in Nimes, France ("serge de Nimes," eventually shortened to "denim"). When the new fabric was treated with indigo dye, it attained its familiar deep blue cover.

Levi never liked the term "jeans" so he called his pants "waist-high overalls." In fact, his company did not use the term—derived from the French word "genes" for a type of cotton trousers—until long after his death.

Levi noticed that miners often complained that the weight of gold nuggets was causing their pockets to tear. Always looking for ways to improve the quality of his pants, Levi and tailor Jacob Davis patented in 1873 the innovation of riveting pocket corners to add strength. By the 1930s, Levi's were worn by everyone from cowboys to school children. The rivets, much appreciated by miners, caused the company problems with other customers, which they quickly addressed. In 1937, the company covered the rivets on the rear pockets in response to complaints that they scratched both saddles and school desks. The rivet at the base of the fly was removed by executive order after company president Walter Haas crouched a little too close to a roaring campfire for a little too long and discovered what the cowboys had been complaining about.

The popularity of Levi's jeans surged again in the 1950s when actor James Dean wore them in the movie *Rebel Without a Cause*. Today, Levi's jeans are sold in more than 70 nations. The company says that they are made with "the choicest fabric, the strongest thread, first-class buttons, rivets, and snaps, precise sewing and careful inspection." The jeans carry a "Levi's promise" card guaranteeing customer satisfaction. With this history of continuous improvement in response to customer needs, it's no wonder that, as the company's slogan puts it, "quality never goes out of style."

closely to the organization's ability to achieve its goals. Some examples are General Electric's implementation of Six Sigma throughout the corporation, and Hewlett-Packard's decision to merge with Compaq. In contrast, process change deals with the operations of an organization. Some examples of process change are a health care organization that discovered weaknesses in the organization's ability to collect and analyze information, followed by a $50 million information system upgrade; or an AT&T division that found that many employees did not recall the division's strategic vision, which prompted managers to increase meetings and interactions with employees to improve communication.

Although change to a business process tends to have lasting effects, the change tends to be narrow in scope. Unlike strategic change, which motivates organization-wide changes in behavior, process change is often confined to a particular unit, division, or function of the organization. For example, changing an organization's process for measuring customer satisfaction usually requires substantive adjustment to a limited number of functional areas, such as marketing or information systems. In Table 11.1, we describe the characteristics of strategic change in contrast with process change. Strategic changes are the ones that impact culture the most.

CULTURAL CHANGE

A major strategic change that organizations must make in pursuing TQ is a change in culture. **Culture** is the set of beliefs and values shared by the people in an organization. It is what binds them together and helps them make sense of what happens in their company (see the box "The Eastman Way" on page 414). Cultures can vary dramatically between one company and another. In some firms, raw ambition is taken for granted, while in others subordination of one's own agenda to the good of the organization is expected. Some companies create a status hierarchy reminiscent of the court of Louis XIV, whereas others downplay status differences.

Culture is a powerful influence on people's behavior; not very long ago most employees at IBM would never wear anything other than a white shirt, whereas most people at Apple Computer wouldn't be caught dead in one. Culture has such power because it is shared widely within an organization, and because it operates without being talked about, indeed, often without even being thought of.

Organizations are in some ways like a circle of high school friends who share strong beliefs about which activities, people, and music are okay, and which are not. A new employee who did something that violated the culture might be told, "That's just not how we do things around here." The employee could be forgiven both for the error and for being perplexed at what was wrong, because the rules of culture are often not written down and must be deciphered.

Despite its intangibility, one can learn about an organization's culture in a number of ways. How people dress and how they address one another provide clues. The layout of offices, plant floors, and lounges may also

TABLE 11.1   STRATEGIC VERSUS PROCESS CHANGE

	Strategic Change	**Process Change**
Theme of change	Shift in organizational direction	Adjustment of organizational processes
Driving force	Usually environmental forces—market, rival, technological change	Usually internal— "How can we better align our processes?"
Typical antecedent	Strategic planning process	Self-assessment of management system
How much of the organization changes?	Typically widespread	Often narrow—divisional or functional
Examples	Entering new markets Seeking low-cost position Mergers and acquisitions	Improving information systems Establishing hiring guidelines Developing improved customer satisfaction measures

reveal what is important in the organization. For example, do managers but not employees have reserved parking spots? Do offices have doors? Are there any private offices? Culture is expressed in the stories and jokes people tell, in how they spend their time at work, in what they display in their offices, and in a thousand other large and small ways. Culture is also reflected by the management policies and actions that a company practices. Therefore, organizations that believe in the principles of total quality are more likely to successfully implement the practices. Conversely, actions set culture in motion. Behavior leads people to think in certain ways. Thus, as total quality practices are used routinely within an organization, its people learn to believe in the principles, and cultural changes can occur.

From this description, it should be clear why firms deciding to pursue total quality need cultural change. If the TQ effort is inconsistent with the organizational culture, it will be undermined. For example, employees in a company in which status is jealously guarded will feel uncomfortable participating on an equal basis in team meetings with individuals from three different levels of management. People who share the belief that stability is the source of business success will be skeptical about continuous improvement. In situations like these, TQ is like an organ transplanted to a poorly matched donor and will be rejected.

A concept related to culture is *organizational climate*. Although some writers interchange the two concepts, many feel that organizational climate is separate from culture. Climate has been likened to an organization's personality—its hopes, attitudes, and biases—in essence, its mood. Some researchers suggest

The Eastman Way[4]

Eastman Chemical Company recognizes that people create quality; this is embodied in a philosophy known as the Eastman Way. The Eastman Way describes a culture based on key beliefs and principles of respect, cooperation, fairness, trust, and teamwork. Developing such a culture depends not only on learning how to recognize and reward behavior, but also understanding the processes and procedures that work against achieving corporate goals.

The wakeup call came in the late 1970s when a key customer told the company that its product was not as good as its competitor's and indicated that if things did not change, Eastman would lose business. Eastman's first realization was that customer feedback was essential to survival. In 1983, the company developed a quality policy and soon after began training in statistical process control, flowcharting, and other basic tools. Production employees were encouraged to post their quality results, which became known as "rat sheets." As one employee stated, "You are asking all of us to post all of our mistakes. How will these things be used?" This clash between the traditional hierarchical, disciplinary organizational culture and the open, honest environment demanded by TQ led to the Eastman Way, which is as follows:[5]

Eastman people are the key to success. We have recognized throughout our history the importance of treating each other fairly and with respect. We will enhance these beliefs by building upon the following values and principles:

__Honesty and integrity.__ We are honest with ourselves and others. Our integrity is exhibited through relationships with co-workers, customers, suppliers, and neighbors. Our goal is truth in all relationships.

__Fairness.__ We treat each other as we expect to be treated.

__Trust.__ We respect and rely on each other. Fair treatment, honesty in our relationships, and confidence in each other create trust.

__Teamwork.__ We are empowered to manage our areas of responsibility. We work together to achieve common goals for business success. Full participation, cooperation, and open communication lead to superior results.

__Diversity.__ We value different points of view. Men and women from different races, cultures, and backgrounds enrich the generation and usefulness of these different points of view. We create an environment that enables all employees to reach their full potential in pursuit of company objectives.

__Employee well-being.__ We have a safe, healthy, and desirable workplace. Stability of employment is given high priority. Growth in employee skills is essential. Recognition for contributions and full utilization of employees' capabilities promote job satisfaction.

Continued

> ***Citizenship.*** *We are valued by our community for our contributions as individuals and as a company. We protect public health and safety and the environment by being good stewards of our products and our processes.*
>
> **_Winning attitude._** *Our can-do attitude and desire for excellence drive continual improvement, making us winners in everything we do.*

that organizations have one overall culture, but many underlying climates, which are specific to different areas. For example, there may be a climate for quality, a climate for safety, a climate for ethics, each of which is driven by different management practices and policies.[6] Thus, although an organization may have a culture that supports teamwork and participation, it may not necessarily have a climate that facilitates the adoption of TQ.

Elements of a Total Quality Culture

The organizational culture needed to support TQ is one that values customers, improvement, and teamwork. In an organization with a TQ-friendly culture, everyone believes that customers are the key to the organization's future and that their needs must come first. If two employees are having a conversation and a customer enters the shop, the conversation ends until the customer is served.

In a culture supportive of TQ, people expect their jobs to change due to improvements dictated by customer needs. They are always looking for better (faster, simpler, less expensive) ways to do things. "Because that's the way we've always done it" is not a valid reason for doing anything. The culture of improvement is exemplified by the Levi Strauss and Eastman Chemical stories.

Employees in a quality-oriented culture instinctively act as a team. If someone is away from her desk and her phone rings, another employee will answer it rather than leave a customer hanging. Organizations where a focus on customers, continuous improvement, and teamwork are taken for granted have a good chance of succeeding at total quality. Most organizations do not have such a culture prior to exposure to TQ; some degree of cultural change is necessary.

These elements, along with several others, are reflected clearly in the Baldrige National Quality Program Criteria for Performance Excellence. The criteria are built upon a set of "core values and concepts":

- visionary leadership,
- customer-driven excellence,
- organizational and personal learning,
- valuing employees and partners,
- agility,

- focus on the future,
- managing for innovation,
- management by fact,
- social responsibility,
- focus on results and creating value, and
- systems perspective.

These values provide a good summary of the cultural elements necessary to sustain a total quality environment and are embedded in the beliefs and behaviors of high-performing organizations.

The existence of a set of cultural values necessary for successful TQ does not mean that all organizations that wish to practice total quality must have the same culture. Many aspects of culture differ greatly from one quality-oriented company to another. Company personnel may prefer to communicate in person or in writing; they may serve smoked salmon and champagne or a bushel of crabs and a keg of beer at the company picnic; they may wear uniforms, gray flannel suits, or jeans. As long as they hold the core values of TQ, quality can find a home in their organization.

Changing Organizational Culture for TQ

Perhaps the first question to address is why organizations decide to pursue a TQ-based organizational culture. A reluctance to pursue TQ often results from some common misconceptions, such as TQ means doing lots of "things" like collecting data and organizing teams, or that it only applies to large companies. TQ does, however, require significant changes in organization design, processes, and culture. Such broad change has been a stumbling block for many companies.

Companies make the decision to adopt the TQ philosophy for two basic reasons:

1. A firm reacts to competition that poses a threat to its profitable survival by turning to TQ.
2. TQ represents an opportunity to improve.

Most firms—even Baldrige Award winners—have moved toward total quality because of the first reason. Xerox, for example, watched its market share fall from 90 percent to 13 percent in a little over a decade; Milliken faced increased competition from Asian textile manufacturers; Zytec Corporation found itself in financial difficulties because of reliance on a single customer. Although they were not facing dire crises, perceived future threats were the impetus for FedEx and Solectron. When faced with a threat to survival, a company effects cultural change more easily; under these circumstances, organizations generally implement TQ effectively. A company will generally have more difficulty gaining support for change when not facing a crisis. This reluctance is a reflection of the attitude "If it ain't broke, don't fix it." In such cases, a company might attempt to manufacture a crisis mentality to effect change.

The biggest dangers lie in the lack of complete understanding and the tendency to imitate others—the easy way out. Many of the experts and consultants have rewritten total quality management around their own discipline, such as accounting, engineering, human resources, or statistics. The "one best model" of TQ may not mesh with an organization's culture; most successful companies have developed their own unique approaches to fit their own requirements. Research has shown that imitation of TQ efforts made by one successful organization may not lead to good results in another.

Building and sustaining a TQ organization requires a readiness for change, the adoption of sound practices and implementation strategies, and an effective organization (see the box "There Is No Instant Pudding").

How can a company change its culture to be more consistent with quality? As with most aspects of TQ, it begins with leadership (see the box "A Sincere Belief and Trust in People").[7] Leaders must articulate to employees the direction in which they want the company to go. They must set an example by expressing TQ values in their own behavior and by recognizing and rewarding others who do the same. The efforts of the new leadership team in a foundry to establish the values of continuous improvement and teamwork are described in this statement by the quality director, whose efforts had been frustrated under the old regime:[8]

> They brought in a people-oriented environment. They made the environment conducive to change and tried to get to the point where employees felt safe to make change. Before, you did what the boss told you to do and if you didn't you're probably going to get fired. Now we have some coaches in place and facilitators, and they want the ideas from the employees and it's a hell of a lot easier with their input.

A great deal of the effort leaders expend in cultural change is devoted to communication. Employees company-wide must be informed of the new values and practices desired. Any early successes of the new approach must also be publicized. This is not always easy, especially when the company's employees are geographically dispersed. In attempting to change the culture at Southern Pacific Lines, railroad executives held 125 "town meetings" at sites where employees worked, sometimes in groups as small as 5 to 10.[9]

In promoting a new culture, leaders also must personally practice behaviors associated with the new culture. This both provides a role model for employees and symbolizes management's sincerity about the new approach. When the Indian soap company, Godrej Soaps, tried to initiate continuous improvement, workers were reluctant to unwrap defective soaps to see how mistakes could be avoided in the future. When informed of this, the managing director said he would go into the plant to unwrap the soaps. As it turned out, he didn't need to do it. When workers heard that the top manager was willing to do this kind of work, they agreed to do it themselves.[10]

None of this should be interpreted to mean that cultural change is easy. On the contrary, it is very difficult, takes several years to complete, and often

"There Is No Instant Pudding"[11]

This is one of Deming's more descriptive phrases in describing American managers' obsession with quick results. Quality takes time. At Armstrong Building Products Operations, the evolution of quality has occurred in several phases since 1983:

Phase I (1983–1985)
- Commitment to try
- Philip Crosby system
- Quality improvement teams

Phase II (1985–1990)
- Process improvement
- Quality plans added to business plans
- Supplier quality management

Phase III (1989–1992)
- Vision clearly defined
- Empowered employees; flatter organization
- Use of Baldrige criteria for self-assessment

Phase IV (1991–1994)
- Product and service leadership
- Baldrige Award applications (1995 winner)
- Business results

Phase V (1994–present)
- High performance change process
- "Nonnegotiable" business strategies
- Achieving value for employees, customers, shareholders

Similarly, ADAC Laboratories began its TQ approach in 1991 by benchmarking other leading organizations, forming a monthly quality committee, developing a commitment to customer satisfaction, investing in field service, and designing a new strategic planning process. In 1992, ADAC developed its vision, began weekly quality meetings, adopted the Baldrige criteria and conducted a self-assessment, and strengthened quality incentives and rewards.

During 1993, the Baldrige criteria were widely deployed, benchmarking was performed in all areas, systematic and comprehensive training programs were started, and quality performance was monitored on a twice-weekly basis. In the next two years, policy deployment was introduced, the ADAC business approach was refined based on TQ and mutual learning principles, the company focused on people-value-added processes, breakthrough improvement became a priority, and ADAC pursued ISO 9000 registration. ADAC received the Baldrige Award in 1996.

A Sincere Belief and Trust in People[12]

One powerful example of the importance of cultural change is the case of Wainwright Industries, a former Baldrige winner. During the 1970s and 1980s, Wainwright lost millions in sales; operations slowed to three days a week; and tensions grew between employees and management. Recognizing the problem lay with management, the CEO made some radical changes. Workers were called "associates," and everyone was put on salary. Associates are paid even if they miss work and they still receive time-and-a-half for overtime. The company has maintained over 99 percent attendance since this change.

Managers shed their white shirts and ties, and everyone from the CEO down wears a common uniform, embroidered with the label *Team Wainwright*. A team of associates developed a profit-sharing plan, whereby everyone receives the same bonus every six months. Everyone has access to the privately held company's financial records. In addition, all reserved parking spaces were removed; walls—including those for the CEO's office—were replaced with glass. Customers, both external and internal, are treated as partners with extensive communication. The most striking example occurred when one worker admitted accidentally damaging some equipment, even though most workers were afraid to report such incidents. The CEO called a plantwide meeting and explained what had happened. Then he called the man up, shook his hand, and thanked him for reporting the accident. Accident reporting increased from zero to 90 percent, along with suggestions on how to prevent them. Wainwright's culture can be summed up as *a sincere belief and trust in people*. One measure of Wainwright's success is that the number of implemented suggestions per person per year exceeds 50, while the previous benchmark that Wainwright identified was 15!

fails.[13] One reason for the difficulty is resistance by middle management. Managers resist change because it creates more work for them when they often feel overburdened and disrupts the steady flow of work in the organization.[14] Getting on board for a change in culture requires managers to acknowledge that the current approach is somehow lacking, despite any of their previous statements to the contrary. They also may be afraid that they will not be able to perform effectively in the new culture.

Often reward systems get in the way of cultural change and must be adjusted for the new culture to take hold. In many companies, telephone operators are rewarded for the speed with which they process calls, rather than for how completely they satisfy the customers who call. Unless this type of reward system is changed, management's pleas to increase customer satisfaction will fall on deaf ears. Willingness to make such changes indicates management's commitment to the new culture.

Managing change often requires a well-defined process, just like any other business process. In fact, an organization that doesn't realize that change is a process probably won't do a good job in TQ. This is critical because about 70 percent of all change efforts fail.[15] Thinking of change management as a process helps to define the steps necessary to achieve the desired outcomes.

It also forces the organization to think of its employees as customers who will be affected by the change. American Express, for example, views its change process as consisting of five steps:[16]

1. Scope the change—why are we doing this?
2. Create a vision—what will the change look like?
3. Drive commitment—what needs to happen to make the change work?
4. Accelerate the transition—how are we going to manage the effort on an ongoing basis?
5. Sustain momentum—what have we learned and how can we leverage it?

People Roles in Organizational Change

Senior management, middle management, and the workforce each have a critical role to play in changing culture. Senior managers must ensure that their vision of TQ is successfully executed within the organization. Middle managers provide the leadership to design the systems and processes. In the end, it is the workforce that delivers quality.

Senior Management

Senior managers must understand how quality can further the mission, vision, and values of the company and its impact on customers and stakeholders. Senior managers must identify the critical processes that need attention and improvement and the resources and tradeoffs that must be made to fund the TQ activity. They must review progress and remove barriers to implementation. Finally, they must improve the processes in which they are involved (strategic planning, for example), both to improve the performance of the process and to demonstrate their ability to use quality tools for problem solving.[17]

Middle Management

Middle management has been viewed by many as a direct obstacle to creating a supportive environment for TQ.[18] Middle managers are often seen as feeding territorial competition, stifling information flow, not developing and/or preparing employees for change, and feeling threatened by continuous improvement efforts. However, middle management's role in creating and sustaining a TQ culture is critical. Middle managers improve the operational processes that are the foundation of customer satisfaction; they can make or break cooperation and teamwork; and they are the principal means by which the workforce prepares for change.

Mark Samuel suggests that transforming middle managers into change agents requires a systematic process that dissolves traditional management boundaries and replaces them with an empowered and team-oriented state of accountability for organizational performance.[19] This process involves the following:

1. Empowerment. Middle managers must be accountable for the performance of the organization in meeting objectives.
2. Creating a common vision of excellence. This vision is then transformed into critical success factors that describe key areas of performance that relate to internal and external customer satisfaction.
3. New rules for playing the organizational game. Territorial walls must be broken, yielding a spirit of teamwork. One new approach is interlocking accountability, in which all managers are accountable to one another for their performance. The second is team representation, in which each manager is responsible for accurately representing the ideas and decisions of the team to others outside the team.
4. Implementing a continuous improvement process. These projects should improve operational systems and processes.
5. Developing and retaining peak performers. Middle managers must identify and develop future leaders of the organization.

The Workforce

The workforce must develop ownership of the quality process. Ownership and empowerment gives employees the right to have a voice in deciding what needs to be done and how to do it.[20] It is based on a belief that what is good for the organization is also good for the individual and vice versa.

At Westinghouse, ownership is defined as ". . . taking personal responsibility for our jobs . . . for assuring that we meet or exceed our customers' standards and our own. We believe that ownership is a state of mind and heart that is characterized by a personal and emotional commitment to approach every decision and task with the confidence and leadership of an owner." Self-managed teams, discussed in Chapter 7, are one form of ownership.

Training, recognition, and better communication are key success factors for transferring ownership to the workforce. With increased ownership, however, comes a flatter organization—and the elimination of some middle managers. Increased ownership also requires increased sharing of information with the workforce and a commitment to the workforce in good times and in bad. This might mean reducing stock dividends and executive bonuses before laying off the workforce during economic downturns. This is what Japanese companies do when the business climate turns south.

Common Implementation Mistakes

A wide range of quality implementation strategies exist, many of which have serious pitfalls. For example, the general manager of a large defense electronics contractor unveiled a major program, then plunged into dealing with the unit's plummeting revenues and layoffs. Quality went nowhere. At Florida Power and Light, John J. Hudiburg drove hard to win the Deming Prize, but created a large bureaucracy in which morale fell as workers and managers had to compile hundreds of pages of analysis. The new CEO reduced the scope of the quality effort. Alcoa's CEO scrapped the company's decade-long continuous improvement strategy, calling it a "major mistake," focusing instead on "quantum" improvements. [21]

Implementation of TQ is often attempted without a full grasp of its nature, and certain mistakes are made repeatedly. The most frequent errors are as follows:[22]

1. TQ is regarded as a program, despite rhetoric to the contrary.
2. Short-term results are not obtained. There may be no attempt to get short-term results, or management may believe that measurable benefits lie only in the distant future.
3. The process is not driven by a focus on the customer, strategic business issues, and senior management.
4. Structural elements in the organization (such as compensation systems, promotion systems, accounting systems, rigid policies and procedures, specialization and functionalization, and status symbols such as offices and perks) block change.
5. Goals are set too low. Management does not shoot for stretch goals or use outside benchmarks as targets.
6. The organizational culture remains one of "command and control," and is driven by fear or game playing, budgets, schedules, or bureaucracy.
7. Training is not properly addressed. There is too little training of the workforce. Training may be of the wrong kind; for example, providing only classroom training without on-the-job reinforcement, or focusing on the mechanics of tools and not on identifying problems.
8. The focus is mainly on products, not processes.
9. Little real empowerment is given and what is given is not supported in actions.
10. The organization is too successful and complacent. It is not receptive to change and learning and clings to the "not invented here" syndrome.
11. The organization fails to address three fundamental questions: Is this another program? What's in it for me? How can I do this on top of everything else?
12. Senior management is not personally and visibly committed and actively participating.
13. The use of teams to solve cross-functional problems is overemphasized to the neglect of individual efforts at local improvements.
14. The belief prevails that more data are always desirable, regardless of relevance—"paralysis by analysis."
15. Management fails to recognize that quality improvement is a personal responsibility at all levels of the organization.

16. The organization does not see itself as a collection of interrelated processes making up an overall system. Both the individual processes and the overall system need to be identified and understood.

Although this list is extensive, it is by no means exhaustive. It reflects the still immature development of TQ. TQ requires a new set of skills and learning, including interpersonal awareness and competence, team building, encouraging openness and trust, listening, giving and getting feedback, group participation, problem solving, clarifying goals, resolving conflicts, delegating and coaching, empowerment, and continuous improvement as a way of life.[23] The process must begin by creating a set of feelings and attitudes that lead to lasting values.

Building on Best Practices

Creating a TQ culture is not rocket science. Although some universal principles apply, a successful quality strategy needs to fit within the existing organization culture. This is why the Baldrige Award guidelines are nonprescriptive; there is no magic formula that works for everyone. At Zytec, for instance, Deming's 14 Points were chosen as the cornerstone of the quality improvement culture. They established a Deming Steering Committee to guide the Deming process and champion individual Deming Points and act as advisors to three Deming Implementation Teams. Motorola, by contrast, invited numerous consultants to propose quality plans, but in the end decided to develop a quality program tailored to their specific needs.

One study of Baldrige winners concluded that each has a unique "quality engine" that drives the quality activities of the organization.[24] These are summarized in Figure 11.1. This is not to suggest that all other aspects of TQ are ignored; they are not. The quality engine customizes the quality effort to the organizational culture and provides a focus for all quality efforts.

Although it is the sincerest form of flattery, imitation may not always be the best strategy for TQ. In fact, it can actually hurt, wasting time and money on the wrong things. Research performed in 1992 by H. James Harrington with Ernst & Young and the American Quality Foundation, called the International Quality Study (IQS), suggested that trying to implement all the best practices of world-class organizations may not be a good strategy.[25] In fact, implementing the wrong practices can actually hurt the organization. The study indicated that only five best practices are "universal," and even then, there is a 5 percent chance that these may not improve performance. They are:

1. cycle-time analysis,
2. process value analysis,
3. process simplification,
4. strategic planning, and
5. formal supplier certification programs.

FIGURE 11.1   QUALITY ENGINES OF BALDRIGE AWARD WINNERS

Company	Quality Engine	Focus
IBM Rochester	Market-driven quality	Customer needs determined early in the planning and design process
Motorola	Process control	Defect prevention; Six-Sigma quality
Pal's Sudden Service	Process focus	Everything—from new product introduction to hiring to work systems—viewed as a process that impacts customer satisfaction
Xerox	Banchmarking	Competitive and best-in-class benchmarks
FedEx	Technology	Using technology to speed process and improve customer service
Texas Nameplate	Employee empowerment and involvement	Teams and active participation of employees in all aspects of the business
Clarke American Checks	Strategic planning	Involving all stakeholders in a "First in Service" strategy focused on running and changing the business
Dana Spicer Driveshaft	Measurement	Use of measurements to track and improve quality and to align business strategies

Beyond these, best practices depend on a company's current level of performance. Three measures of performance are ROA (return on assets: after-tax income divided by total assets), which is a measure of profitability; VAE (value added per employee: sales less the costs of materials, supplies, and work done by outside contractors), a measure of productivity; and quality, as measured by an external customer satisfaction index.

Low performers—those with less than 2 percent ROA and $53,000 VAE (in 1996 dollars), and low quality—can reap the highest benefits by concentrating on fundamentals. These include departmental and cross-functional teamwork, training in customer relationships, problem solving and suggestion systems, using internal customer complaint systems for new product and service ideas, emphasizing cost reduction when acquiring new technology, using customer satisfaction measures in strategic planning, increased training for all levels of employees, and focusing quality strategy on "building it in" and "inspecting it in." Among those things that low performers should *not* do is use quality as a basis for senior management assessment, use world-class benchmarking or benchmarking marketing and sales processes, rely on surveys to obtain feedback from customers, emphasize empowerment, and remove quality control inspection.

Medium performers—those with ROA from 2 to 6.9 percent, VAE between $53,000 and $84,000, and medium quality levels—achieve the most benefits from promoting department-level improvement teams, training employees in problem solving and other specialized topics, listening to supplier suggestions about new products, emphasizing the role of enforcement for quality assurance, making regular and consistent measurements of progress and sharing quality performance information with middle management, and emphasizing quality as a key to the company's reputation. Medium performers should not emphasize quality and team performance in assessing senior management, increase training in general knowledge subjects, use cross-functional teams or teams with customers on them to create design specifications, shift primary responsibilities for compliance with quality standards away from the quality assurance function, or select suppliers based on their general reputation.

High performers—with ROA exceeding 6.9 percent and VAE exceeding $84,000—gain the most from providing customer-relationship training for new employees, emphasizing quality and teamwork for senior management assessment, encouraging widespread participation in quality meetings among non-management employees, using world-class benchmarking, communicating strategic plans to customers and suppliers, conducting after-sales service to build customer loyalty, and emphasizing competitor-comparison measures and customer satisfaction measures when developing plans. Practices that could get these firms into trouble include increasing participation in department-level improvement teams, focusing technology on production processes, relying on customer surveys as a primary input for improvement, and using cross-functional teams with customers on them to create design specifications.

These findings contradict the notion that there is one magic quick fix for quality. Rather, companies advance in stages along a learning curve and must design their TQ initiatives carefully to optimize their effect.

SUSTAINING TOTAL QUALITY

Organizations must continually adapt to changing environments, remove antiquated practices, and incorporate new and innovative thinking. This includes self-assessment and the ability to manage knowledge and continually learn.

Self-Assessment

Organizations should begin with a critical self-assessment of where they stand. Such assessment identifies strengths and areas for improvement and determines what practices will yield the most benefit. At a minimum, a self-assessment should address the following:

- *Management involvement and leadership*. To what extent are all levels of management involved?
- *Product and process design*. Do products meet customer needs? Are products designed for easy manufacturability?
- *Product control*. Is a strong product control system in place that concentrates on defect prevention, before the fact, rather than defect removal after the product is made?

- *Customer and supplier communications.* Does everyone understand who the customer is? To what extent do customers and suppliers communicate with each other?
- *Quality improvement.* Is a quality improvement plan in place? What results have been achieved?
- *Employee participation.* Are all employees actively involved in quality improvement?
- *Education and training.* What is done to ensure that everyone understands his or her job and has the necessary skills? Are employees trained in quality improvement techniques?
- *Quality information.* How is feedback on quality results collected and used?

Many self-assessment instruments that provide a picture of the state of quality in the organization are available.[26] Most self-administered surveys, however, can provide only a rudimentary assessment of an organization's strengths and weaknesses. The most complete way to assess the level of TQ maturity in an organization is to evaluate its practices and results against the Malcolm Baldrige National Quality Award criteria by using trained internal or external examiners, or by actually applying for the Baldrige or a similar state award and receiving comprehensive examiner feedback (see the box on Hartford Hospital). Understanding one's strengths and opportunities for improvement creates a basis for evolving toward higher levels of performance.

Of course, many companies, especially smaller firms, that are just starting on a quality journey should begin with the basics, for example, a well-documented and consistent quality assurance system such as ISO 9000, which was discussed in Chapter 2.

Leveraging Self-Assessment: The Importance of Follow-Up[27]

Although some research suggests a positive relationship between the conduct of self-assessment and performance outcomes, other evidence suggests that many organizations derive little benefit from conducting self-assessment and achieve few of the process improvements suggested by self-study. This lack of follow-through might seem a bit surprising. Why would organizations take the time to conduct a self-assessment and then not follow up on the results? After all, improvement opportunities usually offer significant gains in organizational effectiveness and competitive performance. Some managers may not follow up because they truly do not sense a problem—despite information suggesting otherwise. Often, however, managers get the message but choose not to respond. Many managers react negatively or by denial: "These are wrong," "This is not how it is here," and "These [examiners] missed the boat" are often heard. Such remarks are particularly likely when the report suggested that the organization was a less-than-stellar performer in areas perceived as strengths by senior managers.

Other mangers may not know what to do with the information. Managers possessing little understanding of how the organization operates may not

Alignment through Assessment[28]

Hartford Hospital used a Baldrige assessment to guide its improvement efforts. The hospital needed to align its processes with the rapidly growing managed care environment, leverage internal clinical financial strength, and align employee and department goals with each other and the strategic goals of the organization. Using the Baldrige Health Care criteria, a month-long assessment was completed in 1996. The analysis revealed that the hospital had numerous strengths and many opportunities for improvement. Most areas of the hospital were not aligned with each other, leading to a disconnect between the strategic plan and many of the operational units, processes, and personnel. Major systems, such as human resources, leadership, and planning, were functioning independently of each other. Measures of performance were not trended and did not lead to improvement activities. Performance improvements were ad hoc, lacking priority, and not driven by the strategic plan.

Six initial performance improvement projects involved improving the leadership structure, linking information with the strategic plan, improving deployment of the strategic plan, improving human resource allocation, planning business and programs, and centralizing complaint management processes. The success of the project exceeded all expectations. Despite closing more than 15 percent of its beds, Hartford Hospital has not lost any market share, and it has received numerous recognitions as one of Connecticut's outstanding hospitals.

know which levers to pull in order to effect change or simply do it to appease their superiors. Typical comments include, "There's some good stuff here, but I have no idea where to go from here," and "It's hard for me to understand how to turn this [assessment report] into action." After reading his copy of the feedback report, the head of one manufacturing company muttered, "Well, we've satisfied [the boss's demand for conducting the self-assessment] for another year. Now we can put this all away and get back to business."

Following up requires senior leaders to engage in two types of activities: action planning and subsequently tracking implementation progress. Managers must take a positive approach to self-assessment findings, no matter how unpleasant they might appear—"Okay, what should we do to improve these areas?" Positive reactions often reinforce long-held but suppressed views about how the organization functioned. For example, at a meeting where results were being presented to the top management team, the chief engineering manager, on hearing of low evaluations related to the organization's communications processes, exclaimed, "I've been telling you guys this for years! Maybe now you'll believe me that we need to do something." The action plan identifies particular activities necessary to address the improvement opportunities. Effective action plans share some common characteristics. First, key actions to address the opportunities must be identified. A meeting to discuss the findings with key employees is often an excellent way to begin. Once identified, action plans should be documented and the who, what, when, where, and how of each action item specified. A draft version of the action plan should be communicated to inform those directly affected and gain their cooperation. Finally, the action plan should be reviewed to ensure that it effectively addresses the key opportunities identified by the self-assessment findings.

Many managers consider their job finished when action plans are set in motion. However, planned changes are rarely implemented as initially intended. Moreover, people responsible for implementing the plans may need to use encouragement or involvement in order to effectively execute their portions of the intended change. Change implementation demands a second component of effective follow-up—tracking the progress of action plan execution—to provide managers with crucial feedback on whether the intervention is effective. To leverage self-assessment findings, managers must do four things:

1. *Prepare to be humbled.* "Humbling" is a word we often hear from managers who have recently digested assessment findings. Many of them have trouble believing that the performance levels of the organization are as low as they appear. Managers can temper their expectations by learning about the self-assessment activities and experiences of other organizations. Hearing it from peers, through phone calls to colleagues, and attending conferences, permit managers to learn firsthand about the self-assessment experiences of others.

2. *Talk though the findings.* Follow-up can be enhanced when the top management team discusses the self-assessment findings. Discussing the issues, concerns, and ideas can generate greater shared perspective among executives and improve consensus.

3. *Recognize institutional influences.* Managers should be sensitive to the institutional forces working on their self-assessment activities, such as pressures from customers. Institutional influence can be covertly transmitted through the literature, presentations, and conversation that managers encounter. During the planning phase of the assessment, frank discussion about the environmental motivators of the project can sensitize managers to these outside influences.

4. *Grind out the follow-up.* Even though follow-up activities may not be as exciting as plotting competitive strategy or entertaining customers, they provide infrastructure for realizing the process improvements possible from self-assessment.

Knowledge Management and Organizational Learning

One Hewlett-Packard manager noted, "The fundamental building material of a modern corporation is knowledge." H. James Harrington observed, "All organizations have it, but most don't know what they know, don't use what they do know and don't reuse the knowledge they have."[29] Six Sigma efforts build a vast supply of knowledge within an organization, but knowledge is perishable, and if it is not renewed and replenished, it becomes worthless.

Knowledge assets refer to the accumulated intellectual resources that an organization possesses, including information, ideas, learning, under stand-ing, memory, insights, cognitive and technical skills, and capabilities. **Explicit knowledge** includes information stored in documents or other forms of media. **Tacit knowledge** is information that is formed around intan-gible factors resulting from an individual's experience, and is personal and content-specific. These two aspects represent the "know how" that an orga-nization has available to use, invest, and grow. Employees, software, patents, databases, documents, guides, policies and procedures, and technical draw-ings are repositories of an organization's knowledge assets. Customers, sup-pliers, and partners also may hold key knowledge assets. Knowledge assets have become more important than financial and physical assets in many organizations. Process improvement requires new knowledge to result in better processes and procedures. Increasing the knowledge of the organiza-tion, both in an individual sense as well as for the organization as a whole, is the essence of learning. Knowledge can easily be lost if information is not documented or when individuals are promoted or leave the organization.

Knowledge management involves the process of identifying, capturing, organizing, and using knowledge assets to create and sustain competitive advantage. Knowledge management differs from *information management* in that information management is focused on data whereas knowledge man-agement is focused on information. A knowledge management system allows intangible information to be managed as an organizational asset in a manner similar to tangible assets. Skandia, a large Swedish financial services company, internally audits its intellectual capital every year for inclusion in its annual report. An effective knowledge management system should include the following:

- A way of capturing and organizing explicit as well as tacit knowledge of how the business operates, including an understanding of how current business processes function.
- A systems-approach to management that facilitates assimilation of new knowledge into the business system and is oriented toward continuous improvement/innovation.
- A common framework for managing knowledge and some way of vali-dating and synthesizing new knowledge as it is acquired.
- A culture and values that support collaborative sharing of knowledge across functions and encourages full participation of all employees in the process.[30]

The transfer of knowledge within organizations and the identification and sharing of best practices often set high-performing organizations apart from the rest. Many organizations perform similar activities at different locations or by different people. Just consider a large organization with many Six Sigma black- and master-black belts. What happens when one individual develops an innovative practice? How is this knowledge shared among others performing similar jobs? In most organizations, the answer is that knowledge is probably never shared.

Continuous improvement and organizational change are difficult to achieve without creating a "learning organization," a term popularized by Peter Senge, a professor at the Massachusetts Institute of Technology (MIT). He defines the learning organization as: ". . . an organization that is continually expanding its capacity to create its future." For such an organization, it is not enough merely to survive. "Survival learning" or what is more often termed "adaptive learning" is important—indeed it is necessary. But for a learning organization, "adaptive learning" must be joined by "generative learning," learning that enhances our capacity to create.[31]

Art Schneiderman, who had worked with Senge and spent a long career with Analog Devices, offers the following simple definition of organizational learning: ". . . the acquisition, application, and mastery of new tools and methods that allow more rapid improvement of those processes whose improvement is critical to the success of the organization."[32]

Senge repeatedly points out, "Over the long run, superior performance depends on superior learning." The concept of organizational learning can be thought of as the process of moving through the four stages of learning that we described at the very beginning of this chapter. Effective learning requires an understanding and integration of many of the concepts and principles that are part of the TQ philosophy. It can help avoid repeating mistakes, build sensitivity, and better adapt to a changing world, and help to improve operations by understanding the weaknesses in the past and how to correct them.[33]

Organizational learning is considered a fundamental practice in the Baldrige criteria, which defines it as "continuous improvement of existing approaches and processes and adaptation to change, leading to new goals and/or approaches."[34] The criteria view learning as having four distinct stages:

1. planning, including the design of processes, selection of measures, and deployment of requirements;
2. execution of plans;
3. assessment of progress, taking into account internal and external results; and
4. revision of plans based on assessment findings, learning, new inputs, and new requirements.

In the Leadership category, for example, the requirement of Organizational Performance Review focuses organizations to provide a picture of their "state of health" and examine how well they are currently performing and also how well they are moving toward the future. This review capitalizes on the information generated from the measurement and analysis of business results and is intended to provide a reliable means to guide both improvement and change at the strategic planning level.

Many companies learn from Baldrige winners (see the box on Texas Instruments). Scott McNealy, CEO of Sun Microsystems, for example, invited

---

Organizational Learning at Texas Instruments

Many firms use self-assessment against the Baldrige criteria as a means of organizational learning. Thus, it is not surprising that perhaps the best examples of learning organizations are Baldrige winners. In pursuing their TQ efforts that eventually led to the award, they have continually and systematically translated the examiner feedback into improvements in their management practices.

A vice president at Texas Instruments Defense Systems & Electronics (DS&E) Group noted that "participating in the Baldrige Award process energized improvement efforts."[35] By 1997, just before its purchase by Raytheon, DS&E had reduced the number of in-process defects to one tenth of what they were at the time it won the Baldrige. Production processes that took four weeks several years before were reduced to one week, with costs 20 to 30 percent less.

DS&E's approach began in 1994, when the Texas Instruments Corporation launched the TI Business Excellence Standard (TI-BEST), an assessment and improvement process that grew out of DS&E's Baldrige Award experience.[36] The process is applied to TI businesses around the world. The four steps of TI-BEST are:

1. define business excellence for your business;
2. assess your progress;
3. identify improvement opportunities; and
4. establish and deploy an action plan.

The TI approach to business excellence is achieved through the core principles of total quality discussed in Chapter 1 and a focus on operational excellence through achieving customer satisfaction with processes and teamwork and empowerment. The approach is implemented by an annual improvement process (Strategic Planning) and measured by a balanced scorecard involving customer, process, HR, and financial measurements and indicators.

TI is one of only two semiconductor companies in the world to have gained market share in each of the four consecutive years prior to 1997, and during that time jumped from last place to first in return on net assets, compared to Intel, Motorola, and National Semiconductor.

three CEOs of Baldrige winners (FedEx, Motorola, and Xerox) to visit his company to discuss their quality processes. From those meetings came the core principles and strategies that Sun uses today. The key lessons that Sun learned were:

- Quality must be elevated to the level of a "core management process."
- Quality must be the first agenda item of every executive management and board meeting.
- Quality can be managed only if it is measured.
- Quality starts with the employee.
- Achievement in quality must be a factor in compensation.

In explaining this approach, McNealy noted that "Sun was launched as a company in 1982, just about the time that Xerox was starting its Leadership Through Quality process. We wanted to learn as much as we could about what worked and what didn't work before we started solving problems that had already been solved."[37]

One of the indicators of a true learning organization is the ability to identify and transfer best practices within the organization, sometimes called **internal benchmarking** (see the box on Royal Mail on page 433). This is one area where even the most mature organizations falter, even those that are adept at external benchmarking. The American Productivity and Quality Center (APQC) noted that executives have long been frustrated by their inability to identify or transfer outstanding practices from one location or function to another. They know that some facilities have superior practices and processes, yet operation units continue to reinvent or ignore solutions and repeat mistakes.[38]

APQC suggests that although most people have a natural desire to learn and share their knowledge, organizations have a variety of logistical, structural, and cultural hurdles to overcome. These include:

- organizational structures that promote "silo" thinking in which locations, divisions, and functions focus on maximizing their own accomplishments and rewards, or, as Deming called it, suboptimization;
- a culture that values personal technical expertise and knowledge creation over knowledge sharing;
- the lack of contact, relationships, and common perspectives among people who don't work side by side;
- an overreliance on transmitting "explicit" rather than "tacit" information—the information that people need to implement a practice that cannot be codified or written down; and
- not allowing or rewarding people for taking the time to learn and share and help each other outside of their own small corporate village.

Internal benchmarking requires a process: first, identifying and collecting internal knowledge and best practices; second, sharing and

Neither Rain nor Sleet nor Dark of Night Keeps the Royal Mail from Learning[39]

One example of an internal best practice learning process is Royal Mail, the largest business unit within the Post Office Group in the United Kingdom (UK), which handles an average of 64 million letters per day using approximately 160,000 people at 1,900 operational sites throughout the UK. Each potential good practice (a term used to recognize that a practice may not be the best, but is good enough to provide significant performance gains) requires formalized documentation that includes a description of the practice; names and telephone numbers of the contacts; date; process diagram; description of the major steps, who performs them, and what is needed to do the work; implementation resources; and risks and barriers. These are scrutinized by a panel for evaluation of their potential for transferability to other parts of the business.

The panel characterizes the good practice as either mandatory, where all units and staff are required to adopt it, or recommended, where application is optional, depending on local conditions. Royal Mail uses six measurements for evaluating its approach:

1. the number of potential national good practices reaching national process groups;
2. the proportion of national good practices becoming confirmed good practices;
3. the extent of implementation;
4. the cycle time from first submission to entry in the national database;
5. the benefit gained compared to the anticipated benefit; and
6. satisfaction from members of the national and business unit process groups.

understanding those practices; and third, adapting and applying them to new situations and bringing them up to best practice performance levels. Technology, culture, leadership, and measurement are enablers that can help or hinder the process. Many organizations have created internal databases by which employees can share their practices and knowledge. For example, Texas Instruments has a Best Practices Knowledge Base delivered via Lotus Notes, Intranet, and TI's mainframe systems. Information is often organized around business core and support processes. Cultural issues include how to motivate and reward people for sharing best practices and establish a supportive culture. As with any TQ effort, senior leadership has to take an active role. This can be done by tying initiatives to the company's vision and strategy, communicating success stories at executive meetings, removing implementation barriers, reinforcing and rewarding positive behaviors, leading by example, and communicating the importance of best practice sharing with all employees. Finally, measuring the frequency of use and satisfaction with best practices databases, linking practices to financial and customer satisfaction, focusing on cycle time to implement best practices, and measuring the growth of virtual teams that share information are ways in which the organization can monitor the effectiveness of its approaches.

Perhaps a more difficult thing for organizations to do is to accept assistance from outside the organization—the "Not Invented Here" syndrome. General Electric, for instance, suddenly asked Southwest Airlines to allow them to help their business become more efficient and cost-effective. GE offered to send over a Six Sigma black belt to work at no cost on a problem involving a component made by another company. Southwest balked, reluctant to share private information about one supplier with another, and many managers were unwilling to accept the rigid scientific approach of Six Sigma into the freewheeling Southwest culture. Nevertheless, Southwest relented and GE's black belt helped eliminate the failures of the part. Since then, Southwest has let dozens of other GE folks work on projects such as financial analysis and invoice flow.[40]

Although this story focused on organizational learning at Southwest, the underlying reason is a push from GE to share its best practices throughout the supply chain to its customers. Dubbed "At the Customer, For the Customer," or ACFC in GE jargon, this initiative is designed to add more customer value and differentiate the company from its competitors. Continuous improvement can be a unique corporate strategy.

ORGANIZATIONAL CHANGE IN ACTION

Many organizations have made substantial changes in their organizations that reflect continuous improvement, breakthrough improvement, and learning. In this section, we highlight some of their approaches.

Boeing

Many organizations have attempted to change their cultures to become more responsive to customer needs. Boeing is a good example of a company in a difficult competitive situation that has undertaken this task.[41] Boeing has been a fixture in the aerospace industry since Bill Boeing built his first airplane—a single-engine seaplane—in 1916. Boeing's planes were heavily involved in World War II, with almost 7,000 produced by Boeing and another 13,000 produced by other manufacturers using Boeing designs. In modern times, approximately half the commercial jets in the world have been produced by Boeing; the company contributes substantially to the U.S. balance of trade by exporting planes all over the world.

Not content to rest on its corporate laurels, however, Boeing was among the early leaders of the quality movement in the United States, implementing quality circles in 1980. (Quality circles are groups of workers who meet for an hour or so each week to work on quality problems and they were a forerunner of total quality efforts in many companies.) Managers at Boeing quickly recognized, however, that the corporate culture would need to be changed if quality efforts were to be successful, and they began a process to do so. This process consisted of five steps:

1. identify norms that currently guide behaviors and attitudes;
2. identify the behaviors necessary to make the organization successful for tomorrow;
3. develop a list of new norms that will move the organization forward;
4. identify the culture gaps—the difference between the desired norms and actual norms; and
5. develop and put in place an action plan to implement the new cultural norms. These new norms will replace the old ones, and this transition will be monitored and enforced.

Boeing backed up this commitment to cultural change with a great deal of training, surveying of employees and customers, and executive commitment. Today the company faces tremendous challenges, including a decline in demand for military aircraft, competition from Airbus Industries (the European airplane consortium) and a very weak global market for jets. Its quality-oriented culture, however, based on customers, continuous improvement, and teamwork, should help it to stay competitive for years to come.

As Boeing's John Black reflected:

> This process of continuous improvement, to which we are committed, is not one that can suddenly be grafted onto a company. Every organization must make it their own. Top management leadership must be provided, and all management must be brought on board. Only when all the people are committed and the process is locked in for the long term, will it achieve the breakthrough that it is capable of providing for us—the key to economic success in the future.

Organizational Change for Six Sigma

As we indicated throughout the preceding chapters, a fully implemented Six Sigma process is a strategic approach that is driven and supported by top management, but is deployed throughout the organization at every level. Several key principles are necessary for effective implementation of Six Sigma:[42]

*   *Committed leadership from top management.* In most companies, Six Sigma represents a major cultural shift, and changing an organization's culture

requires intimate involvement by top leadership. Motorola's former CEO Bob Galvin passionately led the Six Sigma effort with aggressive goals: 10-fold reduction in defects in the first three years, and 100-fold improvement in the next three years. Managers at GE participate in hands-on approaches such as personally spending time in every Six Sigma training wave, speaking and answering questions for students, dropping in (usually unannounced) on weekly and monthly Six Sigma reviews, and making site visits at the manufacturing and call-taking operations to observe firsthand the degree to which Six Sigma in ingrained in the culture.

- *Integration with existing initiatives, business strategy, and performance measurement.* Six Sigma should not be pursued just because other companies are doing it. It should have a clear justification in terms of a company's mission and strategic direction. However, with its focus on customers and the bottom line, this integration usually is not too difficult. At companies like GE and Allied Signal, Six Sigma has been extended to all areas of the company, such as product development and financial services. For example, GE first identifies all critical customer performance features and subjects them to a rigorous statistical design process, thus designing products for Six Sigma levels.

- *Process thinking.* As one of the foundation principles of total quality, a process focus is, not surprisingly, a necessary prerequisite. Mapping business processes is one of the key activities in Six Sigma efforts, as is a disciplined approach to the information gathering, analysis, and problem solving.

- *Disciplined customer and market intelligence gathering.* The ultimate goal is to improve those characteristics that are most important to customers; thus knowledge of customer needs is vital. Approaches that we discussed in Chapter 4 are essential to help focus Six Sigma projects on customers.

- *A bottom-line orientation.* Six Sigma projects must produce real savings or revenues in both the short term and long term. Most Six Sigma projects are designed to be completed within three to six months. GE has a financial analyst certify the results of every project.

- *Leadership in the trenches.* Within GE, Six Sigma includes a diverse population of technical and nontechnical people, managers, and others from key business areas who work together as a team to attack a problem using the DMAIC approach. All employees participate, not just those that hold the "belts."

- *Training.* Although many companies that embraced total quality provide employees with only basic awareness training, Six Sigma companies train nearly everyone in rigorous statistical and problem-solving tools. GE's Green Belt training is delivered to all GE employees and is available in strategic locations across the world. It is typically rolled out over a four-month period and is scheduled to help facilitate the trainee in leading a "green belt project" to not only yield savings but also practice in a real-life situation what is being learned in the training.

- *Continuous reinforcement and rewards.* Six Sigma companies have significantly changed performance measurement and reward systems. At GE, 40 percent of executive incentives are tied to Six Sigma goals and progress. Before any savings are credited to an individual, the Black Belt overseeing the project must show that the problems are fixed permanently. All employees, even executives, who want to be considered for promotion must be trained in Six Sigma and complete a project. Some companies also pool the savings at the business unit level and share the savings with the Six Sigma team members.

A succinct way of describing a successful game plan for implementing Six Sigma is to consider Iomega, the global producer of PC storage devices: *invest in people, make data-based decisions, and achieve and measure results* (see the box on Motorola). The company credits Six Sigma for taking responsibility for quality out of the hands of a few specialists and spreading it throughout the company. Inventory and incoming bad material were both decreased by 80 percent, technical support call wait time was reduced from 80 minutes to 2 minutes on average, and direct labor productivity increased by 65 percent since the Six Sigma program started in 1998, producing more than $120 million in savings through 2001.[43]

ORGANIZATIONAL CHANGE AND ORGANIZATION THEORY

A large amount of research and writing in organization theory (OT) focuses on organization change. Some of the more prominent organizational models include: Weisbord's six box model, Nadler and Tushman's congruence model, the McKinsey seven-s model, Tichy's change framework and TPC (technical, political, cultural) matrix, and the Burke-Litwin model. Few change models have been rigorously validated. Rather, the validity of most change models has been tested less formally, usually through consultant-based applications with clients and through comparison to empirical observation. The plethora of change models in use suggests that there are many viewpoints of how organizational change is achieved. However, the success by which a number of these models have been employed by scholars and consultants in empirical situations suggests that a number of these viewpoints are valid.

One commonality among these change models is a teleological perspective of organizational change. Van de Ven and Poole[44] suggested that teleology was one of four categories of change process theory. Teleological change theory posits that organizations change through an iterative process of goal

The Second Generation of Six Sigma at Motorola

Although Motorola introduced the concept of Six Sigma back in 1986, it is significantly different today. Motorola's "second generation" Six Sigma is an overall high-performance system that executes business strategy.[45] Its results are evident in Motorola's Commercial, Government, and Industrial Solutions Sector division receiving a Baldrige Award in 2002. Their new approach to Six Sigma is based on the following four steps.

1. *Align executives to the right objectives and targets.* This step means creating a balanced scorecard of strategic goals, metrics, and initiatives to identify the improvements that will have the most impact on the bottom line. Projects are not limited to traditional product and service domains but extend to market share improvements, better cash flow, and improved human resource processes.

2. *Mobilize improvement teams around appropriate metrics.* Teams use a structured problem-solving process to drive fact-based decisions; however, the focus on defects and defects per million opportunities (dpmo) sigma levels is less important, particularly in human intensive processes such as marketing and human resources. For example, the definition of a defect as "employee performance that falls below a certain level" can be controversial and be easily manipulated. Continuous measures such as invoice delivery time or credit approval response time are replacing count-based measures such as the number of overdue invoices or the percentage of dissatisfied customers.

3. *Accelerate results.* Motorola uses an action learning framework methodology that combines formal education with real-time project work and coaching to quickly take employees from learning to doing. Project teams receive support from coaches on a just-in-time basis. Projects are driven to be accomplished quickly, rather than over a long period of time. Finally, a campaign management approach helps integrate various project teams so that the cumulative impact on the organization is, in fact, accelerated.

4. *Govern sustained improvement.* Leaders actively and visibly sponsor the key improvement projects required to execute business strategy and review them in the context of outcome goals. An important step is for leaders to actively share best practices and knowledge about improvements with other parts of the organization that can benefit.

Six Sigma continues to be Motorola's method of choice for driving bottom line improvements. More efforts will be focused on product design that enhances the overall customer experience across the value chain. As such, Six Sigma projects increasingly involve key customers, suppliers, and other business partners.

setting, implementation, evaluation, and revision. Unlike other theories of change that suggest the environment as the dominant change force, teleology represents change as a deliberate undertaking by individuals affiliated with the organization.

The organizational learning literature makes a fundamental distinction between single- and double-loop levels of learning. Single-loop learning is the most common level of learning, and encompasses the organization's ability to perceive deviations from perceived performance and "fix" them. Single-loop learning occurs, for example, when managers detect a problem in implementing a specific strategic initiative and then take action to correct the deviation. Most diagnostic management control systems exhibit single-loop learning characteristics. Double-loop learning is more sophisticated, as the organization must review the underlying assumptions that created the problem to be "fixed" in the first place, and adapt a better set of assumptions to support future performance.

Research suggests that organizational learning is enhanced when people gather for "dialog." Dialog is defined as a sustained collective inquiry into the processes, assumptions, and certainties that compose everyday experience. An important consequence of effective organizational dialog is the reduction of "defensive routines," which are policies, practices, or actions that prevent people involved in a group activity from being embarrassed or threatened, and, at the same time, prevent people from learning how to reduce the causes of embarrassment or threat. Defensive routines can adversely impact the organization's ability to implement large-scale strategic change. In one research experiment, executives learned to overcome defensive routines by engaging in dialog that forced the managers to articulate their underlying assumptions and reservations about particular strategic decisions to be implemented in their organizations. After the experiment, most managers reported that their strategies were being implemented more effectively.[46]

TQ Perspectives

This section compares the TQ perspective on organization change to the organizational theory literature. Given the amount of work in this area, this section will only identify a few of the major ideas in the literature on organization change and show how they relate to total quality. Organizational behavior and organization theory textbooks generally have at least one chapter on organization change, which can be consulted for further details on this research. TQ will be compared to organization theory in terms of the reasons for change, the source of change, the nature of change, the difficulty of change, and how to manage change. The overall conclusion is that, despite some differences in focus, the research on change conducted by organization theorists is a rich source of information for those embarking on the changes required by total quality.

The Reason for Change

The reason behind TQ-oriented change is quality improvement for customer satisfaction. This has not been a major focus of the OT literature on change, which has focused primarily on changes intended to improve productivity and/or improve job satisfaction. Of course, many quality-oriented changes may improve productivity or job satisfaction, but that isn't usually their main objective.

The Source of Change

The source of most change considered in OT is top management. In general, top management responds to changes in the organizational environment, such as increased competitiveness or declining demand. This parallels the cultural change aspect of TQ. In fact, the OT literature on change is most relevant to cultural change, as opposed to continuous improvement or process redesign.

Types of Change

The types of changes considered in OT theories partially overlap with TQ-oriented changes. In particular, OT theories that deal with changes in values and norms are relevant to the transformations associated with cultural change in TQ. Other types of change featured in OT theories, such as the introduction of new technology, are not as directly relevant to TQ. (Reengineering, however, often involves the application of some type of information technology.)

Furthermore, the changes discussed in the OT literature tend to differ in two important ways from TQ-oriented change. First, they tend to be limited in scope, usually to one or two departments, and even to only a few aspects of the work of these departments. Second, they tend to be limited in duration, with the idea being to get the change over with and get on with organizational life. This may apply to cultural change (and to some extent to process redesign), but is very different from continuous improvement. Indeed, the management of continuous change over a long period of time has not been addressed often by OT research and presents a clear opportunity for research.

One of the earliest studies of organization change was conducted by Coch and French in a Virginia factory that produced pajamas.[47] In this study, a change in procedure was made in three different ways. In one group, the workers themselves devised the change. In a second group, workers appointed representatives who devised the change. In a third group, the new system was imposed on the workers by management.

The study found that the change was much more successful in the more participative groups; this study is often cited as support for the need for employee participation in organizational change. What is interesting from a TQ perspective is that it is a study of process redesign and, in the participative groups at least, of process redesign initiated by the people actually doing the work. Thus, it anticipates by 40 years the kinds of changes that have become commonplace among firms practicing total quality. True to the limits in the thinking at the time, however, the improvement was a one-shot deal. Continuous improvement was an idea whose time had not yet come.

TQ and the OT literature agree on the difficulty of successfully changing organizations and on the fact that "resistance to change" is often the underlying problem. OT research has made significant progress in identifying why organization members resist change and even in identifying various methods for dealing with this problem.[48] Resistance is at least as likely to come from managers as from lower-level employees.

The whole idea of resistance, however, flows from a concept of change mandated by top management. Managers or workers are unlikely to resist a process change that they themselves have devised. For such changes, the literature on resistance to change seems off the mark.

Perhaps the literature on population ecology provides a more helpful perspective on the difficulty of organizational change in the TQ context.[49] From this perspective, worker resistance is not to blame for the difficulty of change. Rather, the structures and systems that management has created are at fault. For example, the hierarchical organization structure of most firms makes it difficult for them to adapt effectively to environmental changes such as the evolution in customer demand. This idea is consistent with Deming's theory that problems are more often related to system imperfections than to worker inability or lack of motivation.

Population ecology theorists generally argue that the difficulty of changing structures, authority, reward systems, and so forth, renders most organizations unsuccessful in their change efforts. Writers on TQ often have commented on the major impediments such structures and systems create, but have gone on to identify ways in which such obstacles can be removed. This difference in prognosis should not mask the fundamental agreement between the ecological OT perspective and TQ on the importance of structural and systemic impediments to change.

From the ecological perspective, change in a set of similar organizations often comes about by ineffective organizations going out of business and being replaced by new ones, rather than by changing from ineffective to effective. Clearly both processes occur. Many organizations that did not provide the quality customers demanded are no longer with us, whereas others (Xerox is an excellent example) have managed to transform themselves in order to survive. Needless to say, the battle between transformation and extinction continues to be fought every day in many firms throughout the world.

Many of the principles for managing change derived from the OT literature apply directly to total quality change. Some of these principles are as follows:

1. *It is necessary to "unfreeze" people's attitudes and behavior before they can be changed.*[50] This principle, a staple of the OT understanding of change, relates directly to TQ. Before organizations can change in the direction of

practicing TQ, people must see why the current approach is inappropriate or incomplete and what problems of competitiveness and customer dissatisfaction this causes. Cultural change in TQ is often the vehicle for unfreezing behavior.

2. *Change can only succeed with effective leadership.* One early proponent of this view was Thomas Bennett.[51] Bennett identified the need for leaders to deal with the emotional aspects of the change for subordinates, the need for clear goals, and the importance of logical problem-solving processes. These and other aspects of the leader's role identified by OT theorists clearly are relevant to TQ.

3. *Change agents must manage interdependence.* Few things in organizations—for example, jobs or technology—can be changed without affecting other things—structures or processes. Many OT theorists of change recognized this fact and based their theories on the need to identify and manage the interdependence among organizational phenomena.[52] This applies directly to process redesign and is consistent with Deming's emphasis on organizations as systems.

4. *Effective change must involve the people whose jobs are being changed.* This point was noted in reference to the Coch and French study. Although a variety of rationales for the importance of participation have been advanced, its significance for reducing resistance is an article of faith among organization change theorists.[53] This is probably the point of greatest overlap between OT and TQ. The "participation" and "involvement" championed by OT theorists as much as 50 years ago have become so widely accepted in industry that they have evolved into today's concepts of "empowerment" and "self-management."

5. *Refreezing is needed to make gains permanent.* Research in OT has concluded that steps are needed to lock in the changes that have been made.[54] This point has not been lost upon the TQ community, as many organizations are now becoming concerned about maintaining, as opposed to creating, change. Many of the recommendations of the OT literature, especially the need to monitor and revise change efforts continually, are quite relevant to TQ.

REVIEW AND DISCUSSION QUESTIONS

1. Describe some personal experiences in which you traveled through the four stages of learning described in this chapter.
2. Briefly describe the three kinds of organizational change practiced in total quality efforts.
3. You probably have, unfortunately, heard the term "dysfunctional family" in news stories about our society. What might the term "dysfunctional corporate culture" mean?

4. Describe the culture of an organization you have worked in or are familiar with. What is valued in this culture? Do you think this culture provides fertile ground for total quality? Why or why not?

5. Will an organization's culture be the same throughout or will it vary from department to department? Why?

6. How do the values stated in "The Eastman Way" promote a total quality culture?

7. Find and examine five Internet Web sites for large corporations. What do these sites tell you about the company's culture?

8. For each of the core values of the Baldrige criteria, describe some practices that you would expect to see high-performing organizations implement.

9. Download the latest version of the Baldrige criteria from the NIST Web site (http://www.quality.nist.gov) and discuss how the core values and concepts underlying the Baldrige criteria are reflected in each category of the criteria.

10. Managers can enforce rules about what people do and say at work. But can they enforce a culture? If yes, how can they do it? If no, what does this say about the limits of managers' ability to ensure quality?

11. A major stumbling block in implementing TQ in the United States has been the traditional adversarial relationship between unions and management. What should be the role of both unions and management in building a TQ culture?

12. What might the "learning organization" concept mean to a college or university?

13. How might internal benchmarking be applied within your college? What types of activities would be appropriate?

CASES

The Yellow Brick Road to Quality[55]

In the film *The Wizard of Oz*, Dorothy learned many lessons. Surprisingly, managers can learn a lot also. For each of the following summaries of scenes in the film, discuss the lessons that organizations can learn in pursuing change and a TQ culture.

A. Dorothy was not happy with the world as she knew it. A tornado came along and transported her to the Land of Oz. The tornado dropped Dorothy's house on the Wicked Witch of the East, killing the witch. "Ding, dong, the witch is dead!" rang throughout Munchkinland, but Dorothy had enraged the dead witch's sister. Dorothy only temporarily lost her home support provided by family back in Kansas. All is not good, however, in the Land of Oz. Dorothy's problem is to find her way home to Kansas. Her call to action was precipitated by a crisis—the tornado that transported her to an alien land.

B. In the throes of a Kansas tornado, Dorothy is transported to an unfamiliar land. Immediately, she realizes her world is different and the processes and people she encounters are different, yet bear some similarity to her Kansas existence. She is lost and confused and uncertain about the next steps to take. She realizes she is in a changed state—the Land of Oz—and must devise a plan to get home.

C. Dorothy is a hero for killing the Wicked Witch of the East. Glinda the Good Witch sends Dorothy on her way to meet the Wizard of Oz who will help her get back to Kansas. The Wicked Witch of the West tries to get Dorothy's newly acquired ruby slippers, but to no avail. Dorothy and Toto leave for Oz via the Yellow Brick Road. Along the way, they are joined by the Scarecrow, the Tin Man, and the Lion. Through their teamwork, they provide mutual support to endure the vexing journey. They overcome many risks and barriers on the way to Oz, including a field of poppies that puts them to sleep, flying monkeys, and a haunted forest.

D. Dorothy and her entourage finally reach Oz and meet the Wizard. Rather than instantly granting their wishes, the Wizard gives them an assignment—to obtain the Wicked Witch's broom. They depart for the West.

E. Charged with the task of obtaining the broom, Dorothy and company experience several encounters with near disaster, including Dorothy's incarceration in the witch's castle while an hourglass counts the time to her death. In a struggle to extinguish the Scarecrow's fire (incited by the Wicked Witch), Dorothy tosses a bucket of water, some of which hits the Witch and melts her. Dorothy is rewarded with the broomstick and returns to Oz.

F. Returning to Oz, the group talks with the Wizard, expecting him to help Dorothy return to Kansas. After defrocking the Wizard, they find out he does not know how. The Wizard tries to use a hot air balloon to return and accidentally leaves Dorothy and Toto behind upon takeoff. Glinda arrives and helps Dorothy realize she can return to Kansas on her own with the help of the ruby slippers.

G. Dorothy awakens from her dream and experiences a new understanding and appreciation for her home and family in Kansas. "Oh, Auntie Em, there's no place like home."

The Parable of the Green Lawn[56]

A new housing development has lots of packed earth and weeds but no grass. Two neighbors make a wager on who will be the first to have a lush lawn. Mr. Fast N. Furious knows that a lawn will not grow without grass seed, so he immediately buys the most expensive seed he can find because everyone knows that quality improves with price. Besides, he'll recover the cost of the seed through his wager. Next, he stands knee deep in his weeds and tosses the seed around his yard. Confident that he has a head start on his neighbor, who is not making much visible progress, he begins his next project.

Ms. Slo N. Steady, having grown up in the country, proceeds to clear the lot, till the soil, and even alter the slope of the terrain to provide better drainage. She checks the soil's pH, applies weed killer and fertilizer, and then distributes the grass seed evenly with a spreader. She applies a mulch cover and waters the lawn appropriately. She finishes several days after her neighbor, who asks if she would like to concede defeat. After all, he does have some blades of grass poking up already.

Mr. Furious is encouraged by the few clumps of grass that sprout. While these small, green islands are better developed than Ms. Steady's fledgling lawn, they are surrounded by bare spots and weeds. If he maintains these footholds, he reasons, they should spread to the rest of the yard. He notices that his neighbor's lawn is more uniform and is really starting to grow. He attributes this to the Steady children, who water the lawn each evening. Not wanting to appear to be imitating his neighbor, Mr. Furious instructs his children to water his lawn at noon.

The noon watering proves to be detrimental, so he decides to fertilize the remaining patches of grass. Since he wants to make up for the losses the noon watering caused, he applies the fertilizer at twice the recommended application rate. Most of the patches of grass that escape being burned by the fertilizer, however, are eventually choked out by the weeds.

After winning the wager with Mr. Furious, Ms. Steady lounges on the deck enjoying her new grill, which she paid for with the money from the wager. Her lawn requires minimal maintenance, so she is free to attend to the landscaping. The combination of the lawn and landscaping also results in an award from a neighborhood committee that determines that her lawn is a true showplace.

Mr. Furious still labors on his lawn. He blames the poor performance on his children's inability to properly water the lawn, nonconforming grass seed, insufficient sunlight, and poor soil. He claims that his neighbor has an unfair advantage and her success is based on conditions unique to her plot of land. He views the loss as grossly unfair; after all, he spends more time and money on his lawn than Ms. Steady does.

He continues to complain about how expensive the seed is and how much time he spends moving the sprinkler around to the few remaining clumps of grass that continue to grow. But Mr. Furious thinks that things will be better for him next year, because he plans to install an automatic sprinkler system and make a double-or-nothing wager with Ms. Steady.

(© *1994 American Society for Quality. Reprinted with permission.*)

Discussion Questions

1. Within the context of the continual struggles to create a "world-class" lawn and "world-class" business, draw analogies between the events when total quality is implemented.

2. Specifically, translate the problems described here in business language. What are the implementation barriers to achieving total quality?

Westerfield Construction[57]

Westerfield Construction hired a new quality manager, Kelly Deters, to help integrate its quality system into everyday business operations. One of her initial projects was to lead the development and implementation of a customer service life cycle (CSLC), which is the identification, analysis, involvement, management, data sharing, and evaluation of all the contact points between the company and its customers, along with strong feedback mechanisms.

Deters began by assessing the readiness of the organization for change. She determined that the executive team was able to inspire others and act as role models, and were strong and effective leaders. The company had a functioning quality council of executive and middle managers, whose purpose was to review and become personally involved in selected change initiatives. Communications among the team, middle managers, and employees had improved significantly, largely because of frequent open forums that were initiated by the CEO. Deters concluded that the firm's strategy supported its mission and vision, and that organizational culture supported change in the company. These factors all pointed to a favorable environment for change, leading her to believe that she would be able to successfully implement the CSLC.

Because the CSLC was cross-functional, it touched almost every part of the organization, including some that did not recognize their relationship with other parts of the company. Deters built a cross-functional team of employees to review the business plan and customer strategies to provide context and alignment with the vision and company strategy. She also had a consultant train the team in the use of the seven management and planning tools. Resources were available to the team for benchmarking outstanding organizations with established CSLCs. Sufficient budget, time, and other resources were also provided to her by the executive team. The CSLC team used the tools prior to developing an action plan for implementation. They developed measures to monitor the effectiveness of the CSLC and drive continuous improvements. She decided to phase in the implementation in two functional areas that had strong existing customer relationships: estimating and project management. Within six months the CSLC was operational and the team was rewarded for its efforts; each team member was given a day off with pay, and the company newsletter ran articles about customer service, satisfaction, and the progress of the CSLC team. An executive manager was given the responsibilities for managing the new process, and before the team disbanded, lessons learned were identified and shared for future projects.

Discussion Questions

1. In examining the process that Deters used to manage the development and implementation of this project, what factors contributed to her success?

2. Try to develop a model in the form of a flowchart that characterizes an effective change process based on this case.

ENDNOTES

1. Quoted in E. F. Cudworth, "3M's Commitment to Quality as a Way of Life," *Industrial Engineering*, July 1985.

2. Matthew W. Ford and James R. Evans, "Baldrige Assessment and Organizational Learning: The Need for Change Management," *Quality Management Journal*, Vol. 8, No. 3, 2001, pp. 9–25.

3. Based on *Everyone Knows His First Name* by Levi Strauss & Company.

4. Adapted from Weston F. Milliken, "The Eastman Way," *Quality Progress*, Vol. 29, No. 10, October 1996, pp. 57–62.

5. Source: "To Be the Best," Eastman Chemical Company publication ECC-67, January 1994. © 1996 American Society for Quality. Reprinted with permission of Eastman Chemical Company.

6. See, for example, B. Schneider, *Organizational Climate and Culture*, Jossey-Bass, 1990; and B. Schneider, S. K. Gunnarson, and K. Niles-Jolly, "Creating the Climate and Culture of Success," *Organizational Dynamics*, Vol. 23, Summer 1994.

7. For a more detailed look at leadership's role in total quality, see Chapter 9.

8. Interview with Richard Garula.

9. J. M. Delsanter, "On the right track," *TQM Magazine*, March/April 1992, pp. 17–20.

10. Kiron Kasbekar and Namita Devidayal, "Improvement Is Not All Smooth Sailing," *The Times of India*, January 8, 1993.

11. Henry A. Bradshaw, "From Leadership to Customer Satisfaction: The Total Quality Management System," Presentation Material from the 1996 Regional Malcolm Baldrige Award Conference, Boston, June 6, 1996, and Doug Keare, "Lessons Learned and Quality Journey," Presentation Notes, 1997 Quest for Excellence Conference, Washington, D.C.

12. Gregory P. Smith, "A Change in Culture Brings Dramatic Quality Improvements," *The Quality Observer*, January 1997, pp. 14–15, 37.

13. Dan Ciampa, *Total Quality: A User's Guide to Implementation*, Reading, Mass.: Addison-Wesley, 1992, cautions about trying to change culture.

14. Several reasons for managerial resistance to change are outlined by J. M. Juran in *Juran on Leadership for Quality*, New York: Free Press, 1989.

15. Michael Beer and Nitin Nohria, "Cracking the Code of Change," *Harvard Business Review*, May–June 2000.

16. Janet Young, "Driving Performance Results at American Express," *Six Sigma Forum Magazine*, Vol. 1, No. 1, November 2001, pp. 19–27.

17. Arthur R. Tenner and Irving J. DeToro, *Total Quality Management: Three Steps to Continuous Improvement*, Reading, Mass.: Addison Wesley, 1992.

18. Mark Samuel, "Catalysts for Change," *TQM Magazine*, 1992.

19. Samuel, "Catalysts for Change."

20. James H. Davis, "Who Owns Your Quality Program? Lessons from the Baldrige Award Winners," College of Business Administration, University of Notre Dame (n.d.).

21. *Business Week*, "Where Did They Go Wrong?" October 25, 1991.

22. Leadership Steering Committee, *A Report of the Total Quality Leadership Steering Committee and Working Councils*, Procter & Gamble Total Quality Forum, November 1992.

23. Thomas H. Patten, Jr., "Beyond Systems—The Politics of Managing in a TQM Environment," *National Productivity Review*, 1991/1992.

24. Davis, "Who Owns Your Quality Program?"

25. "Special Report: Quality," *Business Week*, November 30, 1992, pp. 66–75; and H. James Harrington, "The Fallacy of Universal Best Practices," Report TR 97-003, Ernst & Young, 1997.

26. See, for example, Mark Graham Brown, "Measuring Up Against the 1997 Baldrige Criteria," *Journal for Quality and Participation*, Vol. 20, No. 4, September 1997, pp. 22–28.

27. Matthew W. Ford and James R. Evans, "Managing Organizational Self-Assessment: Follow-up and Its Influencing Factors," Working Paper, College of Business, Northern Kentucky University and College of Business, University of Cincinnati. See also Matthew W. Ford, "A Model of Change Process and Its Use in Self Assessment," Doctoral Dissertation, Unviersity of Cincinnati, 2000.

28. Mark S. Leggitt and Rhonda Anderson, "Linking Strategic and Quality Plans," *Quality Progress*, October 2001, pp. 61–63.

29. H. James Harrington, "Creating Organizational Excellence—Part Four," *Quality Digest*, April 2003, 14.

30. Chuck Cobb, "Knowledge Management and Quality Systems," *The 54th Annual Quality Congress Proceedings*, 2000, American Society for Quality, 276–287.

31. Peter M. Senge, *The Fifth Discipline: The Art and Practice of the Learning Organization*, New York: Doubleday Currency, 1990, p. 14.

32. Arthur M. Schneiderman, "Measuring Organizational Learning," Unpublished note; http://www.schneiderman.com/.

33. Thomas H. Lee, "Learning, What Does It Really Mean?" *Center for Quality of Management Journal*, Vol. 4, No. 4, Winter 1995, pp. 4–14.

34. See Matthew W. Ford and James R. Evans, "Baldrige Assessment and Organizational Learning: The Need for Change Management," *Quality Management Journal* 8, 3, pp. 9–25, 2001.

35. Ann B. Rich, "Continuous Improvement: The Key to Success," *Quality Progress*, Vol. 30, No. 6, June 1997.

36. Brad Stratton, "TI Has Eye on Alignment," *Quality Progress*, Vol. 30, No. 10, October 1997, pp. 28–34.

37. Larry Hambly, "Sun Microsystems Embeds Quality into Its DNA," *The Quality Observer*, July 1997, pp. 16–20, 45.

38. Carla O'Dell and C. Jackson Grayson, "Identifying and Transferring Internal Best Practices," APQC White Paper, 2000 (www.apqc.org/free/whitepapers/cmifwp/index.htm).

39. Mohamed Zairi and John Whymark, "The Transfer of Best Practices: How to Build a Culture of Benchmarking and Continuous Learning—Part 1," *Benchmarking: An International Journal*, Vol. 7, No. 1, 2000, pp. 62–78.

40. Diane Brady, "Will Jeff Immelt's New Push Pay Off for GE?" *Business Week*, October 13, 2003, pp. 94–98.

41. Based on John R. Black, "Boeing's Quality Strategy: A Continuing Evolution," The *Quest for Competitiveness: Lessons from America's Productivity and Quality Leaders*, Y. Krishna Shetty and Vernon M. Buehler (eds.), New York: Quorum Books, 1991.

42. Jerome A. Blakeslee, Jr., "Implementing the Six Sigma Solution," *Quality Progress*, July 1999, 77–85; © 1999. American Society for Quality. Reprinted with permission; and Kim M. Henderson and James R. Evans, "Successful Implementation of Six Sigma: Benchmarking General Electric Company," *Benchmarking: An International Journal* 7, No. 4 (2000), 260–281.

43. Robert A. Green, "Seeking Six Sigma Standardization," *Quality Digest*, August 2001, 49–52.

44. A. H. Van de Ven and M. S. Poole, "Explaining Development and Change in Organizations," *Academy of Management Review*, Vol. 20, No. 3, pp. 510–540.

45. Matt Barney, "Motorola's Second Generation," *Six Sigma Forum Magazine* 1, No. 3 (May 2002), 13–22.

46. C. Argyris, "Strategy Implementation: An Experience in Learning," *Organizational Dynamics*, Vol. 18, No. 2, pp. 5–15.

47. L. Coch and J. P. French, "Overcoming Resistance to Change," *Human Relations*, Vol. 1, 1948, pp. 512–532.

48. For a summary of this material, see J. P. Kotter and L. A. Schlesinger, "Choosing Strategies for Change," in J. J. Gabarro (ed.), *Managing People and Organizations*, Boston: Harvard Business School Publications, 1992, pp. 395–409.

49. See, for example, H. A. Aldrich, *Organizations and Environments*, Englewood Cliffs, N. J.: Prentice Hall, 1979.

50. K. Lewin, "Forces Behind Food Habits and Methods of Change," *Bulletin of the National Research Council #108*, 1947, pp. 35–65. See also E. Schein, "Organizational Socialization and the Profession of Management," *Industrial Management Review*, 1968, pp.1–16.

51. See Thomas R. Bennett III, *Planning for Change*, Washington, D.C.: Leadership Resources, 1961.

52. See, for example, Harold J. Leavitt, "Applied Organization Change in Industry: Structural, Technical, and Human Approaches," in W. W. Cooper, H. J. Leavitt, and M. W. Shelly (eds.), *New Perspectives in Organizational Research*, New York: Wiley, 1964.

53. For an interesting (and now classic) discussion of this issue, see P. R. Lawrence, "How to Deal with Resistance to Change," *Harvard Business Review*, May/June 1954.

54. See Schein, "Organizational Socialization," *Industrial Management Review*. See also, P. S. Goodman and J. W. Dean, Jr., "Creating Long-Term Change," in P. S. Goodman (ed.), *Change in Organizations*. San Francisco: Jossey-Bass, 1983.

55. David M. Lyth and Larry A. Mallak, "'We're Not in Kansas Anymore, Toto' or Quality Lessons from the Land of Oz," *Quality Engineering*, Vol. 10, No. 30, 1998, pp. 579–588.

56. Adapted from James A. Alloway, Jr., "Laying Groundwork for Total Quality," *Quality Progress*, Vol. 27, No. 1, January 1994, pp. 65–67. © 1994 American Society for Quality Control. Reprinted with permission.

57. Based on Gregory S. Shinn, "Intentional Change by Design," *Quality Progress*, May 2001, 46–51.

BIBLIOGRAPHY

This bibliography is a sampling of the hundreds of books that have been published in response to the quality revolution. They are arranged in the following categories:

1. Malcolm Baldrige National Quality Award
2. Six Sigma
3. Deming philosophy
4. Employee involvement/human resources
5. General reference
6. Management
7. Case studies of quality practices
8. Service organizations
9. Tools

Many others can be found by visiting the American Society for Quality Web site: http://www.asq.org, and the Online Quality Resources bookstore at http://www.quality.org.

Malcolm Baldrige National Quality Award

Brown, M. G. *Baldrige Award Winning Quality: How to Interpret the Malcolm Baldrige Award Criteria* (13th edition). White Plains, N.Y.: Quality Resources and ASQ Quality Press, 2004.

Cartin, Thomas J. *Principles and Practices of Organizational Performance Excellence.* Milwaukee: ASQ Quality Press, 1999.

Conyers, John G., and Ewy, Robert. *Charting Your Course: Lessons Learned During the Journey Toward Performance Excellence.* Milwaukee: ASQ Quality Press, 2004.

Haavind, R. *The Road to the Baldrige Award.* Boston: Butterworth-Heinemann, 1992.

Hutton, David W. *From Baldrige to the Bottom Line: A Road Map for Organizational Change and Improvement.* Milwaukee: ASQ Quality Press, 2000.

Six Sigma

Breyfogle, Forrest W., III, James M. Cupello, and Becki Meadows. *Managing Six Sigma.* New York: Wiley-Interscience, 2001.

Breyfogle, Forrest W. *Implementing Six Sigma: Smarter Solutions Using Statistical Methods, 2nd Edition.* Milwaukee: ASQ Quality Press, 2003.

Brue, Greg, *Six Sigma for Managers.* New York, McGraw-Hill, 2002.

Chowdhury, Subir. *Design for Six Sigma: The Revolutionary Process for Achieving Extraordinary Profits.* ASQ Quality Press, 2002.

Eckes, George, *The Six Sigma Revolution.* New York: John Wiley & Sons, 2001.

George, Michael L., *Lean Six Sigma: Combining Six Sigma Quality with Lean Speed.* New York: McGraw-Hill, 2002

Pyzdek, Thomas, *The Six Sigma Handbook, Revised and Expanded*. New York: McGraw-Hill, 2003.

Stamatis, D. H. *Six Sigma and Beyond: Foundations of Excellent Performance*. Boca Raton, Fla.: St. Lucie/CRC Press, 2002.

The Juran Institute. *Juran Institute's Six Sigma Breakthrough and Beyond: Quality George, Michael L. Performance Breakthrough Methods*. Milwaukee: ASQ Quality Press, 2003

Deming Philosophy

Aguayo, R. *Dr. Deming: The American Who Taught the Japanese About Quality*. New York: Simon & Schuster, 1990.

Deming, W. E. *Out of the Crisis*. Cambridge, Mass.: Massachusetts Institute of Technology Center of Advanced Engineering Study, 1982.

Gabor, A. *The Man Who Discovered Quality: How W. Edwards Deming Brought the Quality Revolution to America—The Stories of Ford, Xerox, and GM*. New York: Times Books, 1990.

Joiner, Brian L. *Fourth Generation Management*. New York: McGraw-Hill, 1994.

Killian, C. S. *The World of W. Edwards Deming*. Washington, D.C.: SPC Press Books, 1988.

Mann, N. R. *The Keys to Excellence: The Story of the Deming Philosophy*. Los Angeles: Prestwick Books, 1989.

Neave, H. R. *The Deming Dimension*. Knoxville, Tenn.: SPC Press, 1990.

Scherkenbach, William W. *Deming's Road to Continual Improvement*. Knoxville, Tenn.: SPC Press, 1991.

Walton, M. *Deming Management at Work*. New York: G.P. Putnam's Sons, 1990.

Employee Involvement/Human Resources

Cooksey, Clifton, Richard Beans, and Debra Eshelman. *Process Improvement: A Guide for Teams*. Arlington, Va.: Coopers & Lybrand, 1993.

Grazier, P. B. *Before It's Too Late: Employee Involvement . . . An Idea Whose Time Has Come*. Chadds Ford, Pa.: Teambuilding, Inc., 1989.

Kinlaw, Dennis C. *Developing Superior Work Teams*. Lexington, Mass.: Lexington Books, 1991.

Knouse, Stephen B. *Human Resource Management Perspectives on TQM: Concepts and Practices*. Milwaukee: ASQ Quality Press, 1996.

Kohn, A. *No Contest: The Case Against Competition*. Boston: Houghton Mifflin, 1986.

Ryan, K. D., and D. K. Oestreich. *Driving Fear Out of the Workplace: How to Overcome the Barriers to Quality, Productivity, and Innovation*. San Francisco: Jossey-Bass Publishers, 1991.

Scholtes, P. R. *The Team Handbook*. Madison, Wisc.: Joiner and Associates, 1988.

Shuman, Jeffrey, Janice Twombly, and David Rottenberg (Contributor), *Everyone Is a Customer: A Proven Method for Measuring the Value of Every Relationship in the Era of Collaborative Business*. Milwaukee: ASQ Quality Press, 2002.

Wellins, Richard S., William C. Byham, and Jeanne M. Wilson. *Empowered Teams*. San Francisco: Jossey-Bass, 1991.

General Reference

Evans, J. R., and W. M. Lindsay. *The Management and Control of Quality* (6th ed.). Cincinnati: South-Western Publishing Company, 2005.

Feigenbaum, A. V. *Total Quality Control* (3rd ed., revised). New York: McGraw-Hill Book Company, 1991.

Forsha, H. I. *The Pursuit of Quality Through Personal Change*. Milwaukee: ASQC Quality Press, 1992.

Juran, J. M., and F. M. Gryna. *Juran's Quality Control Handbook* (4th ed.). New York: McGraw-Hill Book Company, 1988.

Juran, J. M. *A History of Managing for Quality*. Milwaukee: ASQC Quality Press, 1995.

Juran, J. M. *Juran on Planning for Quality*. New York: Free Press, 1988.

Juran, J. M. *Juran on Quality by Design*. New York: Free Press, 1992.

Juran, J. M. *Architect of Quality: The Autobiography of Dr. Joseph M. Juran*. Milwaukee: ASQ Quality Press, 2003.

Tenner, A. R., and I. J. DeToro. *Total Quality Management: Three Steps to Continuous Improvement*. Reading, Mass.: Addison Wesley, 1992.

Townsend, P. L. and J. E. Gebhardt. *Quality in Action: 93 Lessons in Leadership, Participation, and Measurement*. New York: John Wiley & Sons, 1992.

Walsh, L., R. Wurster, and R. J. Kimber (eds.). *Quality Management Handbook*. New York: Marcel Dekker, Inc., and ASQC Quality Press, 1986.

Management

Berry, T. H. *Managing the Total Quality Transformation*. New York: McGraw-Hill, 1991.

Blanchard, Ken. *The Heart of a Leader: Insights on the Art of Influence*. Tulsa, Okla.: Honor Books, 1999.

Bossidy, Larry, Ram Charan and Charles Burch. *Execution: The Discipline of Getting Things Done*. New York: Crown Books-Random House, 2002.

Bowles, J., and J. Hammond. *Beyond Quality: How 50 Winning Companies Use Continuous Improvement*. New York: G.P. Putnam's Sons, 1991.

Brocka, B., and M. S. Brocka. *Quality Management: Implementing the Best Ideas of the Masters*. Homewood, Ill.: Irwin, 1992.

Chawla, Sarita, and John Renesch, eds. *Learning Organizations: Developing Cultures for Tomorrow's Workplace*. Portland, Ore.: Productivity Press, 1995.

Cobb, Charles G. *From Quality to Business Excellence: A Systems Approach to Management*, ASQ Quality Press, 2003.

Crownover, Dale. *Take It to the Next Level*. Dallas, Texas: NextLevel Press 1999.

Dixon, G., and J. Swiler. *Total Quality Handbook: The Executive Guide to the New American Way of Doing Business*. Minneapolis, Minn.: Lakewood Books, 1990.

Fitzsimmons, James A., and Mona J. Fitzsimmons. *New service development: creating memorable experiences*. Thousand Oaks, Calif.: Sage Publications, 2000

Garvin, D. A. *Managing Quality: The Strategic and Competitive Edge*. New York: Free Press, 1988.

Hudiburg, J. J. *Winning with Quality: The FPL Story*. White Plains, N.Y.: Quality Resources, 1991.

Imai, M. *Kaizen: The Key to Japan's Competitive Success*. New York: McGraw-Hill Publishing Company, 1986.

King, B. *Hoshin Planning: The Developmental Approach*. Methuen, Mass.: GOAL/ QPC, 1989.

Neely, Andrew, Chris Adams, Mike Kennerley. *The Performance Prism: The Scorecard for Measuring and Managing Business Success*. New York: Financial Times-Prentice Hall, 2002.

Schmidt, Warren H. and Jerome P. Finnigan. *The Race Without a Finish Line*. San Francisco: Jossey-Bass, 1992.

Senge, P. M. *The Fifth Discipline: The Art and Practice of the Learning Organization*. New York: Doubleday Currency, 1990.

Shecter, E. S. *Managing for World-Class Quality: A Primer for Executives and Managers*. New York: Marcel Dekker, Inc., and ASQC Quality Press, 1992.

Whiteley, R. C. *The Customer-Driven Company: Moving from Talk to Action*. New York: Addison-Wesley Publishing Company, Inc., 1991.

Case Studies of Quality Practices

Brown, Mark Graham. *Keeping Score: Using the Right Metrics to Drive World-Class Performance*. Milwaukee: ASQ Quality Press, 1995.

Camp, Robert C. *Business Process Benchmarking: Finding and Implementing Best Practices*. Milwaukee: ASQ Quality Press, 2000.

Hiam, A. *Closing the Quality Gap: Lessons from America's Leading Companies*. Englewood Cliffs, N.J.: Prentice Hall, 1992.

International Quality Study: A Definitive Report on International Industry-Specific Quality Management Practices (Automotive Industry Report). Cleveland, Ohio: Ernst & Young and American Quality Foundation, 1992.

International Quality Study: A Definitive Report on International Industry-Specific Quality Management Practices (Banking Industry Report). Cleveland, Ohio: Ernst & Young and American Quality Foundation, 1992.

International Quality Study: A Definitive Report on International Industry-Specific Quality Management Practices (Computer Industry Report). Cleveland, Ohio: Ernst & Young and American Quality Foundation, 1992.

International Quality Study: A Definitive Report on International Industry-Specific Quality Management Practices (Health Care Industry Report). Cleveland, Ohio: Ernst & Young and American Quality Foundation, 1992.

Lefevre, H. *Government Quality and Productivity-Success Stories*. Milwaukee: ASQC Quality Press, 1990.

Peters, T. J., and R. H. Waterman, Jr. *In Search of Excellence: Lessons from America's Best-Run Companies*. New York: Harper & Row Publishers, 1982.

Weinstein, Art, and William C. Johnson. *Designing and Delivering Superior Customer Value: Concepts, Cases, and Applications*. Milwaukee: ASQ Quality Press, 1999.

Welch, Cas, and Pete Geissler. *Applying Total Quality to Sales*. Milwaukee: ASQ Quality Press, 1995

Service Organizations

Denton, D. Keith. *The Toolbox for the Mind*. Milwaukee: ASQ Quality Press, 1999.

DiPrimio, A. *Quality Assurance in Service Organizations*. Radnor, Pa.: Chilton Book Company, 1987.

Drewes, W. F. *Quality Dynamics for the Service Industry*. Milwaukee: ASQC Quality Press, 1991.

Heskett, J. L., W. E. Sasser, Jr., and C. W. L. Hart. *Service Breakthroughs: Changing the Rules of the Game*. New York: Free Press, 1990.

Kyrillidou, Martha, and Fred M. Heath. *Measuring Service Quality*. Champaign, IL: University of Illinois Graduate School of Library and Information Science, 2001.

Lash, L. M. *The Complete Guide to Customer Service.* New York: John Wiley & Sons, 1989.

Lefevre, H. L. *Quality Service Pays: Six Keys to Success.* Milwaukee: ASQC Quality Press and Quality Resources, 1989.

Lele, M. M., and J. N. Sheth. *The Customer Is Key: Gaining an Unbeatable Advantage Through Customer Satisfaction.* New York: John Wiley & Sons, Inc., 1987.

Rosander, A. C. *Deming's 14 Points Applied to Services.* New York: Marcel Dekker, Inc., and ASQC Quality Press, 1991.

Rosander, A. C. *The Quest for Quality in Services.* Milwaukee: ASQC Quality Press and Quality Resources, 1989.

Spechler, J. W. *When America Does It Right: Case Studies in Service Quality.* Norcross, Ga.: Industrial Engineering and Management Press, 1988.

Tschohl, J. *Achieving Excellence Through Customer Service.* New York: Prentice Hall, 1991.

Zeithaml, V. A., A. Parasuraman, and L. L. Berry. *Delivering Quality Service: Balancing Customer Perceptions and Expectations.* New York: Free Press, 1990.

Tools

Allen, Derek R., and Morris Wolburn, *Linking Customer and Employee Satisfaction to the Bottom Line*, Milwaukee: ASQ Quality Press, 2002.

Automotive Division: Statistical Process Control Manual. Milwaukee: American Society for Quality Control, 1986.

Basic Training in TQM Analysis Techniques. Springfield, Va.: U.S. Department of Commerce, National Technical Information Service, 1989.

Bauer, John E., Grace L. Duffy, and Russell T. Wescott, Eds. *The Quality Improvement Handbook.* Milwaukee: ASQ Quality Press, 2002

Bemowski, Karen and Stratton, Brad (editors). *101 Good Ideas: How to Improve Just About any Process*, ASQ Quality Press, 1998.

Brassard, Michael. *The Memory Jogger Plus+.* Methuen, Mass.: GOAL/QPC, 1989.

Clements, R. B. *Handbook of Statistical Methods in Manufacturing.* Englewood Cliffs, N.J.: Prentice Hall, 1991.

Evans, James R. *Statistical Process Control for Quality Improvement: A Training Guide to Learning SPC.* Englewood Cliffs, N.J.: Prentice Hall, 1991.

Gitlow, H., S. Gitlow, A. Oppenheim, and R. Oppenheim. *Tools and Methods for the Improvement of Quality.* Homewood, Ill.: Irwin, 1989.

Harrington, H. J. *The Improvement Process: How America's Leading Companies Improve Quality.* New York: McGraw-Hill Book Company, 1987.

Harrington, H. James and Kerim Tumay, *Simulation Modeling Methods.* New York: McGraw-Hill, 2000.

Ishikawa, K. *Guide to Quality Control.* Tokyo: Asian Productivity Organization, 1982.

Leebov, W., and C. J. Ersoz. *The Health Care Manager's Guide to Continuous Quality Improvement.* American Hospital Association, 1991.

Marsh, S., J. W. Moran, S. Nakui, and G. Hoffherr. *Facilitating and Training in Quality Function Deployment.* Methuen, Mass.: GOAL/QPC, 1991.

Mazur, G., J. B. ReVelle, and S. Nakui. *Quality Function Deployment: Advanced QFD Application Articles.* Methuen, Mass.: GOAL/QPC, 1991.

Mears, Peter. *Quality Improvement Tools and Techniques.* New York: McGraw-Hill, 1995.

Mizuno, S., ed. *Management for Quality Improvement: The Seven New QC Tools.* Cambridge, Mass.: Productivity Press, 1988.

Moran, J. W., R. P. Talbot, and R. M. Benson. *A Guide to Graphical Problem-Solving Processes*. Milwaukee: ASQC Quality Press, 1990.

Morse, W. J., H. P. Roth, and K. M. Poston. *Measuring, Planning, and Controlling Quality Costs*. Montvale, N.J.: National Association of Accountants, 1987.

Nikkan Kogyo Shimbun, Ltd./Factory Magazine, ed. *Poka-Yoke: Improving Product Quality by Preventing Defects*. Cambridge, Mass.: Productivity Press, 1988.

Ott, E. R. *Process Quality Control: Troubleshooting and Interpretation of Data*. New York: McGraw-Hill Book Company, 1975.

Pyzdek, T. *Pyzdek's Guide to SPC: Volume One/Fundamentals*. Tucson: Quality Publishing, Inc., and ASQC Quality Press, 1990.

Pyzdek, T. *Pyzdek's Guide to SPC: Volume One/Fundamentals (Workbook)*. Tucson: Quality Publishing, Inc., and ASQC Quality Press, 1989.

Pyzdek, T. *Pyzdek's Guide to SPC: Volume One/Fundamentals (Workbook for Services)*. Tucson: Quality Publishing, Inc., and ASQC Quality Press, 1992.

Pyzdek, T. *An SPC Primer: Programmed Learning Guide to Statistical Process Control Techniques*. Tucson: Quality America, Inc., 1987.

Smith, Gerald F. *Quality Problem Solving*. Milwaukee: Milwaukee: ASQ Quality Press, 1998.

Swanson, Roger. *The Quality Improvement Handbook*. Delray Beach, Fla.: St. Lucie Press, 1995.

Wilson, P. F., L. D. Dell, and G. F. Anderson. *Root Cause Analysis*. Milwaukee: ASQC Quality Press, 1993.

INDEX